Global Civil Society 2007/8

Martin Albrow, Helmut Anheier, Marlies Glasius, Monroe E Price, Mary Kaldor, editors-in-chief

Fiona Holland, managing editor

⑤SAGE Los Angeles•London•New Delhi•Singapore
www.sagepublications.com

SAGE Publications Ltd
1 Oliver's Yard
55 City Road
London EC1Y 1SP

SAGE Publications Inc.
2455 Teller Road
Thousand Oaks, California 91320

SAGE Publications India Pvt Ltd
B1/I1 Mohan Cooperative Industrial Area
Mathura Road
New Delhi 110 044

SAGE Publications Asia-Pacific Pte Ltd
33 Pekin Street # 02-01
Far East Square
Singapore 048763

British Library Cataloguing in Publication data

A catalogue record for this book is available from the British Library

ISBN 978-1-4129-4800-5
ISBN 978-1-4129-4801-2

Typeset by People, Design Consultants
Printed in Great Britain by Cromwell Press, Trowbridge, Wilts
Printed on paper from sustainable resources

Front cover illustration: Hassan Karimzadeh, graphic designer and cartoonist. Hassan lives in Tehran, Iran and has contributed to the 'Voices of Global Civil Society: Cartoonists, Comic Strip Artists, and Graphic Novelists' exhibition, a taste of which forms Chapter 9 of this volume.

ACKNOWLEDGEMENTS

The production of the Yearbook depends on the support, advice and contributions of numerous individuals and organisations. We endeavour to acknowledge them all in these pages. The final publication of course remains the responsibility of the editors.

Consultations
Global Framing of Democracy Workshop, Annenberg School for Communication, University of Pennsylvania, 2-3 November 2007, Philadelphia, USA
In conjunction with Annenberg School for Communication, University of Pennsylvania; supported by the Westminster Foundation for Democracy, Rockefeller Brothers Fund, and the University of Pennsylvania's Annenberg School for Communication, Middle East Center and Christopher H Browne Center for International Politics.

Participants: Susan M Abbott, Alain Ambrosi, Maziar Bahari, Sylvie Beauvais, Pinar Bilgin, Clifford Bob, Peter Busse, Neera Chandhoke, Weixing Chen, Cibelle Colmanetti, Kate Coyer, James Curran, James Deane, Michael X Delli Carpini, Paul Falzone, Shahid Fiaz, Allison H Fine, Christopher Finlay, Peter Funke, Marlies Glasius, Alfonso Gumucio-Dagron, Susan Haas, Kathleen Hall, John Hartley, Mark Harvey, Matthew J Hill, Fiona Holland, Armine Ishkanian, Thomas Jacobson, Alagi Yorro Jallow, Mary Kaldor, Kaitira Kandjii, Weiping Kang, Thomas Keenan, Wael Khalil, Iain King, Dennis Kinsey, Antonio Lambino, Jocelyn Landau, Dina Matar, Elzbieta Matynia, Anna McCarthy, JoAnn McCarthy, Drusilla Menaker, Sean O'Siochru, Monroe E Price, Vincent Price, Marc Raboy, Michael Serazio, Hakan Seckinelgin, Sabine Selchow, Nicole Stremlau, Malek Triki, Lokman Tsui, Joseph Turow, Magdalena Wojcieszak, Dieter Zinnbauer.

Other input
Guest boxes
Bart Cammaerts, Ronald J Deibert, Kunda Dixit, Nicole Doerr, Hojjat ol-Islam Hasan Yousefi Eshkevari, Zsofia Farkas, Tarek Ghanem, Arne Hintz, Todd Lester, Christian Pentzold, Manuel Plaza, Rafal Rohozinski, Hakan Seckinelgin, Sabine Selchow, Guobin Yang.

Chronology correspondents
Mustapha Kamel Al-Sayyid, Leighton Andrews, Baris Gencer Baykan, Nick Buxton, Giuseppe Caruso, Hyo-Je Cho, Bernard Dreano, Louise Fraser, Iuliana Gavril, Nihad Gohar, Vicky Holland, Deborah James, Jeffrey Juris, Bjarne Kristoffersen, Silke Lechner, Leeshai Lemish, Otilia Mihai, Alejandro Natal, Esther Nagle, Imogen Nay, Katarina Sehm Patomaki, Mario Pianta, Oscar Reyes, Asthriesslav Rocuts, Ineke Roose, Thomas Ruddy, Amade Suca, Katharine Talbot, Kate Townsend, Caroline Watt, Duccio Zola.

Research and editorial assistance
Muhammad Altamash, Julia Chan, Wonyoung Choi, Chris Dance (indexer), Nicole Doerr, Marcus Lam, Ian le Poidevin, Max McColl, Marco Moraes, Libby Morgan, Carole Pearce (copy editor), Barbara Piotrowska, Sabine Selchow, Sally Stares (data programme), Jill Timms (chronology), Hila Yogev (data programme).

Others who provided assistance or support
Joel Fischer, Union of International Associations; LSE's Anju Begum, Judith Higgin and Michael Oliver.

Design and production
People, Design Consultants: Christine Bone, Andrew Harrison, Andrew Stocks. Panos Pictures: David Arnott, Teresa Wolowiec, Zoe Slotover.

Administrative support
Sylvie Beauvais, Harriet Gallagher, Jocelyn Guihama, Jennifer Otoadese, Joanna Stone.

Financial support
We gratefully acknowledge the financial support of the following:
Aventis Foundation
Robert Bosch Foundation
Compagnia di San Paolo
Victor Phillip Dahdaleh
Stichting Democratie en Media
Ford Foundation
LSE
Charles Stewart Mott Foundation
Rockefeller Brothers Fund
UCLA School of Public Affairs
Westminster Foundation for Democracy

Contents

COMMUNICATIVE POWER

RECORDS

CONTENTS CONTINUED

Boxes

Figures

Maps

Tables

Records

CONTRIBUTORS

Martin Albrow is a sociologist whose books include *Max Weber's Construction of Social Theory, Do Organizations Have Feelings?, Sociology: the Basics,* and the prize-winning *The Global Age.* Formerly he was founding editor of the Journal *International Sociology,* President of the British Sociological Association and Chair of the Sociology Panel for the British universities Research Assessment Exercise. Emeritus Professor of the University of Wales, he is currently a Visiting Fellow at the Centre for the Study of Global Governance, LSE, and an editor-in-chief of *Global Civil Society 2006/7* and *Global Civil Societ 2007/8.*

Helmut Anheier is Professor of Public Policy and Social Welfare at the University of California, Los Angeles, where he directs the Center for Civil Society, and the Center for Globalization and Policy Research. He is also a Centennial Professor at the Centre for the Study of Global Governance, LSE. His work has focused on civil society, the non-profit sector, organisational studies and policy analysis, and comparative methodology. He is a founding editor of the *Journal of Civil Society* and author of over 250 publications in several languages. His present research examines the emergence of new organisational forms in global civil society, the role of foundations, and methodological aspects of social science research on globalisation.

Clifford Bob is associate professor of political science at Duquesne University. He is the author of *The Marketing of Rebellion: Insurgents, Media, and International Activism* (Cambridge University Press 2005), which won the 2007 International Studies Association Best Book Award. In addition, he has published in such journals as *Foreign Policy, American Journal of International Law, Social Problems,* and *Mobilization,* as well as in various edited volumes. Bob's research interests include human rights, social movements, and globalisation. He is currently working on three book projects: *Globalizing the Right-Wing:Conservative Activism and World Politics; Blasphemy beyond Borders:The Globalization of Umbrage*; and an edited volume, *Rights on the Rise:The Struggle for New Human Rights.*

Nick Couldry is Professor of Media and Communications at Goldsmiths, University of London and taught media, communications and culture at LSE between 2001 and 2006 where he directed a major ESRC-funded project on 'Media Consumption and the Future of Public Connection'. He is the author or editor of seven books including *Listening Beyond the Echoes: Media, Ethics and Agency in an Uncertain World* (Paradigm Books 2006), *Media Consumption and Public Engagement: Beyond the Presumption of Attention* (Palgrave 2007, with Sonia Livingstone and Tim Markham) and *Contesting Media Power* (Rowman and Littlefield 2003, co-edited with James Curran). He is Director of the recently formed Centre for the study of Global Media and Democracy at Goldsmiths.

James Deane is Head of Policy Development at the BBC World Service Trust. Formerly he was Managing Director of the Communication for Social Change Consortium, and before that Executive Director of the Panos Institute, in which role he established independent, regional Panos Institutes in Southern Africa, Eastern Africa and South Asia, and similar institutes in West Africa and the Caribbean. Deane has written widely on media, information and communication technologies, and other social communication issues. He was the organiser of the Global Media Forum at the Global Knowledge conference in Malaysia in 2000, the convenor of the Bellagio Symposium on Media, Freedom and Poverty, and the Bellagio Symposium on Communication and the Millennium Development Goals (both in 2004). He has provided formal strategic advice and consultancies to DFID, Sida, Norad, Danida, Swiss Development Cooperation, the World Bank, WHO, Unicef, Unesco, UNDP, UNAIDS, UNFPA, IFAD, FAO, the Rockefeller Foundation, and the Stop TB Partnership.

Miguel Darcy de Oliveira is Special Advisor to former President Fernando Henrique Cardoso and Research Coordinator for the Project on Civil Society and Democracy at the Fernando Henrique Cardoso Institute in Brazil. A graduate of the Brazilian Diplomatic Academy and of the Geneva Institute of Advanced International Studies, he was exiled for his opposition to the military dictatorship in Brazil. Founder and former director of CIVICUS: the World Alliance for Citizen Participation, he is co-author of the CIVICUS report on the status of civil society, *Citizens: building global civil society.* De Oliveira is founder and director of the Brazilian NGOs IDAC, Comunidade Solidária and COMUNITAS, and co-chair of the Civil Society Working Groups in the Club de Madrid International Summit on Terrorism, Democracy and Security. He is also an NGO leader and civil society activist in the fields of democracy and citizen participation.

Marlies Glasius is a lecturer in global politics at the London School of Economics and Political Science (LSE). She recently published *The International Criminal Court: A Global Civil Society Achievement* (2006). Other publications include *A Human Security Doctrine for Europe: Project, Principles, Practicalities,* with Mary Kaldor (Routledge 2005), and *Exploring Civil Society: Political and Cultural Contexts,* with David Lewis and Hakan Seckinelgin (Routledge 2004). Glasius studied English Literature and International Law at the University of Amsterdam. She holds a PhD with distinction from the University of Utrecht in association with the Netherlands School of Human Rights Research. She has been working at LSE since 2000, as managing editor of the Global Civil Society Yearbook (2001-2003), as coordinator of the Study Group on European Security (2003-2004), and as lecturer in management of non-governmental organisations (2004-2006). She is a research associate at the Centre for the Study of Global Governance, and continues to be an editor-in-chief of the Global Civil Society Yearbook. Her present research interests include global civil society, economic and social rights, human security, and social forums.

Amber Hawkes, a recent Masters graduate from the UCLA School of Urban Planning, now works at an urban design and planning firm in Los Angeles. She was a graduate research assistant at the UCLA Center for Civil Society and worked on the 2007 and 2008 *Cultures and Globalization Series.*

Jonathan Haynes is Professor of English at the Brooklyn Campus of Long Island University. A former Fulbright Senior Scholar at the University of Nigeria-Nsukka, Ahmadu Bello University, and the University of Ibadan, he was Director of the Friends World Program West African Center in Kumasi, Ghana. With Onookome Okome he co-authored *Cinema and Social Change* in West Africa (Nigerian Film Corporation 1996) and edited *Nigerian Video Films* (Ohio University Press 2000). He has also written two books on English Renaissance literature. He has published numerous articles on Nigerian and Ghanaian video films; more are forthcoming in A*frica Today, Film International, Postcolonial Text, the International Encyclopedia of Communication,* and in *African Cinemas* edited by Josef Gugler.

Armine Ishkanian is a Lecturer in Social Policy at the Centre for Civil Society and a Research Associate at the Centre for the Study of Global Governance, LSE. Her research focuses on civil society, democracy building, gender and development. Her regional expertise is on the countries of the former Soviet Union with a particular focus on Armenia. Her forthcoming book, *Democracy-building and Civil Society in post-Soviet Armenia* (Routledge 2008) addresses the challenges of democracy building in Armenia and the broader post-Soviet region.

Mary Kaldor is Professor of Global Governance at LSE and Co-Director of the Centre for the Study of Global Governance, LSE. She has written widely on security issues and on democracy and civil society and is a founder and editor-in-chief of the Global Civil Society Yearbook series. Her recent books include *Global Civil Society: An Answer to War* (Polity Press 2003) and *New and Old Wars: Organised Violence in a Global Era* (1999). Most recently she co-edited *A Human Security Doctrine for Europe: Project, Principles, Practicalities,* with Marlies Glasius (Routledge 2005). Kaldor was a founder member of European Nuclear Disarmament (END), and founder and Co-Chair of the Helsinki Citizen's Assembly. She is Convenor of the Study Group on European Security Capabilities established at the request of Javier Solana.

Hagai Katz is Lecturer at the Department of Business Administration at the School of Management at Ben Gurion University of the Negev in Beersheba, Israel, Chief Research Officer at the Israeli Center for Third-sector Research, and a Research Associate at the UCLA Center for Civil Society. He has published extensively on the non-profit sector in Israel and on global civil society. Katz is editor of the Yearbook's Data Programme.

Thomas Keenan teaches literary theory, media studies and human rights at Bard College, where he directs the Human Rights Program. Among his publications are *Fables of Responsibility: Aberrations and Predicaments in Ethics and Politics* (Stanford University Press 1997) and an edited volume on media theory, with Wendy Chun, called *New Media, Old Media* (Routledge 2005). His current manuscript is called *Live Feed: Crisis, Intervention, Media,* about the new media and contemporary conflicts. With Andras Riedlmayer, he started International Justice Watch (JUSTWATCH-L), an Internet discussion list on war crimes and transitional justice. He has served on the boards of WITNESS and the Soros Documentary Fund.

Denisa Kostovicova is Lecturer in the Government Department/Development Studies Institute and a Research Associate at the Centre for the Study of Global Governance, LSE. Her present research interests include nationalism and democratisation in the global age, post-conflict reconstruction and security, civil society and state weakness, and European integration of the Western Balkans. She has also studied the role of education in identity formation and ethnic reconciliation in Serbia and Kosovo. Her publications include *Kosovo: The Politics of Identity and Space* (Routledge 2005), and 'Old and new insecurity in the Balkans: Learning from the EU's involvement in Macedonia' in *A Human Security Doctrine for Europe: Project, Principles, Practicalities*, edited by Kaldor and Glasius, (Routledge 2005). She also co-edited a special issue of *Ethnopolitics*, 'Transnationalism in the Balkans', with Vesna Bojicic-Dzelilovic.

Marcus Lam is a PhD student in the Department of Social Welfare at the UCLA School of Public Affairs and a graduate research assistant at the UCLA Center for Civil Society. He is editorial assistant for the *Journal of Civil Society*. In additional to diffusion models, his research interests include the regional non-profit sector in Los Angeles County, social enterprises, and organisational factors related to HIV testing. He holds a Masters in Public Policy from UCLA and a BA In Public Policy from Occidental College.

Victor Pickard is a doctoral candidate in the Institute of Communications Research at the University of Illinois, Urbana-Champaign. He holds an MA in communications from the University of Washington where he wrote his Masters' thesis on and volunteered for the Seattle Independent Media Center. His research explores the intersections of media politics, communications policy, and democratic theory, and has been published in a number of academic journals, including: *the Journal of Communication; Global Media and Communication; Media, Culture & Society; New Media and Society; Journal of Communication Inquiry; International Journal of Law and Policy;* and *Critical Studies in Media Communication*. Currently he is writing a dissertation on the normative foundations of democratic communications policy.

Monroe E Price is Director of the Project for Global Communication Studies at the Annenberg School for Communication at the University of Pennsylvania. Price, who was Dean of Cardozo from 1982 to 1991, graduated magna cum laude from Yale, where he was executive editor of the *Yale Law Journal*. He clerked for Associate Justice Potter Stewart of the US Supreme Court and was an assistant to Secretary of Labor W Willard Wirtz. He was founding director of the Program in Comparative Media Law and Policy at Wolfson College, Oxford, and a Member of the School of Social Sciences at the Institute for Advanced Study in Princeton. Price was a senior fellow of the Media Studies Center in spring 1998. He was deputy director of California Indian Legal Services, one of the founders of the Native American Rights Fund, and author of *Law and the American Indian*. Among his many books are a treatise on cable television, *Media and Sovereignty*, and *Television, The Public Sphere and National Identity*.

Vincent Price is the Steven H Chaffee Professor of Communication and Political Science at the Annenberg School for Communication, University of Pennsylvania. He was formerly chair of the Department of Communication Studies at the University of Michigan, where he also served as a Faculty Associate with the Center for Political Studies in the Institute for Social Research. Price earned his doctorate at Stanford University and has published extensively on mass communication and public opinion, social influence processes, and political communication. He served as editor-in-chief of *Public Opinion Quarterly* and on a number of journal editorial boards. His research on media framing of issues, the measurement of media exposure and political information, social identification processes, and third-person effects of mass communication is widely cited; and his book *Public Opinion* has been published in five languages and used in graduate and undergraduate courses throughout North and South America, Europe, and Asia. His most recent research, funded by grants from the National Science Foundation and the Pew Charitable Trusts, focuses on the role of political conversation, particularly web-based discussion, in shaping public opinion.

Sabine Selchow is a PhD candidate in the LSE Department of Government, under the supervision of Mary Kaldor and Ulrich Beck. In her thesis, Sabine takes a constructivist approach to 'the global' and explores the extent to which contemporary (national) policy decisions are 'global'. Sabine studied Development Studies at the LSE, and

American literature and culture at Freie Universitaet Berlin, Germany and at Duke University, USA. She holds a Masters degree (M.A.) in North American Studies and Communication Studies from Freie Universitaet Berlin.

Jill Timms is a Research Assistant at the Centre for the Study of Global Governance, LSE. She coordinates the Chronology of the Global Civil Society Yearbook and is completing her doctorate research on corporate social responsibility at the Department of Sociology, LSE. Her research interests include corporate citizenship, anti-corporate groups, labour activism and social forums. Her publications include 'Trade Union Internationalism and a Global Civil Society in the Making', co-authored with Peter Waterman, in *Global Civil Society 2004/5* (Sage 2005) and 'The Role of Social Forums in Global Civil Society: Radical Beacon or Strategic Infrastructure', co-authored with Marlies Glasius, in *Global Civil Society 2005/6* (Sage 2006).

DEMOCRACY AND THE POSSIBILITY OF A GLOBAL PUBLIC SPHERE

Martin Albrow and Marlies Glasius

Set in contrast to the manipulated mass opinion and ideological conflicts of the Western nation state, Jürgen Habermas found in the eighteenth century a model of rational communication and rational-critical debate that he called the public sphere. 'Private people come together as a public', as he defined that sphere, challenged the state to engage with them in reasoned argument (Habermas 1989 [1962]: 27). Parallel with and necessary to the economic interests of civil society, communication was also subject to rational principles. Since his intervention full and free communication has become ever more salient. It outstrips the principle of representation in contemporary efforts to reconstruct democratic theory.

As Habermas stressed, the public sphere has been in a permanent state of transformation as underlying social and economic conditions have changed, and even as he wrote Marshall McLuhan (1962) was exemplifying that by writing of the 'global village' that the new media technology made possible. Since then, advances in technology have given us global mass media and permitted private worldwide communication. Along with those developments civil society has become global. At the same time, as Mary Kaldor emphasizes in Chapter 2 of this volume, representative democracy in nation states has advanced throughout the world. Yet there is no global counterpart to national democratic institutions.

Without that counterpart the democratic nature of global communication appears very open to question. Did the private video recording and global dissemination of the last living moments of Saddam Hussein, as he was led to execution, help to undermine the authority of the new representative democracy of Iraq by publicising the deep factional loathing that tears at Iraqi society? Or does it show that institutions imposed by force of arms are vulnerable to an even stronger force of global public opinion?

Global civil society has reacted to the harassment that accompanied the execution with almost universal indignation. Arguably, this was a vast global audience of disgusted observers communicating their abhorrence of the violence. But the interpretation of what was objectionable about the execution has diverged widely. British newspaper readers objected to the 'pornographic ghoulishness' of photographs and footage of the hanging (Mayes 2007: 29). In Kerala, South India, the main Muslim party and the locally powerful Communist party called a strike in response to Saddam's execution, even before the news about its vicious implementation had broken (Sebastian 2006). What was being objected to here was not the death penalty per se but either the victimisation of Muslims or the victimisation of everyone poor and non-Western, depending on your ideological outlook. In Latin America, as in India, in undoubtedly free and vibrant media environments, Saddam turned into Che Guevara.

And should the reactions to the Iraq war really be interpreted as an expression of the soft power of free and equal communication through the new media? The Bush Administration has provoked an un-reflexive anti-Americanism that is not the sole domain of civil society, but is hijacked and instrumentalised by political leaders as diverse as Hugo Chavez, Mahmoud Ahmadinejad and Jacques Chirac. Saddam Hussein, one of the worst dictators of the twentieth century, becomes a martyr in the process.

The Saddam images fed into a debate that immediately became global. But it has no global institutional locus. Is this the new global public sphere, where a global public opinion takes shape? Do the new communication possibilities realise democracy beyond the nation state or does the very proliferation of media channels result in a fragmentation that undermines any public sphere? Habermas re-centred the issue of democracy in the nation state on the possibilities of full and free communication in the public sphere. We ask whether developments in the media of communication and their use now require us to rethink democracy for global society. If we do now have a global public sphere can we be sure that democracy will inspire its debates? These are our concerns in *Global Civil Society 2007-8*.

Communication, as Selchow reminds us in Chapter 11, is one of the primary human impulses. The sophistication of human communications defines and sets human beings apart from other species. As such, it is also foundational to any socio-political formation human beings create. Even Trappist monks would interrupt their silence to conduct necessary managerial meetings.

Because free speech is the antidote to thuggery (the pen is mightier than the sword, and the blog may be mightier than the missile), communication tends in political science to have positive connotations and be associated with dialogue, exchange of views, learning, and even democracy. Not so in media studies. There, we are constantly reminded of the use of communication as manipulation and spin, whether in nominally democratic or in authoritarian political settings. The multiple uses to which human communication can be put, which may even be in the eye of the beholder, have not fundamentally changed with the advent of global communications technology. But it may have eroded the force of monolithic messages from a single (state or religious) entity.

As academics, we may be inclined to equate communication with language, but this Yearbook has attempted to both describe (in language) and display powerful non-linguistic forms of global communication. Chapter 10 describes the use of fiction in semi-commercial Nigerian videos opening up a range of social issues, as well as the use of 'documentary' videos by radical Islamic militants to propagandise violent action in Iraq. Chapter 9 is devoted to a selection of very diverse cartoon art. These art works alert us to the problematic nature of the term 'global', highlighted by Selchow, which is constantly used in different combinations in the pages of this book. The selection is 'global' in that artists from different parts of the globe are represented, although certainly not every corner of the globe. More importantly, their messages transcend national boundaries, but at the same time we should be alert, as we discovered in the selection, that they are not universal: each of us will interpret them or respond to them differently, even if those cultural differences do not neatly map onto political borders. As such, they are precisely a reflection of the complex and contradictory

tendencies we try to capture with the inadequate term 'global'. We can illustrate this by the very term 'global democracy': do we mean democracy for the world's population as a single political unit, for some an ideal aspiration, or do we mean democracy in its different national and local settings worldwide? We trust we shall make clear which it is in each context.

Democracy in a global age

Kaldor draws our attention to the paradox that democratic institutions spread worldwide in the latter part of the twentieth century but have also suffered a 'hollowing-out' in the process. While in the 1980s and 1990s more and more states became nominally democratic and it has become a virtual taboo to espouse any other political system, there have been severe declines in the number of political party members, in attendance at party conferences, and in voter turnout in most established democracies. Anticipating the electorate at large, democratic theorists had already become increasingly disillusioned with representative democracy, calling it 'thin' or 'procedural' democracy (Pateman 1970; Bessette 1980; Cohen and Rogers 1983; Barber 1984).

Kaldor connects this paradox to globalisation. In the first place democratisation, in the sense of a spread of formal procedures, accompanies the expansion of Western market institutions and guarantees participation in the global economic system. A cynical reading is that this has nothing to do whatsoever with 'rule by the people' Adherence to certain democratic procedures has become a badge of respectability, and more especially marketability, for state participation in the global neo-liberal order. Moreover integration into that order means that parliamentary democracy suffers the erosion of the substance of democratic participation and choice (see for instance Held 1995; McGrew 1997; Scholte 2001; Anderson 2000). David Held (2002) uses the phrase 'overlapping communities of fate' to express the fact that those who are affected by certain decisions are no longer found neatly in a single political entity controlled by a democratic process.

Ishkanian describes potently in this volume how such integration has taken place at the civil society level. Western governments in the last 15 years have sought to reinforce democratic legitimacy in nation states by co-opting organised civil society. Based on a particular reading of de Tocqueville (ignoring his concern for social equality), influential scholars like Putnam, Fukuyama and Larry Diamond asserted a direct connection between the existence of numerous associations and the vibrancy of democracy. Applying such theories to transition countries, where they might not find the 'right' type of associations for promoting Western-style democracy, donor agencies would in Ishkanian's term 'genetically-engineer' NGOs through training and project funding. Under these conditions of global communication, the types of aid projects Ishkanian describes have provoked a backlash against the twin projects of 'building civil society' and 'democratisation', often and justly perceived as a form of neo-imperialism.

But globalisation does not only take the form of enforced integration into Western governmental models. Even before the 1990s when Richard Falk (1993) gave recognition to globalisation from below, there were plenty of empirical examples of democratisation as the result of successful efforts of social movements in Eastern Europe, Latin America, and South Africa building transnational links and appealing to transnational norms in order to defeat the authoritarian state (Keck and Sikkink 1998; Kaldor 2003; Glasius 2003). This volume provides an example of those transitions: in Chapter 6 de Oliveira charts the transformation in Latin America where NGOs and social movements spearheaded the struggle for democracy in the 1970s and 1980s, but where now the vitality of what he calls the 'classical notion of civil society', its organised form, has declined. But they have left a legacy of democratisation at the very personal level: 'today, ordinary people tend to be more intelligent, rebellious and creative than in the past.' They are constantly called upon to make value judgments and life choices where previously there was only conformity to a pre-established destiny. This enhanced capacity of individuals to think, deliberate and decide is a consequence of the decline in diverse forms of authority based on religion and tradition. As he says, 'democracy is always work in progress, an unfinished journey.'

The Latin American case suggests that the very bonding of civil society to representative democracy propagated by Western capacity-building projects may already be inappropriate for the new social and economic conditions of the early twenty-first century. Perhaps partly because of a tradition of ideological resistance to the hegemonic power from which the project mainly emanated, Latin America appears to have been less affected by the growth of genetically-engineered civil society than other parts of the world such as Eastern Europe, Central Asia and Africa. But de Oliveira finds that the institutional and organisational legacy of earlier democratic struggles is now subject to the challenges from an informed communicating public for whom new media of communication offer unprecedented opportunities to make their views known, and who demand openness and transparency. He now sees the main contest between authoritarian populism and an informed autonomous and diverse citizenry. Public disaffection with representative democracy runs deep and recent years have been marked by frequent depositions of elected leaders. Less-than-democratic populist leaders like Chavez exercise 'a sort of fascination over large sectors of Latin American civil society still enraptured by the revolutionary myth'. That fascination is enhanced, we might add, by the ability of the leader to project national identity through global media.

At the same time globality does not merely undermine liberal democracy in nation states. Kaldor and Kostovicova in Chapter 5 show how illiberal regimes are equally vulnerable to global connections. In their responses to the pressures of globalisation, most of these regimes have moved far away from the monolithic Orwellian ideal type. Instead of aspiring to eliminate civil society and monopolise communication, which is simply no longer possible, they tolerate some forms of civil society organisation as well as some forms of transnational communication. They either try to contain and control civil society, relegating it to the role of social policy sub-contractor, or found their own organisations, but without the old aspiration to a complete monopoly. In the realm of communications, Iran, Saudi Arabia or China now try to 'get the message out', becoming, in Monroe Price's term, sellers in the market for loyalties (see Chapter 3). These changed parameters may also have consequences for the old debate as to whether to isolate or engage rogue states. The 2008 Beijing Olympics, for instance, has become an occasion for bringing attention to a plethora of human rights-violating aspects of Chinese domestic and foreign policy (see Box 5.1 in Chapter 5).

On the other hand, the murder of Russian journalist Anna Politkovskaya suggests that in some of the self-declared democracies of the twenty-first century there are those prepared to violate even the right to life in order to prevent exposure of murky dealings at the top. However, while protests against her murder were sparse in Russia itself, the murder of Hrant Dink in Turkey (see Box I.1) sparked an intense, if perhaps elliptical, debate that went to the heart of Turkish identity. A third journalist, Alan Johnston of the BBC, who had been kidnapped in the Gaza strip by a local gang and released through the mediation of Hamas, serves as another reminder that threats to free speech are now more diverse and complex, but no less daunting, than old-fashioned jailing by a dictatorial regime.

Civility now has to be entrenched globally before it can be guaranteed nationally and locally, but the guarantors of civility in the old nation state, a legal system, rights, a judiciary, police, political representation and administration under the law, have no global equivalents. Democratic behaviour then has to be lodged at a deeper level than in institutions alone.

Even before globalisation was widely recognised as a key contributory factor in the decline of democratic participation, political theorists were seeking a more satisfying normative underpinning for democracy than majority rule expressed in periodic elections, constructing models of radical, participatory or deliberative democracy (Barber 1984; Blaug 1999; Bessette 1980; Cohen and Rogers 1983; Gutmann and Thompson 1996). The most famous and broadly inspirational of these conceptualisations is probably Habermas' conception of the public sphere as a space of communication and deliberation where citizens identify and discuss social problems, forming a 'public opinion', which in turn informs the decision making of political actors (Habermas 1989; 1992; 1996). In such conceptions, the effectiveness of communicative action, not the density of associations, is the key measure of democracy.

In developing his theory over three decades culminating in *Between Facts and Norms* (German edition published 1992) Habermas built in lots of ifs and buts; in particular he was pessimistic about the role of the mass media in relation to the public sphere ideal. Since then, the development and use of new information and communications technologies has fuelled an enthusiasm for the notion of the public sphere that goes far beyond Habermas' own very cautious endorsement. A search on Google Scholar,

itself a product of these new technologies, for social science articles containing the phrase 'global public sphere' renders over four hundred results, few of which moderate the phrase with a question mark.

Apart from the notes of caution inserted by Habermas and others concerning the application of the ideal-typical concept of the public sphere to reality, the new enthusiasts also tend to miss the fact that for Habermas, and even in the seminal work on civil society by Cohen and Arato (1992), the only imaginable relevant context was the state. Their public spheres end neatly at the border, civil society is national, and the formation of public opinion only relates to decision making by government and parliament. Habermas saw 'the potential for self-annihilation on a global scale' (1989 [1962]: 235) as adding emphasis to Kant's call for a 'cosmopolitan order', but this was only within the frame of a world of nation states.

In this issue of the Yearbook we aim to encourage the reconsideration of communication in democracy in a world where global civil society challenges states to develop deeper relations with all their people and to respond to issues that transcend national boundaries. As Kaldor's Chapter declares, the deepening of democracy nationally and locally requires a negotiation of a global social contract. Democracies cannot escape global conditions, but the mere fact of global communication does not provide for such a contract. We have, therefore to examine the relations of democracy and communication in principle if global civil society is to contribute to democracy beyond the nation state.

In our institutions and in our thinking, world communication and democracy have historically been bonded in a set of complex and often contradictory relations. As we said at the outset, Habermas pointed to the continual transformation of the public sphere. One stage in that process was 'the plebeian public sphere' that flourished in the French Revolution (1989 [1962]: xviii). One can trace that back to what he calls Rousseau's 'democracy of unpublic opinion' (1989 [1962]: 98), a mass of popular prejudices. Given the fact that the mass media today reflect just that so much of the time, it will help our appreciation of the fraught relationships between the mass media and democracy, and the limits on full and free communication, if we retrieve some of their roots in Rousseau and his successors who framed the theory of modern public opinion

Public, community and communication in Western modernity

The dependency of democracy on communication is not a new theme. Indeed so fraught was it for the old democratic model of the modern sovereign state that it was frequently suppressed as a premise as well as in practice. We need initially, therefore, to give some attention to that context just to gain perspective on how the new communication media challenge the old model.

For brevity's sake let us simply take two paradigmatic contributions to modernity's thinking about communication and democracy. The first is from the mid-eighteenth century in Europe at the beginning of the coalescence of the modern nation-state order. The second, which references the first, is immediately after the First World War of 1914-18 when the potential for self-destruction of that order had become apparent.

The attempt to force Iraq to be free is at first glance startlingly evocative of Jean Jacques Rousseau (1712-88) and his *Social Contract* (1762). As a citizen of the free republic of Geneva he was proud to think it followed in the best traditions of classic Greek democracy, but he feared the emerging mass national state was not going to secure the same kind of citizen attachment and involvement. He therefore made the early outstanding revolutionary appeal for a re-ordering of society to create a cohesive national state out of a mass population. He called for the whole people of a nation to be sovereign, constitutive of the state and bearer of a general will, constraining the dissenting individual 'which means nothing else than that he shall be forced to be free' (1895:113). (However, we note, that does not speak of one state imposing freedom on another.)

He understood communication was foundational and his approach was radical. Citizens had to be knowledgeable. They also had to share 'manners, customs, and above all opinion – a province unknown to our politicians, but one on which the success of all the rest depends' (1895: 148). The wise legislator provided for the unity of religion and the state, in which respect 'Mohammed had very sound views: he thoroughly unified his political system' (1895: 222). Rousseau concluded by advocating a civil religion avowing the deity, permitting many faiths and outlawing only religious intolerance.

It was the direct relationship of the individual to the collective and corporate existence of the state that Rousseau exalted. It meant that he severely restricted the scope of intermediate associations: 'It is important then, in order to have a clear declaration of the general will, that there should be no partial association in the State, and that every citizen should express only his own opinion' (1895: 124). The general will depends on the people coming to a resolution 'when adequately informed and without any communication among the citizens' (1895: 122)

For our ideas of civil society and democracy today, the restrictions he imposed on free association and speech are breathtaking. Moreover we should note that Rousseau was contemptuous of the British representative government system of his day, should we be inclined to see that as modestly democratic for the time, precisely because it encouraged plural interests. He viewed it as faction breeding, divisive and anti-egalitarian.

There could be no legitimate collective interest apart from that of the sovereign people as a whole. We can thus discern in Rousseau already, modernity's fatal ambivalence towards communication: a way to disseminate the right ideas or the source of dissidence and discontent. Ironically his beloved democratic Geneva got the message only too well, promptly ordered his arrest and the burning of his book. The other elements in Rousseau's thinking are all palliatives for the fatal totalitarianism that infects his model republic. Recognising the illiberal danger he strove to thwart popular tyranny by asserting the need for rights, equality and civil liberty. He required the sovereign power to observe strict limits within its overall duty to protect its citizens and since him we have indeed come to regard rights, equality and liberty as necessary to, even constitutive of democracy itself. Yet his overriding concern to create a model not so much for democracy, which he regarded as suitable only for 'a nation of gods' (1895:160), but for a republican national state, a collective entity based on a direct relation with its citizens, provided a direct line to the excesses of the French Revolution and beyond. Rousseau speaks to our time in many different ways. His insistence on rights, equality and liberty is a permanent and strengthening feature of contemporary political discourse and, as a touchstone of democracy, it far outweighs the idea of representation that has fallen into as much disrepute with the public of today as it had for Rousseau. His idea of the general will has few admirers, but his

Box I.1: A brief anatomy of a journalist's murder

On the afternoon of Friday 19 January 2007 a Turkish journalist of Armenian descent, Hrant Dink, was assassinated in Istanbul, outside of the offices of *Agos*, the weekly newspaper he edited. Internationally, commentators drew a comparison between Dink's murder and that of Anna Politkovskaya in Russia. Both journalists were awarded the '2007 IPA Freedom Prize - Special Award' posthumously in May 2007 by the International Publishers Association.

Nationally, Dink's murder sparked an intense debate, which focused generally on Armenian-Turkish relations and specifically on the perennial question of whether a genocide was committed in 1915 by the Ottoman administration against the Armenian population. Initial and subsequent reactions to the murder reflect the changing public discourse, which can be charted by examining media sources in the two-week period between the murder, the funeral and its immediate aftermath.

On the afternoon of the murder, the print media - through their Internet editions - were already broadcasting the news, with photos from the murder scene where there had been an immediate reaction by thousands of people who held a candlelit vigil in front of the newspaper office. One of the advantages of Internet newspapers editions is their provision for readers to post comments, and from the hundreds of comments posted that day the general shock and condemnation of the murder was clear. On one hand many people said that although they disagreed with Dink's views on the issue of the genocide, the act of murder was unacceptable in a civilised society. Others said that though they really did not know who Dink was or what he stood for, the killing of another journalist or intellectual represented the loss of another of Turkey's 'good children'. In this way they placed Dink with other journalists and scholars who have been assassinated in Turkey in the last 25 years. Such comments on Internet sites posted in this period generally agreed that Dink's murder was a conspiratorial act to hurt Turkey, which had been committed against all Turks and the country. Then, on the same day, media sources and television news channels broadcast the image of the suspected murderer caught on CCTV. Recognised by his family, the police caught the suspect later that weekend.

On Tuesday 23 January Dink's funeral took place in Istanbul attended by over 100,000 people, many of whom carried placards with the statement, 'We are all Armenians' or 'We are Hrant Dink'. Media coverage of this stimulated another change in people's views. While they condemned the murder still, they questioned the appropriateness of such slogans, and instead said, 'We are all Turkish'. Some questioned the sincerity of those who attended the funeral, suggesting perhaps that people were trying to create a good impression for the European Union and the US. Some asked, 'How many of these people had attended the funerals of soldiers killed in south eastern Turkey and claimed that they are Ahmed, Mehmet or Ali?'

In order to assess popular mood, the national daily, *Hürriyet*, conducted a nationwide survey through its website, asking the question: 'Was the slogan "We are all Armenian", right or wrong?' On 25 January, it was reported that, of the 320,958 people who responded, 52.2 % said it was wrong and 47 % said it was not wrong. There were thousands of comments posted on the websites of various newspapers about this issue, most of which questioned the rationale of this slogan and expressed their unhappiness about it, asserting their position in terms of Turkish national identity. Among the thousands of comments posted on websites, those who agreed with the slogan were not strongly represented.

The next major focus of media coverage on 1 February was a video of the suspect pictured between two police officers, holding a Turkish flag. Still photos taken from the video appeared in newspapers, galvanising another huge response on websites. The video and still images were presented by broadcast and print media as a scandal: a murderer, who had committed a crime against society, was associated with the national symbol. In other words, the images offended a broad spectrum of people, including those who had reacted against the slogans and those who joined the funeral. Also, the assassin's earlier statement, that he had committed the crime because of news about Dink that had stirred his nationalistic feelings, created an important debate. Many argued that while they too had a strong national identity and feelings, killing someone because of their views did not play any part in that identity.

Throughout this period another set of issues regularly appeared among the Internet comments, which illustrates another aspect of the media's role in public debate. If Dink was such a patriot and working for the good of the country, these commentators asked, why was he not presented in the media as such before the murder. Others questioned the role of the media in conducting what they saw as inflammatory public opinion surveys. The former comments refer to an earlier episode, which led to Dink's six-month suspended sentence in October 2006 under the controversial Article 301 of the Turkish Penal Code for the crime of 'insulting Turkishness'. In this period his comments on the genocide and the need for open debate about taboo topics in Turkey were treated sceptically by the media.

The public responses to the murder and how these were presented in the media demonstrates various roles played by the media. While different types of media act as a medium for participation in public debates, newspapers also contribute to the substance of the discussion as civil society actors. This is evident in newspaper websites and on YouTube where over 400 entries were posted after the murder. In the aftermath of the murder, new media provided public forums for broader discussion, which being virtual, allowed people outside Turkey to comment. The role of media as a public forum is a more subtle and long-term process. One aspect of this role can be observed in the way events are reported from the moment of the murder up until the above-mentioned survey. Another aspect can be seen from the ways in which the media have reported Dink's earlier trial, debates on the genocide issue, the trials of writers Orhan Pamuk and Elif Şafak under Article 301in 2006, and pressures from the EU on these issues. Under these conditions, in terms of the comments that appear on websites, it is not clear whether the media are merely conduits for people's views, or whether the way they frame the debate has an entrenching influence on nationalism in society.

Hakan Seckinelgin, Lecturer in International Social Policy, Department of Social Policy, LSE anxieties about information, free association and shared values anticipated the dilemmas of a unitary nation state.

Fast forward to the 1920s and we find those dilemmas the focus of a famous exchange between Walter Lippman (1889-1974), regarded by many as the founder of media studies (Carey 1989), and John Dewey (1859-1952), the leading philosopher representative of American pragmatism. They addressed precisely the failings of the large-scale nation state that Rousseau had sought to forestall.

One hundred and sixty years of experience bore out Rousseau's worst fears. Human beings could effect democracy in small communities but both Lippman and Dewey saw it failing in 'the Great Society'. This was the title of the book (1914) by Graham Wallas (1858-1932), the first Professor of Political Science at the LSE, who viewed representative democracy as unable to create the same cohesion. He argued that specialised fields of knowledge and work became ever more complex and distant from citizens and each other, and that interest groups competed to exercise influence on government. Wallas addressed his book to Lippman, who had earlier attended his discussion class at Harvard. Lippman responded to him with his book *Public Opinion* (1922) seeking to find a remedy for the ills that he saw as coming to disastrous culmination in the Great War of 1914-18. The public opinion of the great national societies was a partial, compressed, distorted picture of a world beyond reach, formed into stereotypes to fit self-perceived interests, then easily manipulated and led into war.

The small rural community that inspired Jefferson's vision of democracy, 'guided somewhat by Jean Jacques Rousseau' (Lippman 1922: 267) confined consent and community within the frontiers of self-governing groups and correspondingly assumed that the only knowledge necessary was that available to a village jack-of all-trades. But the knowledge required for a mass democracy in industrial society in Lippman's view necessitated a new political science, one that would inform the people's representatives and responsible administrators through a system of intelligence bureaux devoted to gathering and analysing social data. Expert judgement was to replace stereotype and public opinion was to be educated to the point of understanding its purpose.

Dewey agreed with the diagnosis, but not the remedy. 'Till the Great Society is converted into a Great Community, the Public will remain in eclipse. Communication can alone create a great community' (Dewey 1927: 324). His communication was grounded not in public information but in 'relations of personal intercourse in the local community' (1927: 371). The articulate public Dewey called for depended on a responsive and vivid art of communication. It would take charge of the machinery of transmission and circulation, thus creating the free and enriching communion known as democracy (1927: 350).

Eighty years ago Dewey sounded utopian but his dispute with Lippman anticipates so many of the contested issues of our own day that we cannot simply regard it as of merely antiquarian interest. They may have written in a world dominated by competing imperialisms and intensifying conflict between nation states. But their formulations still intimated theoretical possibilities for a world that might, in the future, be organised in a different way.

Public spheres beyond the state

Translated now to the global level, in some ways Lippman's 'network of intelligence bureaus in politics and industry' (1922: 394) anticipates well the global policy networks of government officials, multilateral institutions and think tanks. But for many, including Noam Chomsky (Chomsky and Herman 1988), he is also the spokesperson for manipulated and manufactured public opinion. This is the dark interpretation of the phenomenon Monroe Price points to in Chapter 3, the way nation states are working hard to domesticate global broadcasting entities. States may even find global suppliers of news and information more congenial occupiers of airtime than homegrown opposition and, in a world where they accept the dominance of the global economy, less destabilising.

On the other hand Dewey, in spite of his nostalgic communitarianism, in our time of digital, interactive, Internet-based technology seems to speak as the animating spirit of civil society-led global communication. His local community was not cut off from the wider world by national boundaries. It was to be the vital node for transmitting democratic values. Anticipating Habermas, he declared 'The Great Community in the sense of free and full intercommunication' will only work through translocal associations that feed into the intimate unions.

'Democracy must begin at home' (1927: 367-8). 'Fraternity, liberty and equality isolated from communal life are hopeless abstractions' (1927: 329).

We can argue whether Dewey would have considered web chat groups to be local but his sense of the mutual determination of technology and discourse should guard us against any tendency to treat new models of democracy as the reflex of technology. We can trace a direct line from him, through Habermas to the thinking about deliberative democracy that predates the Internet (Dryzek 1990, 2000; Held 2006: 231-55). But clearly, Dewey did not conceptualise democracy in exclusively national terms. The limits of such conceptualisations manifest themselves in two directions. First, as Ricardo Blaug has pointed out, the very abstracted preoccupation with the national level erodes the credibility of such theories. Little attention is paid to the actual small-scale group practices the theories are built on, the practices on which Dewey built his hopes. '[S]uch a lack is particularly troubling in deliberative democratic theory ... precisely because such fora are appealed to in order to provide the fair discursive input required for the state to be legitimate.' (Blaug 1999: 131)

Second, in their original version these 'island-polity' theories do not help in rescuing democracy under conditions of globalisation. But it appears that the concepts can be taken beyond the imagination of their creators. The current popularity of the notion of the public sphere, and of civil society conceived as having a primarily communicative political function, appears to be precisely related to processes of political globalisation. The fact that these are political concepts rooted not in the state but in society makes it possible and even desirable to begin thinking of them outside any necessary context of the state. Fraser advances this line of thinking by arguing that perhaps participatory democracy does not need a single public sphere, but multiple ones that contest each other (Fraser 1992).

Keane describes global public spheres as:

sites within global civil society where power struggles are visibly waged and witnessed by means other than violence and war: they are the narrated, imagined non-violent spaces within global civil society in which millions of people at various points on the earth witness the powers of governmental and non-governmental organisations being publicly named, monitored, praised and condemned, defying the old tyrannies of time and space ... [but] few of these are reducible to the dynamics of rational-critical argumentation about matters of sober truth and calm agreement. (Keane 2003: 169)

A recent volume edited by Peter Wagner has pointed out that, once Hegel is left out of the picture, there is in fact a historical tradition of civil society theory less predicated on the state. It defines civil society as 'a virtual space for deliberation that contains a plurality of yet undecided possibilities.' Civil society does need political institutions to consolidate and enforce decisions, but 'it is equally central...to think about this question in problematic terms. Civil society's need for institutions opens possibilities to which the already constituted contemporary state is only one of the many responses' (Wagner 2006: 231-232). However, it is not sufficient to just take the concepts of 'civil society' and 'public sphere' as found in the state-based tradition and stick the word 'global' in front of them. Selchow shows how such 'natural' usage of 'global' may only entrench what are primarily national outlooks, as in the US government's 'global war on terror'. Far more theoretical and empirical research is necessary before we can begin to understand how, or even whether, civil society in its communicative, legitimising aspect might function under the current much more confused political dispensation. We are, however, convinced that the old conceptual usages confined to nation states are now of strictly limited relevance.

In Chapter 6, de Oliveira urges national politicians to change their tune and engage differently with emancipated citizens and their technologies. We doubt whether they have the ability to do so. It is not just a matter of personality or style of governance: to some extent, they simply inhabit the wrong framework. First, is doubtful whether it would be possible under any circumstances to reform the command-and-control structure that is paradigmatic of the modern state into a more dynamic, horizontal, network-driven political structure. Second, the crisis of representative democracy cannot be separated from globalisation processes. Contemporary national governments have neither the capacity to deal with border-crossing phenomena that nowadays affect almost every area of politics, nor do they have the policy space to deviate significantly from neo-liberal prescriptions. It is therefore inadequate to think of the public spheres and public debates de Oliveira describes primarily in national terms. Instead they can begin to be a response, from global civil society, to the 'overlapping communities of fate' problem in contemporary politics.

The fact that we are only beginning to theorise the relationship between global civil society and the global public sphere expresses itself in the loose and varied use of the two expressions in the emerging literature. In Habermas, the associations of civil society are mediators between private individuals and the public sphere, distilling, transmitting, institutionalising discourses and inserting them into the public sphere (Habermas 1996: 367). In Keane on the other hand, just quoted above, multiple global public spheres are located inside global civil society. For Kaldor, the global public sphere is 'a global space where non-instrumental communication can take place' (Kaldor 2003: 8), while global civil society is the medium through which the social contract is negotiated. Eventually, after perhaps another decade of scholarship, this conceptual jumble on the relationship between our three key terms, global civil society, global public sphere and democracy will crystallise itself into more sharply defined positions. At this point, where we are all collectively groping towards a clearer comprehension of the emerging concepts and realities, we have left the field completely open for each author in this Yearbook to formulate their own understanding of the concepts and their interrelations.

Most authors in this volume treat both global civil society and the global public sphere either as an existing reality, or at the least as an achievable ideal. But are such assumptions at all justified? Critiques of global civil society have been aired in many previous Yearbooks. Here, we give some attention to the trenchant critiques of the notion of the 'global public sphere'.

Critiques of the global public sphere

In Habermas' ideal public sphere, 'access is guaranteed to all citizens' (1989: 136). But access is in fact limited in many ways. First there are those who explicitly exclude themselves from deliberative fora they deem illegitimate. As Iris Marion Young puts it, they typically 'make public noise outside while deliberation is supposedly taking place on the inside',

although sometimes they 'invade the houses of deliberation and disrupt their business' (Young 2001: 673). These disrupters, well-known figures in global civil society, can still be considered as part of the public sphere. They do after all 'aim to communicate specific ideas to a wide public' (2001: 676). They do, however, test the limits of the public sphere-related conception of civil society, particularly when the method of disruption is violent (see Albrow and Anheier 2006). Much more numerous are those who cannot participate.

First, access to global public spheres is still restricted by governments (see Chapter 5). Beyond deliberate obstruction by states, there is a wider problem with participation. As Ricardo Blaug puts it wryly:

Whether due to there being simply too many of us, to the excessive complexity and interdependence of the problems we face, to a perceived inefficiency of deliberation, or to a perceived lack of ability and motivation on the part of the demos, democratic theorists since Plato have taught us that the people, while being sovereign, require structures that limit their participation (Blaug 1999: 132).

The UN Panel on UN-Civil Society Relations follows in this tradition. It describes participatory democracy as a process in which 'anyone can enter the debates that most interest them, through advocacy, protest, and in other ways' (UN 2004: paragraph 13). But a few pages later it acknowledges that there are practical constraints: 'if the United Nations brought everyone relevant into each debate, it would have endless meetings without conclusion' (2004: paragraph 23).

Not only is participation limited, it is typically limited in ways that confirm existing power imbalances: 'under conditions of structural inequality, normal processes of deliberation often in practice restrict access to agents with greater resources, knowledge, or connections to those with greater control over the forum' (Young 2001: 680). Even at the very local level, Young sums up a number of barriers to participation by 'anyone with an interest':

Even when a series of public hearings are announced for an issue, people who might wish to speak at them need to know about them, be able to arrange their work and child care schedule to be able to attend, be able to get to them, and have enough understanding of the hearing process to participate. Each of these abilities is unevenly present among members of a society. (Young 2001: 680)

These constraints are of course multiplied at the global level. Discussions of inequality of access to public debates often focus rather crudely on geographical representation. The 'North' is over-represented, the 'South' muted. But many more subtle exclusions also operate. Almost without exception, the 'voices of global civil society' belong to an English-speaking, university-educated, computer-literate middle class. Within that class access to information is limited again by the commercial logic of websites and search engines. As Vincent Price points out in Chapter 1, Google channels the bulk of users to a set of sites produced mainly by the big media corporations. James Deane in Chapter 8 provides an extensive review of the tendencies towards the appropriation of communicative power and the consequent contraction of the public sphere. He highlights the use of the 'war on terror' to restrict freedom of expression, the concentration of media ownership, dependency on advertising, and a growth in the number of outlets that actually stifle genuine diversity of opinion.

As if universal access was not a tall enough order, a functioning public sphere also requires that all voices must be equally able to make themselves heard. As Benhabib has formulated it:

each participant must have an equal chance to initiate and to continue communication; each must have an equal chance to make assertions, recommendations, and explanations; all must have equal chances to express their wishes, desires and feelings; and finally, within dialogue, speakers must be free to thematize those power relations that in ordinary contexts would constrain the wholly free articulation of opinions and positions (Benhabib 1992: 89).

Inequalities in status based on gender, race, class, education or income are to 'bracketed', i.e. for the purposes of the dialogue they are to be treated as if they did not exist.

Finally, the public sphere requires the actors in it (to a greater or lesser extent, depending on the theorist) to be willing to abide by particular rules of process, and display a certain measure of respect for each other. At the minimum this would involve a rejection of using violence against each other. The nation state was to some extent capable of enforcing such respect, and excluding those who would not follow the rules of the process. In global civil society there is no such enforcement, and contributions to our book clearly show that conceptualisations of actually existing global civil society as prepared to voluntarily observe such rules are naïve. The National Rifle Association, discussed by Clifford Bob in Chapter 10, may be willing to abide by rules of non-violent debate, even if its ultimate aim is to arm everyone, but for the producers and publishers of *Jihad* videos, described by Thomas Keenan in the same Chapter, violence itself is the means of communication.

Much academic critique has been addressed to removing any lingering notion that these ideal conditions existed, or exist today, in liberal democracies (Fraser 1992; Benhabib 1992; Young 2001). The notion that equal access, equality of expression and mutual respect can exist in the uneven and fragile spaces of actually existing global civil society seem preposterous by comparison. These conditions can indeed only exist among a 'nation of gods'. They do not obtain on earth or in cyberspace.

Finally, even if an ideal-typical public sphere were taking shape in global civil society, one may wonder how it could eliminate the tendency to concentrate power. Instead of the kind of formal equality of access that the ideal type of the global public sphere requires, what is developing, in Monroe Price's analysis, are precisely the kind of inequalities of power that correspond to the formal equalities of market capitalism. Everyone going around expressing opinions, even freely and equally, is not enough. A democratic theory must also have something to do with decision making. In Habermas' conception, public opinion was somehow informing governmental decision making. How this link operated was always a problematic aspect of the theory, but it has not been theorised at all for the messy power landscape of political globalisation.

Building a global public sphere

These critiques seem to undermine the possibilities for new democratic forms based on civil society-as-communication. But there may be a rescue from a quarter that political theorists tend to neglect: actually existing global civil society. The ideal of a public sphere, or multiple spheres, of decision making based on communication and deliberation, has escaped from the clutches of the theorists into the real world. Global civil society as-is may not correspond to the ideal of a public sphere where free and equal deliberation takes place between all global citizens. But what one does find in global civil society is some adherents to the ideal, and numerous shaky attempts to practice it.

The new social movements of the 1970s already showed some affinity with this ideal, causing Habermas to revise his view of the public sphere from something once briefly glimpsed in the Enlightenment that could never return, to a 'less pessimistic assessment' of an ideal for which one could strive in practice (1992: 457). Since then, the newer global movements that have emerged have even more explicitly sought their salvation in an alternative politics of communication. The 'hacker ethic' of the first generation of computer geeks launched a wholesale attack on the foundations of modernity: the work ethic, the notion of private property, and command-and-control structures of governance (Himanen 2001). But the most enduring characteristic of that ethic has been the emphasis on 'open access' and free flows of information and communication, which has to date determined the architecture of the Internet. Beside this paramount achievement, the broad movement has spawned numerous other civil society initiatives built on the same norms, including the earliest internet worked email networks, the free software and open source movements, the Indymedia centres, Wikipedia. These are all expressions of, and contributions to, 'an emerging techno-political ethos' (Juris 2005) in global civil society. This ethos has now spread far beyond the original Western left-wing hacktivists: Box I.2 describes how the resistance of a single couple of Chinese homeowners to property developers became a *cause celebre* by moving from the blogosphere into the Chinese and Western mainstream media.

But the ideal has not only inspired cyberspace. The opening phrases of the World Social Forum Charter, now adopted by hundreds of regional, national and local social forums, could have been written by Habermas or Benhabib themselves. According to the Charter, a social forum 'is an open meeting place for reflective thinking, democratic debate of ideas, formulation of proposals, free exchange of experiences' etc. As the social forums chapter in *Global Civil Society 2005/6* put it, they 'give rise to uneven attempts to practise politics in horizontal, network-based ways that are meant to be more participatory and democratic than conventional structures' (Glasius and Timms, 2006: 190). Six years on from the first World Social Forum, our data suggest that the majority of social forums tend to survive, and new ones continue to be founded. (see map in record 9) Deliberative democracy has flown off the pages of the theorists' scholarly works and become a real-life aspiration for civil society activists.

In their transnational practices and focus on global issues, such as Darfur, climate change, or the Iraq war, these activists enact themes that have been central to theories of public opinion formation. As Vincent Price points out, the discursive model of public opinion formation sees it 'as part of a multifaceted social response to the widely shared problems recognised as issues.' The highly differentiated nature of this public with civil society activists as leaders and mass audiences is entirely congruent with global opinion formation under globalised conditions.

Moreover that discursive model has its impact in turn on the practices of NGOs, sensing the demands of a global public opinion and responding to the urgings of activists. In Chapter 7 Helmut Anheier's and Amber Hawkes' review of the shifting locus of accountability shows the backlash against the gross excesses of capitalist organisations like Enron has gathered pace and extended to NGOs, and joined up with a broader sense of social accountability that informs debate about new kinds of democracy for a globalised world. The self-critique of capitalist organisations looks suspiciously like the demand for participatory democracy and the checks and balances that advocates of communicative power to the people have long demanded. We might say 'suspiciously like' of course, because this rapprochement between the agents and critics of the global corporation looks very like a replay of the earlier compact between governments and NGOs. The rise of private equity that bypasses the constraints on public corporations suggests new power strategies by the owners of capital. We may now be moving to a new stage of the continuing struggle to sustain democracy: a kind of democracy-lite in the form of accountability being forced upon and embraced by the corporate sector.

It is in the practices of activists themselves where

Box I.2: 'China's Last Nailhouse'

In 1999, the term blog – literally 'web-log' – was coined. Since then, blogging has burgeoned - an estimated 75.2 million blogs have been indexed by Technorati (Technorati 2007). Blogging is enabled by the standard format software of the Web 2.0 user generated content platform, which allows anyone with a computer and Internet access to create, and easily update, their personal website or diary. It is not only the number of bloggers around the world, but the nature of this new sphere of communication that has important implications for global civil society, the mainstream media, governments of all political hues, and democracy.

One of the most beneficial and important effect of blogs must be the provision of alternative sources of information to the mainstream media, particularly in countries where traditional print and broadcast outlets may be censored (Pain 2005). The window bloggers open on events not covered by state-controlled media is of interest to activists, journalists and ordinary citizens alike, both within and beyond the country concerned. The fact that journalists in the mainstream media pay attention to blogs, and vice versa, and that newspapers and broadcasters encourage readers and listeners to respond and engage in online debates, indicates the extent to which the interactivity of the blogging phenomenon is changing how we communicate.

In non-democratic contexts, where blogging has proved a particularly attractive tool for dissidents and activists, the targeting of bloggers has increased in the last five years (see Boxes 5.4 and 5.5 in Chapter 5 of this volume). In such contexts, it would be easy to portray the blogger-state relationship as one of David and Goliath in the battle for freedom of expression, but the reality is more complex. Extremist views and incivility are inevitable in a system that is neither regulated nor mediated. Some commentators (admittedly mainstream journalists) argue that backbiting and lack of purpose is stalling the development of the blogosphere, which according to journalist Tim Dowling, is 'a seemingly intemperate, foul mouthed, grotesquely misogynistic community where no-one can spell and everyone is blessed with a surfeit of time' (Dowling 2007).

Such issues have met with two main responses. First, the creation of blog 'consolidators', which select blogs from around the world, aggregate them, and encourage debate that is regulated. Global Voices Online (URL) is one such initiative, founded in 2004 by Harvard Law School's Berkman Center for Internet and Society, which welcomes comments from anyone but moderates posts to weed out spam, hate speech and pornography. Second, and more ambitious, are proposals for self-regulation, most recently by Tim O'Reilly (who coined the phrase Web 2.0) and Jimmy Wales (founder of Wikipedia). They proposed a 'Blogger Code of Conduct', 'to promote personal expression and constructive conversation,' with kite-marks for those who comply (Blogging Wikia URL). However, this idea met with a predictable response from those who believe the lack of regulation is a key principle of the blogosphere (see for example Freedland 2007).

With so many and varied effects, it may be too soon to evaluate definitively the impacts of this young and evolving sphere of communication. However, its rich complexities and often unexpected effects encourage examination of a single, much-blogged incident in 2007, selected from a myriad possible examples, in the hope of better understanding some of the implications of the blogosphere – in particular for ordinary people.

'China's Last Nail House'[1] was first reported by bloggers in China on 27 February 2007. They relayed the story of couple Wu Ping and Wang Yu who since 2004 had fought against the demolition of their modest house to make way for a new development in the city of Chongqing, south west China[2]. Bloggers differed over the history and details of the story. But there was greater consensus about one thing: Wu Ping's feisty resistance of the developer and the authorities in defence of her rights made for a compelling story. Striking photographs of the slim, ramshackle building, perched atop the last unexcavated sliver of land in the midst of a huge construction site, doubtless kindled people's curiosity and appeal for the media – the house, adorned variously with protest banner and Wang Yu waving the Chinese flag, could be seen clearly from Chongqing's railway station.

From Chinese blogs, the story entered the mainstream media, both local and national, print and broadcast. Even the state run *China Daily* reported the story (URL). An illustration of the seamless traverse of information between

---

[1] *Ding zi hu literally 'nail house' in Chinese, refers to a household or person who refuses to vacate their home to make way for property development. Nail houses literally stick out like nails in an otherwise modern environment, and their owners, just like nails, refuse to be beaten down, to give in. See* http://www.virtual-china.org/2007/01/shanghais_stron.html

[2] *Many blogs, in English and Chinese, posted this story. For English language blogs, see* http://venture160.wordpress.com/2007/03/08/chinas-most-incredible-holdout/#comment-7 http://www.globalvoicesonline.org/2007/03/22/china-homeowners-hold-their-ground/

mainstream media and blogosphere was provided by blogger 'Matt', of *The Coffee House* (URL), who translated and posted the *Peering Into the Interior* post of 8 March (itself a translation of the *Southern Metropolis Daily* report), only to find the Chongqing Nail House pictured in Britain's *Daily Mirror* on 14 March (and in Metro Online edition of 11 March URL). 'Amazing how news stories go from obscurity to a global audience in a relatively short time frame these days. It's the Google thing ... and now anyone can play reporter!' says Matt (*The Coffee House* URL). This was the beginning of what was dubbed 'a media frenzy' over an incident that had been 'frothed up like crazy on the Web', according to Chongqing Mayor Wang Hongju (Gaofeng 2007). Newspapers and broadcasters around the world featured the story including, to name a few, *The New York Times*, *The International Herald Tribune*, the BBC, CNN, *The Globe and Mail*, and *The Guardian*. And in the 1,380,000 hits Google returns for 'China's last nail house' there must be many more media reports .

Debates in the blogosphere about this mainstream coverage ensued, not all of them complimentary. However, despite frequent disparagement from both sides, the relationship between bloggers and journalists is perhaps more mutually beneficial than either are prepared to admit – at the very least, as illustrated above, information flows rapidly between these spheres, adding to knowledge and magnifying interest. A catalyst to the 'Last Nail House' story spiraling around the world was Zola Zhou, 26, who arrived in Chongqing to investigate further, inspired by a self-professed sense of justice and the fear that coverage would be soon be censored (*Zuola* URL). John Kennedy, of Global Voices, translated the 23 March blog of Zhou, dubbed the 'nation's first citizen reporter':

As everyone knows, some reports of news like this which involves the government will surely never be reported, and [online] stories will be deleted at the request of unknown 'relevant departments'. There had been a Sina blog reporting 24 hours a day on the situation, but that blog later disappeared. That's why I realised this is a one-time chance, and so from far, far away I came to Chongqing to conduct a thorough investigation, in an attempt to understand a variety of viewpoints. (Kennedy 2007)

Indeed, the Chinese government reportedly attempted to suppress mainstream media coverage of the story and blocked online access to it via Google (Qiang 2007). Zhou's thorough and insightful investigation, during which he stumbled upon an unexpected discovery, may have contributed to the authorities' concern about the implications of the extensive media coverage (Global Voices URL). He found that people from as far away as Zhuhai, Chengdu, Xian and Shanghai, had come to Chongqing in the hope of publicising their stories of lost homes, inadequate or no compensation, and sometimes forced evictions. Among them was Mr Chen, from Zhuhai, Guangdong, who told Zhou that his home was torn down after residents were lured out of the building and beaten; and Ms Lui, of Chongqing, who protested against the inadequate compensation for her house in Huaxin village, Yu district (Global Voices URL).

Mr Chen heard about Chongqing's Nail House on Phoenix Television. It seems that the extensive coverage and passage of a new law guaranteeing private property rights (which Wu Ping used in her defence), galvanised others who felt similarly wronged to vent their feelings in a bid for redress. According to Yang Zhizhu, assistant professor at the China Youth University for Political Science, 'It was precisely the universality across the country of this brutal eviction and demolition, of insufficient or delayed compensation, that generated such sympathy and support for the "toughest nail house"' (quoted by Bandurski 2007). Struggles between residents and developers are common in China's rapidly developing cities, and the implications of the agreement reached eventually over the Chongqing Nail House for citizens' rights and the public sphere were discussed widely online and in print.

In addition to catalysing ordinary citizens in China, the Chongqing saga encouraged the exchange of similar experiences over the blogosphere. For example, 'Louise' describes a struggle between Brooklyn developers and residents:

The situation is not that different here in Brooklyn, USA. Developers want to seize six homes that residents claim are part of the Underground Railroad of the Civil War era. The City has tried all sorts of tactics to discredit the residents. It seems like the same story gets repeated over and over: 'selfish and possibly crazy holdouts preventing progress.' (Virtual China URL)

The blogosphere is a communication space where the struggles over rights, hitherto defined as national, involve an appeal to an aspiration for transnational, or global, standards.

Fiona Holland, Centre for the Study of Global Governance, LSE

[1] *As of 15 April 2007.*

we find responses adequate to the challenge posed by the unprecedented levels of the power of capital. For instance, as Victor Pickard describes in Chapter 10, Indymedia is committed to radical democratic practices in its networks both locally and globally, yet whether this is adequate to the task of democratising global governance is open to question when, as Clifford Bob shows, the same technologies are open to the National Rifle Association and, as Thomas Keenan describes, are central to the idea of global *Jihad*. Deane shows that activists are now going beyond attempts to practice deliberative democracy within their own spaces, to address global governance structures with the new norm of a 'right to communicate.' Yet that right has to be guaranteed in some way and the dilemmas around which the debate between Lippman and Dewey revolved, between management of information, individual participation and democratic decision making, are ever more acute in a world confronted with global issues that require collective responses. Global civil society is forced to engage with state structures if it is to secure their democratisation. It has to take communicative democracy to the centre of state power if it is to build global governance and redress the inequalities that stand in the way of adequate action on a global scale.

The climate change debate: evidence for a global public sphere?

The climate change debate is an interesting case for the hypothesis of a global public sphere, in that mutual accusations of shutting down debate are an integral part of the debate itself. There is no doubt that the environmental mainstream would in fact like to close part of the debate, namely that part that still questions whether climate change is occurring and whether it is caused by human behaviour, in order to move on to discussing policy and behavourial change. Continuing to give air to the climate change sceptics gives politicians somewhere to hide, and obstructs progress on the latter half of the agenda. But from the vantage point of the public sphere as a form of democratic practice, any attempt to shut down other voices is problematic. What, if any, should be the limits to what can be debated in a global public sphere, and who sets the limits? Holocaust denial is criminalised in many countries, although in Iran it is government policy. But can climate change denial really be likened to Holocaust denial? Climate

sceptics see such equivalence as only a first step, and warn darkly of eco-dictatorship, predicated on the notion that human beings will not adapt their consumptive behaviours willingly.

In an ideal-typical public sphere, attempting to shut down the 'whether' debate would not only violate the rules, but also be unnecessary. Faced with all the available evidence presented on both sides, the freely deliberating public would naturally make the 'right' choice, and public opinion would move on to discussing remedies. In Europe, the debate is indeed moving in that direction. According to de Oliveira's optimistic assessment, if the debate remains open and vibrant, no 'eco-fascist' measures will be required: in energy consumption as in other areas, the public, having understood what is necessary, is capable of profound behavioural change (see Chapter 6). This remains to be seen.

Of course, the climate change debate does not fulfil the ideal requirements of universal access and equality of voices anywhere in the world. But it is important to note that it is much more unequal in some places than in others. In the United States, the Union of Concerned Scientists found that ExxonMobil had funnelled nearly $16 million between 1998 and 2005 to a network of 43 'climate sceptic' advocacy organisations in order to influence the debate (Union of Concerned Scientists 2007). Additionally, a majority of climate scientists working at federal agencies surveyed reported constraints in climate-related work, documenting 435 incidents of political interference over the past five years (Monbiot 2007). In such circumstances it takes the crowbar of a former US Vice-President's feature documentary to even open the debate.

How, or whether, the climate change debate is developing in other parts of the world is more difficult to assess. A poll by Worldpublicopinion.org renders some surprising results, which would appear to negate any relationship between general openness of the political climate and inclination to take action on climate change. According to this poll, Indians are least concerned, followed by Russians. Among the Chinese polled, on the other hand, 42% approve immediate action even at significant cost, and another 41% believes the problem needs to be tackled gradually with low cost policies (Worldpublicopinion.org 2007a). However, as Vincent Price warns, global polls of this kind come with severe methodological health warnings, the usual problems of methodological variation, leading questions, and unrepresentative samples being compounded by cultural differences of understanding. And Africans, expected to experience the worst consequences of climate change, are not included in the poll.

It does seems likely that there are multiple global public spheres when it comes to climate change, partly determined by political boundaries and partly by political predilection, but they do stand in connection with each other. The reports of the Intergovernmental Panel on Climate Change, for instance, may be presumed to penetrate into the different spheres. The subject has in all likelihood gone beyond the level of the attentive public, and begun to impinge on the awareness of what Price calls 'mass audiences'. While the debate on 'whether' is polarised into two camps, the debate on remedies is far more varied, lively, and indeed deliberative. However, participation is very uneven, causing actors in global civil society to do much perilous speaking 'on behalf of' potentially threatened populations in parts of Africa or the Pacific islands. Meanwhile, it is clear that, probably due to a combination of influential reports and unusual weather, the climate change debate has experienced a sudden elevation to the higher regions of political agendas. To what extent policy and citizen behaviour will be affected remains open.

Conclusion

In the networks and forums surrounding global issues, civil society finds a powerful way to challenge governments and has discovered the full potential of rights to free speech and association that hitherto were national preserves. Even as governments resist the possibility of developing representative democracy for the globe, so the communicative democracy of civil society gains in legitimacy.

The possibilities this opens for the development of new models of democracy for the global age is one of the most exciting frontiers of knowledge and practice. Industrial society and nation states produced parliaments, elections and representation as modernity's characteristic institutional form, both in liberal or totalitarian states. Whether the global information society will generate an equivalent institutional locus for democracy is the big issue that this Yearbook leaves open.

By addressing this issue civil society, as we now

know it, may find that it is the answer and not as Rousseau thought the problem. Even he conceded grudgingly that if there had to be private associations of citizens in the state, then it would be better for there to be more rather than fewer, 'that the people may not be deceived' (1762 [1895]: 124). It is the associational diversity of civil society that provides the basis for communicative democracy and a fertile contrast with the monolithic citizen-state relationship of representative democracy.

On past experience the new institutions will only develop and become adequate for the tasks ahead if global civil society debates democracy and communication for itself and the world at large as explicitly as did theorists of democracy for the modern age that has past. The Yearbook is our contribution to promoting that debate.

REFERENCES

Albrow, Martin and Helmut Anheier (2007) 'Violence and the Possibility of Global Civility' in Mary Kaldor, Martin Albrow, Helmut Anheier, Marlies Glasius, (eds) *Global Civil Society 2006/7*. London: Sage.

Allott, Daniel (2007) 'A Real (Military) Solution To Darfur'. *Weekly Standard*, 25 March. http://www.cbsnews.com/stories/2007/03/23/opinion/main2601005.shtml

Anderson, Kenneth (2000) 'The Ottawa Convention Banning Landmines, the Role of International Non-governmental Organizations and the Idea of International Civil Society'. *European Journal of International Law*, 11/1: 91–120.

Barber, Benjamin (1984) *Strong Democracy: Participatory Politics for a New Age*. Berkeley: University of California Press.

Bandurski, David (2007) 'Chinese media and Web users discuss the winners and losers following demolition of China's "toughest nail house"', 4 April. China Media Project, Hong Kong University.

Benhabib, Seyla (1992) 'Models of Public Space: Hannah Arendt, the Liberal Tradition, and Jurgen Habermas' in Craig Calhoun (ed) *Habermas and the Public Sphere*. Cambridge, Mass: MIT Press.

Bessette, Joseph (1980) 'Deliberative Democracy: the Majority Principle in Republican Government' in Robert A. Goldwin and William A. Schambra (eds) How Democratic is the Constitution? Washington: American Enterprise Institute for Public Policy Research.

Blaug, Ricardo (1999) *Democracy, Real and Ideal: Discourse Ethics and Radical Politics*. Albany: State University of New York Press.

Blogging Wikia, http://blogging.wikia.com/wiki/blogger%27s_Code_of_Conduct

Carey, John (1989) *Communication as Culture: Essays on Media and Society.* London: Routledge.

China Daily (2007) '"Nail house" in Chongqing demolished', 3 April. http://www.chinadaily.com.cn/china/2007-04/03/content_842221.htm

Chomsky, Noam and Herman E (1988) *Manufacturing Consent: The Political Economy of the Mass Media*. New York: Pantheon.

Cohen, Jean and Andrew Arato (1994) *Civil Society and Political Theory*. Cambridge, Mass: MIT Press.

Cohen, Joshua and Joel Rogers (1983) *On Democracy: Toward a Transformation of American Society*. Harmondsworth: Penguin.

Dewey, John (1927) [1981] *The Public and its Problems* in *John Dewey: The Later Works*, 1925-53, vol. 10. Carbondale: Southern Illinois Press.

Dryzek, John (1990) Discursive Democracy: Politics, Policy and Science. Cambridge: Cambridge University Press.

Dryzek, John (2000) *Deliberative Democracy and Beyond: Liberals, Critics, Contestations*. Oxford: Oxford University Press.

Dowling, Tim (2007) 'Comedy of manners', *The Guardian*, 14 April.

Falk, Richard (1993) 'The Making of Global Citizenship' in J. Brecher, J.B. Childs and J. Cutler (eds) Global Visions: Beyond the New World Order. Boston: South End Press.

Fraser, Nancy (1992) 'Rethinking the Public Sphere: A Contribution to the Critique of Actually Existing Democracy' in Craig Calhoun (ed) *Habermas and the Public Sphere*. Cambridge, Mass: MIT Press.

Freedland, Jonathan (2007) 'The blogosphere risks putting of everyone but point-scoring males', *The Guardian*, 11 April.

Gaofeng, Lu (2007) 'Media Overexcited in "Nail House"' *China Youth Daily*, 29 March posted and translated by David Bandurski 'China Youth Daily editorial calls for greater professionalism in Chongqing "nail house" reports', China Media Project, Hong Kong University. http://cmp.hku.hk/look/article.tpl?IdLanguage=1&IdPublication=1&NrIssue=1&NrSection=100&NrArticle=828

Glasius, Marlies (2003) 'Global Civil Society: Theories and Practices' in Paul van Seters, Bas de Gaay Fortman and Arie de Ruijter (eds) Globalization and Its New Divides. Alblasserdam: Dutch University Press.

Glasius, Marlies and Jill Timms (2006) 'Social Forums: Radical Beacon or Strategic Infrastructure?' in Marlies Glasius, Mary Kaldor, Helmut Anheier (eds) Global Civil Society 2005/6. London: Sage.

Global Voices Online, http://www.globalvoicesonline.org

Gutmann, Amy and Dennis Thompson (1996) *Democracy and Disagreement*. Cambridge, Mass: Belknap Press.

Habermas, Jürgen (1989 [1962]) *The Structural Transformation of the Public Sphere*. Cambridge: Polity Press.

— (1989) 'The Public Sphere: An Encyclopedia Article'. In Stephen Eric Bronner and Douglas MacKay Kellner (eds) *Critical Theory and Society: A Reader.* London: Routledge.

— (1992) 'Further Reflections on the Public Sphere' in Craig Calhoun (ed) *Habermas and the Public Sphere*. Cambridge, Mass: MIT Press.

— (1996) *Between Facts and Norms: Contributions to a Discourse Theory of Law and Democracy*. Cambridge: Polity Press.

Held, David (1995) *Democracy and the Global Order: From the Modern State to Cosmopolitan Governance*. Cambridge: Polity Press.

— (2002) 'Globalization After September 11th'. Global Transformations website, Polity Press. http://www.polity.co.uk/global/after_sept11.htm

— (2006) *Models of Democracy*. 3rd edition. Cambridge: Polity Press.

Himanen, Pekka (2001) *Hacker Ethic*. Random House.

Juris, Jeffrey S (2005) 'The New Digital Media and Activist Networking within Anti-Corporate Globalization Movements'. Annals of the American Academy for Political and Social Science, No. 597, January. 189-208.

Kaldor, Mary (2003) *Global Civil Society: An Answer to War*. Cambridge: Polity Press.

Kaldor, Mary, Helmut Anheier and Marlies Glasius (2004) 'Introduction' in Helmut Anhier, Marlies Glasius and Mary Kaldor (eds) *Global Civil Society 2004/5*. London: Sage.

Keane, John (2003) *Global Civil Society?* Cambridge: Cambridge University Press.

Keck, Margaret and Kathryn Sikkink (1998) 'Transnational Networks on Violence against Women in Margaret Keck and Kathryn Sikkink, *Activists beyond Borders: Advocacy Networks in International Politics.*

Kennedy, John (2007) 'China: Nation's first citizen reporter?', Global Voices Online, 30 March. http://www.globalvoicesonline.org/2007/03/30/china-nations-first-citizen-reporter/

Lippman, Walter (1922) *Public Opinion.* London: George Allen & Unwin.

McLuhan, Marshall (1962) *The Gutenberg Galaxy.* Toronto: Toronto University Press.

McGrew, Anthony (1997) The Transformation of Democracy? Globalization and Territorial Democracy. Cambridge: Polity Press.

Mayes, Ian (2007) 'Open Door: the readers' editor on coverage of the execution of Saddam Hussein,' *The Guardian*, 8th January.

Metro, http://www.metro.co.uk/news/article.html?in_article_id=40673&in_page_id=34&ito=newsnow

Monbiot, George (2007) 'There is Climate Change Censorship - and it's the Deniers who Dish it out'. *The Guardian*, 10 April.

Pain, Julien (2005) 'Bloggers, the New Heralds of Free Expression' in *The Handbook for Bloggers and Cyber-Dissidents,* Reporters Without Borders, September. http://www.rsf.org/IMG/pdf/handbook_bloggers_cyberdissidents-GB.pdf

Pateman, Carole (1970) *Participation and Democratic Theory.* London: Cambridge University Press.

Qiang, Xiao (2007) 'Chinese Government Forbids Coverage of the "Nailhouse" Story', *China Digital Times*, 23 March. http://chinadigitaltimes.net/2007/03/chinese_govern ment_forbidden_media_reports_about_the_na.php

Rousseau, Jean-Jacques (1762) [1895] translated by H. Tozer. *The Social Contract or Principles of Political Right.* London: George Allen & Unwin

Scholte, Jan Aart (2001) 'Civil Society and Democracy in Global Governance' (CSGR Working Paper No.65/01). Warwick University: Centre for the Study of Globalisation and Regionalisation.

Sebastian, Don (2007) 'Saddam Hussein lives on in Kerala', *Daily News and Analysis*, 31 December. http://www.dnaindia.com/report.asp?NewsID=1072152

Technorati (2007) 'State of the Blogosphere', April. http://technorati.com/weblog/2007/04/328.html

The Coffee House, http://environmentdebate.wordpress.com /2007/03/08/one-chinese-mans-battle-to-save-his-environment/

United Nations (2004) *We the Peoples: Civil Society, the United Nations and Global Governance.* Report of the Panel of Eminent Persons on United Nations-Civil Society Relations. UN Doc. A/58/817.

Union of Concerned Scientists (2007) *Smoke, Mirrors & Hot Air: How ExxonMobil Uses Big Tobacco's Tactics to Manufacture Uncertainty on Climate Science.* http://www.ucsusa.org/global_warming/science/exxonmobil-smoke-mirrors-hot.html

Virtual China, http://www.virtualchina.org/2007/03/ another_chinese.html

Wagner, Peter (ed) (2006) *The Languages of Civil Society.* New York: Berghahn.

Wallas, Graham (1914) *The Great Society: A Psychological Analysis.* London: Macmillan.

Worldpublicopinion.org (2007a) 'Poll Finds Worldwide Agreement That Climate Change is a Threat; Publics Divide Over Whether Costly Steps Are Needed'. 13 March. http://www.worldpublicopinion.org/pipa/pdf/mar07/CCGA+_ClimateChange_article.pdf

World Social Forum Charter of Principles, http://www.forumsocial mundial.org.br/main.php?id_menu=4&cd_language=2

Young, Iris Marion (2001) 'Activist Challenges to Democracy', *Political Theory*, Vol.29, No.5, October.

Zuola, http://www.zuola.com/weblog/

CHAPTER 1

DEMOCRACY, GLOBAL PUBLICS AND WORLD OPINION
Vincent Price

Democracy, global publics and world opinion

'In politics communication makes possible public opinion', wrote the prominent American sociologist Charles Horton Cooley in 1909, 'which, when organized, is democracy'. At the dawn of the last century, observing a rapidly developing system of global communication based upon 'the telegraph, the newspaper and the fast mail' (1909: 85), Cooley discerned an important connection between the revolution in communication and the rise of democracy, arguing that the latter was promoted, not because of changes in the formal Constitution, but rather 'as the outcome of conditions which make it natural for the people to have and to express a consciousness regarding questions of the day' (1909: 86). Ever the optimist, he opined that popular education and progressive developments in the media would enlarge and quicken social organisation, fostering an international consciousness in literature, science and politics, and promising 'indefinite enlargement of justice and amity'.

Although his optimism strikes one as rather naïve and proved, if nothing else, to be ill-timed – within a decade of Cooley's writing, Europe, Asia and North American would plunge into World War I – his words nonetheless have quite a modern ring, echoing the sometimes breathless language one encounters today in discussions of the global revolution in communication, the ascendancy of new forms of global civil society and the consequent upsetting of national structures.

One is often impressed with the thought that there ought to be some wider name than democracy for the modern movement, a name that should more distinctly suggest the enlargement and quickening of the general mind, of which the formal rule of the people is only one among many manifestations. The current of new life that is sweeping with augmenting force through the older structures of society, now carrying them away, now leaving them outwardly undisturbed, has no adequate name. (Cooley 1909: 86–7).

Even if what Cooley wrote a century ago was perhaps not entirely justified, such language may be appropriate in 2007. Developments in digital and network technologies have been particularly dramatic over the past several decades, helping to create widely dispersed and decentralised systems of communication that are nonetheless thoroughly interconnected, with media flows increasingly crossing national and continental boarders. The largely centralised, national, limited-channel mass media systems of the twentieth century have given way to much more variegated, multi-channel systems embracing a wide range of alternative media reaching across geopolitical borders. These changes in communication are generally viewed as significant for their democratising potential and are linked in various ways to a flowering of civil society on an increasingly global scale, and to an expansion of popular political participation.

On the other hand, present optimism may seem to readers a century hence just as naïve and ill-timed as Cooley's. As Kaldor argues in this volume, despite the diffusion of free market economic practices and national elections, people are increasingly subject to the effects of commercial and political decisions made outside their countries, let alone their local communities (see Chapter 2 of this volume). Hence the propagation of democratic procedure may not signal a true expansion of popular influence over collective action.

What can be stated perhaps more confidently, Kaldor proposes, is that the congruence has broken down between the state, its people, economy and territory. With the worldwide expansion of media and commerce, nations around the world are increasingly subject to informal but consequential global constraints. National governments forced to contend with an expanding web of international agreements are less able to control flows of information and opinion and, in the face of global social norms and pressures, must now take into account not only public opinion within their borders, but the opinions of

How does global public opinion shape state actions?

external constituencies as well. States have always been responsive to informal public pressure, but usually within their own jurisdictional boundaries: foreign pressures were usually mediated almost entirely by states. Now international pressures are felt more directly through externally controlled media, organised non-governmental groups, attentive international publics and their opinions.

The rise of so-called 'public diplomacy' illustrates the emergent order, testifying both to the perception of global public opinion as a powerful new field of political forces and to the predictable impulse of states to gain control over these forces. Traditional diplomacy used to be a matter of governments engaging one another through a system of formally negotiated contacts, with embassy officials representing state interests in the host countries. Public diplomacy, by contrast, is oriented toward informal constellations of individuals and non-governmental organisation (NGOs). 'Global public opinion,' explains the website of the UK Foreign Policy Centre (2007), 'is increasingly a strategic concern for states acting on the world stage'. The expanding reach of communication networks enables such opinion to form and influence state behaviour. However, communicative influence flows in both directions, for as the Centre points out, new media

systems increasingly provide governments 'with the ability to bypass heads of foreign states to pursue their foreign policy agendas'.

How then, might we understand global publics and world opinion and their role in constraining or shaping state actions? The purpose of this chapter is twofold. First, we explore the concept of world opinion. Drawing from discursive conceptualisations of publics and public opinion, we distinguish global publics from global civil society. The latter is primarily a structural concept, represented by a variety of non-state institutions and organisations, while the former is of a more virtual and ephemeral nature, a complex function of widespread discussion and emergent patterns of association. Second, we turn to global media systems, examining the ways in which world publics depend upon these systems for their modes of interaction and development. Here we briefly consider recent trends in communication and their implications for the behaviour of publics on a global scale.

Conceptualising world opinion

Are 'world opinion' or 'global public opinion' merely rhetorical expressions, or do they express important sociological realities? In a fundamental way, the concepts are imaginary in nature and yet they may have quite real manifestations and effects. At its core,

the idea of world opinion refers to a means of informal social control, whereby the ability of leaders, organisations or governments to act as they wish rises or falls, expands or constricts, due to their perceived standing or reputation among interested publics around the globe. Both the reputational standing and the publics involved are in the order of 'useful fictions', widely believed and hence taken into account in calculations about what can be done, by whom, with what possible political consequences.

Imaginary aspects of world opinion

Since its earliest deployment, the idea of public opinion has retained a dual character, referring to the imagined views of imagined communities, but also to the very real power of such imaginings to constrain, and even to direct, state actions. With the diminuition of European royal power during the eighteenth century, both monarchs and their opponents began to invoke 'the public' as a new source of authority and legitimacy for their competing claims (Ozouf 1988; Baker 1990). The term was at that time, like the world public of today, ill-defined and without a readily identifiable sociological referent. Though it was linked with the viewpoints circulating among educated men of financial means, it often acquired (as in the writings of Rousseau in 1762/1968) an abstract and almost superhuman quality as an expression of the common will, divined through reasoned debate and framed as the paramount source of political legitimacy.

Central to the concept was the widening reach of political information and discussion though newspapers, pamphlets and other media, which brought an increasingly diverse group of non-state actors into closer familiarity with state affairs. Coupled with the growth of the merchant classes and a growing awareness of the monarchy's dependence upon these classes for financial support, the reach of the political media fostered a growing awareness of a new, virtual assembly of citizens who asserted the right to have their opinions on state affairs taken into account. According to Peters (1995), the European Enlightenment transformed the classical, Athenian assembly of the people into a mass-mediated, fictive body constituted by newspapers that could bring people together, not in physical space, but in shared conversations at a distance. Today, such virtual assemblies are constituted by a wide range of media – radio, television, print media, the Internet and worldwide web as well as mobile telephony – and have consequently grown beyond national and regional dimensions, acquiring transnational and transcontinental scale.

To acknowledge the virtual and imaginary qualities of world opinion, however, is not to deny that the concept captures new empirical realities as well. As Peters (1995: 16) put it in discussing the Enlightenment, 'in acting upon symbolic representations of "the public" the public can come to exist as a real actor'. The eighteenth-century concept of public opinion had more than merely rhetorical qualities: it signalled the emerging social customs, manners and later, shared political views of an ascendant class of literate and well-read European merchants, courtiers and intellectuals congregating in new popular institutions such as salons and coffee houses (Speier 1950). World opinion today signals the social customs, perceptions and opinions of more diverse classes of people throughout the world, following global events and issues and congregating in Internet exchanges, demonstrations and, occasionally, world forums.

A public or a crowd?

Sociological aspects of world opinion

When sociological writers of the late nineteenth and early twentieth centuries began to give public opinion more systematic attention as a phenomenon of social behaviour, they framed the public as an elemental, spontaneously developing collective that arises in reaction to an issue and which is organised into factions through discussion over time. Park (1904/1972) distinguished the public from the crowd, another spontaneous form of collective action organised through communication (as described, for instance, by LeBon 1895/1960). Both were social groupings that were loosely organised in reaction to some common object of attention or concern, and that thus lacked features characteristic of a society, such as shared norms, to direct their collective action. Both took shape through communication among members. However, their defining means of organisation differed, in Park's view. In a crowd, the organising principle is a dominant, widely shared emotion, communicated from one person to another via imitation and contagion. Crowds are thus uniform and impulsive in their action. In a public, on the other hand, the organising principle is disagreement, communicated through discussion. The public actively decides its action through debate.

Park argued that publics and crowds are alike in one key respect: they are proto-societal forms of collective action resulting when societal norms and structures are not in place to direct behaviour. The public is, particularly in its earliest forms, an ephemeral grouping rather than a social organisation per se; however, in the course of acting the public becomes increasingly organised through shared attention, discussion, opinion formation and political action. Factions emerge, coalitions form and interrelated processes of ideological and social organisation unfold as shared viewpoints become associated with definable subgroups (Price 1992).

The twentieth century brought considerable sociological attention to a third form of elemental collective behaviour, the mass (Kornhauser 1959). Like the crowd and the public, the mass is proto-societal in nature, constituted though communication and generating its own emergent norms (Blumer 1946). However, in contrast to the crowd, which is constituted through shared emotion, or the public, which is constituted through debate and discussion, the mass is generated merely through giving shared attention to the same object, person or event. This shared attention is all that aggregates people into a mass; they respond as anonymous individuals according to their diverse needs and interests, and do not interact to determine a course of action. Consequently masses form no common will, as do publics or crowds. Masses, for this reason, tend to be quite heterogeneous in their make-up, being largely contiguous with the audiences of various media of mass communication. Whether or not global media systems today have fostered the growth of worldwide crowds or publics, they almost certainly have expanded the size of mass audiences attending to, for instance, World Cup football, the Olympics, international politics, popular celebrities, and disasters both natural and man-made, such as the 2001 terrorist attacks on the World Trade Center or the 2004 Indian Ocean tsunami.

Temporal and spatial aspects of world opinion

According to the discursive model (Foote and Hart 1953; Price 1992), public opinion is understood as developing through each of these various forms of communication – mass attention, public discussion and emotional contagion – unfolding over time as part of a multi-faceted social response to widely shared problems recognised as issues. There are inevitably fuzzy boundaries to the crowds, publics and masses surrounding any single issue, boundaries that are continuously reconfigured as the problem is at first recognised, then becomes the object of media attention, the subject of discussion, the focus of more formal policy debates and, eventually, the object of organised collective action.

The discursive model proposes that the public is highly differentiated in terms of the roles various members play in the processes of public debate and decision. A small minority plays a distinct leadership role, aggressively pursuing its favoured actions, while at the other end of the participatory continuum are much larger mass audiences that do little more than receive information about the issue and retain some

of it. Price and Neijens (1997) distinguish six different types of actors in public debate, arrayed roughly from the smallest and most active groups to the largest and least active aggregates. Political leaders, policy experts and interest groups comprise the 'elites', both within and outside the sphere of formal government who play active roles throughout all the phases of decision making (we place NGOs and public advocacy groups in the last of these categories). Members of the press serve as critical conduits for information and opinion exchange between these elites, as well as to their followers in attentive publics, made up of people following the issue, discussing it and forming opinions and, finally, to more expansive but minimally engaged mass audiences.

Publics may be conceived then, as a complex blending of active and passive segments, of engaged citizens and mere spectators (Lippmann 1922; Blumer 1946). The size, composition and geographic scope of these segments change across issues and over time. As problems confronting citizens around the world are increasingly global in their nature and effects – immigration, global warming, transnational dislocations of service industries and the like – they should accordingly evoke discursive reactions unfolding on a worldwide scale. Hence a 'world public' is an exceedingly difficult entity to identify precisely. Like all publics, it is loosely organised around a particular issue through communication, includes both active and passive strata, and changes in size, geographic reach and social make-up as it passes into and out of existence with the lifecycle of a given issue (Price 1992: 33).

Publics may also be conceived as a complex blending of stable organisational relationships and newly formed social associations, opinion alignments and political cleavages. Publics can be distinguished from civil society along these lines. The latter refers to a structure of organised group relationships ranging from informal but stable community groups to formal organisations operating as interest groups or advocacy groups, or in modern parlance, NGOs or social movement organisations.[1]

Public discussion and opinion formation naturally follow existing channels of social organisation, but issues divide and recombine these organised relationships in new ways. Global publics are, in this sense, at the leading edge of global civil society. They are highly variable in their composition, depending upon the issue at hand, and they change in size and shape as issues are first recognised, understood, debated and decided upon. The discursive opinion-formation process unfolds in two interrelated ways: one is primarily ideological in nature and has to do with the various perspectives or frames of reference on an issue as these come to be widely understood by members of a public, and the other is primarily sociological in nature and has to do with the 'sides' of an issue, defined by the types of people and groups adopting different positions. Once a particular issue has been debated and decided, communication about it gradually dissipates.

However, the highly active and organised groups within the public can continue to function, taking on quasi-institutional forms as advocacy groups or developing, through continued successive coalitions arising through public debate, into political parties representing views on multiple issues. As Price (1992) notes, the organisational remnants of one issue become the backdrop for the next. Publics allow political organisations to adapt and change and they also permit new associations to be formed. World publics thus have the effect of globalising existing national parties through, for example, coalitions such as the Global Greens, for advocacy of environmentalism and grassroots democracy, or the International Democrat Union, for advocacy of conservative and Christian democratic values. They also give rise to novel transnational social movements (known as TSMOs; Smith et al. 1997), some of which become formally organised to pursue particular global issues and spanning multiple countries, such as Greenpeace or Amnesty International.

Observing global publics and world opinion

The history of international opinion research stretches back at least 50 years to the founding of World Association for Public Opinion Research, established in 1947 to promote the opinion research around the world and to foster international cooperation and exchange among academic and commercial researchers. However, attempts to assess world opinion have increased dramatically over the past years. Virtually all of these efforts have involved comparative national opinion surveys. For example, the Gallup World Poll, a proprietary venture of the Gallup Organization, carries out random-digit-dial and face-to-face surveys (using clustered sampling designs) in dozens of countries around the world. Gallup completed a poll of the Islamic World with surveys of nine predominantly Muslim countries in 2002 and of 19 sub-Saharan African nations in 2006.

Other efforts along these lines include WorldPublicOpinion.org (URL), launched in 2006 by the Program on International Policy Attitudes of the University of Maryland, which relies upon a network of survey research centres and commercial forms in 25 countries to conduct studies of view across the globe, and the Pew Global Attitudes Project, which recently surveyed 13 countries from March to May 2006. The problems involved in conducting such comparative surveys – stemming from language differences, non-equivalent sampling designs and survey modes, the difficulties of maintaining consistently rigorous fieldwork across vastly different geographical and cultural settings – are considerable, but they can be reduced through careful design and implementation. For example, the World Values Survey, an outgrowth of comparative studies undertaken by the European Value Systems Study Group beginning in the late 1970s (Moor 1995), is now a formal consortium of member organisations that agree to field a common questionnaire (a translation from a standard English version upon which the entire member group has agreed) and adhere to a set of shared technical and methodological specifications.

These efforts have been significant and highly informative, for example, in assessing how the populations of many nations perceive other countries or the degree to which they oppose the US-led war in Iraq. However, they assess mass opinion, as conceptualised above, and hence capture only one aspect – and perhaps not the most telling aspect – of world opinion. As the modern field of public opinion research emerged and gained prominence in the latter part of the twentieth century, and particularly as it adopted probability-sampling and survey methods as its main research techniques, it evoked persistent criticism for having implicitly embraced mass opinion rather than

---

1 This conceptualisation of global civil society in structural terms helps to distinguish it from publics, crowds and masses, as explicated here. Others have adopted more expansive definitions of global civil society, subsuming all the proto-societal processes of primary interest here. As Anheier et al. (2001: 17) note, 'part of the attraction of the term "global civil society" is that different people feel at home with different conceptions of it'.

*'Issue publics' follow particular issues closely, demanding
responsiveness and accountability from political leaders*

public opinion as its primary object of study (Blumer
1948; Bogart 1972; Graber 1982).

Alternatively, analysts have sometimes turned to
studies of elites or organisational leaders, attempting
to examine opinion among those who have a
significant stake or influence in the matter at hand.
Just such an effort is now underway by the
commercial firm Environics, under the auspices of the
2020 Fund, to identify and survey stakeholders
concerned with globalisation and its underlying
economic, environmental and social equity challenges
(2020 Fund 2007). The traditional sociological
conception of the public related above, frames it not
as any fixed geopolitical entity, however, but as a
loosely organised subset of the mass, akin to what is
sometimes known in political science as an 'issue
public' or 'special public' (Almond 1950; Key 1961;
Converse 1964). These are people who follow
particular issues with close and relatively continuous
attention, engage political leaders and the media over
these issues and demand some degree of elite
responsiveness and accountability.

How are we to define these fluid segments of the
world population? Typical and reasonable starting
points involve identifying those who are most
knowledgeable about the particular issue at hand,
those with the most intense opinions, or those who
vote with their feet by getting involved in political
action (Devine 1970; Krosnick 1990). However, Price et
al. (2006) found in a recent study of health care reform
in the US that that knowledge about health care,

strong opinions on health care issues and health-
related political activity were relatively independent,
pointing to a need for a very careful consideration of
how membership in issue publics might be variously
defined and studied. All three of these dimensions are
implicated in political movements. Knowledge
facilitates the reception and comprehension of
information and enables the effective advocacy of
one's position. But in the absence of well-formed
opinions and motivations to engage politically,
knowledge may not translate into effective public
opinion. For both theoretical and practical reasons
then, we are well advised to avoid overly simplified
observational models of issue publics.

Beyond general population surveys, we can also turn
to content analyses of world media (Rusciano et al.
1997), interviews with non-governmental elites (in
NGOs and businesses) and data monitoring of Internet
exchanges (such as in blogs and discussion boards).
No matter what observational techniques are used,
over time arrays of data are necessary to capture
dynamic public opinion processes and to establish the
manner in which it interacts with state policy outputs.
These observational tasks may well seem daunting to
the point of near impossibility; though we do well to
bear in mind that the assemblage of elaborate cross-
national poll data, which is becoming increasingly
routine today, would have seemed similarly fantastic
just a few decades ago.

Conceptualising the role of global media systems

The discursive model accords communication
systems and practices a number of central roles in
the development of publics and public opinion. In their
watchdog role, the media act as surveillance agents,
monitoring the behaviour of political elites, alerting
audiences to potential problems and enabling
attentive publics to form around elite disagreements.
Even more critically, they act as a means of
correlating and coordinating disparate internal
responses to these problems by bringing together
contrasting views, offering a forum for airing the
debate through which the public develops and helping
opinion coalitions to form (Laswell 1948). Less
obviously but no less important, the media perform
these same functions for political elites (Price 1992).

Media characterisations of opinion in the attentive
public, for example, may serve to help correlate the

public's responses, but at the same time they also serve a surveillance function for political elites (by allowing them to monitor the public's behaviour). Likewise, news of about other political actors permits political elites to learn about, understand and react to one another (and hence correlating elite responses to problems). Thus, the same piece of news or information conveyed by the media may perform different functions for different actors in the process, depending upon one's point of view. By conveying information from elites to publics and vice versa and by connecting popular wishes to elite decisions the media serve a linkage function (performing on a continual and informal basis, though much less precisely, what electoral systems seek to accomplish).

Without some mass system of communication, only relatively small attention aggregates could ever form around particular objects, events, or issues. The broader the reach of media systems, the larger the potential scale of attention and interest aggregation. The more interactive and conversational the system, the greater its potential to facilitate interest aggregates that begin to talk, to form and to exchange opinions, that is, to form publics in the sense outlined above. The global reach and conversational capacities of contemporary media systems should, at least in theory, foster international or global public awareness, opinion formation and political participation – just as Cooley proposed a hundred years ago.

On the matter of scale, there is little doubt that the increasingly global reach of the media has produced correspondingly large attention aggregates (for example, the World Cup draws a television audience in the hundreds of millions). Whether global media systems foster public debate, however, or facilitate the formation and development of autonomous world publics, are much more difficult questions to address. Critics have raised a number of concerns about how well twentieth-century mass media carried out these public functions, and these concerns are useful to bear in mind. To many analysts and observers, the press – particularly the commercial news media – has been far more dedicated to gaining audience attention than to serving as an effective watchdog, much less a vital forum for free-flowing disagreement and debate or as an agitator spurring widespread public action (Laswell 1948; Carey 1978).

© Mark Henley/Panos Pictures

Can the great society be a great community?
The democratic character of public communication and opinion formation can be difficult to maintain even in small decision-making bodies, as status and knowledge differences emerge, where those with unpopular views may prove reticent, and where racial, religious, or other cleavages prevent open and equitable exchanges (Mansbridge 1983). As communication systems expand, as participants in that system become heterogeneous and widely dispersed and as the problems at stake become more specialised and distant, the difficulties become all the more significant.

A fair, open, bottom-up discursive process incorporating widespread popular participation is

2 *Writings of the nineteenth and twentieth centuries tended to valorize the public as rational and deliberative, defining it as a kind of counter-concept to the crowd, which was thought to reflect baser emotional impulses that tended to corrupt public opinion (Price 1992). The privileging of rational discourse has been heavily criticised by scholars of many stripes, including feminist scholars, who argue that this bias often serves elite interests and marginalises as unreasonable critical views expressed emotionally. As noted above, the discursive model of public opinion formation frames it as developing through a confluence of multiple, interacting communicative processes, incorporating discussion, mass attention and crowd behaviour, unfolding over time around issues (see Foote and Hart 1953, or, for a similar argument about understanding crowds in the development of social movements, Oliver 1989).*

GLOBAL PUBLICS AND WORLD OPINION

27

viewed by most as a desirable goal for public communication. Views about the capacities of both the media and of citizens, and hence of the quality of mass-mediated public opinion, however, vary considerably. Early twentieth-century analysts were often fearful that the rational, discursive behaviour of publics, in particular, might be easily subverted by propagandistic emotional appeals and thus that in so many ways publics would devolve into crowds (Park 1904/1972).[2] Lippmann (1922), for instance, expressed profound doubts about the ability of the news media to convey much more than fragmentary and simplistic accounts of the complex issues facing modern citizens, who, in turn, have little time or inclination to acquire accurate knowledge of the political world. He thus placed very little faith in the wisdom of public opinion in the 'great society' (Wallas 1914), which he saw as shallow and based upon incomplete and inadequate stereotypes.

Lippmann argued that collective decision making unfolds best when it is a carefully managed, elite and technocratic affair, with elected leaders and expert policy advisors deciding the course of collective action and then organising public opinion for the masses. Others, while not necessarily more sanguine about the quality of the standard commercial news media, expressed far greater confidence in the capacities of ordinary citizens. In response to Lippmann, Dewey (1927) argued that, while the 'great society' would never possess all the desirable qualities of a local community, a 'great community' of true democratic character was nevertheless achievable. '[T]he essential need' for such a great community, Dewey posited, was improved 'methods and conditions of debate, discussion, and persuasion' (1927: 208). Given 'artful presentations' circulated through a sort of community-based social science, people would – given sufficient education – indeed be able to develop sound, independent opinions and provide useful guidance to policy makers.

Numerous writers on public opinion and the media expressed deep concern, particularly after World War II, that publics had been displaced by mass behaviour. Mass communication, as opposed to true public communication, is characterised by strong vertical (usually downward) flows of information and opinion and weak or non-existent citizen-to-citizen or horizontal exchanges of any meaningful kind. Critics of mid-twentieth-century communication systems

(such as Mills 1956) and of the burgeoning field of opinion polling (Blumer 1948) saw them both as substituting mass opinion for public opinion. The latter is autonomous and emerges from the give-and-take of public discussion, while the former is merely a product of numerous coincidental but uncoordinated individual responses to the mass media. It is thus media-dependent, poorly reasoned and impulsive. Publics fall prey to the media that act as part of a manipulative culture industry (Kellner 2000) which, owing largely to commercial imperatives, constitutes the public, not as an actively deliberating body, but instead as a passive, spectator-like body of political consumers (Ginsberg 1986). Habermas (1962/1989) captured many of these concerns in his influential thesis that the public sphere – an open, sovereign and egalitarian arena of popular debate operating independently of the state and commercial spheres – had largely collapsed in modern welfare states, having been thoroughly suffused with state and commercial influence.

New hopes for global media

Against this backdrop of traditional doubt and concern, recent trends in media systems have given renewed hope for expanded public discourse, freer flows of information and newly invigorated publics. The past decades have witnessed dramatic declines in the cost of producing and distributing messages and, with satellite communications, especially dramatic declines in the sensitivity of cost to geographical distance. As communication bandwidth has expanded, multi-channel media systems have become the norm in many parts of the world, significantly reducing the gatekeeping authority of traditional broadcasting organisations. The social-networking capabilities of new media systems have also facilitated the organisation and coordination of political action across geographical boundaries.

When combined with the liberalisation of media ownership in many nations, these trends have contributed to an apparent blossoming of alternative media willing to challenge mainstream news organisations, along with a growing sense of basic 'rights to communicate' around the world (see chapter 8 of this volume). The ability of ordinary citizens to publish online and to participate in creating and editing news reports using collaborative Wiki software has led to speculation about new forms of grassroots citizen

Will dramatic changes in media systems foster public debate or develop public opinion?

journalism. The success of meet-ups and flash mobs arranged through the Internet or via mobile phones has fuelled predictions of revolutionary changes in social and political organisation (Rheingold 2002; Trippi 2004). An array of e-government and e-democracy initiatives has been launched, with the goal of improving government responsiveness to ordinary citizens and improving public accountability. Advocates of civic journalism and deliberative democracy have been working aggressively to advance a variety of media reforms, including active support for programmes of community discussion sponsored by news organisations, the growth of alternative, community-based and community-operated media and other ways of activating and engaging readers, listeners and viewers.

At the same time, it is unclear for a number of reasons whether recent trends in global media systems will have the hoped-for effects on publics or on the quality of public opinion. First, the deployment of new information and communication technologies (ICTs) will in all likelihood exhibit clear path dependencies (Pierson 2004). Innovation and the diffusion of political and communication practices are likely to follow lines of established cultural compatibility, locking-in on modifications of current practice and compromising potentially valuable alternative designs. Both scholars and practitioners in

the new information society tend to carry a number of implicit assumptions in their largely technocratic and market-focused vision of the future (Pyati 2005; Sarikakas 2004). Emerging economic and structural relationships are viewed as inevitable, with many viewing private–public partnerships as a necessary part of the future. Thus, judgements are likely to be made about the democratic value of ICTs without due consideration of the paths *not* taken – for example, publicly controlled, rather than commercially developed and controlled media.

We may just as easily fall prey to faulty assumptions about the inherent democratic propensities of new, open media systems. Despite a general sense that the Internet significantly expands access to audiences by lowering barriers to market entry, for example, recent studies actually find a remarkable degree of market concentration in audience traffic to political websites. Indeed, Hindman et al. (2003) find that the online audiences may even exhibit more and not less concentration than those of the traditional media such as broadcasting. While the Internet has without question increased access to electronic publishing, Hindman et al. (2003) argue that the rapid expansion of online content has increased the importance of filtering and search mechanisms like Google, channelling the bulk of users to the same restricted set of sites rising to the top of the 'Googlearchy' (sites that are in large part produced by conventional media corporations).

There are other ways in which the new interactive media, despite in theory offering an opening for new voices in public debate, can simply reproduce business as usual. There are of course well-known digital divides between those with and without access to ICTs; but even when such access is equitable, more enduring divides may persist between those knowledgeable or interested enough to engage in politics and those who are, for one reason or another, never drawn into play. Hindman (2006), noting the much touted ability of the 'blogosphere' to counter the mainstream media, finds from an analysis of the top 80 political blogs in the US that these sites are produced by a group that is overwhelmingly male (93 per cent), virtually all white and drawn from the professional ranks of lawyers, political consultants, journalists and policy experts.

Third, the advent of highly flexible, multi-channel media systems, which in principle allow for greater circulation of public affairs information, may conceivably have the effect of reducing rather than expanding the broad distribution of news and information. Recent research by Prior (2002) and others suggests that increasing consumer choice, at least in the US media market, has come largely at the expense of news, the audience for which has been dwindling as entertainment-oriented outlets draw readers, viewers and listeners away in significant numbers. Tewksbury (2003) finds a similar pattern in studies tracking users of news websites. With their newfound freedom to navigate media sites, users tend to seek entertainment and celebrity-related information in place of national or international news and public affairs. At the same time, the remaining audience for public affairs programming has fractured, as people look for news and opinions that match their own ideological commitments and judge the credibility of the press from their own ideological viewpoints (Pew Research Center 2004). Such findings fuel concerns about the centrifugal forces at work in new media systems, which may produce a pattern of one-sided information consumption and a widening gulf between the politically engaged and unengaged and thereby reduce the deliberative character of public opinion.

Finally, changes in media systems are confounded with numerous other global changes, seriously complicating judgments about the effects of communication *per se*. The adaptation of new technologies is ongoing and ever evolving, with ICTs put to many different purposes by myriad users, advocacy groups and governments. This has produced a wide open field of experimental application. Anecdotal stories of success may be found, but these successful deployments of the new media are not easily separated from the larger, democratically oriented efforts in which they are embedded. Thus, the same ends might well have been achieved by other means. The effects of new communication technologies then, are difficult to disentangle from the effects of other ongoing processes, such as the liberalisation of markets, the reform of education, or infusions of foreign subsidies. Communication effects, even if they can be isolated, are also not constant over the course of diffusion. Complex systems are very difficult to observe, given changes in what is done (that is, the introduction of new behaviour), changes in how things are done (performing existing functions in new ways) and changes in who does things and with whom.

There remain then, a number of key questions to address in discussing the nature of the information society. It is unclear at present whether the changes in communication systems will indeed produce entirely new forms of organisation, as Rhinegold (2002) and Trippi (2004) have proposed, or instead, much more modest extensions and refinements of current political practice (as proposed by Bimber 2003). Even less clear is whether these organisations will behave in a democratic fashion. Exactly what sort of leverage can reasonably be exerted by ordinary citizens, vis-à-vis the well-funded and highly organised interests of governmental, commercial and often extra-local or extra-national NGOs?

The road ahead

Elsewhere in this Yearbook authors consider whether globalisation, and in particular the globalisation of the media, has indeed fostered the development of larger, more inclusive publics and a widening of democratic discourse spanning nations and continents. Some propose that global civil society and international media development have served to open authoritarian regimes to greater public influence. Others take a somewhat darker view, focusing on the role of large, well-organised and heavily funded special interest groups in derailing open discourse and thwarting popular desires.

This Chapter has taken a purposefully broad view of

the connection between civil society and democratic practice, framing discursive publics as both 'democracy in practice' and 'civil society in the making.' Efforts to chart the changing contours of global civil society and monitor developments in the worldwide use of television, radio, newspapers and the Internet should continue, as should further development of international mass opinion surveys, stakeholder surveys, comparative content analyses and the like. If we are to understand properly the rise of global public opinion and its putative role in constraining key institutions and global actors, however, these efforts will need to be coordinated around particular issues and designed in such a way that they can be profitably examined as parallel time-series. Mapping the virtual, discursive terrain surrounding issues of global import and better understanding attentive publics and mass audiences worldwide will require both great imagination and sustained collaborative effort. We need more than simply improved snapshot assessments of mass opinion or opinion among the most attentive segments of the population, or NGO leaders or government officials, or of messages distributed via the media. Instead, what is needed is better empirical leverage on the interaction of these various phenomena around particular issues over time – some means of gauging the changing relationships between institutional behaviour, media behaviour and the behaviour of publics, crowds and masses as problems emerge and are contested. The ideal would be a set of linked and comparable observations spanning national borders and assessing comparative beliefs, feelings and opinions across each of these collective constituencies over the life-course of an issue. Such data would permit a dynamic appraisal of the influences flowing bottom-up or top-down, putting to test suppositions of democratic decision making. Data arrays are not presently available, but they are at least no longer inconceivable. Given the substantial costs and logistical difficulty, such data are not likely to emerge without the systematic coordination of the many, varied and inevitably partial efforts now underway worldwide. One hopes the Yearbook has fostered, and will in the future accelerate, coordination of this kind.

2020 Fund (2007) *The Global Stakeholder Panel Initiative on Globalization and Global Governance.* from http://www.2020fund.org/gsp2/2020.htm (consulted 4 May 2007).

Almond, G (1950) *The American People and Foreign Policy.* New York: Harcourt.

Anheier, H, Glasius, M and Kaldor, M (2001) 'Introducing Global Civil Society', in H Anheier, M Glasius and M Kaldor (eds) *Global Civil Society 2001.* Oxford: Oxford University Press.

Baker, K M (1990) 'Public Opinion As Political Invention', in K M Baker *Inventing the French Revolution: Essays on French Political Culture in the Eighteenth Century.* Cambridge: Cambridge University Press.

Bimber, B (2003) *Information and American Democracy: Technology in the Evolution of Political Power.* Cambridge: Cambridge University Press.

Blumer, H (1946) 'Collective Behavior', in A M Lee (ed) *New Outlines of the Principles of Sociology.* New York: Barnes and Noble.

Blumer, H (1948) 'Public Opinion and Public Opinion Polling', *American Sociological Review,* 13: 542–54.

Bogart, L (1972) Silent Politics: *Polls and the Awareness of Public Opinion.* New York: John Wiley.

Carey, J (1978) 'A Plea for the University Tradition', *Journalism Quarterly,* 55: 846–55.

Converse, P E (1964) 'The Nature of Belief Systems in Mass Publics', in D E Apter (ed) *Ideology and Discontent.* New York: Free Press.

Cooley, C H (1909) *Social Organization: a Study of the Larger Mind.* New York: Charles Scribner.

Devine, D J (1970) *The Attentive Public: Polyarchical Democracy.* Chicago: Rand McNally.

Dewey, J (1927) *The Public and Its Problems.* New York: Holt, Rinehart & Winston.

Foote, N N and Hart, C W (1953) 'Public Opinion and Collective Behavior', in M Sherif and M O Wilson (eds) *Group Relations at the Crossroads.* New York: Harper & Bros.

Foreign Policy Centre (2007) *Public Diplomacy.* http://fpc.org.uk/topics/public-diplomacy/ (consulted 9 March 2007).

Ginsberg, B (1986) *The Captive Public*: *How Mass Opinion Promotes State Power.* New York: Basic Books.

Graber, D A (1982) 'The Impact of Media Research on Public Opinion Studies', in D C Whitney, E Wartella, and S Windahl (eds) *Mass Communication Review Yearbook.* Vol. 3. Beverly Hills, CA: Sage.

Habermas, J (1962/1989) *The Structural Transformation of the Public Sphere*: *an Inquiry into a Category of Bourgeois Society* (T Burger, trans.) Cambridge, MA: MIT Press.

Hindman, M (2006) *From Production to From Production to Filtering: Changing Patterns of Online Exclusivity.* Presentation to the Oxford Internet Institute Workshop on 'The World Wide Web and Access to Knowledge' Oxford, February.

Hindman, M, Tsioutsiouliklisz, K and Johnson, J A (2003) '"Googlearchy": How a Few Heavily-Linked Sites Dominate Politics'. Presented at the Annual Meeting of the Midwest Political Science Association, Chicago, IL, March.

Kellner, D (2000) 'Habermas, the Public Sphere, and Democracy: A Critical Intervention', in L Hahn (ed) *Perspectives on Habermas.* Chicago, IL: Open Court Press.

Key, V O Jr (1961) *Public Opinion and American Democracy.* New York: Knopf.

Kornhauser, J A (1959) *The Politics of Mass Society.* New York: Free Press.

Krosnick, J A (1990) 'Government Policy and Citizen Passion: A Study of Issue Publics in Contemporary America', *Political Behavior,* 12: 59–92.

Laswell, H (1948) 'The Structure and Function of Mass Communication in Society', in L Bryson, (ed) *The Communication of Ideas.* New York: Harper & Row.

LeBon, G (1895/1960) *The Crowd.* (R K Merton, ed) New York: Viking.

Lippmann, W (1922) *Public Opinion.* New York: Harcourt Brace Jovanovich.

Mansbridge, J J (1983) *Beyond Adversary Democracy.* Chicago, IL: University of Chicago Press.

Mills, C W (1956) *The Power Elite.* Oxford: Oxford University Press.

Moor, R A de, (ed) (1995) *Values in Western Societies.* Tilberg: Tilberg University Press.

Oliver, P E (1989) 'Bringing the Crowd Back In: The Nonorganizational Elements of Social Movements', *Research in Social Movements, Conflict and Change,* 11: 1–30.

Ozouf, M (1988) '"Public Opinion" at the End of the Old Regime', *Journal of Modern History,* 60: S1–S21.

Park, R E (1904/1972) *The Crowd and the Public and Other Essays,* (ed) H Elsner, Jr (trans.) C Elsner. Chicago, IL: University of Chicago Press.

Peters, J D (1995) 'Historical Tensions in the Concept of Public Opinion', in T L Glasser and C T Salmon (eds) *Public Opinion and the Communication of Consent.* New York: Guilford Press.

Pew Research Center (2004) *News Audiences Increasingly Polarized*: Online News Audience Larger, More Diverse. Washington DC: Pew Research Center for the People and the Press.

Pierson, P (2004) *Politics in Time: History, Institutions, and Social Analysis.* Princeton, NJ: Princeton University Press.

Price, V (1992) *Public Opinion.* Newbury Park, CA: Sage.

Price, V and Neijens, P (1997) 'Opinion Quality in Public Opinion Research', *International Journal of Public Opinion Research,* 9: 336–60.

Price, V, David, C, Goldthorpe, B, McCoy Roth, M and Cappella, J N (2006) 'Locating the Issue Public: the Multidimensional Nature of Engagement with Health Care Reform', *Political Behavior,* 28: 33–63.

Prior, M (2002) 'Efficient Choice, Inefficient Democracy? The Implications of Cable and Internet Access for Political Knowledge and Voter Turnout', in Cranor, L F and Greenstein, S (eds) *Communications Policy and Information Technology: Promises, Problems, Prospects.* Cambridge, MA: MIT Press.

Pyati, A K (2005) WSIS: 'Whose Vision of an Information Society?' *First Monday,* 10(5) May. http://firstmonday.org/issues/issue10_5/pyati/index.html (consulted 30 May 2007).

Rheingold, H (2002) *Smart Mobs: The Next Social Revolution.* Cambridge, MA: Basic Books.

Rousseau, J J (1762/1968) *The Social Contract.* (Cranston, M, trans.) Harmondsworth: Penguin.

Rusciano, F, Fiske-Rusciano, R and Wang, M (1997) 'The Impact of "World Opinion" on National Identity', *Press/Politics*, 2: 71–92.

Sarikakis, K (2004) 'Ideology and Policy: Notes on the Shaping of the Internet', *First Monday*, 9(8) August. http://firstmonday.org/issues/issue9_8/sarikakis/index.html (consulted 30 May 2007).

Smith, J, Pagnucco, R and Chatfield, C (1997) *Transnational Social Movements and Global Politics: Solidarity Beyond the State*. Syracuse, NY: Syracuse University Press.

Speier, H (1950) 'Historical Development of Public Opinion', *American Journal of Sociology*, 55: 376–388.

Trippi, J (2004) *The Revolution Will Not Be Televised: Democracy, the Internet, and the Overthrow of Everything*. New York: Harper Collins.

Tewksbury, D (2003) 'What Do Americans Really Want to Know? Tracking the Behavior of News Readers on the Internet', *Journal of Communication*.

Wallas, G (1914) *The Great Society*. London: Macmillan.

WorldPublicOpinion.org (URL) http://www.worldpublicopinion.org/pipa/about.php?nid=&id=

CHAPTER 2

DEMOCRACY AND GLOBALISATION

Mary Kaldor

Our international engagement, our democracy promotion, our development assistance, our public diplomacy - all of these efforts are vital to our nation's defense and well-being. [...]When democracy is in retreat, America is vulnerable; and when democracy is on the march, we are more secure.[...]And so when we talk about it among senior staff, I don't ever talk about the competition or the conflict between our democracy promotion and our interests. I think you would be hard-pressed to hear that I've ever said that, because I see them as one.

Condoleezza Rice 2007

With domestic actions being increasingly constrained by international actions, individuals can only meaningfully participate in the decisions that affect them, if these international processes are democratic.

Joseph Stiglitz 2007

The last three decades of the twentieth century witnessed the global spread of democratic institutions. In 1974, when the Portuguese dictatorship was overthrown, there were only 39 countries classified as democratic by Freedom House out of a total of 145 countries. By 1997 this had increased to 117 out of a total of 191 countries. In other words, whereas roughly a quarter of the countries in the world were classified as democracies in 1974, this had increased to over 60 per cent by 1997 (Diamond 1999). Democratisation spread from Southern Europe (1970s) to Latin America and East Asia (1980s), and to Central and Eastern Europe and Africa from 1989 to the early 1990s. Although some of these countries have moved out of the democratic category, others have joined them, especially post-conflict countries, where elections are often held as an exit strategy for the international community. Samuel Huntington (1991) dubbed this recent spread of democracy as the 'third wave' of democratisation.[1]

In this Chapter, I argue that the spread of democratic institutions has to be understood in the context of globalisation. Common rules and procedures provide an institutional basis for the global connectedness of states. This is what Condeleezza Rice is hoping for; to create partners for the United States on the global stage. But the spread of rules and procedures is not the same as the spread of substantive democracy, by which I mean the possibility for ordinary people in different parts of the world to influence the decisions that affect their lives. Despite the spread of formal democracy, substantive democracy is under erosion everywhere, in the UK as

well as other countries. I argue that this has something to do with globalisation. If we are to renew the democratic process, then it is not just a matter of spreading the formal procedures of democracy, it also requires new fora which provide access for ordinary people to all levels of governance (local, national, global) and a new responsiveness at all levels of governance to public debate and deliberation, as the quotation from Joseph Stiglitz makes clear. In other words, it requires the possibility of negotiating a global social covenant.

Interestingly, most of the literature on what is known as democratic transition focuses on the national level. Within the globalisation literature, there is a lot of discussion of the global democratic deficit but this is rarely taken into account in the democratisation literature. This is why the gap between formal and substantive democracy is usually explained in terms of the legacy of authoritarianism or the weakness of democratic culture, despite the fact that the gap characterises older Western democracies as well as newly democratic countries.

In developing this argument, I start by elaborating the distinction between formal and substantive democracy. I then discuss the spread of formal democracy and argue that this has to be understood primarily as a process of global integration, the way in which the practices and institutions needed to participate in the global market and in global decision

---

[1]   *The first two waves, both of which ended with a reverse wave, were 1828 to 1926 and 1943 to 1964.*

making are constructed. The various techniques of democracy promotion determine the terms of integration. The more bottom-up the approach, the more the emphasis is on dialogue and communication, the more favourable the terms and the greater the possibilities for substantive democracy. Global civil society, I suggest, is the mechanism for reconciling national and global levels and deepening substantive democracy. In the last section, I will discuss the need for a global framework for democracy and some of the steps that could be taken to advance substantive democracy at different levels.

Democracy is not just about free and fair elections

Formal versus substantive democracy

A few years ago I undertook an evaluation of the EU's democracy programmes in Central and Eastern Europe. This included organising seminars in which participants were asked what they understood by the term democracy. When a seminar was organised in Brussels, the participants firstly emphasised elections, and secondarily, institutions like an independent judiciary, the separation of the legislature from the executive, or even an active civil society. When the seminars were organised in the newly democratic Central and East European countries, the answers were much more subjective. 'It means that bureaucrats are our servants, even if they do not realise it', said a Polish woman. 'It means that we have to take individual responsibility for decisions and decide for ourselves what we think about political issues instead of following what we are told', said a young Georgian. And a Romanian girl talked about the new opportunities to choose a life, to be able to travel and to follow one's own interests.

This difference between democracy as a set of procedures or institutions and democracy as the expression or framework for a more subjective notion of freedom has been widely discussed in the literature on political thought. There have always been varying usages and definitions of the term 'democracy'. As George Orwell pointed out:

[N]ot only is there no agreed definition but the attempt to make one is resisted from all sides...The defenders of any kind of regime claim that it is a democracy and fear they might have to stop using the word if it were tied down to any one meaning. (1957: 149).

For de Tocqueville, democracy had essentially two meanings: one was a political regime that was accountable to the people and defined in terms of a range of institutional and procedural mechanisms; the other was a condition of society characterised by its tendency towards equality. This societal democratic condition, the 'habits of the heart', could not be reduced to the formal institutional aspects of democracy. He travelled to America to observe this societal condition and was much impressed by what he called 'democratic expedients' such as lively newspapers, local government and above all, the practice of association. According to de Tocqueville 'if men are to remain civilised or to become so, the art of associating together must grow and improve in the same ratio as the equality of conditions is increased' (1945: 118).

By formal democracy, I mean the framework of rules and institutions that provide the necessary conditions in which members of a community can shape their own lives to the extent that this does not conflict with others (Held 1995). These institutions encompass an inclusive citizenship, the rule of law, the separation of powers (executive, legislature and judiciary), including an independent judiciary capable of upholding a constitution, elected power holders, free and fair elections, freedom of expression and alternative sources of information, associational autonomy, and civilian control over the security forces (Kaldor and Vejvoda 1998). By substantive democracy, I mean a process, which has to be continually reproduced, for maximising the opportunities for all individuals to shape their own lives and to participate in and influence debates about public decisions that affect them.

This difference between procedural and substantive democracy is paralleled by two other distinctions often drawn in democratic theory. One is the distinction between popular or direct democracy and liberal or representative democracy. Athens is the paradigmatic example of direct democracy, while liberal representative models emerged at the end of the eighteenth century in Western Europe and North America (Held 2006). The latter was often called the republican model because it drew on the experience of Republican Rome and the city states of Italy. Until the twentieth century, democracy tended to be equated with direct democracy. For this reason, political theorists were sceptical of democracy because they feared that if every citizen participated directly in decision making, it would lead to what we now call populism, decisions based on fear and prejudice rather than the public use of reason. The liberal democratic model was supposed to resolve this problem by electing representatives who would engage in rational debates about key decisions. The representatives were not supposed to express particular positions or special interests; they were supposed to debate the public good. In his famous speech to the electors of Bristol, Edmund Burke pointed out that:

Parliament is not a Congress of Ambassadors from different and hostile interests; which interests each must maintain, as an Agent and Advocate, against other Agents and Advocates; but Parliament is a deliberative Assembly of one Nation, with one Interest, that of the whole; where, not local Purposes, not local Prejudices ought to guide, but the general Good, resulting from the general Reason of the whole. (Burke 1774)

The other distinction that parallels that between formal and substantive democracy is that between democracy as a method and democracy as a goal. For Joseph Schumpeter, democracy was viewed as a relatively efficient method of choosing a government, which he likened to a steam engine or a disinfectant. He defined this method as 'that institutional arrangement for arriving at political decisions in which individuals acquire the power to decide by means of a competitive struggle for the people's vote' (1961: 269). The idea that political contestation is likely to produce the best outcome in terms of decision making is the political counterpart of the economic

idea that competition in the marketplace will lead to economic efficiency. This Schumpeterian view of democracy contrasts with the idea that democracy is an end in itself, a process through which individuals can realise their aspirations.

Liberal representative models of democracy and the notion of democracy as a method of choosing a government tend to emphasise procedures and institutions both as defining characteristics of democracy and as safeguards against what Kant called 'democratic despotism'. But while procedures and institutions are the necessary condition for substantive democracy and while it seems true that nothing better than the liberal representative model of democracy has been invented, these are not sufficient to ensure that individuals can influence the conditions in which they live. Undoubtedly, attempts to represent the 'social condition' as the pre-eminent 'substantive value', as in the former Communist countries, led to tyranny in the twentieth century. On the other hand, formal procedures can easily be subverted or 'hollowed out' without an underlying normative commitment to democracy embedded in society.

The global spread of democracy

The 'third wave' of democracy gave rise to great optimism in the 1990s and ideas like Francis Fukuyama's 'end of history' expressed the conviction that the world was finally discovering that liberal representative democracy, combined with free markets, constituted the best possible system of governance. As Gia Nodia, a Georgian democracy specialist, put it:

The most basic contention that lay at the basis of third-wave optimism was the notion that democracy is now the only "normal" political regime – the only game in the global village, if you will. At the end of the day, democracy is the only political regime that is fully compatible with modernity. (quoted in Carothers 2004: 193)

Yet despite the spread of democratic institutions, there remains a big gap between formal and substantive democracy. Many of the countries classified as democracies perform poorly on Freedom House's freedom scores, which are made up of a combination of political rights and civil liberties. In many countries, democratic procedures that have been specified in laws and constitutions are only partially implemented. Thus newly emerging democracies may be characterised, in varying combinations, by a weak rule of law, the lack of an independent judiciary, limitations on freedom of speech and association, ethnic or religious exclusion, election fraud, and presidential domination. These procedural weaknesses are often associated with substantive weaknesses, including the tendency for political parties to extend control over different spheres of social life in ways that limit political participation, especially in former Communist countries; a tendency for the government to control the electronic media and restrict registration of NGOs; a politicised and clientilistic administration; various forms of racist or xenophobic sectarianism which may provide a basis for populism; and a widespread sense of personal insecurity that undermines the ability and readiness to debate public issues owing to inadequate law enforcement and an undeveloped judiciary. Participation is also often limited, as evidenced by low voter turnouts, low membership of political parties, and widespread apathy, disillusion and cynicism. Indeed, the introduction of democratic procedures, especially elections, may lead to conflict, state failure and/or elective dictatorship, and only a very few countries in Central and Southern Europe or South America have escaped this fate.

Thomas Carothers, in a widely quoted article, 'The End of the Transition paradigm', suggests that most so-called transition countries have actually entered a 'political grey zone' characterised by two broad types – 'feckless pluralism' (Latin America) or 'dominant power politics' (the post-Communist world, Africa and the Middle East) (Carothers 2004: 193). A number of other terms have been used to describe these types of polity, including illiberal democracy, pseudo democracy, cosmetic democracy, façade democracy, semi-democracy, or virtual democracy.

The gap between formal and substantive democracy is usually explained in terms of the legacy of authoritarianism. And this is an important factor. The anomie, submissiveness and passivity of individuals, the experience of patronage and clientilism, the suspicion of parties, politicians and bureaucrats, the pervasiveness of exclusivist ideologies – these can all contribute to a profoundly distorted and traumatised 'societal condition'. But one or two authors point out that the gap, while larger in newly emerging democracies, can be found in older democracies as

well. Thus Carothers talks about the 'syndrome of post-modern fatigue with democracy and perhaps politics itself' (Carothers 2004: 150). So the legacy of authoritarianism cannot be the whole explanation.

Others point to the 'simultaneity' problem - the fact that the transition to democracy is taking place at the same time as the transition from a statist planned economy to a market system. The introduction of economic liberalisation and privatisation has often led to dramatic falls in income and deterioration in public services, as well as increased inequality. These all contribute to dissatisfaction with the political class (see Bozoki in Kaldor and Vejvoda 1998; also Elster, Offe and Preuss 1998).

But what is rarely discussed in the literature on 'transition' or newly emerging democracies is the global context. Those who write about democratisation tend to analyse the process almost entirely within a national or comparative framework. Yet the spread of democratisation has coincided with the speeding up of the process known as globalisation – growing interconnectedness in political, economic, or cultural spheres. Theorists of globalisation point to the global democratic deficit which results from the speeding up of globalisation (Archibugi, Held and Köhler 1998). In the context of globalisation, democracy, in a substantive sense, is undermined. This is because, however perfect the formal institutions, so many important decisions that affect people's lives are no longer taken at the level of the state. Democracy assumes congruence between the state, the people, the economy and territory. Yet this congruence no longer exists. Increased migration means that 'the people' cross boundaries and live in multicultural global cities. The economy is increasingly global, shaped by the decisions of global companies, free floating speculators, and international financial institutions. States have to take into account a range of international agreements, which constrain national choices (Held et al. 1999).

This applies to all countries to a greater or lesser degree. What is the meaning of elections when, for example, decisions about the size of budgets, environmental regulations, or war and peace are taken in Washington, Brussels or New York? In other words, is not the gap between formal and substantive democracy that we observe in the newly emerging democracies merely a symptom of globalisation that affects all democracies at national level?

The spread of democracy, it can be argued, is both a consequence and a cause of globalisation. The opening up of authoritarian states resulted from market pressures, increased communication (travel, radio and television, and more recently mobile phones and the Internet), and the extension of international law. In the 1970s and 1980s, the failure of the statist model of development, the drying up of economic aid, and the growth of indebtedness, contributed to growing disaffection and to demands, often from outside donors, to introduce democratisation measures to legitimise painful economic reforms. In some countries, for example Communist countries, frustrated bureaucrats saw an opportunity to translate political positions into economic wealth. These impulses towards democratisation from above were paralleled by pressure from below as communication with the outside world helped to nurture nascent civil societies especially under the rubric of human rights laws, formally adopted by non-democratic states. But while economic, political, technological and legal interconnectedness may have contributed to democratisation, the processes of political and economic liberalisation, in turn, further speeded up global integration.

Indeed, it can be argued that the spread of democratic procedures is essentially a form of global integration. It is a way in which the institutions and practices necessary to participate in the global system are established. These can range from regulations governing foreign investment and trade, to the political legitimacy required to be considered a serious actor in the various fora of global governance. The Human Rights Report of the British Foreign and Commonwealth Office argues that the increased commitment to democracy promotion is driven by a twin logic 'because it is the right thing to do and because we have a direct interest in building the conditions for sustainable global security and prosperity while fostering reliable and responsible international partners' (quoted in Youngs 2006: 212).

Whether global integration also leads to substantive democracy, however, depends on whether individuals are able to influence the terms of global integration. In many cases, the newly emerging democracies are offered standard recipes for transition, all of which are adopted by competing political parties. Indeed the language of transition is often reminiscent of the language of authoritarianism, as supposedly technical solutions are offered to social and economic problems and the pain of transition is treated as merely medicine needed to reach some promised utopia. The Communists called on people to tighten their belts and work harder so that they could attain socialism; nowadays people are told much the same things in the hopes of reaching the nirvana of capitalism. Citizens experience their rulers as distant and manipulative as in former times. Moreover, the lack of choice in the new democracies often leads to an emphasis on religious and ethnic difference as a way of winning votes in the absence of any progressive alternative to the standard transition recipe.

There are, of course, important differences among the newly emerging democracies. Some countries, especially in the Balkans and Africa, have disintegrated under the impact of liberalisation. Ian Bremmer's book *The J Curve* (2006) suggests that it is during the transition from authoritarianism to democracy that the risk of instability is greatest. Other countries in Southern and Central Europe are considered relatively successful. Part of the explanation has to do with specific legacies and experiences in the past and part has to do with economic factors. But if we understand the spread of democratic institutions as a form of global integration, then these differences also have to do with the terms of global integration - the extent to which newly emerging democracies are able to shape their position in the global system. And these, in turn, depend on the various instruments through which democracy is developed. The more that democratic institutions are introduced as a result of pressure from above, the less favourable the terms are likely to be. Conversely, the more that democracy is the outcome of the actions of individuals wanting to influence the conditions of their lives, the better the terms of global integration and the more substantive is democracy. Joining the EU was very important for

Central and Southern European countries because it strengthened significantly their ability to influence the terms of their integration in the global system.

Techniques of democracy promotion

During the Cold War, the left were generally suspicious of democracy promotion; it was seen as part of Cold War rhetoric and neo-colonial interventionism. The general presumption during this period was one of non-interference in the internal affairs of other countries. In the 1970s and 1980s however, peace and human rights groups became increasingly active in opposing dictatorships, especially apartheid and the military dictatorships in Latin America. Those opposed to the Cold War division of Europe began a strategy of 'détente from below', linking up with opposition groups in Eastern Europe (Kaldor 2003a).

The typical approach of Western activists was to support local civil society groups - the African National Congress (ANC) in South Africa, human rights groups in Latin America, groups like Solidarity or Charter 77 in Central Europe - both morally and materially, helping with literature and campaign materials, publicising their cause, protecting local dissidents through public disclosure, demonstrating or travelling to the region in solidarity. The debates with local groups led to the development of joint strategies including pressure on Western governments to use various instruments to oppose repression and dictatorship. Hence the sanctions on South Africa, the human rights legislation introduced in Congress in relation to Latin America, and the insistence on respect for the Helsinki Final Act in Europe. These were all examples of what Keck and Sikkink (1998) call the 'boomerang effect'.

Even before the 1989 revolutions in Central and Eastern Europe, Western governments and international institutions joined the bandwagon. The democratisation of much of the post-Communist world further reduced the international resistance to governmental involvement in democracy promotion. The difference between the approach of governments and international institutions and the approach of civil society groups has to do with the mix of democracy promotion tools. Broadly speaking, it is possible to distinguish three types of tools.

The first type of tool is administrative. Administrative tools consist of coercive pressure by

A poster about democracy on a school wall in Afghanistan

governments and international institutions on other governments; they are pressures 'from above'. They include Neo-Conservative efforts to bring about 'regime change' as in Afghanistan and Iraq, sanctions on South Africa, Iraq, Serbia and North Korea, as well as various forms of conditionality attached to aid. The European Union always attaches a democracy clause to agreements with third countries. During the 1990s, international financial institutions (IFIs) insisted on political and economic reforms as a condition for loans.

The second type of tool is money. It has been estimated that some US$2 billion a year is spent on democracy assistance, mainly by the United States and Europe, though it is increasing and the true figure is probably much higher (Youngs 2006). Democracy assistance tends to cover such areas as elections and election monitoring, security sector reform, justice including transitional justice, public service reform, support for political parties and parliamentary institutions, public service reform, local government, and support for media and civil society. US assistance is both public and private – the Open Society Foundation (founded by George Soros) is probably the biggest single funder of democracy programmes. After 9/11, the US increased official democracy assistance from $800 million in 2000 to $1.4 billion in 2005 (Mathieson and Youngs 2006). European funding is primarily public. The Organisation for Economic Cooperation and Development (OECD) calculates that the EU spending accounts for some 1.4 billion Euros a year .

The third type of tool is communication and dialogue. Essentially this means engaging both government and civil society in debates among themselves and with outsiders. This was mainly what the peace and human rights groups did in the 1970s and 1980s and it is also sometimes the job of diplomats. As the EU's External Affairs Commissioner, Chris Patten put great emphasis on political dialogue within the EU framework.

The effectiveness and/or benefits of different techniques have never been systematically assessed. There are, however, many criticisms of current techniques. It is often argued that the administrative and financial techniques are counter-productive because democracy cannot be imposed or bought from the outside. External military intervention can destroy regimes but it cannot build democracy - the consequence is more likely to be state failure, as in Iraq or Afghanistan. Sanctions, as in Iraq, Serbia or North Korea, weaken the state and, simultaneously, allow the state to mask its weaknesses by helping to mobilise political support against the external enemies who impose sanctions. Money may lead to the formation of artificial NGOs which squeeze the space for genuine grassroots initiatives. It may foster corruption or train people who then use their new skills to find jobs abroad. It may discredit those who receive the funds who may then be accused of being 'enemies' (see Chapter 4 of this volume).

A related criticism is that administrative tools and money are directed less at the democratic process and more at establishing pro-Western governments. Thus the United States favoured its own expatriate allies in Iraq, while it failed to respect the results of elections in Palestine because they were won by Hamas. The sanctions on Serbia and Iraq were not aimed at promoting democracy as such, rather they were about foreign policy goals: the elimination of weapons of mass destruction in Iraq, and stopping ethnic cleansing in Bosnia and Kosovo in the case of Serbia. The repressive regimes in Saudi Arabia or Uzbekistan are not subjected to the same kind of external pressures because of their pro-Western orientation. Indeed, the more muscular approach to democracy promotion often conflates pro-democracy with pro-Western.

There is much in these arguments but they are not always true. Sometimes military intervention can help provide security and the conditions for a political process that can lead to democracy; the UK intervention in Sierra Leone in 1999/2000 might be one such example. Sanctions do seem to have worked in South Africa and it often said that targeted sanctions against Milosevic and his cronies were a major reason for his capitulation at the end of the NATO bombing. Funding for independent radio in Serbia or for young people's resistance movements like *Otpor* (Serbia) or *Pora* (Ukraine) helped to contribute to the colour revolutions. Moreover, while Pora was pro-Western, this was not true of Otpor. The success of sanctions against South Africa, it can be argued, was because they were a response to civil society pressure and could not, therefore, be used by the South African government to mobilise public opinion against those who imposed the sanctions. In Sierra Leone, civil society strongly supported both the British and the United Nations interventions.

What is really important, however, is communication. It can be argued that the empowerment of civil society comes not from resources or capacity building but from access to decision-makers and participation in public deliberation. There are no blueprints for democracy promotion. While experiences and methods can be offered, what fits any particular situation is a complex political set of compromises that are the outcome of an ongoing process rather than externally provided standard recipes.

When the US and the UK invaded Iraq in 2003, they assumed that they would be welcomed. They had talked to exiles and to politicians in Northern Iraq - the relatively free Kurdish part of the country. But they had not talked to those in Iraq who were at the time offering other advice. These included underground movements and parties such as the Al Da'wa Party (Shi'ite Islamist), the Communist Party, the General Union of Students (GUSIA), and the League of Iraqi Women who did a lot to support the widows of the victims of Saddam's regime. There were also artists who met and talked at the *Hewar* (Dialogue) gallery, established by a well-known artist who left the Ba'ath Party at the time of the invasion of Kuwait. The Wednesday group, composed of current and ex-Ba'athists, met every Wednesday to discuss political and intellectual issues even after one of their members was arrested and executed (Said 2005). Among both Sunni and Shi'ite clerics, there were those who were trying were to create more open space within the mosques by leveraging Saddam's emphasis on religion in the last few years of his rule, in a strategy reminiscent of the Catholic Church in Poland.[2]

These underground groups were suggesting a

strategy similar to the opening up of Eastern Europe. For example, they proposed that the UN run the oil-for-food programme instead of allowing it to be channelled through the government, which had turned the programme into a device for the ruling clique to sustain their incomes. They also favoured the return of the weapons inspectors, not merely because this would be more likely to bring the weapons of mass destruction (WMD) programme under control, but because the presence of the inspectors made them feel more safe. The worst atrocities would not, they believed, be carried out under the noses of the inspectors. They pointed out that the 1991 ceasefire resolution not only covered security issues like the elimination of WMD but also commitments to human rights and political pluralism. They suggested that these commitments should receive more emphasis; for example, human rights monitors could have accompanied the weapons inspectors (Kaldor 2003b).

This is not to say that communication necessarily means taking local advice. Often that advice is conflicting and may involve special pleading. But communication and dialogue are both key to empowering civil society and shaping democracy strategies. Money and administrative instruments can be useful where they are a response to bottom-up demands. But they are less likely to be effective where they are based on exporting particular models of democracy or supporting particular pro-Western factions.

Communication has to be ongoing and continuous if 'opening up' is to lead to substantive democracy. It is not just a matter of communicative engagement designed to bring about a-once-and-for-all 'regime change'. Rather the toppling of dictators is one moment in the continuous process of constructing the practices and institutions needed for global integration. Whether this makes things worse, for example through the spread of 'new wars' or transnational crime, or whether it makes things better, by leading to substantive democracy, depends on the extent to which pressure from below is mobilised to influence the terms of global integration. For example, can civil society mobilise together with counterparts in other countries on issues like debt repayment, trade agreements, or the terms of membership in international organisations like the Council of Europe or NATO? In other words, communication has to cover broad global issues such as social justice, human rights, environmental

Pro-democracy campaigners in Hong Kong, China

responsibility, and not just the issue of formal democratic institutions.

The role of global civil society

The Neo-Conservatives often point to Israel as the only democracy in the Middle East. One can quibble about the claim. Should not Turkey or Lebanon be counted as democracies, even if, in the case of Lebanon, it is organised on a consociational basis? Elections are held in Iran, even though, in the last elections, many reformist candidates were disqualified. All the same, there is no doubt that elections in Israel are more free and fair than anywhere else in the Middle East, and debates in the Knesset and in Israeli civil society are as lively as anywhere else in the world. Palestinians often say that they have learned about democracy from watching Israeli television. Yet what does it mean to have a democracy based on an exclusive notion of community, that is to say an exclusive Jewish state? A much more extreme example is South Africa under apartheid. Mamdani (1996) argues that during the colonial period in Africa, civil and political rights were reserved for the Europeans while a coercive reinvented tribal law was imposed on the 'natives'. South Africa, under apartheid, he argues, represented the generic case of this type of dualism between citizen and subject. During the apartheid years, white South Africans held free elections and debated among themselves and claimed they were the only

2   *Members of the Council of Sunni Clerics whom I met in May 2004, told me how they had come to the conclusion that they could never defeat Saddam Hussein through a coup; instead, from 1999 onwards, they developed a strategy, together with their Shi'ite counterparts, of slow strangulation (Kaldor and Said 2003).*

democracy in Africa, even though blacks were excluded and repressed.

These examples highlight a more general problem with democracy. Representative democracy is necessarily exclusive. It is territorially based and whether citizenship is based on residency, as in civic notions of citizenship, or on race and ethnicity, as in the examples above, it necessarily excludes non-citizens, those who are not permanent residents or those of a different ethnicity. In a world where territorial boundaries matter less and where communities are no longer congruent with territory, the exclusive character of democracy helps to explain the limitations on substantive involvement in democracy. Should not Iraqis, for example, be able to vote in American elections? Should not British citizens be able to influence conditions in Pakistan since so many minority groups in the UK come from that country.

In contrast to democracy, civil society is no longer territorially bounded. Like democracy, civil society is one of those terms that has very many definitions and the discussion about definitions is part of what civil society is about. I define civil society as the medium through which social contracts or bargains are negotiated between the individual and the centres of political and economic authority. Civil society is a process of management of society that is 'bottom-up' rather than 'top-down', and that involves the struggle for emancipatory goals. Civil society, of course, includes reactionary groups as well – people struggling to preserve traditions or those who have exclusive agendas – but it is the site where all these issues are debated and negotiated. Civil society makes possible governance based on consent where consent is generated through politics. Substantive democracy is only possible where procedural

democracy is accompanied by and indeed constructed by a strong and active civil society.

Up until 1989, the definition of civil society was territorially bounded. Moreover, civil society was considered to exist only in part of the world – primarily north west Europe and North America. The reinvention of the concept of civil society in the 1970s and 1980s was linked to the wave of new social movements that developed after 1968 – the generation described by Ulrich Beck (1998) as 'freedom's children'. These movements operated outside formal party politics and were concerned with new issues – gender, environment, peace and human rights. They were harbingers both of more radical demands for democracy – autonomy, participation, self-organisation – but also growing global consciousness, the sense of a common humanity. They also made use of the emerging infrastructure of globalisation - air travel and improved information and communications technology.

The language of civil society that expressed these aspirations was reinvented simultaneously in Latin America and Eastern Europe, in societies struggling against authoritarianism and militarism, although the East European discourse is better known. In both cases, there was a similar emphasis on human dignity and on 'islands of engagement'. The intellectuals in both regions understood civil society as something distinct from the state, even anti-state, a rolling back of the state in everyday life. And they linked this idea with transnational concerns – opposition to the Cold War and to National Security Doctrines that were prevalent in Latin America, and the belief that the reinvented concept of civil society had global relevance. In both cases, these ideas expressed a practical reality: on the one hand, the growth of international legal instruments that could be used to criticise the state and, on the other hand, involvement in transnational networks of activists with North America and Western Europe, which helped to protect these islands of engagement and through which these ideas were debated, refined and exported.

At a moment when democracy at a national level appears to be 'hollowing out', the informal political sphere is increasingly active through NGOs. This includes those operating at local levels and those with global brand names like Oxfam, Human Rights Watch or Greenpeace, as well as a new wave of global social movements like the Social Forums, the anti-war movement or Islamist and other national or religious movements.[3] Moreover new types of informal policy making are being pioneered on big global issues like social justice, climate change or war. These are being tackled through consumer practices (fair trade or carbon miles) or through volunteering (delivering humanitarian aid, acting as civilian monitors).

Democracy in a substantive sense depends on the possibilities for closing the gap between the political class chosen on the basis of nationally based formal democracy and global civil society. On the one hand, this would mean that efforts to establish democratic procedures at local and national levels should be the outcome of debates at local levels although external models, ideas, and experiences could be taken into account. In other words a substantive democracy in a given territory is the outcome of a social contract negotiated among those territorially defined individuals who are constructing a democracy, even though they are influenced by or have links with external actors. In this situation, external actors can help to provide the political space needed for domestic deliberation. On the other hand, closing the gap would also mean that any agreements about democratic procedures reached at local and national levels should be supplemented by a process of negotiating a global social contract, necessary to create the conditions for substantive democracy at the local and national level. Substantive democracy is only possible if people live in a relatively secure environment so that they make decisions without fear and without coercion and if they have some control over the allocation of resources or are able to take preventive measures in the event of environmental risks. In other words, they need to be directly involved in deliberation about the big global issues of our time - human security, social justice, or climate change.

Deepening democracy

What are the practical implications of this argument for those attempting to deepen democracy, to enhance substantive democracy at local, national and global levels? What would count as substantive as opposed to procedural democracy? What would it mean to promote democracy as an end in itself, rather than in order to make America safe or to improve the functioning of global markets?

First of all, administrative tools and money need to be guided by communication, by debates at local, national and global levels. The aim of substantive democracy promotion is to help create and protect political spaces where projects and procedures can be discussed and negotiated. Bureaucrats tend to favour 'capacity-building' and measurable outcomes. Yet the most important role that outsiders can play is facilitating discussions and meetings and responding to local agendas. This may mean less rather than more funding. But it does require more ambitious efforts to create channels through which ordinary people and the associations they form can have access to political authority at all levels.

At global levels, this means new forms of accountability for multilateral institutions – mechanisms through which organisations like the IMF, the World Bank, or the United Nations have to engage with and take seriously local opinions. At national levels, it means fostering interactions between governments, municipalities and civil society, helping to overcome taboos, bringing factional groups together, stimulating a notion of public interest, and empowering those organisations that are engaged in public policy like gender issues or human rights, as opposed to sectarianism. Capacity-building assistance has been poured into Iraq and much has vanished through security costs and corruption. Yet what is really needed in Iraq is a broad dialogue, especially involving those groups like the Iraqi women's network or humanitarian organisations that are outside the current factional intrigues.

Secondly, governments may not be the best institutions for imposing administrative measures or spending money because they are more likely to be guided by national self-interest and to favour particular factions, whatever Condoleezza Rice may say about America's interests in democracy. Administrative measures should only be adopted within a multilateral framework and after civil society consultations. Money could be better spent at arms length by independent public bodies, who are accountable to civil society. The UN Democracy Fund, established in 2005, is a possible

---

3   For information and mapping of global civil society, see the annual Global Civil Society Yearbook series: Global Civil Society 2001, 2002, 2003, 2004/5, 2006/7, the first four editions of which are available at http:www.lse.ac.uk/Depts/global/researchgcspub.htm and more recent editions are available from Sage Publications.

model for such an approach, provided that it is relatively autonomous from national governments and EU and international institutions, and that it includes representatives of civil society in emerging or potential democracies, as well as from donor countries, in its decision-making processes.

The evaluation of democracy assistance is another mechanism for ensuring that assistance is guided by 'bottom-up' concerns. Instead of formal benchmarks, stakeholder meetings including recipients and their peers could be used to assess the utility and effectiveness of democracy assistance. Such stakeholder meetings also represent ways to foster debate about democracy promotion in specific contexts.

Thirdly, and perhaps most importantly, democracy promotion means imaginative responses to demands from global civil society. The best form of empowerment is success, the knowledge that engagement leads to meaningful outcomes. Action designed to fulfil an emerging global social contract or covenant - the consequence of numerous debates, campaigns and arguments taking place all over the world - offers a political project that can help to recast democracy at local and national levels. A good example of what is meant by this is the enlargement of the European Union. The European Union can be understood a new type of multilateral organisation at a regional level, promoting, as it were, regional public goods. Membership of the European Union for newly emerging democracies has become an appealing political project that does take democracy forward. In the same way, a global social covenant could offer a political project for 'civilising' globalisation and pressing for global public goods like resource redistribution or global action to tackle climate change, which represents an alternative to backward-looking sectarianism.

Democracy promotion that merely covers procedures is a necessary condition for democracy in a substantive sense. But the 'political grey zone' that has been created so far is unsustainable. The alternative to democracy in a substantial sense is not a return to classic authoritarianism; closed societies are no longer an option (see Chapter 5 of this volume). Rather it is the politics of fear based on various forms of populist exclusion, state weakness and, in the final instance, 'new wars' and terror. The London bombing illustrated what might be described as the 'perverse boomerang effect' when disaffected minorities make common cause with those with similar nihilistic political positions elsewhere. Reinvigorating democracy, both at home and abroad, means both a bottom-up process of communication and, at the same time, taking seriously an ambitious global agenda.

REFERENCES

Archibugi, Daniele, Held, David and Köhler, Martin (eds) (1998) *Re-imagining Political Community. Studies in Cosmopolitan Democracy.* Cambridge: Cambridge University Press.

Beck, Ulrich (1998) *Democracy without Enemies.* Cambridge: Polity Press.

Bremmer, Ian (2006) *The J Curve: A New Way to Understand Why Nations Rise and Fall.* New York: Simon and Schuster.

Burke, Edmund (1774) *Selected Works of Edmund Burke.*

Carothers, Thomas (2004) *Critical Mission: Essays on Democracy Promotion.* Washington DC: Carnegie Endowment for Peace.

de Tocqueville, Alexis (1945/1835) *Democracy in America.* New York: Vintage Books.

Diamond, Larry (1999). *Developing Democracy: Toward Consolidation.* Baltimore and London: John Hopkins University Press.

Elster, Jon, Offe, Claus and Preuss, Ulrich K (1998) *Institutional design in Post-communist Societies: rebuilding the ship at sea.* Cambridge: Cambridge University Press.

Held, David (2006) *Models of Democracy*, third edition. Cambridge: Polity Press.

Held, David, McGrew, Anthony, Goldblatt, David and Perraton Jonathan (1999) *Global Transformations: Politics, Economics and Culture.* Cambridge: Polity Press.

- (1995) *Democracy and the global order: from the modern state to cosmopolitan governance.* Cambridge: Polity Press.

Huntington, Samuel (1991) *The Third Wave: Democratisation in the Late Twentieth Century.* Norman: University of Oklahoma Press.

Kaldor, Mary (2003a) *Global Civil Society: An Answer to War.* Cambridge: Polity Press.

- (2003b) 'In Place of War: Open Up Iraq', OpenDemocracy http://www.opendemocracy.net/conflict-iraqwarquestions/article_974.jsp

Kaldor, Mary and Vejvoda, Ivan (1998) *Democratisation in East and Central Europe.* London: Pinter.

Kaldor, Mary and Yahia Said (2003) 'Regime Change in Iraq', Discussion Paper 26, Centre for the Study of Global Governance, November.

Keck, Margaret and Kathryn Sikkink (1998) *Activists beyond borders : advocacy networks in international politics.* Ithaca, NY: Cornell University Press.

Mamdani, Mahmoud (1996) *Citizen and Subject: Contemporary Africa and the Legacy of late Colonialism.* Princeton: Princeton University Press.

Mathieson, David and Richard Youngs (2006) 'Democracy promotion and the European left: Ambivalence Confused?' FRIDE Working Paper 29, Madrid, December.

Orwell, George (1957) *Selected Essays.* London: Penguin Books with Secker and Warburg.

Rice, Condoleezza (2007) 'Remarks On Transformational Diplomacy' Washington, DC, 8 February. http://www.state.gov/secretary/rm/2007/feb/80989.htm

Rosenau, James (1997) *Along the Domestic-Foreign Frontier: Exploring governance in a turbulent world.* Cambridge: Cambridge University Press.

Said, Yahia (2005) 'Civil Society in Iraq', in Anheier, Helmut, Glasius, Marlies, Kaldor, Mary (eds) *Global Civil Society 2004/5*, text box in the Introduction. London: Sage.

Schumpeter, Joseph (1961) *Capitalism, Socialism and Democracy.* London: George Allen and Unwin.

Stiglitz Joseph (2007) personal communication, the Symi Symposium, Papandreou Foundation, Paros.

Youngs, Richard (ed) (2006) *Survey of European Democracy Promotion Policies 2000-2006.* http://www.fride.org/eng/Publications/publication.aspx?item=1049

CHAPTER 3

CIVIL SOCIETY AND THE GLOBAL MARKET FOR LOYALTIES
Monroe E Price

Introduction

My purpose in this chapter is to suggest a particular mode of thinking about media and global civil society: ways in which major groups that seek to mould opinion around the world interact with each other, with states and corporations, with domestic regulatory systems and with international organisations and structures. I start with an approach I developed in a book called *Television, the Public Sphere, and National Identity* (Price 1995) and expanded in *Media and Sovereignty: The Global Information Revolution and its Challenge to State Power* (Price 2002). There I described the existence of a 'market for loyalties', in which large-scale competitors for power, in a shuffle for allegiances, often use the regulation of communications to organise a cartel of imagery and identity among themselves. In the retrospectively simple state-centred version of a market for loyalties, government is usually not only the mechanism that allows the cartel to operate, but is often part of the cartel itself. Management of the market yields the mix of ideas and narratives employed by a dominant group or coalition to maintain power. For fulfilling that process – or attempting to do so – control over participation in the market has been, for many countries, a condition of political stability.

Some version of this market, I contended, has existed everywhere and at all times. What differs in today's market is the range of participants, the scope of boundaries of relevant markets and the limitations on the regulatory bodies capable of establishing and enforcing rules for participation and exclusion. The question for this chapter is how to define a global version of such a market and the role of civil society players within it. Put differently, one may ask how a new array of global voices and forces seeks to arrange or manipulate law and technology so that their messages can reach target audiences and have a competitive edge.

Behind all this lies a significant factor that enables civil society to be 'global', indeed, may force it to be global: the changing nature of communications technology and practice. Transformation in communications technologies has always had implications for organisational strategies in the sale and consumption of goods, in the political process and finally in the large-scale formation of public attitudes. Changes in strategy are intensified when technology shifts are combined with large political upheavals, altered demographies and changed concepts of law. Satellites, the Internet and other methods of exploiting new production and distribution technologies are exactly the phenomena that undermine old cartels and are the predicate for forming new ones. Brands become global, films are conceived in a worldwide market, banks become massive and transnational, religions think of multi-state markets, nations see themselves in global competition for hearts and minds and even museums think widely across boundaries. Many groups – the International Committee to Ban Landmines and Falun Gong are examples that demonstrate the wide spectrum – increasingly have a global focus because they realise that a widely distributed consensus, among elites or among broader segments of society, is often essential for their growth and success.

All these actors in the global theatre, if they wish to deepen or expand allegiances, must determine how best to gain access to markets and how to have sufficient entry to exploit the shifts in communications technologies and policies that are taking place. Media globalisation and the accompanying growth of new information technologies shake up access to the political cartel by eroding existing barriers to entry. At the same time, these changes can yield a crisis of domestic law and policy, especially if the new entrants (or entrants who have been long repressed) present threats to control, stability, territorial integrity and national identity.

In this construct of a market for loyalties, the 'sellers' are all those for whom myths and dreams and history can somehow be converted into power and wealth – classically, states, governments, interest

groups, businesses and others. Increasingly and especially as the platform expands to the global, these include organised elements of civil society – transnational groups that exist outside the boundaries of a state but use new marketing mechanisms to enter existing but restricted domestic markets. Organisations of various political and ideological stripes fit into this definition. Environmental and humanitarian organisations, supporters and opponents of gun control, advocates of particular religions or ideologies, foundations committed to shifts in the availability and circulation of medicines: all these and more seek to extend their global reach and to transcend existing legal and technological restraints that limit their ability to reach potential audiences. These groups compete not only with traditional domestic sellers, such as political parties, but also with other experienced and talented purveyors of loyalties, including the civil society and interest groups already mentioned, as well as companies that, through traditional advertising and more subtle forms of persuasion, seek to reinforce the rising tide of commercialisation and consumption.

The 'buyers' are the citizens, subjects, nationals and consumers – recipients of the packages of information, propaganda, advertisements, drama and news propounded by the media. The consumer pays for one set of identities or another in several ways, including with their attention (an increasingly valuable commodity) and with other modes that are attributes of loyalty or citizenship. Payment, however, is not expressed in the ordinary coin of the realm: it includes not only compliance with tax obligations, but also obedience to laws, readiness to fight in the armed services, intensity of dedication to a particular cause and even continued residence within the country. Buyers also pay with their own sense of identity (Price 1994: 667–70). In a globalised world these buyers are still often locked within a specific state, even as their available group of suppliers are transnational (and increasingly, as the power to produce and impart information is democratised, buyers also have roles as sellers).

Prising open the state-centered market

It is easiest to understand the functioning of such a market for loyalties in the traditional context of a single state. One can make the general claim that much domestic broadcast regulation is an effort in a society to maintain or adjust the distribution of power among those who are dominant, with due recognition for subsidiary groups. In a state, re-regulation, or the incentive to change media law and policy, occurs when the cartel of political allegiances can no longer maintain its position of civil dominance. This may seem like a churlish description, especially of societies that pride themselves on free and open markets – the liberal ideal of a marketplace of ideas. But even in such societies, the process of opening and closing reflects ideas of dominance.

A contemporary example of this phenomenon is the slow rate of diffusion in the US of Al-Jazeera English (the counterpart to the original Al-Jazeera channel), which was launched in November 2006. Although the

broadcaster is, strictly speaking, not a civil society organisation, it is a platform for those, including civil society players, who seek to influence political attitudes and shape public opinion. In the US Al-Jazeera English has encountered enormous difficulty in being carried by cable providers, and is currently only available through satellite TV and the Internet. In Canada, the 2004 Canadian Radio-television and Telecommunications Commission (CRTC) ruling that approved the carriage of the Arabic-language Al-Jazeera placed onerous and exceptional conditions on the privilege of cable television systems to carry it (CRTC 2004). A market for loyalties analysis would ask what formal and informal efforts restricted pathways open to such a channel.

An older example dealing with a domestic seller in the market of loyalties and the question of access to mainstream television channels, is also suggestive. In 1970, the civil society organisation, Business Executives' Move for Vietnam Peace, complained to the Federal Communications Commission (FCC) that the broadcaster CBS had refused it the right to buy time to broadcast spot announcements expressing the group's views on Vietnam. The FCC ruled that a broadcaster was free to refuse all 'issue' advertising. An intermediate court reversed this decision, saying that 'a flat ban on paid public issue announcements is in violation of the First Amendment, at least when other sorts of paid announcements are accepted' (Columbia Broadcasting System v. Democratic National Committee 1973). The court remanded the causes to the FCC to develop regulations governing which, and how many, editorial advertisements could

be aired. In a 1973 decision, however, the Supreme Court upheld CBS, ruling that an American broadcaster was not a 'common carrier' that had to accept messages that were the equivalent of paid editorial advertisements (Columbia Broadcasting System v. Democratic National Committee 1973). This decision maintained an institutional status quo that limited entry, and characterised an era of scarce channels and tight gatekeepers – a model that has far from disappeared.

Because every state provides a different, almost idiosyncratic model of the market for loyalties and different rules of access for new entrants, a comparative study is useful. Some countries, in their baseline approaches, have had highly organised plural approaches. The Netherlands and Lebanon are examples. In the Netherlands, a complex but aesthetically fascinating system built on pillarisation in society, including separate, publicly financed schools for those of different religious commitments. Radio, then television followed with separate producing organisations and public allocations of time for specific religious and social entities (Catholic, Protestant, social democratic and others). Shares of time on channels were allocated according to a complex formula and many were quite explicitly excluded. Belgium has a similar system.

In Lebanon, chaos and relatively free entry into the media sphere, characteristic of the civil war period, ended with a pacted agreement that allocated television channels (and the principal political offices in the land) on the basis of 'confessions' or plural power groupings (Maronite Christian, Sunni and Shiite Muslim) that still persists. Totalitarian societies have exercised near monopolies in the market for loyalties with calibrated modes of barring entry for any competing voice.

In states with a significant and autonomous public service broadcaster, the nature of access for elements of civil society has been different. Public service broadcasters have been more likely to seek out the viewpoints of civil society groups (though as monopolies, and because of their historic relationship to national power structures and their political sensitivities, they are hardly providing open access, or access available to all). In some states, public service broadcasting has sought a structured voice for civil society groups, sometimes through quota representation on the staff or in programming, and sometimes through representation on a governing board, both forms of political pluralism.

Because of these and other differences, variously constructed markets for loyalties have offered more or fewer opportunities for elements of civil society to enter and compete. Dominant players are always interested in preserving their share in the allegiances of audiences and citizens. Even where, as in the Netherlands, the voices heard and positions represented were finely calibrated and broadly inclusive, limitations and exclusions existed. A pillarised society that organised schools, media and other public goods along plural lines had to have a method for determining which entities would have entitlements and which would not. Rules and structures always provided a barrier to entry (see Humphries 1996). And these barriers have a tendency to collapse when, as in the case of the Netherlands, technologies of transmission made a mockery of restrictions. It is stating the obvious to note that where forces of preservation are in conflict with forces of transformation:

> potential changes in power and control over the
> established electronic media – either as a result
> of new media or as a result of changes in the world
> surrounding the media – do lead to initiatives in
> favour of keeping the old pattern as well as to
> initiatives in favour of new patterns of power
> and control. (McQuail and Siune 1986: 16)

Finding new ways to engage audiences

When we shift from a focus on the state to the transnational, the question of how civil society engages with domestic and international systems emerges more clearly. We must ask how access to previously excluded spaces is achieved by global civil society organisations and movements. Specifically, what do these groups do, in fact, to break cartels or otherwise increase their capacity to be effective, and how do states and cartels respond? Put differently, how do such groups invoke laws (even if not authoring them), deploy useful new technologies (even if not controlling them) and muster force (even if it is outside their direct capacity)?

It is relevant that the market for allegiances is not a zero sum game. The buyer can absorb many loyalties with differing intensities. He or she can be loyal to the King, increasingly believe in democratic values, be a

The Netherlands Image and Sound Institute: broadcasting restrictions in this pillarised society collapsed in the face of new technologies of transmission

devout Muslim, wear blue jeans and love consumer culture. The issue here is not how the messages are received and gain adherence, but rather what steps are taken so that audiences have access. Guobin Yang, using Margaret Keck and Kathryn Sikkink's analysis (Keck and Sikkink 1998), argues, 'in information politics, advocacy networks generate politically usable information and move it to where it will have the most impact' (Yang 2006). It is that effort to shift and achieve platforms for usable information that is the essence of the growth at the global level of this competition by civil society organisations.

In a globalised media world, efforts to gain access intensify as competition emerges among those who supply different ideologies or ideas, such as environmental groups and contrarily-minded industrial interests, or groups that have competing notions of economic justice, religious beliefs (Huntington 1993) or the use of small weapons (see Bob in Chapter 10 of this volume). From a perspective of control over competing ideologies, the rush for various states to have a satellite channel presence is evidence of this competition.

Invoking international norms, overcoming barriers

Laws are made at the national level, but norms and pressures increasingly come from the global. Tacit or explicit arrangements among states, or between states and multinational corporations or non-governmental organisations (NGOs) may be designed to affect the nature of a global market in cultural and political attitudes and facilitate the predominance of one ideology over another. Thus, while the apparent determinant of the relationship between regulation and control remains the nation state, communication avenues in any given state are increasingly a matter of international action or pressure, justified under the aegis, for example, of stability, trade or human rights.

Historically, rules, practices and other decisions, both legitimate and arbitrary, and often arguments based on scarcity, have blocked avenues for certain civil society groups (both homegrown and foreign) in specific markets for loyalties. In particular, access by controversial civil society groups to platforms presented by traditional media has often been made difficult, if not impossible. Important advocates in global civil society will often hold views that are unpopular in the target society they are trying to penetrate. Those in authority will (and in some instances should) characterise those views as undermining national security or identity, as opposed to longstanding and significant cultural norms, and as inconsistent with the views of dominant economic and political actors. Indeed, the very motive for organising transnationally may be to alter attitudes among specific publics. Transnational sellers, linked to minority local counterparts, often argue for ethical and legal outcomes that deserve to be heard but are out of sync with prevailing mores. In this context, global strategies can offer what Keck and Sikkink describe as a 'boomerang effect,' allowing groups to circumvent domestic indifference or pressure by transferring debate to the international level (Keck and Sikkink 1998: 12; Della Porta and Tarrow 2004). Positing this kind of restricted market and suggesting these limitations on some players only raises the questions of what techniques are available to civil society groups that wish to expand their capacity to reach audiences globally: what they do, in fact, to break cartels or otherwise increase their capacity to be effective.

The point of this chapter is to describe the way such a shift from a state-centered to a transnational market for loyalties serves to reduce these limitations or alter the theatre in which limitations operate. Of course, this is just a shift: there have always been transnational efforts to affect the structure of the market. As Margaret Blanchard notes, the 'free-press crusade' during the Second World War sought to export the American ideal of freedom of the press:

If journalists could only manage to export the blessings that the American free-press system brought to the United States, then, indeed, the world would be assured of democracy and peace.
(Blanchard 1986: 1)

More recent, transnational 'neutral' intermediaries include Article 19, Reporters sans frontiers and the Global Internet Policy Initiative. International media development efforts frequently focus on developing the infrastructure – including technical capacity such as computers, websites and transmitters, as well as business structure – that will allow entry by global civil society and the increased dissemination of content. These efforts often rely on government funding for such work (Price et al. 2002).

As civil society groups think more and more about how globalisation affects their speech-related needs, they support changes in the infrastructure of communications that permit greater ease of multi-site access. Intermediaries begin to foster and advocate, often under neutral auspices, policy structures that permit global advocates to be more effective in achieving their goals. Obviously, the new sellers favour a multichannel universe, one that expands the numbers of platforms locally because of altered technologies (such as satellite to home and satellite to cable). Over time, and accelerating with the arrival of satellite broadcasting, new technologies empower transnational sellers in the market for loyalties to reach domestic buyers. The globalisation of the media alters the locus and operation of the market for loyalties. Openness is expanded: old vehicles become more attuned to the opportunities available to the transnationalised civil society players and new vehicles are created to deliver a broader message. From a Western standpoint, the expansion of the BBC World Service, the support of BBC Online, the entry of France 24 and new uses of digital public broadcasting channels in Europe and globally are examples of such new entrants as vehicles for delivery. But channels to reach diasporic communities in Europe count here as well. These vehicles complicate the task of domestic gatekeepers and challenge government controls on the gatekeeper. Entities outside the state, such as multinational corporations, other states and identity-related groups, also participate in the market for loyalties when they advocate the use of technology or the adoption of international norms that would facilitate or require the expansion of members in the cartel of ideological or identity presenters. An example of this is the Kurdish diaspora's efforts to pressure Turkey for increased respect for human rights and the protection of minorities through the EU as a condition of its accession the EU (Eccarious-Kelly 2002; European Commission 2005).

Pressures for unimpeded access

Civil society groups see themselves as committed to liberalising access and expanding the number of players in the market for loyalties. Except in specific instances ('hate speech' is discussed below), they do not perceive the need for a legal framework in which they can help to exclude competitors. For that reason (among others) an important technique for breaking cartels of sellers in the market for loyalties and allowing space for new voices comes through pressure for the strengthening of international free speech norms, such as the Universal Declaration of Human Rights' Article 19. Civil society groups benefit from a global infrastructure that allows broader, less impeded dissemination of their messages, and access to important domestic platforms.

Without question, implanting free speech norms benefits a new cohort or those who have learned to take advantage of the altered legal and technological circumstances, as well as citizens promising (and perhaps delivering) access to a variety of information sources that constitutes enhancing the 'right to receive'. By the same token, such norms provide opportunities for those disparate, dissenting and plural points of view from outside to have clearer opportunities to influence opinion (the 'right to impart).' As part of this, global civil society groups promote a legal regime that compels the opening of media systems. Put simply, they do so on the proper belief that a more open system makes their voice more likely to be heard (Blanchard 1986). Take the global campaign of the great, prototypically global, civil society organisation, Article 19 (established to advance the Article of the Universal Declaration of Human Rights). Article 19's campaign is supported by

global civil society advocates who hope for legal frameworks that would be more sanguine for their capacity to persuade.

Inventing new platforms

But reliance on law is cumbersome. Legal norms must set clear and enforceable limits on the restrictive actions of gatekeepers and enforceability must be effective. Devices in which civil society players have unmediated access have more appeal to these new entrants than does reliance on law. The use of direct mail efforts (in societies where mail is an inexpensive and unmonitored form of message delivery) is an example. And in the Internet world the capacity to establish a website, to enter chat rooms and to develop a presence on newly created platforms, provides another method of relatively (in many societies and, at least, for the moment) unmediated access. The increased number of satellite channels serves to expand opportunities, but the capacity of cable operators to select (where signals are so redistributed) means that there are gatekeepers who can pick and choose partly based on message.

In their relentless search for unmediated modes of delivering information and persuading audiences, global civil society builds new and powerful platforms to disseminate its messages. Woodstock was an early emblem of this mode, which was linked to global civil society by Sir Bob Geldof and Live Aid (and continued with Live 8). The event itself can become a medium; its link to celebrity is the means of circumventing the

The 2008 Olympics in China creates opportunities for greater leverage by civil society

normal obstacles to entry. The notoriety of the event becomes an argument, often compelling, for the message (embodied in the event) to be transmitted through traditional media outlets. Alternate modes of distribution, such as documentary film festivals, are another part of the armament for civil society groups seeking to more effectively enter the global market for loyalties. Here the work of Sundance Film Festival and the Sundance Institute in highlighting films that address global social issues should be noted.

Hijacking platforms and piggy-backing

In addition to creating new platforms, global civil society can appropriate existing platforms (the larger the platform, the more appealing) and turn the message from that of its sponsors to those of the global civil society groups. Daniel Dayan, co-author with Elihu Katz of *Media Events* (Dayan and Katz 1992), has called this a 'hijacking' of a platform. The 1999 World Ministerial Conference of the World Trade Organization was the hallmark recent event, exemplifying at least a piggy-backing on a platform created for one general narrative to convey yet another. Embedded in this idea are a variety of notions: that platforms (or certain platforms) provide opportunities for exposure, that there is some accepted narrative (even if this is illusionary) that is being crowded out or violated, and that it is possible to tell, sometimes in advance of the event, who the contenders are for the hijacking process.

The Olympic Games, and in particular the 2008 Olympics, are an important example of this phenomenon, offering opportunities for alliances among disparate groups that make up global civil society to alter allegiances. China is using the Games to influence public opinion at home and abroad; at the same time, environmental and human rights groups, both inside China and internationally, are using the occasion to alter this official representation (and, as a result, policies in China).

The Olympics offers opportunities to raise the profile of human rights and other groups concerned with China. With the raised profile come new opportunities to bring leverage to bear – Olympic boycotts at one extreme. Because of the platform, the Games provide an opportunity to characterise, to create representations and to alter the pressure points of global public opinion and the global public sphere (see Box 5.1 in Chapter 5 of this volume). One dramatic example of this was an effort to 'shame' China into altering its UN Security Council position on UN troops for Darfur by raising the specter of labelling 2008 the 'Genocide Olympics'. A powerful Open Letter by Eric Reeves, a professor at Smith College and Sudan activist, set the tone:

It's time, now, to begin shaming China – demanding that if the Beijing government is going to host the premier international event, the Summer Olympic Games of 2008, they must be responsible international partners. China's slogan for these Olympic Games – 'One world, one dream' – is a ghastly irony, given

Beijing's complicity in the Darfur genocide (see the website for China's hosting of the Olympic Games at http://www.olympic.org/uk/games/beijing/index_uk.asp). The Chinese leadership must understand that if they refuse to use their unrivaled political, economic, and diplomatic leverage with Khartoum to secure access for the force authorized under UN Security Council Resolution 1706, then they will face an extremely vigorous, unrelenting, and omnipresent campaign to shame them over this refusal. (Reeves 2007)

Hollywood soon joined the pressure campaign. After urging from Mia Farrow, Steven Spielberg, who is serving an artistic advisor for the Games, wrote a letter to President Hu Jintao in April, urging him to use China's influence constructively. The following week there was some movement in China's policy, with a Chinese official visiting Sudan to press the government to accept a UN peacekeeping force (Cooper 2007).

Such versatility and experimentation become necessary qualities for global civil society as it copes with media transformations. To innovate effectively and circumvent existing barriers to entry in the market for loyalties, global civil society must creatively use new communications technologies, as well as heritage technologies. Audio-cassettes provided a means of entry for unpopular ideas to an otherwise closed market in Iran. An analysis by Ian Liston-Smith for BBC Monitoring (Liston-Smith 2006) addresses modes by which, in Africa, the introduction of mobile phone networks suggested new possibilities for receiving news unavailable via local media and helping coordinate activism by human rights and social justice organisations. SW Radio Africa employed mobile phone text messaging to overcome the blockage of news by the government of Zimbabwe; a station operated by a London-based group of Zimbabwean exiles was routinely jammed by the Zimbabwean authorities but they circumvented the barrier by text service. NGOs also used mobile phones more frequently for delivery of information.

Creating new barriers

Still there are cartels and efforts to limit those who can enter the market. Especially in Europe, governments are establishing rules that govern what channels, suspected of conveying hate speech, can be carried by European-based satellite providers. After

Huge speakers on the fortified island of Kinmen, Taiwan, broadcast 2km across the water to China

the French regulatory agency, the CSA, determined that Al-Manar, the Lebanese Hizbollah satellite channel, should not be transmitted into Europe on Eutelsat (on the grounds that its programming was anti-Semitic), the EU orchestrated an elaborate system of cooperation to decide who would have jurisdiction to exclude channels (EUROPA 2005).

New technologies are also sites for the exercise of state efforts to exclude various proponents in the global civil society arena. Satellite receiver dishes are prohibited or limited in many states because of the government's inability to control what information transmitted over them comes into the society. For similar reasons, the Internet becomes a site for surveillance and a target of sophisticated blocking or filtering manoeuvres.

Few modern and democratic governments or policy makers would articulate a policy of regulatory reform saying explicitly that it was designed to keep them and their cohort in power. In contrast, an authoritarian society with a monopoly on information might have less difficulty marrying rhetoric to reality. Threats to the monopoly must be defeated; making that explicit may be part of the ideology of control. In 2000, Ayatollah Ali Khamenei ordered Iran's reformist parliament to abandon its effort to change the country's restrictive press laws, stating:

> If the enemies infiltrate the press, this will be a big danger to the country's security and the people's religious beliefs ... I do not deem it right to keep silent ... The bill is not legitimate and not in the interest of the system and the revolution. (Abdo 2000)

While some states diligently and pervasively seek techniques to limit entry, partly to keep global civil society organisations at bay, not all states have the resources and organised intelligence to do this. One example is 'failed states' that lose control over their media space – and their ability to resist external views – as force is exerted against them. This is the case in Afghanistan and Iraq, where the US has used specially equipped military transport plans (Commando Solo) for radio and TV broadcasts (Allen 2003).

Conclusion

It is hardly the case that all developments in the globalising of the media are in the service of civil society. The impulse to allow new entrants into the cartel and to encourage a media that reflects an expanded set of suppliers in the market for loyalties is matched by an impulse to prevent destabilisation. Furthermore, powerful traditional players – states themselves, religious groups, elements concerned with economic issues – strikingly seek to control entry into the market for loyalties (sometimes seeking to enter, sometimes seeking to block the entry of others).

One result is the domestication of the global broadcasting entities. States may prefer certain global suppliers of news and information because they may be less threatening than homegrown opposition channels. Theodor Adorno and Max Horkheimer (1972) long ago pointed to the political impact of assembly-line, standardised entertainment, arts and education. They recognised that a vast industrialised culture industry could benefit a ruling class by separating the masses from critical perspectives and

socialist ideas. Commercialisation may undermine historic cultures, but it is less subversive and, in the short run, less destabilising and therefore more appealing than a market in which civil society messages are effective. A media space filled with commercials is thus often preferable, from the perspective of the status quo, to one crowded with opposing alternate identities, such as stations of Islamic fundamentalists in Egypt, Basque separatists in Spain, or Kurdish nationalists in Turkey. In this sense, in some circumstances, it can benefit the government to allow the gestation and entry of attractive commercial supply material, as the powerful influences exerted by this material may make it more difficult for competing national identities to emerge. In a similar vein, the measured inclusion of transnational civil society actors provides an image of openness and progress, and is not necessarily destabilising.

The world is engaged in a vast re-mapping of the relationship of the state to images, messages, and information within its boundaries. National governments, international agencies, multinational corporations, human rights organisations and individuals are involved in this process. All is under construction, yielding a thorough shaking and remodelling of communications systems. Global civil society, along with other actors, tests new and modified techniques aimed at shaping and regulating, if not mastering, the market for speech and allegiances while using or responding to forces that seem to undercut traditional patterns of sovereignty.

As imagery becomes a supplement to or substitute for force, the way media structures are shaped becomes a matter of multilateral and international concern. Global civil society has a stake in the ease of reception of messages around the world: this is why international speech norms are so much a part of their agendas. Pressure to affect public opinion regardless of boundary has always been a preoccupation of those holding or seeking power (Fejes 1986; Nordenstreng and Schiller 1993; Fisher 1987; Frederick 1986). In these ways, the international media environment in which global civil society must act is an increasingly interdependent site for the development and application of formal and informal rules that shape common narratives. In this space ideologies compete and groups forge allegiances that ultimately help shape public opinion and determine the course and very persistence of governments and nations themselves. Those involved in the competition for power and particular outcomes learn to exploit the interplay between conflict, instability and ideology.

In all of this, there is a shift away from the singularly inward forms of state control to outward-looking, regional or multilateral approaches, and away from law and regulation toward negotiation and agreement. The tentacles of influence by one state over the media of another are hardly new, but the process of interaction through treaty or agreement on the flow of ideas, information and sheer data, is every day intensifying. In times of conflict, bombs now supplement more traditional forms of propaganda and new modes of surveillance are enabled by sophisticated software. How states respond to the new media environment influences the profile and the capacities of global civil society. At the same time, state response is in some part a function of the actions of global civil society. One aspect of what makes civil society global is the accumulated set of understandings and the taxonomy of responsiveness to these roiling forces in media production and distribution.

Abdo, Geneive (2000) 'Iran's Leader Stamps on Freedom: Ayatollah Tells Mps to Spike Their Reformist Press Bill', *The Guardian*, 7 August.

Allen, Mike (2003) 'U.S. Uses Iraqi TV to Send Its Message', *The Washington Post*, 11 April.

Adorno, Thoedore and Horkheimer, Max (1972) *The Dialectic of Enlightenment*. New York: Herder and Herder.

Blanchard, Margaret A (1986) *Exporting the First Amendment: The Press-Government Crusade of 1945–1952*. New York: Longman.

Bob, Clifford (2008) 'Conservative forces, communications and global civil society: toward conflictive democracy' in Martin Albrow, Helmut Anheier, Marlies Glasius, Monroe Price and Mary Kaldor (eds) *Global Civil Society 2007/8: Communicative Power and Democracy*. London: Sage.

Columbia Broadcasting System v. Democratic National Committee (1973) 412 US 94. http://supreme.justia.com/us/412/94/case.html (consulted 11 June 2007).

Cooper, Helene (2007) 'Darfur Collides with Olympics, and China Yields', *The New York Times*, 14 April.

Canada Radio-television and Telecommunicatins Commission (CRTC) Broadcasting Public Notice (2004) 'Requests to Add Al Jazeera to the Lists of Eligible Satellite Services for Distribution on a Digital Basis,' CRTC 2004–51, 15 July. http://www.crtc.gc.ca/archive/ENG/Notices/2004/pb2004–51.htm (consulted 17 May 2007).

Dayan, Daniel and Katz, Elihu (1992) *Media Events: The Live Broadcasting of History*. Cambridge, MA: Harvard University Press.

Della Porta, Donatella and Tarrow, Sidney (eds) (2004) *Transnational Protest and Global Activism*, Lanham: Rowman and Littlefield Publishers.

Eccarious-Kelly, Vera (2002) 'Political Movements and Leverage Points: Kurdish Activism in the European Diaspora,' *Journal of Muslim Minority Affairs* 22(1): 91–118.

EUROPA (2005) EU Rules and Principles on Hate Broadcasts: Frequently Asked Questions http://europa.eu/rapid/pressReleasesAction.do?reference=MEMO/05/98&format=HTML&aged=0&language=EN&guiLanguage=en (consulted 17 May 2007).

European Commission (2005) *Turkey Progress Report*. http://ec.europa.eu/enlargement/turkey/key_documents_en.htm (consulted 17 May 2007).

Fejes, Fred (1986) *Imperialism, Media and The Good Neighbor: New Deal Foreign Policy and United States Shortwave Broadcasting to Latin America*. Westport, CT: Ablex Publishing.

Fisher, Glen (1987) *American Communication in a Global Society*. Westport, CT: Ablex Publishing.

Frederick, Howard H (1986) *Cuban-American Radio Wars: Ideology in International Telecommunications*. Westport, CT: Ablex Publishing.

Humphreys, Peter J (1996) *Mass Media and Media Policy in Western Europe*. Manchester: University of Manchester Press.

Huntington, Samuel L (1993) 'The Clash of Civilizations?' *Foreign Affairs*. Summer 72(3): 22–49.

Keck, Margaret E and Sikkink, Kathryn (1998) *Activists Beyond Borders: Advocacy Networks in International Politics*. Ithaca, NY: Cornell University Press.

Liston-Smith, Ian (2006) 'Analysis: Africa Embraces Mobile Phone for News, Political Activism', *BBC Monitoring World Media*, 15 December.

McQuail, Denis and Siune, Karen (eds) (1986) *New Media Politics: Comparative Perspectives in Western Europe*. London: Sage.

Nordenstreng, Kaarle and Schiller, Herbert I (eds) (1993) *Beyond National Sovereignty: International Communication in the 1990s*. Westport, CT: Ablex Publishing.

Price, Monroe E (1994) 'The Market for Loyalties: Electronic Media and the Global Competition for Allegiances', *Yale Law Journal* 104: 667–705.

— (1995) *Television, the Public Sphere and National Identity*. Oxford: Clarendon Press.

— (2002) *Media and Sovereignty: The Global Information Revolution and its Challenge to State Power*. Cambridge, MA: MIT Press.

Price, Monroe E, Davis Noll, Bethany, and De Luce, Daniel (2002) *Mapping Media Assistance*. World Bank–USAID Paris meeting, Programme in Comparative Media Law and Policy. http://pcmlp.socleg.ox.ac.uk/archive/MappingMediaAssistance.pdf (consulted 11 June 2007)

Reeves, Eric (2007) 'An Open Letter to Darfur Activists and Advocates'. http://www.sudanreeves.org/Article152.html (consulted 16 May 2007).

Universal Declaration of Human Rights, Article 19. http://www.unhchr.ch/html/menu3/b/a_ccpr.htm (consulted 15 May 2007).

Yang, Guobin (2006) 'Activists Beyond Virtual Boarders: Internet-Mediated Networks and Informational Politics in China', *First Monday*. Special Issue Number 7, September. http://www.firstmonday.org/issues/specia111_9/yang/index.html (consulted 15 May).

CHAPTER 4

DEMOCRACY PROMOTION AND CIVIL SOCIETY

Armine Ishkanian

Introduction

In his testimony to the US Senate Foreign Relations Committee hearing on the role of non-governmental organisations in the development of democracy Ambassador Mark Palmer argued that 'achieving a 100% democratic world is possible over the next quarter century – but only with radical strengthening of our primary frontline *fighters of freedom*' (emphasis added). Palmer characterises these 'frontline fighters of freedom' (i.e. non-governmental organisations – NGOs) not only as having assisted 'a massive expansion in freedom' but as being the 'heirs of Mahatma Gandhi, Martin Luther King and Lech Walesa' (Palmer 2006). While few scholars of civil society would describe NGOs in such laudatory language, such thinking has fuelled democracy promotion efforts since the late 1980s. At that time, the idea that civil society is critical to development, democratisation and successful transition became quite prominent among donors and policy makers, because of their growing enthusiasm for the idea of civil society, a certain disillusionment with the over-concentration on aid to state institutions, and the belief that through civil society 'democratic forms' could be transformed into 'democratic substance' (Carothers 2000).

Civil society strengthening subsequently became a central part of democracy promotion programmes implemented in both transition and developing countries. Since 1989 very large sums of money have been spent by international development agencies, private foundations and other actors on strengthening, building, nurturing and supporting the institutions of civil society, training civil society activists and funding their projects as a means of promoting democracy. In the former socialist countries, the aims of 'democracy promotion' and 'programmes strengthening civil society' have been to assist the transition from socialism as well as to support good governance and free and fair elections, human rights and the rule of law. In developing countries, in addition to these aims, it was hoped that promoting democracy and civil society strengthening would also enhance aid effectiveness and support efforts to reduce poverty. In conflict or post-conflict areas, promoting democracy is seen as a tool for preventing or reducing conflict (Kaldor et al. 2007: 110). In addition to all these aims, after September 11, democracy also came to be seen as vital in countering terrorism.

Since the early 1990s, programmes strengthening civil society, in particular American, have excluded political associations and parties (i.e. political society) in an attempt to appear non-partisan and to avoid accusations of 'playing politics' (Ottaway and Carothers 2000: 12). Instead, although donors have recently sought to expand the definition of civil society to include more actors than just NGOs, in practice civil society was often equated with the development and growth of NGOs and as a result, the infusion of donor funding and focus on civil society strengthening throughout the 1990s led to an unprecedented and exponential growth in the numbers of NGOs worldwide. Many have referred to this as the 'NGOisation' of civil society.

Nearly two decades have passed since the collapse of the Berlin Wall there is widespread acknowledgement that democracy promotion efforts in various regions, including the former Soviet Union, sub-Saharan Africa and the Middle East, have failed to produce democratic regimes, and that the anticipated vibrant, independent civil societies do not exist. Even in countries where democracy promotion efforts are considered a success (for example, Eastern Europe) there is growing cynicism towards civil society (Hann 2004: 47). Furthermore, there is a rising backlash against democracy promotion as the euphoria and optimism that accompanied the collapse of Communism and the end of the Cold War have been replaced by disillusionment. In spite of the emerging pessimism and backlash, donors and policy makers describe democracy as a universal value and right (Ferrerro-Waldner 2006; McFaul 2004: 148; UN Democracy Fund [UNDEF] URL). Such is the popularity of democracy today that even 'despots' (Rieffer and Mercer 2005: 385) and 'tyrants' (McFaul 2004: 151) who are suspicious of Western-led democracy promotion, pretend to be democrats or claim they are charting an evolutionary (or revolutionary) transition to democracy.

Of the various strands of democracy promotion, in this chapter I focus on civil society strengthening programmes and ask the following questions. First, can democracy be promoted through civil society strengthening, and second, given that democracy appears to have near universal appeal and acceptance (at least at the level of rhetoric), why has there been a backlash against democracy promotion that targets civil society? My reasons for focusing on civil society strengthening programmes instead of programmes that are aimed at election monitoring or state institution building are twofold. First, civil society strengthening was viewed as an end itself as well as a means of furthering the other components (such as human rights and free and fair elections) within the democracy promotion agenda. Second, the current backlash against democracy promotion is almost entirely directed at civil society strengthening programmes and involves legal and extralegal measures aimed at constraining, co-opting, coercing or closing foreign-funded NGOs (Gershman and Allen 2006: 38; Howell et al. 2007). Foreign funding of NGOs is increasingly being described as a form of interventionism and neo-imperialism, and as the creation of a fifth column.

I begin by examining why democracy promotion and civil society strengthening became a central part of donor aid programmes in the 1990s, before discussing the achievements and challenges of democracy promotion. In doing so, I consider several explanations and arguments suggested by policy makers and scholars as to why democracy promotion has not been as successful as anticipated and hoped for in the post-Cold War euphoria. I consider a range of arguments and although I recognise that authoritarian legacies and culture shape perceptions, understandings and practices, I argue that the manner in which civil society and democracy were defined and operationalised as well as the current conflation of democracy with regime change in certain contexts, such as Iraq and Venezuela, have significantly affected democracy promotion efforts.

Why democracy promotion and civil society strengthening?

Academic debates

Although he did not use the term civil society, Alexis de Tocqueville was the first to attribute the importance of associationalism and self-organisation

Nigeria, election time

for democracy (Kaldor 2003: 19). In the late twentieth century, de Tocqueville's work became quite popular among some American scholars, including Robert Putnam, Francis Fukuyama and Larry Diamond, and it was subsequently also influential in policy circles. The neo-Toquevillian position is that democracy is strengthened, not weakened, when it faces a vigorous civil society (Putnam 1994) and that successful transitions to democracy are possible only if civil society or 'something like it' either predates the transition or is established in the course of a transition from authoritarian rule (Perez-Diaz 1993: 40). The belief that civil society is a bulwark against the 'monstrous state' (Weffort 1989: 349) and a counterweight to state power (Rueschemeyer et al. 1992: 6) supported the emphasis on civil society promotion in US foreign aid programmes, and what some describe as the 'democracy aid industry' (Encarnacion 2003: 709). While these neo-Tocquevillian theories linking civil society to democracy became a key element of the post-Cold War zeitgeist and subsequently quite fashionable

The public sphere: a space to discuss, learn and exchange

among certain donor agencies, they are not universally accepted among academics.

On the contrary, there are scholars who argue that democracy can be weakened by civil society (Berman 1997; Bermeo and Nord 2000) and that the nature of civil society is far more important than the existence of civil society alone (Bayart 1986; White 2004). Sheri Berman, in particular, has pointed out the dangers of an active civil society, which can lead to illiberal regimes. Through an analysis of the collapse of the Weimar Republic, Berman argues that the active participation of citizens in civil society led to the weakening of democracy and the rise of the Nazi party (Berman 1997: 408). She maintains that middle-class tension and frustration sparked the growth and activism in voluntary associations and that their participation subverted republican virtue (Berman 1997: 417). She contends that what is needed is a shift away from the normative view of civil society to a more politically neutral view, in which civil society or associationalism are neither 'inherently good nor inherently bad, but rather dependent' on the wider political context (1997: 426–27).

David Rieff also criticises the 'dogma holding that civil society strengthening is the key to creating and sustaining a healthy polity' (Rieff 1999). He views the rise in popularity of civil society in the late 1980s and 1990s as being part of wider trend of the privatisation of the state and the shrinking of overseas aid budgets, and argues for a greater focus on the nation state than on civil society.

While the neo-Tocquevillian position was influential in donor policy circles, it should be recalled that the Latin American and Eastern European intellectuals, dissidents and activists were far more inspired and influenced by the ideas of Italian Marxist Antonio Gramsci. For Gramsci, civil society was more than political economy. He questioned the economism of the Marxist definition and went on to invert Marx's vision by arguing that ideologies come before institutions and that ideology is the force capable of shaping new histories (Bobbio 1988: 88). Gramsci placed the emphasis on civil society's politically relevant cultural dimension (Cohen 1999: 214) and considered civil society as the space for the (re)production and contestation of hegemonic as well as counter-hegemonic discourses. In both Eastern Europe and Latin America civil society referred to autonomy and self-organisation, with an emphasis on withdrawal from the state and the creation instead of 'islands of civic engagement' (Kaldor 2003: 193).

In the 1980s Jürgen Habermas' work on civil society also became quite influential in academic circles. Habermas' notion of the communicative public sphere envisaged a space where people could discuss matters of mutual concern and learn about facts, events and others' opinions (Habermas 1996). As opposed to de Toqueville's vision in which public opinion was treated more as 'a compulsion toward conformity', for Habermas public communication had the potential to provide the space in which the general or public interest could be rationally and critically discussed (Habermas 1992: 133). Although Habermas saw this potential in the ideal model of the public sphere, he also expressed concern with the colonisation of the 'lifeworld' that undermined the progressive potential of the project (Howell and Pearce 2002: 57). Nevertheless, Habermas went on to search for the emancipatory possibilities of civil society and subsequently triggered a debate, which continues today, about civil society, democracy and conceptions of the public sphere.

While scholars continue to debate the virtues, relationship and contributions of civil society to democracy (Chandhoke 1995), in the 1990s donors began actively supporting civil society strengthening programmes, driven by the belief that the relationship between civil society and democracy is natural and inevitable (Howell and Pearce 2002: 51). Driven by policy influenced by neo-Tocquevillian thinking, it was believed that through financial and technical assistance to civil society, democracy could be built. When conducting interviews with donors in Armenia in 2002–3, I was struck by the fact that none of my respondents from donor agencies who were engaged in democracy promotion programmes ever questioned *whether* civil society should be strengthened as part of their democracy building efforts; the question was always *how* it could best be done. Indeed, as the transitions progressed in all the former socialist countries, the radical democratic ideas and visions of civil society that had emerged in the 1980s dissipated, giving way to more established and less revolutionary neo-liberal ones. Subsequently, civil society became a project that was implemented in the name of democracy building, which eventually led to the projectisation of civil society (Sampson 2002). While this approach has led to the phenomenal growth in the number of NGOs, it has not generated genuine participation or public debate. The following quote, cited by Timothy Garton Ash from an Eastern European colleague, sums up the projectisation which occurred in the 1990s: 'We dreamed of civil society and got NGOs' (Garton Ash 2004).

It is important to note that although most bilateral and multilateral donors have some institutional mechanism for engaging with or supporting civil society strengthening, not all explicitly focus on democracy building or democracy promotion programmes. In the next section I consider the different stances of the key bilateral and multilateral, as well as non-state donors that have been involved in civil society strengthening for democracy promotion.

Donor approaches to democracy promotion

US democracy promotion

Although the US has been engaged in democracy promotion since the 1980s through a focus on election monitoring, civil society strengthening became a significant part of US foreign policy following the collapse of the socialist regimes (Ottaway and Carothers 2000). Since then, civil society assistance has come to be considered 'a centrepiece of America's international outreach' (US Senate 2006: 1) and 'a matter of principle' (Tobias 2007). This position is reflected in the fact that since the early 1990s, more money has been spent on civil society assistance than on any other sector of USAID democracy assistance[1]

(Finkel et al. 2006: 33). From 1990–2003, most USAID democracy assistance was sent to the countries in Eurasia ($5.77 million) with the lowest levels of aid going to Africa ($1.29 million) and Asia ($1.29 million) (Finkel et. al. 2006: 33–4). US-funded civil society assistance has largely been directed at NGOs, because the USAID position in the early 1990s was to provide vigorous support for local NGOs, which would 'be a critical element of civil society strengthening' (USAID 1999: v). Although the earlier strong focus on NGOs has shifted somewhat and civil society is now defined more broadly, the assumption persists that 'a strong civil society is desirable and makes democratic practices and traditions more likely to flourish' (USAID 1999: xi). As US Senator Joseph Biden stated in the 2006 Senate Foreign Relations committee hearing on NGOs, 'we must understand that an election does not a democracy make...*A democracy must rest on the foundation of a strong civil society*' (Biden 2006, emphasis added).

Funding in this area increased following September 11 when democracy promotion became a distinct national security concern and 'key objective of US foreign policy' (USAID URL). While the official US position is clear *vis à vis* civil society and democracy promotion, the approach of the European Union and various leading European bilateral donors toward democracy promotion in general and civil society strengthening in particular is more 'vague' (Schmid and Braizat 2006: 3) and 'opaque' (Youngs 2006: 8).

European democracy promotion

While democratisation is by no means a new departure for the EU or European bilateral donors, Richard Gillespie and Richard Youngs contend that the US began focusing more systematically on democratisation slightly earlier than the EU and that effective co-ordination of EU democracy promotion efforts has been conspicuously absent (Gillespie and Youngs 2002). They maintain that until the late 1990s, the lack of mechanisms for marrying national initiatives to overall common guidelines on democracy presented a serious challenge to effective concerted European action (Gillespie and Youngs 2000: 6). Discussions on transatlantic democracy building efforts have

---

1 *For instance, while civil society aid was $2,438.2 million from 1990–2003, governance and rule of law programmes received $1,457.6 million and $1,218.5 million respectively (Finkel et al. 2006: 33).*

Police survey a public protest in Uzbekistan

intensified following September 11 (Schmid and Braizat 2006: 4), but as Jeffrey Kopstein points out, following the war in Iraq, many European leaders and the European public remain suspicious of democracy promotion, interpreting it as 'a repackaged commitment to the unilateral use of force as well as justification for war and occupation' (Kopstein 2006: 85).

Presently, the EU is intensifying its democracy promotion programmes. Of the three strands of EU democracy promotion that include enlargement, the European Initiative for Democracy and Human Rights (EIDHR), and the European Neighbourhood Policy (ENP), the EIDHR is the EU structure that most specifically targets civil society. Created in 1994 and with a current annual budget of €100–130 million, the EIDHR supports human rights, democratisation and conflict prevention activities. EIDHR is seen as more flexible than other EU institutions and policies concerned with enlargement in that it can act entirely independently of national governments in partner countries and work with a wider range of actors, including parliaments, political foundations and civil society organisations, but it has been criticised for failing to have a real impact because it lacks administrative flexibility, requires long lead times and tends to favour the capital-based NGOs, known as the 'capital darlings' (European Foundation for Democracy 2006: 6).

A survey of European bilateral and multilateral democracy promotion policies from 2001–6 by the Fundacion Para Las Relaciones Internacionales y el Dialogo Exterior (FRIDE) also found that there was sufficient complexity and diversity to make it difficult to speak of 'the European approach' (Youngs 2006: 25, emphasis in original). Of the seven countries surveyed (Denmark, France, Germany, The Netherlands, Spain, Sweden and the UK), there was variation in the levels of 'democracy-related competence' and 'manpower allocated specifically to democracy promotion responsibilities remained limited', with Sweden having the most clearly articulated democracy promotion policies (Youngs 2006: 16–17). While various European bilateral donors, including the UK Department for International Development (DFID) and the Swedish International Development Co-operation Agency (SIDA), actively support and engage with civil society actors through their programmes, they tend to view democracy as a means by which to eliminate or overcome poverty (DFID URLa; URLb) or as a means for achieving peace, justice and human rights (SIDA 1997). Democracy is not discussed as a matter of principle or centrepiece of policy, as in the US context discussed above.

Moreover, there is relatively less focus on civil society as a key pillar of democracy promotion among European bilateral and multilateral donors as compared to the US. Indeed organisations such as the US National Endowment for Democracy (NED) (URL), which focus heavily on civil society promotion, were described as 'pushy' by some respondents in the FRIDE report (Youngs 2006: 18). Even the Organisation for Security and Co-operation in Europe's Office for Democratic Institutions and Human Rights is far more focused on legislative processes, legal training, rule of law and political parties than on civil society.

The UN approach

Even though democracy is not a precondition for UN membership and the word 'democracy' does not appear in the UN charter, since 2005 the UN has also made a foray into democracy promotion. According to Newman and Rich,

> It is not one of the stated purposes of the United Nations to foster democracy, to initiate the process of democratisation or to legitimise other actors' efforts in this field [democracy promotion]. (Newman and Rich 2004: 5)

Although various UN agencies, including the UN Development Programme and the Office for the UN High Commissioner for Refugees, have engaged with civil society through their programme activities or civil society consultative fora, including the Conference of Non-Governmental Organizations in Consultative Relationship with the UN (CONGO),[2] the establishment of the UN Democracy Fund[3] (UNDEF) in July 2005 was the first time that a separate structure was created in the UN specifically to promote democracy. Of UNDEF's six funding priority areas, three focus on civil society and provide funding for civil society empowerment, civic education and citizens' access to information. Although this demonstrates a focus on civil society in democratisation, there are concerns as to how UNDEF will decide on funding to NGOs and other civil society organisations that are critical of a member state's authority. According to the executive head of UNDEF, Magdy Martinez Soliman, active democracy

promotion is only a recent admissible part of the UN mandate and one that has been problematic because it can eventually go against the will of the non-democratic representative of a member state (Martinez-Soliman 2006: 2). There is concern with maintaining a balance between respecting national ownership on political transitions while providing external support to democrats and democratic values, so that democracy assistance is not seen as regime change or interference. For this reason, Martinez-Soliman argues that democracy assistance from the UN should be provided only at a member state's request, otherwise democracy promotion in hostile environments can create 'the kiss of death' – bolstering the authoritarians' argument that democrats are not representative of the national community and are supported from abroad.

Non-state actors and democracy promotion

In addition to bilateral and multilateral agencies, non-state actors, including private foundations, Northern NGOs, private service contractors, political parties and others have been involved in democracy promotion. There are differences among these various actors in terms of their objectives and missions, as well as levels of financial independence and autonomy. Some organisations, such as the Open Society Institute (also known as the Soros Foundation) and the Ford Foundation, are funded by private endowments and consider democracy promotion as an integral part of their mission. They have been actively engaged in democracy promotion and civil society strengthening. Meanwhile NGOs or quasi-NGOs such as the US-based NED and National Democratic Institute for International Affairs, or the UK-based Westminster Foundation for Democracy (URL), which are also committed to promoting democracy around the world, have less financial independence than the aforementioned private foundations and are dependent on government funding.[4] For instance, NED receives an annual appropriation from the US Congress through the Department of State (NED URL), while the Westminster Foundation is an independent body that receives £4.1 million annual funding from the UK Foreign and Commonwealth Office (URL). In addition to these various types of foundations, there are also

---

2   *The Conference of Non-Governmental Organizations in Consultative Relationship with the UN (CONGO) is an independent, international, not-for-profit membership association of NGOs that facilitates the participation of NGOs in UN debates and decisions.*

3   *The UNDEF is a voluntary UN Trust Fund under the overall management of the UN Secretary General with an Advisory Board of 17 members, including representatives from the largest member state contributors.*

---

4   *It should be noted that these NGOs are also engaged in raising funds from individual donors as well as corporations.*

political parties or organisations affiliated to political parties that engage in democracy promotion. In Germany, for instance, there are a number of organisations, including the Friedrich Ebert, Friedrich Naumann, Heinrich Böll and Konrad Adenauer foundations that are associated with various political parties and that have been active in democracy promotion. Finally, among non-state actors, there are the private service contractors or consulting companies (such as Planning and Development Collabrative International and Development Alternatives, Inc. url), which procure contracts and carry out democracy promotion, civil society strengthening and governance on behalf of and based on the specifications of their clients. USAID, in particular, provides a significant amount of contracts to such consulting companies and private service contractors. In 2004 alone it provided US $8 billion to contractors engaged in carrying out international development projects throughout the world (USAID 2006).[5]

While the levels of financial and operational autonomy vary, it is important to recognise that similar to the bilateral and multilateral approaches discussed above, there tends to be a strong commitment among all the aforementioned non-state actors to the belief that civil society is important for democracy building. So, given the involvement of such diverse actors, what has been the impact of democracy promotion through civil society strengthening? Democracy promotion has had mixed results.

Achievements of democracy promotion programmes

Many of the democracy promotion success stories are about the countries in Central and East Europe, although South Africa and the Philippines are also mentioned (Gaventa 2006; Hawthorne 2004: 5). The EU enlargement and accession process has come to be seen not only as the EU's first major experience of democracy promotion, but also as one of the most successful cases of democracy promotion in general. Integration into the EU is often described as an effective tool of democracy promotion because it provided incentives for the leadership of democratising countries to pursue internal changes

(McFaul 2004: 157). Certainly, great strides have been made and many democratic institutions and practices have been established in the countries of Central and East Europe. However, this did not happen overnight and enlargement is not an approach that can be replicated elsewhere. Moreover, the 'return to Europe' has been more complicated than would initially appear. Examining democratisation processes in Central and Eastern Europe, Mary Kaldor and Ivan Vejvoda recognise the establishment of formal democratic institutions and maintain that there is hope for the development of substantive democracies in these countries. They contend that the process of democratisation, in substantive terms, is 'underway' (Kaldor and Vejvoda 1997: 80). While acknowledging the successes of Eastern European countries in establishing democratic institutions and practices, it is important to also recognise that the development of democracy and the growth of Eastern European civil societies (namely, an increased number of organisations) has not necessarily been translated into greater citizen engagement or participation (Celichowski 2004: 77), or led to greater benefits for various social groups (Hann 2004: 46).

The exponential growth in numbers of NGOs worldwide is also often cited as evidence of the success of democracy promotion efforts. Indeed, there has been a 'global associational revolution' (Salamon and Anheier 1997) and the number of civil society organisations has dramatically grown worldwide since 1990. Civil society organisations, and in particular NGOs, are actively engaged with governments and intergovernmental bodies on issues of global and national importance through awareness raising, advocacy and lobbying. These organisations work on a wide spectrum of issues, including poverty reduction, debt relief, human rights, women's rights, the environment and others. Although there are questions about civil society impact on policy making, the ability of civil society actors to introduce issues onto national and global political agendas, to influence public debates, and to name and shame actors who do not deliver on their promises, should not be underestimated. Consultations with NGOs, as well as the growing complaints about the power of NGOs from politicians and business leaders, attest to the fact that civil society organisations are actively engaged in public debates and policy advocacy at the national and global levels.

---

5   *The report did not indicate how the $8 billion was broken down among programme areas.*

Women and men queue separately to vote in Afghanistan

While the growth and presence of NGOs is undeniable, increased activism should not necessarily be seen as the result of democracy promotion programmes for two reasons. First, much of the civil society activism at the global level comes from organisations based or operating in the global North; far fewer Southern organisations are engaged in lobbying and advocacy at the global level. It still tends to be the 'usual suspects' (that is, well-established, Northern-based organisations) that are engaged in global activism and included in consultations with intergovernmental organisations. For instance, only 251 of the 1,550 NGOs associated with the UN Department of Public Information come from the global South; the remainder are NGOs from the global North (Wild 2006).

Second, although the numbers of NGOs have dramatically increased in developing and transition countries, the reality is that the vast majority of these NGOs are almost entirely dependent on foreign support. This dependence not only raises concerns about their long-term sustainability and impact but also raises questions about their legitimacy, probity and accountability. In other words, are these NGOs considered legitimate actors locally? These considerations are often ignored and the growth in the number of NGOs is frequently cited by donors as a sign of success. This is due to the fact that it is easier to count the number of organisations and to cite increased numbers as evidence of the impact and success of donor programmes. For instance, the 'Lessons in Implementation: The NGO Story' report published by USAID in 1999 examines the lessons learned in 'building civil society in Central and Eastern Europe and the New Independent States'. The report acknowledges that the immense amount of aid led to an 'explosive growth of local NGOs' (USAID 1999: 3), citing growth as one of the eight success indicators.[6] The need for demonstrating success is driven by the pressures on all actors engaged in democracy promotion, whether donors or recipients, to demonstrate effectiveness and to give account to their own funders. However, since it is difficult to measure the impact of democracy-building efforts on people's behaviour and attitudes, often what is considered and presented as signs of success are the formal or procedural democratic mechanisms and institutions.

The minimalist or procedural definition of democracy is identified as originating with Joseph Schumpeter (1947), who argued that democracy at the conceptual level is the existence of citizens holding their rulers accountable and the existence of procedures by which to do so. This narrow approach focuses on the formal institutions of democracy and does not consider social and economic inequalities and how they affect participation, access and decision making. While procedural democratic institutions and mechanisms are necessary and in fact represent an a *priori* safeguard against the abuses of power and for the development of substantive democracy (Kaldor and Vejvoda 1997: 63), there are many managed[7] democracies where the procedural elements are present but where substantive democracy is absent. Consequently while recognising the successes, we must be cautious in prematurely proclaiming the triumph of democracy promotion efforts, consider the challenges and ask why a backlash against civil society strengthening is emerging.

---

6   *Other indicators include the increased managerial competence of local NGOs, the establishment of regional linkages, strengthened sectoral infrastructures, improved prospects for NGO financial sustainability, improved legal and regulatory frameworks governing NGO sector operations, learning by local NGOs of professional grant making systems and procedures and, finally, the benefit to women and minority groups as well as reflecting social concerns and public policy issues important to women and minorities through the establishment of NGOs (USAID 1999: 5–6; see Box 4.1).*

---

7   *'Managed democracy' (upravlyayemaya demokratiya) is a phrase that was introduced by the Russian authorities in the early 2000s and is now being increasingly used to describe the situation in other former Soviet states (such as Kazakhstan and Kyrgyzstan). It refers to a situation in which the formal/procedural institutions and practices (for example, elections) of democracies exist but are controlled and managed by the authorities (Colton and McFaul 2003).*

DEMOCRACY PROMOTION AND CIVIL SOCIETY

Box 4.1: En-gendering democracy: the 2002-04 anti-domestic violence campaign and democracy building in Armenia

Following the collapse of communism, support for women's organisations in the post-socialist states in Eastern Europe and the former Soviet Union became a significant component of democracy promotion and civil society strengthening programmes. Donors, including USAID, the Ford Foundation, the German Marshall Fund, the Eurasia Foundation and the Open Society Institute, shared the belief that there was a direct link between democratisation and women's advocacy groups (Ghodsee 2004; Hemment 2004; Henderson 2003; McMahon 2002; Richter 2002). Furthermore, the pressure to liberalise the economy and to privatise state welfare delivery often meant that women, traditionally involved in caring for children, the disabled and the elderly, assumed a greater share of this burden in the face of shrinking public services. By the end of the 1990s, women's NGOs represented a significant proportion of NGO activism in the former Soviet countries (Berg 2004; Hemment 2004; Henderson 2003; Ishkanian 2004; Olson 2003; Richter 2002; Tohidi 2004), and at the same time domestic violence became a popular funding initiative among donors. In September 2002 the USAID Mission in Armenia made available US $476,367, which was divided among six Armenian NGOs. This funding was part of the USAID Democracy Program (USAID 2002: 32–34) and the six grants represented the first direct USAID grants to Armenian NGOs (USAID 2002).

Although the issue was being discussed in global forums and funding was becoming more readily available in the mid-1990s (Sen 2003), domestic violence was still a taboo subject in many post-Soviet countries, including Armenia. Unlike in the USA or Europe, where the issue of domestic violence was first raised and addressed by local women's organisations and groups of battered women (Keck and Sikkink 1998: 174), in Armenia there was no broad-based grassroots movement pushing for recognition of the problem. Most of the women's or human rights NGOs that worked on the issue did not begin doing so until the announcement of large grant programmes (Ishkanian 2004).

Domestic violence had not been recognised locally as a social issue that could be addressed by law enforcement, hotlines and shelters until it was identified as such by Western donors and experts; and therefore the problem, as well as the proposed solutions (i.e. hotlines, shelters), were perceived as being artificially imported and imposed. This perception led to widespread civil society criticism of and resistance to the efforts of the six NGOs involved in the 2002–04 USAID-funded campaign. Although much of the criticism was directed at specific policy solutions, such as shelters, the metanarrative of the critique was directed at the influence of donors and the post-Soviet transition policies (i.e. liberalisation and privatisation) more generally.

As the campaign unfolded, the greatest challenge for these NGOs became countering the persistent civil society resistance to and critique of the campaign, which alleged that the issue was being imposed by donors and that the six NGOs' involvement was motivated by greed and grant-seeking. This led the six NGOs to devote a significant amount of time demonstrating the existence of domestic violence existed in Armenia, arguing that they were not working on the issue because of the grant money, and explaining that they considered local cultural practices and beliefs while designing their programmes. In addition, they sought to legitimise their work by framing domestic violence as a human rights issue and maintaining that addressing the problem was a critical component for democracy building. The crux of their argument was to define domestic violence as a human rights violation and to contend that since the protection of human rights are a necessary, if not obligatory, component of democracy building, the anti-domestic violence campaign was contributing to democratisation processes in Armenia. During interviews, in public addresses, and in their publications the leaders of the six NGOs often made the connection between their work and the larger goal of democracy promotion.

When I visited Armenia in 2005 I found that donor interest had shifted to other topics and that all but one of the shelter programmes had closed due to lack of funding. One of the six NGOs involved even denied any involvement in the 2002–04 campaign (Ishkanian, forthcoming). There was broad consensus among the other NGOs involved that, even though the anti-domestic violence campaign had not fully overcome the resistance and criticisms encountered from the outset, at least it had accomplished the difficult task of introducing the topic to the public and generating discussion about the issue. Less successful were the technical solutions, such as shelters and hotlines, employed by NGOs to try to combat the problem.

Hotlines were not successful in Armenia for a number of reason, including the costs of phone calls (there were no toll-free numbers during the campaign); the absence or poor provision of telephone services in some rural areas; the lack of privacy in most households; and the fact that sharing problems with a stranger over the phone is a alien concept. Meanwhile, shelters, which may be successful in developed countries with welfare systems that provide public assistance, unemployment benefits, health insurance, subsidised housing and free schooling, did not work in Armenia, where these provisions are either not present or not functioning. All that a shelter can do in Armenia is to provide counselling and housing for up to four weeks, leaving the question of what happens to a woman when she leaves a shelter unanswered. Without viable employment, affordable housing and subsistence benefits, often the only options for women are to return to their husband or their parental household. The lack of alternatives and public assistance meant that shelter programmes were viewed by many women as untenable.

The technical solutions such as hotlines and shelters that were implemented ignored the socio-economic problems, including poverty, unemployment and multi-generational households living in cramped conditions, which exacerbate and at times provoke incidences of domestic violence, as well as the fact that Armenia has a weak social welfare system. They were thus implemented in the place of more ambitious programmes that would address the structural and economic inequalities and provide more long-term and sustainable solutions. Unless the broader issue of access to services and a more robust welfare system are addressed, short-term, temporary, technical solutions such as shelters will not solve the suffering of the victims of domestic violence.

Armine Ishkanian, Lecturer in Social Policy, LSE

Challenges and obstacles to democracy promotion

Cultural barriers

In analysing why the transitions to democracy have not yielded the expected results, a common claim is that a society's propensity or 'fitness' for democracy is predicated on its cultural and geographic proximity to the West (Nodia 2002; McFaul 2002). Ernest Gellner (1994), for instance, argued that the concept of civil society is inapplicable in certain contexts, including in non-Western patrimonial societies and in tribal societies (Gellner 1994). He questioned whether civil society could exist in Islamic societies. Others, such as Elie Kedourie or Serif Mardin, have also claimed civil society is a Western dream that does not translate well into Islamic terms (Mardin 1995, quoted in Sajoo 2002) or that Muslims have nothing in their own political traditions that is compatible with Western notions of democracy (Kedourie 1992). Meanwhile, in the context of the post-socialist countries in Eastern Europe, 'transitologists' often 'invoke "culture", that amorphous, omnibus concept' as an explanation for why certain Western policies or blueprints have been resisted (Burawoy and Verdery 1999: 14). For instance, in Bosnia, culture or ethnic mentality were cited as reasons for the inability to embrace civil society development and democratisation. David Chandler discusses the disparaging ways in which the Bosnian people and society were viewed by some international actors and internationally funded local NGOs. They perceived Bosnian society as 'deeply sick', 'feudalistic' or as 'the flock' (Chandler 2004: 240–1). He argues that this focus on the perceived incapacities of Bosnians is only one side of the story and that greater attention must be paid to the 'failing within international democratisation practice itself' (Chandler 2004: 228).

Such sweeping generalisations and claims that blame culture for the lack of democracy or progress are hardly new; they are examples of the interpretations that have been used to explain the failure of development and modernisation programmes since the 1950s. Michael Herzfeld criticises the 'misuse of the culture concept' in the media and among some academics who decry 'Balkan nationalism' and 'religious fundamentalism', all the while failing to recognise their own, Western cultural fundamentalisms. Yet, as Herzfeld adds, rejecting the essentialisation of other cultures does not legitimate meting out the same treatment to the 'West', and for treating the West as a generic bogey (Herzfeld 2001: 152). Such views, Herzfeld maintains, not only essentialise the 'other' but they also essentialise 'the West'. For this reason it is important to recognise that the culture concept is also (mis)used by authoritarian leaders who argue that democracy or human rights are incompatible with local traditions and values.

From African dictators in the 1970s to Asian government officials in the 1990s there have been two sets of arguments: first, democracy is a luxury that can and should only come after a certain stage of economic development and stability has been achieved; and second, democracy is a Western individualistic value that is not compatible with more 'traditional' or kin-based societies. These arguments held great sway in the 1990s until the financial crisis in Asia undermined the 'Asian values' position and silenced most of its supporters (Thompson 2001: 154).

While I would argue that cultural beliefs and ideologies are certainly important and do affect individuals' understandings and behaviour, I am sceptical of the essentialising discourses that view culture as an unproblematic, monolithic and static entity. Furthermore, I find quite problematic the tendency in some of the works on culture as a mitigating factor to democratisation to speak of the 'other' as being affected by culture, whilst claiming to be objective and thereby ignoring how one's own behaviour and understandings are also influenced by cultural beliefs. I argue that if the cultural argument is to be applied, it is necessary to examine critically the cultural attitudes and biases of both donors and recipients.

Authoritarian legacies

In addition to arguing that culture is a barrier to democracy promotion, some policy makers and scholars have maintained that the authoritarian legacies in various countries mitigate the development of a vibrant civil society and democracy (Brzezinski 2002: 196; Gershman and Allen 2006; McFaul 2002: 264; Nodia 2002: 203). In an article co-written with Michael Allen, the President of NED, Carl Gershman, suggests that the failures of and backlash against democracy promotion are a 'by-product of so-called hybrid regimes' (Gershman and Allen 2006: 37).

'Pure Victory' reads the fruit juice advert above Russians commemorating the 1917 October Revolution

Hybrid regimes, according to Gershman and Allen, are those that have certain formally democratic procedures, including the holding of relatively free (if not fair) elections and allowing civil society organisations to function. In other words, hybrid regimes are procedural democracies where the substantive elements are either weakly constituted or missing. Clearly, societies do not exist in a vacuum and it very important to examine and understand how the past has influenced and continues to influence the present. In discussing the lack of civic participation or democracy in Arab countries, there is a tendency to argue that decades of authoritarian rule have left a legacy of 'widespread political apathy' (Hawthorne 2004: 10). Meanwhile, in the post-Soviet states certain practices (such as corruption and clan-based rule), which were common under Communism, persist and have influenced how the current policies have been interpreted, adapted, and operationalised.

While recognising the importance of history, I would argue it is important not to attribute all of the present problems to the legacies and memories of the past. In the field of democracy promotion in particular, Cold War ideologies have influenced and shaped the design and implementation of policies and practices. In the 1990s these ideologies had engendered the notion that everything created prior to the collapse of communism was either 'not true civil society' or

that it was polluted and contaminated by the Communist legacy and had to be purged before true civil society and democracy could flourish (Mandel 2002). The reality is far more complex and it is worth considering how the past is interpreted and instrumentalised by different parties under different circumstances.

For instance, in recent years there has been growing selective remembrance (that is, forgetting about the political repressions and lack of freedoms) and intensifying nostalgia for the 'stability' of the Soviet past and a questioning of the benefits of democracy, which is linked in the minds of many post-Soviet citizens with the introduction of the shock therapies that led to poverty, gross inequality, social exclusion, gangster capitalism and the rise of the oligarchs (see Box 4.2). Democracy promotion in Eastern Europe was also affected by the close association between democracy and market reform programmes. Because the rapidly implemented market reforms and shock therapies of the early 1990s led to vast inequality, poverty and social exclusion, people soon became disillusioned, not only with the market reforms but also with the associated programme of democracy building.[8]

---

8   *I am grateful to Mary Kaldor for drawing my attention to this point.*

Box 4.2: *Nashi* (Ours)

What is Nashi?

Nashi (Ours) is a pro-government, patriotic Russian youth movement that was created in March 2005. Since then, it has rapidly grown throughout Russia and presently has over 200,000 members, of which 10,000 are regular activists or Nashi 'commissars' (Konovalova 2007). The majority of Nashi members are in their late teens or twenties and for some membership is a path to career advancement. The movement's activities include organising voluntary work for members in orphanages and helping restore churches and war memorials, organising educational and training programmes, and organising demonstrations and rallies. Critics, including Russian opposition activists as well as Western observers, argue that the movement is the Kremlin's attempt to co-opt the youth, control dissent and to prevent a 'colour revolution' from occurring in Russia. Given that youth groups played an instrumental role in organising mass demonstrations in Serbia in 2000 (*Otpor* – Resistance), Georgia in 2003 (*Kmara* – Enough) and Ukraine in 2004 (*Pora* –High Time), the establishment of and support for Nashi is seen as a pre-emptive measure, especially in view of the 2008 presidential elections. Although Nashi has been described as a neo-*Komsomol* (Communist Youth Movement) movement that, similar to its Soviet predecessor, trains and grooms its members for leadership positions, it does so by using the forms (demonstrations, sit-ins), techniques (master classes, trainings), and language (of rights, participation) of civil society organising.

Sovereign democracy and the Nashi manifesto

According to its manifesto, Nashi's aims are to support Russia's development as a global leader in the twenty first century through economic, social and cultural means rather than through military and political domination. The key theme throughout the manifesto is sovereignty, which is interpreted as the freedom and independence to set the 'rules of the game' in one's own country and the rejection of Western (i.e. American) hegemony. The manifesto also rails against and calls for the liquidation of 'oligarchical capitalism', crediting President Vladimir Putin as the first to have challenged the oligarchs' power, for strengthening the state, and for turning Russia into a global power. Nashi pledges its support for Putin's policies and vows to work toward these goals in a variety of ways, including through the creation of a 'functioning civil society'. Criticising the existing 'liberal' civil society as being the 'worst advertisement for democracy', the manifesto claims that Nashi will promote civil debates, work with multiple stakeholders (such as government, business, etc) to promote Russia's economic and social development, fight against fascism and intolerance towards ethnic minorities, campaign against violence in the army, and restore people's faith in Russia's future (URLa).

Nashi's manifesto is greatly influenced by the work of Kremlin ideologue, Vladislav Surkov, and his idea of sovereign democracy (*suverennaya demokratsiya*), which rejects the notion of a single type of democracy (i.e. American) and argues that each country should have the freedom and sovereignty to develop its own form. Indeed the only 'sources' cited on the movement's website are Surkov's works (URLb). The concept of sovereign democracy is a critique of Western democracy promotion efforts which were implemented following the collapse of the Soviet Union.

The idea of sovereign democracy as espoused is currently spreading beyond Russia. In July 2006 the Nashi Rossiya-Uzbekistan movement was established in Uzbekistan (Saidazimova 2006). Meanwhile, Dariga Nazarbaeva, the daughter of President Nursultan Nazarbayev of Kazakhstan, praised sovereign democracy as sign of freedom. She said:

> For a long time, we trod a path to democracy guided by maps prepared in the West. But times are changing. We see more and more countries and peoples in the world refusing to live according to identical patterns set up for them by someone else. Even the failure of the European constitution, was in defence of the national and the home-grown... In defence of sovereignty (Kimmage 2006).

Demonstrations, mass mobilisations and education

While opposition groups, including members of the 'Other Russia' (*Drugaya Rossiya*) coalition, have faced harassment from police and had their rallies and meetings disrupted by security forces, in contrast Nashi's actions, such as mass mobilisations and educational activities, have not been obstructed and have instead received support.

In the past two years Nashi has organised numerous high profile demonstrations. In 2006 members of Nashi spearheaded a campaign against the British Ambassador in Moscow, Anthony Brenton, because he had attended an opposition conference organised by the 'Other Russia' coalition. Brenton's appearance at this conference sparked a series of protests led by Nashi including demonstrations in front of the Ambassador's official residence and disruptions at public events where Brenton was due to speak. Nashi claimed it wanted Mr Brenton to apologise for having shown support for what the movement defined as extremist and nationalist groups.

On 17 December 2006, over 70,000 Nashi members dressed as Father Christmas, Snow Maiden or elves took to the streets of Moscow to celebrate the 60th anniversary of the Soviet victory against the Nazis in the Battle of Moscow. The day before, a rally was held with heavy police reinforcements to commemorate more than 200 journalists killed in Russia in the past 15 years. Only 200 people attended this commemoration.

In April and May 2007, Nashi members began to hold daily protests in front of the Estonian embassy in Moscow following the removal of the Bronze Soldier of Tallinn statue. The removal of this statue is described on the group's website as evidence of state-sanctioned fascism in Estonia.

In addition to these high profile demonstrations, Nashi provides educational and ideological training to its members. Those who successfully complete the training and pass the exams become Nashi commissars. The commissars are the most active members who receive even further education and training, and are groomed for leadership positions. In the various provinces Nashi activists also organise master classes, lectures, and educational competitions for high school students.

Nashi and democracy promotion

Nashi is growing against the backdrop of criticism in Russia about how the country fared in the wake of the collapse of the Soviet Union and what it perceived as its humiliation and loss of status globally. According to Steven Pifer, a senior adviser with the Centre for Strategic and International Studies in Washington:

Moscow's combative stance is widely seen as a reaction to the humiliation many Russians felt in the 1990s, when the country was emerging from the Soviet collapse...Russia was also subject to frequent Western lectures about how best to rebuild its society and government. There is this lingering perception that in the 1990s the West somehow took advantage of Russia. (Whitmore 2007)

Indeed there is a growing backlash against democracy promotion and civil society strengthening in the way it was introduced by Western donors and NGOs in the 1990s (Carothers 2006; Howell et al. 2007). While derided for his autocratic policies in the West, Putin currently enjoys widespread public support in Russia. His popularity is based on the perception that he has restored Russia's pride and place in the world and that he is challenging the hegemony of Western powers including the US and Britain. In a scathing critique of democracy promotion, Putin made the following remarks at the G8 Summit in St Petersburg:

If you look at newspapers of 100 years ago, you see how, at the time, colonialist states justified their policies in Africa or in Asia. They talked of their civilising role, of the white man's mission. If you change the word 'civilising' to 'democratisation', you find the same logic, you can read the same things in the press today. (BBC 2006)

According to Russian political analyst, Pyotr Romanov, one of the implicit items on the summit's agenda was the issue of the independence and sovereignty in relations between democratic countries. He writes, 'In a unipolar world dominated by the United States and its desire to be "generous" to humankind by forcing the North American worldview on it, this issue was bound to surface at bilateral talks within the G8 and during joint discussions' (Romanov 2006). Such criticisms of Western democracy promotion are becoming more widespread in Russia and other former Soviet countries (including Kazakhstan, Uzbekistan, etc.) and Nashi, which draws on Soviet and post-Soviet era models of organising, is both a recipient as well as purveyor of these neo-Cold War ideologies.

Armine Ishkanian, Lecturer in Social Policy, LSE

Genetically-engineered civil society

Katherine Verdery (1996) contends that since the demise of communism, Western capitalist societies have come to believe that they have a monopoly on truth and can therefore dispense wisdom about how to build the 'proper' forms of democracy and capitalism. This, the critics charge, led to the promotion of a single (i.e. Western) model of civil society that ignores other traditions and understandings (Parekh 2004: 22). According to Thomas Carothers, 'Democracy promoters pass through these countries [in Africa, Asia and the Middle East] on hurried civil society assessment missions and declare that "very little civil society exists" because they have found only a handful of Westernised NGOs devoted to non-partisan public-interest advocacy work on the national side' (Carothers 1999: 248). Since donor-defined civil society (that is, professional NGOs) did not exist in many places or was believed to have been tainted, donors engaged in a process of building society from scratch (Mandel 2002: 282).

This led to the promotion of a particular model of civil society and democracy, and encouraged the creation of what I refer to as 'genetically-engineered civil societies.' With the injection of external funding (the growth hormones), these genetically engineered civil societies experienced spectacularly rapid growth that would have not occurred organically. Similar to genetically modified crops, they also began to colonise and squeeze out all indigenous competitors, becoming the dominant type in their environment. In the process, in many places existing civil society lost its diversity and was reduced to professionalised NGOs that were engaged in advocacy or service delivery and that supported, in theory if not in practice, liberal Western values. Through this approach, which has also been termed 'institutional modelling' (Carothers 2000), organisations and actors were rewarded on the basis of their success in imitating that particular model and its associated discourses.

Subsequently, groups that did not replicate these practices and discourses, such as nationalist organisations and activist groups, were ignored or marginalised by donors and soon came to view themselves as real civil society, in contrast to the donor-created and- supported NGOs. In Latin America, as Jenny Pearce (2004) discusses, this led to divisions between organisations that considered themselves builders, and those that considered themselves critics, of democracy building. The critics (social organisations) not only view the builders (professionalised NGOs) as having been co-opted by the state, but also consider them as advocates of the neo-liberal economic agenda (Pearce 2004: 63). Sabine Freizer also differentiates between the donor-supported 'neo-liberal' and the 'communal' civil societies that have developed in Tajikistan and Uzbekistan, and discusses the lack of mixing of goals and approaches between these parallel forms (Freizer 2004). She points out the lack of grassroots support or recognition for such neo-liberal organisations. Such developments have led to discussions about the unintended consequences of civil society strengthening programmes in many parts of the world and concerns that NGOs are donor driven, upwardly accountable and disconnected from their own communities and constituencies (Abramson 1999; Adamson 2002; Bruno 1997; Glasius et al. 2004; Hann 2004; Helms 2003; Hemment 2004; Henderson 2003; Howell and Pearce 2002; Ishkanian 2003, 2004; Mendelson 2002; McMahon 2002; Pearce 2004; Obadare 2004; Sampson 2002; Wedel 2001).

In addition to the funding of projects and organisations, a major component of the technical aspect of democracy promotion programmes involved the capacity building and training of trainers. Capacity building has been used to teach individuals a series of skills, including how to create and manage NGOs, how to apply for grants, how to prepare reports and so on. Having participated in a number of capacity building exercises designed for NGO activists in Armenia, I found that training, in addition to teaching a particular skill (for example, how to fundraise) also implicitly communicated the donors' expectations by teaching local actors which topics were open to discussion and which kinds of knowledge and discourses were considered valuable. While never criticising them publicly, many NGO members I interviewed in Armenia complained that the training often provided superficial, one-size fits all answers to problems, and information that was not applicable to the local context. They also resented the large sums spent on the trainers' per diem, their five-star hotel stays and business air travel. In neighbouring Georgia, where many of the same policies and trainings were also implemented, a Georgian NGO leader writes,

Teaching democracy? Representatives of NGOs in the Democratic Republic of Congo learn about democracy and elections

Some [Western] specialists come without the slightest knowledge of the countries they are advising. The latter generously share the American experience in organizing election campaigns and fundraising for candidates for state legislatures, or perhaps the Indian experience of community-building in traditionally caste-bound villages. I do not deny that all the information may be of some theoretical interest to some local specialists, but I will say that in Georgia the practical use of all those lectures, seminars, and training sessions was pretty much nonexistent ... Expert knowledge of India, combined with complete ignorance of Georgia ... was both insulting and humorous, neither facilitating the learning process nor contributing to the reputation of the international experts. (Haindrava 2003: 77)

The popularity of capacity building continues unabated. The following excerpt from the USAID (2004) 'A Year in Iraq: Building Democracy' report demonstrates the importance ascribed to capacity building. As part of the US democracy promotion effort in Iraq, a former official from Colorado was asked to write a guide explaining how to run a meeting, how to encourage people to speak and contribute, and how to resolve disagreements and reach decisions through compromise. The guide was translated into Arabic and distributed to all members of local councils in Iraq. In order to assess how these lessons had been absorbed, a district council meeting was observed. According to the report:

At the district council meeting, the Iraqi experiment in democracy seemed to be running off the tracks when a couple of council members began shouting their opinions around the table, appearing to be angry enough to come to blows. (USAID 2004: 12)

The USAID observer was told not to worry by an Iraqi council member, who explained that the shouting was only theatrics and that it would not disrupt the process. While seemingly accepting that this was 'the Iraqi way', the authors express their satisfaction that 'the shouting soon gave way to constructive debate; the council agreed on some issues and deferred others before it adjourned peacefully' (USAID 2004: 12).

Although donor policies are indeed an important factor, we must not disregard the agency and the role of the NGO leaders and members in developing or transition countries who, for various reasons, ranging from a sincere belief in the values of civil society and democracy to the more banal, pragmatic need to make a living, embraced the models, discourses, ideologies and projects promoted by donors. In the context of economic upheaval, impoverishment and crises, this led to some opportunistic use of aid funding. The misuse of aid money is hardly a shocking revelation: however, the actual misappropriation or perceived misuse of funds intended for democracy and civil society promotion not only has a negative impact on how NGOs are perceived (such as corrupt and opportunistic), but also on how the ideas they promote are received.

DEMOCRACY PROMOTION AND CIVIL SOCIETY

Box 4.3: Civil society and democratisation in the 'colour revolutions'

The 'colour revolutions' were a series of protest movements that emerged in several post-socialist countries following fraudulent elections by authoritarian governments. They took the form of massive street demonstrations that led to the overthrow of the ruling regimes by new coalitions committed to political reform and democratisation

The revolutions are so-named because of their non-violent resistance and the symbolic use of colours or flowers by supporters. NGOs, in particular youth and student activist groups, played a key role in organising the street demonstrations and creative non-violent resistance. The colour revolutions refer to the Rose Revolution in Georgia (2003), the Orange Revolution in Ukraine (2004), and the Tulip Revolution in Kyrgyzstan (2005). Some scholars also consider the Serbian Bulldozer Revolution of 2000, which led to the overthrow of Slobodan Milošević, as an influential forerunner of the colour revolutions. This revolution was led by *Otpor* (Resistance), which became an important knowledge source for, and trainer of, the subsequent movements.

In Georgia, following fraudulent elections in November 2003, and galvanized by the *Kmara* (Enough) youth movement and the Liberty Institute, protestors thronged the streets of Tbilisi carrying roses – a symbol of non-violence. Georgia's Rose Revolution forced President Eduard Shevardnadze to resign; and he was replaced by Mikhail Saakashvili after new elections in March 2004.

In Ukraine, as rumours of fraudulent second round elections circulated, opposition leader Viktor Yushchenko called for mass public protests. Wearing orange or carrying orange flags, the colour of Yushchenko's campaign coalition, demonstrators poured onto the streets and squares. The youth movement *Pora* (High Time!) coordinated the mass protests, acts of civil disobedience, sit-ins and general strikes during the Orange Revolution. The movement resulted in a re-run of the election and Yushchenko's victory.

Kyrgyzstan's Tulip Revolution of 2005 was led by a new movement, *Kelkel* (Renaissance), which was modelled on Otpor and Pora. In the wake of fraudulent elections, activists seized control of several towns in southern Kyrgyzstan and called on President Askar Akaev to resign. The demonstrations spread to the north of the country, and when a 10,000 strong demonstration, led by Kelkel, was attacked by Akaev supporters, a riot broke out and the presidential palace was stormed. The violence of the Tulip Revolution, in which at least three people were killed, contrasted with the peaceful change of the other colour revolutions.

Common features
The experiences of the first democratic revolutions offered a model, which was spread by NGOs and adapted according to local circumstances by social movements. Four key characteristics of the colour revolutions have been identified:

1. civil society organisations' use of fraudulent elections to mobilise against regimes
2. foreign support for the development of local democratic movements
3. the organisation of radical youth movements using unconventional protest tactics and non- violent resistance
4. the importance of transnational linkages (Beissinger 2005).

1. All of the colour revolutions were electoral revolutions, and used the occasion of a stolen election to organise mass protests led by a coalition of civil organisations. For example, the Orange Revolution's central civic organisation was Pora, whose yellow wing - named after the colour of their symbols - formed part of the Freedom of Choice Coalition, which was active in election monitoring. This coalition organised massive protests in cities across Ukraine; the largest, in Kiev's Independence Square, attracted an estimated 500,000 participants, which was unprecedented.

2. The financial support of foreign donors and mainly American NGOs was critical to the emergence of local democratic movements (Wilson 2006). Through the democracy promotion programmes in Ukraine prior to the Orange revolution, the United States spent an estimated $65 million, which was channelled mainly

through foreign NGOs to Ukrainian NGOs and social movements (Beissinger 2005). In Georgia, the local branch of the Soros Foundation supported Kmara's election support programme with $350,000, and other NGOs also received significant financial and organisational support from the National Democratic Institute (Stojanovic 2004).

3. The rise of radical youth organisations influenced the tactics of the movement. Due to the young age composition of NGOs, the internet became a major location, not only for mobilisation and the diffusion of information, but for humour and ridicule of the authorities (Kuzio 2006). For example, the intellectual abilities of Ukrainian presidential candidate Victor Yanukovych were ridiculed in youth NGO circles and on websites after it emerged the 'Professorship' listed on his CV was fictitious (Chornuhuza 2005). In addition to this humour, the Ukrainian movement's activities were infused with a carnivalesque atmosphere; for instance, the hymn of the Orange revolution was downloaded 1.5 million times from the internet in 2004 (Kuzio 2006). Non-violent resistance was common to all the colour revolutions – a tactic inspired by the work of Gene Sharp (1993), the guru of non-violent resistance in the West, and then disseminated by NGO training centres (Beissinger 2006).

4. The successful operations of the main NGOs could not have developed without the experience of others, and the transnational linkages that allowed those lessons to be shared. For instance, the Soros Foundation supported a trip by Georgian civil society activists to Belgrade where they met with Otpor activists and learnt about non-violent resistance techniques. This inspired the creation of Kmara, which grew into a broad-based movement of 3000 students (Beissinger 2006). Before the Orange Revolution, 14 Pora leaders were trained in Serbia at the Centre for Non-Violent Resistance, an organisation created by Otpor activists to teach youth leaders how to organise a movement, how to motivate voters, and how to develop mass actions. Pora also provided summer camps in civil disobedience training for its members (Yablokova 2004).

Diffusion

The success of each revolution provided impetus for neighbouring countries in the post-Soviet region. Democratic youth groups such as 'Walking Without Putin', the Red Pora or the Orange Moscow, were formed in Russia, while in Belarus, the youth movement Zubr (Bison) became more active in this period. Similar movements emerged later in Azerbaijan and Kazakhstan, the activists trained often by Pora. Youth movements modelled on Otpor were also created in Albania, Egypt, and Zimbabwe. The so-called 'Cedar Revolution' in Lebanon also gained some inspiration from the Orange and the Rose Revolutions.

Despite the spread of the colour revolutions, the role of NGOs in the emergence of these revolutions has been highly criticised by academics on one side, and governments in the region on the other. The primary critique has been that NGOs are foreign agents of Western democracy promotion; for example, some argue that the Orange Revolution was 'made in the USA' (Wilson 2006: 3). The colour revolutions have also engendered a backlash against civil society in several authoritarian regimes (Carothers 2006; Howell et al. 2007), with the result that some NGOs have been closed down by the authorities. For instance, the Soros Foundation no longer operates in Belarus, Russia, Turkmenistan, and Uzbekistan because of the growing hostility of those governments towards what is perceived as assistance to 'revolutionary organisations' (Beissinger 2005). Finally, some analysts doubt that in the long term these revolutions will influence the process of democratisation significantly. Before the national elections in Kazakhstan, President Nursultan Nazarbaev criticised Western interference through NGOs:

They [parliament] have seen the dangers that arose in neighbouring countries when foreign N.G.O.s insolently pumped in money and destabilized society. The state was defenceless against this. (Karajkov 2005:1)

A Russian law passed in 2006 portrays 'NGOs as imported, unnatural, un-Russian implants' (Kuzio 2006: 12). In 2006, Kazakhstan modified its law on NGOs to control their activities and require consent for foreign financing (Wilson 2006). Similar legislation and regime propaganda is also evident in Belarus. The increasing isolation of authoritarian regimes and the greater oppression of civil society organisations offers little chance for a successful democratisation in the region.

However, others argue that unless there is a genuine domestic mass movement against an authoritarian regime, foreign support will have little effect (Wilson 2006). Moreover, most of the original protest campaigns were funded domestically. The majority of the foreign finance went on training and maintenance. According to Amchuk (2004) the cost of organising the protest in Kiev's central square was equivalent to US $3.8 million, which was raised without foreign support. Beissinger (2006), Herd (2005) and others agree that the financial support of Western countries and NGOs was crucial, but that these revolutions emerged from domestic dissatisfaction and were not instigated from abroad.

Finally, some critics argue neither the goals nor the outcome of the colour revolutions were revolutionary, or led to dramatic regime change (Jones 2006). In the Rose Revolution people did not expect the resignation of Shevardnadze; they were more concerned with transparency of the government, removal of the old nomenclature and more reforms. After the revolution, changes including new constitutional amendments in favour of the executive, and increased accountability of the administration, did not lead to radical transformations. As Jones says: 'And has the Rose Revolution over the last two years transformed itself into a 'Rosy Revolution', based on public relations rather than genuine democratic change?' (2006: 7). The long-term impact of the colour revolutions on democracy building remains to be seen.

Zsófia Farkas, postgraduate student in NGOs and Development, LSE

I recognise the diversity of civil society actors' motivations and I do not wish in any way to portray all NGO actors as being driven by economic incentives. However, the fact remains that in the 1990s, creating or joining NGOs became an economic survival strategy from countries as far apart as Albania to Zambia, thanks to the influx of donor aid (Celichowski 2004: 75; Ishkanian 2004; Mandel 2002: 286; Obadare 2004: 159; Sampson 2002: 307). These so-called 'grant-eaters' (Ishkanian 2003: 29), 'civil society entrepreneurs'(Obadare 2004: 159) or 'profiteers' (Kaldor et al. 2007: 111) cashed in on the 'gold rush' by engaging in civil society strengthening programmes. Of course individuals adapt, manipulate and negotiate ideologies, discourses and projects to fit their needs, but within the context of aid encounters they very rarely publicly question the validity of these approaches and ideas, even if they do so privately and off the record. Whereas I understand the potential costs of speaking out (including losing funding and being labelled a troublemaker), unfortunately, silence has often been interpreted by donors as a sign of acceptance of the *status quo*.

Therefore I argue that donors' definitions of democracy and civil society, and the operationalisation of civil society, have affected local processes of democracy and have raised questions about the viability of externally driven democracy promotion programmes.

Conflating democracy promotion with regime change

Finally, in recent years the crisis of democracy in the West has made democracy promotion much more difficult as claims of undemocratic behaviour in others are met with charges of hypocrisy. The *ex post facto* justification for the Iraq war as a form of democracy promotion has meant that democracy promotion has been confused or conflated with regime change. At present, suspicion about and resistance to US democracy promotion activities in developing and post-socialist countries is at an all-time high (Carothers 2006). Far from having won hearts and minds in the Middle East, it appears that the US justification for the war in Iraq has 'given democracy promotion a bad name' (Halperin 2006). The perceived presence of the US 'shadowy guiding hand' in the colour revolutions has also intensified the criticism and scepticism toward democracy

promotion in the former Soviet states. Four years on from the first colour revolution (that is, the Rose Revolution in Georgia), optimism has declined and democratic development remains under serious question in all the countries that experienced a colour revolution (Beissinger 2006; see box 4.3). Following these revolutions, allegations of interventionism and imperialism have intensified as the authorities in many former Soviet states attribute the 'directive' and 'top down approaches' to foreign meddling in what they consider internal political affairs.

Such criticisms are not limited to Iraq or the former Soviet states. For instance, US support for the NGO *Súmate* (Join Up) in Venezuela, which has received support from NED and USAID, is described by critics as having been created with the sole purpose of getting rid of President Hugo Chavez and replacing him with someone who is on friendlier terms with the US (Gindin 2005; see Box 4.4). William Robinson describes the objectives of US democracy promotion in Venezuela as undermining authentic democracy by

gaining control over popular movements for democratisation, keeping a lid on popular democracy movements, and limiting any change that may be brought about by mass democratisation movements so that the outcomes of democracy struggles do not threaten the elite order and integration into global capitalism. (Robinson and Gindin 2005)

Although at times these critics tend to ignore some of Chavez's authoritarian policies, they do articulate the growing questioning of the motives behind American democracy promotion.

Increasingly there are arguments that democracy promotion and civil society aid are beginning to be used in the way that human rights became a cynical tool in the Cold War, where violations in Brazil under military rule or Pinochet's Chile were ignored because these regimes were anti-Communist and part of the 'free world' (Kaldor 2003: 52). Today the double standards of supporting 'friendly tyrants' in Saudi Arabia, Pakistan and Egypt, as well as claims about extraordinary rendition and the use of torture in Abu Ghraib and Guantanamo Bay, are compromising democracy promotion efforts and feeding into the emerging backlash against civil society and democracy promotion.

Conclusion

'Democracy is not instant coffee' stated Benita Ferrerro-Waldner, the European Commissioner for External Relations and ENP in a recent speech (2006). Her comment represents the pragmatic attitude that has replaced the euphoria and optimism of the early 1990s. After nearly two decades of democracy promotion, donors remain committed to civil society strengthening, but they are re-evaluating their earlier approaches and formulating new strategies. In this period of reckoning, we are faced with questions of how and whether democracy should be promoted through externally funded programmes. Is continued civil society strengthening the way forward? What about support to state actors? Or political parties?

The results of democracy promotion thus far have been varied. Indeed, democracy has been (re)established in many countries. Moreover, if we consider the spread of formal or procedural democracies, then democracy promotion programmes can be and are deemed a success.[9] However, if we consider the development and spread of substantive democracies, then it is clear that donor-supported democracy promotion and civil society strengthening programmes have not met with great success because, although the mechanisms and institutions have been created, we are not witnessing greater civic participation, engagement and inclusion. It is not uncommon to hear about 'virtual' and 'managed' democracies. In many instances donor civil society strengthening programmes, while leading to the exponential growth of NGOs, have also thwarted natural political processes and imposed a particular model of democracy and civil society. This tendency has led to an 'abortion of local processes of change' (Hann 2004: 46) and tamed social movements (Kaldor 2003). Some even suggest that donor civil society strengthening programmes risk 'inhibiting and ultimately destroying the most important purposes of civil society ... the freedom to imagine that the world could be different' (Howell and Pearce 2002: 237).

These concerns, however, are only part of the story. The reality is far more complex because, in spite of the taming, co-optation, and backlash, there is still much emancipatory potential left in civil society and it is important not to deny the agency of civil society actors around the world for challenging hegemonic discourses and powerful actors, as well as contesting oppressive regimes.

As the development of civil society and, indeed, democracy is no longer solely restricted to national boundaries, outside actors, be they foreign donors, diasporic networks or global civil society activists, cannot be excluded from the equation. Global actors are implicated in and shape national/local processes in a multitude of ways, including providing financial assistance, training, and supporting exchanges and education abroad. Actually existing global civil society is complex and contradictory (Kaldor et al. 2007: 119); it can contribute to peace, stability and justice just as it can foment conflict, instability and exclusion. While some global civil society actors (such as NGOs) are engaged in democracy promotion through civil society strengthening programmes, this is not the most important contribution of global civil society. The greatest contribution of global civil society is its potential to enhance communication by creating 'islands of engagement' (Kaldor 2003: 160), where diverse actors will find opportunities for discussion, participation and debate. If global civil society can do this and also encourage greater self-reflection by Northern actors about the state of their own democracy (and not only discussions about the status of democracy in the South), then it will go a long way in revitalising and reinvigorating democracy and of course, civil society.

Acknowledgements

The author would like to thank Martin Albrow, Marlies Glasius, Mary Kaldor and Hakan Seckinelgin for their useful comments and suggestions on previous drafts of this chapter.

---

9 *For instance, a recent USAID-commissioned study, 'Effects of U.S. Foreign Assistance on Democracy Building: Results of a Cross-National Quantitative Study,' used Freedom House and Polity IV measures to examine the impact of US democracy promotion programmes worldwide. As one of the authors of the study said, 'We found that when the United States spends money to promote democracy in foreign countries, it works' (Finkel et al. 2006). The authors of the report attribute the growth of democracy to US assistance and write, 'USAID Democracy and Governance obligations have a significant positive impact on democracy, while all other US and non-US assistance variables are statistically insignificant' (Finkel et al. 2006: 83, emphasis added).*

Box 4.4: *Súmate* (Join Up): promoting and defending democracy in Venezuela

Súmate (Join Up) is a private non-profit association, founded by opposition activists, Alejandro Plaz and María Corina Machado, and a group of Venezuelan citizens in 2002, with the objective of promoting individual liberty and the free exercise of citizen's constitutional rights. Today, the organisation has more than 30,000 volunteers.

Plaz and Machado were employed in the private sector until they founded Súmate, Plaz was a senior partner for McKinsey & Company in Latin America, and Machado worked for a car parts manufacturer (National Review Online 2006).

According to Golinger (2005), Súmate's mission is to 'promote a recall referendum against President Chávez, a participatory instrument introduced in Venezuela's Constitution of 1999, with the support of the Chávez government. However, Súmate describes its mission as being to '...promote, defend, facilitate and support the complete exercise of political rights the Venezuelan Constitution grants to every one of its citizens' (Súmate URL). Its stated goals and values are:

- The guarantee of civil and political freedom and rights
- Impartial and independent citizen participation in democratic processes
- Professional volunteerism with a high level of citizen participation
- Organisational transparency and efficacy

Súmate has engaged in a number of activities in its effort to promote and defend democracy in Venezuela, including the collection and processing of signatures for the recall referendum; the collection and processing of the signatures for a constitutional amendment; and the design, planning and coordination of the *Firmazo* (the Big Signing) of February 2003. In addition, Súmate runs several projects that include the consolidation of the national web of volunteers, the diagnosis and analysis of the permanent national electoral registry, the planning and execution of the parallel manual counting of the votes to strengthen transparency and trust in electoral processes, and educational projects implemented through its numerous volunteers (Súmate 2004).

Because of Súmate's open objections to the many steps President Hugo Chávez has taken to consolidate his power, the organisation has been described as an 'enemy of the people' by the Venezuelan government (O'Grady 2005). Both founders, Plaz and Machado, are being accused of a conspiracy 'to alter the Republican order' under the Venezuelan Penal Code, and are currently awaiting trial. Other active members, such as Luis Enrique Palacios and Ricardo Estévez, face the same charges, but as accomplices. The Prosecutor Ortega Díaz has requested the maximum penalty for the crime of conspiracy, which is 16 years.

Critics argue that Súmate is not an impartial organisation, even though Súmate describes itself as a civil association that is not concerned with who governs but rather with safeguarding democracy in Venezuela. The criticism surrounding Súmate stems largely from the perception that it is funded and influenced by foreign actors. The conspiracy charge mentioned above, for instance, is linked to the grant received by the US National Endowment for Democracy (NED). In September 2003, Súmate signed a contract with the NED for a US$53,400 grant for the implementation of a programme of non-partisan elections education. However, only $31,000 was used by the organisation to develop its educational project and the rest of the grant was returned to the NED. (O'Grady 2005).

In addition to the NED grant, Súmate has also received funds from the German Konrad Adenauer Foundation, USAID and the Canadian Embassy (interview with Súmate 2007).1 The USAID grant was part of the agency's programme, launched in August 2002, to provide assistance to maintain democratic stability and strengthen Venezuela's fragile democratic institutions (USAID/OTI 2006).

Súmate's director, Alejandro Plaz, says that only 5% of the organisation's total funding comes directly from foreign entities. In an interview held in May 2007, he said:

Súmate's funding comes primarily from Venezuelan citizens concerned with the current situation our country is living. Deposits are made through several national bank accounts the organistion owns, for as little as $1, if desired, by any one who wishes.

Aside from the arguments about foreign funding, critics point to the relationship between Súmate's leaders and the Bush administration. For example, a meeting between Machado and President Bush in the White House in 2005, caused an outcry and criticism from the government in Caracas. Venezuela's foreign minister, Alí Rodríguez Araque, called the meeting 'a provocation', and the interior minister, Jesse Chacón, called Machado 'a puppet of the CIA', continuing the heated rhetoric that has characterised the relationship between the Bush administration and Venezuela's president (Ceaser 2005).

A protestor demonstrates against President Hugo Chavez

Golinger (2005) states the Venezuelan government believes the promotion of a recall referendum against the President, though within the constitutional rights of all Venezuelans, is inherently a partisan act. According to the Venezuelan government, Súmate was specifically 'promoting' and campaigning for a referendum against President Chávez, with the goal of prematurely terminating his mandate, utilising the funding from the NED, along with additional grants from USAID and funds from the National Democratic Institute and the International Republican Institute, both entities financed by NED and USAID (Golinger 2006).

The recall referendum held in August 2004 was defeated with a 59% 'NO' vote, and even though the US based Carter Center (2005) concluded the results were accurate, the European Union observers could not monitor the referendum because of the restrictions imposed upon them by the Venezuelan government (de Cordoba and Luhnow 2004). An exit poll by Penn, Schoen & Berland Associates (PSB), in which Súmate personnel participated, predicted Chávez would loose by 20%, whereas the election results showed him winning by the same percentage. Schoen said of the referendum, 'I think it was a massive fraud' (Barone 2004).

The Venezuelan democracy, Súmate points out, was set up with a separation of powers, an independent judiciary, civil rights and provisions for free and fair elections. Súmate believes that the electoral processes under Chávez have not been transparent and fair, stating that the Venezuelan National Electoral Council (*Consejo Nacional Electoral*, CNE) is biased and controlled by the government. They also believe the Venezuelan state does not possess a clear separation of powers, which futher complicates the issue of transparency in electoral and other democratic processes (interview with Súmate 2007).

Venezuela's National Assembly approved a preliminary draft NGO law with provisions similar to those in Uzbek and Russian legislation. Venezuela would require all local civic organisations to register as legal entities with a new regulatory body, in addition to complying with existing civil code and tax laws. Registered groups would have to provide detailed information on donations and donors. The Venezuelan government would monitor and control all international contributions to civil society groups. Instead of using state banks, the government would establish a regulatory board to filter donations. This 'agency for international cooperation' would have full discretion to issue or withhold funds based on the government's own criteria. It could also give money to causes that donors never intended to sponsor (Johnson 2005). Huguette Labelle (2006), Chair of Transparency International, states:

> strong democracies are built on a solid foundation of freedom: freedom to speak out, to organise and to operate without government interference. This law's excessive regulation would undermine those basic rights. The role of civil society, to help protect the interests and rights of society in general, would be hindered.

According to Amnesty International, President Chávez 'must respect the right of non-governmental human rights organizations to carry out their legitimate work, such work is underpinned by international human rights treaties which the Venezuelan government has willingly pledged to uphold' (Amnesty International 2004).

Súmate's experience illustrates the pertinent and often contentious issues for civil society organisations seeking to promote democracy: donor interventions, agendas, and influences; and sovereignty and nationalism (Howell and Pearce 2002). If an NGO is partly funded by international institutions with clear links to the US government does it mean a foreign government is meddling in another's internal affairs, thus breaching its sovereignty? Where does one draw the line between promoting democracy and foreign intervention on domestic affairs?

Manuela Plaza, postgraduate student in NGOs and Development, LSE

REFERENCES

Abramson, David M (1999) 'A Critical Look at NGOs and Civil Society as Means to an End in Uzbekistan', *Human Organization*, 58(3): 240–50.

Adamson, Fiona B (2002) 'International Democracy Assistance in Uzbekistan and Kyrgyzstan: Building Civil Society from the Outside?' in Sarah E Mendelson and John K Glenn (eds), *The Power and Limits of NGOs: A Critical Look at Building Democracy in Eastern Europe and Eurasia.* New York: Columbia University Press.

Amchuk, Leonid (2004) 'Aleksandr Tretiakov: U nas ne bylo amerikanskikh deneg. Na revoliutsiiu perechislili 20 millionov griven'. [We did not have American money. The revolution cost 20 million griven.] www2.pravda.com.ua/archive/?41222-1-new (consulted 22 December 2004).

Amnesty International Report (2004) http://web.amnesty.org/library/Index/ENGAMR530012004?open&of=ENG-VEN (consulted 19 May 2007).

Barone, M (2004) 'Exit polls in Venezuela'. US News & World Report. http://www.usnews.com/usnews/opinion/baroneweb/mb_040820.htm (consulted 19 June 2007).

Bayart, Jean-François (1986) 'Civil Society in Africa', in Patrick Chabal (ed), *Political Domination in Africa.* Cambridge: Cambridge University Press.

BBC (2006) 'Putin rebuffs 'colonialist' West', 12 July. http://news.bbc.co.uk/go/em/fr//1/hi/world/europe/5172794.stm (consulted 14 June 2007).

Beissinger, Mark R (2006) 'Promoting Democracy: Is Exporting Revolution a Construtive Strategy?' Dissent Magazine. http://www.dissentmagazine.org/article/?article=155 (consulted 28 March 2007).

Beissinger, Mark R (2005) 'Structure and Example in Modular Political Phenomena: The Diffusion of Bulldozer/Rose/Orange/Tulip Revolutions'. http://polisci.wisc.edu/~beissinger/beissinger.modrev.article.pdf

Berg, Andrea (2004) 'Two Worlds Apart: The Lack of Integration between Women's Informal Networks and Nongovernmental Organizations in Uzbekistan', in Carol Nechemias and Kathleen Kuehnast (eds), *Post-Soviet Women Encountering Transition: Nation-Building, Economic Survival, and Civic Activism.* Baltimore, MD: Johns Hopkins Press and Woodrow Wilson International Center for Scholars Press.

Berman, Sheri (1997) 'Civil Society and the Collapse of the Weimar Republic', *World Politics*, 49(3): 401–29.

Bermeo, Nancy and Nord, Philip (eds) (2000) *Civil Society Before Democracy: Lessons from Nineteenth Century Europe.* Boulder, CO: Rowman & Littlefield.

Biden, Joseph R (2006) 'Statement of Senator Joseph R. Biden, Jr. Hearing on Non-Governmental Organizations and Democracy Promotion', US Senate Committee on Foreign Relations, 8 June. http://www.senate.gov/~foreign/testimony/2006/BidenStatement060608.pdf (consulted 20 March 2007).

Bobbio, Norberto (1988) 'Gramsci and the Concept of Civil Society', in John Keane (ed) *Civil Society and the State: New European Perspectives.* London: Verso.

Brzezinski, Zbigniew (2002) 'The Primacy of History and Culture' in Larry Diamond and Marc F Plattner (eds), *Democracy after Communism.* Baltimore, MD: Johns Hopkins University.

Bruno, Marta (1997) 'Playing the Co-operation Game,' in Sue Bridger and Frances Pine (eds), *Surviving Post-Socialism: Local Strategies and Regional Responses in Eastern Europe.* London: Routledge.

Burawoy, Michael and Verdery, Katherine (eds) (1999) *Uncertain Transitions: Ethnographies of Change in the Post-Socialist World.* Lanham: Rowan & Littlefield.

Carothers, Thomas (1999) *Aiding Democracy Abroad: The Learning Curve.* Washington, DC: Carnegie Endowment for International Peace.

— (2000) 'Democracy Promotion: A key focus in a new world order', Issues of Democracy, 5(1) May. http://usinfo.state.gov/journals/itdhr/0500/ijde/carothers.htm (consulted 28 March 2007).

— (2006) 'Responding to the Democracy Promotion Backlash'. Testimony, US Senate Committee on Foreign Relations, 8 June 2006. http://www.carnegieendowment.org/publications/index.cfm?fa=view&id=18416&prog=zgp&proj=zdrl,zme (consulted 20 March 2007).

— (2006) 'The Backlash against Democracy Promotion', *Foreign Affairs*, March/April.

Carter Center (2005) 'Observing the Venezuela Presidential Recall Referendum: Comprehensive Report'. http://www.cartercenter.org/news/documents/doc2023.html (consulted 19 June 2007).

Ceaser, M (2005) 'Anti-Chávez leader under fire: María Corina Machado is due in court Wednesday on treason charges', *The Christian Science Monitor.* http://www.csmonitor.com/2005/0705/p06s01-woam.html (consulted 19 June 2007).

Celichowski, Jerzy (2004) 'Civil Society in Eastern Europe: Growth Without Engagement', in Marlies Glasius, David Lewis and Hakan Seckinelgin (eds), *Exploring Civil Society: Political and Cultural Contexts.* London: Routledge.

Chandler, David (2004) 'Democratization in Bosnia: The Limits of Civil Society Building Strategies', in Peter Burnell and Peter Calvert (eds), *Civil Society in Democratization.* London: Frank Cass.

Chandhoke, Neera (1995) *State and Civil Society: Explorations in Political Theory.* New Delhi: Sage Publications.

Chornuhuza, O (ed) (2005) *Tak! Ukrayintsi Peremahayut Smiyuchys.* VUS: Kyiv.

Cohen, Jean (1999) 'Trust, Voluntary Association and Workable Democracy', in Mark Warren (ed), *Democracy and Trust.* Cambridge: Cambridge University Press.

Colton, Timothy J. and McFaul, Michael (2003) *Popular Choice and Managed Democracy: the Russian Elections of 1999 and 2000.* Washington, DC: Brookings Institution Press.

de Cordoba, J and Luhnow, D (2004) 'Venezuelans Rush to Vote on Chavez: Polarized Nation Decides Whether to Recall President After Years of Political Rifts', *Wall Street Journal* (Eastern edition). (consulted 18 June 2007).

Development Alternatives Inc. (URL) http://www.dai.com/work/practice_detail.php?pid=6

(consulted 14 June 2007).

DFID (URLa) 'Making Democracy Work for Poverty Reduction'. http://www.dfid.gov.uk/pubs/files/election.pdf (consulted 20 May 2007).

— (URLb) 'The Civil Society Challenge Fund'. http://www.dfid.gov.uk/funding/civilsocietyguidelines06.asp (consulted 20 May 2007).

Encarnacion, Omar (2003) 'Beyond Civil Society: Promoting Democracy after September 11', *Orbis* 47(4): 705–20.

European Foundation for Democracy (2006) 'The EU Approach to Democracy Promotion in External Relations: Food for Thought'. http://www.democracyagenda.org/modules.php?mop=modload&name=Upload&file=index&op=getit&fid=15 (consulted 25 April 2007).

Ferrerro-Waldner, Benita (2006) 'Remarks on democracy promotion' delivered at the conference, 'Democracy Promotion: The European Way', European Parliament's Alliance of Liberals and Democrats for Europe, Brussels. http://www.alde.eu/fileadmin/images/photo_library/2006/20061206_democracy_promotion/061207_benita_ferrero_speech_on_democracy_promotion.doc.pdf (consulted 14 June 2007).

Finkel, Steven E, Aníbal Pérez-Liñán, Mitchell A Seligson and Dinorah Azpuru (eds) (2006) 'Effects of US Foreign Assistance on Democracy Building: Results of a Cross-National Quantitative Study'. http://www.usaid.gov/our_work/democracy_and_governance/publications/pdfs/impact_of_democracy_assistance.pdf (consulted 28 March 2007).

Freizer, Sabine (2004) 'Central Asian Fragmented Civil Society: Communal and Neoliberal Forms in Tajikistan and Uzbekistan' in Marlies Glasius, David Lewis and Hakan Seckinelgin (eds), *Exploring Civil Society: Political and Cultural Contexts* London: Routledge.

Garton Ash, Timothy (2004) 'The $65m question: when, how – and where – should we promote democracy? First we need the facts', *The Guardian*, 16 December.

Gaventa, John (2006) 'Triumph, Deficit or Contestation@ Deepening the 'Deepening Democracy' Debate'. http://www.ids.ac.uk/ids/particip/information/WP264Summary.pdf July (consulted 28 March 2007).

Gellner, Ernest (1994) *Conditions of Liberty: Civil Society and Its Rivals.* London: Hamish Hamilton.

Gershman, Carl and Allen, Michael (2006) 'The Assault on Democracy Assistance', *Journal of Democracy*, 17(2): 36–51.

Gillespie, Richard and Youngs, Richard (2002) 'Themes in European Democracy Promotion', *Democratization*, 9(1): 1–16.

Ghodsee, Kristen (2004) 'Feminism-by-Design: Emerging Capitalisms, Cultural Feminism and Women's Nongovernmental Organizations in Post-Socialist Eastern Europe', *Signs: Journal of Women in Culture and Society*, 29(3): 727–53.

Gindin, Jonah (2005) 'Bush and SUMATE', Znet. http://www.zmag.org/content/showarticle.cfm?ItemID=8000 (consulted 25 April 2007).

Glasius, Marlies, David Lewis and Hakan Seckinelgin (2004) 'Exploring Civil Society Internationally', in Marlies Glasius, David Lewis and Hakan Seckinelgin (eds), *Exploring Civil Society: Political and Cultural Contexts.* London: Routledge.

Golinger, Eva (2006) *The Chávez Code: Cracking US Intervention in Venezuela.* Olive Branch Press: Massachusetts.

— (2005) 'The Sumate Case: How the NED violates sovereignty and self-determination in Venezuela.' http://www.venezuelanalysis.com/articles.php?artno=1500 (consulted 18 June 2007).

Habermas, Jürgen (1992) *The Structural Transformation of the Public Sphere.* Cambridge: Polity Press.

— (1996) *Between Facts and Norms: Contributions to a Discourse Theory of Law and Democracy.* Oxford: Polity Press.

Haindrava, Ivlian (2003) 'H E L P !!' *in Centers for Pluralism – Networking for Democracy: 10 Years.* Institute of Statehood and Democracy. http://www.idee.org/JournalFINAL.pdf (consulted 15 June 2007).

Halperin, Morton H (2006) 'Democracy Promotion as Policy: Online Debate', Discussants Paul J Saunders and Morton H Halperin. http://www.cfr.org/publication/10784/ (consulted 20 March 2007).

Hann, Chris (2004) 'In the Church of Civil Society' in Marlies Glasius, David Lewis and Hakan Seckinelgin (eds), *Exploring Civil Society: Political and Cultural Contexts.* London: Routledge.

Hawthorne, Amy (2004) 'Middle Eastern Democracy: Is Civil Society the Answer?' *Carnegie Papers Middle East Series.* Washington, DC: Carnegie Endowment for International Peace.

Helms, Elissa (2003) 'Women as Agents of Ethnic Reconciliation? Women's NGOs and International Intervention in Postwar Bosnia–Herzegovina', *Women's Studies International Forum*, 26(1): 15–34.

Hemment, Julie (2004) 'The Riddle of the Third Sector: Civil Society, International Aid, and NGOs in Russia', Anthropological Quarterly 77(2): 215–41.

Henderson, Sarah L (2003) *Building Democracy in Contemporary Russia: Western Support for Grassroots Organizations.* Ithaca, NY: Cornell University Press.

Herd, G P (2005) 'Colorful Revolutions and the CIS: "Manufactured" versus "Managed" Democracy?' Problems of Post-Communism, 52(2): 3-18.

Herzfeld, Michael (2001) *Anthropology: Theoretical Practice in Culture and Society.* London: Blackwell.

Howell, Jude and Pearce, Jenny (2002) *Civil Society and Development. A Critical Interrogation.* Boulder, CO: Lynne Rienner.

Howell Jude, Ishkanian, Armine, Obadare, Ebenezer, Seckinelgin, Hakan and Glasius Marlies (2007) 'The Backlash against Civil Society in the Wake of the Long War on Terror', *Civil Society Working Paper 26*, Centre for Civil Society, London School of Economics. http://www.lse.ac.uk/collections/CCS/pdf/CSWP/CCS_WP_Howell_26.pdf (consulted 14 June 2007).

Ishkanian, Armine (2003). 'Is the Personal Political? How Domestic Violence Became an Issue in Armenia's NGO Sector in the Late 1990s', *Berkeley Program in Soviet and Post-Soviet Studies.* http://repositories.cdlib.org/iseees/bps/2003_03-ishk (consulted 14 June 2007).

— (2004) 'Working at the Global–Local Intersection: The

Challenges Facing Women in Armenia's NGO Sector,' in Carol Nechemias and Kathleen Kuehnast (eds), *Post-Soviet Women Encountering Transition: Nation-Building, Economic Survival, and Civic Activism*. Baltimore, MD: Johns Hopkins Press and Woodrow Wilson International Center for Scholars Press.

— (Forthcoming 2007) 'En-gendering Civil Society and Democracy-Building: the Anti-Domestic Violence Campaign in Armenia', *Social Politics*, 14(4), December.

Johnson, S (2005) 'Venezuela's New Chokehold on Civil Society', The Heritage Foundation. http://www.heritage.org/Research/LatinAmerica/em1005.cfm (consulted 12 January 2007).

Jones, S F (2006) *'The Rose Revolution: A Revolution without Revolutionaries?'* Cambridge Review of International Affairs, 19(1): 33–48.

Kaldor, Mary (2003) *Global Civil Society: An Answer to War.* Cambridge: Polity Press.

— Kostovicova, Denisa and Said, Yahia (2007) 'War and Peace: The Role of Global Civil Society', in Mary Kaldor, Martin Albrow, Helmut Anheier and Marlies Glasius (eds), *Global Civil Society Yearbook 2006/7*. London: Sage.

— and Vejvoda, Ivan (1997) 'Democratisation in Central and Eastern Europe' in *International Affairs*, 73(1): 59–82.

Karajkov R (2005) *'NGO Bashing'*, Worldpress.org. http://www.worldpress.org/Europe/2178.cfm

Keck, Margaret and Sikkink, Kathryn (1998) *Activists Beyond Borders : Advocacy Networks in International Politics*. Ithaca, NY: Cornell University Press

Kedourie, Elie (1992) *Democracy and Arab Political Culture*. Washington, DC: Washington Institute for Near East Policy.

Kimmage, Daniel (2006) 'Kazakhstan: 'Sovereign Democracy' in Almaty and Moscow. http://www.rferl.org/featuresarticle/2006/07/6129be69-8044-4ead-a401-3ac4d549a134.html (consulted 14 June 2007).

Konovalova, Evgeniya (2007) 'Reactionary Revolutionaries' in Transitions Online, 11 May 2007. http://www.tol.cz/look/TOL/article.tpl?IdLanguage=1&IdPublication=4&NrIssue=217&NrSection=3&NrArticle=18717 (consulted 14 June 2007).

Kopstein, Jeffrey (2006) 'The Transatlantic Divide over Democracy Promotion', *Washington Quarterly*, 29(2): 85–98.

Kuzio, Taras (2006) 'Civil society, youth and societal mobilization in democratic revolutions', *Communist and Post-Communist Studies*, 39(3): 365-386.

Lukas, Carrie (2006) 'Women the World Should Know', *National Review Online*. 8 March. http://www.nationalreview.com/symposium/symposium200603080944.asp (consulted 20 June 2007).

McFaul, Michael (2002) 'A Mixed Record, an Uncertain Future', in Larry Diamond and Marc F Plattner (eds), *Democracy after Communism*. Baltimore, MD: Johns Hopkins University Press.

— (2004) 'Democracy Promotion as a World Value', *Washington Quarterly*, 28(1): 147–63.

McMahon, Patrice C (2002) 'International Actors and Women's NGOs in Poland and Hungary' in Sarah E Mendelson and John K Glenn (eds), *The Power and Limits of NGOs: A Critical Look at Building Democracy in Eastern Europe and Eurasia*. New York: Columbia University Press.

Mandel, Ruth (2002) 'Seeding Civil Society' in C Hann (ed), *Postsocialism: Ideals, Ideologies and Practices in Eurasia*. London: Routledge.

Mardin, Serif (1995) 'Civil Society and Islam' in J A Hall (ed) *Civil Society: Theory, History, Comparison*. Cambridge: Cambridge University Press.

Martinez-Soliman, Magdy (2006) 'Challenges to Democracy Promotion', text of speech delivered at Club of Madrid Rapid Response Meeting, Pocantico, New York, 19 July.

Mendelson, Sarah E (2002) 'Conclusion: The Power and Limits of Transnational Democracy Networks in Postcommunist Societies' in Sarah E Mendelson and John K Glenn (eds), *The Power and Limits of NGOs: A Critical Look at Building Democracy in Eastern Europe and Eurasia*. New York: Columbia University Press.

Nashi (URLa) 'Ideology – Manifesto' http://www.nashi.su/ideology [in Russian] (consulted 14 June 2007).

Nashi (URLb) 'Ideology – Sources' http://www.nashi.su/ideology/sources [in Russian] (consulted 14 June 2004).

National Endowment for Democracy (url) http://www.ned.org/about/faq.html#Is%20NED%20part%20of%20the%20U.S.%20Government (consulted 20 May 2007).

Newman, Edward and Roland Rich (2004) *The UN Role in Promoting Democracy: Between Ideals and Reality*. Tokyo: United Nations University Press.

Nodia, Ghia (2002) 'How Different are Postcommunist Transitions?' in Larry Diamond and Marc F Plattner (eds), *Democracy after Communism*. Baltimore, MD: Johns Hopkins University Press.

Obadare, Ebenezer (2004) 'Civil Society in West Africa: Between Discourse and Reality' in Marlies Glasius, David Lewis and Hakan Seckinelgin (eds), *Exploring Civil Society: Political and Cultural Contexts*. London: Routledge.

Olson, Lara (2001) 'Women and NGOs: Views from Conflict Areas in the Caucasus', *New Bridges to Peace Occasional Papers*. Washington, DC: Women in International Security.

O'Grady, Mary Anastasia (2005) 'A Young Defender of Democracy Faces Chávez's Wrath', *Wall Street Journal*. (consulted 19 June 2007) http://www.hacer.org/current/Vene009.php (consulted 18 June 2007)

Planning and Development Collaborative International (URL) http://www.padco.aecom.com/MarketsAndServices/38/56/index.jsp (consulted 14 June 2007).

Ottaway, Marina and Carothers, Thomas (2000) *Funding Virtue: Civil Society Aid and Democracy Promotion*. Washington, DC: Carnegie Endowment for International Peace.

Palmer, Mark (2006) 'Promotion of Democracy by Nongovernmental Organizations: An Action Agenda', Testimony. US Senate Foreign Relations Committee, June 8. http://www.senate.gov/~foreign/testimony/2006/PalmerTestimony060608.pdf (consulted 20 March 2007).

Parekh, Bhikhu (2004) 'Putting Civil Society in Its Place' in Marlies Glasius, David Lewis and Hakan Seckinelgin (eds), *Exploring Civil Society: Political and Cultural Contexts*. London: Routledge.

Pearce, Jenny (2004) 'Collective Action or Public Participation?: Civil Society and the Public Sphere in Post-Transition Latin America' in Marlies Glasius, David Lewis and Hakan Seckinelgin (eds), *Exploring Civil Society: Political and Cultural Contexts.* London: Routledge.

Perez-Diaz, Victor (1993) *The Return of Civil Society: the Emergence of Democratic Spain.* Cambridge, MA: Harvard University Press.

Putnam, Robert (1994) *Making Democracy Work: Civic Traditions in Modern Italy.* Princeton, NJ: Princeton University Press.

Richter, James (2002) 'Evaluating Western Assistance to Russian Women's Organisations' in Sarah E Mendelson and John K Glenn (eds), *The Power and Limits of NGOs: A Critical Look at Building Democracy in Eastern Europe and Eurasia.* New York: Columbia University Press.

Rieff, David (1999) 'Civil Society and the Future of the Nation-State', *The Nation.* 22 February: 11–16.

Rieffer, Barbara Ann J and Mercer, Kristan (2005) 'US Democracy Promotion: The Clinton and Bush Administrations', *Global Society*, 19(4): 385–408.

Robinson, William and Gindin, Jonah (2005) 'The United States, Venezuela, and 'Democracy Promotion': William I Robinson interviewed. *Open Democracy* 4 August. http://www.opendemocracy.net/democracy-protest/venezuala_2730.jsp (consulted 28 March 2007).

Romanov, Pyotr (2006) 'G 8 and Sovereign Democracy', *Ria Novosti* 17 July. http://en.rian.ru/analysis/20060717/51480097.html (consulted 14 June 2007).

Rueschemeyer, Dietrich, Stephens, Eveyln and Stephens, John (eds) (1992) *Capitalist Devleopment and Democracy.* Chicago, IL: University of Chicago Press.

Sajoo, Amyn B (2002) 'Introduction: Civic Quests and Bequests' in Amyn B Sajoo (ed), *Civil Society in the Muslim World.* London: IB Tauris and Institute of Ismaili Studies.

Saidazimova, Gulnoza (2006) 'Uzbekistan: New Pro-Russian Youth Movement Launched', 14 July. http://www.rferl.org/featuresarticle/2006/07/271b4fea-f527-4638-8467-a52f0c730838.html (consulted 14 June 2007).

Salamon, Lester M, and Anheier, Helmut K (1997) *Defining the Nonprofit Sector: A Cross-national Analysis.* Manchester: Manchester University Press.

Sampson, Steven (2002) 'Beyond Transition: Rethinking Elite Configurations in the Balkans' in C Hann (ed), *Postsocialism: Ideals, Ideologies and Practices in Eurasia.* London: Routledge.

Schmid, Dorothee and Braizat, Fares (2006) *The Adaptation of EU and US Democracy Promotion Programmes to the Local Political Context in Jordan and Palestine and their Relevance to Grand Geopolitical Designs.* EuroMesco research project published by Institut français des relations internationales and Center for Strategic Studies.

Schumpeter, Joseph Alois (1947) *Capitalism, Socialism and Democracy.* New York: Harper and Brothers.

Sen, Purna (2003) 'Successes and Challenges: Understanding the Global Movement to End Violence Against Women' in Mary Kaldor, Helmut Anheier and Marlies Glasius (eds), *Global Civil Society 2003.* Oxford: Oxford University Press.

Stojanovic, D (2004) 'Nonviolent Revolution for Export from Serbia', *Associated Press*, October 31.

Súmate (2004) 'Preliminary report: The presidential recall referendum'. http://web.sumate.org/documentos/PrelimRRP1-2%20main%20text2.pdf (consulted 23 April 2007).

— Who we are (*Quienes somos*)http://web.sumate.org/quienes_somos.asp (consulted 22 April 2007).

Swedish International Development Co-operation Agency (SIDA) (1997) Justice and Peace: SIDA's Programme for Peace, Democracy and Human Rights. http://www.sida.se/shared/jsp/download.jsp?f=Part+1+JusticePeace97.pdf&a=2085 (consulted 20 May 2007).

Thompson, Mark R (2001) 'Whatever Happened to 'Asian Values'?' *Journal of Democracy*, 12(4): 154–65.

Tobias, Randall L (2007) Democracy and the New Approach to US Foreign Assistance. http://www.usaid.gov/press/speeches/2007/sp070117.html (consulted 20 March 2007).

Tohidi, Nayereh (2004) 'Women, Building Civil Society, and Democratizationin Post-Soviet Azerbaijan' in Carol Nechemias and Kathleen Kuehnast (eds), *Post-Soviet Women Encountering Transition: Nation-Building, Economic Survival, and Civic Activism.* Baltimore, MD: Johns Hopkins Press and Woodrow Wilson International Center for Scholars Press.

Transparency International (2006) 'Unrestricted civil society is critical to fight against corruption', press release. Berlin/Caracas. http://www.transparency.org/news_room/latest_news/press_releases/2006/2006_07_26venezuela_ngo_freedom (consulted 19 June 2007).

UN Democracy Fund (UNDEF) (URL) Brochure http://www.un.org/democracyfund/Docs/UNDEF_brochure.pdf (consulted 25 April 2007).

USAID/OTI (2006) 'Venezuela Field Report', April-June. http://www.usaid.gov/our_work/crosscutting_programs/transition_initiatives/country/venezuela/rpt0307.html (consulted 13 January 2007).

USAID (1999) *Lessons in Implementation: The NGO Story – Building Civil Society in Central and Eastern Europe and the New Independent States.* Washington, DC: USAID.

USAID (2002) *United States Assistance to Armenia,* USAID Mission to Armenia. Yerevan: Printinfo.

USAID (2004) 'A Year in Iraq: Building Democracy', 28 June. http://www.usaid.gov/iraq/pdf/AYearInIraq_democracy.pdf (consulted 2 April 2007).

USAID (2006) 'USAID Primer: What We Do and How We Do It'. http://www.usaid.gov/about_usaid/PDACG100.pdf (consulted 20 May 2007).

USAID (URL) 'Promoting Democracy and Good Governance'. http://www.usaid.gov/our_work/democracy_and_governance/ (consulted 28 March 2007).

USAID (2002) Mission to Armenia, Press Release on USAID Grants Program to Help Victims of Domestic Violence, October 18, 2002 Domestic Violence. http://www.usaid.gov/am/pr10_02_DV.html (consulted 20 May 2007).

US Senate (2006) '*Nongovernmental Organizations and Democracy Promotion: 'Giving Voice to the People'*, A Report to the Members of the Committee on Foreign Relations United States Senate. 22 December.

http://www.fas.org/irp/congress/2006_rpt/democracy.pdf
(consulted 20 March 2007).

Verdery, Katherine (1996) *What Was Socialism and What Comes Next?* Princeton, NJ: Princeton University Press.

Wedel, Janine R (2001) *Collision and Collusion: The Strange Case of Western Aid to Eastern Europe 1989–1998.* New York: St. Martin's Press.

Weffort, Francisco C (1989). Why Democracy? in Alfred Stephen (ed) *Democratizing Brazil: Problems of Transition and Consolidation.* New York: Oxford University Press.

Westminster Foundation for Democracy (url) http://www.wfd.org/pages/home.aspx?i_PageID=1811 (consulted 20 May 2007).

Whewhell, Tim (2006) 'The Kremlin's New Commissars', *BBC Newsnight*, 12 July. http://news.bbc.co.uk/2/hi/programmes/newsnight/5169610.stm (consulted 14 June 2007).

White, Gordon (2004) 'Civil Society, Democratization and Development: Clearing the Analytical Ground' in Peter Burnell and Peter Calvert (eds), *Civil Society in Democratization.* London: Frank Cass.

Whitmore, Brian (2007) 'Russia: Culture of Fear Back with a Vengeance', 1 June. http://www.rferl.org/features/features_Article.aspx?m=06&y=2007&id=A391FBA0-7C40-413A-8E25-5AF107BA4F18 (consulted 14 June 2007).

Wild, Leni (2006) 'The Darker Side of Global Civil Society', *Open Democracy*, 3 April. http://www.opendemocracy.net/democracy-think_tank/civil_society_3413.jsp (consulted 25 April 2007).

Wilson, A (2006)'Ukraine's Orange Revolution, NGOs and the Role of the West', *Cambridge Review of International Affairs*, 19(1): 21-32.

Yablokova, Oksana (2004) 'Youthful Pora Charges Up the People', *Moscow Times*. December.

Youngs, Richard (2006) *Survey of European Democracy Promotion Policies 2000–2006.* Madrid: Fundacion Para Las Relaciones Internacionales y el Dialogo Exterior (FRIDE).

CHAPTER 5

GLOBAL CIVIL SOCIETY AND ILLIBERAL REGIMES
Mary Kaldor and Denisa Kostovicova

At night every light that is on in Tehran shows that somebody is sitting behind a computer driving through information roads.
Iranian cyber-dissident

My back is someone else. People can't trust each other. People can't even trust their wives or children.
North Korean émigré recently arrived in the United Kingdom

Agreeing to disagree is a prerogative only of those who live under a democratic system. Under an authoritarian regime, disagreeing can be seen as a crime. This makes life for us rather difficult. Sometimes dangerous. But certainly not dull.
Aung San Suu Kyi

Introduction

Zimbuyer.com is a UK-based website that allows Zimbabweans living in the UK to purchase groceries and other items such as satellite dishes for friends and relatives back home, using the Internet and mobile phones, and thus avoid the costs of run-away inflation. The ordered goods are delivered by hand to households in Harare, Chitungwiza and Bulawayo. There are several other websites that offer similar services. For example, Mukuru.com is a UK-based platform through which money can be transferred (at the black-market rate), as well as payments for fuel and mobile phone airtime. Likewise, Beepee Medical Services, based in the UK, allows the diaspora community to pay for doctors' appointments, prescription drugs and surgery for people in Zimbabwe; the service was set up by a Zimbabwean doctor in the UK and has staff working full-time in Zimbabwe.

These websites could be regarded as a form of economic dissidence, which is just as important as the various forms of political dissidence in creating space in illiberal regimes. Whether we are talking about people smuggling in North Korea, the tourist market in Cuba, or blogging in Iran and China, increasing interconnectedness has weakened the state's ability to exercise administrative, economic and even ideological forms of control. Individuals, groups and networks use their global links to break out of the constraints imposed by authoritarian or repressive regimes.

The authors would like to thank Julia Chan, Wonyoung Choi and Sabine Selchow for their assistance with this chapter, and those people around the world who responded to our questionnaire.

This Chapter is about global civil society in illiberal regimes. We define illiberal regimes in terms of the spaces that exist for what might be described as civil society. And we ask whether and how these spaces are opened, closed or transformed in the context of globalisation. The Chapter is based on a study of civil society in six countries: China, North Korea, Burma, Belarus, Iran and Saudi Arabia; and we also refer to Cuba, Russia and Zimbabwe. Each case study was based on a survey of available literature and websites, personal interviews and interviews via email. Our main argument is that globalisation, even in the most closed authoritarian systems, has led to some form of involuntary pluralisation and that different types of illiberal regimes are based on various forms of this involuntary pluralisation. Pluralisation is not the same as democratisation and global connections may help both to dismantle and to strengthen illiberal regimes.

We start with a critique of the literature on illiberal regimes and the failure of most scholars to take globalisation into account. We then describe the ideas, the forms of activism and the spaces that characterise civil society in different illiberal regimes, and their global connections. We show that the idea of separation between the outside and inside does not hold. Rather, they are interconnected and embodied in civil society that is both local and global at the same time.

The nature of illiberal regimes

Remarkably little has been written about totalitarian and authoritarian regimes since the fall of Communism. The main preoccupation of scholars in recent years has been the process of democratisation rather than the nature of contemporary illiberal regimes.

Linz and Stepan, in their classic book on the transition to democracy, identified five modern regime ideal types: democracy, authoritarianism, totalitarianism, post-totalitarianism and sultanism (derived from Weber's extreme patrimonialism), which they described in terms of the defining characteristics of pluralism, ideology, mobilisation and leadership.

Of particular interest for our argument is their perspective on pluralism and, more specifically, the space of civil society in these regimes. According to Linz and Stepan, there is no civil society in sultanistic and totalitarian regimes due to the extensive power of the sultan or the party respectively. Totalitarian regimes were characterised by a pervasive ideology that, at their height, controlled even private spaces. By contrast, they argue that there is limited pluralism in authoritarian and post-totalitarian regimes. In the former, pluralism is mostly social and economic, with limited political pluralism. In the latter, there are various degrees of a 'second culture' or 'parallel society' that is limited and persecuted, but nonetheless a potent and independent political alternative (Linz and Stepan 1996: 38-54).

Implied in these definitions is the assumption that it is the state that grants or at least tolerates these liberties and, hence, free spaces. The state is understood as an all-powerful institution capable of controlling society. Yet it was always the case that the state is the expression of a set of social relations and the degree of control depends on the way that such relations are regulated. The difference between democratic and non-democratic regimes has to do with whether control is based on consent or coercion; usually state control depends on a mixture of consent and coercion. In democratic societies, control is based largely on consent, which in turn is the outcome of a debate within civil society. In non-democratic societies control is based on a mixture of submissive consent and coercion. We would contend that in the age of globalisation it is increasingly difficult, though not of course impossible, to exercise control on the basis of submissive consent and coercion. The consequence is that, contrary to the image of the all-powerful state, illiberal regimes are often also weak regimes.

The assumption that the state is all-powerful is linked to the tendency to focus on domestic factors and to treat external influences as add-ons,

Porous borders: North Koreans wave to Chinese across the Amnok River, the border between their countries

exogenous rather than endogenous determinants of democratic developments. Because of their focus on domestic factors, the analysts of 'troubled' democratisation tend to emphasize the legacy of the past more than the contemporary global context.

By contrast, we introduce globalisation into the analysis of democratisation, or, put more modestly, into the opening up of illiberal regimes. From this vantage point, the distinction between the external and internal does not hold. Instead, globalisation becomes internal to the changes in illiberal regimes. Our argument is that contemporary illiberal regimes are being pluralised involuntarily under the complex pressures of globalisation. The nature of these illiberal regimes changes as civil society spaces are carved out, either in the virtual world or in physical space or as a combination of both these spheres.

Involuntary pluralisation is a result of the impact of global political, economic and cultural/media forces. The state's ability to exercise control has been undermined both in a functional and spatial sense: in its ability to deal with challenges like the HIV and AIDS epidemic or environmental crisis, and in the increasing porosity of national borders and the 'infiltration' of global criminal networks that bypass the state, as illustrated by smuggling people out of North Korea.

Illiberal regimes have found themselves affected both by progressive and regressive globalisation. Commonly, when we think about globalisation and democratisation, the focus has been on the impact on norms and human rights, which was so important in Latin America and Communist Europe (Keck and Sikkink 1998; Kaldor 2003). Schmitter has pointed out that 'this world beneath and beyond the nation state

Box 5.1: The 2008 Beijing Olympics: a 'once-in-a-lifetime opportunity' for global civil society

Controversy and much public debate followed the 2001 decision of the International Olympic Committee (IOC) to grant China the 2008 Olympics. Britain's *Guardian* called the decision 'the most controversial one in the history of the IOC', and US Democrat Tom Lantos said that it 'truly boggles the mind. The decision will allow the Chinese police state to bask in the reflected glory of the Olympic Games despite having one of the most abominable human rights records in the world' (in Chaudhary 2001). Olympic Watch (URL), an initiative set up by Timothy Garton Ash and other public figures, warned that the decision was 'an important and risky step with far-reaching potential consequences. At stake is nothing less than the Olympic idea of peace, friendship and solidarity'. Clearly, despite the promising 2008 Olympic slogan 'One World. One Dream', many facets of China's (domestic) policy simply do not match the Olympic ideals as promoted in the Charter of the Olympic Movement.

Human rights abuses in general, the persecution of Falun Gong practitioners in particular, censorship and the control over the media, the oppression of civil society, the systematic destruction of Tibetan culture, the excessive use of the death penalty in an environment which does not guarantee access to appropriate legal defense and fair trial, and widespread abusive labour conditions are just the most obvious contradictions between Chinese political reality and Olympism, which Roche links to 'key elements of the rhetoric and mission of post-war internationalism embodied in the United Nations and the Universal Declaration of Human Rights' (2002:169). In a report about China's 'execution frenzy' during which 2,960 people were sentenced to death just months before the 2001 IOC meeting in Moscow, Amnesty International points out:

> *Ironically, sports stadiums were the last places where many of those condemned to death were taken, to be subjected to ritual humiliation in front of large crowds, just before being executed. In the past stadiums like the Beijing's Workers' Stadium, which may be used as the Olympic football venue in 2008, have hosted such macabre events.* (Amnesty International URL)

Some even went as far as to draw a comparison to the 1936 Olympics: following the example of Nazi Germany in 1936 and the Soviet Union in 1980, Communist China will use the games as a powerful propaganda instrument destined to consolidate its hold on power. (French politician quoted in Chaudhary 2001).

On the other hand, many, such as IOC executive director Francois Carrard, saw the decision as a 'bet that in the coming seven years up to the 2008 Olympic Games, the interaction, the progress and the development in many areas can be such that the situation in China can be improved'. China's yielding to international protests against the planned beach-volleyball competition in Tiananmen Square was considered a step in the right direction.

The IOC decision put China under an extraordinarily bright and global spotlight. Oscillating between actual world politics, explicit national(ist) rivalries and the promotion of world peace and human solidarity, the Olympic Games are per se highly political and symbolic events. Xu wittily adopts von Clausewitz' famous statement to suggest that sport is 'the continuation of politics by other means' (2006: 91). And the first Olympic Games in China are particularly special. Firstly, there is hardly any host country that is more controversial than China, and hardly any host country more eager than China to utilise the event to present a positive image of its society. Secondly, China is one of the most promising markets for Olympic sponsors, which adds another dimension to the commercialisation that has characterised recent Olympic Games. Closely related to this is the fact that, more than ever, the Olympics will be a global media spectacle. Whereas the founder of the Olympic Movement Baron Pierre de Coubertin, had to provide VIP treatment for journalists in order to get any coverage of the first modern Olympic Games in 1896 at all (Slater), the US channel NBC is paying US $894 million to carry the 2008 event (Sandomir 2001). Thirdly, the Beijing Games will take place in an era that is characterised by a 're-styling of politics' (Corner and Pels 2003), in which the relation between politics and media is significantly (re)shaping political practice; and in which 'celebrity politicians' (Street 2004) and celebrities as global civil society activists are the most glamorous signposts of these 'spectacular' times. In particular, the 2008 Games are embedded within the context of a growing communicative power of global civil society thanks to new forms of comunication outlined in this volume. In this respect, the 2008 Beijing Olympics offers a unique chance for global civil society activists to promote their concerns and to globally stage their protests: a 'once-in-a-lifetime opportunity' according to Nicholas Bequelin of Human Rights Watch (Reuters 2007).

Most human rights groups have an explicit Olympia agenda. Human Rights Watch, for instance, highlights three issues on its Beijing 2008 website: censorship, forced eviction and labour rights; a banner 'Light a Torch for Human Rights in China' can be downloaded (URL). A number of campaigns and coalitions have been established in response to the Beijing Olympics, such as the above mentioned Olympic Watch and the Collectif Chine JO 2008 (URL), which includes, for example, the International Federation for Human Rights (FIDH), and Reporters Without Borders; in addition, countless individual websites and blogs advocate variously free speech, access to the Internet, human rights, fair labour conditions and even boycotts of the Games.

Among the hundreds of videos critical of the Beijing Olympics on You Tube is one posted by noolympics (URL) that includes a tragic-comic take on the Olympic logo, which ends with the announcement: 'Olympic Gold for mass execution: China!' The video then goes on to show footage of what appears to be clashes between official forces and protesters in China. Various activist groups have hijacked the Olympic symbol and the 2008 Beijing logo in order to make their points, including the Students for a Free Tibet who changed the official Olympic slogan into: 'One World. One Dream. Free Tibet'. They also adopted/reclaimed one of the official Olympic mascots, the Tibetan antelope, which Chinese organisers had named YingYing, arguing that it was being used as a 'propaganda tool to cover up [China's] military occupation of Tibet' (URL). They renamed YingYing, Yingsel, produced stickers advocating a free Tibet, and created a website on which she explains: 'I've defected from the Olympic team because I can no longer stand being used as a puppet to cover up China's destruction of my homeland'.

One of the most interesting global civil society campaigns is the use of the Olympics to highlight China's relationship with the Sudanese government, and to hold the Olympics host responsible for not putting pressure on Khartoum to allow an adequate UN peacekeeping force into Darfur. The genocide in Darfur has long been a focus of global civil society activism in general and of (US) celebrity activism in particular. The Not On Our Watch campaign (URL), launched in spring 2007 by members of the film crew of Ocean's 13, George Clooney, Brad Pitt, Matt Damon, Don Cheadle and Jerry Weintraub, is just the latest example of Hollywood's attention to an issue that has become 'Hollywoodised' (Glaister 2007). In March 2007 Mia Farrow and her son Ronan Farrow, published an article in *The Wall Street Journal* entitled 'The Genocide Olympics' (Farrow and Farrow 2007), in which they refer to China's extraordinary position to influence the Sudanese Government, and argue that 'China is bankrolling Darfur's genocide'. 'There is now one thing that China may hold more dear than their unfettered access to Sudanese oil: their successful staging of the 2008 Summer Olympics,' they wrote. In order to take advantage of this point of leverage they ask the Olympic sponsors to put pressure on China, warning that the Olympic slogan 'One World. One Dream' might become the 'Genocide Olympics'.

Indeed, this catchphrase has not only provoked media attention but spread quickly: in mid-June 2007 it generated more than 71,000 hits in a google.com search. The Farrows also criticised Steven Spielberg, founder of the Shoah Foundation and artistic advisor for the Olympic ceremonies, comparing him to the director of the Nazi propaganda film about the 1936 Olympics, Leni Riefenstahl. This broadside was successful: Spielberg publicly regretted his lack of awareness of the link between China and the genocide in Darfur. Four days later he wrote to China's President Hu Jintao. At the beginning of April 2007 China dispatched a senior official to Sudan in order to encourgae the Sudanese government to allow UN peacekeeping forces into the region, and to visit refugee camps in Darfur. *The New York Times* and other papers credited China's reaction to the campaign, which showed 'how a pressure campaign, aimed to strike Beijing in a vulnerable spot at a vulnerable time, could accomplish what years of diplomacy could not' (Cooper 2007).

However, while China's move was a first important step, further action, such as sanctions, have not (yet) followed. For global civil society, the campaign to shame China has moved on: on 11 June 2007 Mia Farrow, together with Sudan-expert Eric Reeves, launched the campaign Olympic Dream for Darfur with the goal of ensuring a UN protection force to privide verifiable security for civilians and humanitarian workers in Darfur (URL). To achieve their aim, the campaign plans an Olympic Torch Relay on 8 August 2007 'through countries that define the history of genocide [...] Rwanda, Armenia, Bosnia, Germany, and Cambodia', which will start at the Darfur-Chad border and end in Hong Kong.

It remains open if China's intervention in Sudan is 'more of a commercial than a humanitarian nature', as Norwegian Deputy Foreign Minister Raymond Johansen argues (in Fabricius 2007), and it is impossible to predict a significant long-term shift of China's policies with regard to Sudan. It would be naive too, to assume that the 2008 Beijing Olympics and the global civil society activism surrounding it, will turn China into a human rights advocate.

Nevertheless, there is no doubt the campaign linking China to the genocide in Darfur by naming and framing the 2008 Beijing Olympics, the 'Genocide Olympics', triggered the change in attitude towards Khartoum. In this sense the campaign is a prime example of the communciative power of global civil society actors in their role as 'signifying agents' (Snow and Benford 2000), and of the potential of new media to launch a 'viral' and 'potent, creative, focused and uncontrollable' campaign (Reeves 2007). It is also an example of the logic of contemporary (celebrity) politics and the impact of the Hollywoodisation of certain political issues. While Darfur, which has become the top issue on the list of contemporary (US) celebrity activism, is the clear winner in the global civil society race for pressuring China on the grounds of being the host of the mega sports spectacle, other issues have not (yet) received similar attention.

Sabine Selchow, Research Officer, Centre for the Study of Global Governance, LSE

© Nicolas Righetti/Panos Pictures

President Kim Il Sung presides over a performance in the Mangyongdae Schoolchildren's Palace, North Korea

has played an especially significant role in the international promotion of democracy' (1996: 29). And even today, under the global gaze and pressure put by human rights activists, illiberal regimes have sometimes been forced to give in, and, for example, free political prisoners, as is happening now in China (see Box 5.1).

However, our case studies show that regressive globalisation, especially involvement in the illicit global economy (whether criminal, informal, or in extremist transational networks), is forcing regimes to open up, although this process may not be the same as democratisation. In the Balkans or the Caucasus, for example, powerful transnational networks involved in people smuggling, drugs, or other forms of organised crime, are linked into the state and help to sustain a combination of state weakness and repression (Kostovicova and Bojicic-Dzelilovic 2006). In Saudi Arabia, until recently, the main form of opposition consisted of groups linked to extreme global Islamism, with powerful global outreach through the Internet and other new forms of communication.

Like their democratic counterparts, illiberal states have understood the need to change and adapt in the face of globalisation. It is possible to distinguish three main forms of control exterted by the state. The first is administrative, the exercise of the rule of law and/or repression. While repressive regimes can and do imprison political dissidents and use torture and other inhumane treatments, it can be argued that physical repression is less effective than in the past, partly because of the difficulty of controlling the spread of weapons or knowledge of bomb-making, and partly because of international pressure. To an increasing extent, the implementation of a rule of law or of administrative measures depends on consent.

The second is economic. Totalitarian or sultanistic regimes exercised total control over the economy. Today, economic control is exerted through patronage, for example, through oil rents, as in the majority of authoritarian regimes, or through predation, as in Zimbabwe. The growth of global markets, such as China's, creates autonomous economic spaces that require a political response lest they open the floodgates for freedom, as happened in the former Soviet Union. The third form of control is through communication or, as Joseph Nye puts it, soft power (2004). In the global era, this may be the most critical form of control. New forms of communication such as the Internet and the electronic media are inherently global, and these connections can help and hinder illiberal regimes in promoting their ideology.

Today, most illiberal regimes are populist, mobilising consent around powerful nationalistic or religious ideologies. They use modern communications to promote their messages and they thrive on external hostility or pressure. Bush's phrase the 'axis of evil', for example, has helped to substantiate the anti-imperialist claims of regimes in Iran and Venezuela. Paradoxically, these same communications offer space for debate and discussion that is often difficult to close down. Ending illiberal regimes is not simply 'a matter of wiring enough people'; nonetheless the Internet is bound to be a factor in their opening up, along with other vital processes of 'traditional' liberalisation, such as civic education, building local governments and so on (Kalathil and Boas 2003: 135-153).

It is difficult to introduce a new set of categorisations for today's illiberal regimes because each regime has different characteristics. Thus both Iran and Saudi Arabia are dominated by their religious establishments but in Iran the religious institutions preside over and interfere with more or less 'normal' democratic institutions, while in Saudi Arabia, the total control of the monarchy and the tribal system was only very recently tempered by the introduction of minor, and many would say cosmetic, reforms. In both countries there is a form of gender apartheid and the role of ominous groups like the Committee for the Promotion of Virtue and the Suppression of Vice in Saudi Arabia, and the Monkerat (morals police) in Iran rigidly enforce gender segregation and/or women's dress codes. China, North Korea and Cuba are all nominally communist. Yet China is probably the most successful capitalist economy in the world today, while Cuba's income depends largely on Western tourism, which opens up autonomous economic space. Even in North Korea, new forms of communication and illicit economic relations as well as nuclear diplomacy are penetrating what appears to be the last bastion of totalitarianism. Zimbabwe and Belarus both seem to be characterised by mad leaders, but while Lukashenko has managed to sustain a relatively orderly repressive society, Mugabe's government has degenerated into spreading predation that is completely unable to control a burgeoning civil society. In Burma, brutal violence against the Burmese and ethnic minorities, and pervasive control by the military junta of all aspects of state and society give this dictatorship totalitarian characteristics.

In all these regimes, civil society expands and contracts as the regime passes through cycles of reform and repression. The more that civil society takes advantages of openings, the less able the regime is to close them again. Thus Iran experienced a brutal period of repression after the revolution. The sweeping victory of Khatami in the 1997 presidential elections and of reformists in the parliamentary elections of 2000 ushered in a 'Prague Spring' with talk of civil society, rule of law and a 'Dialogue of Civilisations'. The victory of the hardliner Mahmoud Ahmadinejad in the 2005 presidential elections led to a wave of arrests, executions (including of people under 18), and closures of civil society spaces. Despite the crackdown by religious authorities and the removal of reformists from the government, the debates did have a deep impact on Iranian institutions; above all, as one person interviewed put it, the reform period 'demystified Islam and separated Islam from Absolutism'. There is a parallel here with the hollowing out of Marxist-Leninism in the last years of communism.

Civil society

What is a civil society in an illiberal regime? The survey of ideas, activism and spaces of civil society in the illiberal regimes selected for this study tells us that civil society is least likely to resemble the liberal Western conception of civil society as a space between the family, market and state. It may be a family affair, as with the activism of China's most famous dissident couple; we may talk about 'market dissidents' in Cuba

Iranian President Mahmoud Ahmadinejad celebrates the 28th anniversary of the Islamic revolution

or North Korea, about societal autonomy created by NGOs that were originally created by the state to further its control; or we can count those dark elements in society who embrace ideologies more extreme and repressive than the ideology of the ruling regime (Salame 1994).

It is more helpful to view the autonomy of civil society in terms of its impact. Civil society activists from Burma to Iran have demonstrably undermined to various degrees the state's ultimate claim to political control over society, which is the essence of illiberal regimes and their survival. One Iranian theorist defines civil society as 'the sphere of social discourses, trends and autonomous social movements that attempt to regulate society' (Amiramachi 1996). According to this definition, we can identify something that could be called civil society in every illiberal regime that exists today, ranging from economic dissidents in North Korea to the very lively range of different opinions, movements, organisations and spaces that exists in Iran, even after the recent elections and the retreat of the reform process, and in Zimbabwe.

Civil society in an illiberal regime is shaped and constrained by its own repressive political environment as well as complex global connections. Autonomous initiatives are exercised at a great risk, including persecution, imprisonment, torture and even death. Nonetheless, they do take place, though how and where they do are as different as the regimes they challenge. In the next section, we provide an overview of the ideas, activism and spaces of civil

Burmese leader Aung San Suu Kyi

society, which reveals the diversity of challenges they can present against even the most repressive state in the context of globalisation.

Ideas

The ideas guiding civil society activities in illiberal regimes can be grouped as follows:

1. Ideas informed by Western liberal thought and a commitment to political and civil liberties.

2. Ideas that are about reforming the system framed within the dominant discourse of the regime.

3. Ideas about specific issues such as environmentalism, women's rights, poverty, or HIV and AIDS that can be framed both within a liberal discourse and within the dominant regime discourse.

4. More extremist ideas than those of the regime. The pervasiveness of these more extremist positions within some illiberal regimes dispels the notion of civil society as a solely progressive and liberal space.

1. Western liberal ideas

This group of ideas is pursued by Western liberals in a non-Western setting who campaigned for democratisation based on the defence of the political and civic rights. They are a small but visible minority threatened with severe persecution by their rulers. Their language is the language of democracy, rights and the rule of law. Perhaps the embodiment of this set of ideas is Aung San Suu Kyi, who has become a global symbol for a non-violent struggle for democracy and against repression in Burma, on a par

with the South African leader Nelson Mandela. For most of the time since the 1990 electoral victory of her National Democratic League (NLD), which the military junta refused to recognise, Aung San Suu Kyi has been under house arrest for her beliefs. The Lady, which is how the Burmese call her in deference, describes what she is fighting for:

When we ask for democracy, all we are asking is that our people should be allowed to live tranquilly under the rule of law, protected by institutions which will guarantee our rights, the rights that will enable us to maintain our human dignity, to heal long festering wounds and to allow love and courage to flourish. Is that such a very unreasonable demand? (Suu Kyi 1997: 205).

Similarly, there are Chinese dissidents who have put the struggle for democracy and political rights at the forefront of their activism. Xu Wenli, known as the 'godfather of dissent' in China was involved and imprisoned for involvement in the 'Democracy Wall' movement in the 1970s. The wall was a notice board for dissident views. In 1998 he tried to establish the China Democratic Party, the first opposition party in China, directly undermining the regime's soul. Subsequently jailed for 13 years and released early on medical grounds, Xu Wenli joined a growing number of Chinese dissidents in exile. However, the political struggle and its persecution in China has continued, exemplified by Hu Jia and his wife Zeng Jinyan. Their latest house arrest and ban on foreign travel is part of a crackdown on human rights activists in the run-up to the 2008 Olympic games in Beijing (see Box 5.1). Hu Jia began as an HIV/AIDS activist in the 1990s. However, he soon realised that social challenges in China could not be tackled without first addressing politics, and consequently turned his efforts to the struggle for the freedom of speech and the press.

2. Reformist ideas

Alongside the dissenters who mount a direct political challenge to the regime, there has been a foment of ideas that challenges the regime on its own terms, both in religious or ideological terms. Such ideas are often framed in terms of the discourse of Islam in Iran and Saudi Arabia, for example, as well in terms of 'rightful resistance' in China.

In Iran many of the radicals who made the 1979

revolution became the backbone of the reformist movement in the 1980s. Particularly important has been the Islamic reform movement or the New Religious Thinking that argues that Islam, in particular Shi'ism, depends on human interpretation. Hojjat ol-Islam Hasan Yousefi Eshkevari has been an outspoken and influential critic of the current Iranian version of theocracy. After speaking at a conference in April 2000, he was condemned to death for 'apostasy' and 'war against Islam', a sentence that was later commuted to five years in prison. In Box 5.2 Eshkevari outlines his thinking in the context of current Islamic perspectives.

The missing Imam in Shi'ism implies that no one has a direct line to God. Rules that are said to be Islamic are, in practise, the result of Islamic jurisprudence, that is constructed by men. Every individual is able to interpret the right 'way', i.e. *Shari'a*, and there is no 'objective interpretation of divine law, independent of historical, geographical and socio-cultural context' (Amiramachi 1996).

The dominant group within the Iranian religious discourse are the secularists, who want to separate politics and religion and dismantle the *velayat-e fiqih* (the religious institutions that 'supervise' democracy). Particularly important was the Republican manifesto of Akbar Ganji, written from prison, where he spent eight years as a result of his investigation into the involvement of government officials into the murder of hundreds of intellectuals and journalists during the 1990s. As was the case with East Europeans, a critical change in the thinking of the Iranian reformists has been the rejection of revolution and the belief in gradual change towards a more open society, 'instead of seeking radical change in the name of a holistic utopia' (Hooglund 2002).

Similar ideas are espoused by Islamic reformers in Saudi Arabia, often supported by the Shi'ite minority in the East of the country. The Islamic refomers, who were among the signatories to the Petition for a Constitutional Monarchy in December 2003 along with liberal reformers, argue that Islam and democracy are compatible and religion has to be interpreted by human beings, and what is moral behaviour therefore varies in different periods of history.

Another method of challenging the system within the existing paradigm is the analysis of local reforms in rural China in terms of 'rightful resistance'. This concept has been applied in other contexts, for

All Burma Students' Democratic Front student army and Karen people on the Thai-Burmese border

example in East Germany during Communism when activists challenged power structures by 'taking the state at its word' (O'Brien and Li 2006: 16-17). Recent grassroots activism in rural China has been triggered by socio-economic changes and media development. 'Rightful resisters' have challenged local authorities for not delivering on their promises. These rights mainly have to do with policy implementation, and not with the struggle for wider civil and political rights to association, expression and participation. Nonetheless, O'Brien and Li argue that rightful resistance has created a new class of activists, and has led to the rise of rights consciousness, and the emergence of 'rights talk' and 'rights defense' (2006: 126-7).

3. Specific issues

This set of ideas has to do with specific issues and how they relate to broader questions of political and civil rights. In many illiberal regimes, environmentalism or humanitarianism is tolerated and movements of this type, as in the former Soviet Union and East and Central Europe, become new spaces within which novel ideas can be generated. In Burma, for example, a new concept of 'earth rights' has been developed to capture a nexus between environmental protection and human rights.

The construction of the Yadana gas pipeline linking gas extraction off the Burmese coast to a power plant near Bangkok illustrates how environmental and human rights issues converged. This project caused environmental degradation and human rights violations. Karen and Mon minorities opposed the project, which went ahead with the support of the Burmese military. The Karen Human Rights Group documented forced labour, forced relocation, rape and summary execution of Karen villagers.

Box 5.2: The New Religious Thinking in Iran

As a Muslim cleric who belongs to the New Religious Thinking in Iran, I would like to say a few words about the recent thinking of Jürgen Habermas on the interaction and understanding between believers and unbelievers, particularly given the importance of this subject, the special place of Habermas as a critical and secular intellectual, the growth of violence in the world and the need for peace and tolerance.

To start with, let me point out that in the world of Islam (even among the European Muslims), there are four active Islamic-social tendencies:

1. **Traditional Muslims**: followers of traditional, non-political Islam, who pay little attention to the modern world and are largely content to lead a life on the basis of belief and Sharia.
2. **Cultural Traditionalists**: adherents of traditionalist and non-political Islam, who accept the old culture and civilization of Islam as a valuable historical heritage, and do this through a philosophical-mystical and at times juristic-theological approach; they are intent on keeping this heritage and at most introducing it to the modern world. The thinkers of this tendency do not tolerate any serious criticism of Islam or of current Muslim culture and knowledge. They are revivalist (*mojadded*) not reformist (*motajadded*).
3. **Dogmatic fundamentalists**: followers of political, fundamentalist Islam who are essentially intent on the revival of Islamic political authority in the mould of the 'Islamic Caliphate', and are not much concerned with its culture and civilization. The theorists of this tendency not only see colonialism, and the West's political domination, to be the enemy of religion and an obstacle to the realization of Islamic Caliphate and Empire, but they often as a whole consider the modern culture and civilization of the West to be in contradiction with (their understanding of) Islam and the interests of the Muslims. Their aims are political, and in their struggle to defeat the Western world they use all available means.
4. **Islamic intellectuals and adherents of the New Religious Thinking** who seek to realise a modern Islamic civilization. The theorists of this tendency believe that this can be achieved by the revival of authentic religious belief, by trimming the accretions from the religious domain, the rationalization of the totality of the religious system, criticism of historical Islam and traditional Islamic knowledge in the light of the latest human philosophical and scientific theories; and eventually the 'reconstruction' of Islamic thought.

If we consider the differences among these tendencies, it is evident that the main audience addressed by Habermas and others who are keen on peace, tolerance and dialogue among religions, civilizations and cultures, is in fact the New Religious Thinkers, not the Traditional Muslims nor the Cultural Traditionalists nor the Dogmatic Fundamentalists. This is so because, first, the New Thinkers are the only Islamic tendency that accepts the fundamental principles of modernity and its products (such as science, critical reason, democracy, freedom, justice, human rights and so on). They see them as being basically Islamic, or at least compatible with Islam. Secondly, impelled by their intellectualism and by relying on modern critical reason, they simultaneously engage in a critique of Islamic tradition and heritage (i.e. historical Islam) and a critique of some of the foundations and products of modernity. But it must be added that their critique of tradition and modernity is positive and constructive, not negative and destructive. Thirdly, the main project of the New Muslim Thinkers is the modernization of Islam not the Islamization of modernity, and they see the way to the realization of this project to be in making links with free thinkers, by criticism, dialogue, tolerance and understanding, not by force, imposition, war and violence. In fact, the acceptable Islam of the New Thinkers is critical Islam and a synthesis of tradition and modernity.

Critical Islam rests on the following basis:

1. Rational criticism (criticism of everything, including religion, the pathology of religious history and rituals, Islamic law (*fiqh*) and reasoning (*ijtihad*).
2. Human emancipation from the four prisons (the prisons of nature, society, history and the self).
3. Exposing the different faces of power (including the power of the clergy over people's lives and their hold on politics and government, and the power of men over women).
4. Dialogue and mutual understanding and learning.

This type of critical Islam, which became known in Iran with Ali Shariati, is close to the critical theory that is known as the Frankfurt School. In view of the place of the 'public sphere' in critical theory, we can propose that the most suitable place for debating the truth, authority and legitimacy of religion, is the public sphere. While welcoming Habermas' recommendations, I say that one thing that the modern and secular world can learn from religion is the spiritual interpretation of the world and humanity that modernity is lacking. Muhammad Iqbal of Pakistan, in the early decades of the twentieth century, in his critique of the modern and non-religious world and what it lacks, said that the biggest deficiency of the modern world is that it has been emptied of its spiritual element. For this reason, new religious thinkers such as Iqbal, and Shariati in Iran, tried to compensate for this lack by designing a modern worldview and anthropology that is also *towhidi*, spiritual and ethical (i.e. an Islamic humanism).

In the light of these considerations, I suggest that religious thinkers and intellectuals of all religions, secular intellectuals and even anti-religious but democratic intellectuals, should strengthen their intellectual and cultural relations with the New Religious Thinkers all over the world (including Iran). Experience has shown that in the world of Islam, any lasting change is impossible or at least difficult without taking account of religion. Habermas's correct recommendation is that religious people, in order to secure their survival in the modern world, must be able to 'translate' their thoughts in such a way that they are meaningful for the secularists. In this case, new Muslim thinkers are the ones that have the logical and ethical capacity for dialogue and mutual understanding with the world. They are also able to pave the way for social and political change by changing the thoughts and minds of Muslims. At the same time, this does not mean that one should not have a dialogue with the Traditionalists and even the Fundamentalists; it is important to leave the door open for dialogue with any tendency.

But it must be pointed out that, attempting to solve the problem of violence in the world and to fight terrorism, whether its Islamic version or otherwise, by sheer violence and oppression is not only impossible, but ends up playing to the interests of the fundamentalists and strengthening the seekers of violence. The intellectuals and politicians in the West must pay attention to the deep roots of violence in the world, especially among the Muslims.

It appears that several factors have been at work in the rise and growth of violent fundamentalism in the world of Islam.

1. The dominance of Western colonialism in the Muslim world in the course of several centuries.
2. Euro-centrism and the constant actual and ideological humiliation of Muslims and Muslim societies.
3. The failure of modern or semi-modern social movements in Muslim societies and their suppression by secular governments and politicians.
4. Poverty, increasing deprivation and the growth of class differences and the North-South gap.
5. The continuation of old despotisms in the Muslim Middle East.
6. The weakness of Islamic intellectualism and New Religious Thinking in the Muslim countries.

Without due attention to these root causes, and without offering practical and logical ways, any solution or action will be unsuccessful or at least insufficient. It is not right, on the pretence of fighting against violence, terrorism and fundamentalism, to fight against the basis of religiosity and religious values and principles. It is not possible to eliminate modernity and its products from the lives of religious people, nor is eliminating religion either possible or useful; even if it were possible, it could not be achieved except by violence and suppression, which would also mean the destruction of all the philosophical, anthropological foundations and privileges of the modern and secular world. One cannot expect much from statesmen and the holders of power, but peace-seeking and democratic intellectuals must by no means abandon the path of understanding and dialogue; in the same way, Muslims must not give in to extremists. According to Habermas, in liberal secular Western systems, religious people (mostly Muslims, particularly after Sept 2001) are subject to various psychological and social pressures (even physical abuse). Believers are often expected to draw an absolute line between the private and public realms, and to render the public realm entirely to the government. But is this really possible? A secular government is right to expect religious people to accept the principle of democracy and the neutrality of the government and political system with respect to the beliefs and thoughts of all people, and to have equal respect for the rights of every citizen. But why shouldn't religious people have the right to express their religious and ethical teachings in the public sphere, even in political matters and in seeking to secure the basis of freedom and justice, and in criticizing the status quo? In particular, it must be pointed out that secular or liberal governments should not patronize religious people, or even worse, insult their religious sanctities (as happened recently with the unacceptable cartoons in Denmark).

In conclusion, I believe that the revival and reinforcement of authentic religious-centred values and ethical rules, including those of Islam in the modern time, will certainly help in the spread of peace, justice, tolerance, love, serving human beings, respect for law and democratic rules. Of course it will also help the growth of freedom and the spirit of justice.

Hojjat ol-Islam Hasan Yousefi Eshkevari

This is an edited version of remarks by Hojjat ol-Islam Hasan Yousefi Eshkevari at the School of Oriental and African Studies on 12 May 2006, which were translated by Ziba Mir-Hosseini and Richard Tapper, to mark the launch of Islam and Democracy in Iran: Eshkevari and the Quest for Reform. *London: I B Tauris 2006.*

Publication of their reports exposed the use of sexual violence as a regime strategy for intimidating and terrorising opponents of the pipeline (Doyle and Simpson 2006).

In both Iran and Saudi Arabia, new ideas about the role of women have been developed within the Islamist discourse. Thus women campaigning for greater rights in Saudi Arabia point out that Muhammad was committed to equality and that his wife Khadiga was a successful businesswoman. They point out that there is nothing in the Koran that says that women must not drive or must cover their faces. Similarly, in Iran it is argued that discriminatory laws against women contradict the fundamental Islamic belief in justice and equality (Mir Hosseini 2006). In particular, women are supposed to have a privileged position as mothers yet they do not enjoy fundamental rights (Gheytanchi 2001).

In Zimbabwe, it is women who have provided the inspiration for the civil disobedience movement. Women of Zimbabwe Arise (WOZA), a movement with 35,000 both male and female members, has adopted the slogan 'Tough Love'. The idea that the power of love can conquer the love of power comes out of Zimbabwean traditions and norms. The argument is that 'Tough Love' is the disciplining love of a parent; women practice it to press for and to bring dignity back to Zimbabweans. Political leaders in Zimbabwe need some discipline, it is argued, and who better to dish it out than mothers? Tough Love is used as a 'people power' tool to press for better governance and social justice. Annual marches held on Valentine's Day demonstrate the power of 'Tough Love' (URL).

4. Extremist ideas

Alongside the liberal, the reformist and the issue-based ideas, civil society harbours extremist ideas as well. There is a tendency to believe that it is regimes that are bad and people that are good. But as was revealed after the end of Communism, prejudice and hatred are bred in authoritarian regimes just as much as a belief in democracy. There are extreme nationalists in Russia and Belarus and extreme Islamists in Iran and Saudi Arabia. In Iran, for example, in January 2007, the government closed down a fundamentalist website Baztub, which had accused Ahmadinejad of betraying the revolution because he watched a female dance show at the recent Asian games in Qatar.

In Saudi Arabia, the main opposition, at least during the 1990s, was extremist Wahabism, which distinguishes itself both from mystical Islam and from Shi'ism. These conservatives argue that modernity and westernisation is threatening the true Islam both globally and locally, and that the royal family is failing to protect and promote the values of Islam. The Gulf War of 1991 was a turning point for these groups – the deployment of American troops in Saudi Arabia was considered a betrayal of Islam. Key issues are the defence of global Islam, opposition to corruption and demands for redistribution, and opposition to the American presence in Saudi Arabia, especially in the holy places.

Activism

By definition there is only a limited space for political activism in illiberal regimes. However, a close look at movements, NGOs and associations, reveals a busy civil society engaged in a spectrum of activities ranging from those that are political and persecuted by the regime, to those that are humanitarian and supported by the state. Women and youth groups are particularly important social forces in all our case studies.

Women

In Iran, discriminatory laws were introduced within weeks of the 1979 revolution, including the right of men to divorce unilaterally, lowering the age of marriage for women to nine years, imposing a rigid dress code for women, introducing strict gender segregation, and inflicting violent punishments such as flogging and stoning. Since the revolution, prohibitions on 'immoral behaviour' are enforced by the Revolutionary Guards, other paramilitary groups of the Ministry of the Interior, and by the Monkerat.

A vibrant women's movement developed during the 1990s, particularly around the magazine *Zanan*. It includes both Islamic and secular women and brings together rich and poor women. It has succeeded in prohibiting stoning and in reversing some laws, such as the rules on divorce. The daughter of Iran's former president Ali Akbar Hashemi Rafsanjani, Faezeh Hashemi, played an important role as a member of parliament (1996-2000) in defending women's rights. Shirin Ebadi's Campaign for Equality became famous around the world after she won the Nobel Prize. Despite the crackdown, women's groups are still very active, as illustrated by the One Million Signature Campaign to end discriminatory laws, which was launched in 2005.

In Saudi Arabia, in 1991, a large group of educated women drove their cars into the centre of Riyadh. They were harassed, threatened and publicly denounced. Subsequently the government announced travel restrictions on women. Women have become more outspoken in the last few years. The broadcaster Rania al-Baz allowed her face to be photographed after her husband beat her. A businesswoman addressed the Jeddah Economic Forum with her face uncovered. In 2004, a petition signed by 300 people demanded greater rights for women, and women protested their exclusion from the municipal elections. The government's defence was based on logistics, the difficulty of registering women, rather than on principle, and it has been agreed that women would be allowed to vote in future elections

In China, women have been critical in raising awareness of state repression. Particularly important has been the role of the 'Tiananmen Mothers'. A group of mothers who lost their loved ones in the 1989 Tiananmen Square massacre got together with the aim of seeking justice from the regime. They were harassed, threatened, put under surveillance and some were detained by the Chinese authorities. The Internet was critical to their cause. They informed the Chinese public about their cause, publishing open letters, declarations and other information. In 2002 they were nominated for the Nobel Peace Prize. Transnational connections with human rights groups abroad were critical for ensuring the early release of three mothers arrested for 'harming national security' in 2004 (Tai 2006: 106-108).

Youth

Young people are often singled out as a political threat by illiberal regimes, one might say not without good reason. While thriving on and learning from transnational connections facilitated by information and communication technologies, they have challenged their respective regimes in numerous creative and humorous ways. Their activism has managed to capture and mobilise popular support.

In Iran, young people's movements include non-political movements of young people who want to be able to meet the opposite sex freely in public places or dress as they please, as well as those who make more

Youthful dissent: young Iranians want to dress as they please and meet the opposite sex in public

explicitly political demands, especially among student groups. Unemployment is also an important factor in young people's protest. In Burma, university students were a critical force in the 1988 pro-democracy demonstrations that were brutally suppressed, but they are still defiant and active. Despite the regime's repression of dissent, some 1,000 people gathered to mark the birthday of the imprisoned student leader Min Ko Naing in October 2006 (Yeni 2006).

In Belarus as well, the regime has been particularly afraid of youth activism. Grassroots movements of youth groups and unregistered NGOs, such as *Malady Front* (Youth Front) and *Zubr* (Bison as the country's national symbol) have flourished, even as their members have been imprisoned. They have launched campaigns like 'Enough!' modelled on the Serbian youth movement *Otpor* (Resistance), organising street actions or satirising the regime. They collaborate with the young Ukranian activists, in *Pora*, National Alliance, and *Svoboda*, learning from their role in the Ukraine's Orange Revolution (Schipani-Aduriz and Kudrytski 2005; see Chapter 4 of this volume).

NGOs and associations

Across the spectrum of illiberal regimes there is a myriad of NGOs and associations in some places and hardly any in others. For example, they number some 8,000 in Iran, hundreds of thousands in China but cannot be counted in Belarus because of the government's policy of 'judicial liquidation', a series of repressive administrative measures that aimed to 'root out' civil society. In some countries NGOs cover

Box 5.3: China's environmental movement in the making

An environmental movement has been in the making in urban China since the mid-1990s. Its main feature is the development of grassroots environmental non-governmental organisations (ENGOs). Since the launching of the first ENGO in 1994, over 200 have been founded. In addition, according to a survey by the All-China Environment Federation (2006), there were 1,116 college student environmental associations and 1,382 government-organised ENGOs as of 2005. The grassroots ENGOs are relatively independent from the state and come closest to the common understanding of civil society organisations as autonomous, non-profit, and voluntary associations.

These grassroots ENGOs have launched many campaigns. The first major campaign was about the protection of the snub-nosed golden monkey. In 1995, when environmental activists learned of a local government's plan to cut an old forest - a habitat of the endangered monkey - they organised a petition and succeeded in stopping the plan. Another national campaign was launched in 1998 to protect the Tibetan antelope. And since 2003, Chinese environmentalists have been engaged in a sustained campaign to stop dam-building on the pristine Nu River in southwest China. A sign of its initial success was the government's decision in 2004 to suspend the project, subject to environmental impact assessment.

Besides public campaigns, Chinese ENGOs organise a broad range of activities. In Beijing, Friends of Nature run environmental education projects in elementary schools. Global Village of Beijing produces environmental television programs and work with the municipal government to build green communities. Green Earth Volunteers hold a monthly 'Environmental Journalists' Salon' to educate media professionals about environmental reporting. Green River in Sichuan province runs an environmental monitoring station on the Qinghai-Tibet plateau. In Yunnan, Green Watershed leads a citizens' movement to protect rivers. The list goes on.

The archetypal movement in modern Chinese history – recall the student protests in 1989 – was mounted as direct challenge against the state and its delegates. It adopted confrontational tactics, invariably met with repression and never developed legitimate movement organisations. The emerging environmental movement differs markedly. It does not challenge central state power, but instead targets business and consumer behavior and, at times, local government authorities. It has a legitimate organisational base and uses non-confrontational tactics. Its participants are well-educated urban professionals concerned with quality of life issues rather than apocalyptic visions. These features are typical of environmental movements elsewhere (for example, see Dalton 1994). They bring China's environmental movement closer to the world. Independent from the state in finance, administration, and personnel appointment while embedded in Chinese social and political conditions (Ho 2007), the grassroots organisations leading the movement represent the vanguard of an incipient Chinese civil society.

How to explain its development? First, Chinese environmentalists are skilled social actors in negotiating the political context. This context offers both opportunities and constraints. State actors have anxieties about non-state organisations getting out of control. This ambivalence is reflected in the implementation in 1998 of national regulations for the registration and management of social organisations. Its stringent articles, such as the requirement for a sponsoring institution, make registration a daunting and often futile process. The political constraint partly explains why they are engaged in non-confrontational activities such as workshops, seminars, exhibitions, field trips, and media campaigns. It also partly explains why ENGOs have evolved into a variety of hybrid types. Some groups register as business entities while others operate without registration.

The good news is that the 1998 regulations give legitimacy, at least to those organisations that can manage to register. And of course, China's much publicised national policy of sustainable development and the associated 'greening of the state' (Ho 2001) also offer political space for the growth of ENGOs. Increasingly, for example, environmental activists are making use of legal instruments such as environmental impact assessment laws to push their agendas.

Second, in negotiating the state, Chinese environmentalists have some valuable resources and skills. One skill is transnational competence (Koehn 2006: 379) such as the ability to communicate in English and knowledge about international NGO culture and practices. International awards given to Chinese environmentalists certify their transnational competence. Well-known leaders of environmental NGOs, such as Liang Congjie of Friends of Nature, Liao Xiaoyi of Global Village of Beijing, and Yu Xiaogang of Green Watershed, have all received major international awards. Furthermore, Chinese environmentalists are well connected with the mass media, another major resource. Many are media professionals themselves. Green Camp, Green Earth Volunteers, Green Plateau, Tianjin Friends of Green, and Panjin Black-Beaked Gull Protection Association, are all led by journalists or former journalists. Friends of Nature has influential journalists in its membership. These media professionals serve as direct linkages between the mass media and the environmentalists.

The two kinds of resources are mutually generative. Transnational competence is conducive to building connections with the global community, thus generating more social capital. Connections with the mass media give them easy access to the otherwise politically controlled media channels. Such access can translate into media visibility, which then becomes a source of cultural prestige.

Transnational competence is especially important in an age of globalisation. Indeed, globalisation is the third contributing factor in the growth of China's environmental movement. The global discourse of sustainable development, multilateral and bilateral aid programs, global and transborder environmental issues, and even the 1995 NGO Forum held in Beijing in conjunction with the UN World Conference on Women, have all helped to shape China's environmental movement. Above all, international ENGOs have given much-needed support to their counterparts in China. According to the survey mentioned above, there were 68 international ENGOs with offices in China as of 2005. For example, Greenpeace and Natural Resources Defense Council both opened offices in China in 1997. The Jane Goodall Institute started operating a Roots & Shoots program in Beijing in 2000 and now has offices in Shanghai and Chengdu. These international organisations influence Chinese environmentalism through exemplification and hands-on instruction as well as by providing funding, expertise, and prestige. Mei Ng, former director of Friends of Earth (Hong Kong), was proud of her organisation's contribution in this respect, stating:

I am glad to have dedicated the last nine years' work in China to transfer the NGO experience, which could serve as a useful reference for the budding green movement in Mainland China.... It is encouraging to witness the establishment of increasing numbers of school and individual environmental groups around the country in the last five years. I see myself as a green seed sower. (Ng n.d.)

China's environmental movement is an urban phenomenon among a relatively well-educated segment of the population. Its quiescent character does not reflect what is happening in rural areas, where there are violent forms of environmental protest. Nor does it reflect other parts of the contentious urban scene - the increasing frequency of demonstrations and strikes among workers and relocated citizens. Yet it does represent a broad trend of building civil society bases for collective action through legitimate channels, for besides environmental groups, NGOs working on many other issue areas have also flourished (see, for example, Howell 2004).

Organisational development is the main success story of China's environmental movement. Yet in the long run, the preoccupation with organisational development may hinder the movement's political potency, because to sustain organisational growth, activists have to operate within the range of the possible. As scholars of environmental movements have often noted, more formal and institutionalised organisations tend to adopt cooperative approaches (della Porta and Andretta 2002). As in so many other instances, here again we encounter the paradox of institutionalisation.

Guobin Yang, Barnard College

the whole spectrum of opinion; in others, only pro-government NGOs are allowed to exist.

In Saudi Arabia, religious charities became the breeding ground for extremist Islam during the 1990s and only recently has the government imposed restrictions, which have affected moderate charities as well. A few NGOs and associations are also tolerated. These have included the establishment of professional syndicates where women have been allowed to stand and vote, for example, the Saudi National Agency of Engineers, the Chambers of Commerce, and an organisation for journalists.

In Iran, there are many pro-government groups, such as Ansar-e Hizbullah, Muslim Students following the Imam, and the Tehran Militant Clergy Association. There are also pro-reform groups like the Office of Strengthening Unity among students, and opposition groups. And there are groups representing minorities who are discriminated against (such as Arab, Kurdish, Azeri, Christian and Bahai).

Whether in Iran, Burma, Belarus, Saudi Arabia or China, the regimes themselves have resorted to the creation of NGOs. In Burma, the state created its own 'civil society', embodied by the Union Solidarity and Development Association (USDA). Its focus on the youth is an important element in its campaign to forestall the dissent among young people, especially after the 1988 pro-democracy demonstrations. Like USDA, the Belarussian Republican Youth Union (BRSM) seeks to appeal to youth, but also intimidates and harasses the regime's opponents at universities and schools. BRSM is known as Lukamol, a combination of Lukashenka and Komsomol, the Youth Communist League from the Communist Period. In Saudi Arabia, two human rights bodies have been established by the government although they have no autonomy and could not, for example, defend the signatories of the Petition for a Constitutional Monarchy, some of whom were arrested and imprisoned.

The state-led creation and/or tolerance of NGOs also often has a functional justification: to offload services onto the non-state sector and to fill in gaps in service provision. In Iran, the grassroots response to the humanitarian crisis after the Bam earthquake, and NGOs specialising in dealing with drug addiction or poverty play a critical role. In China, 'civil society' has been allowed to assist the state in service provision where the state and market cannot deliver (Chong 2005), for example fighting the HIV and AIDS epidemic or environmental degradation (see Box 5.3).

In both China and Iran, the government has maintained a restrictive legal environment in order to 'contain and control' the civil society, lest it should provide a political challenge to the state (Zengke 2007). Despite this, many NGOs have managed to bypass the government's restrictions in different ways, gain some autonomy, and even challenge government policy. For example, in big cities such as Beijing and Shanghai, Homeowners Committees represent the increasing number of homeowners who have taken developers or local governments to court for infringing their rights.

Spaces

The clandestine printing and dissemination of Samizdat editions with dissidents' works and ideas during Communism in Eastern Europe illustrates the necessity and power of communication for civil society activists and their struggle against non-democratic regimes. The arrival of the Internet, with websites, blogs and emails, and of other information and communication technologies, such as mobile phones and SMS, have revolutionised the opportunities to communicate dissent. At the same time, it has given illiberal regimes another sphere in which to practise repression. Although the Internet is a significant space, it is one of many.

The Internet and other new technologies

The Internet has provided an unprecedented space for dissent for civil society and a dilemma for rulers. As Taubmann says: 'efforts to sanitize the Internet are hampered by the fact that the features of the Internet that cause problems for nondemocratic rulers are the same features that make the technology so attractive' (1998: 256) and, one might add, necessary in order to participate in the global economy. (See Box 5.4 for an exploration of efforts to control the Internet).

Until recently, in Iran the Internet offered a freer space than the print media. By 2001 there were some 1,500 Internet cafés, and there are now between 70,000 and 100,000 bloggers. Some 7.5 million Iranians are estimated to surf the net, more as a proportion of the population than any other Middle Eastern country except Israel. The government has not been able to enforce its own regulations effectively for a number of reasons, including its own lack of expertise, and because the Internet is largely provided by commercial

© Nikolai Ignatiev/arabianEye

providers. In addition, the government uses the Internet to propagate its own Islamic discourse. According to several clerics the Internet is a 'gift to spread the word of the prophet' (Rahimi 2003).

The use of the Internet by reformists include a former prostitute whose weblog exposed the 'underworld life of Iranian society'(Rahimi 2003); the intellectual Akbar Ganji who posted his Republican Manifesto; and Ayatollah Montezeri, the 82 year old dissident cleric once in line to be Supreme leader, who uploaded his 600-page memoir in December 2000, which criticised the ideological foundation of the Islamic state and opposed the 'dogma' of velayat-e fiqih.

However, since 2003, the Iranian regime has stepped up its attack on the space provided by the Internet. Some 450 Internet cafes have been shut down, dozens of websites have been closed down, including popular Western sites like Amazon, YouTube and the New York Times (in 2007), and many bloggers have been arrested. Egyptian bloggers have also been targeted by the state – see Box 5.5.

In Saudi Arabia, the Internet has also become a space utilised by both government and opposition. As in other Islamist countries, the religious establishment regards the Internet as an important forum to propagate its message. The Saudi regime interdicts many popular western websites; nevertheless technically-savvy people can find ways to circumvent these restrictions. No one knows who runs the Committee Against Corruption website (URL). According to its mission statement, it was inaugurated by 'people with strong ties to the business community in the US and Saudi Arabia'.

In China, virtual technology provides a way to side step restrictions on public gatherings and social activism. It has become a 'hotbed of collective action', a site for making cyber-protest and organising cyber-gatherings. The death of young graphic designer and student Sun Zhigang, in Guangzhou in March 2003, illustrates the power of the Internet. Arrested on his way to an Internet café for not having a residency permit, he was taken to a local detention centre for beggars and vagrants. Three days later he was found dead in a local hospital. A local reporter published the story on the his paper's Internet edition. It led to a nationwide public outcry. Pressure built up through online postings in chat rooms, blogs, online petitions and protest letters. It resulted in charges against government officials and police officers, financial

compensation to the family and eventually the repeal of the out-dated law on urban vagrants (Tai: 159-268).

Since the introduction of the Internet in China, the government has played a 'cat and mouse' game, using various approaches to control it, including regulation, self-censorship, 'cyber police', surveillance, a crackdown on internet cafes, and the building a 'Great Firewall' around China (Endeshaw 2004). However, having learnt from its inability to stop the use of satellite dishes in China, it has not tried to ban Internet access. A Chinese official compared the Communist Party's strategy towards the Internet to the Chinese people's historic struggle to control the Yellow river. According to him, the proper technique is not to try stopping the water but to guide it in the right direction (Cody 2007).

In Burma, restrictions on the Internet are physical, such as restrictions on where people can open email accounts (only in hotels, government offices and businesses), and technical, such as blocking access to Yahoo and Google. Still, people can use a handful of Internet cafes to surf and to sidestep government restrictions. A journalist from Burma with whom we corresponded said:

> There are Internet café owners who are asked by military intelligence to monitor the users and inform the officials if they try to look at the banned sites. But many Internet users are still reading banned sites with the help of proxy software and sites. Internet connection starting installation fee is about US$ 2,000. But in cafes, hourly usage costs only US$ 0.6. While I am trying to send this letter to you, I am using a proxy web to use gmail illegally in a café and sometimes we need to spend one hour to send a letter.

Like the youth movement *Otpor* in Serbia and *Kmara* in Georgia, Belarus' *Zubr* has relied on mobile

Box 5.4: Controlling the Internet

The Internet was once seen as a boon to civil-society led democratisations and the spread of liberal values on a global scale. Increasingly today, the Internet is as complex as the societies in which it is embedded, and a forum for economic, criminal and political struggle.

During the latter half of the twentieth century, and in particular during the Internet 'DotCom' heyday of the mid-to-late 1990s, a unique combination of historical, technological, and social forces came together fortuitously to create an open Internet environment. With the end of the Cold War, the spread of Western-led techno-optimism, and an unprecedented economic boom fueled by new technologies, governments were willing to take a 'hands-off' approach and delegate Internet design choices to networks of engineers and computer scientists. These engineers and scientists held both a technical and political philosophy that encouraged openness, which in turn complemented the hope (and belief) of policy elites (particularly in the United States) that such a hands-off approach to the Internet was the best way to encourage continued innovation and rapid economic growth.

But beneath the euphoria and democratic openness of the Internet, a 'dark side' of was lurking. The open networked communications environment also enabled deep and often divisive challenges to political and economic authority. Some of these took the form of organised street demonstrations against capitalist globalisation. More serious was the facilitation of networked forms of militancy and extremism, most vividly illustrated in the Al-Qaeda terrorist network. It also allowed the illegal trade in copyrighted material and the spread of what many societies perceived to be pornography, cultural decadence, and hate speech. The hands-off approach to the Internet adopted by political elites was bringing about unintended and increasingly negative implications.

The 'DarkNet' comes of age

Since the mid-1990s the Internet has served civil society as a means to circumvent state authority by providing a platform for networking, advocacy and mobilisation. Notable cases, such as the 1999 anti-globalisation riots in Seattle, and Zapatista rebellion in Chiapas, Mexico, 1994-1996, drew media attention to what many civil society actors were already aware of: the latent potential power of global networking for local causes. But civil society actors were by no means the only ones to benefit from being globally connected and omnipresent. By the new millennium, criminals, militants and others seeking voice, fame or economic gain had colonised cyberspace and presented a new challenge to states and global order.

The 'social netwars' first described by David Ronfeldt and John Arquila in their analysis of how the Zapatistas circumvented the armed might of the Mexican military (Arquilla, Ronfeldt and Fuller 1998), are now a significant feature of all contemporary conflicts – economic, criminal and political. Mexican and Colombian gangs regularly post videos of grisly gangland executions to the popular site YouTube (see for example Watson 2007). These videos are used to intimidate competitors, bolster their image, and often to serve as a warning to those who resist demand for ransom in cases of kidnappings. In Afghanistan and Iraq, the battle with insurgents over 'hearts and minds' is as often fought in cyberspace as in physical engagements. Insurgents film attacks, often from several camera angles, and produce vignettes with powerful propaganda resonance. Consequently, the Internet has emerged as the 'great equalizer' where even the smallest groups can greatly amplify their strategic effect in a 'battlespace' that military and police forces are ill equipped to contest (see Keenan in Chapter 10 of this volume). A recent study of Iraqi insurgent media carried out by Radio Free Europe concluded that their 'product' was increasing in reach and sophistication. It is progressively finding traction and appeal in the mainstream Arab press. Moreover, the study concludes that 'there is little to counter this torrent'(Kimmage and Ridolfo 2007).

But criminals and militants are not the only ones shaping the future Internet. Increasingly, individuals acting alone or as a group can have an effect previously thought to be restricted to states. In May 2007, the removal of a statue from a park in Estonia led to an acrimonious row between Russian and Estonian nationalists.[1] The conflict spilled over into cyberspace where, in the words of Hillar Aarelaid, chief security officer of the Estonian Computer Emergency Response Team (CERT), a 'cyber-riot' ensued that at one point threatened a complete shut down of Estonian banking and telecom systems.[2] The degree of disruption was astonishing and worrying, as it appeared to have occurred in a self-organised fashion rather than as a consequence of a planned and coordinated campaign.

As a consequence, the variegated terrain of cyberspace is now increasingly contested as states attempt to enforce nationally defined rules on conduct in cyberspace, in order to render it less 'ungoverned'. Borders, checkpoints and 'fences' are being built, but with mixed results (Deibert and Villeneuve 2004). In part the very nature of cyberspace, as a technical human-made domain dependent on cooperation for its very existence, makes the issue of traditional sovereignty built on the basis of defensive borders, difficult to conceptualise, much less enforce. However, this has not stopped states from trying.

Borders and checkpoints in cyberspace

A 2007 study by the OpenNet Initiative (ONI) found that 25 of 41countries surveyed engaged in some form of technical filtering of the Internet (Deibert, Palfrey, Rohozinski and Zittrain 2007). More worryingly, the testing revealed that the content targeted for censorship included political expression, social themes, and topics deemed dangerous to national security. However, very few of the countries limited their filtering to a narrowly defined set of targeted subjects. Instead, a majority filtered a broad set of topics, suggesting that filtering regimes, once put into place, generally 'creep' beyond their initial mandate. The lack of legal norms and public oversight over filtering contributes to increasingly non-accountable practices while the technical nature of filtering often leads to the mis-recognition of content, which is therefore blocked - for example, maternal healthcare sites have been classified as pornography.

The ONI study also suggested that filtering is a fast-moving and evolving trend. First generation filtering relied on passive means where lists of banned websites were loaded into routers such that requests to the servers hosting those websites were denied. These methods, used by countries such as China, Iran, and Saudi Arabia, are relatively unsophisticated and easy to defeat.[3] Moreover, they are also difficult to hide. As ONI testing revealed, it is relatively easy to determine what content is being filtered, and by whom. As a result, countries engaging in first generation filtering have been quickly targeted by advocacy groups and labeled as 'pariahs'. It is therefore hardly surprising that first generation methods are being supplanted by 'second generation' strategies designed to be more stealthy, dynamic and sophisticated.

Filtering '2.0'

Evidence gathered by ONI points to several emerging trends that characterise second generation filtering strategies. First, the value of information is fixed in time, and therefore filtering does not have to permanent, but present only when a particular kind of information has greatest value (or potential for disruption). This is particularly true during elections, when interest in media reporting and political communications is heightened, and where the consequences of an electoral loss may have major repercussions. In two cases, the February 2005 election in Kyrgyzstan (which led to the toppling of President Askar Akayev in the 'Tulip revolution'), and during the 2006 presidential elections in Belarus, ONI documented 'just in time' filtering against key opposition media and political sites. This filtering differed from first generation strategies in two ways; first, it was applied temporarily, in these cases

---

[1] *For more information concerning the bronze statue of Tallinn incident, see http://en.wikipedia.org/wiki/Bronze_Soldier_of_Tallinn*
[2] *Author interview with Hillar Aarelaid, Vihterpalu, Estonia, June 2007.*
[3] *Proxy software, such as Psiphon, which are based on social network principles, provides an easy-to-use solution that can confound many national firewall systems. See, for example, BBC Online (2006) 'Web censorship 'bypass' unveiled', 27 November. http://news.bbc.co.uk/2/hi/technology/6187486.stm*

during the election period; and second, in the method used to apply it. In the Kyrgyzstan and Belarus cases, access to sites was disrupted through offensive means, by attacking web servers hosting information services using denial-of-service attacks, which flooded the servers with requests rendering them unable to respond. In the Kyrgyz case, these attacks were accompanied by an ultimatum to the Internet Service Provider (ISP) hosting the websites, demanding that they be removed (OpenNet Initiative 2005). In the case of Belarus, denial-of-service attacks were accompanied by other tactics, such as introducing deliberate errors in domain name servers (which are necessary for finding servers on the Internet), and once temporarily shutting down all Internet access in Minsk (Rohozinski 2006). There are indications that these second generation techniques are not restricted to technologically sophisticated states. During 2007, Ethiopia, Uganda, and Cambodia shut down access to SMS services during politically sensitive times, presumably in recognition that these technologies offer a means for opposition movements to mobilise (Zuckerman 2007).

Another trend of second generation filtering emerging from ONI research is the specific targeting of critical resources, rather than broad-brush censorship of whole categories of content. This form of filtering is also closely linked to surveillance. In several countries, notably Egypt, a combination of surveillance and selective prosecution is used to effectively curtail bloggers, and specific minority groups (especially the gay and lesbian community) (Abbas 2007). The message being sent by the state is that you cannot hide in cyberspace. It is a clear warning to anyone seeking the anonymity of cyberspace to voice political criticism or express alternative lifestyles: you can be found, and you can be prosecuted.

At third emerging, but as of yet unverified, trend, is that countries can buy 'pre-filtered' Internet access from countries that apply these practices on their national segments. In 2004, ONI research revealed that an ISP in Uzbekistan demonstrated the same patterns of filtered content as that used by China Telecom. Further investigation revealed that the ISP purchased its connectivity from China Telecom. Similar patterns, albeit on a lesser scale, were highlighted by the 2007 ONI survey, which found that several CIS countries that buy their access through a Russian-based ISP shared similar filtering patterns (Rohozinkski 2007). Evidence is preliminary, but the idea of outsourcing national filtering to a third country has appeal in that it provides a plausible pretext for denying culpability, or at least the ability to deflect criticism by blaming a third party. It is also perhaps indicative of a broader trend in the Internet as regional powers, such as Russia, China and potentially India, increasingly control larger parts of the 'core' global Internet infrastructure.

Lastly, second generation filtering is increasingly multifaceted, reflecting the growing importance of the Internet to economic life as well as politics. The Internet is opening up areas of commercial interest previously the preserve of state monopolies. For this reason, many countries block new services, such as Internet telephony, ostensibly to protect national providers from competition, and to retain lucrative licensing and revenue streams.

Balkanization, or an increasingly competitive and militarised commons?

As the Internet continues to grow and evolve as a universal platform for communication, pressures to contain, control and dominate cyberspace will continue to develop. At present, the tendencies seem to point in two directions. On the one hand there is the possibility that the Internet will become increasingly Balkanised, and divided among tightly controlled national networks. This possibility, however, is unlikely given that few countries are large enough to support a truly autarchic Internet economy, and doing so would mean that many of the advantages of a globally connected Internet would disappear. The fact remains that only large and powerful countries like China - which may soon eclipse the US as the largest country in cyberspace - seem content to pursue 'great firewalls' to defend and control national cyberspace at great expense and effort.

---

4   *Although this document remains classified, an unclassified powerpoint summary was circulated in mid-2006.*

The second tendency points to an increasingly competitive cyberspace commons where states, individuals, civil society and 'dark nets' jostle for agency and advantage. In this scenario, states will more aggressively defend their interests in cyberspace without concern for blockading their national borders from information flows. States like the US acknowledge that they now fight on a level playing field against sophisticated network actors who are adapt at operating in global cyberspace It is therefore no coincidence that the US National Military Strategy for Operations in Cyberspace (2006), which remains classified,[4] defines cyberspace as a domain equal in importance to land, air, and sea, and one in which the US must seek appropriate tools for war fighting, and superiority (Wynne 2006).

Which outcome will prevail is a matter for future historians. But it is clear that the Internet has evolved into a domain capable of supporting a sophisticated social and political ecosystem – a domain that seems destined to shape the great geopolitical struggles of our century.

Ronald J Deibert, University of Toronto, and Rafal Rohozinski, University of Cambridge, are principal investigators of the OpenNet Initiative, a collaborative research project between the Universities of Cambridge, Harvard, Oxford and Toronto, which aims to identify and document Internet filtering and surveillance, and to promote and inform wider public dialogue about such practices.

phones, text messaging, and emails to organise rallies in the capital. In North Korea, illegal sales and the spread of transistor radios without a fixed tuning dial are lifting the information blockade imposed by the regime. Defectors from North Korea have been able to get in touch with families back home thanks to the penetration of the Chinese mobile network in border towns (Jeffries 2006: 93). And family connections were rekindled thanks to video-conference telephoning between relatives separated after the Korean war of the 1950s (Jeffries 2006: 76-80).

Our interviewees also confirm the significance of transnational media, whose impact was demonstrated in the Communist period. In Iran, the Iranian service of Voice of America, Radio Free Europe and National Iranian Television, based in Los Angeles, play an important role.

Newspapers, magazines and journals

Despite its increasing availability in illiberal regimes such as Cuba, Burma and China, Internet access is restricted to elites and a handful of dissidents in urban areas. Magazines and journals continue to be crucial spaces for dissent. In Iran, the ideas of the religious reformer Abdul-Karim Soroush were first expressed in the magazine *Kiyan*. The women's magazine *Zanan* has also been important. At the same time, many magazines and journals have been closed down by the state, especially during the Khatami period, and many journalists arrested. In 2006, Iran's most popular daily *Shargh* was closed down. In Belarus, the unregistered underground newspaper *Right to Freedom* is provides information for civil society groups. In Burma, a number of weekly and monthly papers are owned and run by independent journalists and writers. Accused of supporting the opposition and exiles, the media is strictly monitored by the generals. However, journalists do manage to circumvent censors and publish their ideas by focusing on issue-specific stories, such as those related to the environment.

Economic spaces

Autonomous spaces in illiberal regimes are being carved out both by the legal and shadow global economy. Even North Korea, dubbed the Hermit Kingdom, has not been impervious to economic globalisation. The economic crisis, exacerbated by the Great Famine of 1996-1999, and the growth of

corruption among the country's officials, including border-guards, facilitated a migration of an estimated 100,000 North Koreans into China in the last decade. There they remain as illegal labourers, doing casual and unskilled work in restaurants, construction and farms, or work as domestic maids. Though underpaid, they make a significant amount of money compared to what they would earn in North Korea, and they use any opportunity to send money back home, even returning to visit the families left behind (Lankov 2004).

Cross-border smuggling and trafficking has an explicit gender aspect. The shortage of brides due to the migration of young women into urban areas and China's one child policy, has produced a lucrative business in young Korean women. Its underside has been massive human rights violations (Davis 2006). Many women who enter into an agreement to be sold for marriage find themselves at the mercy of traffickers, forced to work in the sex industry, physically maltreated, or even killed for resisting. Others are lured by promises of a job in China. One victim was reported as saying, 'it is better to find a man, any man, than to starve to death in North Korea' (quoted in Davis 2006: 133).

From Cuba and China to Burma and North Korea, tourism has been a potent yet contradictory force. While it opens up countries to outsiders, it also provides a welcome cash flow for regimes and a source of black market income for guides, minders, and others who are permitted to work in tourism. Even North Korea has become tourist destination, its rarity value attracting Chinese tourists and the occasional American or Briton. Like journalists, tourists are assigned minders to prevent a corrosive political impact on the locals (*The Economist* 2007a).

Religious spaces

Religious venues provide another forum for communication. In Iran and Saudi Arabia, religious institutions may be dominated by hardliners but nevertheless they do provide spaces for reformers as well. Just as the Church provided space in Poland and East Germany in Communist times, so religious institutions, even where the regime is fiercely secular, can sometimes carve out spaces. Buddhist monks organised in sangha (order of monks) were involved in the Burmese pro-democracy movement. During the 1988 demonstrations they negotiated with the military and later put pressure on the regime to recognise the results of the 1990 elections by refusing to accept alms or perform religious ceremonies for military families. Their defiance led to a clampdown on the monasteries, including a law banning all independent sangha organisations. Some still exist, like Malon Rice Donation Group, a Buddhist religious group that has been donating rice to Buddhist monks, nuns and the poor for over 100 years. Merciless repression of Falun Gong members in China, including a ban on the 'evil cult' in 1999, demonstrates the government's anxiety about a non-governmental organisation outside its control. Falun Gong - 'Law of the Wheel'- which claims to have 70 million followers worldwide, is a sect, also popularly referred to as a cult and spiritual organisation, that follows a combination of Buddhist and Taoist beliefs, and practises traditional breathing and mediation exercises, and above all harbours religious devotion of Master Li, its founder. The 1999 ban was prompted by the sudden and unexpected public action of 10,000 believers who surrounded government buildings to protest the arrest of their leaders. Falun Gong's owes its survival in China to the Internet, which enables a global reach through a network of websites and branches and teaching centres around the world. For example, the Friends of Falun Gong USA have been campaigning against the ban that included human rights walks, public rallies, phone calls into China, and a public relations campaign (URL). Elsewhere, for example in Iran and Saudi Arabia, courageous reforming clerics provide spaces for debate within some mosques.

Other public and private spaces

Concerts, football matches, parks, teashops, or art galleries all in different ways offer potential public spaces for free expression. In Iran, many young people want to participate in music festivals and sporting events, especially football. They want to do what young people do in the West, to meet in public parks or cafes. There are several groups of women sporting fans. For example, there is a campaign among women to be allowed to cycle. In the Burmese cities of Rangoon and Mandalay, intellectuals, artists and scholars meet in teashops even though there are restrictions on what they can say.

And, of course, in all but the most repressive regimes (perhaps only in North Korea), people are able to talk freely within the confines of their homes.

A traditional Burmese teashop, Rangoon

And sometimes it is in private homes that dissent is expressed through discussion or lectures and performances. In Burma, three comedians, the Moustache Brothers, who have been banned from public venues and imprisoned previously, performed a traditional Burmese vaudeville in a private home that ridiculed the military regime.

In Saudi Arabia too, there are obviously some informal spaces within the home, although even homes are usually segregated. The group of women who protested their exclusion from the municipal elections hold a weekly cultural salon in their homes. Azar Nafisi's enthralling book *Reading Lolita in Teheran* describes the conversations in a women's reading group in Iran.

Underground

When none of these spaces are available, political dissent becomes secret and goes underground, risking yet more repression for the dissenters. In Burma, after the suppression of the 1988 demonstrations, and the 1990 contested election, a number of activists went into hiding and engaged in underground activism. These activists are held in high regard by ordinary Burmese for risking their lives. Nonetheless, due to the secrecy of the struggle, their ideas are restricted to a closed circle of supporters. Similarly, in Belarus, activism has been pushed underground by regime repression. NGOs and groups, which no longer have legal status, operate illegally, leaving them vulnerable to greater repression by the regime. In China too, underground resistance has been a response to the government's crackdown on

Box 5.5: Egyptian bloggers, the state and civil society

The story of the Egyptian regime and bloggers is a significant, multifaceted and illuminating account of how an absolute and hard-hearted state deals with the noisy march of activism into the new possibilities and frontiers of cyberspace. It is an experience that can be read in many lights, from media, international politics and activism, to mass psychology and literature, and from which important lessons and insights can be drawn. Between creativity and acute repression, Egyptian bloggers have been able to swiftly jump between virtual and physical space, sometimes saving themselves from the state's iron fist, sometimes not. In so doing, they have opened the way for a new era for Egyptian civil society, in both normative and practical terms. This contribution aims to outline the relationship between Egyptian bloggers and the state, with a special eye for the relevance of this relationship, its different experiences, and various impacts on Egyptian civil society actors.

From May 2005, Egypt – the state, its people and, until then, its forcefully numbed civil society – became aware of a new reality. For the first time, the Egyptian regime prepared for multi-party elections in order to create a cosmetic democratic reform, especially in the eyes of its macho ally, the US. Opposition groups dismissed this empty and tactical move by the government, and called for a boycott on voting day. The government hired thugs to organise pro-government rallies, who beat up anti-government protesters in downtown Cairo and sexually harassed female activists.

Little did activist Wael Abbas know that day that he would be setting the stage for the role of Egyptian civil society as an alternative and reliable media provider, pulling the carpet from underneath the government's media monopoly. He used his mobile phone to document the state-sponsored violence against protesters, and recorded a testimony of one of the thugs, who admitted he had been paid by the government. Wael then uploaded the story to his blog (misrdigital.tk), thus instigating a practice that is now widely used and even endorsed by the some of the world's biggest news providers.

Wael broke new ground striving for civil society concerns, receiving half a million hits on his blog in two days and offering substantial evidence against the government's shameless denial of the incident. This, however, did not suffice to save him from being arrested the next day. He was freed shortly after. Since then, providing alternative news – not just information on social and political issues – to local and international communities has become a quintessential function of Egyptian bloggers' electronic activism; news that otherwise would have been buried by the noisy drums of the one-party state media.

Bloggers have brought to the fore awareness about issues like police torture, state-sponsored violence, electoral frauds, labour strikes, and sectarian violence. They also caused a public frenzy when reporting on the infamous group assault of women at the end of Ramadan 2006, which had been scandalously neglected by the state police. Such silenced issues that shame the government were unheard of in the media before.

One of the most important roles of bloggers now is the provision of alternative news for Egyptian activists, intelligentsia, diasporas, and opposition and international media outlets, from promising new Egyptian opposition papers and independent satellite channels, to Al-Jazeera. The popular, leftist 'meta-blog' of the activist couple Alaa and Manal (manalaa.net) is the top of the list. Alaa was arrested for six weeks after being dragged from a pro-democracy demonstration; he continued to blog determinedly from his cell. At the moment, Alaa is an aggregator of Egyptian blogs, an important resource of Egyptian blog life, which can be found at omraneya.net (Arabic/English).

The second significant role of Egyptian bloggers is their local and international mobilisation, which encompasses a wide spectrum, from ordinary Egyptian citizens, activists, and intellectuals, to NGOs, diasporas, international organisations and watchdogs. It must be stressed that Egypt's blogging activism emerged from a public movement going electronic, not from an isolated island of virtual activists. The movement of *Kifaya* (Enough), a wide umbrella for opposition groups and activists that was galvanised by opposition to the President's extension of his term of office, is the child of an electronic petition, per se. In addition to mobiles and emails, blogs have been a source of information on organised rallies, campaigns and activism-related lectures. It is no coincidence then that six bloggers were removed by police from a demonstration in support of the independence of the judiciary, which they had helped to organise. One of them, Mohammed al-Sharqawi (sharkawy.wordpress.com), was blindfolded, beaten and sexually abused with a cardboard tube by the police, an experience he reported in his blog, which sparked a spirited public discussion about police practices.

One of the biggest events in the Egyptian blogosphere involved Abdul Kareem Suleiman Amer, who blogs under the pseudo name Karim Amer. Amer was sentenced to three years for insulting Islam and inciting sedition, and one year for insulting the Egyptian President. The incident not only created havoc in the media, it illustrated the ability of bloggers to organise and mobilise with other activists in Washington DC, New York, Chicago, Paris, Ottawa, London, Berlin, Rome, and Bucharest, in order to lobby for his release.

Bloggers' activism and coordination with international organisations has also been a focus and function. Unfortunately it has proved a source of danger. In addition to Amer, the widely-covered arrest of Abdul-Moneim Mahmud, a blogger, journalist and editor of the website of the banned (yet tolerated) Muslim Brotherhood, is a case in point. After he was freed he wrote on his blog that he was arrested - without warrant - on the night he met with a delegation from Amnesty International, and chiefly for that reason.

Egyptian bloggers face a raft of obstacles and dangers. In an accident that draws legitimate parallels with the practice of burning of books in the Middle Ages and the struggles for freedom of expression, pro-government judge Abdel Fattah Mourad filed a lawsuit calling for the closure of 50 blogs and websites claiming that they 'defame Egypt's image, insult the president, and harm national interests'. In addition to persecution, arrest, and even torture in some cases, bloggers are threatened with the closing down of their web pages. There is evidence that the government exercises censorship by influencing Internet Service Providers and search engine companies; for example, the website of the Muslim Brotherhood does not open from one particular ISP.

Bloggers also face tarnishing campaigns through the pro-state media, who call them 'immature', 'traitors', 'sellouts', and 'agents of America', a set of stigmas that aim to strip them of any credibility in the eyes of the public. An immediate problem and potential danger is the personal nature of their challenge to the authorities because, as blogger Nora Younis says, they 'have put a name and a face to state security torturers and therefore the battle became personal' (norayounis.com).

Unlike other less fortunate, less technologically savvy and less vocal activists, Egyptian bloggers are privileged to have attracted many ears and eyes, especially in the West. Their experience has been widely covered internationally. Younis, in her post 'War on Bloggers Unfolds', explains:

[blogger] Sandmonkey quitting echoed for [appealed to] foreigners more than Egyptians. Bloggers enjoy wide readership among embassies, diplomats, scholars and policy makers all over the world. If you want to know about Egypt but can't sit at a cafe and chat with people; you read the blogs. (norayounis.com)

Other bloggers - especially women - have quit after being summoned to the state security offices. Nonetheless, despite being in the spotlight, their cause languishes, a state of affairs they share with other besieged civil society actors. And, although they brought to public and international awareness many novel stories and hidden facts, so far, unfortunately, little has changed on the grounds of action, which are occupied by the state's territorial despotism, whether in physical or the virtual space.

Tarek Ghanem, writer, translator and editor of Islamica Magazine

Internet cafes. The establishment of illegal Internet cafes has been connected with the informal economy. For example, illegal cafes sprang up in Shanxi province, southwest of Beijing, in the wake of the Internet café ban introduced by the authorities in mid-2006. When asked how it was possible, the owner said the secret was in the relationship with the police (Cody: 2007).

Diaspora and global cities

Diasporas continue to play a complex role in the opening up of illiberal regimes. Exiled dissidents, such as those from China and Burma, are critical for maintaining the struggle for democracy and human rights in their homeland. However, global diasporas are contested spaces, and they harbour proponents and opponents of liberalisation. Diasporas have been able to exercise political power through economic leverage. Until recently, the Korean diaspora in Japan, numbering some 600,000, played a part in bolstering the regime through profits made in pinball arcades that were channelled to North Korea (*The Economist* 2007b).

London has become an important venue for the Saudi opposition. London is host to the Committee for the Defence of Legitimate Rights, responsible for the Memorandum of Advice in 1991, and its splinter group the Movement for Islamic Reform. London is also host to Saudi establishment newspapers and Middle East Broadcasting, owned by the royal family, which are more liberal than media in Saudi Arabia. Similarly, Lithuania and the Ukraine have proved havens for Belarussian civil society. Banned from universities at home, Belarussians organised a parallel university in Vilnius, while both Lithuania and the Ukraine have been critical for enabling Belarussian NGOs to

operate their programmes, hosting activities organised by Belarussians.

Conclusion

In all illiberal regimes, it is possible to identify some kind of space – underground or open, private or public, virtual or real, at home or abroad – for autonomous activity. The kind of people and groups who fill those spaces are not necessarily democrats. On the contrary, in illiberal regimes, especially those of long-standing, criminals and economic dissidents, right-wing nationalists, anti-imperialist populists or religious fundamentalists are probably more widespread than democrats. Most of these spaces are constructed out of global connections. Trading links, both legitimate and illicit, tourism and travel, new forms of communication, especially the Internet and mobile phones, provide the basis for new nodes in the global system in which some people are able to organise themselves and act independently of the state.

In other words, it is very difficult, in the context of globalisation, to sustain closed authoritarian regimes, even in the most repressive systems like North Korea, Burma or Saudi Arabia. This is what we mean by involuntary pluralisation. The implication is that governments increasingly depend on consent as well as coercion. But consent is not the same as democracy. Globalisation is both regressive and progressive. Today's authoritarian regimes depend on the global economy because they are oil states, need other forms of international business like tourism, or they are linked to criminal networks as well as other authoritarian regimes. And they use modern communications to mobilise consent around radical nationalist or religious ideologies.

The dominant approaches to democracy promotion adopted by Western governments are based on rather traditional analyses of illiberalism, developed during the Cold War. They presuppose a clear distinction between internal and external and they assume that overthrowing the government - 'regime change' - will lead to democracy. One approach is what we call the geo-political approach. These are aggressive forms of democracy promotion based on military and economic threats. This approach echoes the Western method of dealing with Communism during the Cold War and is characteristic of the Bush policy towards Iran, Syria,

North Korea, Cuba and Venezuela. This approach often tends to reinforce illiberalism. It contributes to xenophobic popular sentiment and reinforces the dominant ideology in the way that Cold War ideologies of anti-communism and anti-imperialism were mutually self-reinforcing. Our North Korean interviewees who have recently arrived in the UK said, 'US is the enemy. Everything that goes wrong is because of the US' and 'Famine is because of the US'. Similarly, Most Iranian dissidents take the view that American policy helps to strengthen the hardliners in government and vice versa; Bush and Ahmadinajad are seen as mutually supporting each other. As one Iranian commentator said:

> The regime's greatest strength has been its claim to be the only country in the Middle East standing up to the United States. The nuclear question, particularly the way it has been spun in Teheran, has permitted the regime to emerge as the champion of Iran's sovereign rights, even in the eyes of many Iranians who despise their leaders. (Milani 2005:49)

Moreover, air strikes or sanctions weaken legitimate institutions and encourage illicit, underground or criminal networks that benefit extremist and authoritarian factions. This is what happened in Milosevic's Serbia or Saddam Hussein's Iraq.

Another approach is the provision of money for democracy promotion. Such assistance can be beneficial provided it is aimed at creating the enabling conditions for a democratic civil society. Too often it is spent on trying to overthrow regimes, as in the colour revolutions, or in constructing artificial NGOs, which can easily be dubbed 'enemies of the regime' (see Chapter 4 of this volume). In Iran, for example, few NGOs are willing to accept the money announced by Condoleezza Rice to promote Iranian democracy. On the other hand, support for legitimate spaces, such as independent or external media, universities, culture and sport, especially where these enable international exchanges, can be very helpful.

But most important in empowering and enabling those civil groups who favour democracy is communication and dialogue – making use of the spaces that exist to engage in a debate based on reason rather than promoting ideology. Both outside pressure and money can sometimes be useful provided it is guided by a debate of this kind and is supported and even promoted by local democratic reformers. This is what our interviewees who corresponded with us from the heart of illiberal regimes said. What matters to them is contacts and ideas.

Explaining their goal to set up the nucleus of a future journalism school and an association to defend the rights of journalists, our Burmese correspondent told us:

> We welcome all the cooperation and assistance from the outside and also would like to participate in activities such as conferences, seminars, workshops, etc. We would love to connect the civil society in our country with global mainstream civil society movements. We would also like to welcome anyone who wants to come to this country in order to strengthen civil society and develop the media industry.

The best prospect for democratising illiberal regimes is through liberalising civil society spaces and stimulating a debate and deliberation. Of course globalisation does provide an unprecedented opportunity for doing this even if it also opens up illiberal spaces. As a Chinese student told us: 'Globalisation is our only hope for democratisation'.

Abbas, W (2007) 'Big Brothers: In Egypt, blogging can get you arrested - or worse', *Slate http://www.slate.com/id/2166146*

All-China Environment Federation (2006) 'Survey Report on the Development of Civic Organizations in China'.

Amirahmadi, Hooshang (1996) 'Emerging Civil Society in Iran', *SAIS Review* 16(2).

Arquilla, J, Ronfeldt, D, Fuller, G, & Fuller, M (1998) *The Zapatista Social Netwar in Mexico*. Santa Monica, RAND - Arroyo Center.

Arendt, Hannah (1989) 'What is Authority?' in Richard T. Garner and Andrew Oldenquist (eds) *Society and the Individual: Readings in Political and Social Philosophy.* Belmont, CA: Wadworth Publishing Company.

Chaudhary, Vivek (2001) 'Olympic reaction: 'This decision will allow a police state to bask in reflected glory', *The Guardian* 14 July.

Chong, Agnes (2005) 'Chinese Civil Society Comes of Age', 22 September. www.opendemocracy.net

Cody, Edward (2007) 'Despite a ban, Chinese youth navigate to Internet cafes', *The Washington Post*, 9 February.

Cooper, Helene (2007) 'Darfur Collides With Olympics, And China Yields', *The New York Times*, 13 April.

Corner, John and Pels, Dick (eds) (2003) *Media and the Restyling of Politics*. London: Sage.

Dalton, Russell (1994) *The Green Rainbow*. New Haven: Yale University Press.

Davis, Kathleen (2006) 'Brides, bruises and the border: The trafficking of North Korean women into China', SAIS Review, Vol. XXVI, No. 1: 131-141.

Deibert, R J and Villeneuve, N (2004) 'Firewalls and Power: An Overview of Global State Censorship of the Internet' in M Klang and A Murray, A (eds) *Human Rights in the Digital Age*. London, Cavendish Press.

Deibert, R, Palfrey, J, Rohozinski, R and Zittrain J (eds) (2007) *Access Denied: The Practice and Policy of Global Internet Filtering*, Cambridge, MIT Press.

della Porta, Donatella and Massimiliano, Andretta (2002) 'Changing Forms of Environmentalism in Italy: The Protest Campaign on the High Speed Railway System', *Mobilization* 7(1): 59-77.

Doyle, Timothy and Simpson, Adam (2006) 'Traversing more than speed bumps: Green politics under authoritarian regimes in Burma and Iran', *Environmental Politics*, Vol. 15 (5): 750-767.

The Economist (2007) 'North Korea through Chinese eyes: All the misery of Maoism with none of the redeeming features', 24 May.

The Economist (2007) 'Pyongyang's cashflow problem', 13 January.

Endeshaw, Assafa (2004) 'Internet regulation in China: The never-ending cat and mouse game', *Information & Communications Technology Law*, Vol. 13 (1): 41-57.

Farrow, Mia and Farrow, Ronnan (2007) 'Genocide Olympics' *The Wall Street Journal*, 28 March.

Frolic, Michael B (1997) 'State-led civil society' in Timothy Brook, Michael B Frolic (eds) *Civil Society in China*. Armonk, NY and London: M E Sharpe.

Gheytanchi, Elham (2001) 'Civil Society in Iran: Politics of Motherhood and the Public Sphere', *International Sociology* 16(4):557-576.

Ho, Peter (2007) 'Embedded Activism and Political Change in a Semi-authoritarian Context', in Peter Ho and Richard Edmonds (eds) *China's Embedded Environmentalism: Opportunities and Constraints of a Social Movement.* London: Routledge.

Hooglund, Eric (2002) *Twenty years of Islamic revolution : political and social transition in Iran since 1979.* Syracuse, NY: Syracuse University Press.

Howell, Jude (2004) 'New Directions in Civil Society: Organizing Around Marginalized Interests', in Jude Howell (ed) *Governance in China*. Lanham: Rowman and Littlefield.

Jackson, Steve (2007) 'China to eradicate queue-jumping', BBC News, 11 February.

Jeffries, Ian (2006) North Korea: *A guide to economic and political developments.* New York and London: Routledge.

Kalathil, Shanthi and Boas, Taylor C (2003) *Open Networks Closed Regimes: The Impact of the Internet on Authoritarian Rule*. Washington, DC: Carnegie Endowment for International Peace.

Kaldor, Mary (2003) *Global Civil Society*. Cambridge: Polity.

Keck, Margaret and Sikkink, Kathryn (1998) *Activists beyond Borders: Advocacy Networks in International Politics*. Cornell: Cornell University Press.

Kimmage, D and Ridolfo K (2007) *Iraqi Insurgent Media: The War of Ideas and Images,* Washington DC: RFE/RL Special Report.

Koehn, Peter H (2006) 'Fitting a Vital Linkage Piece into the Multidimensional Emissions-Reduction Puzzle: Nongovernmental Pathways to Consumption Changes in the PRC and the USA', *Climatic Change* 77: 377–413.

Kostovicova, Denisa and Bojicic-Dzelilovic, Vesna (2006) 'Europeanizing the Balkans: Rethinking the Post-communist and Post-conflict Transition', *Ethnopolitics*, 5(3):223-241.

Lankov, Andrei (2004) 'North Korean refugees in Northeast China', *Asian Survey*, 44(6):856-873;

Linz, Juan J and Stepan, Alfred (1996) *Problems of Democratic Transition and Consolidation: Southern Europe, South America, and Post-Communist Europe.* Baltimore and London: The Johns Hopkins University Press.

Mackay, Duncan and Chaudhary, Vivek (2001) 'Human rights alarm as Beijing wins race for 2008 games', *The Guardian*, 14 July.

Milani, Abbas (2005) 'U.S. Foreign Policy and the Future of Democracy in Iran', *The Washington Quarterly* 28(3):41–56.

Mir-Hosseini, Ziba (2006) 'Muslim Women's Quest for Equality: Between Islamic Law and Feminism', *Critical Inquiry* 32.

Mol, Arthur and Carter, Neil (2006) 'China's Environmental Governance in Transition', *Environmental Politics* 15(2): 149-170.

Ng, Mei (n.d.) 'Message from Mei Ng, Director of Friends of the Earth (HK)' www.foe.org.hk/welcome/geten.asp?id_path=1,%2011

Nye, Joseph (2004) *Soft power: the means to success in world politics.* New York: Public Affairs.

O'Brien, Kevin J and Li, Lianjing (2006) *Rightful Resistance in Rural China.* Cambridge: Cambridge University Press.

OpenNet Initiative (2005) 'Special report: election monitoring in Kyrgyzstan'. http://opennet.net/special/kg/

Rahimi, Babak (2003) 'Cyberdissent: The Internet in

Revolutionary Iran', *MERIA Middle East Review of International Affairs* 7(3): September.

Reeves, Eric (2007) 'On China and the 2008 Olympic Games: An open letter to Darfur activists and advocates', 10 February. http://www.sudanreeves.org/Page-10.html

Reuters (2007) 'Beijing Games become catch-all for causes', 13 June.

Roche, Maurice (2002) 'The Olympics and 'Global Citizenship'', *Citizenship Studies* 6(2):165-181.

Rohozinski, R (ed) (2006) 'The Internet and elections: The 2006 Presidential elections in Belarus (and its implication)', Open Net Initiative, Internet Watch 001.

Rohozinski, R (2007) 'Internet Filtering in the Commonwealth of Independent States' in Deibert, R, Palfrey, J, Rohozinski, R and Zittrain J (eds) *Access Denied: The Practice and Policy of Global Internet Filtering.* Cambridge MA: MIT Press.

Salame, Ghassan (eds) (1994) *Democracy without democrats?: the renewal of politics in the Muslim world.* London: IB Tauris.

Sandomir, Richard (2001) 'Olympics: TV/Marketing - You'll Be Looking Live At Some Morning Events', *The New York Times*, 14 July.

Schipani-Aduriz, Andres and Kudrytski, Alyaksandr (2005) 'Banana revolution and banana skins', Transitions On-line, 7 September. http://www.tol.cz.

Schmitter, P C (1996) 'The influence of the international context upon the choice of national institutions and policies in neo-democracies' in L Whitehead (ed) *The International Dimensions of Democratization:* Europe and the Americas. Oxford: Oxford University Press.

Smith, Craig S (2001) 'Olympics: Joyous Vindication and a Sleepless Night', *The New York Times,* 14 July.

Snow, David A and Robert D Benford (2000) 'Framing Processes and Social Movements: An Overview and Assessment', *Annual Review of Sociology,* 26.

Street, John (2004) 'Celebrity Politicians: Popular Culture and Political Representation' *The British Journal of Politics and International Relations* 6(4).

Suu Kyi, Aung San (1997) *Letters from Burma.* London: Penguin Books

Tai, Zixue (2006) *The Internet in China: Cyberspace and Civil Society.* New York and London: Routledge.

Taubman, Geoffry (1998) 'A not-so World Wide Web: the Internet, China and the Challenges to Nondemocratic Rule', *Political Communication* 15: 255-272.

Watson, J (2007) 'Mexican drug gangs spread fear through Internet, newspaper ads, messages tacked to dead', Associated Press, 12 April.

Wynne, Michael W (2006) 'Cyberspace as a Domain In which the Air Force Flies and Fights', speech delivered to the C4ISR Integration Conference, Crystal City, Va, 2 November. http://www.af.mil/library/speeches/speech.asp?id=283

Xu, Xin (2006) 'Modernizing China in the Olympic spotlight: China's national identity and the 2008 Beijing Olympiad.' *The Editorial Board of the Sociological Review* 2006:90-107.

Yang, Guobin (2005) 'Environmental NGOs and Institutional Dynamics in China', *The China Quarterly*, 181: 46-66.

Yeni (2006) 'Activists celebrate "Silent Birthday"', *The Irrawaddy,* 18 October. www.irrawaddy.org.

Zengke, He (2007) 'Institutional barriers to the development of civil society in China', *Discussion Paper* 15, China Policy Institute, The University of Nottingham.

Zuckerman E (2007) 'Mobile Phones and Social Activism: Why cell phones may be the most important technical innovation of the decade', Techsoup.org. http://www.techsoup.org/learningcenter/hardware/page7216.cfm

Websites (consulted 19 July 2007)

Amnesty International, http://web.amnesty.org/wire/september2001/china

Collectif Chine JO 2008, http://pekin2008.rsfblog.org

Committee Against Corruption, http://www.geocities.com/saudhouse_p/faq.htm#remember

Falun Gong, http://www.fofg.org/

Human Rights Watch, http://www.hrw.org/campaigns/china/beijing08/

International Olympic Committee, www.ioc.org

manalaa.net

misrdigital.tk

Noolympics, http://www.youtube.com/watch?v=J8siFEJktZs

norayounis.com

Not On Our Watch, http://www.notonourwatchproject.org/

Olympic Charter, http://multimedia.olympic.org/pdf/en_report_122.pdf

Olympic Dream for Darfur, http://www.dreamfordarfur.org/

Olympic Watch, www.olympicwatch.org

sandmonkey.org

speaksfreely.net

Women of Zimbabwe Arise, http://wozazimbabwe.org/?page_id=4

CHAPTER 6

DEEPENING DEMOCRACY IN LATIN AMERICA
Miguel Darcy de Oliveira

Twenty years after the transition from military dictatorship to the rule of law, democracy is in crisis in Latin America. This crisis is also raising questions and forcing a reappraisal of the role played by civil society in strengthening democracy in the region. The manifestations and causes of this crisis, as well as how to deepen democracy in order to safeguard it, are the focus of this chapter.

Challenges and threats to democracy in Latin America

From the early 1980s to the mid-1990s, Latin American countries led the so-called second wave of democratisation, following Southern Europe in the mid-1970s and preceding Eastern Europe, East Asia and parts of Africa in the late 1980s and 1990s. For two decades the peaceful transition from authoritarian to democratic rule after decades of repressive military dictatorship and, in Central America, outright civil war, was deemed a success story. The only exception in the region to this democratic trend was Cuba.

This is no longer the case. Over the last five years democracy has been put to severe test. Since the turn of the century, more than a third of Latin American countries – Paraguay (in 2000), Peru (2000), Argentina (2001), Venezuela (2002), Bolivia (2003 and 2005), Ecuador (2000 and 2006) – have experienced situations of acute political risk. In several cases, widespread public protest led to the downfall of elected presidents. Alberto Fujimori in Peru, Fernando de la Rúa in Argentina, Gonzalo Sánchez de Lozada and Carlos Mesa in Bolivia, and Jamil Mahuad and Lucio Gutiérrez in Ecuador were removed from office by a combination of social protest in the streets and political action by parliaments. In Paraguay the military played a key role in the impeachment of President Raul Cubas Grau. In Venezuela, a farcical coup d'état, promoted by military and civil sectors with US support, led to the temporary overthrow of President Hugo Chávez, who was soon reinstated, with the full support of democratic leaders and public opinion throughout the region. To this list might be added situations of extreme tension in the political system that did not reach breaking point: Nicaragua in 2004 and 2005, when President Enrique Bolaños was threatened with impeachment; Honduras in 2005 when authorities delayed announcing the winner of the presidential elections; Brazil in 2005 when the government of Luiz Inacio Lula da Silva was undermined by a wave of political scandals; and Mexico in 2006 when the opposition candidate, López Obrador, aggressively contested in the streets the legitimacy of Felipe Calderon's election to the presidency.

The recurrence and intensity of these political crises and risky situations indicate the fragility of Latin American democracies. Latin America has entered a new historical phase of crisis, inflection and political change. Democracy is again at the centre of the public agenda. It will be safeguarded – and this will be my main contention in this chapter – only if it is strengthened and deepened.

With the exceptions of Chile, Uruguay and, surprisingly, Colombia, despite the permanent threat to political and civil liberties posed by the drug cartels and the Revolutionary Armed Forces of Colombia – People's Army (FARC) guerrillas, there is throughout the region a deep and widening public disaffection vis-à-vis political institutions. All opinion polls corroborate the deficit of trust and the pervasive sense of fatigue affecting political parties, parliaments and governments.[1] Democracy, therefore, must be made to work or apathy, cynicism and disenchantment will facilitate the resurgence of authoritarianism under old or new disguises.

In Chapter 2 of this volume, Mary Kaldor argues for a concept of substantive democracy as something deeper or 'thicker' than formal democracy:

By substantive democracy, I mean a process, which has to be continually reproduced, for maximising the

---

[1] A region-wide opinion poll conducted in 2006 by Latinobarometro indicates that although 54 per cent of Latin Americans believe there can be no democracy without political parties, only 19 per cent have any trust in political parties.

opportunities for all individuals to shape their own lives and to participate in and influence debates about public decisions that affect them. (Kaldor 2008)

Democracy, to be sure, requires the respect for basic political rights and civil liberties, such as a multiparty political system, free and fair elections, freedom of expression and organisation. But this is what we might call a thin, or minimalist concept of democracy as opposed to a thick, or wider definition (Kekic 2007). Democracy is more than the sum of its institutions and procedures. In a substantive sense, democracy is embedded in society, nurtured and enhanced by a vibrant civil society and a civic culture of participation, responsibility and debate. That is why democracy is always a work in progress, an unfinished journey, a process rooted in the history of any given society. That is also why it cannot be imposed from the outside and is never achieved once and for all.

So far, no Latin American country has relapsed into dictatorship. However, the proliferation of corruption scandals and the rising levels of criminal violence combined with the persistence of poverty and inequality are at the root of a profound sense of disconnection between people's aspirations and the capacity of political institutions to respond to the demands of society. The root causes of this growing political instability are to be found in the deep political, economic and social changes undertaken by Latin America over the last two decades. Every country in the region, with the exception, again, of Cuba, underwent not one, but two, radical transformations: the transition from dictatorship to democracy, and the opening up of closed and stagnant economies. Democracy authorised the full expression of long repressed demands for social change. For most countries, however, the restoration of political and civil liberties went hand-in-hand with times of economic and social hardship. The oil crises and huge debts of the 1980s drove national economies to the verge of bankruptcy. The combination of rampant inflation and economic stagnation threatened the very fabric of social life.

The crisis of the Latin American developmentalist model of the 1960s and 1970s, based on internal markets and import substitution, coincided with the sweeping changes brought about by globalisation. A state-centred vision of national development, deeply ingrained in Latin American political culture and

Supporters of Mexico's opposition candidate López Obrador took to the streets in 2006

institutions, came into sharp conflict with the demands of global competitive capitalism. Internal needs and external pressure led to a second drastic process of change: the reform of the state and the opening up of closed national economies to global trade, privatisation and fiscal adjustment. Globalisation, however, is not only an economic or technological process. It is also a political, social and cultural phenomenon. It is not only about financial flows and goods being exchanged in the global market arena. Globalisation is also about information, values, symbols and ideas. The modernisation of the economy and the emergence of open, democratic societies thus represented a profound historical change, both in the patterns of development and in the social dynamics of Latin American countries.

To be sure, in most countries, growth resumed after the lost decade of the 1980s. Wealth, however, remained unevenly shared. Inequality and high levels of poverty persisted. Many young people live in despair, with no sense of future. This frustration, combined with the incapacity of the political democracy to improve, quickly and significantly, people's standards of living is certainly one of the root causes of the prevailing widespread sense of hopelessness. The legitimacy crisis affecting political institutions has been dramatically compounded by the proliferation of corruption scandals and the rising levels of criminal violence and incivility, especially in the region's large cities. Human security is at risk in Latin America, anywhere and at any time.

DEEPENING DEMOCRACY IN LATIN AMERICA

The democratic transition in Latin America created the rules and institutions of democracy, but in most countries respect for due process and rule of law is in danger, at best. Mistrust of politicians, political parties, parliaments and the judiciary is paving the way for the resurgence in several countries of forms of authoritarian populism that were thought to be relegated to the past. Nothing is more expressive of this all-encompassing rejection of the political establishment than the call – *que se vayan todos* (they all must go) – that punctuated the street demonstrations in Argentina, leading to the overthrow of three successive presidents in a few days. In some countries, such as Venezuela, the traditional political system literally fell apart. In others, the crisis of legitimacy gave rise to new actors and demands for radical change.

The resurgence of authoritarian populism

The notion of populism has been used to characterise the policies of countries such as Venezuela, Bolivia, Ecuador, Nicaragua, and even Argentina. Many interpret the recent string of electoral victories by charismatic leaders as a historical turn to the Left in Latin American politics. A core component of Latin American neo-populism is the reaffirmation of the central role of the state. Its leaders vocalise a strident

anti-imperialist and anti-globalisation message but abstain from defining the utopian way towards the new society. President Chávez has resorted to the old Cuban rallying cry of *Patria o muerte, venceremos* (Fatherland or death, we shall overcome!) to promote his Bolivarian Revolution. In his inaugural speech in January 2007, President Rafael Correa of Ecuador made a distinction between *una época de cambios* (an epoch of change) and *un cambio de época* (a change of epoch) to underline his radicalism. President Evo Morales' *indigenismo* appeals to the ethnic and cultural identities of Bolivia's indigenous population as the foundation of his concept of a new society based on non-Western values.

However, in their call for radical political, economic and social change, today's populist leaders differ significantly from Getulio Vargas in Brazil and Juan Perón in Argentina, whose populist regimes shaped Latin American history in the mid-twentieth century. These charismatic leaders appealed directly to the urban masses, ensuring their political allegiance through an extension of labour legislation. They despised representative democracy, promoting the redistribution of resources but not seeking to change the prevailing social and economic order. Perón was strongly anti-American, unlike Vargas, but neither ever entertained an anti-market stance. Their reliance on an authoritarian state was more pragmatic than ideological.

The new populists have in common with their predecessors a strong reliance on mobilising the masses against internal and external enemies, as well as on policies of income redistribution through social programmes. However, they do not hide their hostility towards the markets and political pluralism. Populist leaders speak to people's hearts and mobilise powerful symbols and emotions in response to real or imaginary grievances. They build on the climate of frustration and disillusionment that makes people think that the way to the future is a return to the past – even though it is a romanticised past that, in fact, has never existed.

This direct association of a charismatic leader with 'the people' and 'the nation' undermines the foundations of democracy. It brings with it an inevitable propensity to impose, always for the greater good of the people and the nation, controls by the state over society. This is what is happening in Venezuela, where civil society and the mass media are

Enraptured by the revolutionary myth: a Venezuelan supporter of Hugo Chavez dressed as Che Guevara

already subjected to restrictions and interference. In Venezuela, Bolivia and Ecuador, mechanisms of direct democracy are being used to grant unlimited power to the presidency, by-passing parliament and undermining representative democracy.

Populism is, however, more than just a risk to representative democracy. It is also and foremost a risk to substantive democracy. The imposition of increasing controls by the state over society directly contradicts the gradual building and strengthening of open societies in Latin America. It also exercises a strong fascination over large sectors of Latin American civil society that are still enraptured by the revolutionary myth. It is important to remember that the dream of a radical transformation of the established order remains alive throughout the region in social movements ranging from the neo-Zapatistas of Subcomandante Marcos in Mexico to the Landless Peasant Movement in Brazil, not to mention the narco-guerrilleros of Colombia who still see themselves as revolutionaries. The triumphal reception accorded to President Chávez at the fifth World Social Forum at Porto Alegre in 2005 is an eloquent example of the incantatory power for non-governmental organisations and social movements of the rhetoric of anti-Americanism and anti-globalisation.[2]

The forces of renewal: the rise of informed and empowered citizens

Latin America is at the threshold of a new historical cycle in which the fault-lines will be defined by the contrast between old models and new ideas, authoritarian regression and the deepening of democracy. This is a situation fraught with risks but also with challenges and opportunities. Widespread disaffection towards the political system coexists with the emergence of new forms of citizen participation and civic culture that may well prove to be the best antidote to the resurgence of populism. Latin American societies have changed drastically in the last few decades. These changes have deeply affected the relationship between civil society, the state and democracy. NGOs and social movements were at the forefront of the struggle for democracy in the 1970s and 1980s. With the traditional channels of participation – political parties, unions – having been blocked by the dictatorship, the only available alternative was the creation of small circles of

2   *It is hard to equate the resurgence of populism with the strengthening of the Left in Latin America. Presidents Ricardo Lagos and Michelle Bachelet of Chile, or Tabaré Vázquez of Uruguay, by virtue of their personal history and political philosophy, stand much further to the Left than Hugo Chávez, and they clearly reject his anti-American and anti-globalisation rhetoric.*

freedom at the community level. This kind of grassroots work represented a break with the Latin American tradition of looking to the state and at labour relations as the strategic reference point for political and social action. With their backs turned to the state, social activists have promoted an immense variety of local initiatives that combine the struggle for civic rights and freedom with concrete projects to improve people's daily quality of life. This flexible, bottom-up approach was profoundly democratic, insofar as civil society organisations grasped emerging demands, gave a voice to new actors, empowered communities, tested innovative solutions and pressured governments.

This is less true today, for a number of reasons that it is very important to underline. It is citizen action that gives life to civil society, and citizen initiatives are as diverse as the public issues at stake and the energy of those who mobilise around them. Civil society is not homogeneous. It is not a realm of the good, guided by pure and noble values, contrasting with the evils of the state and the market. Civil society has no controlling or regulatory body to set action agendas or a consensus about what to do. Citizens do not ask for permission to act nor do they conform to any pre-established hierarchy of priorities. They create their own, constantly evolving, agenda.

And yet, some activists see in the plurality of initiatives, actors and causes intrinsic to civil society a risk of fragmentation and dispersion of energies. For an important segment of organised Latin American civil society, the way to restore unity of vision and purpose lies in a closer alignment with leaders such as Chávez, Morales or Correa, who are seen as standard bearers of a Latin American socialism for the twenty-first century.

This subordination of the diversity of citizen action to the political imperatives of a uniform, state-centred strategy of radical social transformation challenges civil society's constituent freedom and autonomy. Citizen participation is multiple, fluid, diverse and, in a way, it is precisely in its lack of organisation – a reflection of the growing complexity and fragmentation of contemporary societies – that its strength resides. Civil society is not, nor can it be, a political party. Its goal is not to achieve or exercise state power. Nobody speaks for civil society, nor has the power or capacity to define who is part of it or who is excluded from it. It is, by its very nature, a contested political space, an arena of debate and innovation, criss-crossed by the conflicts and controversies present in society. It cannot be appropriated by any single political project. Its most visible face is made from organisations and movements. However, today, this organised dimension, no longer accounts for the range and diversity of citizen action. This classical notion of civil society has to be reframed and enlarged to take into account emerging actors, processes and spaces.

The decline in the role played by organised civil society as a driver of democratic change and the concomitant rise of informed and empowered individuals and networks is a significant trend that calls for further scrutiny. It has to do with the emergence of open and complex societies as well as with the opportunities for participation and dialogue that have been opened up by the new information technologies. Today, ordinary people tend to be more intelligent, rebellious and creative than in the past, in so far as they are constantly called upon to make value judgments and life choices, where previously there was only conformity to a pre-established destiny. This enhanced capacity for individuals to think, deliberate and decide is a consequence of the decline in the forms of authority based on religion or tradition. Each of us is daily confronted in our private life with choices that are no longer dictated by a supreme authority nor regulated by law.

The experience of our bodies and sexuality, the decision to get married or not, to maintain the marriage or opt for separation, to have children or not to have them, to interrupt an undesired pregnancy or not to do so, to exercise the right to die with dignity – all these questions are now open to choice. Even the preservation of a loving relationship requires constant care of the other partner, who is also endowed with desires, aspirations and the capacity to make choices of his or her own. In the past, tradition and religion determined identities that were destinies. Today, identity is the end-result of our choices. Each individual tries to be or to become what he or she really is. But, in contemporary society, to quote the Portuguese poet Fernando Pessoa, 'each one is many'. Identities are as multiple and fluid as our own repertoire of experiences and belongings.

Alain Touraine observes that 'the public space is emptying at the top and filling up at the bottom' (Touraine and Khosrokhavar 2000: 31). This formulation keenly grasps the double phenomenon of the withering away of

Citizens are increasingly expressing their identities: left, Quechua women march for equal rights in Peru and right, transsexuals demonstrate in Mexico City

institutional politics and the dominance of everyday concerns in people's lives. These profound changes that shape contemporary societies are increasingly visible and relevant in Latin American. What is missing is the analysis of the significance for democracy of this emergence of a critical mass of informed and empowered citizens. Anthony Giddens uses the concept of 'active trust' to define the ethos of participation and responsibility at the core of the democratisation of everyday life:

> In almost all spheres of life we have moved from passive to active trust as the main bond of social cohesion. Active trust is trust that has to be won from the other and others; where there is two-way negotiation rather than dependence; and where that trust has to be consistently renewed in a deliberate way. (Giddens 2007: 116)

Today, citizens tend to have multiple, overlapping identities and interests. Ethnic origin, age group, religious creed, sexual orientation, and consumption patterns have become a more powerful source of identity than social status. We all become what we desire to be by resisting whatever negates our freedom, and in the incessant search to give our own life meaning. This process opens up new linkages between personal life and public debate, individual freedom and collective responsibility. The process of self-construction is inseparable from the dynamic of social transformation. Citizens capable of making up their minds, deliberating

and taking stands, are at the root of a second phenomenon of great significance for the strengthening of substantive democracy: the rising power of public opinion to shape and influence public debate.

A society less organised but more connected and interactive

Manuel Castells was one of the first to underline the change represented by the transition from a public sphere anchored in political institutions to a public sphere structured around the communication system, which he understood both as media and new information technologies (Castells 1996). Individuals increasingly elaborate their opinions and choices based on they way they live and what they see. If their perception and experience bear no relation to the message of politicians, the inevitable outcome is growing disbelief and mistrust.[3]

The other aspect of this demand for accountability is people's capacity to see through and reject demagogical gestures, empty words and promises as false solutions to complex problems. George Papandreou, leader of the Panhellenic Socialist

---

[3] *The global opposition to the web of lies underpinning the invasion of Iraq, and the exemplary reaction of the Spanish people, who punished the government of Jose Maria Aznar for its attempt to manipulate information about the perpetrators of the Madrid terrorist attack in March 2004, are two recent and eloquent examples of the call for truth and transparency as a paramount political value.*

O IMPORTA DE QUE LADO VOCÊ ESTÁ. **USE CAMISINHA.**

MINISTÉRIO DA SAUDE · GOVERNO FEDERAL

An innovative safe sex campaign by the Brazilian Government

Movement (PASOK) in Greece, says people want a new relationship with power. As they experience a sense of greater freedom and autonomy in their daily lives, they also want to be respected in their ability to understand problems, to take a stand and to act (Barnett 2004). Informed citizens no longer accept the role of passive audience. They want to be actors, not spectators. They want to speak and to be heard. They want the truth to be told to them in a straightforward way, and they want to be sure their contribution will be taken into account.

Consider the case of Brazil, a country with a low level of formal education but with extended access to information through television. There are several examples in recent history of situations in which citizens showed that they are fully capable of understanding complex problems, evaluating arguments, overcoming prejudice and coming up with innovative answers. To the astonishment of many, ordinary people overwhelmingly supported President Cardoso's *Plano Real* (Real Plan) of 1994, to stabilise the currency and curb inflation, support that actively contributed to its success. The national plan to combat the spread of HIV and AIDS generated profound changes in mindsets and patterns of behaviour, thanks to information messages reaching out to all segments of the population in the clearest possible language. Faced in 2001 with the immediate risk of acute power shortages, again people reacted in a surprising way by voluntarily changing their energy consumption patterns on a much broader scale than had been requested by government policy makers.

Similar examples can be found in other countries of the region. Their common message is that when leaders acknowledge the capacity of ordinary people,

when knowledge and information are provided about what is at stake, when credible calls are made for citizen participation and involvement, the popular response tends to be extensive and vigorous. The surprising result of the October 2005 referendum in Brazil on the prohibition of the sale of arms and munitions can also be understood in the light of these new forms of participation and deliberation. Concern with urban violence and criminality is by far the top priority in all public opinion polls. Brazil comes second only to Venezuela in the number of people killed by guns. Imposing legal restrictions on the commercialisation of guns and ammunition had long been a demand of groups concerned with human rights and urban violence. Sensitive to pressure by the media and public opinion, Congress approved legislation severely restricting the gun trade with the provision that the law should be ratified by the people in a national referendum, scheduled for 2005. A couple of months before the vote, opinion polls estimated popular support of ratification to be 75 per cent of the electorate. The Yes campaign was backed by an overwhelming majority of politicians, religious and civic leaders, opinion makers and the media. The outcome seemed a foregone conclusion.

And yet the unexpected happened. The virtual consensus in favor of gun control started to be challenged in blogs and websites. A variety of arguments opened up a process of heated discussion. Opponents denounced the approved legislation as a false, simplistic solution to the complex, dramatic problem of violence, arguing that it reduced government responsibility to ensure public safety. Others spoke about risks to individual freedom and civic rights. Blogs and virtual communities were created overnight. Friends and colleagues shared emails about contrasting points of view. Ideas were confronted in an extensive conversation that spread to the workplace and many households. People who usually took stands along clear-cut idelological lines started to defend conflicting opinions. With the opening up of television prime time for both sides to argue their case and with mandatory voting, the debate expanded to the entire population.

Voters listened to the arguments and evaluated them based on their personal experience of violence and criminality. Citizens felt challenged to elaborate and sustain their views and possibly to change their mind. In a matter of weeks, there was a massive shift in national opinion against ratification: gun control was rejected by 64 per cent of the electorate. Enlightened public opinion and political analysts were stunned. On the one hand, the broad discussion preceding the vote showed the untapped potential of the Internet in a developing country as a space for horizontal communication and public debate. On the other hand, the outcome expressed ordinary people's capacity to confront arguments with their own experience and make up their own minds about complex and emotional issues. This example also demonstrates that citizens tend to be much more creative and innovative than politicians in handling new technologies. Blogs, emails, cell phones and Internet sites are becoming enabling tools for a new type of communication: personal, participatory and interactive. Society is apparently less organised but it is more connected and participatory.

The main hurdle to overcome in the path to substantive democracy is not, therefore, disinformation or apathy on the part of the population. It is politicians' incapacity to understand, respect and trust the capacity of the citizenry – or at least, the extreme difficulty they experience in trying to do so. Latin American countries such as Brazil, Colombia, Chile and Mexico are unjust and yet vibrant societies, marked by high levels of social mobility and new forms of citizen participation. The dynamism of such societies calls for more efficient and less arrogant actions by the state, based on dialogue not monologue, partnership not imposition, argument not empty rhetoric, and autonomy not bureaucratic centralism.

New actors, processes and tools for public debate are making the interaction between citizens and political institutions much more unpredictable and complex. Democracies are evolving into a space for collective dialogue and public deliberation. What matters today is not a fluid 'will of all', but the participation of all concerned in the deliberation. The legitimacy of the decision-making process will increasingly depend on its openness and transparency. This transformation is a formidable challenge to the democratic imagination. Increasing citizen participation and deliberation calls for a radically new style of political leadership. Democracy is a long process of incremental change and it now involves many actors: media, public opinion and parliament. There is no longer space – even though the ardent expectation is always there – for a heroic

Latin Americans citizens are proving more adept than politicians in handling new communications technologies

gesture by the leader that, in a stroke, responds to the people's needs. The democratic leaders will be those open to dialogue and committed to harnessing the energy and creativity of an informed society.[4]

Citizen participation, civic culture and substantive democracy

In complex systems, order is not imposed from the top down by a centre of command and control. Neither does social change occur according to uniform and pre-established strategies. Change is an ongoing process that occurs simultaneously at multiple points. Personal freedom and technological innovation release creative social energy. Pioneering actions, innovative experiences, exemplary projects and unexpected interactions take many shapes, flow along multiple pathways and radiate at great speed. These decentralised initiatives produce an impact on the system as a whole, generating a critical mass of new ideas, messages, proposals, knowledge and experiences. Connectors and communicators amplify and re-transmit these innovations in a continuous dynamic of experimentation, learning, feedback, reorganisation and expansion. Power is moving from the centre to the periphery, from vertical command and

---

4   In his political memoirs Fernando Henrique Cardoso (2006) says that if there is one lesson he learnt in his eight years as president of Brazil, it is that, in today's world, political leadership is never gained once and for all. 'Votes in an election, even dozens of millions of them, are not enough. The day after, one has to start almost from scratch'. Trust and legitimacy must be constantly nurtured and renewed. It is no longer possible for the leader to impose without negotiating, to decide without listening, to govern without explaining and persuading.

control structures to horizontal networks and collaborative platforms. Communication is increasingly participative, interactive and collaborative.

In this rapidly evolving context, the transformation of society is a collective process of changing mindsets, practices and structures, not the result of an act of unilateral political will. The responsibility of the democratic leader is to grasp the challenges, break new ground and show the way forward. There is a growing call for truth, respect and transparency. Either the leader inspires and mobilises around a vision of the future or the loss of power is inevitable.

So far these new forms of citizen action and civic culture have not revitalised the political system. If the gap between politics and society remains unbridged, they may – paradoxically – contribute to further undermine representative democracy. To acknowledge the emergence of these new processes of social participation and communication does not imply their idealisation. Freedom and innovation go hand-in-hand with uncertainty and risk. In any one situation, the appeal of populism is as strong as the disaffection towards the political system. The risks of authoritarian regression are as real as the perspectives for strengthening democracy through citizen participation and civic culture. Much will depend on the capacity of democratic leaders and empowered citizens to interact in a constructive way, as they have done in Brazil, to create the most successful developing country programme to fight HIV and AIDS (de Oliveira 2001) or in the Colombian cities of Bogotá and Medellín to fight violence with the resources of citizen conviviality (Mockus 2002). The paramount contributions of Latin America to global civil society and to the global spread of democracy are to preserve the freedom and autonomy of civil society and to deepen democracy at the national and regional level.

The arguments presented in this chapter are an invitation to the debate and a reaffirmation of the value of democracy, understood as the exercise by citizens of their capacity to deal with the questions and influence the decisions that affect their lives, and the future of society.

REFERENCES

Barnett, Anthony (2004) 'Parties for Everyone?' Interview with George Papandreou. *openDemocracy*, 9 December 2004. http://www.opendemocracy.net/democracy/article_2262.jsp (consulted 2 July 2007).

Castells, Manuel (1996) *The Rise of the Network Society: The Information Age – Economy, Society and Culture,* Vol 1. Malden, MA: Blackwell.

Cardoso, Fernando Henrique (2006) *A Arte da Política* [The Art of Politics]. Rio de Janeiro: Civilização Brasileira.

de Oliveira, Miguel Darcy (2001)'Globalização e Democracia em Tempos de AIDS' [Globalisation and Democracy in Times of AIDS], in *Globalização, Democracia e Desenvolvimento Social* [Globalisation Democracy and Social Development], Programa das Nações Unidas para o Desenvolvimento/Centro Brasileiro de Relações Internacionais, 2001: 41–59.

Giddens, Anthony (2007) *Europe in the Global Age*, Cambridge: Polity Press

Kaldor, Mary (2008) 'Democracy as a Global Integration Project' in Martin Albrow, Helmut Anheier, Marlies Glasius, Monroe Price and Mary Kaldor (eds) *Global Civil Society 2007/8: Communicative Power and Democracy.* London: Sage.

Kekic Laza (2007) 'The Economist Intelligence Unit's index of democracy: The World in 2007'. *The Economist.*

Mockus, Antanas (2002) 'Cultura Ciudadana, Programa Contra La Violencia en Santa Fé de Bogotá, Colombia, 1995–1997' [Civic Culture, Program Against Violence in Santa Fé de Bogotá, Colombia, 1995–1997] , Banco Interamericano de Desarrollo, División de Desarrollo Social, Documento SOC-127. http://www.economist.com/media/pdf/DEMOCRACY_INDEX_2007_v3.pdf (consulted 29 May 2007).

Touraine, Alain and Khosrokhavar, Farhad (2000) *La Recherche de Soi: Dialogue sur le Sujet.* Paris: Fayard.

CHAPTER 7

ACCOUNTABLITY IN A GLOBALISING WORLD: INTERNATIONAL NON-GOVERNMENTAL ORGANISATIONS AND FOUNDATIONS

Helmut Anheier and Amber Hawkes

Introduction

Demands for better governance and greater accountability have increased significantly in recent years at both national and transnational levels and across public, private and non-profit sectors. Originally, accountability, referring in a general sense to having to answer for one's behaviour, was a core concept of public administration and has been exported to other fields. The scandals that have rocked the business world, governments and non-profit organisations alike seem to have undermined public trust in many institutions. Prominent examples include the Enron debacle of 2002, mismanagement in the reconstruction of Iraq, corruption charges in the UN's Oil for Food Programme, the veracity of Greenpeace's information in the Brent Spa case in the mid-1990s, questions about the use of funds raised by the American Red Cross in the aftermath of 9/11 and issues about the transparency of some non-governmental organisation (NGO) operations after the 2004 tsunami in South East Asia.

Such incidents have brought the issue of accountability closer to the public eye. At the same time, they demonstrate the role of the media in detecting and publicising accountability issues. As the flows of media grow in scope and reach, the ability of interested bodies to hold guilty parties up to public scrutiny increases. As a result of congressional action, the Sarbanes–Oxley Act of 2002 (Mintz and Vail 2003; Board Source and Independent Sector 2003) became a milestone for the accountability debate among NGOs and non-profit organisations generally. Larger non-profit organisationss and foundations are anticipating the implications of the Sarbanes–Oxley Act, which requires independent and financial audit committees, certified financial statements, policies on conflicts of interests and disclosure, and introduces protection for whistle-blowers. What is more, some states like California have introduced regulations that apply to tax-exempt organisations and others, like New York, have turned the keen eye of the Public Prosecutor's Office to philanthropic organisations.

Members of International Advocacy NGOs, a group made up of 11 large NGOs including Save the Children, Oxfam, and Amnesty International, adopted the INGO Accountability Charter in summer 2006 (International Non-Governmental Organisations Commitment to Accountability 2006), which includes many aspects of the Sarbanes–Oxley Act (see Box 7.1). Similarly, in May 2007, the European Foundation Centre and the US Council on Foundations issued the *Principles of Accountability for International Philanthropy* (European Foundation Centre and the US Council on Foundations 2007) to guide funders in making better decisions in pursuing their international missions and objectives and to provide a framework that will encourage and assist more foundations to get involved internationally (see Box 7.2). While the INGO Charter and the *Principles of Accountability for International Philanthropy* can be seen as steps forward, they also highlight some of the biggest challenges in defining and enforcing accountability in a globalising world, for instance, those centred around the multiplicity of stakeholders and the difficulty of enforcement and liability, which will be discussed later in this Chapter.

An additional challenge to NGOs working internationally came with the major change in the geo-political climate after the terrorist attacks of September 11, 2001. Legislation and guidelines issued by the US government and the subsequent declaration of a 'war on terror' by President Bush, put a much higher accountability burden on non-profit organisations than in the past. Issued first in 2002 by the US Department of the Treasury under the authority of the Patriot Act and updated since, the *Anti-Terrorist Financing Guidelines: Voluntary Best Practices for US-based Charities* address foundations and cross-border philanthropy. This measure takes the first step to put in place detailed regulations governing the operations of financial institutions, including foundations and NGOs. Similar and sometimes more stringent measures have been discussed at the European Commission, the Council

A doctor examines the X-ray of a TB patient in Kenya

of Europe and the OECD (Anheier and Daly 2005) with regard to financial audits and the review of foreign organisations.

While these are major developments that will add to the 'accountability burden' of foundations in particular, it is equally important to recognise that the accountability challenges go beyond the regulatory compass of the Sarbanes–Oxley Act and anti-terrorist legislation. In fact, they are part of a wider, and perhaps chronic, 'accountability syndrome' facing cross-border organisations in a globalising world. Examining this accountability syndrome for transnational civil society organisations is the core purpose of this Chapter.

While many accountability issues can be broadly applied across all sectors, transnational civil society faces specific challenges in terms of governance, responsibility and liability. Indeed, we see the accountability challenges of transnational civil society closely linked to the process of globalisation itself. On the one hand, globalisation is characterised by democratic deficits and governance problems: disparate societies and communities engage each other and are made to interact with greater frequency and intensity, yet without adequate global supervisory mechanisms. On the other hand, accountability for international NGOs is increasingly related to the cross-national dispersion of democratic values and the public expectations that come with them. In this model, global civil society organisations act as proactive instruments for exposing and demanding transparency and accountability across sectors.

Hence global civil society is on both sides of this problem: having normalised the previously alien notion that all kinds of power-holders, not just governments, have an obligation to 'render account' to stakeholders and the global public, international NGOs, as prominent actors of global civil society, also epitomise internal and external deficits in the form of disconnects between donors, members and beneficiaries. To whom these organisations should be accountable and through what mechanisms and enforcement, are questions central to this discussion.

The main argument

At the core of accountability is what economists call the principal-agent problem. How can owners (the principals) ensure that managers (the agents) run the organisation in a way and with the results that benefit the owners? In the business world, the owners/shareholders delegate the oversight authority to a board of directors. The board is then charged with

Box 7.1: INGO Charter

The heads of 11 large international non-governmental organisations endorsed the International Non-Governmental Organisations Accountability Charter (INGO Charter) in June, 2006. Signatories were ActionAid International, Amnesty International, CIVICUS: World Alliance for Citizen Participation, Consumers International, Greenpeace International, Oxfam International, the International Save the Children Alliance, Survival International, International Federation Terre des Hommes, Transparency International and the World YWCA. The INGO Charter, which is voluntary and not exclusive, outlines an accountability and governance framework for the participating organisations. Its mission states:

This Charter outlines our common commitment to excellence, transparency and accountability. To demonstrate and build on these commitments, we seek to:

- *identify and define shared principles, policies and practices;*
- *enhance transparency and accountability, both internally and externally;*
- *encourage communication with stakeholders; and*
- *improve our performance and effectiveness as organisations.*

The Charter defines the concept of stakeholders (including those whose rights the organisations seek to advance, ecosystems, members, donors, staff, regulatory bodies and the media) and outlines its guiding principles:

- respect for universal principles (such as freedom of speech and assembly)
- independence
- responsible advocacy
- effective programmes
- non-discrimination
- transparency (reporting and auditing, and accurate information)
- good governance
- ethical fundraising (the rights of donors, use of donations, gifts-in-kind and agents)
- professional management (financial controls, evaluation, public criticism, partners, human resources, bribery and corruption, respect for sexual integrity and whistleblowers).

The next steps for the INGO 11 will be to consider reporting mechanisms and review the Charter, along with issues of liability and enforcement.

Source: INGO Accountability Charter (2005), http://www.amnesty.org/resources/downloads/INGO_Accountability_Charter.pdf

the responsibility to make sure that management acts in accordance with the principal's goals and interest. In the public sector, voters (the electorate) elect politicians who then exercise oversight over public sector performance; in addition, the media, agencies like the US Government Accountability Office, and many interest organisations monitor the conduct of government.

By contrast, in non-profit organisations and philanthropic foundations in particular, the situation is undetermined and it is unclear who should be regarded as, or function as, the owner, particularly in cases where the members do not exercise direct democratic control. Trustees are not owners in the sense of shareholders, and while different parties could assume or usurp the role of a principal, such a position would not rest on property rights but on some form of politically negotiated or imposed legitimacy.

The key to understanding the governance and accountability requirements of non-profit organisations is to recognise the special importance of multiple stakeholders rather than owners.

The application of the principal–agent dynamic is limited in the non-profit world, where information about performance is not as clearly and keenly demanded, required, assembled and analysed to the same extent as in the for-profit and public sectors due to weaker signals and incentives in the former. In other words, accountability is less linked to incentives in response to owner/stakeholder signals than in the other sectors, which makes information management and sharing potentially problematic.

However, in a transnational context, the weak signal/incentive problem that applies as well to domestic accountability assumes a new quality. We also argue that in transnational contexts, accountability is increasingly becoming a problem in search of a solution, rather than a solution in response to problems that are well understood and accepted by stakeholders. What is more, it is increasingly difficult for non-profit organisations that operate cross-nationally to be or become accountable relative to growing public and political expectations. Ultimately, the accountability syndrome of transnational civil society organisations embeds accountability in legitimacy.

There are several features of this syndrome, some of which are well known and certainly not new, including the presence of multiple jurisdictions with divergent oversight regimes, reporting systems, professional claims and expertise and the overall 'culture' of accountability and transparency (van Veen 2001; the International Center for Not-for-Profit Law URL). Other factors are less understood, particularly when they begin to interact with the former, including the presence of multiple stakeholders and the notion that accountability goes well beyond donor–recipient relations (Jordan 2004; Bendell 2006). Many stakeholders today have stronger voices and are heard more frequently than in the past. They generate accountability claims and demand their enforcement, as a result of several processes that include a greater political mobilisation and awareness in many parts of the world, the emergence of a global civil society and a value shift in many countries from generalised institutional trust to the culture of the audit society (Power 1997a).

Illustrating the accountability syndrome

The Aventis Foundation (AF) is a French–German corporate foundation of the Sanofi–Aventis pharmaceutical corporation located in Frankfurt, Germany. Its main areas of interest are health related, in particular public health and the intersection of society, culture and health behaviour. One of the AF projects funds the German Diabetes Association for developing and launching an awareness campaign for increasing public knowledge about the relationship between lifestyle choices (such as nutrition and exercise), obesity and diabetes. The Foundation and the Association work closely with public health authorities, other relevant organisations (largely professional associations in the fields of health, education and nutrition) and advertising agencies. What are the accountability issues in this case?

Assuming that the AF as well as other relevant organisations receiving foundation funds, in particular the German Diabetes Association, file the appropriate tax returns, disseminate information about the project in ways deemed adequate domestically, and also assuming that stakeholders believe that the project is transparent by local standards, there should be no intrinsic issues about accountability. The AF is accountable according to law and public expectations. The fact that Sanofi–Aventis manufactures diabetes drugs would not be seen as something to be questioned; on the contrary, most stakeholders would see the support of public health efforts to generate greater awareness about diabetes as an exemplary act of good corporate citizenship and enlightened corporate philanthropy.

Against the diabetes case, a purely domestic project, consider another AF grant – this time a transnational project in the sense that it involves devolved authority and responsibilities across borders. The project is 'TB Free,' which aims at reducing tuberculosis (TB) infection rates in South Africa by involving local communities through volunteers, traditional healers, grassroots groups, churches and so on, to (a) help administer and complete the treatment course for TB patients as part of a so-called 'directly observed treatment system' (DOTS), (b) fight the stigma attached to TB at the community level and (c) create better public awareness about the disease and its relationship with HIV/AIDS.

As a foreign foundation, the AF decided to establish and work through a non-profit organisation created for the purpose of the project called 'TB Free', in a partnership that includes the Nelson Mandela Foundation and with the Government of South Africa as the main public sector partner, to set up up training centres for DOTS as well as for administering AF funds locally. The Foundation signed a contract with the National Department of Health to make sure that the government would take over the programme after five years and ensure its long-term sustainability. Parallel to, and independent of, setting up TB Free, the Sanofi–Aventis corporation bid for a government contract to sell anti-TB drugs to the South African health authorities, successfully outbidding competitors like Sandoz from Switzerland (which supports a smaller project of this kind in Soweto), and those from other countries, including India.

Box 7.2: European Foundation Centre and Council on Foundations

The following principles of accountability were developed by a Joint Working Group of the European Foundation Centre and the Council on Foundations, Brussels, 2007.

Principles of accountability for international philanthropy

Cross-border philanthropy is exciting and rewarding, with benefits far outweighing the challenges. In view of the distinct complexities facing independent funders working across national borders, the European Foundation Centre (EFC) and the Council on Foundations created a joint working group to develop a set of principles of accountability specifically for international philanthropy. The result is this voluntary, aspirational document that is intended to educate, guide and help EFC and Council members be more accountable and effective in their cross-border activities. In early 2005 the Working Group undertook the extensive process of consulting members of the two organisations as well as other philanthropic networks and experts. In addition, consultations were held with groups of grantees and philanthropic partner organisations in Latin America, Eastern Europe, and Africa, including a three-day workshop with 25 African non-governmental organisation (NGO) leaders in South Africa. The Working Group recognises that legal compliance, fiduciary responsibility, and administrative oversight are essential components of philanthropic accountability. These 'givens' are therefore not the focus of this document. The Working Group's primary concern was to come up with a set of principles and good practice options addressing the issue of accountability to mission, grantees, and partners and, ultimately, to the intended beneficiaries of transnational philanthropic activity.

The Seven Principles of Accountability for International Philanthropy are:

1. Integrity
Engage in international philanthropy in a way that is in line with and truthful to your mission, values, vision, and core competencies. Show that you are genuine in your intentions throughout all aspects (programmatic, operational, and financial) of your international work. Be honest and transparent with your stakeholders.

2. Understanding
Take the time to research and understand the political, economic, social, cultural, and technological context in which your international philanthropy will take place. Tap into expertise that already exists, including at the local level, and develop a philanthropic strategy that is realistic and appropriate.

3. Respect
Avoid cultural arrogance by respecting cultural differences and human diversity. Recognise local knowledge, experience, and accomplishments. Be modest about what you know, what you can accomplish with the resources you have, and what you have yet to learn. When visiting international grantees and partners, always keep in mind that you are a guest in someone else's country.

4. Responsiveness
Listen carefully to your international grantees and partners in order to understand and respond adequately to their needs and realities. Be open and prepared to adjust your original objectives, timeline, and approach to the local context and capacity—resist the temptation to impose your own models or solutions. Build a relationship of trust with your international grantees and partners and with the communities where you work.

5. Fairness
Be reasonable and flexible in what you require from your grantees and partners, ensuring that your demands are proportionate to the level, purpose, and nature of your support. Be mindful of their possibly limited capacity to deal with multiple funders, and do not demand of them what you would not demand of yourself.

6. Cooperation and Collaboration
Recognise that international work calls for a high level of cooperation and collaboration among funders themselves and with a variety of actors, including non-governmental organisations (NGOs), businesses, governments, and multilateral organisations. Strive to work collaboratively in order to maximise resources, build synergies, boost creativity, and increase learning and impact.

7. Effectiveness
Assess whether your international philanthropy is effective by engaging in a process of mutual learning with your peers, grantees, and partners. Demonstrate how your international philanthropy contributes to the achievement of your organisation's mission and the advancement of the public good. Plan for sustainability and commit to staying long enough to be effective.'

Source: European Foundation Centre and the Council on Foundations (2007: 8, 11–12)

The result is a complex public–private partnership that works rather well and is beginning to show results (TB Free URL; Aventis Foundation URL). At the beginning, however, the project faced major and chronic accountability challenges, and managing them consumed a considerable amount of managerial effort and resources. These tensions were often between 'doing the project,' and 'accounting for it' to different stakeholders, especially at the local level in South Africa. Being accountable is a way of building legitimacy. It becomes an investment into something that, while legally granted, has to gain political acceptance, even legitimacy, across a broad spectrum of actors and interests, as shown below.

Early on, three major organisational project components were put in place that together laid the foundation for the accountability infrastructure of the project. The first was reconciling the German and South African legal requirements for the transfer (from Germany to South Africa) and disbursement (inside South Africa) of funds. The second was establishing overall and local responsibilities vis-à-vis government and public health officials, and the third was securing a local legitimacy base for TB Free (the Nelson Mandela Foundation).

As a result, the project developed several important accountability lines: in TB Free (which operates a central office in Midrand, Gauteng, and in

the country's nine provinces where TB Free centres operate) and in the AF in Germany; between TB Free and three layers of government (local, provincial and national); between TB Free and the Nelson Mandela Foundation and between TB Free and the AF. Next in importance are the secondary accountability lines between the AF and Sanofi–Aventis, the Nelson Mandela Foundation and the Government of South Africa, as well as internal governmental accountability.

Moreover, the project required several tertiary accountability lines that were not fully anticipated at the beginning of the project. One was the relationship between hospital staff and the DOTS volunteers, many of whom are traditional healers practicing African medicine; Western-trained doctors required the traditional healers to report to them but did not have to reciprocate. Another was the relationship between medical nurses and the DOTS volunteers: the former either felt threatened or over-burdened by the latter in a health crisis in which there is an acute scarcity of resources. Added to all this was the highly politicised nature of the TB–HIV/AIDS policy field in South Africa; the tensions that existed at that time between the Nelson Mandela Foundation and the government in power; and the presence of other pharmaceutical corporations, foundations, NGOs and government entities involved in related programmes and projects.

The challenge of being accountable to, and among, multiple stakeholders is thus clear.

Accountability and global governance

The difference between domestic and transnational accountability arises from the complexity in attempting to promote change across borders. In the transnational arena, questions of legitimacy are raised because the funding and impetus for projects originate from a foreign source. Civil society actors working across borders typically want to change current conditions in the foreign country towards some kind of improvement or to develop better capacity to deal with problems of many kinds. Because of this, relationships among stakeholders are likely to undergo some form of transformation or tension that may or may not have been anticipated.

At its core, this difference is largely a result of what is known as the global governance problem, that is, weak, patchy, loosely coupled and sometimes contradictory policies, regulatory frameworks and enforcement institutions relative to the needs of stakeholders, as well as actual and potential accountability failures (Held 2003). Global governance refers to the

government, management and administration capabilities of the United Nations, World Bank and other international organisations, various regimes, coalitions of interested nations and individual nations when they act globally to address to various issues that emerge beyond national borders. (Yakota 2004) The governance debate is about the efficacy of this system in ensuring 'a degree of co-operation sufficient to bring about order in human affairs' (Smith and Stacey 1997).

In transnational arenas, accountability exists in a world of multiples (including jurisdictions and legal systems, reporting and oversight regimes and stakeholders) dispersed across countries and cultures. Consequently, accountability tends to be fluid – even ambiguous – in terms of the expectations and standards involved, both legally and politically complex and, given the emerging nature of global civil society, subject to change. What is more, there are no quick policy fixes in sight, although a number of policy options exist. We explore this argument and its implication below in a series of four theses.

Thesis 1: Accountability is the problem, not the solution

We need to rethink accountability and move away from a position that sees accountability as a fix, as we do at domestic levels, towards an understanding of the endemic accountability problems of many types of non-profit organisations, epitomised by independent grant-making foundations. These foundations are among the freest institutions of modern societies: free in the sense of being independent of market forces and the popular political will. This enables foundations to ignore political, disciplinary and professional boundaries if they choose, to take risks and consider approaches that others cannot. As quasi-aristocratic institutions they flourish on the privileges of a formally egalitarian society and, while they exist in a democracy, foundations are themselves not democratically constituted.

As others have pointed out, foundations have no 'demos' or membership equivalent, and no broad-based election of leaders takes place that would aggregate preferences and hold those elected accountable. Unlike firms in the marketplace, membership-based non-profit organisations or government agencies, foundations have no equivalent set of stakeholders that would introduce a system of checks and balances. Grantees have little influence, and no explicit vehicles for redress and grievance. Expressing primarily the will of the donor or deed, the organisational structure of a foundation does not typically allow for broad-based participation and decision making outside the limited circle of trustees. In a domestic context there is usually a supervisory or regulatory office looking after foundations. By imposing certain rules and regulations for the establishment and operations of foundations, countries try to compensate for the lack of checks and balances and accountability. The Sarbanes–Oxley Act is as an example of this regulatory compensation. However, cross-nationally, the regulatory regimes and the institutions involved, together with the extent and frequency of reporting and audits vary widely (van der Ploeg 1999; van Veen 2001), as does the balance countries are able to strike between encouraging foundation growth and activities on the one hand, and controlling, even curtailing, them on the other.

The point is that in a domestic context today, we tend to have some sort of workable congruence between the regulatory frameworks in place to demand, channel and enforce accountability in relation to the accountability deficit of foundations in legal and political space. By contrast, we do not have similarly adequate accountability agreements and mechanisms in place when it comes to transnational activities. To grasp the scale of this problem, consider what kind of accountability exists of the large-scale activities of the Bill and Melinda Gates Foundation in addressing HIV/AIDS in Africa with a budget that exceeds that of the World Health Organisation (WHO) in the same field. Compare the complex governing structure of WHO and its elaborate accountability regime with that of the Bill and Melinda Gates Foundation. Consider also the activities of US foundations supporting democratisation movements such as anti-apartheid organisations in South Africa during the 1980s and 1990s, or the activities of the Open Society Institute in Central and Eastern Europe during the 1990s and in Central Asia and Russia today. Who empowered or entitled Ford, Gates or Soros to become active in supporting causes and addressing problems abroad, many of which are transnational in nature? In whose name and for whom are they active? At a formal level, legitimacy questions are not problematic at all; accountability becomes an issue only when it relates to the highly politicised arenas that characterise global problems such as HIV/AIDS, poverty, economic and democratic development or environmental degradation. In such fields, multiple jurisdictions and stakeholders (typically with different accountability expectations and standards), high levels of politicisation and legitimacy challenges, the impact of anti-terror legislation and other developments, make it increasingly difficult to be accountable.

Thus, in the context of globalisation, accountability is a persistent and growing problem in search of a solution rather than a solution in response to a problem, in part because it relates to questions of legitimacy. Accountability becomes part of the global political economy: some stakeholders have more voice than others and are the preferred audience of accountability for legitimacy reasons; some jurisdictions are more 'hands off' and others are more controlling, even restrictive; some audits in some countries are demanding, others are easy. Accountability becomes a political issue that reflects power differentials among stakeholders, and an economic issue that reflects transaction and compliance costs.

Thesis 2: Accountability expectations increase while global governance institutions weaken

Not only are we dealing with the very high transaction and compliance costs of full accountability but also with a need for strategic answers on behalf of boards and management that go beyond the technical aspects of accountability to anticipate complex scenarios that combine legitimacy, governance and accountability, as illustrated by the TB Free project above. Accountability has become a major policy issue because the lack of accountability is believed to have many negative consequences, as the debacles in the business and non-profit worlds have shown, including corruption, lower efficiency and effectiveness, greater inequities and other negative externalities that have to be borne by the public at large. Several forces, some at cross-purposes with each other, are at work in this context:

Role of the media

The expectations of being (or having to be) accountable are rising among stakeholders and across borders. This seems to have increased in recent times, coupled with lower institutional confidence (Power 1997a), perhaps because of the increase in democracy and associated values, greater awareness of the media and the role of the media, and institutionalised suspicion of watchdog groups, among other reasons. Unethical behaviour is often uncovered by responsive media entities rather than by formal audit bodies and other traditional authorities, even in developed democracies. The media thus acts as a watchdog, even monitoring the formal auditing authorities themselves.

The implications that this has on public expectations of accountability are profound. Though this type of media-based accountability offers certain benefits, especially because of the growing capabilities of globalising mass communication streams and technologies, relying on the media as the prime watchdog is not dependable, because media bodies themselves can have political and economic motivations, and can lack access to relevant information. Furthermore, reports from small media outlets may be ignored or overlooked, while larger, more politically embroiled mainstream media sources supply the bulk of accountability reports. The question of who should regulate the regulators comes into play here. Another complication is that while media-based accountability implies aspects of liability (because a public that is aware of corruption is more likely to act to punish the guilty party), it does not guarantee actual enforcement.

Enforcement
Because of globalisation and corresponding governance problems, accountability is more difficult to enforce than in the nation-state frameworks of the past (Held 2003). Being accountable in a transnational context implies relatively high transaction and compliance costs. The capacity of organisations for being or becoming unaccountable is often greater than their capacity to enforce accountability.

Detection
While globalisation expands opportunities for being unaccountable, it also increases the likelihood of detection due to improved communication and the denser network of the media, information technologies such as the Internet, watchdog organisations and the rise of transnational civil society institutions (see for example, Kaul et al. 1999).

Policy void
A policy void is created as globalisation challenges conventional accountability mechanisms and practices, and civil society and the public at large simultaneously demand more accountability (see Kaldor et al. 2003). As a result of these processes, accountability becomes easily entangled with legitimacy questions about the role and performance of foundations and other non-profit organisations.

Thesis 3: Accountability is a multi-dimensional concept that requires unpacking before becoming a useful policy concept and management tool
The use of accountability in transnational contexts has led to multiple definitions and meanings. Indeed, Koppell (2005) suggests that conflicting expectations borne of disparate conceptions of accountability undermine organisational effectiveness; he proposes a five-part typology of accountability: transparency, liability, controllability, responsibility, and responsiveness.

1. Transparency: did the organisation reveal the facts of its performance? Transparency is an important tool for assessing organisational performance and includes giving access to audit results, internal reports, and other evaluation documents to the press, the public, and other interested parties.

2. **Liability: did the organisation face consequences for its performance?** This dimension attaches consequences for an organisation's performance. Liability can come in the form of setbacks, such as diminished budget authority and increased monitoring or positive reinforcement, such as cash bonuses to employees and other rewards.

3. **Controllability: did the organisation do what the principal desired?** Many analyses of accountability focus on this dynamic of controllability: how much control the stakeholder has over the organisation or principal, for example, the view that government bureaucracies, as their representatives, should carry out the will of the public.

4. **Responsibility: did the organisation follow the rules?** This aspect of accountability includes being lawful, adhering to professional or industry standards and behavioural norms, and being morally sound.

5. **Responsiveness: did the organisation fulfill the substantive expectations?** Responsiveness works horizontally and refers to the levels of attention that organisations give to their clients and stakeholders' needs and demands. It implies accountability outwards rather than upward.

Koppell's five dimensions of accountability are not mutually exclusive: the first two, transparency and liability, are foundational supporting concepts on which the other three aspects of accountability rest. Each dimension denotes a particular aspect of accountability: while a US foundation can be transparent about its grant-making to recipient X in country Y for the purpose of Z, and may indeed be responsible for the grant and perhaps even liable, it may neither have the controllability nor the necessary responsiveness in place to prevent abuse. This suggests that we should approach accountability from a more refined perspective that includes the organisation and its many diverse stakeholders. One organisation can have overlapping accountabilities on different levels.

Applied to the TB Free case above, Table 7.1 offers

Table 7.1: Accountability dimensions and stakeholders in the TB Free project

Stakeholders	Transparency: reveal performance?	Liability: face consequences?	Controllability: principal control?	Responsibility: follow rules?	Responsiveness: meet expectations?
Aventis Foundation	Yes	No	Yes	Yes	
TB Free	Yes	Yes	Yes	Yes	
Local DOTS Training Centres	Yes	Yes	Yes	Yes	
National Department of Health	No	No	No	Yes	To be seen, as project is ongoing
Regional Departments of Health	Yes	No	No	Yes	
Nelson Mandela Foundation	No	No	No	Yes	
Sanofi-Aventis Corporation	Yes	No	Yes	Yes	

a schematic overview of the various accountability dimensions, following Koppell, for a number of stakeholders. Each cell could be further differentiated according to project needs and information requirements:

• The primary target or addressee involved, for example, the German tax authorities for the liability of the AF, as opposed the South African tax and public health authorities for TB Free.

• The range of demands and strength of expectations in terms of transparency, liability, controllability, responsibility and responsiveness, for example, what are the expected responsibilities of the Nelson Mandela Foundation and how responsive to accountability demands is it expected to be?

• The actual performance in terms of the five accountability dimensions, for example, how transparent is the National Department of Health in relation to its project responsibilities, or to what extent have the local training centres been able to control the flow of information relevant for discharging its accountability obligations?

A somewhat different typology was introduced by Radin and Romzek (1996). They differentiate between the source and the degree of control of accountability. This yields four basic accountability types, as shown in Table 7.2.

Hierarchical accountability can be seen in organisational roles such as supervisory relationships, standard operating procedures, and the monitoring of agency or employee performance. Obedience is the key concept here. Legal accountability implies supervision and monitoring activities by an actor external to the agency or organisation, such as an auditor or legislative review body. There is little room for discretion in these two types of accountability, but the monitoring that does occur is sporadic. Professional accountability comes from within the organisation or agency in terms of standards and expectations. Political accountability comes from external sources that have a low degree of control. These external sources/stakeholders have expectations of the agency, but the agency or individual can decide how much they want to respond to the expectations of such external stakeholders. The role of the media as monitor fits in the Radin and Romzek framework here.

Table 7.2: Types of accountability relationships

Source of control	Source of control	
	Internal	**External**
High	Hierarchical accountability	Legal accountability
Low	Professional accountability	Political accountability

Thesis 4: We should encourage innovation around accountability

NGOs are not alone in seeking solutions to the accountability syndrome of organisations working transnationally. Different actors, including international organisations like the World Bank and transnational corporations, are seeking new ways and means of accountability, trying to create what Selznick (1994: 397) called 'regularized forms of openness' that could make transnational organisations more sensitive and porous to information needs about their performance, and at the same time also generating a feeling of ownership and control for stakeholders. As Bovens (2005) explains, accountability is important for three main reasons. First, it is an essential component of the democratic process in which voters/stakeholders are made aware of the conduct of the organisational body in question. Second, it helps prevent corruption and abuses of power, and third, it leads to improved policies and decision-making processes.

The field of accountability is currently a crowded one, containing many models that attempt to set standards but with no actor/coalition strong enough to impose its will. Table 7.3, from the UN Non-Governmental Liaison Service (NGLS) Development Dossier on Accountability (Bendell 2006), shows just some of the accountability mechanisms that NGOs currently use. Some methods are pure window-dressing, others are sincere; some are naïve, others well-grounded and workable. Most initiatives work outside informal networks of accountability such as those practiced by the media and watchdog groups, though some, such as One World Trust's Global Accountability Partnership Initiative (GAP), acknowledge the role of the media in disseminating information about an organisation to facilitate transparency.

Tables 7.4 and 7.5 present examples of accountability initiatives for international NGOs in terms of the five Koppell dimensions and the Radin/Romzek framework. What is immediately apparent in these applications is that the accountability initiatives for NGOs differ in scope, target, method and motivation. Most initiatives, however, lack specific enforcement mechanisms. While transparency and responsibility are dynamics that are included in almost every accountability initiative, liability and enforcement are not. These are especially contentious topics in the accountability debate for the non-profit sector, because creating instruments of enforcement puts the control of organisations into the hands of a third party and usurps many of the rights that non-profit organisations rely on to do their work. The question remains of who this third party should be.

Thesis 5: We should move from an NGO-centred notion of accountability to an understanding of social accountability, even moral accountability in a broader sense

Social accountability is an approach in which citizens and civil society organisations participate directly or indirectly in exacting accountability from private and public institutions, including NGOs. Businesses, governments and NGOs are held accountable for their actions and the social, political, or environmental impact they may have. Social accountability refers to a broad range of actions and mechanisms that citizens, communities, independent media and civil society organisations can use to hold public officials and civic leaders accountable (Malena et al. 2004). Such mechanism include participatory budgeting, public expenditure tracking, monitoring of public service delivery, investigative journalism, public commissions and citizen advisory boards. They complement and reinforce conventional mechanisms of accountability

Table 7.3: Types of voluntary NGO accountability mechanisms

Accountability Mechanisms	Definition	Example
Elections	Elections of board members by NGO members	World Development Movement (WDM), Friends of the Earth (FOE)
Board Appointments	Appointment of independent board members from key stakeholder groups	World Wide Fund for Nature (WWF)
Monitoring and Evolution	Assessing performance against a set of pre-defined goals for the funded activity	A requirement of most bilated aid agency funded projects (OECD-DAC)
Standards and Codes of Conduct	Documented statements of how an organization and its staff should operate adopted by one or a collection of organizations	Human Accountability Project (HAP-I), People In Aid
Certifications	Auditing organizations against, and endorsing them as in conformity with, specific standards or codes	Société Générale de Surveillance (SGS) NGO Certification, Philippine Council for NGO Certification
Ratings	Assessing organizations against a standard or code, and rating their performance, whether requested or not	Global Accountability Project (GAP), Charity Navigator
Reporting	Publishing of performance sometimes against using a specific standard, to a specific organization or the public	Financial reports are required in most countries, and most large NGOs publish annual reports on progress, for donors or members
Dialogue and Participation	Involvement of affected persons in decision making on, or implementation of, specific projects	ActionAid

Source: Bendell 2006

Table 7.4: Accountability initiatives for NGOs using Koppell's framework

				Transparency	Liability	Controllability	Responsibility	Responsiveness
InterAction	△	□	↔	2	4	3	1	5
One World's GAP[a] (also for TNCs)	△		■ O	1	-	3	-	2
Global Reporting Initiative	△		■	1	-	3	2	3
Keystone Reporting	△		■	1	-	2	3	2
Draft EC Code	△	□	O	1	[b]	-	2	-
Humanitarian Accountability Partnership Int.	△	□	■	1	-	2	3	4
WANGO	△	□	■	1	5	4	2	3
Independent Sector	△	□	■	1	-	-	2	3
MANGO: Who Counts	△		■	1	-	-	2	3
SA8000 (also for TNCs)	△	□	■	1	-	-	2	-
Sphere Project				1	-	2	4	3
People in Aid		□		1	-	-	2	3

Note: Nos 1 to 5 indicate the relative importance of this indicator to the initiative, with '1' indicating the highest and 5 the lowest importance, based on our qualitative assessment of the available material. – in the cell indicates that the initiative does not address the corresponding accountability dimension. See Box 7.3 for information on the initiatives named here, and for other accountability initiatives of interest.

Key to symbols
[a] The GAP framework can also be applied to the accountability of transnational corporations.
[b] Although liability controls are not explicit in the code, they are implied in it.
□ the organization relies on some sort of certification process
△ the initiative emphasizes reporting
O the initiative was created by a government agency
↔ the initiative incorporates within it a component of sharing best practices, information exchanges, and meetings between NGOs,
■ and/or training opportunities regarding accountability.

such as political checks and balances, accounting and auditing systems, administrative rules and legal procedures.

Social accountability affirms and operationalises direct accountability relationships between (a) citizens and the state, (b) citizens and businesses, (c) businesses and the state and (d) NGOs and relevant stakeholders (Social Accountability International URL). The globalising media plays an increasingly dynamic role in this, not only helping to broaden the capabilities of social accountability movements but also as an actor itself in holding the parties in question to account.

Social accountability both complements and enhances conventional mechanisms of accountability so that internal (state) and external (social) mechanisms of accountability could be mutually reinforcing. Similarly, while social accountability emphasises vertical bottom-up action, it also reinforces accountability mechanisms that are vertical, top-down (from regulatory agencies or boards) and horizontal (from peers or other similar organisations) as people demand more access to information. Another key feature of social accountability mechanisms is their use of a range of formal and informal rewards and sanctions, including public pressure.

Social accountability has become an important policy issue for three reasons (Malena et al. 2004). The first is the crisis of democratic governance and the growing disillusionment among citizens with governments that they perceive as unresponsive and given to corruption and favouritism (World Bank 2001). In many developing countries the effectiveness of conventional mechanisms of accountability such as elections has proved to be limited, as has the capacity of governments to hold businesses accountable. Social accountability mechanisms are intended to allow ordinary citizens to access information, voice their needs and demand accountability between elections, and to strengthen calls for greater corporate social responsibility and business ethics. Emerging social accountability practices enhance the ability of citizens to move beyond mere protest toward engaging with bureaucrats, politicians and business leaders in a more informed, organised, constructive and systematic manner, thus increasing the chances of effecting positive change.

Second, social accountability is an important tool for increased development effectiveness by improving public service delivery and more informed policy design, particularly in the context of new public management (NPM). As governments fail to deliver services and to adhere to terms of contracts or formulate policies in a discretionary and non-transparent manner, social accountability mechanisms promote dialogue, consultation and learning. In particular, as NPM frequently involves the privatisation of public functions, social accountability mechanisms become important in monitoring non-profit as well as for-profit service delivery.

Third, social accountability initiatives can lead to empowerment, particularly of poor people, for instance, through the expansion of individual freedom of choice and action. By providing critical information on rights and entitlements and soliciting systematic feedback from poor people, social accountability mechanisms provide a means to increase and aggregate the voice of disadvantaged and vulnerable groups. With the rise of information and communication technologies, this ability increases. An enhanced voice empowers the poor and increases the chance of greater responsiveness by the state to their needs.

In a recent article Kaldor (2003) introduced the notion of moral accountability to complement what she calls measures of procedural accountability. Indeed, most, if not all of the accountability measures referred to in this chapter and presented in the various boxes, are procedural in nature, including social accountability. What sets moral accountability apart, and thereby elevates the debate to a normative level, is the value base of NGO activities and the extent to which NGOs live up to the standards they set for themselves and for others. Moral accountability arises from the mission of the organisation (Kaldor 2003) and is closely related to its legitimate right to speak for and on behalf of others. Put simply, if an NGO seeks to promote democracy and the rule of law, it must itself be democratically organised and soundly governed. Otherwise, the organisation faces accountability deficits and can easily be affected by the accountability syndrome described earlier that will threaten its legitimacy.

Accountability and democracy-as-debate

An increasing number of different accountability frameworks exists (as depicted in Box 7.3), especially for organisations and foundations working internationally. The accountability syndrome facing global civil society actors is a by-product of the governance problems of a globalising world. Accountability regimes are tied to a world of nation states but economy and society, and increasingly civil society and philanthropic institutions, no longer fit into this framework. Anti-terrorist legislations in the USA and Europe, laws like the Sarbanes–Oxley Act and the multiplication of watchdog groups add to the accountability complexity of transnational civil society. While we may feel uncomfortable with the multiplicity of accountability initiatives in our increasingly globalised world, there is no single approach that can appropriately dictate how every organisation should seek accountability. A multi-pronged approach to accountability is more appropriate. A first step towards finding solutions is to acknowledge, as we have argued in this Chapter, that accountability is a growing problem that requires a strategic political perspective rather than a procedural, regulatory point of view alone. We also need to see accountability more broadly in relation to negotiated legitimacy and institutional trust, rather than in terms of proven impact, efficiency and fiduciary compliance. Indeed, as Kaldor (2003) suggests, the balance among different accountability approaches used will differ across types of NGOs and fields of activity, in particular in the relative emphasis given to procedural and moral accountability.

In this respect, NGOs will certainly benefit and

learn from the various accountability projects and approaches presented in Tables 7.4 and 7.5. However, the various options are unlikely to offer a quick fix on their own for addressing the accountability syndrome. By contrast, when taken together with other measures, they may indeed offer ways forward. Among these are:

• to acknowledge that full accountability lies beyond what NGOs can and should do. Instead, external bodies or agents should be encouraged to offer accountability services to stakeholders on a for-profit or not-for-profit basis, to increase the mechanisms available to organisations and the public. One option

Table 7.5: Accountability initiatives for NGOs using the Radin/Romzek framework

	Hierarchical	Legal	Professional	Political
InterAction	X		X	X
One World's GAP	X		X	
GRI	X		X	
Keystone Reporting	X		X	
Draft EC Code	X	X	X	
HAP-I	X		X	
WANGO				
Independent Sector	X		X	
MANGO: Who Counts	X		X	
SA8000	X	X	X	X
Sphere Project	X		X	
People in Aid	X		X	

Note: A blank cell means that the particular accountability initiative does not have that particular dimension of accountability.
See Box 7.3 for information about the initiatives named in this table.

ACCOUNTABILITY IN A GLOBALISING WORLD

Box 7.3: Examples of accountability initiatives

Active Learning for Accountability and Performance in Humanitarian Action (ALNAP URL). ALNAP is an international, inter-agency forum, established in 1997 after a mutli-agency evaluation of the Rwandan genocide. The network currently has 51 full members and 450 observer members. ALNAP's annual Review of Humanitarian Action monitors the performance of humanitarian action through its members' evaluation reports, as well as the quality of these evaluations using an ALNAP quality pro forma, and it works with agencies to improve their evaluation skills.

Association of Leaders of Local Civic Group (SLLGO). This Polish non-profit and non-partisan organisation has put together a manual on local government transparency (SLLGO 2006), which discusses cooperation between local governments and the third sector. Specifically, the manual explains how local governments should implement transparent rules for distributing public funds to public service organisations and how they can establish a monitoring and evaluation system.

Australian Council for International Development Code of Conduct (ACFID URL). The Council is an independent national association of Australian NGOs working in the field of international aid and development. The ACFID Code of Conduct lays out standards for public reporting and fundraising. Currently over 110 organisations have signed the code; being a signatory is a prerequisite for applying for Australian

Government funds through AusAID.

Bank Track (URL). Bank Track is a network of civil society organisations and individuals who monitor the private financial sector. The network runs international accountability campaigns, conducts research, produces reports and educational materials, operates training programmes for NGOs that are monitoring the financial sector, and gives related direct support.

Canadian Council for International Cooperation (URL). The Council comprises around 100 civil society organisations that must comply with a code of ethics. The Code deals with matters such as finance accountability, governance, management practices and fundraising, and is operates through a self-certification scheme in which organisations can assess their own levels of compliance. An Ethics Review Committee advises them indirectly (but does not take any disciplinary action).

Central and Eastern European Working Group on Notprofit Governance. The working group developed a Handbook of NGO Governance (Wyatt 2004), which lays out ideal governance practices for non-profit organisations in Central and Eastern Europe. It includes information on board structure, delegation of duties, roles of staff members, organisational missions, evaluation, codes of conduct, conflict of interest, audits and reporting, among other topics, and includes an implementation checklist for organisations. The Handbook can be applied to not-for-profit sectors around the world and has been translated into many languages.

Credibility Alliance (URL). The Credibility Alliance is a grouping of over 450 civil society organisations in India who are dedicated to accountability and transparency. The organisation has created credibility alliance norms of good governance, which are voluntary and self-regulated standards. For an organisation to belong to the Alliance it must adhere to standards that include basic legal requirements, optimal governance structure, management and human resource standards and required reporting. The Alliance is currently developing a formal accreditation mechanism.

EC Code (EC 2005). The recommendations regarding a code of conduct for non-profit organisations to promote transparency and accountability best practice is a voluntary initiative that was drafted in 2005. It focuses solely on the financial accountability and annual reporting of organisations in the voluntary sector and strives primarily to guard against the exploitation of organisations by terrorism.

Ethical Corporation (URL). The Ethical Corporation, founded in 2001, is an independent publisher and conference organiser that focuess on issues surrounding corporate ethics. The Corporation is owned primarily by First Conferences Ltd, an independent, privately owned London-based media company.

Extractive Industries Transparency Initiative (EITI URL). The initiative supports improved governance in resource-rich countries through the verification and full publication of company payments and government revenues from oil, gas and mining. It works to build multi-stakeholder partnerships in developing countries in order to increase the accountability of governments. The assumption underlying EITI is that good governance is a precondition for converting the large revenues from extractive industries into economic growth and poverty reduction.

Global Reporting Initiative (URL). An international network of business, civil society, labour and professional institutions with a reporting framework (G3 Guidelines) that is applicable to organisations regardless of size, sector or location. The Guidelines include principles, guidance and standard disclosures that can be voluntarily adopted.

Government Accountability Project (GAP URL). A whistleblower protection agency created in the late 1970s as a public interest group, GAP deals with government and corporate accountability.

Help Argentina (URL). This non-profit organisation has a self-evaluation tool that allows organisations to analyse their programmes qualitatively in order to become more transparent. Help Argentina created the tool in April 2007 with the support of the Tinker Foundation and the World Bank Small Projects Fund.

Humanitarian Accountability Partnership International (HAP-I URL). HAP-I, the humanitarian sector's first self-regulatory body, is a partnership of 15 member agencies. The HAP 2007 standard in humanitarian accountability and quality management lays out principles for humanitarian action and benchmarks for performance and verification for organisations to become certified. The initiative focuses on accountability to beneficiaries.

Independent Sector (URL). Independent Sector is a leadership forum for charities, foundations and corporations that has an accountability checklist for NGOs to assess their own accountability. The checklist includes criteria such as staff and board training, the publication of a code of ethics and values, a conflict of interest policy, independent auditing of financial statements and a whistleblower policy.

InterAction (URL). InterAction is the largest alliance of US-based international development and humanitarian NGOs such as the Christian Children's Fund, the Aga Khan Foundation, Action Aid International, Catholic Relief Services, Heifer International, Oxfam, United Way and others. All InterAction member organisations (over 160) have to certify their compliance with private voluntary organisation (PVO) standards, which cover topics like management practices, financial integrity, communications and reporting.

International Advocacy NGOS. The INGO Accountability Charter (2005 URL) is a voluntary accountability charter for international advocacy NGOs adopted in summer, 2006. Members include 11 large NGOs such as Save the Children, Oxfam, and Amnesty International. The charter outlines governing principles, such as respect for universal human and social rights, responsible advocacy, non-discrimination, transparency in reporting and auditing, ethical fundraising and professional management.

ISEAL Alliance 2006 (URL). The International Social and Environmental Accreditation and Labelling Association of voluntary international standard-setting organisations (from private and manufacturing industries) focuses on social and environmental issues. ISEAL helped to develop a code of good practice for setting social and environmental standards, to which all ISEAL members adhere and are evaluated against through self-assessment and peer review.

Keystone Reporting (URL). Keystone offers an open source model for civil society accountability that can be adapted by each organisation according to their needs. The model covers self-assessment techniques, stakeholder engagement methods, monitoring and evaluation and reporting techniques.

Management Accounting for Non-governmental Organisations (MANGO). This charity launched its Who Counts (URL) campaign in April 2005. MANGO helps NGOs to strengthen their financial management by providing training and guidelines for best practice. The campaign encourages NGOs to implement transparent and comprehensive financial reporting to beneficiaries.

NGOWatch (URL). The American Enterprise Institute (AEI) for Policy Research and the Federalist Society developed NGOwatch.org. This evolving website provides NGO- monitoring tools and related information. In 2003 AEI and the Institute for Public Affairs (Australia) held a conference on NGOs, 'the growing power of an unelected few', from which NGOwatch emerged. Instead of advocating a particular accountability initiative, NGOwatch lists information about hundreds of NGOs, with links to their websites and their tax forms. Critics of NGOwatch call the project 'a clear example of a right-wing campaign designed to monitor and critique "liberal" U.N.-designated NGOs' (The Political Research Associates 2004: 3).

One World Trust (URL). This organisation focuses on education and research in relation to three main areas: sustainable development, accountability, and peace and security. One World runs the global accountability project (GAP), a framework that considers accountability in four dimensions: transparency, participation, evaluation and complaints and response. Inter-governmental organisations, transnational corporations, international NGOs, and other organisations, can use the GAP framework internally to increase their accountability. In addition, it can be used by stakeholder groups to advocate for the accountability of these organisations.

Pakistan Centre for Philanthropy (PCP URL). The PCP non-profit certification programme is the first of its kind in Pakistan and, in fact, in the whole of South Asia. It evaluates an organisation's governance and the transparency of its financial management together with the effectiveness of its programme delivery. Certification is awarded after a desk review and a field visit, with scoring done by professionals, followed by a review by an evaluation panel (two members of which are from the the Pakistani government).

Parliamentary Network on the World Bank (PnoWB URL). This international network of parliamentarians strives to increase transparency and accountability in the World Bank and other multilateral and bilateral donor organisations. The PNoWB runs annual conferences, dialogues, and field visit programmes, and has national and regional chapters. It has run a parliamentarians' implementation watch since 2002, which produces updates, connects parliamentarians with NGOs, private sector organisations and the media, creates action plans and builds the capacity of parliamentarians to enforce and pursue the goal of accountability in the World Bank and other similar organisations.

People in Aid (URL). People in Aid is a support organisation for a global network of development and humanitarian assistance agencies. The code of good practice in the management and support of aid personnel (People in Aid 2003) helps these agencies enhance the quality of their human resources management in terms of health, safety, security, training, communication, leadership, policies and practices. It is geared towards all development and humanitarian relief organisations and is the result of collaboration between international and national NGOs from around the world.

Philippine Council for NGO Certification (URL). The Council was initiated by six large Philippine NGOs and is a private non-profit organisation that certifies other non-profit organisations in terms of their financial management and accountability. The Council is authorised by the Department of Finance to carry out this certification process. NGOs can apply for certification, are evaluated and if successful, awarded certification for three to five years.

Social Accountability International (SAI URL). SA8000 is a standards and verification system mainly for private business but also for any organisation with a supply chain, such as a non-profit organisation. The programme relies on certification by certain SAI-accredited bodies and deals with workplace standards. It is based on International Labour Organization conventions, the Universal Declaration of Human Rights and the UN Convention on the Rights of the Child, and covers topics like child labour, forced labour, health and safety, and freedom of association. SA8000 mandates certain management requirements, involvement by stakeholders, public reporting through SA certified facilities and annual reports, training partnerships, and complaints and appeals processes.

South African NGO Coalition (URL). The Coalition, created in 1995, is the largest grouping of NGOs in South Africa. Its members adhere to a code of ethics, which covers such matters as values, governance, accountability, management and human resources, finance and resources.

Sphere Project. The project was developed by the Red Crescent Movement, the Red Cross and other humanitarian NGOs and includes the a handbook, the Humanitarian Charter and Minimum Standards in Disaster Response (2004) which lays out what people affected by disasters should expect from humanitarian assistance and how accountability in disaster response can be enhanced.

Standards for Excellence (USA). As part of an initiative by the Standards for Excellence Institute, the Standards include a certification component and are based on a code developed by volunteers several years ago from the not-for-profit sector. The Standards cover eight principle areas, such as conflict of interests, missions and programmes, fundraising and transparency, which lay out how responsible non-profit organisations should operate. Over 60,000 copies of the Standards Code have been distributed. Non-profit organisations can use the Code as a guide for best practice; versions of the code tailored to the needs of different US states also exist.

World Association of NGOs (WANGO). WANGO is an international support organisation uniting NGOs worldwide, with members in over 150 countries. The code of ethics project was initiated by WANGO in 2002 and the current version of the code was completed in March 2005. It lays out a series of guidelines that an organisation should follow to be accountable, in terms of governance structures, human rights, fundraising, mission statements, human resource development, reporting and public information, partnerships and financial and legal responsibility.

would be for foundations or government funders to allocate a portion of each international grant to this purpose, perhaps by adding a line item to the project budget.

• to require international organisations to play a greater role and encourage the UN, EU and similar bodies to address the accountability syndrome under conditions of weak global governance. Discussions in Europe to establish the legal instrument of a European Association/Foundation, and having the European Commission serve as regulator and supervisory body, is one example of this option.

• to introduce and encourage the use of standards (ISO) for international NGO activities based on established and proven good practices. This option entails that foundations and organisations will engage in the necessary research and fact-finding needed for developing best practices and standards, and also that they will think about appropriate ways and means of certification and auditing.

• to develop transnational NGO audits, conducted by independent institutions (public or private) that mediate between 'general principles of control and accountability which have a populist basis, and internal procedures capable of uniting technical and moral competence' (Power 1997b: 21).

• to view accountability in the broader context of social accountability. An example of this is that organisations can run versions of town hall meetings and forums at regular intervals to give relevant stakeholders the opportunity to share information, ask questions, voice concerns and make suggestions about such matters as the project's goals, performance and accountability. Such forums are also a good way to detect potential conflicts, and for discussing and settling them in an open manner. Related to this is the need to investigate both the potentials and limitations of the media as accountability monitor and transparency enforcer.
There is, of course, a bridge between social/moral accountability and democracy, in particular the notion of democracy-as-debate. Indeed, of the five types of accountability Koppell identifies, transparency and responsiveness relate most directly to this conception and, as it turns out, are among the most popular of the initiatives we have looked at. By contrast, controllability, which is closest to the traditional conception of democracy-as-representation, does not fare so well and shows the inherent weakness of civil society organisations in this respect. Thus, if social accountability approaches could be developed into the direction of democracy-as-debate and therefore more into the direction of moral accountability, the accountability syndrome we have identified in this chapter could move from an emphasis on technocratic supervision and control to more devolved and open transnational accountability networks.

Acknowledgements

We would like to thank Marlies Glasius, Martin Albrow, Mary Kaldor and Fiona Holland for their helpful comments on earlier versions of this draft, Eugen Mueller, of the Aventis Foundation, for making the case study of TB Free possible and for supporting the background research, and the UCLA Center for Civil Society for logistical assistance.

Anheier, Helmut and Daly, Siobhan (2005) 'Philanthropic Foundations: A New Global Force' in Helmut Anheier, Mary Kaldor and Marlies Glasius, *Global Civil Society 2004/5*. London: Sage.

Association of Leaders of Local Civic Groups (SLLGO) (2006) *Local Governments Transparency. Enhancement of Public Funds Distribution Standards Final report from the activities undertaken in the period: 1st April 2005 –31st August.* http://www.lgo.pl/uploads/download/Attachment%201_final%20report%20Local%20Governments%20Transparency.doc (consulted 5 July 2007).

Australian Council for International Development, *Code of Conduct.* http://www.acfid.asn.au/code-of-conduct (consulted 5 July 2007).

Aventis Foundation (url) TB Free.Powerpoint presentation www.aventis-foundation.org/_de/projekte/civilsociety/tbfree/download/Aventis_TBFree_South_Africa.ppt (consulted 6 Juy 2007).

Bank Track, http://www.banktrack.org/ (consulted 5 July 2007).

Bendell, Jem (2006) *NGLS Development Dossier: Debating NGO Accountability*, New York and Geneva: UN Non-Governmental Liason (NGLS). http://unngls.org/pdf/NGO_Accountability.pdf (consulted 6 July 2007).

Board Source and Independent Sector (2003) *The Sarbanes–Oxley Act and the Implications for Nonprofit Organisations*. Washington, DC.

Bovens, M (2005) 'Analysing and Assessing Public Accountability: A Conceptual Framework'. Paper presented at the accountable governance: an international research colloquium, 20–22 October, Queens University. Belfast.

Canadian Council for International Cooperation, *Code of Ethics*. http://www.ccic.ca/e/002/ethics.shtml (consulted 5 July 2007).

Credibility Alliance, *Code of Ethics*. http://www.credall.org.in (consulted 5 July 2007).

Dombrowski, K (2006) *Overview of Accountability Initiatives.* London: One World Trust. Working Paper 100, January.

EC (2005) *Draft Recommendations Regarding a Code of Conduct for Non-Profit Organisations Organisations to Promote Transparency and Accountability Best Practice.* http://ec.europa.eu/justice_home/news/consulting_public/code_conduct_npo/draft_recommendations_en.pdf (consulted 5 July 2007).

Ethical Corporation, http://www.ethicalcorp.com/ (consulted 5 July 2007).

European Foundation Centre and the Council on Foundations (2007) *Principles of Accountability for International Philanthropy.* http://www.efc.be/ftp/public/ic/EFC_COF/EFC_COF_PrinciplesAccountabilityUKV.pdf (consulted 6 July 2007).

Extractive Industries Transparency Initiative, http://www.eitransparency.org (consulted 5 July 2007).

Global Reporting Initiative, *G3 Guidelines.* http://www.globalreporting.org/ReportingFramework/G3Online/ (consulted 5 July 2007).

Government Accountability Project, http://www.whistleblower.org/ (consulted 5 July 2007).

Held, David (2003) *Global Covenant: The Social Democratic Alternative to the Washington Consensus*. Cambridge: Polity Press.

Help Argentina (2007) *Self-evaluation Tool for Civil Society Organisations.* http://www.helpargentina.org/news2.php?id=198#1 (consulted 5 July 2007).

Humanitarian Accountability Partnership International, Humanitarian Accountability *Standards Development Programme.* http://www.hapinternational.org/en/complement.php?IDcomplement=43&IDcat=4&IDpage=74 (consulted 5 July 2007).

Independent Sector, http://www.independentsector.org/issues/accountability/Checklist/index.html (consulted 5 July 2007).

InterAction, http://www.interaction.org/pvostandards/ (consulted 5 July 2007).

IInternational Center for Not-for-profit Law, http://www.icnl.org/knowledge/index.htm (consulted 6 July 2007).

International Non-Governmental Organisations Commitment to Accountability (2006) *Accountability Charter for International Advocacy NGOs.* http://www.ingoaccountabilitycharter.org/about-the-charter.php (consulted 6 July 2007).

International Non-Governmental Organisations Accountability Charter (2005) http://www.amnesty.org/resources/downloads/INGO_Accountability_Charter.pdf

ISEAL Alliance, www.isealalliance.org/code (consulted 5 July 2007).

Jordan, L (2004) *Mechanism for NGO Accountability*. Research Paper Series No. 3. Berlin: Global Public Policy Institute. http://www.gppi.net/fileadmin/gppi/Jordan_Lisa_05022005.pdf (consulted 6 July 2007).

Kaldor, Mary (2003) 'Civil Society and Accountability', *Journal of Human Development*, 4(1): 5-26.

Kaldor Mary, Anheier, Helmut K and Glasius, Marlies (2003) 'Global Civil Society In an Age of Regressive Globalisation', in Marlies Glasius, Helmut K Anheier and Mary Kaldor (eds) *Global Civil Society 2003*. Oxford: Oxford University Press..

Kaul, Inge, Grunberg, Isabelle and Stein, Marc (eds) (1999) *Global Public Goods: International Cooperation in the 21st Century.* New York: Oxford University Press.

Keystone Reporting, http://www.keystonereporting.org/ (consulted 5 July 2007).

Koppell, Jonathan (2005) 'Pathologies of Accountability: ICANN and the Challenge of Multiple Accountabilities Disorder', *Public Administration Review*, 65(1): 94–108.

Malena, Carmen, Forster, Reiner and Singh, Janmejay (2004) 'Social Accountability: An Introduction to the Concept and Emerging Practice', *Social Development Papers*, No. 76. Washington DC: World Bank.

Management Accounting for Non-governmental Organisations (MANGO), http://www.mango.org.uk/whocounts/index.asp (consulted 5 July 2007).

NGO Watch, http://www.NGOwatch.org (consulted 5 July 2007).

One World Trust, http://www.oneworldtrust.org/?display=project&pid=10 (consulted 5 July 2007).

Pakistan Centre for Philanthropy NPO Certification

Programme, http://www.pcp.org.pk/certification.html (consulted 5 July 2007).

Parliamentary Network on the World Bank, http://www.pnowb.org/ (consulted 5 July 2007).

People in Aid (2003) *Code of Good Practice in the Management and Support of Aid Personnel.* London: People in Aid. http://www.peopleinaid.org (consulted 5 July 2007).

Philippine Council for NGO Certification, www.pcnc.com.ph (consulted 5 July 2007).

Political Research Associates (2004) *Public Eye.* http://www.publiceye.org/magazine/v18n1/v18n1.pdf (consulted 12 July 2007).

Power, Michael (1997a) *The Audit Society.* Oxford and New York: Oxford University Press.

Power, Michael (1997b) 'From Risk Society to Audit Society', *Soziale Systeme*, 3(1): 3–21.

Radin, Beryl and Romzek, Barbara S (1996) 'Accountability Expectations in an Intergovernmental Arena: The National Rural Development Partnership', *Publius*, 26(2): 59–81.

Selznick, Philip (1994) 'Self-Regulation and the Theory of Institutions', in Gunther Teubner, Lindsay Farmer and Declan Murphy (eds) *Environmental Law and Ecological Responsibility: The Concept and Practice of Ecological Self-Organisation.* Chichester: John Wiley.

Smith, M Y and Stacey, R (1997) *Governance and Co-operative Networks: An Adaptive Systems Perspective.* New York: Elsevier Science.

Social Accountability 8000 SA8000, http://www.sa8000.org (consulted 5 July 2007).

Social Accountability International, http://www.sa-intl.org/ (consulted 6 Juy 2007).

South African NGO Coalition, http://www.sangoco.org.za (consulted 5 July 2007).

Standards for Excellence (USA) (1998–2004) Standards for excellence: An Ethics and Accountability Code for the Nonprofit Sector. http://www.standardsforexcellenceinstitute.org/public/html/explore_b.html (consulted 5 July 2007).

TB Free, http://www.tbfree.org/ (consulted 6 Juy 2007).

US Department of the Treasury (2002) *Anti-Terrorist Financing Guidelines: Voluntary Best Practices for US-based Charities.* http://www.treas.gov/offices/enforcement/key-issues/protecting/docs/guidelines_charities.pdf (consulted 6 July 2007).

van der Ploeg, Tymen (1999) 'A Comparative Legal Analysis of Foundations: Aspects of Supervision and Transparency', in Helmut K Anheier and Stefan Toepler (eds) *Private Funds, Public Purpose. Philanthropic Foundations in International Perspective.* New York: Springer (Plenum).

van Veen, Wimo (2001) 'Supervision of Foundations in Europe: post-incorporation restrictions and requirements', in Andreas Schlueter, Volker Then and Peter Walkenhorst (eds) *Foundations in Europe: Society, Management, Law.* London: Directory of Social Change.

WANGO (2004) *Code of Ethics & Conduct for NGOs.* http://www.wango.org/download/pdf/CodeOfEthicsV.5.p.pdf http://www.wango.org/activities/codeofethics.aspx?page=0 (consulted 5 July 2007).

World Bank (2001) *World Development Report 2000/2001: Attacking Poverty.* http://web.worldbank.org/WBSITE/EXTERNAL/TOPICS/EXTPOVERTY/0,,contentMDK:20195989~pagePK:148956~piPK:216618~theSitePK:336992,00.html (consulted 6 July 2007).

Wyatt, Marilyn (2004) *Central and Eastern European Working Group on Not-for-Profit Governance.* Budapest: European Center for Nor-for-Profit Law http://www.ecnl.org/dindocuments/18_Governance%20Handbook.pdf (consulted 5 July Active).

Learning for Accountability and Performance in Humanitarian Action, *Review of Humanitarian Action* http://www.alnap.org/ (consulted 5 July 2007).

Yokota, Yozo (2004) 'What is Global Governance?' Keynote lecture given at the National Institute for Research Advancement international forum, global governance – in pursuit of a new international order, July 12–13. Tokyo.

CHAPTER 8

DEMOCRATIC ADVANCE OR RETREAT?
COMMUNICATIVE POWER AND CURRENT MEDIA DEVELOPMENTS
James Deane

Introduction

Issues of information and communication lie at the heart of this edition of the Yearbook. For citizens to participate in democratic life and to exercise democratic choices, they need access to information about the issues that shape their lives, the spaces to discuss and debate those issues openly with others, and the opportunity to make their perspectives and demands heard.

If, as Neera Chandhoke argues (Chandhoke 2002; 2005), civil society is the public space in which people meet, discuss and engage with politics and public policy, then the media is an essential determinant of the success of civil society as a creator of public spaces, and of how effectively people's voices can be heard. Manuel Castells argues that 'media have become the social space where power is decided' (2007: 1).

The link between communication and power, and voice and citizenship is ancient: throughout history, the extent to which citizens have made their voices heard has depended on their ability to exercise communicative power - to exert influence over policies that affect them by communicating, either individually in ways that resonate in the public sphere, or collectively in ways that will pressure those in authority to consider their arguments.

This Chapter will explore how civil society and democratic engagement are mediated through the media and communication technologies, how this is changing and what is driving those changes. It will focus on the efforts - including those of various global civil society actors - to engage and challenge the media by creating alternative forms of mediated communication, and engaging with existing mainstream media. It will also describe how rapid changes in the media present new opportunities for communicative power and action, as well as many new obstacles to a democratic public sphere.

Providing an insight into the relevance of the media for public spheres in the twenty-first century within the context of the Global Civil Society Yearbook requires a global perspective. Mapping the complex, diverse and rapidly changing universe of the media on a global scale in a single Chapter is clearly impossible, but some indication of how the media is reducing and expanding the public sphere can be provided. The Chapter will focus more on the information, communication and media realities of people outside the industrialised world, which have been documented and analysed exhaustively – particularly on the two billion people who live on less than US $2 a day. Countervailing media trends will be examined, some of which contribute to an expansion and enrichment of the public sphere, and others to a contraction and stifling of it. Similarly, interactions between civil society and media that expand the public sphere, and those civil society actions that potentially undermine it, will be explored.

The Chapter makes three main arguments. First, it argues that nearly all the trends outlined are rapidly changing in their character and double edged in their impact, contributing in some ways to an expansion and in others to a contraction of the public sphere, and of the capacity of citizens to make their voices heard. This suggests that a much greater strategic understanding and engagement by civil society organisations in media issues and trends is critical if these organisations are committed to enhancing the plurality and inclusiveness of democratic systems.

Second, the Chapter argues that civil society's relationship with the media is also double edged in terms of its impact on the public sphere. If media is a critical place where power is decided, civil society organisations have an obvious interest in understanding and engaging in processes that shape such power. Civil society actors are, or could be, sources of accountability for media organisations as well as sources of support for media-related attempts to enhance the communicative power of marginalised citizens. Most civil society organisations are often more preoccupied with using media as a conduit for their messages than as a critical component of democracy. This preoccupation can encourage them to appropriate communicative power for themselves through their advocacy initiatives.

Third, the Chapter concludes that international public debates on these issues are hampered by lack of appropriate public fora in which actors from media, civil society, government and business can discuss such issues intelligently, comprehensively and constructively. It calls for a greater investment in spaces for critical and constructive dialogue capable of engaging a broad spectrum of opinion on these issues.

Communicative power and the public sphere

There is a substantial literature on notions of communicative power and communicative action, most famously developed in the context of Jurgen Habermas' argument around the development of the public sphere (Habermas 1983, 1987, 1988, 1989). This Chapter, which is more concerned with trends and actions than concepts, leaves discussion of the many debates around Habermas' and others' work on the public sphere to other contributors to this edition (see for example, the Introduction). However, it does argue that these debates are increasingly relevant in the context of twenty-first century events and trends.

Habermas argued that a public sphere in an idealised form was a space where citizens could discuss their common public affairs and organise against arbitrary and oppressive forms of social and public power. The principles underpinning the public sphere included an open discussion of all issues of general concern, in which discursive argumentation was employed to determine general interests and the public good. The public sphere thus presupposed freedoms of speech and assembly, a free press, and the right to freely participate in political debate and decision making (Kellner 2007).

Discourses on the public sphere, communicative action and power acknowledge the critical importance of the media in determining the character and quality of the public sphere, and the distribution of and access to communicative power in the twenty-first century. This analysis acknowledges the role of the media as a critical determinant of the quality of democratic life, culture and effectiveness (Jacobson 2006). This Chapter explores some of the trends shaping the media's role in relation to communicative power, the public sphere and democracy.

Media and the expansion of the public sphere

During the last two decades, for much of humanity, the public sphere has expanded substantially and the

capacity to contribute to public debate increased. Three main trends have shaped this expansion of the public sphere: first, the wave of media liberalisation that, as part of broader democratic reform movements, swept much of the world after the fall of the Berlin Wall; second, the transformative changes wrought by new technologies; and third, how advocacy and the effective use of communicative power is increasing the pressure for social justice.

Media liberalisation, freedom and expansion

Some of the reverses to press freedom and media pluralism in recent years are outlined below; but the analysis presented in this Chapter is rooted in an acknowledgement of the major expansion of the public sphere over the last two decades. The global wave of media liberalisation that followed the fall of the Berlin Wall, and the associated pressures of globalisation, continues to reverberate on the ever more rapidly changing media landscape of the twenty-first century.

This wave was not uniform, but it did transform state control of communication systems in large parts of Africa, Asia, Eastern Europe and elsewhere. It led to a proliferation of new media actors and the replacement of media monopolies with a profusion of commercial and, in some cases, community and public service media. For a large portion of humanity, media was transformed: once the preserve of government which used it as a tool to control information and maintain power, media now offered opportunities for the creation of fora, and a plurality of sources of news and other information.

COMMUNICATIVE POWER AND CURRENT MEDIA DEVELOPMENTS

Box 8.1: Media, democracy and the public sphere: how community media changed Nepal

2007 marks the tenth anniversary of the setting up of Nepal's first community radio station. What started out as a pilot project has grown into a nationwide movement for grassroots communications culminating in 2006 with radio becoming a critical catalyst in the struggle to restore democracy in the country. Radio Sagarmatha 102.4 FM first came on air in 1997 after a long struggle, years of lobbying by the Nepal Forum of Environmental Journalists to win a licence, and with seed funding from UNESCO. Its aim was to use grassroots communications to empower rural areas and help foster participation and development, but it soon opened the floodgates for dozens of other FM stations. Besides using communication for development, the stations also acted as a medium for conflict resolution during Nepal's insurgency, 1996-2006.

The first community radio stations in Nepal were important in two respects: first, creating awareness about the significant role of grassroots communication in expanding the public sphere; second creating the conditions for democracy and development to thrive. Sagarmatha set up a network of community stations throughout the country for training and exchange of programmes.

Faced with commercial pressures and political interference, Nepali listeners showed there is a tremendous demand for public broadcasting in rural areas for information, entertainment and education. Here, information is at a premium, most listeners want news they can use. The advent of FM radio in Nepal virtually wiped out Hindi Bollywood songs from the airwaves and increased the popularity of Nepali folk and pop. At exam time, radio classrooms have become popular in rural areas where there are few good teachers. With their localised content, radios have given voice to indigenous groups and neglected languages.

The real challenge for the Nepali media came in February 2005 when Nepali King Gyanendra (who had succeeded the throne after a bloody massacre of the Royal Family by the former King Birendra's son in 2001) staged a military coup and, in a meticulously planned move, sent in the army to occupy newspaper offices, radio studios, the server rooms of Internet providers, cable operators and television stations. Mobile telephones were shut down, landlines were cut, no news was allowed on radio and television, and print media was directly censored.

While the phones and television returned after a few weeks and the newspapers began to openly defy censorship, the army singled out radio for special attention. The authorities had realised that the network of community and local FM stations – which by now reached around 65% of the population - had become a powerful tool in forming public opinion and making citizens aware of their democratic rights. They had to control it at all costs.

The army told the stations they could not broadcast news, only music. In response, radio reporters and producers set up the Free Radio Movement. They fought back in creative ways and not without a sense of humour. One radio station in central Nepal started singing the news in popular folk tunes. Another community station in Dang district took its entire studio down to the sidewalk and read the news to passersby every evening at 6pm; soon large crowds gathered and the news-reading ritual became a form of protest. After four months of continuing repression, journalists decided there was nothing left to lose and, starting with Nepal 91.8 FM in Kathmandu, they broadcasted news and current affairs, in defiance of government regulations.

One year after the military coup, anger erupted in the streets. A seven-party alliance, together with the Maoists, launched a people's movement to force the king to back down. As the protests gathered strength, community stations and FM radios across the country relayed the news. They broadcast studio discussions and phone-in programs, providing the protests with broad coverage. This information allowed pro-democracy activists to coordinate demonstrations nationwide, thus magnifying their impact. The military responded with tear gas, rubber bullets and curfews. News of these were relayed live from the streets by radio reporters with mobile phones and transmitted nationwide by FM networks. By mid-April it was clear that the government had lost control. Hundreds of thousands of people were marching to Kathmandu despite curfews and shoot-on-sight orders. An activist media played a major role in keeping the public informed about the demonstrations. It covered extensively the perspectives of leaders of the democratic movement. And although it may have seemed biased, most journalists justified the activism because they said they were fighting for fundamental freedoms.

As the People Power Uprising of April 2006 gathered strength in the streets of Kathmandu, the media played a key role in disseminating the news nationwide. On television, the protests had entertainment value: people battled riot police and went home to watch themselves on the evening news. In many cases television cameras changed reality just by being present at a demonstration. However, it was radio that brought more nuanced coverage, especially to areas of the country where media had less reach and to sections of the population that could not read. In remote areas of Nepal like Jumla district in the west or Taplejung in the east, people walked around with earphones in one ear: they weren't listening to music, but to news transmitted live from Kathmandu and other cities.

Throughout this political transition, community radio stations took the news from the capital to remote rural areas, and brought feedback and reaction of the nation to Kathmandu. Several syndicated services for radio exchange were set up to facilitate this two-way conversation between the centre and periphery. The end result was maximum public participation in the political evolution through horizontal nationwide communication via the FM network. Radio stations read out sections of the constitution to rural audiences in their own language. There were interviews with political leaders, human rights activists and members of civil society. The yearning for an end to the 10-year conflict was so strong among Nepalis that they identified with the demonstrations and got the message that an autocratic king was the biggest obstacle to peace. The slogans changed from 'We Want Democracy' to We will bring peace'.

If it had not been for the 'media multiplier', especially through country-wide networks of radio stations, it is doubtful that the uprising would have gathered the momentum it did. Finally, as demonstrators announced another series of massive protests, King Gyanendra gave in. On 24 April 2006 he announced the restoration of parliament. Since then, Nepal has seen a dramatic transformation of the state structure, which in any other country would have been impossible without widespread violence and loss of life. The king is no longer supreme commander of the army, royal succession will henceforth be determined by parliament, Nepal has been declared a secular state, and the monarchy has been reduced to little more than a tourist attraction.

After the victory of the democratic process, the new administration rewarded radio for its support for democracy by announcing that it would fast-track applications for new FM licenses that the previous royal government had shelved. Seventy new licenses were granted immediately and new applications rose. By the end of 2007 there could be as many as 200 FM radio stations, nearly half owned and run by local communities. Many fragile states have seen significant investment in media development, often driven by external stakeholders and often with mixed results. In Nepal, external investment by organisations like UNESCO was largely internally shaped and driven and its impact has been immense.

However, the challenges for the future are mounting. Are current growth rates in radio too rapid, and has radio become a victim of its own success? Indeed, radio stations are facing a host of second-generation problems: commercialisation, political interference, lack of professional training and business sustainability. Companies and organisations are getting into radio without understanding its technical, managerial and editorial aspects. The state still does not distinguish between commercial and community stations, which means that non-profit cooperatives must pay a four per cent tax on income, and a broadcasting levy. Rural community stations run by volunteers find it hard to sustain themselves. There is a danger they will turn into donor-driven mouthpieces if forced to depend on sponsorship from development organisations. Central government control of the licensing process has brought fears of politicisation: licenses are handed out routinely to politicians or favoured business interests. After the peace process the Maoists joined the government, including former rebel spokesman, Krishna Bahadur Mahara, who is now Minister of Information. There are fears that radio will be used for propaganda rather than public interest information.

Nepal's experience illustrates the importance of media that is connected to grassroots concerns for fostering, catalysing and enriching democracy. The radio movement faces major challenges for the future, but its development builds on strong foundations. Radio Sagarmatha was established with relatively modest support and snowballed into a vibrant community media nationwide. There are few instances in the world where so little money has gone so far.

Kunda Dixit, editor and publisher of the Nepali Times newspaper, Kathmandu

Extracted from *Community Media in the 21st Century: Perspectives and Experiences* (forthcoming, 2007), edited by James Deane, Denise Gray-Felder and Alfonso Gumucio-Dagron.

COMMUNICATIVE POWER AND CURRENT MEDIA DEVELOPMENTS

During this period, there was a greater expansion in both the numbers of media entities and their audiences than at any other time. Despite serious economic difficulties and declining circulations in many Western countries, the number of newspapers has increased substantially globally. Global newspaper circulation has increased by almost 10% over the last five years, according to the World Association of Newspapers, and the number of daily newspaper titles has surpassed 10,000 for the first time (World Association of Newspapers 2007). Most of this increase has occurred in developing countries.

A decade ago, with some exceptions (for example in large parts of Latin America, and in South Africa), television was largely the preserve of industrialised countries and the rich in developing countries. Today, satellite dishes are a prime consumer item in some of the most conflict-ridden areas of the world, particularly the Middle East, where the new channels (most famously Al-Jazeera), have profoundly impacted the public sphere in the Arab world, providing spaces for people to gain insight into political and state actions, and engage in debates around them. Educational soap operas, such as South Africa's award winning *Soul City*, are broadcast to townships where television ownership is common. In Asia, even among the poor, television ownership is rising exponentially; and in many regions of the world it provides the main source of information for people, particularly in industrialised countries. While there remains a gap in television ownership between rich and poor, and urban and rural, these gaps – at least in terms of access – are shrinking rapidly.

Radio remains the most accessed medium in the world, and it is arguably this form of media that has undergone the most significant revolution in structure, content, audience and diversity, with profound impacts on the public sphere in many countries (Girard 2005). In 2004, there were more than five times as many radio sets per hundred people in low income countries than there were television sets. More people in the world have access to a radio signal (96%) than to a television signal (83%) (ITU 2003). According to a major recent study of African media, radio is the most accessible of all media, with both television and newspapers concentrated mostly in urban areas (BBC World Service Trust 2007).

Commercial FM radio has revolutionised broadcasting in many developing countries, transforming broadcast environments from monolithic monopolies to a panoply of new actors. For developing countries, the role of radio in underpinning and enriching democratic debate and processes has been especially significant. Within a decade of liberalising its broadcast policy in 1993, the number of radio stations in Uganda increased from two to nearly a hundred; and the country's FM sector has become famous internationally for its muscular political talk shows and for *Ebimeeza* - public discussions on political issues that are broadcast live.

Liberalisation of media in Ghana produced a smaller number but no less dynamic group of FM radio stations. Their impact in opening up public debate and facilitating the public monitoring of the elections in 2001 (Friedman 2001) and in 2004 (Sakyi-Addo 2007) was particularly significant.

In some of the more mature markets, such as the United States, increased media liberalisation has led to radio ownership becoming increasingly concentrated, and the effect of liberalisation in former closed markets has been a major increase in diversity and pluralism, creating new public spheres of discussion and debate. Later, this Chapter will explore the growing political and commercial pressures on maturing markets which threaten to close down these new public spaces. However, in large parts of Africa, Asia and, to some degree, in the former Soviet Union, Eastern Europe and Latin America, the events that followed the fall of the Berlin Wall have had a major and sometimes a lasting effect on the media and public sphere. In some countries, the effects of these changes are only becoming fully apparent now (see Box 8.1).

While commercial media has benefited most from liberalisation, new policy environments in many countries have also sparked a mushrooming of community media, a trend also facilitated by falling technology costs and a substantial decrease in the price of entry into the radio market (see AMARC URL). The community radio movement in Latin America, which has a long tradition, is experiencing an unprecedented expansion, with hundreds of new licences being issued and the number of community stations reaching perhaps 10,000 across the continent. Peru alone has 4,000 community radio stations and Colombia has issued 500 new licences (Gumucio, forthcoming). In Africa, particularly in Francophone Africa (Sow, forthcoming), the growth in community radio has been almost as dramatic, with thousands of community radio stations across the region.

Where community media has had the opportunity to

Positive feedback: technology change has revolutionised media and vice versa

gain a serious foothold in the broadcast environment, its political and social effects have sometimes been dramatic. Community radio in Nepal, a majority medium reaching nearly 65% of the population, played a central role in mobilising peaceful mass protest against the monarchical dictatorship in the country, and ultimately securing a transition to democracy (see Box 8.1).

Later this Chapter explores the many limits, constraints and setbacks of the media liberalisation wave of the 1990s, as well as many countervailing forces, but it should be acknowledged that, since the last decade of the twentieth century, much of the world's population has witnessed an unprecedented inflation of the public sphere.

Communication technologies

Most current discussions of communicative power focus on the Internet, mobile telephony and other new technologies, and concentrate on what Manuel Castells calls 'the rise of mass self-communication' (Castells 2007: 246). While the revolution in media, particularly in developing countries, has been prompted in large part by a change in politics, policy, economics and society, leading to transformed systems of ownership, it has also been fuelled by, and is itself helping to catalyse, the technology revolution.

Never before have new territories for claiming (and possibly confining) public space emerged as rapidly as

they have over the last two decades, with the emergence of the Internet, and the allied technological revolutions of mobile telephony, satellite broadcasting and communication, and the host of other applications (blogs, vlogs, wikis etc.) that make up what is termed Web 2.0. These issues have been discussed in previous editions of the Yearbook (see Castells et al. 2006; Naughton 2001) and elsewhere in this publication; here attention will be paid to the links between new and traditional media in opening public spaces and enhancing communicative power.

Mainstream media increasingly turn to blogs and podcasts for stories, opinion and inspiration, and are using the same tools as delivery platforms. Social spaces such as MySpace and Facebook enable the instant creation of networks of likeminded people, and activate fluid, dynamic interactions that are beyond – but also can influence - traditional media. Wikis create democratic tools for defining concepts, movements and innovations. The difficulties of censoring such technologies pose a challenge to governments and to mainstream media, which may fear that its reluctance to cover sensitive issues will reduce its credibility as the story becomes available through viral communication networks.

While in the West and established media markets, the Web 2.0 technologies are reshaping media markets and communication opportunities available to citizens,

A radio programme in Guinea Bissau about HIV/AIDS

the effect in resource-poor countries is even greater potentially. Such technologies reduce substantially the price of entry into the media market and they provide an even greater opportunity for unheard, marginalised perspectives to be aired and new public spheres to be created particularly in environments where media freedom is restricted, indigenously produced media content is often prohibitively costly or where existing media markets are too expensive for new independent entrants to survive,

Online public interest journalism is no longer new, with some of the leading online public interest sites demonstrating a capacity to sustain themselves over time, establish a strong brand rooted in public respect and trust, and a lasting influence. Tehelka.com is an independent investigative journalism site in India, founded in 2000, which has been targeted repeatedly by the authorities and equally repeatedly made mainstream news through its exposés. Malaysiakini, another online political website, attracts 160,000 visitors each day, and is celebrating its eighth birthday despite several attempts by the authorities to close it down, including an incident in 2003 when its offices were raided and 19 computers were confiscated, allegedly for a breach of the country's Sedition Act. When Opendemocracy.net was founded in 2001, there were fears this respected web-based fora would prove unsustainable; such anxieties have, at least for now, been dispelled.

Even in the lowest income countries, the links between traditional media and new technologies have transformed media and communication environments from largely vertical communication flows (from political centres of control to disenfranchised citizens) to increasingly horizontally networked patterns of communication. Some of the most powerful effects of new technologies have been felt in developing countries where, in their own right and in constantly reinvented symbiotic relationship with old technologies (particularly radio), they have helped to revitalise public debate. In the last decade, radio content has been transformed in many countries by the talk show, phone-in and discussion programme, many of them made possible by the growing ubiquity of mobile telephony. It has enabled community and other public interest radio stations to form networks within countries and across countries. The massive growth in mobile telephony in developing countries – a phenomenon that will probably have greater implications for democracy and economics in those countries than any other single factor – has opened up traditional media to instant feedback, and interactivity of perspectives and of content with their audiences.

In environments where freedom of expression is under attack or curtailed, independent websites run from within countries, or by diasporic and other related communities, often constitute the only sources of independent and critical analysis. In environments where mainstream media is (or perceived to be) dominated by commercial or political issues, new media sites provide a critical monitoring function of the media (for example, *The Hoot* in India and Mediachannel.org in the US, although such sites have found it extremely difficult to obtain financial support).

Global civil society and communicative power

The degree to which global civil society has been facilitated and enabled by new communication technologies is well documented, including in earlier Global Civil Society Yearbooks. Rather less attention has focused on how the media's reporting of key issues of concern to civil society has also been transformed - and it is the changing character and force of communicative power that has enabled this shift.

The mainstream media continues to be criticised globally for downgrading its coverage of public interest issues, particularly of poverty and marginalisation. Some of the forces shaping reduced journalistic investment in these areas are explored later in this chapter, but at least part of the gap has been filled by a renewed willingness to report on the concerns of civil society, particularly on issues of poverty and marginalisation.

The first years of the twenty-first century ushered in the age of advocacy, a period where the media has been more amenable to stories about critical issues of concern to global civil society arguably than ever before. In few other areas has this been better exemplified than in the global campaign to 'Make Poverty History'.

By the late 1990s, development assistance budgets had been in decline for more than a decade, and media interest in development – at least in the West - was reactive and focused on a fragmented set of issues prompted mainly by famine and disaster. Journalists, production companies and filmmakers found that getting support for development-oriented programming was increasingly difficult; and news organisations in most industrialised countries were cutting back on their international networks of correspondents, particularly in developing countries. Development as an issue was declining on public agendas and financial support was weakening.

This situation has been revolutionised in the last few years. The Millennium Declaration that articulated the Millennium Development Goals (MDGs) provided a clear and proactive framework for global advocacy around a concerted and strategic approach to development. Having spent many years building up their operational and project departments, in part because donors preferred to channel aid through NGOs rather than governments, most major international development NGOs began to focus more on campaigning and advocacy.

Grassroots social movements – most notably on HIV/AIDS – have become increasingly powerful, built largely on their capacity to embarrass and hold governments and international agencies to account through sophisticated public protest and media strategies. This adept use of communications, combined with excellent advocacy campaigns, has transformed networks of people living with HIV/AIDS from the subjects of the response to the pandemic, to agents and strategic shapers of it. In this way, the resources, infrastructure and political commitment galvanised around HIV/AIDS, and other global health issues, such as TB, have increased significantly. The HIV/AIDS global campaign echoed other social movements, for example around debt cancellation, fair trade and against globalisation.

This move has coincided with and increasingly been overtaken by the rapid rise in the communicative power of celebrities to shape media and public agendas around issues of concern to civil society. Rock stars such as Sir Bob Geldof and Bono epitomise the shift in sources of action on development issues, with policy agendas not only represented by but increasingly shaped by figures who have instant access to media. For example, Geldof suggested the establishment of the Commission for Africa, prior to the G8 Summit in 2005, and as one of its 17 commissioners, he played a role in shaping its content. This trend is augmented by massive resources being made available for development work (particularly in health) from new private foundations and individuals, most notably by Bill Gates. The communicative power of such figures is greater than virtually any other development actor, be they implementing agencies, grassroots NGOs or research bodies. In addition, a new generation of US foundations, established by technology entrepreneurs such as Jeff Skoll and Pierre Omidyar, are supporting social entrepreneurship and advocacy.

All development issues now compete for public profile, with the experience of HIV/AIDS, poverty and other causes depending increasingly for political and financial commitment on media visibility and public support. Celebrity ambassadors and endorsers have become a central strategy for many development actors, the massive communicative power of celebrities unleashing unprecedented and previously untapped financial and public support. Having been in decline for decades, development budgets, both formal (through governments) and informal (through NGOs and diasporic networks), are rising faster than at any other time. The use of communicative power in pursuit of a social justice agenda has arguably rarely been so great or so effective.

The contraction of the public sphere and the appropriation of communicative power

Media and the concentration of communicative power

The previous section of this Chapter outlined some of the ways in which the media has undergone a transformative opening worldwide, diminishing the control and influence of government, as a consequence of policy change, social change and technology. This section deals with many of the opposing forces, documenting some of the ways in which public spheres are contracting, and how communicative power is increasingly being either co-opted from citizens or marginalised. Four trends in particular stand out:

1. Newly intensified assaults on freedom of expression, sometimes linked to the war on terror
2. The concentration of communicative power
3. The dependence on advertising and the reduction in public interest reporting
4. A growth in media numbers, but a shrinkage in diversity

1. Freedom of the media is under renewed assault

The number of journalists killed or imprisoned each year is reaching new records, according to Reporters Without Borders (URL). Both terrorism and the war on terror are cited by advocates of media freedom as a cause of media censorship and intimidation. According to the World Association of Newspapers, there is:

a legitimate and growing concern that in too many instances tightening of security and surveillance measures, whether old or newly introduced, are being used to stifle debate and the free flow of information about political decisions, or that they are being implemented with too little concern for the overriding necessity to protect individual liberties and, notably, freedom of the press. (2007:1)

Such advocates argue that the constraints on press freedom arise from new anti-terrorism and official secrets laws, criminalisation of speech judged to justify terrorism, criminal prosecution of journalists for disclosing classified information, surveillance of communications without judicial authorisation, restrictions on access to government data and more strict security classifications. 'All these measures can severely erode the capacity of journalists to investigate and report accurately and critically, and thus the ability of the press to inform,' according to WAN (2007: 1).

Legislative frameworks that guarantee freedom of expression clearly provide an important indicator of communicative power and pluralism, but the existence of new legal and even constitutional guarantees of freedom of expression, and mechanisms for media diversity, are no guarantee that these will be implemented in practice. Historically, the experience of many societies illustrates that while freedom of expression may be guaranteed under the constitution, it can be routinely violated by the government.

Even where freedom of expression exists in theory and in practice, in many poor countries it can be meaningless for everyone except the elite, particularly people in rural areas, who for reasons of cost, media reach, language or other factors, are unable to access information or the means of communication.

In many countries, such as former Eastern Bloc nations, the liberalisation of media has enabled the establishment of media entities, but has not necessarily resulted in a genuinely free and plural media. According to a major review of European countries carried out by the Open Society Institute in 2005, 'freedom of the media soon came to mean first of all freedom to run the media as a private business. Private broadcasters pursuing above all commercial gains rapidly outperformed State broadcasters, which were mostly reluctant or unable to keep up' (OSI 2005: 33).

2. Media ownership is becoming more globalised and concentrated into fewer corporate entities, which exert increasing control across media platforms

This enduring trend towards concentration of media and communication ownership has taken longer to reach the lower value markets of many developing countries, but it is now accelerating. The initial post-1989 explosion in ownership and control of the media in many new democracies and markets is being replaced by a steady consolidation of media systems, as commercial pressures, mergers and acquisitions increasingly focus media ownership on a smaller number of actors. This is evident at the global, regional and national levels.

At the global level, there is an increasing concentration of media and communication industries among a handful of giant corporations. Traditional media conglomerates have increasingly merged with and been joined by new media companies, with Disney, CBS, AOL-Time Warner, News Corporation, Bertelsmann AG, Viacom, Yahoo, Microsoft, Google and General Electric dominating markets – by some estimates around 90% of the media market in the US. Most of these conglomerates have major international operations; for example News Corporation is increasings its foothold in Latin America, through Sky

Latin America, and Asia, particularly in India and China. Many of the Web 2.0 social networking sites are being bought by such corporations; for example, News International has purchased MySpace. The advertising industry, which shapes media markets, is also becoming more globalised; and the emergence of global advertising brands, global consumer cultures (for example, global teenagers) has been well documented (UNDP 1998).

At the regional level, global players are augmented by major regional players. In Africa, South African media companies such as Naspers, and others such as the Nation Media Group, are beginning to shape media ownership throughout the continent. Building on the rapid emergence of an African middle class (rather than simply an elite class), the trend is providing a 'third wind of change' for the continent according to Wallace Chuma of the University of Cape Town. 'Africa has already experienced two "winds of change"', namely the decolonisation process that started in the late 1950s, and the democratisation and deregulation processes that followed the end of the Cold War in the early 1990s (Chuma 2005). In both cases, the media were rapidly influenced by the political upheavals. While these winds

of change were catalysed largely by events and processes outside Africa, the third wind is likely to be driven by pan-African media investment projects from the southern tip of the continent. The changes wrought by this third wind of change seem likely to result in the increasing influence of a few global and regional media players across the continent, the consolidation of the media market, and the pre-eminence of business, sport and entertainment news.

At the national level, concentration of ownership has long been a feature of mature markets; for example, following the US 1996 Telecommunications Act, Clear Channel acquired 1,200 local radio stations across the country. And the trend continues in regions such as Latin America where, for example in Guatemala, four out of six television channels are owned by one businessmen, a Mexican citizen based in Miami. These trends are being challenged, often controversially such as in Venezuela (referred to later in this Chapter). The same trend is taking place in newly democratic countries, as competitive pressures increase broadcast licences, other operational costs rise, and media markets mature.

3. Media is becoming increasingly competitive and advertising dependent, with a reduction in public interest reporting

Competitive pressures ensure that owners, editors and journalists focus coverage on those issues that are of interest to a paying market. A longstanding global trend, this pressure is intensifying in poor countries, where its consequences could be particularly acute. Arguably, the incentives to investigate local issues of poverty, marginalisation and injustice are weakening and the disincentives to doing so are growing, particularly if such coverage threatens to upset those with power or influence. Media owners are increasingly reluctant to exercise courage in the public interest, and the effect on many of those new markets that experienced an opening of public debate following liberalisation, is the beginnings of a steady closing down of public spaces. From Russia to Uganda, where independent media offered new platforms for public debate, there seems to be a stifling of freshly opened public spheres as a result of political pressures and an increased focus on profit.

Indeed, since the fall of the Berlin Wall, the media in many former Soviet countries has undergone a classic Bell curve: rapid transition from dictatorship or a one party state system catalysed free and open debate, facilitated by a confident, diverse and dynamic media movement, but was followed by a stifling of public debate and media diversity through competitive pressures, media consolidation, the growth of consumer culture and the reassertion of central political influence.

The Open Society Institute's 2005 survey of European television illustrates just such a Bell curve, and argues that the investigative reporting and innovative approaches to news gathering and political analysis ushered in by the liberalisation of media have not endured.

Pressure to increase ratings has encouraged a focus on entertainment, with a consequent decline in the status of news journalism. 'In such a precarious environment, and against the background of widespread political interference in programming and economic pressures, self-censorship thrives' (OSI 2005: 71).

Much of the current debate about the role of the media in democratic societies could usefully focus on incentives. Most independent media enterprises need to operate at least on a sustainable financial footing (obvious exceptions are public service and some community broadcasting, as well as those run as loss-making opinion formers by wealthy corporations and individuals). However, in environments of increasingly intense competition between media actors for market share and advertising revenue, the incentive for editors and journalists (let alone proprietors) to cover politically or economically sensitive, or unpalatable, stories are few, both in commercial and political terms. In resource-poor countries, where media systems are often more fragile, markets smaller, penalties for unsettling those in authority sometimes more severe, and the costs involved in undertaking substantial investigative journalism greater, commercial and political realities serve as substantial barriers to public interest reporting.

Public interest media is under increasing pressure, with public service broadcasters (where they exist) facing intense competition, loss of market share and, in many countries, reductions in funding. As media markets fragment and audience share diminishes, even the strongest public service brands – such as the BBC – are struggling to justify licence fees, making it doubtful that such models will be replicated elsewhere. While it is increasingly visible, community media faces a challenge to develop sustainable business models, and the movement is fragile, even when it is effective (see Box 8.2).

4. A growth in media numbers, but not necessarily in media pluralism or diversity

The explosion in media discussed earlier in this Chapter is sometimes taken to indicate greater diversity, plurality and dynamism. However, there is no inherent relationship between the number of media outlets and the plurality of those outlets. Of course, the role and impact of media in a society varies immensely, but the number of outlets provides little guide to their social or political function. Multiple media outlets may just as likely indicate a sophisticated marketing environment as the prevalence of diverse political perspectives.

Nowhere is this more clearly seen than in China. Two decades ago the principal function of media in China was to provide the critical instrument of state control by framing and limiting news and information available to its people. Today, its principal function is the provision of advertising platforms to fuel the country's huge consumer boom, exercised through a media environment transformed by an explosion of television

UNBALANCED NEWS IS ALSO A HUMAN RIGHTS ABUSE

DON'T SIT DOING NOTHING, HELP FIGHT THE WRONGS OF SOCIETY

PEOPLE UNITED FOR PROGRESS (PUP)

and other media channels. Freedom of the press remains heavily curtailed and while a debate continues within the country about the role of a more open media in exposing corruption and providing a more stable business climate (Hilton 2006), the evidence suggests strong reluctance to accept such openness. In such a climate, media focuses mostly on entertainment, beauty, sport and of course state-controlled news.

New technologies and the fragmentation of the public sphere

The Internet has created a limitless matrix through which ordinary people can exercise communicative power, establish shared spaces for discussion and dialogue, and where tapestries of communication between old and new media, traditional and twenty-first century communication networks are constantly rewoven.

However, as media markets fragment and fracture, there are less key reference points and platforms where a clear contestation of ideas within the public sphere can be held. Communities of common interest create spaces for sharing those interests; people with similar views create networks where those views can be shared and reinforced. The advantages of such opportunities are obvious, and have been outlined above, not least in their capacity to create new identities, solidarity, confidence and empowerment of those who are marginalised. There has been less debate about the implications of a communication environment fractured to such a degree that the contestation of ideas and policies is impossible to

sustain. In this context, the public sphere erodes and is replaced by a panoply of individualised private and semi-private spheres.

In such a climate, communicative power may be increased, but the capacity for citizens to assess, evaluate and take informed positions and decisions – not least in elections – becomes far more difficult because the space to weigh up different arguments narrows, thus constraining interpretation. As a result, ideas receive neither due consideration, nor are subject to testing in a genuinely public forum.

In any case, the genuine inclusiveness of new technologies is debatable. The digital divide between those who have access to, or an interest in, new technologies, and those who do not, is an ongoing subject of debate. Even in the age of Web 2.0, there is evidence that media creation and readership using new technologies is drawn from a relatively narrow audience. The top 100 websites receive 62% of the online audience according to an unverified citation on Wikipedia, compared to the top 100 newspapers, magazines, and radio stations, which receive about 30% of their respective audiences on average.

It is not yet clear whether, in such an environment, communicative power will end up being exercised by those with the most marketing muscle, brand recognition and sometimes the most strident views. If there is value in a public debate where a range of perspectives can be aired and challenged, this fragmentation could as well mark the disintegration of the public sphere as the regeneration of it. It seems likely that those brands with high public trust will strengthen their influence on the public debate and become a reference point, if not a platform within an ever more complex and noisy public sphere.

Meanwhile, the optimism for an unfettered and accessible public arena ushered in by the Internet in the mid-1990s - epitomised by the Declaration of Independence of Cyberspace published by the Electronic Frontier Foundation in 1996 (EFF 1996) - has faded, with the rise of censorship. China restricts access to particular websites routinely (see Chapter 5 of this volume), and while those websites highlighted above such as Malaysiakini, have survived, they have been threatened by the authorities and struggle financially.

Civil society, media and the expansion of the public sphere

The trends outlined above demonstrate some of the shifting balances of communicative power. Most of these shifts result from changes in policy, often catalysed by the tectonics of globalisation and international political change, by technology and commercial forces to maximise capital and market share. At the same time, there are also a host of civil society initiatives aimed at rebalancing communicative power in the public interest.

The current communication environment is frequently characterised as one that lends itself to alternative voices finding a platform, an audience and an organisational network capable of creating communicative power. Some of the limitations of such an environment have been touched upon above, but four key areas of civil society activity to improve the public sphere, through and with media, should be outlined.

1. Freedom of expression movements

The international freedom of expression movement, which comprises many international organisations, has become increasingly organised, better resourced and more dynamic. It has needed to, given the increasing worldwide assaults on freedom of expression. The International Freedom of Expression Exchange (IFEX) lists more than 70 members, many working internationally and an increasing number from developing countries. The movement monitors abuses of media freedom, supports independent media movements in countries that face constraints or attacks on press freedom, and develops policy to enshrine and make real rights to freedom of expression. While the movement has embraced members from developing countries, and from a broad range of actors beyond the mainstream media (such as the World Association of Community Radio Broadcasters), relations with civil society organisations are weaker. There are good reasons for this, not least a determination by the media to retain their independence, but both sectors share common concerns, such as increasing pressure from authoritarian regimes.

2. Communication rights in the twenty-first century

A growing international movement – which has sometimes been at odds with those in the freedom of expression movement - is coalescing behind the 'right to communicate'. Such rights go beyond freedom of expression and extend to areas such as democratic media governance, participation in citizen's own culture, linguistic rights, the rights to enjoy the fruits of human creativity, to education, privacy, peaceful assembly and self determination. Central to the right to communicate movement is the right to create one's own media (particularly important for community radio, which continues to be banned or discouraged in many countries). Such rights are also aimed at countering the concentration of media ownership, control of intellectual property and exclusion of minority voices. In effect, the movement is attempting to establish a right to be heard and be listened to.

The history of attempts to establish such rights is contentious and occasionally bitter. The right to communicate was proposed in the 1981 MacBride Report (MacBride 1981), which initiated a global debate around what became known as the New World Information and Communication Order initiative (NWICO), led by UNESCO. The MacBride Commission pointed to the extreme dependency of developing countries on Western news sources, the concentration of Western media ownership that exerted increasing influence in developing and small countries, and the growing information and communication technology gap between the West and the rest (in other words many of the same issues, although often in different form, explored in this Chapter). At this time, developing countries (the Non-Aligned Movement) were in a critical phase of nation building and consolidation or creation of national and cultural identities. They protested that new forms of cultural imperialism (or what could be reasonably termed communicative power) were replacing and augmenting the old forms of military and political power (CRIS 2005).

The NWICO perished in acrimony and prompted the departure of the US and the UK from UNESCO. The reasons for the failure of the initiative were many and complex, including: the ideological context of the Cold War; attempts by several non-Western governments to use communication rights to justify limits or quotas on the media; concerns among Western media that the right could threaten freedom of expression and justify arbitrary limits on media ownership; and the concerns of Western governments that it would undermine intellectual property rights and threaten free speech and free markets.

While many of the contextual realities that led to the NWICO debate becoming so unproductive have disappeared, including the Cold War and the polarisation between developing and developed countries, the problems that sparked it in the first place have become more acute. Partly because of the bitter legacy of the debate, there have been few international fora in which such issues have been discussed seriously since.

However, citizens' movements, NGOs and others have continued to address issues similar to those identified in the MacBride Report. Modern communication for development, and media for development movements are outlined below. Meanwhile, the debate on communication rights is undergoing a renaissance in its own right.

In Latin America, the concept of communication rights provides an important source of inspiration and impetus for the revival of community radio (outlined above), concepts shaped by civil society and academia. At the same time, the recent establishment by Venezuelan President Hugo Chavez of Telesur in Venezuela, the 'new television station of the South', represents a clear challenge to the dominance of private media on the continent and, with an advisory board comprised of intellectuals and academics, is often described as an attempt to realise communication rights. Many of the same tensions that characterised the NWICO debate are re-emerging around the Chavez's attempts to 'rebalance' the media (not least in the government's withdrawal of the licence to RCTV and perhaps other commercial television stations that are accused of inciting rebellion in the country).

While the concept of communication rights is most

vibrant in Latin America, a global campaign for Communication Rights in the Information Society was formed in 2001, and led to significant lobbying at the World Summit on the Information Society, a two-stage UN summit held in 2003 and 2005 (see Box 8.2).

Today, no right to communicate has been established officially, but the campaign continues. At the heart of the debate on communication rights are three sets of issues.

First, the right to communicate is founded on and rooted in the principle of freedom of expression, but is supplementary to it. Nearly all actors involved in this debate argue that freedom of expression is a non-negotiable foundation stone. However, the right to communicate involves not only the right to say, but the right to be heard, and encompasses concepts of listening, understanding, learning, responding and the capacity to create. For some there are tensions between the right to freedom of expression and the right to communicate; and for others, these rights are mutually reinforcing.

Second, there is a question of whether the right to communicate implies the necessity to listen (which in turn could imply compulsion). Many argue, for example, that there is an inherent contradiction in creating a formal right focused largely on ensuring that the authorities enable people to make their voices heard, while at the same time making governments the guarantors of such a right.

Third, and perhaps more profound, is the absence of serious international discussion about the problems that underpin and prompt the communication rights

Box: 8.2: Media and the World Summit on the Information Society: interventions in a policy-making process

Civil society has often been conceptualised and analysed in its interaction with political processes. As Dean argues in this Chapter, in order to influence policies that affect them, citizens need access to information and 'the spaces to discuss and debate those issues openly with others, and the opportunity to make their perspectives and demands heard'. The World Summit on the Information Society (WSIS) offered a prominent opportunity for such an endeavour. As a major forum for transnational policy making in the field of information and communication, it attracted mobilisations and interventions by a wide variety of civil society actors. Among them were community and alternative media activists, including members of the World Association of Community Radio Broadcasting (AMARC) and of Indymedia, as well as representatives of public service media, such as the European Broadcasting Union (EBU), and of commercial media, such as the International Association of Broadcasting (IAB).

These different media actors formed an alliance, the Media Caucus, as part of a broader network of civil society caucuses such as on Human Rights, Internet Governance, and Privacy and Security, each developing and advocating a civil society agenda in their respective areas and bringing it into the WSIS negotiation process. However, with members ranging from grassroots activists to commercial media empires, the media alliance was conflictive and uncovered deeply-rooted divides. The only common denominator, for which the caucus lobbied fiercely and with some success, was freedom of expression. With other objectives eclipsed from the caucus agenda, community and alternative media formed a separate coalition, the Community Media Working Group, and developed their own agenda, which included financial and legal support for these media, access to the airwaves, and communication rights. Meanwhile, those media activists with a more radical agenda and opposed to a government-led summit held parallel events outside the summit compound, such as WSIS?WeSeize!, and articulated a more fundamental critique of current global governance structures, and of the privatisation of knowledge through the intellectual property regime.

Those community and alternative media participating 'inside' the official summit process applied some of the classical repertoire of strategy and action, which has been analysed and conceptualised by social movement studies (Khagram et al. 2002). As civil society actors operating within the WSIS institutional framework, the Community Media Working Group framed their objectives according to the dominant summit theme of enhancing communication technologies for development, focusing on the development aspects of community media, and thus creating bridges to the development-oriented objectives of their target audience, that is, the governments at the negotiation table. They also worked towards expanding the number of allies among government delegations. At the same time, they faced some of the usual challenges of civil society in global policy processes, including the limited openness of the institutional setting and their exclusion from spaces of inter-governmental negotiation, the lack of powerful and committed government allies, dominant interests of state security and business development, physical repression outside the summit compound and the hostility of some governments to civil society concerns - in this case, freedom of expression, citizen participation and self-organised grassroots media. Furthermore, they suffered from the fragmentation of their sector into different types of actors: such as community radios, online activists, larger media organisations and individual software developers, who often had contrasting (or incongruent) political objectives, organisational approaches and ideological backgrounds.

On the other hand, the inside-outside division into institutional and extra-institutional approaches was not as strongly developed as in previous civil society mobilisations; and collaborations between different actors offered an insight into a multi-level strategy between 'inside' and 'outside', between those who lobbied for immediate policy change and those who articulated a broader and more fundamental critique. A small but increasing number of participants from both camps interpreted the different approaches between, for example, the Community Media Working Group and WSIS?WeSeize! not as fundamental ideological dividing lines but as complementary strategies. Bridging the boundaries between media actors with different tactics and thematic focuses, WSIS offered an opportunity to transcend 'predictable spheres of influence' (Calabrese 2004: 323). Furthermore, and in addition to those two spheres, a third strategic approach focused on critical practices and setting up structural alternatives to mainstream communication systems, rather than interacting with the policy process. This 'beyond policy' sphere is well developed among communication-related areas of civil society and constitutes one of their specific characteristics (see Hintz/Milan 2006).

The immediate outcomes of the summit process for media actors were limited. Mainstream media representatives were relieved that freedom of expression and freedom of the press were confirmed. Yet the broader sets of objectives, as advocated by community and alternative media, were either never considered for adoption or were removed from the final WSIS documents. Thus, community media and other self-organised communication projects were hardly mentioned at all: specific requests of legalisation, funding mechanisms and access to airwaves and orbital paths were ignored. No concrete measures were initiated to safeguard media pluralism and the diversity of opinions represented in the media; alternatives to the current intellectual property regime were hardly discussed; and the proposed regulatory environment focused on markets and competition, state security and top-down social management.

However, the summit documents do recognise the environment in which 'third sector' media operate: WSIS language is strongly influenced by values of participation and empowerment (although the summit did not devise any practical steps to strengthen participation), the need for more local content is highlighted, cultural diversity is declared a main objective, and references to the public domain repeatedly blur the dominant market paradigm. Additional conferences that accompanied the WSIS process and dealt with specific issues, such as the conference 'Role and Place of Media in the Information Society in Africa and the Arab States' in 2004, and the 'Asia Media Summit in 2005', provided thorough recognition of community media. Most significantly, community and alternative media raised their profile substantially in the events and discourses around the two WSIS summits. The slogan, 'Create your own media – make your own voice heard' permeated many smaller conferences, presentations and discussions organised by civil society, business and government actors, which complemented official summit proceedings. If these media failed to imprint their mark in the core WSIS documents, they did strengthen their position in the broader discourses on appropriate means of communication and on the role of information in society. Not least through their foundation in grassroots practices, they expressed a vision of the information society that is grounded in bottom-up processes, based on the creative acts of civil society initiatives, and focused on participatory and interactive communication rather than one-way information streams.

Beyond the limited outcomes of WSIS, as well as the latter's promising testing of a 'multi-stakeholder dialogue', which includes civil society (Raboy/Landry 2005), the summit process represented a 'political opportunity structure' (McAdam et al. 1996), which was used by formerly isolated civil society groups to share expertise and experience, create networks and converge their agendas. The vast field of 'third sector' media, including community, alternative, citizens and autonomous media, proved to be fragmented, yet communication between different entities emerged, and the raised profile of these media constitutes an important building block for achieving a more central role in future policy processes. However, coalitions between mainstream and non-mainstream media were fragile, and the inclusion of commercial media in a space dedicated to 'civil society' was frequently questioned. Linking the concepts of 'civil society' and 'media' may encourage the notion that 'civil society media' encompass only specific types of media – generally the non-commercial, non-state 'third media sector' – and not 'the media' as such (Hadl/Hintz 2007).

Arne Hintz, Center for Media and Communication Studies, Central European University, Budapest debate. Issues of growing media concentration, the marginalisation of people living in poverty from debates that shape their lives, the perceived domination of a small number of international news providers, and the role of information and communication in sustainable democratic development – these issues have little place, space or home in international discourse. The World Summit on the Information Society failed to provide that space, and in any case was a forum defined by governments. Whether communication rights - or any other strategy or movement - is an appropriate solution to such issues is rarely subject to a serious debate at international level. This concern extends well beyond social activists and civil society movements as mainstream journalists become increasingly constrained by, and their work shaped according to, the commercial and political imperatives of their owners. No serious international fora exists where a diversity of engaged and concerned actors, from across the ideological spectrum, can address these issues. Without such a forum, the future debate risks continued polarisation (particularly between some freedom of expression advocates and social activists) misunderstandings, unhelpful assumptions, much of it shaped by the sad history of such debates.

3. Alternative media and communicative power

As this Yearbook makes clear, the opportunities for civil society actors to create their own communication platforms – often called alternative media - have never been greater. Many examples of these, such as the Indymedia movement (see Chapter 10 of this volume), are well documented.

'Alternative media' encompasses an extraordinarily broad range, from citizens' networks, community media and the many electronic and web-based entities outlined earlier in this Chapter, to theatre groups, oral testimony initiatives, and wall newspapers, to name a few. In truth, the term tends to define more what it is an alternative to, than what it actually is, leading some to question its value. However, regardless of this terminological debate, alternative media encompasses highly imaginative, dynamic and innovative manifestations of communicative power by ordinary citizens.

In the West, alternative media has been established in response to the unwillingness of the mainstream media to provide spaces and voices to marginalised groups, or those perceived to be outside of mainstream public discourse. It is often articulated as a challenge to the perceived domination of media by international capital, or a set of narrow commercial interests hostile to citizen power (Chomsky 2002).

In most non-Western societies, alternative media has tended to emerge less in response to commercial power and more in response to governmental power, in order to create spaces free of control and censorship by the state. While such distinctions between Western and non-Western societies may simplify a much more complex picture, they do explain, in part, the absence of an integrated and coherent global alternative media movement (another key reason is a lack of resources).

Over the last 40 years, there have been many efforts to establish alternative, non-Western based news and information services, some of which have been successful and achieved impact. The best known and longest lasting, the Inter Press Service (IPS), was established in 1964 as a Southern response to agencies such as Reuters. With strong networks in Latin America, IPS prides itself on breaking stories not normally covered by mainstream media, and on its close links to civil society. It is prominent in many international civil society meetings and conferences. Supported by various development agencies and philanthropic foundations, IPS is one survivor of a substantial number of similar agencies, such as Gemini News and Compass Features, which were not financially viable. In the meantime, regional agencies have become established through an online presence, such as AllAfrica.com.

4. Media for Development

Outlined above are efforts by citizens' movements either to create their own channels of communication, or to establish new rights that enable people to utilise or create such channels. A more coherent set of actions are gaining momentum as media and media support organisations, both national and international, become increasingly organised and effective in developing initiatives to improve public interest media, provide communication opportunities to those living in poverty. The Communication Initiative, an international website (URL), documents thousands of organisations, initiatives, networks and projects designed to improve access to information and build people's capacity to communicate their perspectives.

Much of this Yearbook is concerned with the critical ingredients that make democracies democratic, that make public discourse genuinely public and inclusive, that makes politics work for the most disadvantaged in society and that ensures that social change is shaped by those within societies rather than those determining realities from outside. The international development sector has tended to make such issues secondary to the more tangible interventions of delivering healthcare, education and infrastructure, and the more obviously urgent issues of trade, aid and debt.

However, current development policy increasingly understands the importance of media to the economic and political development of developing countries, and this is leading to a more concerted series of efforts to support it. Most notable among recent steps was the decision by the UK government, outlined in its policy White Paper *Making Governance Work for the Poor* (DFID 2006), to create a new £100 million Governance and Transparency Fund designed to support free media and civil society in developing countries.

The reasons for this new commitment, which is increasingly shared by other multilateral and bilateral organisations, are rooted in an unprecedented consensus that now underpins international development policy. Seven issues underpin this consensus: the importance of national ownership in formulating and implementing development strategies; the necessity for good governance, particularly the capacity of citizens, rather than donors, to hold governments to account for delivery of services; the MDGs as the principal strategic framework for development; globalisation as an overarching context to development; the need for more rights-based approaches to development; the importance of coherence, alignment and harmonisation of development policy; and managing for results.

While all of these issues have major implications for the role of media in developing countries, one in particular stands out. Most donors, led by the UK, are committed to providing funds through budget support to governments. Only by doing so, they argue, can governments become accountable to their citizens for delivery of services, rather than to Western donors, and only then can real democracy take hold (budget support also enables donors to spend large amounts of money with relatively little administration at a time when spending budgets are increasing and administration budgets are being pared down). Increasingly, donors understand that if citizens are to hold government to account in new and poor democracies, capacities for that to happen need to be

A community media project by low caste women in Chitrakost, Uttar Pradesh, India

better developed. Citizens cannot hold governments to account unless they are informed of and have access to information on the issues that shape their lives. The role of the media and of communication structures at all levels (community, sub regional, national, regional and international) is inextricably bound up with how citizens understand and engage in democratic life. The rights and capacities of people, particularly those living in poverty, to voice their own perspectives and have them heard in public debate, particularly through the media, are increasingly recognized as critical to effective governance.

Such Western donor interest in promoting media and civil society in developing countries clearly leaves them open to criticism that they are using such actors as proxy sources of accountability. This has engendered efforts to develop a set of Southern- and particularly African-led agendas on media development. For example, the Strengthening African Media Process, supported by DFID, is expected to reach its conclusions in late 2007. These initiatives are complemented by a series of sector-led initiatives, such as the Global Forum for Media Development, which seek to map out a proactive agenda from media and media support organisations within which external actors – including funders – can operate.

This sphere of media and communication for development is increasingly dynamic. It includes, for example, work on:

- Asserting and developing better access and rights to information, such as enabling people affected by particular policies and initiatives to have access to information about them. A highly successful citizens' movement in India has been particularly effective in gaining legislative and judicial backing for this right.

- Support to media, including media freedom, community media, capacity building and enhancing financial sustainability of independent media, media policy, pro-poor/development focused content, professionalism and ethics in media.
- Strengthening a healthy public sphere, characterised by informed media, a vibrant civil society and decentralised patterns of information exchange.
- The role of communication in informing and generating public debate, and in ensuring the voices of vulnerable and marginalised groups are prominent in such debate; and its allied role in enhancing ownership, accountability and transparency in development policy (such as formulating development, poverty reduction and other related strategies).
- Community empowerment through communication for social change and other dialogue-focused methodologies.
- Communication as part of a rights-based approach to development, and how communication (particularly with and through media) intersects with and enriches civil society voice.

However, while the media for development community and initiatives are increasingly effective, well organised and, hopefully, rooted in Southern frameworks of action, such efforts remain largely marginal and poorly coordinated areas of development policy. Nevertheless, current development contexts and strategies strongly suggest more concerted and increased support for such initiatives in the future.

The appropriation of communicative power

Earlier sections have focused on the role of civil society in supporting public debate, often by creating alternative forms of communicative power and by placing pressure on mainstream media to cover particular issues.

However, as this Chapter illustrates, the relationship between civil society and media is complex, civil society's efforts to enhance media freedom and expand the public sphere face many obstacles, and there are instances of civil society activity eroding the public sphere. While it is not of the same nature or intensity as the competition within the media, civil society

organisations do compete with one another. Such competition creates incentives for civil society organisations to regard the media as a conduit for its messages, rather than as a critical component of the democratic fabric of society. Civil society organisations require a positive public profile and credibility in order to achieve their objectives, and this need has intensified. As a consequence, they have the potential to appropriate communicative power through the media.

The huge success and impact of advocacy and campaigning, and the exercise of communicative power by celebrities and public figures, has been acknowledged above. The social movements that were earlier the principal sources of public pressure for greater attention to be paid to debt, global inequality, poverty and the environment, have been supplanted by a set of new players who are better equipped to exercise communicative power in the twenty-first century. The anti-globalisation protests of Seattle in 1999, the World Social Forums and the many other examples of global civil society action, which have been explored in the Global Civil Society Yearbook series, are now subsidiary sources of global action.

Many events have changed the dynamics, impact and influence of global social movements in the last few years, including, most importantly, Western political reactions to 9/11, the war in Iraq, and the subsequent constriction of spaces for social action; and the partial appropriation of many of these issues by mainstream politics and politicians.

Other influences on global civil society include the appropriation of leadership on central issues of concern by those who command and exercise communicative power – in particular, celebrities. The capacities of rock musicians and of wealthy individuals to mobilise their resources and public support base, to catalyse leadership, and to exert pressure on political processes surrounding issues of concern to global civil society, such as global poverty, has been extraordinary.

Such impact has come at a price, however. It is now more difficult to call a 'movement against poverty' a genuine social movement that is shaped, driven and represented by those most affected by the issues. It is debatable whether the trade justice or global justice movements were ever social movements in this sense; and charities and development organisations have been criticised for many years for representing people living in poverty rather than providing them with a voice. However, they have sought to address such criticisms:

the Jubilee 2000 campaign was perhaps the best example of a genuinely global campaign on poverty rooted in communities throughout the world that were directly affected by debt.

Rather than deriving power from those most affected by particular issues, those leading the current movements on poverty and environment are those able to command communicative power. This is power rooted in their access to and easy capacity to use media to deliver their message. It is not power that is rooted necessarily in a democratic legitimacy or one founded on – or with any kind of accountability to – a large movement of concerned or affected people. This has had the clear benefit of achieving an immense amount. However, there are obvious and major risks.

The first risk is that it is a fragile movement on stilts, with shallow support structures incapable of dealing with setbacks and shifts in political mood. Live 8, the massive global music concert coinciding with the 2005 G8 summit was an event focused not on raising money but on raising public awareness of Africa – but African involvement and representation was limited. Criticism of this feature of Live 8 has been well rehearsed, but it is perhaps emblematic of an event focused on the exercise of communicative power by those best in a position to exercise that power, rather than a deliberate attempt to share and invest others with such power. The opportunity of Live 8 was to provide the Make Poverty History campaign with a set of supporters and voices that could nurture it through the inevitable difficulties that lie ahead. Most opinion polls suggest that public support in the UK for efforts to tackle poverty is very widespread, but also very fragile. While the main justification of celebrity-led campaigns is their ability to reach a large number of people, some evidence suggests that their impact is short lived and shallow. Research in Britain shows public concern about poverty in poor countries reached a high of 32%, in April 2005, prior to the G8 meeting in Gleneagles in June, and two years later has declined to 22%, its lowest level since the study began (Darnton 2007).

The second risk of this style of campaigning is its de-politicisation and over-simplification of complex issues. The Commission for Africa (URL) set out a comprehensive analysis and strategy for action, including the need to tackle highly contentious political issues such as land reform and media policy, but the ensuing public debate focused on levels of development assistance. The need for simple media

Make Poverty History: a new kind of media and celebrity-led civil society campaign?

messages encouraged proponents, including development economists such as Jeffrey Sachs, to highlight the most practical and easily achievable actions (for example, the provision of bed-nets to malarial-affected areas). Complex issues, from macro- economic policy to often difficult policy choices that are required to achieve the Millennium Development Goals (many of which were outlined in the Millennium Declaration and the Report of the Commission for Africa) were lost in the public presentation of the campaign.

In the West, the media and public believe that increased aid to developing countries will and should achieve rapid results, and are ill-prepared for setbacks and slow progress. However sensible the strategy of funnelling development assistance through the national budgets of developing countries, it is likely to lead to news stories of mismanagement and waste. As indicated above, public opinion is fragile and it is questionable whether those who have exerted the most communicative power through the media are able to maintain public confidence and support in the face of negative stories about the use of aid, or slow progress in developing countries.

The third risk is that, parallel to the globalisation of civil society, a globalisation of NGO advocacy is occurring. Such a global process retains credibility and legitimacy when it is rooted in the experience of ordinary people in developing countries. Instead, professionalised advocacy organisations have evolved a development agenda and associated campaigns designed to exercise maximum communicative power through the media. This has clear advantages, in terms of raising the global profile of poverty-related issues, but it risks excluding the very people most affected by poverty. This tendency is reinforced by other factors. As development budgets become increasingly decentralised and budget support mechanisms become the norm, policy and financial priorities are set within developing countries (rather than at donor headquarters), which has clear advantages. But it has effects on how international NGOs operate in developing countries and, in turn, how the media agenda is shaped. By deploying their advocacy resources on issues and experiences within developing countries, in order to gain public and political attention, civil society organisations can dominate media coverage at the expense of indigenous public debate and journalism. In poor countries, public spheres are more limited than in industrialised countries (because the number of and audience for media entities is more limited, and budgets for investigative journalism are more scarce, for example) and such societies can be particularly vulnerable to agendas – even public interest ones – shaped by forces outside the country. If the media and public agendas are shaped more by those with the largest advocacy budgets and access to global celebrities or brands, than by indigenous processes, this risks appropriating, rather than allowing the grassroots exercising of, communicative power.

Conclusion

This Chapter has sought briefly and partially to outline some of the factors and trends relevant to civil society that are shaping who has and does not have access to communicative power in the twenty-first century, and what is expanding and constraining public spheres internationally. This Chapter has sought to demonstrate the complex, contradictory and countervailing media trends shaping the character of democracies in the twenty-first century. It has not been its intention, despite inevitable biases, to reach definitive conclusions or make specific policy

recommendations. The author believes, for example, in the critical role that commercial media can play in invigorating the public sphere, which is also invigorated by community media and public service broadcasting; that globalisation and concentration of media can sometimes bring important benefits, although generally these are greatly outweighed by the problems; that the role of development agencies in strengthening the media is vital, but such support is fraught with problems and inherent contradictions.

The critical questions prompted by this analysis are whether there is a sufficiently serious, focused international debate on the state, role and importance of media and communication in twenty-first century society. If not, how, where, and by whom can that debate be held? Media organisations are often reluctant to engage in discussion about their role because they fear the consequences, for example, on their independence. Governments should not lead such a debate for the obvious reason that it is principally governments that should be held to account by an independent media. International governmental organisations face a similar problem, as debate about NWICO demonstrated. Civil society organisations should be held to account by the media too, and should be wary of making efforts that could be seen as muzzling it. The fact that so many trends are contradictory and complex in their impact, as well as so rapidly moving, heightens the need for civil society (among others) to track, understand and respond to them. This analysis suggests that civil society should focus not only on the media as the conduit for its messages, but increasingly as an enabler of democratic debate and dialogue, and as a critical shaper of the public sphere within which civil society operates. That implies the need for a more determined and informed engagement with debates on the future of the media by civil society. Developing better strategies and spaces for such engagement, and ensuring they do not threaten the independence of the media, is one of the most critical challenges facing democracy, civil society – and of course the media itself - in the twenty-first century.

REFERENCES

AMARC, www.amarc.org

Barlow, J P (1996) 'A Declaration of the Independence of Cyber-space', Electronic Frontier Foundation. http://homes.eff.org/~barlow/Declaration-Final.html

BBC World Service Trust (2007) *African Media Development Initiative Research Summary Report.* London: BBC World Service Trust.

Calabrese, Andrew (2004) 'The Promise of Civil Society: A Global Movement for Communication Rights', *Continuum: Journal of Media & Cultural Studies*, 18(3) 317-329.

Campaign for Rights in the Information Society (2005) *Assessing Communication Rights; A Handbook.* www.crisinfo.org

Castells, M (2007) 'Communication, Power and Counter-power in the Network Society', *International Journal of Communication* 1:1, 238-266. http://ijoc.org/ojs/index.php/ijoc/article/view/46/35

Castells, M, Fernandez-Ardevol, M, Linchuan Qiu J and Sey, A, (2006) 'Electronic Communication and Socio-Political Mobilization: A New Form of Civil Society' in M Glasius, Mary Kaldor and Helmut Anheier (eds) *Global Civil Society* 2005/6. London: Sage.

Chandhoke, N (2005) 'What the hell is civil society?' Opendemocracy, 17 March. http://www.opendemocracy.net/democracy-open_politics/article_2375.jsp

Chomsky, N and Herman, E (2002) *Manufacturing consent: The Political Economy of the Mass Media.* London: Vintage Press.

Chuma, W (2005) 'The Third Wind of Change', *The Mail and Guardian*, 1 December. http://www.themedia.co.za/article.aspx?articleid=261409&area=/media_insightfeatures (consulted 8 January 2007).

The Communication Initiative, www.comminit.com

Darnton A (2007) 'Public Perceptions of Poverty' Omnibus Survey – Wave 6 Findings, Summary Report, 1 June. http://www.bond.org.uk/campaign/ppp.htm (consulted 13 July 2007).

Deane, J (2006) 'Why the media matters: the relevance of the media to tackling poverty' in M Harvey (ed) *Media Matters: Perspectives on Advancing Governance & Development from the Global Forum for Media Development.* Internews/GFMD.

Deane, James, Gray Felder, Denise, Gumucio-Dagron, Alfonso (eds) (forthcoming 2007) *Community Media in the 21st Century: Perspectives and Experiences.* The Communication for Social Change Consortium with AMARC, Swiss Development Cooperation and UNESCO.

DFID (2006) *Making Governance Work for the Poor*, White Paper on International Development. London: DFID.

Friedman, Thomas L (2001) 'Low Tech Democracy' *The New York Times*, 1 May.

Habermas, J (1983 and 1987) *Theory of Communicative Action, Volume 1 and 2.* Boston: Beacon Press.

– (1989) *Structural Transformation of the Public Sphere.* Cambridge, Mass: MIT Press.

– (1998) *Between Facts and Norms.* Cambridge, Mass: MIT Press.

Hadl, Gabi and Hintz, Arne (forthcoming) 'Framing Our Media for Transnational Policy: The World Summit on the Information Society and beyond', in Dorothy Kidd, Clemencia Rodriguez, Laura Stein (eds) *Making Our Media.* Cresskill, NJ: Hampton Press.

Hilton, I (2006) 'Beijing's media chill', Opendemocracy.org, 15 February. http://www.opendemocracy.net/democracy-china/chill_3272.jsp

Hintz, Arne and Milan, Stefania (2006) 'Activist networks in communication governance: Potentials and challenges of their involvement in policy processes', paper presented to the annual conference of the International Association for Media and Communication Research (IAMCR), Cairo, July.

Girard, B (ed) (2005) 'The one to watch: Radio, new ICTs and interactivity'. Rome: FAO and Friedrich Ebert Stiftung.

Gumucio, A (forthcoming 2007) 'Perspectives on twenty-first century community radio in Latin America' in Deane, J (ed), *Community Media in the 21st Century*. Communication for Social Change Consortium with AMARC, Swiss Development Cooperation and UNESCO.

International Telecommunication Union (ITU) (2003) *World Telecommunication Development Report 2003*, Table 1, 19. Geneva: ITU.

Jacobson, T (2006) 'Media Development and Speech in the Public Sphere' in Harvey, M (ed) *Media Matters: Perspectives on Advancing Governance & Development from the Global Forum for Media Development.* Internews/GFMD.

Kellner, D 'Habermas, the Public Sphere, and Democracy: a Critical Intervention'. http://www.gseis.ucla.edu/faculty/kellner/papers/habermas.htm (consulted 3 March 2007).

Khagram, Sanjeev, Riker James V, and Sikkink Kathryn (2002) *Restructuring World Politics: Transnational Social Movements, Networks, and Norms.* Minneapolis: University of Minnesota Press.

MacBride, S (1980) *Many Voices, One World: Towards a New, More Just and More Efficient World Information and Communication Order.* Paris: UNESCO/Kogan Page.

McAdam, Doug, McCarthy John D, and Zald Mayer N (1996) *Comparative perspectives on social movements: political opportunities, mobilizing structures, and cultural framings.* Cambridge: Cambridge University Press.

OECD (2005) 'Paris Declaration on Aid Effectiveness'. www.oecd.org

Open Society Institute (2005) *Television across Europe: Regulation, Policy and Independence.* www.eumap.org

Raboy, Marc, and Landry, Normand (2005) *Civil Society, Communication and Global Governance: Issues from the World Summit on the Information Society.* New York: Peter Lang.

Reporters Without Borders, www.rsf.org (consulted March 8 2007).

Sakyi-Addo K of *JOY FM, Ghana* (2007) presentation at 10th International Roundtable on Communication for Development, 14 February.

Sow, F (fortchoming 2007) 'Community Radio at a Cross roads – A Perspective from Francophone Africa' in Deane, J (ed) *Community radio in the twenty-first century.* Communication for Social Change Consortium with AMARC, Swiss Development Cooperation and UNESCO.

UNDP, Human Development Report 1998. http://hdr.undp.org/reports/global/1998/en/

World Association of Newspapers (2007) 'Newspaper growth defies conventional wisdom', 6 February. http://www.wan-press.org/article12949.html (consulted 8 February 2007).

WSIS, http://www.itu.int/wsis

VOICES OF GLOBAL CIVIL SOCIETY: CARTOONISTS, COMIC STRIP ARTISTS, AND GRAPHIC NOVELISTS

Introduction

Fiona Holland

Their lifeblood is contentious political issues, they are common to many cultures and reach a broad audience. Yet the importance of editorial cartoonists, graphic novelists and comic strip artists is easily overlooked in the study of global civil society - despite, or perhaps because of, the ubiquity of their art form.

Arguably, in an interconnected world, characterised by accelerated and new modes of communication, as well as growing concern about global issues, this graphic form of communication represents an increasingly significant political phenomenon, particularly because it does not rely on language.

Political cartoonists should be considered as important actors in global civil society. Thus, in a Yearbook focused on communicative power and democracy, it is pertinent and timely to highlight their role in provoking debate and catalysing reflection about complex political issues through an eclectic display of cartoons, graphic novel extracts and comic strips that, whether piercing barbs or gentle pokes, are vivid, inventive and compelling.

To that end, we invited contributions and selected works from around the world on seven broad themes of concern to global civil society: Democracy, HIV and AIDS, the Environment, Conflict, Accountability and Transparency of Institutions, Human Rights, and Voices (that is, freedom of expression and the media).

In presenting this diverse selection, we invite readers to consider the following questions, which arose during our discussions about this initiative. What *is* a political cartoon? To what extent are images empowering and have power? How important is this medium of communication in societies with a high degree of illiteracy? Why are there so few women artists? Do cartoons influence people's political priorities and if so, how can we understand this process? What happens in the space between artistic intention and audience interpretation? To what extent can cartooning challenge power holders, particularly in illiberal regimes where the press and freedom of expression may be suppressed?

Ultimately, the key aim of this initiative is to invite discussion and encourage reflection about the role of cartoonists and impact of their work. The debate will continue beyond the pages of the Yearbook in a public exhibition at the London School of Economics and Political Science, 10 October-29 November 2007, and in a series of events at LSE and beyond, between autumn 2007 and spring 2008. For more information, please visit: http://www.lse.ac.uk/Depts/global/2gcsevents.htm

Many people have contributed to this initiative and here we would like to thank those artists who have made this Chapter possible:

Derkaoui Abdellah, Levon Abrahamian, Steve Bell, Thomas Boldt (Tab), Angel Boligan, Cintia Bolio, Matt Bors, Patrick Chappatte, Ali Farzat, Bill Greenhead, Harry Harrison, Hassan Karimzadeh, Keith Knight, Predrag Koraksić (Corax), Andrzej Krauze, Godfrey Mwampembwa (Gado), Paresh Nath, Issa Nyaphaga, Stephane Peray (Stephff), Joe Sacco, Marjane Satrapi, Jonathan Shapiro (Zapiro), Muhammad Zahoor.

Extracts on page 167-169 from *Palestine* by Joe Sacco (Fantagraphics Books 2001), and on 190-193 from *Persepolis: The Story of a Childhood* by Marjane Satrapi (Jonathan Cape 2003).

For advice and assistance, many thanks to Muhammad Altamash, the Yearbook Editorial Committee, Anita O'Brien of the Cartoon Museum, London, and Holli Semetko and Alma Freeman of the Claus M Halle Institute for Global Learning at Emory University. Responsibility for this initiative of course remains with the Yearbook editors.

HEY, THERE'S A LOT OF PEOPLE DOWN THERE...
IS SOMETHING GOING ON?
I want to interject...
I read all about it this morning, didn't I:
It's Silwan, an all-Arab village. A week ago Jewish settlers booted out several Palestinian households, moved in, rolled out the barbed wire, sent up the Star of David... and with Uzis and the Attorney General's green light, who's gonna argue?
AWW, SOMETHING'S ALWAYS GOIN' ON.
And that's why I'm here...
...to see what's going on...
...so I walk down through Dung Gate...
...I walk straight into...
Democracy!
A demonstration!
A counterdemonstration!
A sweet sight for a right-to-assembly nut like me...
Also, I'm a free speech junkie...
And this is Israel!
(okay, annexed land, but let's skip it)
It's 'the Middle East's only democracy'!
And here's both sides of the settler issue for consideration!
PEACE NOW TRAITORS NOW
PEACE NOW
STOP THE SETTLEMENTS
NEGOTIATE
STOP ALL THE SETTLEMENTS

THE WAR ON TERROR

THE WAR ON AIDS

IdiotBOX

Matt Bors

JOHN McCAIN — AIDS MAVERICK

IT'S ALWAYS INTERESTING TO SEE HIM GO AGAINST THE GRAIN. REPORTERS LOB QUESTIONS FIT FOR A THIRD GRADER, THEN SIT BACK AND WATCH THE FUN.

HERE'S ONE FOR YOU, JOHN: **DO CONDOMS HELP PREVENT THE SPREAD OF H.I.V.?**

SNICKER

WHEN QUESTIONING GETS TOO COMPLICATED, McCAIN DEFERS TO THE EXPERTS.

YOU'VE STUMPED ME.

I-I'M SURE I'VE TAKEN A POSITION ON IT IN THE PAST. I HAVE TO FIND OUT WHAT MY POSITION WAS...

I LOOK TO PEOPLE LIKE DR. COBURN. I'M NOT VERY WISE ON IT.

*QUOTE

THE VENERABLE TOM COBURN:

TRICK QUESTION, JOHN. CONDOMS CAN'T PREVENT SOMETHING TRANSMITTED THROUGH THE HAND OF **GOD!**

©2007 WWW.MATTBORS.COM

VOICES OF GLOBAL CIVIL SOCIETY

caglecartoons.com/espanol

GAY MARRIAGE IS AGAINST GOD'S WORD AS HOMOSEXUALITY IS AN ABOMINATION! (LEVITICUS 18:22)

REV. KENNETH MESHOE GIVES THE WORD

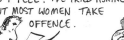

THAT'S PRETTY CLEAR. AS A BIBLICAL AUTHORITY, COULD YOU ADVISE ME ON A FEW OTHER THINGS?

1. WHEN I BURN A BULL ON THE ALTAR, IT IS A PLEASING ODOUR TO THE LORD, BUT MY NEIGHBOURS OBJECT. SHOULD I SMITE THEM?

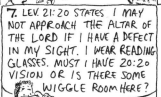

2. IF I SELL MY DAUGHTER INTO SLAVERY AS ALLOWED IN EXODUS 21:7, WHAT IN THIS DAY AND AGE WOULD BE A FAIR PRICE FOR HER?

3. LEV. 15:19 ALLOWS ME NO CONTACT WITH A WOMAN IN HER PERIOD OF MENSTRUAL UNSEEMLINESS. PROBLEM IS, HOW DO I TELL? I'VE TRIED ASKING, BUT MOST WOMEN TAKE OFFENCE.

4. I MAY OWN SLAVES FROM NEIGHBOURING NATIONS (LEV. 25:44). A FRIEND SAYS THIS APPLIES TO ZIMBABWEANS BUT NOT TO BOTSWANANS. WHY CAN'T I OWN BOTSWANANS?

5. MY NEIGHBOUR WORKS ON THE SABBATH. EXODUS 35:2 STATES HE SHOULD BE PUT TO DEATH. MUST I KILL HIM MYSELF?

6. A FRIEND SAYS EATING SHELLFISH IS AN ABOMINATION (LEV. 11:10), BUT A LESSER ONE THAN BEING GAY. I'M NOT SURE. CAN YOU SETTLE THIS?

7. LEV. 21:20 STATES I MAY NOT APPROACH THE ALTAR OF THE LORD IF I HAVE A DEFECT IN MY SIGHT. I WEAR READING GLASSES. MUST I HAVE 20:20 VISION OR IS THERE SOME WIGGLE ROOM HERE?

8. I HAVE HAD MY HAIR CUT, EVEN ROUND THE TEMPLES, THOUGH LEV. 19:27 FORBIDS THIS. CAN I GET EXEMPTION FROM STONING?

9. LEV 11:6 SAYS TOUCHING PIGSKIN MAKES ME UNCLEAN, BUT MAY I STILL PLAY TOUCH RUGBY IF I WEAR GLOVES?

10. MY COUSIN VIOLATES LEV 19:19 BY WEARING GARMENTS MADE OF TWO KINDS OF THREAD (POLY/COTTON). HE ALSO BLASPHEMES A LOT. DOES THE WHOLE TOWN HAVE TO STONE HIM OR COULD WE JUST BURN HIM TO DEATH AT A PRIVATE AFFAIR LIKE WE HAVE TO DO TO PEOPLE WHO SLEEP WITH THEIR IN-LAWS?

I'M SURE YOU CAN CLEAR ALL THIS UP. AND THANKS FOR REMINDING US THAT GOD'S WORD IS ETERNAL AND UNCHANGING!

ZAPIRO
M&G 16-11-06
APOLOGY TO J.KENT ASHCROFT
—adapted and summarized from his letter

OH, ONE MORE THING... ...WHERE DO I FIND LEVITICUS IN THE CONSTITUTION?

No, I am not "torturing" you, I am "de-briefing" you.

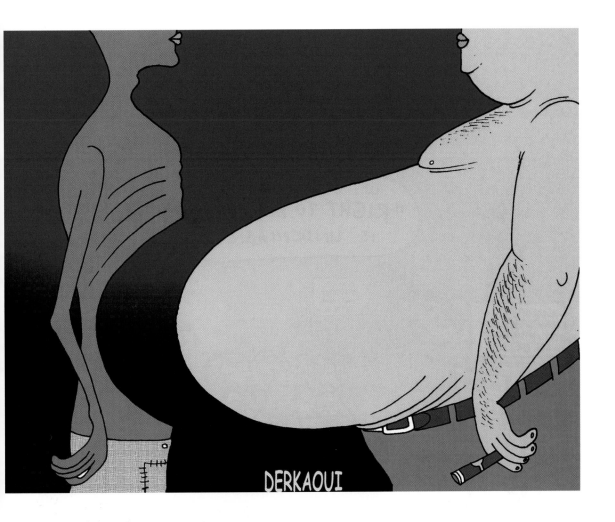

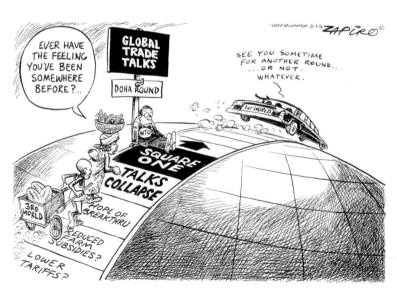

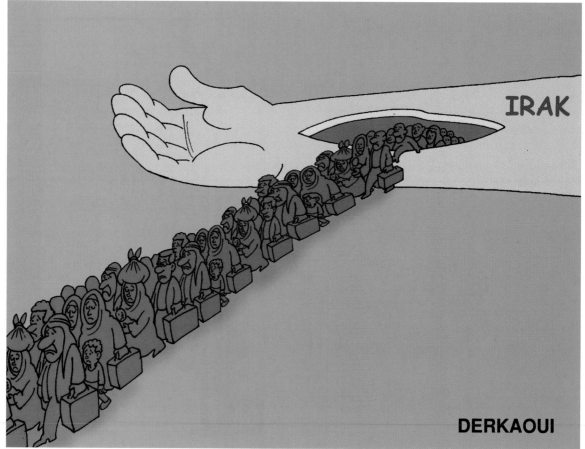

A new form of Warfare:

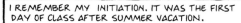

I REMEMBER MY INITIATION. IT WAS THE FIRST DAY OF CLASS AFTER SUMMER VACATION.

WELCOME, GIRLS OF IRAN. THE WAR HAS TAKEN THE FLOWER OF OUR NATION'S YOUTH!

THEN THE LOUDSPEAKERS STARTED TO SING.

BABABABABA ♪ HEY TROOPS OF... BE ♪ READY, ♪ BE READY ♪

LET'S GO CHILDREN, ON THE HEART!

WHACK! WHACK!

AND ALL TOGETHER, WE BEGAN THE SESSION.

IT WASN'T AS BAD AS ONE MIGHT THINK. WE'D SEEN IT BEFORE.

HITTING YOURSELF IS ONE OF THE COUNTRY'S RITUALS. DURING CERTAIN RELIGIOUS CEREMONIES, SOME PEOPLE FLAGELLATED THEMSELVES BRUTALLY.

SOMETIMES EVEN WITH CHAINS.

IT COULD GO VERY FAR.

SOMETIMES IT WAS CONSIDERED A MACHO THING.

AFTER A LITTLE WHILE, NO ONE TOOK THE TORTURE SESSIONS SERIOUSLY ANYMORE. AS FOR ME, I IMMEDIATELY STARTED MAKING FUN OF THEM.

THE MARTYRS! THE MARTYRS!

KILL ME!

SATRAPI! WHAT ARE YOU DOING ON THE GROUND?

I'M SUFFERING, CAN'T YOU SEE?

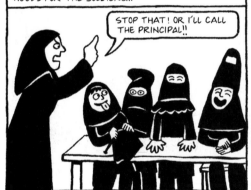

EVERY SITUATION OFFERED AN OPPORTUNITY FOR LAUGHS: LIKE WHEN WE HAD TO KNIT WINTER HOODS FOR THE SOLDIERS...

STOP THAT! OR I'LL CALL THE PRINCIPAL!!

...OR WHEN WE HAD TO DECORATE THE CLASSROOM FOR THE ANNIVERSARY OF THE REVOLUTION...

WHAT ARE THESE GARLANDS?

TOILET PAPER??

YOU'RE AS WORTHLESS AS YOUR DECORATIONS! YOU'RE WORTHLESS!! YOU HEAR ME?! WORTHLESS!!!...

POOPOO

WHO SAID THAT? WHO WAS IT? DOES SHE HAVE THE COURAGE TO STAND UP? IF NOT, YOU'LL ALL BE PUNISHED! WELL? WHO WAS IT??!!?

WE WERE COMPLETELY UNITED.

YOU'RE ALL SUSPENDED FOR A WEEK!

I THINK THAT THE REASON WE WERE SO REBELLIOUS WAS THAT OUR GENERATION HAD KNOWN SECULAR SCHOOLS. OBVIOUSLY, THEY CALLED OUR PARENTS IN.

YOUR CHILDREN HAVE NO RESPECT FOR ANYTHING. NO SELF-CONTROL! THE BASIS OF EDUCATION COMES FROM THE FAMILY!

STOP RIGHT THERE. YOU'RE SAYING THAT WE DON'T KNOW HOW TO EDUCATE OUR CHILDREN?

LISTEN, WE'RE AT WAR. A LOT OF CHILDREN DON'T EVEN HAVE SCHOOL THESE DAYS. YOURS HAVE A RARE OPPORTUNITY. SO YOU SHOULD MAKE SURE THEY'RE WELL-BEHAVED!

WELL-BEHAVED? SO THEY CAN HIT THEMSELVES TWICE A DAY??

SO THEY CAN BE COVERED FROM HEAD TO TOE?

SO THAT THEY CAN BE FORBIDDEN TO PLAY LIKE THE KIDS THEY ARE ??

OH!

ANYWAY, THAT'S HOW IT IS! EITHER THEY OBEY THE LAW, OR THEY'RE EXPELLED!!

AND MAKE SURE THEY WEAR THEIR VEILS CORRECTLY...

IF HAIR IS AS STIMULATING AS YOU SAY, THEN YOU NEED TO SHAVE YOUR MUSTACHE!

MY FATHER ACTUALLY SAID THAT.

CHAPTER 10

MEDIA SPACES: INNOVATION AND ACTIVISM

Clifford Bob, Jonathan Haynes, Victor Pickard, Thomas Keenan and Nick Couldry

Introduction

This Chapter provides an eclectic snapshot of media spaces created by diverse global civil society actors to communicate issues of concern to them and to further their aims. It also catalyses questions about the extent of global civil society's embrace and the characteristics of its members. From the myriad civil society innovations of media spaces and communications technologies around the world, we have selected a kaleidoscope of case studies: advocates of gun control and firearms freedom, Nigerian video-films, Indymedia, and *Jihad* videos, as well as text boxes on film festivals in Africa and political jamming.

The Chapter eschews an exclusive focus on, for example, alternative media in Nick Couldry and James Curran's sense of media production that challenges concentrations of media power (2003). Victor Pickard's analysis of Indymedia does just that. But the Chapter as a whole adopts a broader approach - of media spaces - to explore the extent and variety of global civil society's communicative practices, not all of which have deliberate political intentions, and some of which pursue distinctly undemocratic ends.

Ultimately, the aim is to spotlight the influence of these media spaces on public debate and policy making, or on ideas about identity (whether national, diaspora or religious). To that end, key aspects of these communicative practices are examined: how they are constructed and how they function; the philosophies and values that inform them; the relationships with target audiences, mainstream media and other actors in civil society; and the extent to which they have reclaimed, created anew, or expanded the space for deliberation and debate.

In so doing, two important characteristics of global civil society are highlighted. First, is the creativity of actors, from their adaptation of new technologies and tactical use of mainstream media and political processes, to their art practice, performance and humour. Second is the 'bewildering diversity' of global civil society that, as Nick Couldry points out in the conclusion to this Chapter, encompasses actors from all parts of the political spectrum, whose philosophies, aims and strategies may differ markedly. The diverse array of case studies presented here defies distillation into a single model. Couldry emphasises the importance of linking such communicative practices to processes of decision making if global civil society actors are to have impact and to be sustainable.

Perhaps the most memorable image emanating from this kaleidoscope is that of the public sphere as Play-Doh. But instead of children creating fanciful shapes and strange creatures from this fake dough, it is civil society actors who are constantly kneading, stretching and manipulating it into new communicative forms and expanded media spaces.

Conservative forces, communications and global civil society: towards conflictive democracy

Clifford Bob

In summer 2006, the United Nations faced a major transnational lobbying campaign. In less than a month, it received over 100,000 letters and email messages on a pressing global concern. This rhetorical barrage was not urging action on global warming or the Darfur killings. Rather, the angry writers, mostly members of America's National Rifle Association (NRA), demanded that the UN stop its 'global war' on 'our firearms freedoms' (Stop UN Gun Ban URL). The immediate target was the UN Small Arms Review Conference (RevCon), set up to assess the 2001 Programme of Action on Small Arms, which had established a set of non-binding principles to control illicit arms transfers. But the NRA's involvement in global civil society has been far broader. It has targeted UN activities on small arms and light weapons (SALW) for over a decade, formed linkages with pro–gun organisations in other countries, and actively lobbied the US Congress not only on domestic weapons issues but on overseas arms policy. In so doing, the NRA uses many of the same communication methods as the 'progressive' human rights, environmental, and women's NGOs so closely identified with global civil society. Indeed, while its messages are diametrically opposed to those of the international gun control network, the NRA's communication strategies are quite similar.

Concern over small arms as a global issue first emerged in the early 1990s, as conventional disarmament organisations, domestic gun control groups, UN officials, foundations, and scholars held conferences, began research, and published books on the role of small arms in conflicts and crime worldwide. The NRA and other national gun groups quickly took notice. In 1997, they established a transnational network, the World Forum on the Future of Sport Shooting Activities (WFSA) – two years before pro-control forces formally created the International Action Network on Small Arms (IANSA). WFSA now comprises 38 NGOs from around the world, primarily domestic sporting associations, firearms organisations, and gun manufacturers' groups (WFSA URL). (IANSA claims over 700 member organisations in more than 100 countries, including domestic gun control groups and international development and human rights NGOs [URL]). Just like IANSA, WFSA's most important function is facilitating communication and exchanging ideas through conferences, publications, and a website. As its website declares, WFSA has a 'noble purpose: to further the study, preservation, promotion and protection of sport shooting activities on every continent.' Its 'Project on Myths' refutes 'statistical myths and pseudo-scientific facts' about firearms. Pro-gun groups then use this information to combat control measures. Meanwhile, WFSA's image committee promotes 'a true and accurate portrayal of the time-honored traditions and heritage of sport shooting.' As one part of this, it presents an annual 'Ambassador Award' for a public figure interested in sport shooting who has made the greatest 'social contribution.' The 2006 winner: Italian gun-maker Ugo Gussalli Beretta (WFSA URL).

Most of WFSA's member organisations, like IANSA's, also have vibrant domestic communications networks. The NRA uses books, magazines, radio spots, television programs, and websites to galvanise the four million dues-paying members it claims (LaPierre 2006a: iv). Much of the content now concerns international issues, whether because these are seen as real threats to American gun ownership or as a powerful tool for electrifying the NRA base. NRA Executive Vice President Wayne LaPierre's 2006 book,

The Global War on Your Guns: Inside the UN Plan to Destroy the Bill of Rights, released months before the RevCon, included lengthy chapters attacking the world's 'anti-gunners' and arguing that tragedies like the Rwandan genocide would not have happened if Tutsis had owned guns. One of the NRA's membership magazines, *America's 1st Freedom*, which consistently highlights international issues, recently featured the failures of Australia's strict firearms laws, and an interview with a Brazilian who helped defeat a national referendum banning handgun sales to the country's citizens (see Chapter 6: 120 of this volume). In addition to these mainstream communications technologies, the NRA has a sophisticated website (much of it available in Spanish and English), making its views accessible in print, webcast, and blog not only to members but to gun owners worldwide. While building this foreign following, the NRA also raises international awareness among its domestic constituency, which the American media often stereotypes as 'Red state' and 'redneck'. In short, the NRA is transforming red-blooded American gun owners into a special brand of armed, global citizens. As LaPierre has written, 'let the roar of our voices be heard by all nations, United or not: If you cannot respect our Bill of Rights, you'd best keep your hands off it' (2006a: 226).

In addition to informing and inflaming the pro-gun base, these 'autonomous communication spaces' help WFSA and the NRA influence domestic and global gun policy, which they see as intertwined. WFSA has roster consultative status with the Economic and Social

MEDIA SPACES

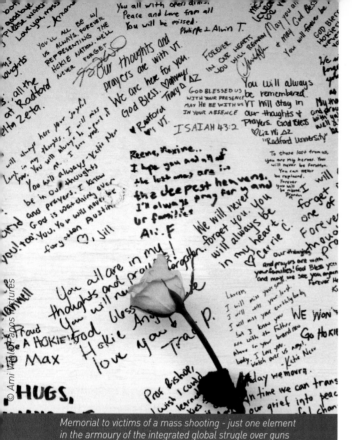

Memorial to victims of a mass shooting - just one element in the armoury of the integrated global struggle over guns

Council, and its member organisations have for years fought IANSA and UN efforts to control trade in small arms. This has included engaging directly with the 'enemy,' not only through research rebutting the pro-control network's ideas, but also through public confrontations, most prominently the 'Great Gun Debate,' an internationally-televised encounter between LaPierre and IANSA Director Rebecca Peters in 2004 (see Box 10.1; both sides now use DVDs or transcripts of the 'Great Debate' to illustrate the dire threat their constituents face). At UN conferences, both pro-control and pro-gun groups seek to shape discourse and shift agendas, using information kits, press releases, and speeches. Representatives from WFSA member organisations, including the NRA, have won seats on country delegations and vigorously lobby other delegates. And both sides have drummed up 'grassroots' campaigns aimed at influencing the UN and attracting media attention. For instance, the July 2006 letter-writing onslaught would have been difficult without the NRA's 'Stop the UN Gun Ban' website, which included pre-written letters available for immediate download and mailing to Kofi Annan, John Bolton, and the chairman of the RevCon. For its part, IANSA and the associated Control Arms group

mounted their own 'Million Faces' campaign, which submitted a photographic petition - said to include over one million participants from more than 160 countries - urging the UN to adopt global arms export standards (Control Arms URL). Ultimately, the RevCon ended in failure, with no action to extend the 2001 Programme of Action's purely voluntary 'goals', themselves the result of US government 'redlines' supported by the NRA.

But the UN is only one arena for this transnational gun activism. Like IANSA, the NRA scours the world for gun-related issues to use in its fundraising and policymaking efforts. In this integrated global struggle, everything from a school shooting in Pennsylvania, and a paramilitary massacre in Bougainville, Papua New Guinea, to the Holocaust is likely to turn up in the contending networks' campaigns. Reciprocally, local groups facing gun control threats at home regularly seek NRA and WFSA aid, just as those suffering gun violence often turn to IANSA. The Brazilian referendum was only a recent example of a pattern visible also in places as far-flung as South Africa, Japan, and Great Britain.

Much of the conflict between pro-gun and pro-control forces is vicious. The groups critique one another's policy positions and allege deception and misrepresentation. Personal attacks are common. So are efforts to exclude the other side from participation or to de-legitimate institutions in which it appears to be making gains. Yet despite contradictory content, the framing of the contending sides' messages, like their media strategies, is quite similar. Both networks portray themselves as moral actors representing the global public interest. Both mix scientific studies and rational arguments with emotional, even histrionic, appeals to their own constituents. Both portray their opponents as so misguided, self-interested, deceitful, even evil, that persuasion, debate, and compromise is impossible. Both identify powerful, shadowy and suspect sources as their foes' bankrollers: for IANSA, the global gun industry is the dark force behind WFSA; for the NRA, George Soros is IANSA's 'sugar daddy,' along with a 'broad collection of left-wing foundations' and European governments (La Pierre 2006a: 8, 11). Both sides seek to strip each other's networks of more moderate members. And both sides highlight the other sides' missteps. For instance, in early 2007 a leaked draft of an NRA fundraising pamphlet, 'Freedom in Peril' drew media accusations of xenophobia, extremism, and racism. In a milder passage, it described the UN and IANSA as 'part of a marching axis of adversaries far darker and more dangerous than gun owners have ever known' (NRA 2007: 1). IANSA quickly responded by placing a link to the online version of this 'scathing attack on gun control advocates, NGOs, the United Nations, feminists and the media' on its website (IANSA 2007). For its part, the NRA has festooned its attacks on IANSA with unflattering outtakes of Rebecca Peters, taken from the 'Great Gun Debate' (LaPierre 2006b; see Box 10.1).

All of this raises questions about how communication technologies affect global democracy - and the nature of global civil society itself. In some ways, the entry of groups such as the NRA and WFSA into the global arena makes for greater democracy. New voices add to the marketplace of ideas. Theorists of global civil society need to open their eyes to this diversity and its implications for democratic practice. For too long, progressive NGOs have identified themselves as 'global civil society,' and sympathetic academics have fueled this perception (Wapner 1996). On this narrow empirical base, elaborate theories of transnational politics have then been erected. This creates the impression that global civil society is thick with like-minded groups harmoniously cooperating to fight corporate greed and state power: they may disagree over strategy, but all fundamentally agree about the world's problems.

The reality is more complex. In many cases, one NGO's solution may be another's problem. Their autonomous and largely closed communication networks make it easy for the rhetorical temperature to rise. Once unleashed, the blogs of war quickly create distrust among contending networks. As a result, direct confrontations, in print or in person, resemble a slanging match more than the rational deliberation and respectful dialogue so dear to many theorists of national and international democracy (Risse 2000; Habermas 2001; Dworkin 2006). Often these controversies serve important purposes for the protagonists: stoking attention to their issues, mobilising their base of support, demonstrating their fighting skills, and securing their organisational leadership. Because activists seek to influence policymakers, rather than making authoritative policy decisions themselves, most have few incentives to restrain their demands or compromise with their foes. At best, political realities may sometimes compel moderation. But with promulgation of new policies and evolving power relations, the opposing sides continue their dueling indefinitely.

For those who view deliberation and dialogue as central to democracy, this strife is troubling. Yet it need not spell the futility of democratic practice at the global level. Indeed, this contentious international reality closely resembles the raucousness of democratic politics within nations. The diversity of values in contemporary societies, and their proponents' passion for them, mean that staid debate signals either an issue's triviality - or the subtle workings of hegemonic power. Instead, what cases like the global small arms and light weapons contest suggest are problems with deliberative democracy theory, both empirically and normatively. Clashes are endemic not just to gun control, but to any number of other global issues, from climate change to family planning. Democratic practice, difficult enough at the global level, must accommodate these profound divergences and the brawling tactics they spur. In turn, democratic theorists must use new tools to understand these realities and strengthen global politics in the face of profound disagreement. While some may cover their ears and wring their hands at the din, it is and always has been a hallmark of political debate. Indeed, as Chantal Mouffe (2005) argues, such conflict is the essence of the political both in domestic and in global arenas.

Notably, however, civil society's conflictive nature does not in itself make it democratic. Neither does the use of communication technologies by all sides in contentious debates. Global civil society remains primarily an arena of elite, not mass, politics. While new communication networks bring a small segment of the public in closer touch with international institutions and issues, the vast majority remain outside the charmed circle (Bob 2005). And even for those inside, the unelected leadership of WFSA, IANSA, and their component organisations, does not represent the 'popular will' or the 'global interest,' notwithstanding declarations to the contrary. Of course, in some ways this too is not fundamentally different from politics in large modern democracies. Professional interest groups dominate and occasional elections provide only the briefest windows for popular preferences to be expressed. But while this may diminish democracies (Skocpol 2003), it does not kill them. The result, democracy with deficits of various degrees, may be the most we can expect at global and national levels.

Box 10.1: The 'Great Gun Debate'

On 12 October 2004 IANSA Director Rebecca Peters and NRA Executive Vice-President Wayne LaPierre went head to head in the 'Great Gun Debate', held at London's King's College and broadcast on pay-per-view television in the US. In the wake of the debate, both sides have used it for their own purposes. An edited transcript is available on the IANSA website, and DVDs of the debate are available from both organisations. Here, extracts provide a flavour of the debate.

Moderator: Do you believe, as you said in the past, that semiautomatic rifles and shotguns have no legitimate role in civilian hands?

Peters: Yes, I do. Semiautomatic weapons are designed to kill large numbers of people. They were designed for military use. Many people have bought them for other purposes, for example, for hunting because they've been available. But there's no justification for semiautomatic weapons to be owned by civilian by members of the civilian population. . . . And not only that, handguns have no legitimate role in civilian hands....

LaPierre: The fact is Ms Peters and IANSA and her UN crowd believe every firearm has no legitimate use. Not just semi-autos but pump actions, shotguns, and any rifle that can shoot over 100 yards. Hunters know that's every hunting rifle out there. Handguns. She doesn't believe handguns have any legitimate use. The truth is there's no such thing as a legitimate role for a firearm. Isn't that your real opinion?

Peters: No. We recognise that hunting, for example, plays an important role in many cultures. You do not need a semiautomatic firearm; you do not need a handgun to kill a deer, to go hunting. We recognise that target shooting is also a sport in many countries. . . You can be a sporting nation without semiautomatic rifles or handguns.

Moderator: How has the NRA been involved in the UN small arms process? In terms of negotiating with the UN how successful have you been?

LaPierre: I think our participation in every way should be defined as the fact we oppose IANSA and the UN's attempt to weaken our Second Amendment to the Constitution of the United States. We're going to get in your way. We're going to fight you folks at every turn. At IANSA, the way we see it, the average people we represent, it's a club of unselected elitists accountable to no one. Our involvement shouldn't be defined as a participant. Our involvement is in opposition. I mean we intend to defeat your intrusion. You want to take foreign money. I know you got George Soros funding IANSA. You've got a bunch of tax-exempt foundations, and you have money from the United Kingdom, by the way, and Norway and Belgium, and a lot of it flowing into IANSA to try to change policy in the United States.

Moderator: Is there a way that the UN would welcome the NRA in . . . this negotiation?

Peters: Well, the NRA has been very involved. As I've said they've had a great deal of influence there. And they do bring some technical knowledge to the process. But that answer of Mr LaPierre sort of demonstrates for me one part of the problem is the preoccupation that Americans have that the world is America. The purpose of IANSA and of activists around the world, in relation to the UN's small arms process, relates to the UN, it relates to the world. . . . And for most people on Earth the rights of Americans are important, but others peoples rights count too. . . . We recently pointed out that governments have an obligation to protect the human rights of their citizens by restricting the proliferation of small arms. They're killing hundreds of thousands of people a year. These are real weapons of mass destruction.

Audience questions: Why do you place such unquestioning trust in governments and the United Nations when you clearly do not trust individuals for the best way to protect themselves and their families?

Peters B: It's called civilisation. Individuals come together. They form societies. They form governments. That's part of the contract that we make. It's a long time gone now since Thomas Hobbes described society as being characterised by a continual fear and danger of violent death and the life of man is solitary, poor, nasty, brutish and short. I have confidence that people coming together into countries are going to operate better than a whole lot of individuals making up their own rules, taking the law into their own hands.

Q: I would like to ask why do you want to export American gun culture to the rest of the world?

LaPierre: . . . What we really are is we're a freedom culture. That's what we're about. We're about the fact that if Ms Peters goes and visits her friend . . . where there are three babies, and there's a knock on the door. You hear somebody. Not a knock, but a pounding on the door. And you hear breaking glass. And someone is coming in that house, either in Australia or here in the U.K. What's she going to do? What does she propose? Is she an expert in martial arts? What gives her that chance to live? That equaliser is the right to have a firearm to protect yourself. And she's got no answer for that. It's global government, some social fantasy. They're going to protect everybody. She's not going to be there at the scene of the crime. She'll be in London or New York or somewhere else. That victim will be there, and that's who I'm concerned about. And that victim ought to always have the choice, whether in the UK or the United States. Rwanda, by the way, how many millions died by machetes? She talked about Rwanda when the UN tuck-tailed and ran. Millions died by machetes. You bet a lot of those individual people in Rwanda would've liked to have a firearm there. It's a freedom we're talking about.

Source: http://www.iansa.org/

Nigerian videos, at home and abroad

Jonathan Haynes

The Nigerian video film industry is now widely recognised as the third largest in the world (for general descriptions, see Haynes 2000 and Barrot 2005). It has done what no film industry in sub-Saharan Africa has ever come close to doing, which is to dominate audio-visual entertainment in its own national market. It has also acquired a remarkable international dimension. Nigerian films are on sale as video cassettes and video compact discs across Africa, and in many places they are regularly broadcast on television. They have followed Nigerians into the African diaspora in Europe, the United States, and elsewhere, and have expanded their audience well beyond the African communities there. Nigerian films are the staple of African Magic, a South African-owned satellite channel with more than a million subscribers in Africa, the Middle East, and Europe. Nigerian films can be bought from dozens of websites in the US, Canada, and Europe and can be streamed from the Internet. The influence of Nigerian films has gone beyond their consumption: they have seeded production of similar films in the Nigerian diaspora in Europe and North America (Haynes 2003a) and in many places in Africa, where they serve as a model and an inspiration for local filmmakers. In several African countries, Nigerians have been involved in co-productions with local artists who are eager to profit from their experience and from their star power (Haynes 2005).

The basis on which all this has grown up is, in comparison with other film industries, peculiar. Nigerian video film production began with artists from the Yoruba traveling theatre tradition, which Biodun Jeyifo (1984) and Karin Barber (1987; 2000) have described as a central instance of the 'African popular arts.' These arts, which include such other forms as popular music and painted decorations on trucks, are produced by and for the heterogeneous masses of African cities. Like other informal sector businesses, they require little capital or technical education, and so are open to all comers, resulting in a crowded and extremely competitive field. Formal sector institutions - the government, banks, and so forth - are largely irrelevant. Socially and culturally, artists of this kind feel themselves to be mediators between the rural/local/'traditional' and the urban/Western/'modern.' In order to survive, they must be in very close touch with popular tastes and desires.

In contrast to the apparatus of cinema, which is capital-intensive and requires considerable technical expertise, and therefore, in the African context, normally requires governmental or foreign support, video technology is cheap, easy to operate, and fits perfectly into the generative structure of the popular arts. This remains the essential structure of Nigerian video production (Haynes and Okome 1998), even though the national marketing of Nigerian films in Igbo and English that took off in the early 1990s was the result of an infusion of personnel from the soap operas made for national television - a more 'formal' environment. The film industry now provides steady work for thousands of people, some of them trained professionals and some who have learned on the job, and it remains open to anyone who can get his or her hands on a video camera. The lack of professional standards is frequently bemoaned by those inside and outside the industry, though the films' grassroots character has also been a source of vitality. The rate of production is now over 1,500 films a year; President Olusegun Obasanjo mentioned the video industry as an important part of the national economy in his 2004 Budget Speech; banks, foreign embassies, and American media conglomerates are now hovering in the wings, trying to figure out how to get involved; but the industry is still based entirely on tiny capital formations. The average budget for a video film is about US $20,000, and almost none run to more than $100,000.

What holds the industry at this level is the extremely leaky distribution system, beset by piracy. Brian Larkin points out that the Nigerian video film industry was actually built on an infrastructure of reproduction and marketing that was created to pirate American, Indian, and Chinese films. Claiming a space for legitimate, regulated commerce is uphill work and the government has been of limited help. As Larkin argues, Nigerian videos are not a case of 'tactical media' in opposition to a mainstream one, but a system that parallels, overlaps, and competes with legitimate media (Larkin 2004). The videos are now the mainstream, having achieved parity with the broadcast media and the press in their hold on the nation's attention. The clear aspiration on the part of everyone in the video film industry is for it to be a mass entertainment business. The extent to which this is a commercial phenomenon and nothing else can hardly be exaggerated. For better and for worse, the videos have no non-commercial dimension, which might allow for more art for art's sake and for a more concerted political orientation (as with African celluloid filmmaking, with its crucial international support), but which might also constrain their nature.

The videos have been an unparalleled success at two classic nationalist projects: import substitution and the projection of a national image in answer to Western media domination and stereotyping. The nationalist mantle has been passed to them perforce, but only with great reluctance and after years of abuse by those in positions of cultural and official power, who saw the video films as technically and artistically sub-standard and as a national embarrassment in their strong tendencies both to imitate Hollywood films and, conversely, to dwell obsessively on dark magical practices, crime, polygamy, and other blemishes on the national image.

As Pierre Barrot points out, the Nigerian film industry is not escapist, as are most other mass entertainment industries. The videos are preoccupied with social problems and motivated by social anxieties. Barrot also suggests that the privacy of the 'home videos' (as they are often called in Nigeria) permits their freedom of expression, even under military rule: because they are primarily viewed in domestic space, they do not provoke the same type of public debates or questions of social responsibility that television programmes or articles in the press would do. 'The only regulatory authority that counts is the consumer himself, who is free to buy or not' (Barrot 2005: 52-53, my translation).

The videos have inherited the 'progressive conservatism' of the Nigerian popular arts (Barber 1987). They are seldom militant in the manner of much of African celluloid cinema, as they do not spring from an activist intellectual class and Nigeria does not have an ideologically coherent political opposition (though see Haynes 2003b). But they have mounted a broad political critique of the ruling elite and of the state of the nation through the forms of popular culture, including, for instance, discourses about the occult,[1] and have treated political matters with increasing directness since the end of military rule in 1999 (Haynes 2006).

Video film production reproduces the major cultural, religious and political division in Nigeria between the Muslim-dominated north and the mainly Christian

On the 'set' in Lagos

© Jacob Silberberg/Panos Pictures

south. Northern Nigeria has its own film industry, mostly based in Kano, which makes films in Hausa (Larkin 1997 2000; Y Adamu 2002; A Adamu et al. 2004). To a remarkable degree, it is a separate phenomenon in terms of production and distribution networks and of aesthetics: the foreign influence that matters most is Bollywood rather than Hollywood, for example. Hausa films have always been surrounded by debates about what was allowable in Hausa culture and in Islam; the introduction of *Shari'a* law in the northern states has hardened the differences with the frequently scandalous English-language films, leading Kano State to institute its own censorship code that forbids any touching between the sexes. To a considerable extent Hausa films are a conscious reaction against English-language Nigerian films and the culture they represent; in southern Nigeria, on the other hand, English-language filmmakers think of their industry as 'Nigerian,' that is to say, national, but there is hardly any consciousness of Hausa films at all. That Nigeria's film culture is so deeply riven is strong evidence of the fragility of the nation.

Northern Nigeria also provides the most dramatic example of the gendered effects of video technology. Respectable women in Hausa society do not go out to cinemas and so they were almost entirely shut out of film culture until the advent of the VCR allowed for viewing in the privacy of home. Hausa video films are sometimes known as 'women's films' because women are the heart of their viewership (Larkin 1997; 2000). All over Nigeria women are considered to be the principle consumers of video films and the ones who most often make decisions about what films to watch. The films have an affinity with domestic space: family melodrama is the predominant form, and the small screens for which they are made favour interior scenes and close-ups.

---

[1] *On occult discourses and modern forms of power, see especially Comaroff and Comaroff 1993, 1999; Geschiere 1997*

'Nollywood' films for sale in Lagos

©Jacob Silberberg/Panos Pictures

In southern Nigeria, artists from the venerable Yoruba traveling theatre tradition maintain a sturdy market share with their videos. To some extent their personnel, themes, and audience overlap with those of the dominant English-language industry, which is largely controlled by Igbo marketers but staffed by people from all the southern ethnicities. Igbo-language production waxes and wanes, and there have been a scattering of films made in Nupe, Efik, Urhobo, Itsekeri, Edo, and other languages, often with financial support from local communities eager to express their ethnic pride in this medium. But 'Nollywood', as the English-language industry has become known, submerges and eclipses such micro-nationalist productions. Business calculations encourage filmmakers to aim at the English-language market, which is the largest. This has led to the creation, through thousands of films, of a shared national image: a set of stereotyped characters, standard images of city and village, common symbols, and typical narratives.

Films in languages other than English have their own export networks, but it is Nollywood films that have had the massive international impact. We need dozens of fieldwork studies of their reception to establish what they mean in the varied contexts in which they are viewed. On television in the Democratic Republic of Congo and in modest video parlours serving the poor in Kenya, interpreters provide translations into local languages and explanations based in local meanings - what are they saying? What influence has the Nigerian example had on the new spate of Wolof-language videos in Senegal? Why the mania for Nigerian films in Guyana and Surinam?

For Nigerians in North America and Europe, the films provide images of home and a means of maintaining their cultural identity within their domestic space, passing that identity on to the next generation, and sharing it with friends. For other Africans abroad, the films provide images of a generalised African modernity and (through the genre of the 'cultural epic') of an African usable past, and express values more like their own than any other available entertainment. Nigerian videos are bolder, more horrifying, and more titillating than any other African culture probably could or would produce, but this extremity helps to sell films. Nollywood is doubtless a homogenising force in the African diaspora.

In the Brooklyn neighborhood where I teach, vendors of Nigerian films report that their biggest customers are African-Americans and Caribbean immigrants. The Caribbean immigrants may feel at home with Nollywood's Third World ethos and production values, but it is remarkable that African-Americans would choose these films, given all their other choices in the saturated American media environment, where movies commonly have $25 million advertising budgets - enough money to finance a thousand Nigerian productions. Nigerian films are never advertised, apart from the trailers included with the films themselves and the occasional film poster in the shops where they are sold, normally shops whose original and main business is selling shoes, electronics, or something else. Often a video monitor sits on the counter, showing a new film, and the salesperson behind the counter offers guidance as each week's wave of new releases washes through the rack behind him. Word of mouth is obviously crucial in moving particular films and in creating interest in the films in general, but the conversations are all private: there are no public spaces associated with Nigerian films.

Barrot claims that the fundamental fact about the Nigerian video industry is the desire of its audience for its own proper form of entertainment, which conjured the whole business into existence with the slenderest of means (Barrot 2005). He means the Nigerian audience, but the point is equally valid, if in a more mysterious way, in Brooklyn and everywhere else. I have written about how badly Nigerian videos fit with the desires of the established North American audience for celluloid African films, including its African-American component, which typically wants images of Africa that convey dignity, cultural richness and purity, and a humane and politically sophisticated response to the continent's misery (Haynes 2000). Classic forms of Afrocentricity might draw African-Americans to Nollywood but probably would not keep them there. A rougher, thoroughly urbanised, actually existing Pan-Africanism sends gangsta rap one way across the 'Black Atlantic' (Gilroy 1993) and Nollywood back the other.

The films' appeal beyond racial boundaries to a wider audience, primarily of immigrants from the Third World, requires an explanation beyond identity politics. The films are rooted in anxiety, the anxiety of a population living in or perched precariously over an abyss of poverty, in a turbulent, aleatory world without a safety net, constantly threatened by violent crime, written off by the authorities, shut out of meaningful political participation by a thoroughly corrupt system, caught in a strong tension between the moral standards of an ancestral village or newer ones based in Pentecostal Christianity and a merciless, amoral urban environment where intimate relationships are stressed and broken by betrayals, witchcraft, temptations of the flesh, and tricks of fate. At the same time fabulous wealth is always visible on the horizon, images of consumer goods rain down on everyone, and a lucky or ruthless few, perhaps able to channel strange hidden powers, are plucked suddenly by fortune into the elite. This is Nigeria, but it is Brooklyn too, and any world city; Nigerian films turn this situation into addictive melodramas, enlivened with laughter and dreams of love, in which much of the world can see itself.

The Indymedia model: strengths and weaknesses of a radical democratic experiment

Victor Pickard

The past decade has witnessed an emergence of global civil society groups defined by their reliance on participatory practices (Polletta 2002), Internet strategies (Pickard, forthcoming), and network social structures (Castells 1996). Indymedia exemplifies all of these trends. What sets Indymedia apart, however, is its commitment to radical democratic practices at both the local organisational and global network levels. The following case study addresses Indymedia's origins, innovations, strengths and weaknesses, and recent developments.

The rise of Indymedia

The November 1999 World Trade Organization protests, a series of events known as 'The Battle of Seattle', left an enduring institutional legacy in the form of the Independent Media Center (IMC, popularly referred to as 'Indymedia'). Emerging from within the global justice movement, Indymedia's roots trace back at least as far as the 1990s media democracy movement, inspired by alternative media groups like Paper Tiger, Free Speech TV, and Accion Zapatista. According to veteran media activist and scholar Dee Dee Halleck, with Indymedia, 'Many different streams came together: the video activist community, microradio pirates, the computer hacker/code writers, the 'zine makers, and the punk music world' (2002: 417-418). Jeff Perlstein, one of the Indymedia co-founders, saw the original idea as using media, especially the Internet, as an activist tool for community self-expression, particularly in under-represented communities. Wanting to challenge the corporate news monopoly on telling their stories, Perlstein says Indymedia's aim was to create 'alternative networks' and a 'community-based people's newsroom' (2001). The original project, then, was to 'be the media' based on radical democratic principles and practices. In its expansion across six continents, the Indymedia movement has since merged with a broad array of local and global struggles and developed new variants, though many of its original objectives remain relatively constant across the evolving network.

The Indymedia model

The IMC model is distinguished by an interactive news website, a global network, and a radical democratic organisation replicated in over 150 sites across six continents (Pickard 2006b). Past scholarship established Indymedia as an anarchic or radical democratic model based on openness, inclusiveness, lateral decision making, non-hierarchy, global justice, and transparency (Downing 2001; Dorothy Kidd 2002; Pickard 2006a). Though one should not over-generalise the distributed and diverse IMC global network, there is remarkable uniformity reflected in common website architecture, a commitment to organisational processes such as consensus-based decision making, and other radical democratic practices codified in a shared manifesto or charter called the 'principles of unity'.

Indymedia first distinguished itself as a radical democratic experiment by its 'open-publishing'

Box 10.2: The African film festival – local entertainment/transnational engagement

For the last seven years, activist Spanish filmmakers have organised the Sahara International Film Festival (SIFF) in Ausserd refugee camp on the border of Algeria and the Western Sahara to raise awareness of the plight of the Saharawi people. In 1976, just after Spain ceded its colony to Moroccan administration, Western Sahara's Polisario Front created a government in exile – the Saharawi Arab Democratic Republic (SADR) – in refugee camps south of the Algerian border town of Tindouf (Wikipedia URL). The Saharawi people wait in these camps with the hope that they will one day be able to return home to the Western Sahara.

At first glance of the sleek SIFF website, the grim reality of life in a border camp is hard to discern. However, SIFF shares a socialist ideology with the films and techniques of filmmakers influenced by 'revolutionary struggles against Neocolonialism that inspired Third Cinema'(Guneratne 2003). Wayne explains the nature and significance of Third Cinema:

> Above all [Third Cinema] designates a body of theory and filmmaking practice committed to social and cultural emancipation. This body of filmmaking is small, indeed tiny, in terms of world cinema output. Yet Third Cinema films are amongst the most exciting and challenging films ever to be made, their political and cultural significance amplified by there proximity and intervention into the major historical processes of the epoch. Third Cinema can work with different forms of documentary and across the range of fictional genres. It challenges both the way cinema is conventionally made (for example, it has pioneered collective and democratic production methods) and the way it is consumed. (Wayne 2001: 5)

In 1970 the Federation of Pan-African Filmmakers (FEPACI) was formed by a small group of intellectuals, the pioneers of African cinema, during the Carthage Film Days in Tunisia, the longest-running film festival on the continent (URL). In 1975 in Algiers, the Charter of African Filmmakers was drafted at the Second FEPACI Congress in an effort to consolidate the role of film in the political, economic, and cultural development of post-colonial African countries (URL). While theoretically under conceptualised, Third Cinema does imply a role for civil society in that 'a cinema of social and cultural emancipation cannot be achieved merely in the political realm of the state' (Wayne 2001).

Today there are between 30 and 40 film festivals in African countries, some annual, others occasional. Often they are hybridised by a variety of users – filmmakers, audience members, and activists in the case of SIFF – whose participation imbues each festival with a different intention, character and outcome. In Event Places, Sabate states that festivals 'are rooted in their place and in turn are place transforming' (2004). For Africa, film festivals have the potential to counter-balance the piracy[1] and informal screenings that constitute the dominant film-viewing experience across the continent. At the same time local filmmakers have an opportunity to meet other film professionals who come from around the world, and thereby expose their work to regional and international entertainment markets. With their convivial nature, festivals often serve as a point of negotiation around sparse distribution networks and contradictory conditions for intellectual property rights, which make it difficult for African filmmakers to profit from screenings in other African countries.

Despite this market orientation, African film festivals often reflect a historical thread connecting ideas of Pan-Africanism and the political project of the Organization of African Unity (now the African Union) with Third Cinema, a theory of film defined by its socialist politics more than its geography (Gabriel 1982).

Stephen Crofts states that the 'export of a given text may shift its variety, as in the common recycling of films from Third and totalitarian cinemas as art cinema' (quoted in Hill & Church 2000). In this way, the staging of SIFF exhibits the versatility of the film festival as a popular Western media format that can 'shift its variety' to become a tool of activism, which in this case moves in the opposite direction from Crofts' idea. This hints at new – and multi-directional – possibilities for the flow of ideas in an era that is termed both post-colonial and neo-colonial. Other examples of film festivals and festival sites with such versatility include:

---

1   *Western audiences may understand this from popular reporting on Nigeria (and Nollywood), and it is endemic in many African countries.*

Rwanda Film Festival – a site of healing

At the 2005 inaugural Rwanda Film Festival (URL) a university theatre in the city of Butare held the first local screening of 'Shake Hands with the Devil', a documentary in which Lieutenant-General Roméo Dallaire, former Force Commander of the UN Mission to Rwanda, publicly apologises for the genocide that had taken place on the same university campus some years earlier. Many of the university students were too young to have witnessed Dallaire's original statement.

Imagine Institute – a site of heritage

Alongside the French-supported Pan-African Film and Television Festival of Ouagadougou (FESPACO URL), Burkinabe director Gaston Kaboré has established the Imagine Institute (URL) for film students in Ouagadougou. 'I believe that a society that is confronted with images and values from abroad on a daily basis will eventually lose its identity and the ability to choose its own destination. Imagine [Institute] is an attempt to wake us up and to keep our inner ears and eyes wide open' (quoted in Vlam n.d).

Zanzibar International Film Festival – a site of collaboration

On the coast of East Africa, the Zanzibar International Film Festival (ZIFF URL) hosts regular meetings of the East African Filmmakers Forum in order to discuss regional cooperation and co-production opportunities, and to embed a regional network of professional organisations and individuals. There are many advantages to a unified approach in East Africa, where there is popular demand for film and television programs in the language Kiswahili.

Many African film festivals are sponsored, at least in part, by philanthropic foundations, multinational corporations, and former colonial governments, which requires the reconciliation of a range of political and economic agendas. ZIFF embodies the dualism of many African festivals, as Anthony explains:

This support was advertised by banners that flew visibly from the heights of the House of Wonders. In this financial sense, therefore, the African Film Festival can be seen as at least partially an extension of globalism in so far as the political economy of film continues to be dominated by Western capital.
(Anthony 2005: 19)

Julia Galindo, of the Polytechnic University of Catalonia, says the festival format 'represents a moment of activity that reflects the social situation at its most exalted point' (quoted in Haskell 2006). With human rights themes such as forced migration, sexual identity, the environment, technological advances, and a generational shift to student festivals and those devoted to short films, the landscape for screening films in Africa holds a pan-continental significance, fiercely dependent and crucial to human development. Wayne echoes this significance and levies is equally between filmmakers and audience:

Social and cultural emancipation needs a much more fundamental and pervasive transformation, and if cinema is to make its own, relatively modest contribution, it too must feel the heat of such transformations, not only as films, but in its modes of production and reception (Wayne 2001:1).

Todd Lester, freeDimensional.net

software, allowing anyone with Internet access to post his or her own news stories for immediate upload onto an IMC website's newswire. Its user-driven news production, collective editing, and open source technology, placed Indymedia in the twenty-first century vanguard for experimenting with Internet-amplified democratic processes. Though the rise of the blogosphere and other facets of the Web 2.0 now eclipse some of its early innovations, Indymedia's radical participatory democracy and global reach continue to make it one of the more significant models to emerge from the Internet. Open source technology and collective editing via wikis further evidence Indymedia's radical democratic model. But Indymedia's most remarkable contribution is arguably its commitment to radical democratic practice, exemplified by consensus based decision-making at the local and global network levels.

The original Seattle IMC followed a spokes council model implemented during the 1999 WTO protests by the Direct Action Network (DAN), a loose coalition of activist groups. With roots in anarchic traditions, the spokes council model empowers small groups to coordinate via temporary representatives. Mediating between autonomous affinity groups, or nodes within a network, this model operates both at the local IMC collective and the global network levels. Based on the notion that sustainability for large networks like Indymedia requires a less bureaucratic and more collectivist system, many IMCs rely on a non-hierarchical collective of smaller volunteer collectives, such as editorial, finance, and tech working groups. New ad-hoc groups may spring up spontaneously to face a particular challenge, though a reliance on volunteer labour makes all IMC collectives prone to activist fatigue. While some IMCs maintain physical spaces where members regularly meet, many issues discussed during face-to-face meetings are negotiated as much - if not more - online. Online discussions take place at the local level on any number of working group or general membership listservs. Network-wide discussions usually unfold over several listservs dedicated to global level discussions, such as 'Communications', 'Finance', 'New IMC' and 'Process'.

All IMCs are mandated by the principles of unity to utilise some form of consensus decision making. The success of this non-hierarchical form of deliberation is based on patient, process-laden discussion, and strong interpersonal relationships founded on trust. At the

Seattle IMC, the consensus process was outlined in a website-linked document entitled 'Detailed Description of Consensus Decision Making', from the online publication, *On Conflict and Consensus* (Butler & Rothstein 1987). Generally, consensus is understood to mean that everyone feels his or her input was considered in the decision-making process. The Seattle IMC's meetings allowed for several levels of consensus and ways to register dissent without derailing the process, including 'reservations' (have concerns), 'non-support' or a state of 'non-disagreement' (the person sees no need for the decision), or 'stand aside' (it may be a mistake, but a person can accept it). Making a 'block' indicates that the person feels the decision goes against fundamental IMC principles. Reaching consensus is sometimes challenging, particularly around contentious issues like membership criteria, financial transactions, and editorial practices.

Indymedia strengths & weaknesses

While the strengths of Indymedia's Internet-enabled radical democratic practices are considerable, they are also fraught with inherent tensions. Indymedia's sustainability issues are discussed in greater depth elsewhere (Pickard 2006b), but a number of other pressure points are well documented. For example, some democratic theorists are quick to note persistent hierarchies in consensus-based decision making (Mansbridge 1983; Young 1996). Gastil (1993) observes that typical drawbacks in small group democracy include long meetings, unequal involvement and commitment, cliques, differences in skills and styles, and personality conflicts. Similarly, Michel's (1915) 'iron law of oligarchy' argues that radical organisations - especially larger groups - tend to become more bureaucratic and conservative over time. In another important critique, Bookchin (1994) argues that beyond intimate small groups, consensus dissuades the creative process of 'dissensus' by pressuring dissenters into silence and thereby gravitating towards the least controversial, mediocrity, and de facto authoritarianism. Similarly, Freeman's (1972) classic critique 'the tyranny of structurelessness' suggests such purported non-hierarchy masks power, allows 'informal elites' to arise, and renders unstructured groups politically impotent.

All of the tensions described above are found in Indymedia practice to some degree. However, increasingly activists are adapting sophisticated tactics to offset oligarchic tendencies. Polletta suggests that contemporary activists are more reflexive than their forbears, constantly re-examining internal structures and processes. Such reflexivity renders implicit power relationships more explicit, and helps illuminate structural power inequities associated with persistent class, race, and gender arrangements. Another corrective measure is the intense focus on process-related issues during and after meetings - what Polletta characterises as 'fetishizing process', which has its own set of drawbacks, such as long meetings. Some activists have decried being 'processed to death'. For example, a 'process v. progress' theme animated debate during Seattle IMC meetings and across the general email list, with some activists arguing for less focus on procedure and more energy devoted to actions like media-making.

Although endless meetings and debates can bog down operations, network organisations arguably make decisions far more quickly and creatively in fast-changing political situations than any organisation with a bureaucratic chain of command. Paul De Armond (2001) illustrated how the Direct Action Network (DAN) was able to prevail during the WTO protests because of their network-based communicative structure comprised of Internet connections and cell phones, while police stymied the traditionally hierarchical labour march. Similarly, Polletta argues that radical democratic practices encourage innovation, solidarity, and dispersion of leadership skills. She explains, 'In a decentralized organization, people can respond better to local conditions and can act quickly on decisions' (2002: 211), thus affording Indymedia adaptability and resistance to state repression.

Polletta also notes, however, that the participatory model becomes strained once membership expands beyond the small group level. Allowing codified processes to become rigid and unyielding to special situations is a potential peril with the Indymedia model. A failure to reach consensus on accepting a Ford Foundation Grant in the fall of 2002 was a spectacular example of network paralysis, though the process arguably prevailed in the end. Consensus on accepting funding for an international IMC conference was blocked due to what some Indymedia activists, particularly members of the Argentina IMC, perceived as repressive historic legacies associated with the Ford Foundation. Additionally, many Indymedia activists were alarmed at North American IMCs seemingly dominating the network decision process (Pickard 2006b).

Radical openness causes similar tensions in the editorial processes governing the open published newswire and featured articles. Editorial policy is not specifically prescribed in the principles of unity and is one of the most important decisions largely left up to individual IMCs. For most IMC websites, the featured articles section takes up the centre, whereas the open publishing newswire is allotted a much smaller space. Unlike the newswire where anyone with Internet access can post news stories, featured articles go through an editorial selection process based on a hierarchical value system and subjective criteria. Indymedia is thus torn between becoming a credible news institution able to challenge corporate mainstream representations, and not wanting to repel journalists resisting mainstream news norms. Dealing with inappropriate posts, such as duplicates, advertisements, and hate speech, is also contentious. Indymedia's openness has allowed hate groups like neo-Nazis to abuse the newswire, causing conflict between those advocating for a truly open, unmanaged newswire, and others who advocate for a more pragmatic approach (Beckerman 2003). Some IMCs deal with this by 'hiding' posts somewhere on the site with an explanation for why they were removed.

In a widely circulated intervention, Whitney (2006), a long-term activist with Indymedia experience in a number of countries, argued that this laissez-faire approach to the newswire combined with shoddy newsgathering was exactly what was ailing Indymedia. On the other hand, NYC IMC's *The Indypendent*, which just celebrated its one hundredth issue, continues to produce reliably good journalism that, if not directly impacting mainstream news media discourse, breaks important local issues eventually picked up by outlets like the *New York Times* (Thompson & Anderson 2007).

Recent Developments

Indymedia's post-Seattle development is something of a mixed legacy, and its direction remains debatable. The continuing dominance of North American white males within the network continues to be a problem. Of the approximately 150 IMCS, about one fourth comes from the Global South. Furthermore, recent research suggests that the global network may be far less active and cohesive than online appearances would suggest (Coopman 2006). Nevertheless, Indymedia's more positive attributes persist. Even Whitney points to IMC journalists in Latin America, Africa, and Asia covering important life and death social issues that no one else approaches. The latter was tragically demonstrated in the Autumn of 2006 when inveterate Indymedia journalist Brad Will was gunned down while covering state oppression of a grassroots uprising in Oaxaca. Other hotspots in recent years where Indymedia often provided the only direct media coverage include the 2003 Bolivian uprising, and the 2005 tumult in Nepal when the King declared martial law and a media blackout (Waltz 2005).

North American Indymedia have undergone important changes as well. One shining example is the large Urbana-Champaign IMC, which conducted a year-long membership fund-drive to purchase the downtown Urbana Post Office building to provide space for a wide array of progressive community projects. Though it continues to court controversy for its non-profit incorporation, paid staffers, and its fiscal sponsorship of the global IMC network, the UC-IMC consistently produces vibrant community journalism via its website, a community radio station, and a monthly newspaper. A stark counter-example is the flagship Seattle IMC, which lost its prime downtown space and much of its membership. As IMCs rise and fall, the earlier rapid expansion of the network seems to have leveled out for the present.

While many tensions plaguing Indymedia have been present in radical politics since time immemorial, today's activists are actualising democratic practices in unprecedented ways. Ranging from open-published news stories to coordinating a vast global network, IMC activists struggle to redefine power relationships while producing news media, instead of replicating the social asymmetries, structural biases, and systemic failures that they passionately resist.

Jihad Video

Thomas Keenan

In a magazine diary of the 2004 American elections, 'The Revolution Will Not Be Blogged', journalist George Packer worries that reporters aren't getting out enough anymore. As in the 1970 Gil-Scott Heron song, the title of which he borrows, Packer expresses a preference for what he calls 'reality,' for getting out there, away from the screen and into the actual world, rather than waiting around for things to be televised, videotaped, emailed, or blogged. 'To see beyond their own little world and get

a sense of what's really going on', he writes, 'journalists and readers need to get out of their pajamas' (Packer 2004). He could have just said, get out.

Get out to where things are happening, turning, revolving. At work here is a powerful if implicit understanding of the temporality of the media and especially of the image. Television and blogs are fundamentally about delay and expectation, about waiting, waiting for something to happen somewhere else. The pathos and the critical force of the trope comes from the sense that the camera always follows the event, arrives afterwards, a little late...that reality comes first; at best the camera records, archives or transmits it, but it's fated to be after-the-fact, secondary, derived.

The suggestion is that one day something will happen, there will be a revolution, and it will happen somewhere, outside, in some street or public square, and that only then, afterwards, the cameras will come along to take pictures of it. Even if cameras do come along with it, they will only be there as witnesses, distributors. We had better not wait.

What if that's the distinction that we can't take for granted anymore, the one between the street and the camera, between 'our own little world' of the screen and the big one out there, where what's really going on, is going on, really? What if the time lag is increasingly being reduced to little or nothing? What about things that happen on screen, that happen only in order to be on screen, that wouldn't happen without a camera and a screen? Today it is indisputable that such events do occur, that revolutions - or at least insurrections, uprisings, violent acts of resistance - are being televised, blogged, videotaped.

In 2007, the most interesting frontline for investigating this phenomenon is what has been called the 'global *jihad*', with its dogged commitment to integrating highly professional media production, particularly on the Internet, into its core activities. The interest is both epistemological and political. *Jihad* media presents a basic challenge to the will-not-be-televised paradigm, and in doing so encourages reflection on what advocates of global civil society had hoped for, or expected, from a more accessible and pluralised media, whether television or the Internet.

Jihad on the web

One night in October 2005, I stayed up late to watch a Zarqawi premiere on the Internet. 'The Expedition of

Omar Hadid"[1] was an hour-long Arabic-language production. It had been announced in the *Jihad* online forums a few days previously, and expectations had been building. When word came of its arrival, our attention was directed to www.omar-hadid.net, where a stylish animated gif, featuring the late Omar Hadid[1], presided over a page composed entirely of download links.

Actually, I did not watch the video that night, I watched its distribution. It was available for downloading in an immense variety of sizes and formats, across maybe 15 links, from a 527 MB DAT file suitable for burning VCDs and DVDs to a micro-version in 3GP format, designed for dial-up access and playback on mobile phones.

The introductory page was designed, it said in Arabic, by 'the Media Department of the Al-Qaeda Organisation in the Land of the Two Rivers [Mesopotamia]', and was dated 'Ramadan 1426'. In other words, the video tape came from Al-Qaeda in Iraq, the *Jihad* insurgent group then led by Jordanian-born Abu Musab al-Zarqawi. It chronicled and honoured a campaign of suicide attacks (or 'martyrdom operations') in Baghdad during April 2005, which had left dozens of Iraqi civilians and a few American soldiers dead. Zarqawi named this campaign, 'The Expedition of Omar Hadid', in honour of his lieutenant, who had been killed in Fallujah the previous November.

The video tape is a relentless catalogue of violence, interrupted only by images of the technical and discursive preparations for that violence, which is announced, claimed, and advertised by its perpetrators. As I watched the site for a few hours that night, I noticed that a feature I'd never seen on a *Jihad* download page before and rarely since: a hit counter at the bottom of the screen, which clicked ever higher as new viewers retrieved their copies. Just before I went to bed, after four hours of distracted attention, I saved a copy of the page, as well as the film, which was trickling in from megaupload.com, sendspace.com, or one of the Japanese open servers popular at the time. The counter read 10,738 downloads.

The basic analytic units of the *Jihad* on the web are the forum and the video file. The agents are dispersed across the Islamic world from Saudi Arabia, Lebanon and Palestine, to Chechnya, Somalia, Algeria and beyond to their comrades in the US, Asia and Europe. They also differ greatly in ideology, theology, and outlook, including Iraqi insurgent armies (mostly Sunni but including some Shiite militias loosely related to Muqtada al-Sadr's Mahdi Army); those with their own media production units; and the Taliban and Al-Qaeda fighters and leaders in Pakistan and Afghanistan (including Al-Qaeda's most important media production unit, As-Sahab).

They appear online in some relatively stable sites, such as theislamsun.com, which hosts the Al-Rashedeen Army in Iraq, and press-release.blogspot.com, which until recently offered multiple daily communiques from the 'Islamic State of Iraq', the successor organisation to Zarqawi's group. But the real action is in the forums, the web-based discussion sites filled with pages of threaded postings and comments, some of which are accessible, others that restrict access, in which news, communiqués and still images are posted and exchanged, and where links to PDF documents, audio and video tapes, mostly hosted by commercial fileservers in the West, are distributed.

The power of contemporary imaging

This is not the advocacy television we grew up with. More than twenty years ago, in Ethiopia and on the concert stages of Live Aid, the world discovered the remarkable power of television and its images to motivate humanitarian concern and action. Bernard Kouchner, one of the French doctors who created the humanitarian organisation, Doctors without Borders, noted that 'where there is no camera, there is no humanitarian intervention' (Kouchner 1991: 210).

These images were so powerful that aid agencies felt obliged to consider their use carefully and even to develop ethical codes to help protect against the risk of exploiting those whom they sought to help. Critics worried about 'disaster pornography'. When television went global and live, as a matter of norm rather than

---

1 *An edited version, with disturbing scenes removed, can be found at:* http://switch3.castup.net/cunet/gm.asp?ClipMediaID=379550& ak=null

Box 10.3: Political jamming

Political jamming is a form of culture jamming that targets not only big corporations but the political in the broad sense (Mouffe 2005) as its object for mockery and activism. The term 'culture jamming' entered popular discourse in 1985 when the 'audio-DaDa' band Negativeland released *JamCon'84*, in which they referred to billboard activists who altered advertising hoardings to produce subversive meanings as the archetypal culture jammer. As Berry so eloquently said, culture jammers 'create with mirrors' (1995).

Jamming is not an entirely new phenomenon. Besides its obvious reference to radio-jamming, it is rooted in surrealism, DaDa-ism, and especially Situationism. This art movement of the 1950s-60s 'situated' art in the context of ordinary life, thereby opposing the elitist perspective of art that is detached from or transcends society and the experiences of 'ordinary' people in everyday contexts. Debord and Wolman (1956 – emphasis added), key actors in the Situationist International, coined the notion of *Détournement,* defining it as 'a *parodic-serious* stage where *the accumulation of detourned elements,* far from aiming to arouse indignation or laughter by alluding to some original work, will express our indifference toward a meaningless and forgotten original, and concern itself with rendering a certain sublimity.'

Culture jammers have appropriated *Détournement* as a form of resistance. A good example is AdBusters, which maintains a website and publishes a magazine of 'subvertissements' or 'demarketing' (Lasn 2000). Peretti (2001) pulled off a now infamous jam by asking Nike to inscribe 'sweatshop' on his custom-made shoes. Nike's refusal and the email discussion swept rapidly around the world via email forwarding and the Internet. Many jams circulate through email forwarding but most culture jams aim to hack into the mainstream media as well. Besides a comprehensive website, AdBusters buys time on mainstream television to air their 'anti-spots'. Billboard activists, such as the Billboard Liberation Front (BLF), who jammed the Apple campaign 'Think Different' into Think Doomed and Think Dissillusioned, use the street as their primary medium of communication, which is then amplified via their website (BLF URL).

The typical culture jam is constructed as a David and Goliath battle of the inventive, funny activists versus the mighty evil corporate world; in essence, as progressive voices struggling for social and cultural justice. While culture jamming is inherently political, political jamming is broader in its scope, going beyond the corporate world and neo-liberalism to target government policies, political adversaries and enemies. Jamming the political is a way of dealing with the messiness of reality, subverting meanings by combining mockery, satire and parody. The use of *Détournement* in political communication is often progressive, but can also ventilate feelings of intolerance, public hatred towards a demonized enemy, and racism towards ethnic minorities.

The following brief case studies illustrate the phenomenon of political jamming:

- Billboard activist Ron English is a master of what he calls the art of subversion. His website contains several examples of political jams: Picasso's famous painting *Guernica* is headlined with the banner, 'The New World Order'; and billboards carry the slogans 'Jihad is Over (If You Want It)' or 'One God, One Party - Republicans for a dissent free theocracy' (Popganda URL). This type of activism shows that the street remains a space for alternative political discourses to be 'advertised' via buying advertising space, which Adbusters does, or by 'hijacking' existing advertisements with subversive messages. In many countries radical activists use stickers or graffiti to voice dissent, subvert mainstream discourse and reclaim public spaces through counter-messages. The Wooster Collective (Wooster Collective URL), the Iranian Graffiti Art Movement (Iran Graffiti URL), and the artist Bansky (Banksy URL) represent such activism.

Source: http://www.popaganda.com

- Prior to the 2003 European and Regional elections in Belgium, an Antwerp-based multicultural radio station, Radio Multipop, supported by a broad coalition of local civil society organisations, launched a campaign to counter that of the North-Belgian extreme right party 'Vlaams Blok'.[1] The counter campaign, 'Hate is no Solution', used the same layout but transformed Vlaams Blok's slogans of 'Less Immigration, More Flanders' and 'Less Crime, More Flanders', into 'More Heart, Less Hate' and 'More Dialogue, Less Hate'. To encourage citizens to display these political jams throughout the city, Radio Multipop printed 40,000 as posters and made them available for download from the Internet, thus demonstrating combined use of the virtual and physical worlds for mobilisation.

- For some, the act of demonstrating becomes a performance in the sense that the Situationists perceived it. Performance is central to activists such as the Yes Men, who pioneered what they call 'identity correction' in which 'Honest people impersonate big-time criminals in order to publicly humiliate them. Targets are leaders and big corporations who put profits ahead of everything else'(Yes Men URL). The Yes Men have famously impersonated a WTO spokesperson promoting 'private stewardry of labour' to an African business conference. And in the guise of Dow Chemical Corporation they pledged on the BBC World Service to compensate victims of the 1984 chemical disaster in Bhopal, India. Another activist group, 'Billionaires for Bush (or Gore)', mounted a successful campaign against corporate control of US politics, which appealed deliberately to the mainstream media and thus the public at large. As one of the activists stated: 'If the media wanted the humour (and they did), they had to take the content too. The materials were catchy and accessible and the action model was easy to DIY. Thus the meme 'spread, replicated, and mutated' (Boyd 2002: 373).

- Photo doctoring is often used to fake images and convey messages opposite to those intended. September 11 2001, and the wars in Afghanistan and Iraq, have provided fertile ground for such illicit political jams (Frank 2004). While some are very critical of Western policies, others voice essentialist and racist discourses, or reinforce the Western hegemonic agenda. Examples of jams that attack Western (often US) policies include George Bush morphed into Osama bin Laden (see below) and a Star Wars film poster re-engineered as 'Gulf Wars, episode II - clone of the attack'. However, more vituperative examples have emerged, such as a plane heading towards the Kaäba in Mecca, entitled 'An Eye for an Eye'; and the détournement of the French sports newspaper l'Équipe, which represented the 9/11 World Trade Centre attack as a goal scored in a deadly football match between religions.

Source: 'Mullah Bush' by Mister Hepburn
(bushspeaks.com)

- The essentialist examples above, which advocate discourses of hate, show that political jamming can easily turn into ridiculing, humiliating or victimising a common enemy or the personification of evil at a given moment in time. At the same time, jamming techniques are increasingly being appropriated as part of 'hip' political communication strategies by political parties, publicity agencies and PR companies, thereby reducing this alternative form of communication to a marketing technique – 'un-jamming' the jam, so to speak.

In our post-modern society, a world of green-wash, spin and other newspeak, Détournement does not always challenge the status quo or strive to extend the rights of citizens. The political jam exposes the impossibility of fixed meanings, whether they are hegemonic or counter-hegemonic; as Debord said, 'In a world which really is topsy-turvy, the true is a moment of the false' (1983 [1967]: 9).

Bart Cammaerts, Lecturer, Department of Media and Communications, LSE

---

1   *Due to a conviction for disseminating persistent racist discourses 'Vlaams Blok' recently changed its name to 'Vlaams Belang'.*

John Shattuck: 'The media got us into Somalia and then they got us out'

exception, the effects multiplied. And so, a decade ago it seemed impossible to discuss the international events of the day - Rodney King and the LA riots, the Gulf War, famine in Somalia, ethnic cleansing in Bosnia, genocide in Rwanda - without reflecting on the seemingly overwhelming role that televised images of violence and suffering played in shaping the way crises unfolded. But opinions were split on just what that role was.

At times it even seemed as if the images were more important than the events. In the foreign policy world, there was excitement, positive and negative, about 'the CNN effect'. 'Surely it exists', said then Chairman of the Joint Chiefs of Staff, General John Shalikashvili, 'and surely we went to Somalia and Rwanda partly because of its magnetic pull' (1995: 115). In Somalia, in 1991, pictures of suffering and starvation proved irresistible for humanitarians, politicians, and generals alike. The United States led an international invasion force that sought to feed and heal the victims of famine by force of arms...and to manufacture a new image for a military that had recently lost its primary reason for being. And the power of images was ratified, however tragically, when the American rescue force was ejected from Somalia two years later by the camcorder pictures of dead American soldiers in the street and a Blackhawk helicopter pilot in captivity.

It seemed that images could make governments undo what previous images had apparently galvanised them to do. 'The media got us into Somalia and then got us out', wrote John Shattuck, former US assistant secretary for human rights and democracy in the Clinton era (1996: 174). The story was obviously more complicated than that (and the counter-example of over-exposed and under-defended Sarajevo can serve as shorthand here) but the message is conventional wisdom today. No major human rights or humanitarian organisation would undertake a major advocacy

campaign, and certainly not one aimed at influencing Northern policy makers, without a comprehensive media strategy.

What the daily torrent of movies from Iraq and the other frontlines have in common, not to mention the homemade videos that American soldiers now routinely upload to You Tube and Live Leak, is the fact that they are conceived, scripted, shot, edited, and distributed by those who feature in them. No third parties, reporters, executive producers, advertisers or network affiliates need be involved. Although, of course, they can be: the Internet reaches into the production and executive suites at Al-Arabiya and BBC World just as easily as it lands on the desktops and cyber cafes of the global *Jihad*. But there exists now, in real life, whatever its blind spots and missed coverage, and all manner of digital divides, a functional, always-on, multilingual and multinational global production and distribution audio-video network.

Its production teams are turning out video tapes at the rate of dozens each week, many of sophistication and high production values. This raises a difficult question. The DIY factor, this user-generated content from the battlefield, differs fundamentally from the paradigm we impute to journalistic coverage of news stories. It is partisan. It advocates, propagandises, seeks to act and encourages action. But does it differ only empirically, or somehow essentially, from the regime of the photo opportunity or the media event? Where would news and politics be without the photo opportunity? The motivation to appear before cameras, and to produce people and events that look good when captured by them, governs not only the behaviour of politicians and celebrities but also humanitarian action and human rights campaigns, as well as military interventions in Somalia, Bosnia, Haiti, Kosovo, and embedded reporters in Iraq. How different is the daily videotaped combat in Iraq and the last testament of the suicide bomber in Algiers?

Two dimensions of contemporary imaging - the photo opportunity and the act of bearing witness - have effectively created a new politics over the last three decades.

Michel Foucault, speaking in 1981, heralded the emergence of an 'international citizenry' (quoted in Keenan 1987: 22), exemplified by Amnesty International and others, which had created a new right, that of private individuals to intervene in the order of international politics and strategies, to uproot the monopoly over reality previously held by governments.

Stuart Hall, writing a couple of years later, saw in the Live Aid and Band Aid concert phenomena nothing less than a new kind of politics, catalysed by global networks of rock music and television. In an important essay, 'The Ethics of Television', Michael Ignatieff (1997) argued that television had not only become the primary connector between people in the rich and poor worlds, but that it was creating a new political space and new political agents - non-governmental organisations - which threatened or promised to take over the traditional monopoly on representation possessed by states, and open up new territories of political action to non-state actors, civil society, a global citizenry.

How? On the screen. Television, Ignatieff wrote, 'is the instrument of a new kind of politics', one in which NGOs seek to circumvent bilateral governmental relations and institute direct political contacts between far-flung people. This notion, exemplified in the paradigms of 'mobilising shame' and 'global witness,' today dominates the 'third sector,' from relief agencies to human rights organisations and community movements. For us, that new politics has been generalised and radicalised. Global civil society is unthinkable without media, without a virtual public space and access to its means of production and distribution. Indeed, under the banners of opening-democratic-spaces and overcoming-the-digital-divide, creating and defending those media zones has become one of the chief preoccupations of the new political movements of our time. The current concern with information and communications technology for development is just one indicator of this phenomenon. But civil society - and the new people politics - is not what it used to be.

'It's a war of perceptions', Army Brigadier General John Custer, Head of Intelligence at Central Command, told CBS News' 60 Minutes. 'They [the insurgents] understand the power of the Internet. They don't have to win in the tactical battlefield. They never will. No platoon has ever been defeated in Afghanistan or Iraq. But it doesn't matter. It's irrelevant' (Pelley 2007).

The 'new politics' of television are increasingly a new new politics of the Internet, and the actors in cyberspace are not just humanitarians and earnest human rights advocates, but protagonists of the restoration of the Caliphate and armed insurgents - maybe even revolutionaries - of the multiform *Jihad*.

All that effort to promote open access and free media, all that connectivity, bandwidth and cyber-infrastructure, all those attempts to overcome the digital divide...and the new new politics has proven remarkably successful.

Conclusion

Nick Couldry

This Chapter has attempted to address the full range of global civil society; the result is a huge, and at first bewildering, diversity. I want to look back over the Chapter, and argue that no less a diversity must be encompassed if the empirical complexity and normative promise of the term 'global civil society' is to be fulfilled. I will end with some suggestions for how our engagement with this diversity can be developed further.

When introducing 'global civil society', the editors of the first Yearbook pointed to an 'underlying social reality' that the term's rising popularity glossed:

the emergence of a supranational sphere of social and political participation in which citizen groups, social movements, and individuals engage in dialogue, debate, confrontation, and negotiation with each other and with various governmental actors – international, national, and local – as well as the business world. (Anheier, Glasius and Kaldor 2001: 4)

From the beginning then, the Yearbook series has recognised a complexity of scale and a heterogeneity of actors, which guarantees that the term 'global civil society' covers multiple dimensions and directions of action. 'Global civil society' as a term may be highly contested and fuzzy (2001: 7-12), but this matters little because of the 'normative aspiration' built into it, particularly in the choice of the word 'global', instead of the more cautious 'transnational' (2001: 17). Since then, the term has been criticised, for example because its reference points are already contaminated by the pre-existing power dynamics of state and markets (Chandhoke 2002), or too detached from 'the daily spaces' in which people act (Sassen 2006: 318). Starting to address those criticisms only increases the complexities that the term embodies.

Four areas of irreducible uncertainty are involved here: first, over what is meant by civil society; second, over what counts as politics; third, over what is meant by 'global' in this context; and fourth, lurking behind these and less explicit, an uncertainty about what it is for media to enable or sustain global civil society. Each of these uncertainties emerges at various points in this chapter, and each is intrinsic, not accidental, to the concept of global civil society.

So, taking civil society first, and even if we leave aside old debates about whether civil society actors must operate outside <u>both</u> market and state, there is a question about what those actors must do to qualify as '<u>civil</u> society'. Marc Williams defines 'civil society' as 'that voluntary sphere in which individuals come together from outside the state and the market *in order to promote common interests*' (2005: 347, added emphasis). If so, we need to ask, how 'common' do those interests have to be, since the wider ambition of the 'global civil society' debate is to identify processes that help broaden *democratic* politics. Just as some fear that Habermas' public sphere ideal may fragment into countless unconnected 'public sphericules' (Gitlin 1998; Sunstein 1999), so too, when looking at possible examples of 'global civil society', we need to ask whether they are connected or at least connectable: if not, as Clifford Bob notes, it may not be a broader civil society or democratic politics that is being built. Uncertainty over the 'civil' inevitably overlaps with long-term debates about the boundaries of the political, as Bart Cammaerts notes in his discussion of 'culture jamming', which is far from traditional electoral politics. Turning to the 'global', the global potential of political debates in the digital media age is a given, but there are many modalities of the global: globality of interactions or networking, globality of the issues or reference-points under discussion, and globality of ultimate political goals (Williams 2005: 350-351). Once again, this chapter illustrates that variety. And finally, if behind the prominence of the term 'global civil society' lie shifts not only in global economics and politics, but also major advances in communications technology (Williams 2005: 353), then there is an uncertainty about how exactly new media – which new media, and in which combinations? – are sustaining global civil society. For, as this Chapter makes clear, we cannot grasp media's contribution simply by looking at 'civil society media', useful though that term might be in some contexts (Hintz 2006).

Thus, in its full ambit, the term 'global civil society' encompasses movements that are not particularly 'civil' (the *jihad* videos discussed by Thomas Keenan), that emerge initially out of national politics (the NRA

discussed by Clifford Bob), that involve an implicit cultural politics rather than an explicit formal politics (Nigerian video-films discussed by Jonathan Haynes) and that challenge existing *media* power as much as political power,[1] sometimes through online networks (Indymedia discussed by Victor Pickard) or through novel combinations of traditional media (Nigerian video films circulating among wider global diasporas).

These complexities are inherent in the term 'global civil society' and the multiple social realities to which it refers. I will describe later how we might take our analysis of this complexity a stage further. First, let us review each case study in a little more detail.

On the face of it, Indymedia is a clear recent example of global civil society: a global network that links various new sites of news, opinion and debate on political issues within a global frame, and in a way, as Pickard illustrates, that was in principle impossible without the Internet. Indeed, the Indymedia network deepens global civil society in two ways, as Pickard shows: first, by offering a new type of media practice, a new type of 'newsroom' much more open to the contributions of non-media professionals; second, by a highly de-centered process of policy making and decision making, which encourages local initiative and adaptability. But this initial success generates major questions for the long-term:[2] how far will Indymedia's implicit challenge to traditional news production values be taken? Under what conditions is Indymedia's distinctive media and political practice sustainable and for whom in particular? These questions become even more acute when, as Pickard notes, we recall that only one fourth of the 150 IMCs worldwide are based in the South, just as 'global civil society' has from the outset been dominated by the North (Anheier, Glasius and Kaldor 2001: 7).

In social and cultural terms, NRA and Indymedia activists would be unlikely to recognise each other as having much in common if they met on the streets of an American city. But the breadth of 'global civil society' as a concept encourages us to look for similar dynamics that may underlie activism from very different points in the political spectrum.[3] As Clifford Bob shows, there

---

[1] *Compare Couldry and Curran (2003) on the contestation of media's symbolic power as a separate dimension of contemporary conflicts.*
[2] *Compare Couldry (2003: 50-51) on these points.*
[3] *Chris Atton (2004) makes a parallel point in favour of the inclusiveness of the term 'alternative media'.*

are important overlaps of method and technique between NRA as an online communicator and the opponents of gun sports and firearm proliferation. These go beyond the obvious value of the web for campaign mobilisation, and include the use of a global issue frame for generating news favourable to their respective viewpoints. But these similarities between online global civil society opponents raise a deeper question, which echoes the uncertainties noted earlier: do we see in the globally framed, digitally enabled gun debate 'global civil society' in action, with positive long-term consequences for democratic expansion, or as Bob suggests, simply a better-resourced *space of conflict* without progress towards greater dialogue or mutual understanding? A recent study of online discussion on immigration and cultural politics in the Netherlands also fails to find signs of genuine 'engagement' online, that is, 'a reflection upon one's own discourse in the light of the other's discourse' (Witschge 2007: 121). It seems clear the presence of mutually exclusive political constituencies on the web is insufficient for genuine 'global civil society'. Thomas Keenan's study of the role of *Jihad* videos in raising the profile of militant groups in many zones of conflict only intensifies this question. As with Indymedia, the Internet's infrastructure is essential to these groups, even if in this case there is no larger network and groups remain highly particularistic. What matters here is not that *Jihad* video represents a form of global civil society – clearly it does not, because this is media where showing and declaration is more important than witness and argument. Rather, the significance of this case study is that it highlights the *normative* force of the global civil society concept: the need for new fora of debate and exchange to *emerge* somehow in the future in an intensely mediatised field of conflict.

Jonathan Haynes' study of Nigerian videos and 'Nollywood' stretches the concept of global civil society in another way, recalling older debates about the political potential of commercial popular culture. On the face of it, Nigerian video culture lies outside 'civil society' because the production and distribution of these films are certainly market operations. The point, as Haynes shows, is how these videos are used by *audiences* in private, often highly gendered contexts, to articulate social issues that find little expression in national or global politics – and for audiences not only in Nigeria but within diaspora populations as far afield as New York. These are videos produced by an industry with low entry costs, and distribution as much by word of mouth as by expensive marketing, and far removed from formal political processes. Yet to dismiss their significance for the longer-term growth of global civil society would be a mistake, because at stake here is the underlying flow of images that are a basic precondition of a working democracy. As the Burkinabe film-director Gaston Kaboré, quoted by Todd Lester, puts it:

> a society that is confronted with images and values from abroad on a daily basis [without others of its own] will eventually lose its identity and the ability to choose its own destination.

Where does this leave us in terms of the concept of global civil society and the questions with which this Chapter started about the emergence and sustainability of new and viable spaces of democratic debate? On the face of it, the heterogeneity of the case studies poses a problem. The media spaces discussed differ in their degrees of 'civility' and politicisation, in their degrees and modes of globality, and in the ways in which media sustain them as spaces. Therefore there is no single model for ensuring either their sustainability or democratic potential.

Following recent work on 'practice' in social theory,[4] we can think of global civil society as a large and complex 'dispersed practice' (Schatzki 1996: 89) held together at most by a shared or analogous set of understandings, rather than by any explicit rules. Dispersed practices may vary considerably in their component parts, but they require certain linkages or articulations if they are to form part of the same practice. To form part of the large and complex dispersed practice we call 'global civil society', the various case studies of this Chapter must show some articulation between their detailed activities of production and engagement, and a wider context where opinions are exchanged and issues recognised as needing common resolution are deliberated upon. How that articulation gets made will vary greatly in particular cases, but it must be there in some form at least. It is this requirement that makes global civil society a critical and normative concept.

---

[4] See Schatzki (1996) and Reckwitz (2002); for an application to research on political engagement, see Couldry Livingstone and Markham (2007: chapter 4).

As we have seen, those articulations may be difficult to find in reality. A question raised by the NRA case study is whether any space yet exists where the NRA and its opponents can address *each other*, and in a way that links to a legitimate decision-making process. The *Jihad* video case study suggests few spaces exist currently online or offline where the declarations and iconography of specific groups can be translated into terms for possible debate and exchange. The cases of Indymedia, the Nigerian video–film industry, and culture jamming seem less problematic, since in each case there is a broader constituency for whom these cultural productions are relevant and resonant, but the issue of articulation arguably arises in a different form: how, if at all, are these processes linked in a regular way to more formal processes of decision-making?[5] If no such links prove sustainable, then the relevance of these practices to global civil society must surely fade too.

For now, we cannot be sure how things will evolve in any of these examples. The NRA is extremely likely to remain a player on the global and national stage; what is less certain is whether it will engage with a wider process of debate and deliberation. Such a shift is unlikely perhaps for *Jihad* groups unless a larger transnational framework for the political resolution of the conflicts they represent emerges. The Nigerian video scene's implicit cultural politics may or may not be sustained by connections to other forms of political and social action, but the trade is likely to continue because of its commercial dynamics. Indymedia's long-term robustness must surely depend, as Natalie Fenton argues for contemporary forms of online activism more generally, on the development of a wider 'social imaginary' that links together the struggles of Indymedia and other actors on the left in a broader narrative of political change (Fenton 2006: 258).

Such uncertainties, however, are not problems with the concept of global civil society. They are simply an index of the scale and multidimensional complexity of the ongoing political, social and media transformations to which this term directs our attention.

---

5   *Compare with Fraser (2005: 85 note 16).*

Adamu, Abdalla Uba, Yusuf M Adamu and Umar Faruk Jibril (eds) (2004) *Hausa Home Videos: Technology, Economy and Society.* Kano: Centre for Hausa Cultural Studies/Adamu Joji Publishers.

Adamu, Yusuf M (2002) 'Between the word and the screen: A historical perspective on the Hausa literary movement and the home video invasion', *Journal of African Cultural Studies* 15.2: 203–213.

Anheier, H, Glasius, M, and Kaldor, M (2001) 'Introducing Global Civil Society' in H Anheier, M Glasius and M Kaldor (eds) *Global Civil Society 2001.* Oxford: Oxford University Press.

Anthony, David H 'African Film Festivals in Focus', Documentary Box no. 24, Yamagata International Documentary Film Festival. http://www.yidff.jp/docbox/24/box24-2-e.html

Atton, C (2004) *An Alternative Internet.* London: Sage.

Barrot, Pierre (ed) (2005) *Nollywood: Le phénomène video au Nigeria.* Paris: L'Harmattan.

Barber, Karin (1987) 'Popular Arts in Africa', *African Studies Review* 30.3: 1-78.

– (2000) *The Generation of Plays: Yoruba Popular Life in Theater.* Bloomington: Indiana University Press.

Beckman, G (2003) 'Edging away from anarchy: Inside the Indymedia collective, passion vs. pragmatism', *Columbia Journalism Review.* 27-30, September/October.

Berry, C (1995) The Letter U and the Numeral 2, *Wired*, Issue 3.01 (Jan).

Bey, H (1985) *The Temporary Autonomous zone, Ontological Anarchy, Poetic Terrorism.* New York: Autonomedia.

Bob, Clifford (2005) *The Marketing of Rebellion: Insurgents, Media, and International Activism.* Cambridge: Cambridge University Press.

Bookchin, M (n.d.) 'What is communalism?' http://www.democracynature.org/dn/vol3/bookchin_communalism.htm (consulted 10 April 2007).

Boyd, A (2002) 'TRUTH IS A VIRUS: Meme Warfare and the Billionaires for Bush (or Gore)', in S Duncombe (ed) *Cultural Resistance: A Reader.* London: Verso.

Brooten, L (2004) 'Digital deconstruction: The Independent Media Center as a process of collective critique', in Berenger, R (ed) *Global media goes to war: Role of news and entertainment media during the 2003 Iraq war.* Spokane, WA: Marquette Books.

Butler, C T and Rothstein, A (1987) *On Conflict and Consensus.* Cambridge, MA: Food Not Bombs. www.consensus.net

Castells, M (1996) *The Rise of the Network Society. The Information age: Economy, Society and Culture, Volume I.* Cambridge, Mass: Blackwell Publishers.

Chandhoke, N (2002) 'The Limits of Global Civil Society' in H Anheier, M Glasius and M Kaldor (eds) *Global Civil Society 2002.* Oxford: Oxford University Press.

Coopman, T M (2006) 'Indymedia: Emergent global media infrastructures', Paper presented at the National Communication Association Convention, San Antonio, Texas, November.

Comaroff, Jean and John Comaroff (eds) (1993) *Modernity and its Malcontents: Ritual and Power in Postcolonial Africa.* Chicago: University of Chicago Press.

– (1999) 'Occult Economies and the Violence of Abstraction: Notes from the South African Postcolony', *American Ethnologist* 26.2: 279-303.

Couldry, N (2003) 'Beyond the Hall of Mirrors? Some Theoretical Reflections on the Global Contestation of Media Power' in N Couldry and J Curran (eds) *Contesting Media Power: Alternative Media in a Networked World.* Boulder, CO: Rowman and Littlefield.

Couldry, N and Curran, J (2003) 'The Paradox of Media Power' in N Couldry and J Curran (eds) *Contesting Media Power: Alternative Media in a Networked World.* Boulder, CO: Rowman and Littlefield.

Couldry, N, Livingstone, S and Markham, T (2007) Media Consumption and Public Engagement: Beyond the Presumption of Attention. Basingstoke: Palgrave Macmillan.

De Armond, P (2001) 'Netwar in the Emerald City: WTO protest strategy and tactics' in D Ronfeldt and J Arquilla, (eds) *Networks and netwars: The future of terror, crime, and militancy.* Washington DC: RAND, National Security Research Division.

Debord, G and Wolman, G L (1956) 'Mode d'emploi du détournement', *Les Lèvres Nues*, No. 8. http://membres.lycos.fr/gviolet/Detournement.html (consulted 2 May 2007).

Debord, G (1983 [1967]) *The Society of the Spectacle.* Detroit: Black & Red. http://www.nothingness.org/SI/debord.html (consulted 2 May 2007).

Downing, J (2003) 'The Independent Media Center Movement and the Anarchist Socialist Tradition', in N Couldry & J Curran (eds) *Contesting Media Power: Alternative Media in a Networked World.* Boulder, CO: Rowman and Littlefield.

Dworkin, Ronald (2006) Is *Democracy Possible Here? Principles for a New Political Debate.* Princeton: Princeton University Press.

Fenton, N (2006) 'Contesting Global Capital, New Media, Solidarity and the Role of a Social Imaginary' in B Cammaerts and N Carpentier (eds) *Reclaiming the Media: Communication Rights and Democratic Media Roles.* Bristol: Intellect Books.

Frank, R (2004) 'When the going gets tough go photoshopping: September 11 and the newslore of vengeance and victimisation', *New Media & Society* 6(5): 633-58

Fraser, N (2005) 'Reframing Global Justice', *New Left Review* second series 36:69-90.

Freeman, J (1972) 'The Tyranny of Structurelessness', *Berkeley Journal of Sociology*, 3: 151-164.

Gabriel, Teshome (1982) *Third cinema in the Third World: The Aesthetics of Liberation.* Ann Arbor: UMI Research Press.

Gastil, J (1993) *Democracy in small groups: Participation, decision making, and communication.* Philadelphia: New Society Publishers.

Geschiere, Peter (1997) *The Modernity of Witchcraft: Politics and the Occult in Postcolonial Africa.* Charlottesville, VA: University Press of Virginia.

Gilroy, Paul (1993) *The Black Atlantic: Modernity and Double-Consciousness.* Cambridge: Harvard University Press.

Gitlin, T (1998) 'Public Sphere or Public Sphericules?' In T Liebes and J Curran (eds) *Media Ritual and Identity.* London: Routledge.

Guneratne, Anthony and Wimal Dissanayake (eds) (2003) *Rethinking Third Cinema.* New York: Routledge.

Habermas, Jürgen (2001) *The Postnational Constellation: Political Essays.* Cambridge: Massachusetts Institute of Technology Press.

Halleck, D (2003) 'Indymedia: Building an international activist internet network', *Journal of the World Association for Christian Communication.*

Haskell, David (2006) 'Festival City', *Urban Design Review*, summer.

Haynes, Jonathan (2000) 'Introduction' in Jonathan Haynes (ed) *Nigerian Video Films. Athens,* OH: Ohio University Press.

— (2003a) 'Africans Abroad: A Theme in Film and Video', *Africa & Mediterraneo* 45: 22-29.

— (2003b) 'Mobilizing Yoruba Popular Culture: Babangida Must Go', *Africa* 73.1: 122-38.

— (2005) 'Nollywood: What's in a Name?' *The Guardian* (Lagos) July 3. .

— (2006) 'Political Critique in Nigerian Video Films', *African Affairs* 105/421: 511-533.

Haynes, Jonathan and Onookome Okome (1998) 'Evolving Popular Media: Nigerian Video Films', *Research in African Literatures* 29.3: 106-28.

Hill, John and Pamela Church Gibson (eds) (2000) *World Cinema: Critical Approaches.* Oxford: OUP.

Hintz, A (2006) 'Civil Society Media at the WSIS: a new actor in global communication governance?' in B Cammaerts and N Carpentier (eds) *Reclaiming the Media: Communication Rights and Democratic Media Roles.* Bristol: Intellect Books.

IANSA (International Action Network on Small Arms) http://www.iansa.org/

— 'NRA publication "dials paranoia level up to 11"' http://www.iansa.org/regions/namerica/paranoid_nra_brochure.htm

Ignatieff, Michael (1997) *The Warrior's Honor: Ethnic War and the Modern Conscience.* New York: Metropolitan/Holt.

Jeyifo, Biodun (1984) *The Yoruba Popular Travelling Theatre of Nigeria.* Lagos: Nigeria Magazine.

Keenan T (1987) 'The Paradox of Knowledge and Power: Reading Foucault on a Bias', *Political Theory,* Vol 15 No 1, February, 5-37.

Kidd, D (2003) 'Indymedia.org: A New Communication Commons', in McCaughey, M and Ayers, M D (eds) *Cyberactivism: Online Activism in Theory and Practice.* New York: Routledge.

Kouchner, Bernard (1991) *Le Malheur des Autres* [The Misfortune of Others]. Paris: Odile Jacob.

Larkin, Brian (1997) 'Indian Films and Nigerian Lovers: Media and the Creation of Parallel Modernities', *Africa,* 67.3, 406-440.

—(2000) 'Hausa dramas and the rise of video culture in Nigeria' in Jonathan Haynes (ed) *Nigerian Video Films.* Athens, OH: Ohio University Press.

—(2004) 'Degraded Images, Distorted Sounds: Nigerian Video and the Infrastructure of Piracy', *Public Culture* 16.2: 289-314. LaPierre, Wayne (2006a) *The Global War on Your Guns: Inside the U.N. Plan to Destroy the Bill of Rights.* Nashville: Nelson Current.

LaPierre, Wayne (2006b) 'The Peters-Principle,' *America's 1st Freedom,* February.

Lasn, K (2000) *Culture Jam: How to reverse America's Suicidal Consumer Binge—and why we must.* New York: Quill.

Mansbridge, J (1983) *Beyond adversary democracy.* Chicago: University of Chicago Press.

Mouffe, C (2005) *On the Political.* London and New York: Routledge.

NRA (National Rifle Association) (2007) 'Freedom in Peril: Guarding the 2nd Amendment in the 21st Century'. http://www.boingboing.net/images/NR-F8_PERILFINAL.pdf

Packer, George (2004) 'The Revolution Will Not Be Blogged', *Mother Jones,* May/June. http://www.motherjones.com/commentary/columns/2004/05/04_200.html (consulted 10 July 2007).

Pelley, Scott (2007) 'Terrorists Take Recruitment Efforts Online', *60 Minutes,* CBS News, 4 March. http://www.cbsnews.com/stories/2007/03/02/60minutes/main2531546.shtml (consulted 10 July 2007).

Peretti, J (2001) 'My Nike Adventure', *The Nation*, 9 April. http://www.thenation.com/doc/20010409/peretti (consulted 2 May 2007).

Perlstein, J (2001) 'An Experiment in Media Democracy', in E Yuen, G Katsiaficas, & B Rose (eds) *The Battle of Seattle.* New York: Soft Skull Press.

Pickard, V (2006a) 'Assessing the Radical Democracy of Indymedia: Discursive, Technical and Institutional

Constructions', *Critical Studies in Media Communication* 23(1) 19-38.

Pickard, V (2006b) 'United yet Autonomous: Indymedia and the Struggle to Sustain a Radical Democratic Network', *Media Culture & Society*, 28 (3) 315-336.

Pickard, V (forthcoming) 'Cooptation and Cooperation: Institutional Exemplars of Democratic Internet Technology', *New Media and Society*.

Polletta, F (2002) *Freedom is an Endless Meeting: Democracy in American Social Movements.* Chicago: University of Chicago Press.

Reckwitz, A (2002) 'Toward a Theory of Social Practices' *European Journal of Social Theory* 5(2): 243-263.

Risse, Thomas (2000) 'Let's Argue! Communicative Action in World Politics,' *International Organization* 54 (1): 1-39.

Ronfeldt & J Arquilla (eds) *Networks and Netwars: The future of terror, crime, and militancy.* Washington DC: RAND, National Security Research Division.

Sabaté, Joaquim, Frenchman, Dennis and Schuster, J Mark (2004) *Event Places.* Cambridge, MA: MIT Press.

Sassen, S (2006) *Territory, Authority, Rights.* Princeton: Princeton University Press.

Schatzki, T (1996) *Social Practices: A Wittgenstinian Approach to Human Activity and the Social.* Cambridge: Cambridge University Press.

Shalikashvili, John (1995) 'Annual Posture Statement' Washington DC, 8 February. http://www.ndu.edu/library/epubs/shali-1995.pdf (consulted 10 July 2007).

Shattuck, John (1996) 'Human Rights and Humanitarian Crises: Policy-making and the Media', in I Rotberg & Thomas G Weiss (eds) *From Massacres to Genocide: The Media, Public Policy, and Humanitarian Crises.* Cambridge, MA: The World Peace Foundation.

Skocpol, Theda (2003) *Diminished Democracy: From Membership to Management in American Civic Life.* Norman: University of Oklahoma Press.

Sunstein (1999) *Republic.com.* Princeton: Princeton University Press.

Thompson, Erin & Anderson, Chris (2007) 'The Indy at One Hundred, http://www.indypendent.org/?p=934 (consulted 10 April 2007).

Waltz, Mitzi (2005) *Alternative and Activist Media.* Edinburgh: Edinburgh University Press.

Wapner, Paul (1996) *Environmental Activism and World Civic Politics.* Albany: State University of New York Press.

Wayne, Mike (2001) *Political Film: The Dialectics of Third Cinema.* London: Pluto P Press.

Whitney, Jennifer (2006) 'Make Media, Make Real Trouble: What's Wrong (and Right) with Indymedia', *Alternative Press Review* 10

(1) 50-57, Spring.

Wikipedia 'Polisario Front'. http://en.wikipedia.org/wiki/Polisario_Front#The_ Sahrawi_Arab_Democratic_Republic

Williams, M (2005) 'Globalization and Civil Society' in J Ravenhill (ed) *Global Political Economy.* Oxford: Oxford University Press.

Witschge, T (2007) *(In)difference online: the openness of public discussion on immigration.* Doctoral thesis at the University of Amsterdam. Amsterdam: University of Amsterdam.

Young, I M (2000) *Inclusion and Democracy.* Oxford: Oxford University Press.

Websites

Banksy, http://banksy.co.uk/

Billboard Liberation Front, http://www.billboardliberation.com/lama.html

Carthage Film Festival, http://www.jccarthage.org/

Control Arms, http://www.controlarms.org/

Imagine Institute, http://www.imagine.bf/

Iran Graffiti, http://irangraffiti.blogspot.com/

PanAfrican Film and Television of Ouagadougou, http://www.fespaco.bf/index_en.html

Pictures on Walls, http://www.picturesonwalls.com/

Popaganda,http://www.popaganda.com/billboards/index.shtml

Press Release, http://press-release.blogspot.com/

Principles of Unity, http://docs.indymedia.org/view/Global/PrinciplesOfUnity

Rwanda Film Festival http://www.rwandafilmfestival.org/

Sahara International Film Festival, http://www.festivalsahara.com/

Stop UN Gun Ban, http://www.stopungunban.net/

The Islam Sun, http://theislamsun.com/rashedeen/

The Wooster Collective, http://www.woostercollective.com/

The Yes Men, http://www.theyesmen.org/

WFSA, http://www.wfsa.net/

Zanzibar International Film Festival, http://www.ziff.or.tz/

CHAPTER 11

LANGUAGE AND 'GLOBAL' POLITICS: DE-NATURALISING THE 'GLOBAL'

Sabine Selchow

Setting the scene: language and politics

Civil society, communication and democracy are inherently and in various respects linked to the issue of language. Most obviously, of course, it is language that distinguishes humans from other creatures and makes them social beings in the first place. Language is an essential ingredient in the formation of individual and collective identities; the exercise of civil rights rests on the linguistic competence of individuals and the concept of the public sphere, which is one of the fundamental structural components for (deliberative) democracy, can hardly be thought of without considering language questions (see Box 11.1). More generally, as long as politics is not about coercion and violence, it is about symbolic action and about language, as one of the critical aspects of communication and social exchange. But language and linguistic signs, and the meanings that are associated with them, are also essential in that they construct social reality.

This Chapter explores the latter understanding of the role of language with regard to politics. It aims to raise awareness of the significance of the term 'global' in contemporary political, public and political studies discourses. Although 'global' has become an important political currency worldwide, it has triggered very little interest, investigation or critical engagement. It has been widely naturalised, which means that it is taken for granted and treated as an 'innocent' or descriptive attribute – both in political practice and in the contemporary political studies discourse. The Chapter illustrates the political dimension of the term 'global' and draws attention to the paradox that, although contemporary political practice seems to be permeated by unilateralism and explicit national interests rather than by (the ideal of) 'global governance', it is increasingly embedded in a 'global' rhetoric. By analysing the use of the term 'global' by US President George W Bush, this Chapter illustrates the importance of taking 'global' seriously in the study of contemporary politics.

To start with, the political nature of linguistic signs in general and the social nature of meanings in particular will be highlighted. This perspective is rarely considered in contemporary political science approaches to world politics, particularly in the Anglo-American political studies discourse.

Words, meanings and politics

Today, it is 'a truism that social reality does not fall from heaven' (Risse 2007: 128); rather, social reality is constructed through language. In this sense, language is not simply a neutral tool for describing an extra-linguistic reality, because it is only through language that this reality emerges, in that it is defined in language, thereby acquiring meaning. It is impossible to know how something 'really' is or was, before its 'distortion' by language, because we cannot think and conceptualise without language.[1] At the same time, language and meaning are much more complicated phenomena than everyday life might suggest; this is because linguistic signs are differential rather than referential. The very existence of some 6,912 different languages reveals that 'things' in extra-linguistic reality do not naturally prescribe what they should be called. Rather, the relation between linguistic signs and their referents is arbitrary and purely conventional. The meaning of a linguistic sign cannot even be thought of as a 'thing' in empirical reality in the first place; rather it is a mind image.

This mind image is itself the product of a process of differentiation between an indefinite number of other meanings; as Terry Eagleton puts it: meaning is a 'constant flickering of presence and absence together' that passes through language like a net (1983: 128). Hence, although everyday communication

---

[1] For this notion and what follows see the theory of structural linguistics as it was developed by Ferdinand de Saussure ([1916] 2000) and the works of his post-structuralist predecessors, such as Jacques Derrida (1976); see also literary theorist Terry Eagleton (1983).

works quite well and it is usually clear what a linguistic sign means, meanings are less stable than they appear initially. Not only are linguistic signs differential rather than referential, and not only is social reality constructed through language, but meanings themselves are the product of social processes; they are based on a constant process of social ratification in communication. This points to the essentially social and political nature of language and meanings that goes beyond the politics of language.

If meanings evolve from within an infinite web of other meanings and are constantly socially ratified in communication, they are the product of social processes which, based on a broad definition of politics as, for example, suggested by Leftwich (1983), makes them political *per se*. Using linguistic signs entails contributing to this social process of meaning production and ratification, through which supposed 'natural' meanings or 'descriptions' of the world are strengthened or challenged. That is why a focus on language in the study of politics is not only interesting with regard to language politics or from a pragmatic perspective, in that language in political practice 'does' something. Rather, terms can even be understood and investigated as nodal points in which collective knowledge and social perceptions of political reality 'appear' (Fraas 2000 in reference to Knobloch 1992).

This is especially true and fruitful when it comes to terms that are more 'abstract' (Fraas 1998) than others, such as 'freedom', 'justice', 'civil society', 'democracy' – and 'global', which is of extraordinary significance in contemporary political discourse.

In contemporary (Anglo-American) political studies, language, in the sense outlined above, is rarely considered a worthwhile object of research in itself. Yet political practitioners seem to be very consciously aware of the construction and political nature of linguistic signs. To find an appropriate label for events and phenomena is an important and an explicit aspect of political practice. This is most obvious when it comes to applying (or avoiding) terms that are associated with (international) law. For example, in 1956 then British Prime Minister Sir Anthony Eden told the House of Commons, 'We are not at war with Egypt. We are in an armed conflict' (Eden 1956). It is further evidenced in the persistent official US use of the term 'unlawful combatants', as opposed to 'prisoners of war', for detainees at Guantanamo Bay, and in the debate about the use of the term 'genocide' for the mass killings in Darfur, in which civil society activists press (Northern) political authorities 'to call a spade a spade' and use the term 'genocide' in order to trigger the associated legal, political and moral consequences.

Box 11.1: Multilingualism and transnational public spaces in civil society

Scene: the arena of a public theatre, Genoa, July 2003. Activists and organisations in the global justice movement have returned to the place where demonstrations against the G8 summit occurred in 2001. Lost in the media cacophony about violence between police and protesters was the role of Genoa as a catalyst for diffusing the idea of cosmopolitanism, inspired by the social forums and communicative democracy practised in the global justice movement (see della Porta and Mosca, forthcoming; Glasius and Timms 2006).

Now, in 2003, the activists are engaged in a social forum process to discuss the future of 'another Europe'. Their meeting, the European preparatory to the European Social Forum (ESF), is just one in a series of regular preparatory sessions. In European preparatory assemblies, such as in Genoa, nearly 400 activists coming together in cities as diverse as Moscow, Sofia, Stockholm, Istanbul and Glasgow, discuss and make collective decisions in a seemingly Babylonian mix of languages. When misunderstandings occur, speakers try to help each other, which can be complicated and takes time. Those who are bilingual switch, for instance, from Italian to French or English; others make their claims in Spanish or Turkish. Most participants listen to simultaneous translations via headphones. Those contributing to the debate are frequently reminded by voluntary interpreters to speak slowly.

As the participants come from such contrasting cultures and speak so many different languages, how democratic can such emerging transnational public meetings and discussion forums in civil society be? To tackle this question, I studied the preparatory assemblies of the ESF between 2003 and 2006. Considering that fewer than half EU citizens speak more than one language (de Cillia 2002) one must take seriously the discriminatory potential of a 'linguistic divide' in Europe (Wodak and Wright 2006). However, evidence from the ESF process, including these transnational meetings, suggests a more pluralistic and procedurally open setting than similar preparatory assemblies at the national level. Based on this unexpected set of results, I concluded that multilingualism in such emerging transnational spaces 'from below' stimulates participative and inclusive decision-making, instead of preventing it. As a result, formerly marginalised groups, such as migrants, find it easier to make their claims and to build alliances in these cosmopolitan European meetings. A better gender balance and the inclusion of migrants in such meetings are just two illustrations of the difference between European and national level meetings (Doerr 2007).

A study of transnational public spaces in movements like the ESF shows that structural obstacles to participation mainly emanate from exclusion based on both non-material and material aspects, such as lacking resources and access to the relevant information to participate. However, in relation to their linguistic diversity, the comparison between European preparatory meetings and those at the national level in Germany and the UK indicates that the European meetings were more democratic internally. In particular, new participants and activists from horizontally organised groups that lacked material resources perceived the European preparatory assemblies to be more transparent and procedurally democratic than the domestic, country-wide preparatory assemblies. This was due to the fact that the difficulties of communication, both political and linguistic, were made explicit in the European meetings and an inclusive procedural setting was created to find common agreement. This is not to say that participants found the European preparatory assemblies particularly open participatory spaces, especially as the ESF process was dominated by a vanguard of professional activists and informal decision making. However, in such multilingual assemblies a 'culture of mutual listening' predominated. Participants made a conscious effort to listen to speakers from different countries and groups and allow them to be heard. In addition to translating, the volunteer network of interpreters, dubbed 'Babels', sensitised participants to the need to speak clearly and to respect the languages, cultures and backgrounds of others.

At the national level, institutions such as Babels and activists with multiple political backgrounds or transnational life histories, for example, those who could mediate between different languages and political cultures, were either absent or were not accorded the importance given to them in the European meetings. In Germany the meetings were dominated by a highly controversial style of decision making, in which a few activists backed by big organisations made the decisions, and in which gender aspects of democracy and groups of migrants or activists that lacked resources, were more easily ignored. In the UK ideological difference created misunderstandings and conflict, which made dialogue and decision making very difficult. In both countries the discussion style of meetings privileged the socio-linguistic codes of traditional 'gatekeepers' in the public sphere, that is, 'powerful actors' 'who speak, write and understand the right language at the right moment' (Wodak 2002). These were mostly professional activists of large, well-funded organisations such as non-governmental organisations, political parties and trade unions.

These findings indicate that the democratic participation of citizens in transnational public spaces in civil society can emerge even in the absence of a shared idiom, common culture or communitarian foundation. In the case of Europe, multilingual public spaces built by non-established civil society actors under the conditions of inclusive procedures and using agents who facilitate access, might be more democratic than national public spaces operating in a single language. This questions theories of citizens' participation and democracy in Europe, in which the public sphere at the national level is often presented as an ideal, homogenous political public (Fraser 2005). I argue that ongoing transnational alliances and spaces created by civil society actors from below might open a window of opportunity for domestically marginalised groups to make their views known to a wider public. For example, activists from different local social forums in the UK have utilised the European preparatory assemblies in order to undermine the strength of influence of groups perceived as dominant at the national social forum process in the UK.

These findings support the idea that a *lingua franca* model in the EU context may be linguistically discriminatory (de Cillia 2002; Kraus 2004; Phillipson 2003), and suggest a conceptualisation of communicative democracy in transnational spaces of civil society that treats linguistic pluralism as a precious resource. Instead of making democratic discourse impossible, a multilingual setting – provided that no single language dominates and an open institutional setting prevails – makes traditional mechanisms of discrimination and exclusion, as experienced in the building of the nation state and its public sphere, more difficult. 'Different languages are problematic without translation, as they are open to manipulation', says Souad, an ESF participant from London:

> However, the main effect of multilingualism is to make everything go more slowly, which is important, because then it gets politically more balanced. The European level is more public and pluralistic; people speak in front of many people who are backed by many movements. (Quoted by Doerr 2007)

Multilingualism can thus be seen as an asset, rather than an obstacle to the democratisation of global civil society.

Nicole Doerr, European University Institute, Florence

An overt awareness of the political significance and nature of words is also apparent in other instances that do not have potential legal consequences, such as US President Franklin D Roosevelt's explicit endeavour to find an appropriate name for the 1939–1945 war:

So I am looking for a word – as I said to the newspapermen a little while ago – I want a name for the war. I haven't had any very good suggestions. Most of them are too long. My own thought is that perhaps there is one word that we could use for this war, the word 'survival'. The Survival War. (Roosevelt 1942a)

As we know, the name 'Survival War' did not take hold. But even 'World War II', which became the common label in the West, was not used worldwide. The Soviet Union, for instance, chose 'The Great Patriotic War', which gave the (supposedly objective) historical event a completely different meaning in that it 'linked the conflict with the struggle against Napoleon ("The Patriotic War")' (Reynolds 2003: 14).

In more recent times, the German Conservative Party, CDU, after its defeat in the 1972 elections, established a 'project group for semantics' whose task it was to develop strategies to, as they called it, 'occupy' terms with meanings according to the party line (Klein 1991).

Elsewhere, the Jubilee2000 campaign consciously chose the name 'Jubilee2000' in order to trigger associations with the 'pattern of the Biblical jubilee of debt remission and freedom for debt slaves which was ordained to occur every fifty years in the old testament' (Jubilee2000 URL). According to Joshua Busby, this was an important aspect of the campaign's success in the US.

After the terrorist attacks on the World Trade Center in New York and the Pentagon Building in Virginia on 11 September 2001 (9/11), the politics of naming (political) opponents took on a new dimension: the frame of the 'global war on terror/ism', established by President Bush as the all-embracing label for much of US post-9/11 politics, has added a new and peculiar value to the term 'terrorist'. The institutionalisation of the 'global war on terror/ism' narrative made it easier for governments, such as the Russian and Columbian administrations, to apply the term 'terrorists' to rebel groups in order to depoliticise them. After 9/11 the Sri Lankan Government saw the chance of labelling the Liberation Tigers of Tamil Eelam (LTTE) not only 'terrorists', a term used by much of the international community anyway, but 'global terrorists', thus situating their struggle against the LTTE within the wider 'global war on terror/ism' campaign and thereby encouraging international support. In contrast, in an attempt to position themselves as political actors and 'freedom fighters', and to challenge their condemnation as 'terrorists', the LTTE explicitly condemned the 9/11 attacks as acts of illegitimate violence (Kleinfeld 2003).

As feminist theorist Dale Spender notes: 'Those who name the world have the privilege of highlighting their own experiences – and thereby identify what they consider important' (quoted in Bhatia 2005: 9).

Political investigations should therefore consider language: in particular, the political investigation of contemporary politics needs to interrogate the term 'global' because it has captured *contemporary* public, political and academic discourses in an unprecedented way.

The 'global'-isation of politics

The term 'global' has become a significant part of the world political lexicon. No political actor can do without it and it is widely used by the general public.

The quantitative dimension of the 'global'-isation of contemporary public and political discourses, the increase of what Robert Holton (1998: 1) calls 'globe talk' has been noted since the 1990s. Martin Albrow, for instance, even uses this observation as one of his arguments to illustrate the birth of a new age, the 'global age' (1996: 80).

However, 'globe talk' is not only about the ubiquity of single terms such as 'globalisation'; the 'global'-isation of public and political discourses is not only about the *quantitative* proliferation of 'glob*'-vocabulary. Rather, it is about the qualitative penetration of language through 'glob*'-words. This pervasiveness is seen in creative word constructions, such as globaphobia (Lawrence and Litan 1997), globo-cop (Lewis 1992), neoglobalism (Gorbachev in Hoffmann 1987), globaldegook (*The New York Times* 1985) and globalution (Friedman 1997). It is further seen in words such as globaloney, anti-globalisation, global-minded and globe-trotting, which in the past were used occasionally, but have since become commonplace neologisms, which means that they have been socially ratified in communication. This social ratification indicates the high degree of social acceptance of 'glob*'-language.

Of all 'glob*'-words, 'global' is the most popular. The use of the term increased more than tenfold in *The New York Times* between 1980 and 2007. But the 'global'-isation of language is not only about quantity. Examples such as Sam Sifton's restaurant review in *The New York Times* illustrates the embeddness of the term 'global' such that its meaning is assumed to be clear:

Oceo's menu is probably best described as post-global. A warm salad of curried chicken, with tiny dumplings flecked with coriander and lemony yogurt sauce, sits beside a delicate salad composed of hearts of palm with earthy pickled mushrooms and a piquant lemon-chili oil. (Sifton 2004)

Apparently, there is no need to explain 'global' or in this case, 'post-global', in a restaurant review; nor in

other cases such as when applied to the former Pope, John Paul II (*The Age* 2005), to poverty in African countries, to the 'war on terror', various 'terrorist groups', the 'environment' and to the 'HIV/AIDS crisis'.

First and foremost, 'global' seems to serve as the linguistic label of the *Zeitgeist*, or spirit of the times. This is seen, for instance, in the increasing appearance of the term in institutional names and official events and conferences, such as 'The Global Fund', 'UN Global Compact', 'Global Alliance for Information and Communication Technologies'. Although the database of the Union of International Associations (URL) shows that the absolute number of civil society groups with the term 'global' in their names is lower than names containing terms such as 'international' or 'world', it also reveals a striking and increasing trend towards 'global' names since the 1990s. However, more interesting than the increasing number of new institutions choosing a 'global' name is the fact that established organisations actually 'global'-ise their existing names. Thus, the Evangelical Missionary Alliance founded in 1958 changed its name to Global Connections in 2000 (URL); the Australian Baptist Foreign Mission of 1913 became Australian Baptist Missionary Society in 1959 and Global Inter-Action (URL) in 2002; Global Impact (URL) was founded as International Service Agencies in 1956; Citizens for Global Solutions started off in 1975 as Campaign for UN Reform; and the International Association on the Political Use of Psychiatry, which was founded in 1980, was renamed Global Initiative on Psychiatry (URL) in 1991.

The settling of the term 'global' in contemporary vocabulary is also seen in the increasing number of 'global' co-occurrences, of which 'global warming' is one of the most prominent. The mainstreaming of 'global warming' was sealed with its entry into the dictionary of new English words in the 1990s (Tulloch 1991). The 'global war on terror/ism' is another popular contemporary term that, in the time since it was introduced by the US administration in September 2001, has become a fixed linguistic short-cut for a complex narrative within which political decisions are framed worldwide, from military engagements in Afghanistan and Iraq to broader issues such as migration and, in the near future, possibly environmental measures (2007 report by the US Centre for Naval Analyses URL). In the US, the

expression the 'global war on terror/ism' became institutionalised through the establishment of the 'Global War on Terrorism Expeditionary Medal' and the 'Global War on Terrorism Service Medal' in March 2003 (US Executive Order 13289); and through the use of the acronym 'GWOT' in official documents which first appeared in a 2002 fact sheet of the US Department of State (URL).

It can be argued that 'global' has become a political currency – the term has become so embedded in the discourse that it is a socially ratified label now, rather than simply a frequently used term. As the earlier mentioned trend of 'global' re-branding and re-labelling indicates, it appears to be important and often essential to be associated with 'global' and to position oneself as 'global', at the same intensifying the 'global-'isation of the discourse. The term 'global' has gained an aura sufficient for it to be perceived as 'doing something' to something; it seems to add value and a certain status. It appears that 'global' gives credibility and importance to things and events; it even seems to be perceived as being able to transform, what Roland Bleiker (2003: 434) calls, the 'chronically tragic', like poverty, into something more 'spectacularly tragic'.

Today, in order to have a chance of reaching the world policy agenda and attracting broad public attention, to a high degree an issue needs to be perceived and ultimately socially ratified as being 'global'. Certainly, if an issue becomes 'global' it has succeeded in getting onto this agenda and powerholders cannot ignore it. Bleiker points out how the 'market-dependent and entertainment-oriented television networks favour heroic and spectacular images' and tragedies' (2003: 434), and in this sense it can be argued that the attribute 'global' appears to add a sense of 'spectacularity' that helps to make

something fit for this context. The term 'global' seems to be strangely embracing; it is used everywhere and appears to appeal to everybody and ultimately seems to refer to everybody.

This is obvious in the institutionalisation of the categories 'global issues' and 'global threats', which have become commonly and officially used to make sense of contemporary social reality. Both labels constitute two indispensable categories in contemporary world politics under which issues are reassembled and gain 'authoritative status'. Today it appears that no political organisation involved in world politics can do without an explicit 'global issues' agenda. Yet a brief look at the list of 'global issues' provided by different organisations reveals the abitrary nature of such selections. While the UN lists 50 issues under the rubric 'Global Issues on the UN Agenda' (URL) covering a pool of concerns from 'Africa' via 'Indigenous People' and 'Outer Space' to 'Youth', the US Under Secretary for Democracy and Global Affairs (URL) calls six issues 'global issues', namely, 'Democracy', 'Human rights and Labor', 'Environment, Oceans and Science', 'Population, Refugees and Migration', 'Women's issues' and 'Trafficking in persons'. Human Rights Watch deals with 27 issues under the label 'global issues', of which the UN, with its 50 'global issues', is one. The Global Civil Society Yearbook series has, to date, covered 16 issues that were introduced in the first edition as 'global issues' (Anheier et al. 2001: 7).[2] The constructed nature of the institutionalised category 'global issues' is further evidenced when one attempts to define what it is about these issues that makes them 'global'. On the UN 'global issues' list, for instance, 'Ageing', 'Youth' and 'Children' seem to be considered 'global issues' because they refer to humanity, and 'Persons with Disabilities' and 'Indigenous People' appear to be considered 'global' because these minority groups exist all over the world. In contrast, the 'global' nature of issues such as 'Iraq' and 'Question of Palestine' seems to evolve from geopolitical perceptions, while the 'global'-ness of the issue 'Outer Space' appears to relate to the

---

2 These are: capitalism, biotechnology, conflict/humanitarian intervention, corporate responsibility, the Statute of the International Criminal Court, oil, democracy, climate change, HIV/AIDS, the movement of labour, UN reform, biological and chemical weapons, violence against women, economic and social rights, water, war and peace.

globe understood as one of many planets in space. The variety of ideas and understandings of the term 'global' behind the apparently uncontested category of 'global issues' could not be more evident.

The communication material of civil society actors, such as that on the websites of, for instance, Greenpeace, Amnesty International, WWF, and Oxfam, further supports the argument that the term 'global' has become a popular political currency. Hardly anybody can do or will do without this term. Similar to the cataloguing of 'global issues', we find categories that have been institutionalised in civil society, such as 'global campaign', 'global call to action', 'global week of action'. However, the ubiquity of the term is not matched by its coherent use. Strikingly, in the communications of actors above, 'global' is often used interchangeably with 'international'. The 'About Us' document of Oxfam International (URL) aptly illustrates this observation:

Oxfam International is an international confederation, comprised of 13 independent non-government organisations dedicated to fighting poverty and related injustice around the world. Oxfam International is a global group of independent non-governmental organisations dedicated to fighting poverty and related injustice around the world.

The apparent lack of awareness of the difference between 'global' and 'international' supports the above assumption that, more than anything, 'global' expresses the *Zeitgeist*. In contrast to the term 'international', not only does 'global' appear to be perceived as less technical, with an almost emotional dimension, it is also simply more fashionable than 'international', adding a sense of 'spectacularity' to things and embodying a sense of (allegedly) embracing and appealing to everybody.

There are two main ways in which Oxfam, Greenpeace, WWF and Amnesty International use 'global'. First, it is used in the sense of 'across the world'. Oxfam's definition of the organisation, described above, falls into this category, as does Amnesty International's 'go global' strategies that imply, for example, that 'all over the world Amnesty International members and activists are campaigning to stop violence against women'. Although they are situated in the North, civil society organisations position themselves as being 'global' in the sense of being active everywhere.

The second use creates and emphasises the (hierarchical) distinction between 'local' and 'global'. Here 'global' refers to a (Northern) audience whose support is requested but, more commonly, it refers to (Northern) governments and international institutions that are being required to act. In contrast, 'local' refers to (primarily) Southern communities and regions. The self-description of WWF illustrates this point:

> The organisation is almost unique in that it has that local presence to global presence – talking to tribes of Baka pygmies in the central African rainforests, through to face-to-face discussions with institutions such as the World Bank and the European Commission.

Similarly, Oxfam's 'global calls' are exclusively and explicitly addressed to primarily Northern donor countries and it is to them that the issue at hand needs to appeal – hence, needs to be perceived as 'global'. Civil society actors and international institutions have adopted the term 'global' with enthusiasm, but the popularity and omnipresence of 'global' is not restricted to the public and political discourse; it has become a significant term in contemporary political studies too.

The 'global'-isation of political studies

Since the 1990s there has been an increasing 'global'-isation of the political studies discourse; the term 'global' has become commonplace among political scientists today. Its striking proliferation and widespread use defies attempts to draw a comprehensive picture of its application but, generally, the term is primarily used as an adjective

- meaning 'worldwide'
- in contrast to 'local', and 'regional'
- in contrast to 'national'
- in contrast to 'transnational' and 'international'
- in linguistic units such as 'global governance', 'global democracy', 'global market' and 'global civil society'; namely, in connection with 'traditional' social and political science concepts.

Here, as in the context of political actors, the last two points in particular reveal that, more than anything, 'global' is applied as an expression of a general *Zeitgeist* rather than as a robust concept. For example, in the Introduction of the first edition of the Global Civil Society Yearbook the editors challenge the notion that the 'global' in 'global civil society' 'sounds too grandiose' by pointing out that alternatives, such as 'transnational', simply understate 'what is really out there' (Anheier et al. 2001: 16). This illustrates the way that 'global' is often used, on the basis that it

'somehow suits and captures' contemporary phenomena without attempting to define why this is, and what the term actually implies. The 'global'-isation of concepts seems to be a reaction to the dilemma of contemporary times, which seem to be 'different in kind'; as many argue we might be experiencing the 'early stage of a profound ontological shift (Rosenau 1996: 248), a 'brave new world' (Bartelson 2000: 192) that challenges established social and political science concepts. The application of the term 'global' to traditional concepts appears to be a way of facing this 'new world'.

This reveals that, in general, in political studies 'global' is mainly used as a derivation of 'globalisation' which, in turn, has come to be 'a talismanic term, a seemingly unavoidable reference point for discussions about our contemporary situation' (Low and Barnett 2000: 54). 'Globalisation', then, is understood in two broad senses in the present discourse: (a) globalisation associated with an increasing interconnectedness and (b) globalisation associated with a growing 'global consciousness'. These two associations, in turn, implicitly lead to two broad understandings of 'global' as worldwide (in a spatial sense) and the 'world as a whole' (in a normative sense).

Given the proliferation of the term 'global' and its multiple uses it is surprising that 'global' is rarely reflected upon critically. The opening sentence of Peter Berger's study of global civil society and religion is symptomatic of the common treatment of 'global':

> Let us assume that we are reasonably clear about what is meant by 'global' and by 'religion'. But what about 'society'? (2005: 11)

The naturalisation of 'global'

In political practice, one of the few fields in which the use of the term 'global' is occasionally the subject of discussion is in the environmental discourse, in particular in the debate about the reform of the environmental activities of the UN and the (dis)advantages of upgrading its Environment Programme (UNEP) into a specialised agency. In this context, there is occasionally the conscious and clear distinction between the terms 'world' and 'global'. While 'world' is used explicitly in the sense of 'universal', 'global' is very consciously used in opposition to 'local' (Esty and Ivanova 2001). As Biermann (2002) mentions, this has provoked rejection of the term in the past – especially by 'developing countries', which fear that the explicit 'global–local' distinction would imply they alone would have to deal with (local) environmental problems such as water pollution, while issues of interest to the 'developed world' are honoured with the term 'global' and hence are privileged. This explicit awareness of the implications of the label 'global' is, for instance, seen in the statement by Indian activist Vandana Shiva that:

> The notion of 'global' facilitates this skewed view of a common future. The construction of the global environment narrows the South's options while increasing the North's. (Shiva 1998: 233)

Other instances in which the use of the term 'global' is explicitly questioned, however, are hard to find. In March 2007 US Democratic staff director Erin Conaton wrote a memo in which she advised her colleagues in charge of the preparation of the US defence authorisation bill to '"avoid using colloquialisms," such as the "war on terrorism" or the "long war," and not to use the term "global war on terrorism"' (*International Herald Tribune* 2007). But her concern focused mainly on the term 'war'. In fact, the public discussion about the linguistic unit 'global war on terror/ism' is an excellent illustration of how much the term 'global' is taken for granted. From the beginning of the conflict there was a debate about the appropriateness of the label the 'global war on terror/ism'. Yet it is the term 'war', rather than the term 'global' that is publicly discussed and questioned, as can be seen, for instance, in Jeffrey Record's examination of the features of the 'global war on terrorism', published by the Strategic Studies Institute, which talks of 'two issues that continue to impede understanding of the GWOT: its incomplete characterisation as a war, and the absence of an agreed upon definition of terrorism' (2004: 2) – omitting 'global' as the third.

This 'naturalisation' of 'global' is also obvious in many parts of the political studies discourse. Although there is an increasing 'global'-isation of the discourse, there is at best rudimentary and sporadic reflection of the various uses of the term. It can be argued, but would need more space for proper elaboration, that so far the 'global'-isation of concepts that so obviously permeates contemporary political studies merely entails a re-labeling, not a profound re-conceptualisation. The (alleged) ontological changes that 'global' is supposed to highlight are rarely reflected in the way the term is added to 'traditional' concepts today.

Peter Berger's symptomatic belief that 'global' does not need further elaboration because one can be 'reasonably clear' about what it means seems to evolve from two things. The first is its derivation from 'globalisation'. While 'globalisation' is subject to rigorous definition, 'global' slips under the radar screen. In fact, it is exactly the popularity and constant focus on 'globalisation' in much of the political studies discourse that blurs the need to investigate 'global' in its own right. This is connected to the second thing, namely, the fact that 'global' is simply considered a neutral term; such that one just needs to look it up in the dictionary. But a brief reflection on the term as such and its dictionary definition reveals the challenges associated with it.

The political dimension of 'global'

The word 'global' is first of all an adjective, and as such it refers to a state of being. According to the *Oxford English Dictionary* (OED) 'global' means:

> pertaining to or embracing the totality of a number of items, categories, etc.; comprehensive, all-inclusive, unified; total; spec. pertaining to or involving the whole world; world-wide; universal. (OED URL)

In this sense it dates back to the late nineteenth century. 'Global' is associated with the term 'globe', which, in the English language, dates back to the mid-sixteenth century when it meant 'the earth'. The term 'globalisation', which entered the (economics) discourse as a neologism through Theodore Levitt's 1983 *Harvard Business Review* article, 'The Globalization of Markets' (Teubert 2002: 157),[3] is listed as one of the derivations of 'global'; it does not have a separate entry but it is defined as 'the act of globalising'. To 'globalise', in turn, is defined as 'to render global'. Hence, according the *Oxford English Dictionary*, both latter terms are derived from 'global'.

The problem with accepting that 'global' is a clear and neutral descriptive term is apparent from a

---

3   Although the term was used before Levitt's 1983 article (see Modelski's work in political studies), Levitt's article is commonly acknowledged as having contributed to its use as a neologism.

Box 11.2: Wikipedia

Wikipedia is the name of one of the most successful inventions in the recent history of the worldwide web. It is an online encyclopaedia that was launched on 15 January 2001 by the US entrepreneur Jimmy 'Jimbo' Wales and the philosopher Larry Sanger as an 'effort to create and distribute a multilingual free encyclopedia of the highest possible quality to every single person on the planet in their own language' (Wales 2005).

Wikipedia is a web-based platform that is potentially global because it is accessible via the Internet and therefore not bounded by national borders. Instead of being a national-territorial project it is divided into separate language editions. Access depends not on nationality but on possession of the requisite language skills and a connection to the Internet. Currently, Wikipedia exists in more than 250 languages and contains a combined total of approximately 7.5 million articles. The English-language version is the largest, containing almost 1.85 million articles (Wikipedia 2007). Fourteen of the other language versions each contain more than 100,000 articles. Wikipedia is therefore the most comprehensive encyclopaedic companion published to date. Apart from that, it ranks among the top ten most visited sites on the Internet. According to the latest survey in April 2007 by the Pew Internet and American Life Project, about 36 per cent of adult US Internet users consult Wikipedia and 8 per cent use it every day (Rainie and Tancer 2007).

Wikipedia is operated by the Wikimedia Foundation, a not-for-profit organisation that relies primarily on private donations and holds regular fundraising events. Its software and content are licensed under the GNU[1] general public licence and the GNU free documentation licence, respectively. These licences give users the rights to copy, redistribute and modify the software, as well as the content of Wikipedia.

The name Wikipedia is made by a combination of 'encyclopedia' and 'wiki'. A Wiki is a type of collaborative website, a set of linked pages that enables documents to be authored collectively. The first application was developed by programmer Ward Cunningham in 1995 and named after the Hawaiian expression *wikiwiki*, meaning 'fast'. Today, Wikis are widely used, for example, in business, universities, schools and libraries. A Wiki provides open access so that anyone can edit documents, allowing users to rewrite, add, remove and link material. Thus, its structure and content are open to editing and evolution. Surprisingly, all forms of activity, even if undesirable, such as 'editorial vandalism', are allowed and there are no software features to prevent problematic user behaviour. Normally, modifications of text are not reviewed. Therefore, by their nature, Wikis are susceptible to vandalism and disruption. Instead of a team of editors that reviews new content, Wikis rely on the concept of soft security: damage is not prevented in the first place, but it is easy to undo. This is possible because every activity is registered and can therefore be monitored and, if need be, reviewed. For that purpose, most Wiki software applications possess additional functions to combat their vulnerability, such as the 'recent changes' page where each alteration is recorded, the 'history of changes', a chronological list of all versions of an article, and the 'diff function' that allows for a comparison of consecutive versions. Moreover, every entry is accompanied by a 'talk page', which is designed to resolve editing conflicts, and to permit planning and other types of coordination.

The functions outlined above are central to the collaborative open content system of Wikipedia. In this way, Wikipedia marks an important step in fulfilling the promise of the Internet to challenge the biased production and distribution structures of the mass media and the asymmetrical relationship between the producer and recipient of media messages. Thus, Wikipedia makes real alternative patterns of knowledge production through its online participation and cooperation.

However, the openess and the absence of formal editorial supervision of Wikipedia has led various critics to question its reliability and accuracy. They argue that it exhibits systemic bias and inconsistency, that articles often lack proper sources, that the same value is attached to expert and lay opinion. Most seriously, Wikipedia is accused of prioritising consensus over authoritative and well-established views, because conflicting viewpoints are given equal weight, which can lead to ambiguity (Matei and Dobrescu 2006).

Several contentious entries have nourished these objections. For example, the Wikipedia biography of former administrative assistant to Robert Kennedy, John Seigenthaler Sr, accused him of involvement in both Kennedy assassinations. This information appeared under his name for 132 days. Writing in *USA Today*,

Seigenthaler (2005) argued that such misleading and false information was a result of user anonymity, because Wikipedia does not require users to disclose their identity. Wikipedia is also subject to corporate and political spin. For example, the Siemens press office, under its then chief executive officer Klaus Kleinfeld, was accused of rewriting passages in the Wikipedia article about him.

Yet some initial comparisons between Wikipedia entries and articles in printed encyclopedias suggest that the levels of accuracy in both are similar. The scientific journal *Nature* (Giles 2005) asked 42 reviewers to examine articles from both the *Encyclopaedia Britannica* and Wikipedia. Only eight serious errors (four from each source) were detected. Smaller errors were also identified: 162 in Wikipedia and 123 in Britannica. In addition, linguistic studies concluded that the language of Wikipedia's co-authored entries is formal and standardised in a way similar to that of traditional encyclopaedias (Emigh and Herring 2005).

Moreover, the users of Wikipedia seek to address the problematic issues of quality and discontinuity of information. Although the project is accessible to all and unregistered visitors can perform most of the key functions, such as editing articles, a few features are restricted to particular user groups. Thus, a hierarchy of users with special access rights has emerged. For example, the administrators can safeguard delicate entries (such as on the Holocaust and George W Bush) to protect them from further editing, or block persistent vandals. Furthermore, Wikipedia has developed a set of policies and guidelines governing editing activities, central to which is the idea of consensus. Its core aim is a collectively produced encyclopaedia – Wikipedia does not have ambitions to publish original research or to be a platform for ongoing debate. Users are expected to respect other contributors and copyright restrictions, avoid bias and add information only if it is based on reliable sources, in relation to which a comprehensive system of rules and advice has been formulated.

An interesting question is why most Wikipedia users obey the norms in this comparatively unregulated online environment, where the enforcement of desirable behaviour remains difficult at best. It has been argued that when users move from peripheral to full participation, their activities and their perception of specific user roles (such as writers, administrators or stewards) are transformed. When novices contribute regularly they become aware of the community and start to learn its rules and guidelines (Bryant et al. 2005). Nevertheless, the motivation to contribute to Wikipedia, which can be time consuming and without financial reward, is still unclear. In contrast to other voluntary online projects, such as the Free and Open Source software development, there is no established public recognition system that could, for instance, be used in job applications. Some have pointed to the low transaction costs of contributing to Wikipedia (Ciffolilli 2003). Additionally, surveys refer to users' identification with the Wikipedia community, and the fulfilment that comes from using one's initiative and a variety of skills (Schroer and Hertel 2007).

Christian Pentzold, University of Technology Chemnitz

---

[1] *GNU is a recursive acronym for 'GNU's Not Unix', chosen because its design is like Unix but differs from this computer operating system in being free software and not containing any Unix code.*

simple reflection on the above definition. If 'global', an adjective, refers to the totality of a number of things, it connotes two things. First, it means that whatever 'global' refers to is either 'global' or not – 'global' refers to a state of being, of totality, hence, by definition, there cannot be degrees of 'global'. This makes comparative expressions such as 'a more global world' (Annan 2000: 14) hard to grasp – or at least intrinsically unclear if one follows the common dictionary definition. By contrast, the term 'globalisation' implies a process (however defined). Accordingly, the process of 'globalisation' can vary and variations can be measured on the basis of the definition of the process and its indicators.

The same applies to the adjective 'globalised'. 'Globalised' refers to the state of being of 'a thing' that has been influenced by the process of 'globalisation'; like the term 'globalisation', 'globalised' implies that varying degrees are possible – hence, a thing can be more or less 'globalised'. The contrast between 'globalised' and 'globalisation' on the one hand and 'global' on the other, reveals the second connotation of the apparently straightforward idea of 'global'. By definition, the attribute 'global' appears readily verifiable, at least easier to verify than attributes that imply degrees. In order to verify and agree that something is 'global' one just needs to know the unit of the items which it refers to. Thus, the second

connotation of the OED definition of 'global' is that it implies a pre-assumption about a pool of items that are then categorised into being either 'all-embracing' (= 'global') or not.

This reflection on the term 'global', as defined by the OED, and its derivations, 'globalisation' and 'globalised', shows that discussing and thinking about 'globalisation' depends ultimately on the definition of the concept. Indeed, discussions about the concept of 'globalisation' fill libraries. Discussions about 'global', on the other hand, do not so much depend on the definition of the term as such, and in this respect (if one takes the dictionary definition) one can actually agree with Peter Berger that it is 'reasonably clear' that the term 'global' refers to some sort of totality of items. Rather, the evaluation of and discussion about 'global' depends on the definition of the pool of items to which the adjective refers. In order to be able to critically discuss, assess and ratify whether something can be reasonably considered 'global', one needs to know the underlying pre-assumed idea to which it refers. Yet, as this chapter argues, there is hardly any critical reflection on the use of 'global' in public, political and political studies discourse.

This lacuna appears to exist because of the general assumption that the underlying unit is clear: as the OED suggests, it is 'the globe'. Indeed, many writers on 'globalisation' start by referring to the dictionary and pointing out the relation between the terms 'globe' and 'global' (for example, Scholte 2005). As is seen, for instance, in Martin Albrow's linguistic elaborations, the 'globe' is then associated with something material:

> It [global] refers back to the globe, but the subtleties of the expansion of the idea depend on the different place given to human agency in a global as opposed to a national context. The nation occupies a contested natural/ideal status; the globe has an undisputed materiality, however, far removed it is from the daily behaviour of those who refer to it in their thoughts and deeds. (Albrow 1996: 81)

Thus, based on the 'natural' unit 'globe', 'global' is then often automatically associated with 'humankind as a whole' and 'everybody around the globe'.

If one accepts the theoretical premises of the political dimension of language sketched here and the nature of linguistic signs and meanings, it is evident that the idea of 'an undisputed materiality' is problematic. But even if one does not sign up to a postmodern theoretical point of view, 'global', in the sense of 'worldwide' as well as 'humankind as a whole', cannot be used in an absolute sense, at least not in a 'natural', descriptive way, because it cannot be empirically verified. Hence, from the beginning there is always an element of construction in it, which means that it is never neutral but always a political statement. 'Global' per se makes whatever it 'describes' a political issue and asks for a revealing of the pre-assumption of the pool of items it is applied to refer to.

With regard to the study of contemporary world politics, the 'naturalisation' of 'global' is particularly surprising. Even if one does not start from the position that terms and language are essentially political in nature, the current critique of 'globalisation theory' in general, and the argument of political scientist Justin Rosenberg in particular (albeit inadvertently), reveal a paradox that readily raises interest and suspicion about the term 'global' and its application in contemporary politics.

The 'global' paradox of contemporary politics
The terrorist attacks of 9/11 and their aftermath, which, to a great extent, have been permeated by the influence of what is called 'the global war on terror/ism' in

general and the US-led military interventions in Afghanistan and Iraq in particular, have triggered much discussion about the state of 'globalisation' (Held and McGrew 2007). In this context, Justin Rosenberg announced that '"the age of globalisation" is unexpectedly over' (2005: 2) – 'unexpectedly' because, for him, the idea of globalisation was never more than a 'craze', the *Zeitgeist* of the 1990s' (2005: 2). Consequently, it was only a matter of time until the 'follies of Globalisation Theory' (Rosenberg 2000) were exposed and the idea of 'globalisation' was revealed as the basis for a 'systematic misinterpretation of the 1990s' (Rosenberg 2005). The fact that this (finally) happened, thanks to 9/11 and its aftermath, according to Rosenberg, is obvious in the 'recent disappearance of this word [globalisation] from Anglo-American media and governmental commentaries [that] has been almost as sudden as its meteoric rise a decade ago' (Rosenberg 2005: 3).

Whether or not one agrees with Rosenberg's overall assessment that 'globalisation theory' is the result of a 'subjective correspondence to the lived experience' (2005: 2) that 'elbowed out the assumptions and resources of more traditional approaches' (2005: 10), and whether or not one is convinced by his praise of Marxism, it is evident that recent political developments suggest a (re)turn to concepts such as 'unilateralism' and 'geopolitics'. Indeed, hopes that 9/11 would strengthen institutions such as the UN and readjust the unilateral direction of the pre-9/11 Bush administration were disappointed – most obviously in the face of the so-called Bush Doctrine and its emphasis on pre-emptive military strategies, as outlined in Part V of the 2002 US National Security Strategy (URL).

Assumptions such as the belief that the US 'military autonomy is decidedly compromised by the web of military commitments and arrangements in which it has become entangled' (Held et al. 2003: 144) simply do not correspond to recent US foreign policy practice. Likewise, the unprecedented scale of civil society mobilisation on 15 February 2003 barely affected the British government's decision to support the invasion of Iraq. In general, the concept of a 'global civil society' still triggers much critique because it does not very obviously resemble everybody's perception of social reality. Rather, contemporary post-9/11 social reality seems to be about 'heightened nationalism, the reassertion of geopolitics, US military hegemony, the strong state and the closing of borders' (Held and McGrew 2007: 1). Yet Rosenberg's assumption that the term 'globalisation' has disappeared from Anglo-American public and political discourse is proved wrong by empirical evidence. As outlined above, 'globe talk' is not decreasing in the 'Anglo-American media and governmental commentaries' at all. In regard to 'globalisation', a study of *The New York Times*, for instance, reveals that during the first five years of the new millennium the term appeared in 2,850 articles, and was used more often than in the last two decades of the twentieth century (1980–1989, 606; 1990–1999, 2164; total = 2770), with a constant rise in its annual use. And, as was outlined above, so did 'glob*'-vocabulary in general; most prominently the term 'global' itself.

Thus, Rosenberg's globalisation critique inadvertently highlights the necessity of taking the term 'global' seriously in that it raises awareness of an (alleged) paradox: although contemporary political practice seems to be permeated by unilateralism and explicit national interests rather than by (the ideal of) 'global governance', it is more than ever embedded in a 'global' rhetoric. This paradox is especially apparent in regard to current US President George W Bush.

For example: George W Bush's 'global' politics

The term 'global' has a history in the US presidents' public papers going back to 1942, when it appeared for the first time in a remark at a press conference by US President Franklin D Roosevelt (1942b). In fact, the term was then used in a context that has become prominent again today; namely, in the context of a 'global war'. In 1942 Roosevelt persuaded US citizens to be more supportive of the 'global war' that the country was fighting against Nazi Germany and its allies:

> The Nation must have more money to run the war. People must stop spending for luxuries. Our country needs a far greater share of our incomes. For this is a global war, and it will cost this Nation nearly $100,000,000,000 in 1943. (Roosevelt 1942c)[4]

The papers of both US Presidents Clinton and George W Bush reflect the above mentioned trend of the striking 'global'-isation of political discourse. By 25 April 2007 President Bush had used the term in a total of 839 public papers.

'We live in a global economy, as you well know' [5]

The first thing that attracts one's attention when reading President Bush's public papers with a particular interest in 'global' is the strategic application of the term.[6] 'Global' is applied remarkably often as a rhetorical device in order to justify a political decision. The reasoning behind this justification is that because something is 'global', something else needs to be done. Through this strategy political actions are framed and justified as political reactions to something 'global' 'out there' which, by default, implies a logic of inevitability. The link between what is (called) 'global' and a particular political decision is explicitly established through terms such as 'therefore', 'because', 'that is why', and 'so'. This rhetorical strategy is used particularly often in regard to economic issues and issues of US competitiveness as in the following examples:

> In other words, we've got to get education right not only because it's a national responsibility but because we're in a global world. (Bush 2006b)

> We got to make sure there's math and science in our high school classrooms so our kids have the skills necessary to compete in this global economy. (Bush 2004a)

The intriguing aspect of this rhetorical strategy is that the term 'global' is not explained. Though it serves as the central component in the justification of political decisions, it is naturalised. President Bush does not reveal what this term actually implies and why and how the 'global' nature of, let's say 'the world' (inevitably) leads to the political decision suggested. In addition, the impression that this 'global' nature leaves no space for alternative political (re)actions is further *actively* constructed as a 'fait accompli' through the use of expressions such as 'see', 'you know', and 'as you well know':

---

4 *Of course, in contrast to Roosevelt's 'global war', George W Bush's war is linked to few, if any, civilian sacrifices, such as tax increases, on the US home front.*

5 *Bush 2006a*

6 *The analysis in this section is based on a computer-assisted analysis of the corpus of all public papers by President George W Bush that include the term, 'global'. The corpus contains 839 documents. The documents were filtered from the online database of the American Presidency Project (url) which holds all presidential papers.*

© Jez Coulson/Panos Pictures

See, this is a global economy, whether people like it or not. (Bush 2006c)

See, we're in a global conflict. (Bush 2006d)

We live in a global economy, as you well know. (Bush 2006a),

culminating in statements such as 'Blair knows what I know – Prime Minister Blair knows what I know, that 'we're in a global war' (Bush 2007). Thus any questioning of the link between the 'global' nature of the world and the proposed policy decisions or President Bush's underlying 'global' world view are ruled out. Yet 'global' is used as *the* argument.

'[G]lobal means global' [7]

The strategic use of 'global' as a justification for policy decisions is fundamental for President Bush's 'global' rhetoric. Though the underlying idea of 'global' is rarely explicitly revealed, a close reading of the papers shows that it is exclusively based on a US perspective. The term, as it is used in President Bush's papers, has nothing to do with 'humankind as a whole', let alone with any kind of 'cosmopolitan' ideal or even the idea of an 'international community', except when it comes to climate change.

The issue of 'climate change' is the only one in which President Bush uses the term 'global' in the sense of 'everybody's responsibility'. Here, again, the term 'global' is strategically used in order to support the current US policy strategy: to remind others that climate change is a 'global' issue, in the sense that everybody is equally obliged to act. Thus, he justifies the 'hesitant' and in some respects even unilateral US position in regard to 'global' climate change initiatives, such as the Kyoto Protocol, by arguing that since it is a 'global' issue, the US is not willing to take significant

steps first, let alone without parallel action by developing countries, in particular China and India. This is illustrated in the following remark at a press briefing:

When you're talking about global emissions, that means – global means global. So everyone is emitting up into the air. And if there are no actions taken by the major developing countries, like China and India ... you're going to put the American economy at a great disadvantage. (Perino 2007)

From 'global terrorism' to 'global war'

An analysis of 'global' co-occurrences offers further insight into the ways in which the term 'global' is applied and the ideas associated with it.

Prior to the terrorist attacks of 9/11 the most frequent 'global' co-occurrences were 'global economy' and 'global trade', both in President Bush's papers and in the 2000/1 President Clinton's papers. This changed after 9/11. 'Global economy' was replaced by 'global terror', followed by 'global terrorism'. Though it is unsurprising that the frequency of the use of terms such as 'terrorism' and 'terror' increased after 9/11, because the 9/11 attacks were interpreted as 'terrorist attacks' by the US administration, there is nothing 'natural' about its co-occurrence with the term 'global'. So what does the 'global' 'do' and mean in these contexts?

First of all, as noted above, 'global' is very much based on a US perspective. Immediately after the terrorist attacks of 9/11 'global' was used in the sense that something 'global' had attacked the US. Since 'terror' and 'terrorism' was 'global', the US was no longer safe and needed to take measures to defend itself against a 'global' threat, a threat of 'global reach'. In this context, the term 'global' referred to the nature of the 'new' threat: in fact the 'global' was very much associated with 'American' in the sense that this new 'global' threat was perceived as 'global' only when it suddenly reached American soil. The reaction was to fight against this 'global' threat by launching a war against 'global' terror/ism:

Today I am pleased to issue the National Strategy for Combating Terrorism. This strategy outlines the effort our Nation is making to win the war against global terror. (Bush 2003)

America will not rest; we will not tire until every terrorist group of global reach has been found, has

---

[7] Perino 2007

been stopped, and has been defeated. (Bush 2002a)

... our Nation is just beginning in a great objective, which is to eliminate those terrorist organizations of global reach. (Bush 2002b)

At the end of 2004 a shift in rhetoric is noticeable. From October 2004 onwards, 'global terror' which was until then the most frequent use of the term 'global' is replaced by 'global war'. The shift in the use of 'global' can be traced to a particular event, the Presidential debate between John F Kerry and George W Bush on 30 September 2004 (Bush–Kerry 2004). During this debate John F Kerry is asked about his position on the concept of pre-emptive war, to which he answers:

The president always has the right, and always has had the right, for preemptive strike. ... But if and when you do it, Jim, you have to do it in a way that passes the test, that passes the global test where your countrymen, your people understand fully why you're doing what you're doing and you can prove to the world that you did it for legitimate reasons.

Asked for his position, President Bush responded:

Let me – I'm not exactly sure what you mean, 'passes the global test,' you take preemptive action if you pass a global test. My attitude is you take preemptive action in order to protect the American people, that you act in order to make this country secure.

From then on 'the war against global terror/ism' became the 'global war against terror'. At first sight, this may appear to be a minor rhetorical shift, but actually it signals a significant shift of perspective and attitude. Suddenly, it is not the threat that is 'global' but the American action that is justified as being 'global', which implies a more offensive position following the attitude that '[i]n our time, terrible dangers can arise on a short moment anywhere in the world, and we must be prepared to oppose these dangers everywhere in the world' (Bush 2005b):

And so long as I'm sitting here in this Oval Office, I will never forget the lessons of September the 11th, and that is that we're in a global war against coldblooded killers. (Bush 2005c)

We are now waging a global war on terror – from the mountains of Afghanistan to the border regions of Pakistan, to the Horn of Africa, to the islands of the

Philippines, to the plains of Iraq. We will stay on the offense, fighting the terrorists abroad so we do not have to face them at home. (Bush 2005a)

A shift in the use of key vocabulary can be generally seen as impacting on political identity and can read as a predictor of tendencies in future (foreign) policy (for example see Hellmann et al. 2005). In regard to President Bush's application of the term 'global' two things can be observed: first, a shift to a more offensive position is evident, which gives us reason to assume that US foreign politics will further shift towards unilateralism and a foreign policy that is based on an extreme national interest. Second, this foreign policy is (nevertheless) embedded in a 'global' rhetoric, in which a systematic and strategic use of the political currency 'global' is supposed to make US foreign policy discourse applicable to the 'global discourse' in general, which, to some extent, obscures its narrowly US-focused premises.

Conclusion

This Chapter has argued that the term 'global' constitutes a significant political currency today. Contemporary public, political and academic discourses are characterised by the use of the term 'global' in new ways and to an unprecedented degree. Yet because reflection on the diverse applications of, and ideas associated with, the term is rare, it is naively assumed that the proliferation of the term 'global' means that 'global' is 'global'. The term 'global' is naturalised, and taken for granted. Where it is interrograted, it usually centres around the idea of 'worldwide', reflecting the *Zeitgeist*, 'everybody around the world', 'humankind as such' and a sense of 'cosmopolitanism'. This 'naturalisation' of the term 'global' is problematic, though, because the idea(s) associated with it potentially challenge traditional perceptions of socio-political reality and address the important social coordinates of 'we' and 'them'; at the same time they (potentially) blur power relations and particular interests in that they cover them in (supposedly) all-embracing, 'global' terms.

Based on a post-structuralist understanding of the relation between reality and language, and based on the premise that the meanings that construct social reality are products of social processes, it should be acknowledged that whatever is brought into the discourse inevitably affects it by shaping the basis on

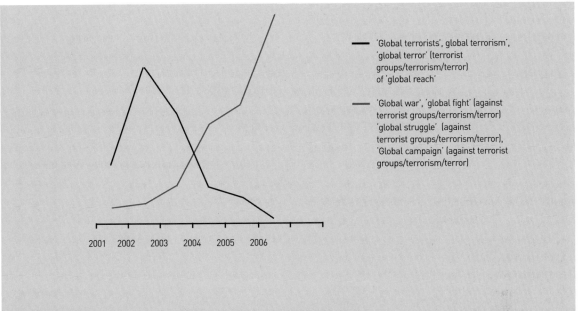

Figure 11.1: The development of the main use of the adjective 'global' in US President Bush's public papers between 11 September 2001 and 31 December 2006, illustrating the shift in Autumn 2004

which future communication and reality construction is built. This is especifically true for strong and influential (political) voices, such as that of the US president, but also of prominent civil society groups. Hence, the investigation of contemporary 'global' politics comes with the imperative to investigate the term 'global' as the significant, discourse-shaping term.

With regard to the use of the term 'global' by prominent civil society groups, this Chapter illustrates that their use of the term is primarily associated with a feeling of the *Zeitgeist*, but also with 'the North'. Hence, it could be argued that major civil society groups are discursively supporting a traditional idea of a world order in which (Northern) nation states are the predominant actors. The analysis of the term 'global' in President Bush's public papers shows how the term is used strategically as part of a policy attitude which is profoundly nationally focused or US-centric. The analysis of his use of the term revealed a shift in the rhetoric that indicates the strenghtening of the US's unilateral position under a 'global' roof.

Overall, this Chapter advocates a greater openess towards the analysis of language in the investigation of contemporary world politics. Since the term 'global' has become a valuable political currency worldwide it needs to be critically addressed through further analyses of what it implies and which coordinates of 'we' and 'them' are established, both in the context of political discourses and with regard to political studies. The term 'global' has become too important and influential to continue taking it for granted.

Albrow, Martin (1996) *The Global Age*. Cambridge: Polity.

Anheier, Helmut, Marlies Glasius and Mary Kaldor (eds) (2001) *Global Civil Society 2001*. Oxford: Oxford University Press.

Annan, Kofi (2000) *'We the Peoples' The Role of the United Nations in the 21st Century*. New York: United Nations Publications.

Bartelson, Jens (2000) 'Three Concepts of Globalization', *International Sociology*, 15(2):180–96.

Berger, Peter (2005) 'Religion and Global Civil Society,' in Mark Juergensmeyer (ed). *Religion in Global Civil Society*. Oxford: Oxford University Press.

Bhatia, Michael V (2005) 'Fighting Words: Naming Terrorists, Bandits, Rebels and other Violent Actors', *Third World Quarterly*, 26(1): 5–22.

Biermann, Frank (2002) 'Strengthening Green Global Governance in a Disparate World Society: Would a World Environment Organisation Benefit the South?' *International Environmental Agreements: Politics, Law and Economics*, 2: 297–315.

Bleiker, Roland (2003) 'Aesthetisising Terrorism: Alternative Approaches to September 11', *Australian Journal of Politics and History*, 49: 430–45.

Bryant, Susan L, Forte, Andrea and Bruckman, Amy (2005) Becoming Wikipedian: Transformation of Participation in a Collaborative Online Encyclopedia. *Proceedings of the 2005 International ACM SIGGROUP Conference on Supporting Group Work*, 9–9 November. Sanibel Island. http://portal.acm.org/citation.cfm?id=1099205&coll=ACM&dl=ACM&CFID=15151515&CFTOKEN=6184618&ret=1 (consulted 30 June 2007).

Bush, George W (2002a) 'Remarks at a Reserve Officers Association Luncheon'. 23 January.

— (2002b) 'Remarks Following Discussions With Prime Minister Ariel Sharon of Israel and an Exchange With Reporters' 7 February.

— (2003) 'Statement on the National Strategy for Combating Terrorism'. 14 February.

— (2004a) 'Remarks in a Discussion in Nashua, New Hampshire'. 30 August.

— (2005a) 'The President's Radio Address'. 9 July.

— (2005b) 'Commencement Address at the United States Naval Academy in Annapolis, Maryland'. 27 May.

— (2005c) 'Interview With the London Times'. 29 June.

— (2006a) 'Remarks to the American Council of Engineering Companies'. 3 May.

— (2006b) 'Remarks at Waldo C Falkener Elementary School in Greensboro, North Carolina'. 18 October.

— (2006c) 'Remarks on Energy in Pottstown, Pennsylvania'. 24 May.

— (2006d) 'Remarks at a Nevada Victory 2006 Rally in Elko, Nevada'. 2 November.

— (2007) 'Remarks to the World Affairs Council of Western Michigan and a Question-and-Answer Session in East Grand Rapids, Michigan'. 20 April.

Bush–Kerry (2004) 'First Bush–Kerry Presidential Debate'. 30 September.

Ciffolilli, Andrea (2003) Phantom Authority, Self-Selective Recruitment and Retention of Members in Virtual Communities: The Case of Wikipedia, in *First Monday*, 8(12). http://www.firstmonday.org/issues/issue8_12/ciffolilli/index.html (consulted 30 June 2007).

de Cillia, Rudolph (2002) 'Europäische Sprachenpolitik – Anspruch und Wirklichkeit. Ausgabe "EU: Sprachenvielfalt und Mehrsprachigkeit"', *Die Union – Jahreszeitschrift für Integrationsfragen*, 1(2): 29–41.

della Porta, D and L Mosca (2007) 'In movimento: "Contamination" in action and the Italian Global Justice Movement', *Global Networks*, 7(1): 1–27.

Derrida, Jacques (1976) *On Grammatology*. Baltimore and London: Johns Hopkins University Press.

Doerr, Nicole (2007) 'Is "another" public space actually possible? Deliberative democracy and the case of "women without" in the ESF process', *Journal of International Women's Studies*, Special Issue on the Forum Social Mundial. 8(3): 71–87. http://www.bridgew.edu/soas/jiws/April07/Doerr.pdf (consulted 10 July 2007).

Eagleton, Terry (1983) *Literary Theory: An Introduction*. Oxford: Blackwell.

Eden, Sir Anthony (1956) Speech, House of Commons, 4 November.

Emigh, William and Herring, Susan C (2005) Collaborative Authoring on the Web: A Genre Analysis of Online Encyclopedias. *Proceedings of the 38th Hawaii International Conference on System Sciences (HICSS'05)*. Waikoloa. http://ieeexplore.ieee.org/ie15/9518/30166/01385436.pdf?arnumber=1385436 (consulted 30 June 2007).

Esty, D C and M Ivanova (2001) *Making Environmental Efforts Work: the Case for a Global Environmental Organization*. Working Paper 02/01, New Haven: Yale Center for Environmental Law and Policy.

Fraas, Claudia (1998) 'Interpretations- und Gebrauchsmuster abstrakter Nomina – ein korpusbasierter Beschreibungsansatz', *Deutsche Sprache*, 26(3): 256–72.

— (2000) Begriffe – Konzepte – kulturelles Gedächtnis. Ansätze zur Beschreibung kollektiver Wissenssysteme, in H D Schlosser (ed) *Sprache und Kultur*. Frankfurt: Peter Lang.

Fraser, Nancy (2005) 'Die Transnationalisierung der Öffentlichkeit' [The transnationalisation of the public sphere]. www.republicart.net (consulted 1 September 2006).

Friedman, Thomas L (1997) 'Foreign Affairs; Berlin Wall, Part 2,' *The New York Times*, 22 December.

Giles, Jim (2005) 'Internet Encyclopedias Go Head to Head', Nature, 438 (7070), 900–1. http://www.nature.com/news/2005/051212/full/438900a.html (consulted 30 June 2007).

Glasius, Marlies and Jill Timms (2006) 'The role of social forums in global civil society: radical beacon or strategic infrastructure?' in M Glasius, M Kaldor, and H Anheier *Global Civil Society 2005/6*. London: Sage.

Held, David, Anthony McGrew, David Goldblatt and Jonathan Perraton (2003) *Global Transformations: Politics, Economics and Culture*. Cambridge: Polity Press.

— and Anthony McGrew (2007) 'Introduction: Globalization at Risk?' in David Held and Anthony McGrew (eds) *Globalization Theory: Approaches and Controversies*. Cambridge: Polity Press.

Hellmann, Gunther, Baumann, Rainer and Wagner Wolfgang (2005) *Deutsche Außenpolitik. Eine Einführung*. Wiesbaden: VS Verlag für Sozialwissenschaften.

Hoffmann, Erik (1987) 'Soviet Foreign Policy from 1986 to 1991: Domestic and International Influences', *Proceedings of the Academy of Political Science*, 36(4): 254–72.

Holton, Robert (1998) *Globalization and the Nation State*. London: Macmillan.

International Herald Tribune (2007) 'Republicans, Democrats Spar Over Use of Term 'Global War on Terror' to Include Iraq Action', 4 April.

Klein, Josef (1991) 'Kann man 'Begriffe besetzen'? Zur linguistischen Differenzierung einer plakativen politischen Metapher', in Frank Liedtke, Martin Wengeler and Karin Boeke (eds) Begriffe besetzen: *Strategien des Sprachgebrauchs in der Politik*. Opladen: Westdeutscher Verlag.

Kleinfeld, Margo (2003) 'Strategic Troping in Sri Lanka: September Eleventh and the Consolidation of Political Position', *Geopolitics*, 8(3): 105–26.

Kraus, Peter A (2004) 'In Vielfalt geeint? Europäische Identität in der Zwickmühle', *Internationale Politik*, 6: 723–31.

Lawrence, Robert Z and Robert E Litan (1997) '*Globaphobia: the Wrong Debate Over Trade Policy*'. Policy Brief 24, Brookings Institution. http://www.brookings.edu/comm/policybriefs/pb24.htm (consulted 2 May 2007).

Leftwich, Adrian (1983) *Redefining Politics: People, Resources and Power*. London: Methuen.

Levitt, Theodore (1983) 'The Globalization of Markets', *Harvard Business Review*, May/June.

Lewis, Flora (1992) 'A Globo-Cop No Longer', *The New York Times*, 1 August.

Low, Murray and Clive Barnett (2000) 'After Globalisation', *Environment and Planning D: Society and Space*, 18(1):53–61.

Matei, Sorin A. and Dobrescu, Caius (2006): Ambiguity and Conflict in the Wikipedian Knowledge Production System. Paper presented at the 2006 International Communication Association (ICA) Annual Meeting, Dresden, http://www.matei.org/ithink/papers/ambiguity-conflict-wikipedia/ (consulted 7 July 2007).

Perino, Dana (2007) 'Press Briefing by Dana Perino.' 2 April.

Phillipson, Robert (2003) *English-only Europe? Challenging Language Policy*. London: Routledge.

Record, Jeffrey (2004) *Bounding the Global War On Terrorism*. University Press of the Pacific.

Rainie, Lee and Tancer, Bill (2007) Data Memo, Pew Internet and American Life Project. http://www.pewinternet.org/pdfs/PIP_Wikipedia07.pdf (consulted 30 June 2007).

Reynolds, David (2003) 'The Origins of the Two 'World Wars': Historical Discourse and International Politics', *Journal of Contemporary History*, 38(1): 29–44.

Risse, Thomas (2007) 'Social Constructivism Meets Globalization' in David Held and Anthony McGrew (eds) *Globalization Theory: Approaches and Controversies*. Cambridge: Polity Press.

Roosevelt, Franklin D (1942a) 'Remarks to the Governing Board of the Pan American Union'. 14 April.
— (1942b) 'Excerpts from the Press Conference'. 24 April.
— (1942c) 'Fireside Chat'. 7 September.

Rosenau, James N. (1996) 'The Dynamics of Globalization: Toward an Operational Formulation', *Security Dialogue*, 27(3): 247–62.

Rosenberg, Justin (2000) *The Follies of Globalisation Theory: Polemical Essays*. London: Verso.
— (2005) 'Globalization Theory: a Post Mortem', *International Politics*, 42: 2–74.

Saussure, Ferdinand de (1916/2000) *Course in General Linguistics*. London: Duckworth.

Scholte, Jan Aart (2005) *Globalization: A Critical Introduction*.

2nd ed. Hampshire: Palgrave.

Schroer, Joachim and Hertel, Guido (2007) Voluntary Engagement in an Open Web-based Encyclopedia. Wikipedians, and Why They Do It. http://opensource.mit.edu/papers/Schroer_Hertel_Wikipedia_Motivation.pdf (consulted 30 June 2007).

Seigenthaler, John Sr (2005) A False Wikipedia 'Biography', *USA Today*. http://www.usatoday.com/news/opinion/editorials/2005-11-29-wikipedia-edit_x.htm (consulted 30 June 2007).

Shiva, Vandana (1998) 'The Greening of Global Reach', in Gearoid O. Thuatail, Simon Dalby and Paul Routledge (eds) *The Geopolitics Reader*. London: Routledge.

Sifton, Sam (2004) *The New York Times*, 19 March.

Teubert, Wolfgang (2002) 'Die Bedeutung von Globalisierung', in Oswald Panagl and Horst Stürmer (eds) *Politische Konzepte und verbale Strategien*. Frankfurt: Peter Lang.

The Age (2005) 'Divided Legacy of the World's First Global Pope'. 3 April, http://www.theage.com.au (consulted 1 June 2006).

Tulloch, Sara (1991) *The Oxford Dictionary of New Words: a Popular Guide to Words in the News*. Oxford: Oxford University Press.

Wales, Jimmy (2005) Wikipedia is an Encyclopedia, Mail from 8 March 2005. http://lists.wikimedia.org/pipermail/wikipedia-l/2005-March/020469.html (consulted 30 June 2007).

Wikipedia (2007) Statistics. http://www.en.wikipedia.org/wiki/Special:Statistics (consulted 30 June 2007).

Wodak Ruth (2002) 'Europäische Sprachenpolitik und europäische Identität. Ausgabe "EU: Sprachenvielfalt und Mehrsprachigkeit"' *Die Union – Jahreszeitschrift für Integrationsfragen*, 1: 7–22.

Wodak, Ruth and Scott Wright (2006) 'The European Union in Cyberspace: Multilingual Democratic Participation in a Virtual Public Sphere?' *Journal of Language and Politics*,5(2): 251–75.

Websites (consulted 2 May 2007)
Citizens for Global Solutions, http://www.globalsolutions.org/
Global Connections, http://www.globalconnections.co.uk/
Global Impact, http://www.charity.org/
Global Initiative on Psychiatry, http://www.gip-global.org/
Global Inter Action, http://www.globalinteraction.org
Global Issues on the UN Agenda, http://www.un.org/issues/Jubilee2000,
http://www.jubileeresearch.org/analysis/reports/world_never_same_again/contents.htm
Oxfam International, http://www.oxfam.org
Oxford English Dictionary, http://www.oed.com
The American Presidency Project database, http://www.presidency.ucsb.edu
The National Security Strategy of the United States (2002), http://www.whitehouse.gov/nsc/nssall.html
Union of International Associations, http://www.uia.org/
US Centre for Naval Analyses, http://www.cna.org
US Department of State, http://www.state.gov/coalition/cr/fs/12753.htm
US Under Secretary for Democracy and Global Affairs, http://www.state.gov/g/

DIFFUSION MODELS AND GLOBAL CIVIL SOCIETY

Helmut Anheier, Hagai Katz and Marcus Lam

Each edition of the Yearbook includes a Chapter that explores methodological approaches to global civil society from different social science perspectives. These Chapters are motivated by a belief that understanding globalisation requires approaches outside the conventional system of social science data reporting and analysis: globalisation creates new institutions, organisations, networks and communities, and their corresponding cultural and behavioural patterns, including problems of many kinds, that transcend traditional policymaking. These institutions, patterns and problems not only cut across the nation state and related units, but they increasingly create and reflect social realities that are sui generis.

Globalisation is more than the 'sum' of national societies and economies or their international aspects. It is something qualitatively and quantitatively different, and something that ultimately challenges the assumed equivalence between nation state, domestic economy, and national society. In our opinion (Centre for the Study of Global Governance 2001; Center for Civil Society 2006) as well as those of others (Beck 2002; Detlef 2006), this has profound implications for social science methodologies that require fresh approaches and innovative thinking in exploring how available social science methods can be applied to the study of globalisation.

Consequently, beginning with its inaugural edition, each Yearbook takes on a distinct methodological issue or approach: we have addressed the operational definition of global civil society (Anheier 2001), developed the Global Civil Society Index (Anheier and Stares 2002), presented geographic information systems (Anheier and Katz 2003), and introduced social network analysis (Anheier and Katz 2004) to the study of global civil society. More recently we proposed applying comparative historical methodologies such as event structure analysis, qualitative-comparative analysis and fuzzy sets approaches to examine global civil society (Anheier and Katz 2005; Katz, Anheier and Lam 2006).

In this edition of the Yearbook, we look at diffusion models and related approaches, and illustrate their utility for understanding the essential features of global civil society: the dynamics of information flows, the spread of ideas and innovation, behavioural patterns, forms of organising, advocacy and protest. Diffusion can take place between centres and peripheries, elites and more marginal groups, and among actors who find themselves in coalitions or caught in conflict with each other. Diffusion is not necessarily top-down or from centre to periphery. On the contrary, many innovations take place at the crossroads, if not at the margins, of social systems rather than their centres. Indeed, in the context of globalisation, with an increase in cross-border exchanges of institutions and knowledge, diffusion often takes place via horizontal channels rather than hierarchical ones.

What in the previous paragraph may appear, at first sight, as rather abstract social processes are in fact the lived reality of a globalising world: for example, reactions to the publication of the cartoons depicting illustrations of Muhammad in the Danish newspaper *Jyllands-Posten*, on 30 September 2005, illustrate an instance of diffusion facilitated by globalisation, here in the field of media and communication: local reactions to a provincial publication, at first somewhat isolated and sparse, achieve national and then transnational prominence, and ultimately high policy salience across the globe, with protests turning increasingly violent, creating significant property damage, leaving many people dead, and affecting relations between Denmark, the EU and 'the West' on the one side, and Islam and the Arab world on the other. Other examples include the spread of suburban riots in French cities to other parts of Europe in 2005/6, the organisation of the global anti-Iraq protests in February of 2003, or the copycat effects of protest tactics (for example, the series of self-immolation protests against war, or the spread of demonstrations outside the homes of executives in the cosmetics industry).

Of interest here are questions such as, how is information disseminated among individuals and organisations that may or may not be connected with each other? What is the role of outside actors such as the media in pushing innovations and changes in groups or organisations? What links people and organisations in order to create common responses, or encourages copycat behaviour? What is behind the rapid diffusion of rumours and misinformation in some cases, and their containment in others? Why are some innovative ideas widely adopted while others are not? How do protest movements spread transnationally, and why do some turn violent while others remain peaceful?

Of course, these are complex questions, and we will not be able to answer them fully. What we seek to explore are aspects relating to the patterns and dynamics of diffusion processes involved in each question, and the basic empirical fact underlying these questions: globalisation facilitates the diffusion of information, values and behavioural patterns, and vice versa. The questions also imply that diffusion occurs neither evenly nor at equal pace across units, time and space; on the contrary, there are distinct patterns of diffusion that involve different thresholds of adoption and dissemination, thereby yielding characteristic processes, structures and outcomes.

Indeed, the notion of diffusion is frequently evoked in the globalisation literature, either implicitly or explicitly: prominent examples include Giddens (1990) and Harvey (1989), who argue that a general time-space compression makes interactions among previously unconnected entities more instantaneous and less likely to be held up by distance. Such compression also makes diffusion patterns less predictable than in the past. Other factors and consequences of diffusion, such as ease of information flows, new communication technologies, exchange of ideas, trade, cooperation and conflict are often mentioned, which Held et al. (1999) describe in terms of interaction extensity, intensity and volume. Similarly, the metaphor of the 'woven world' by Yergin and Stanislav (1998) expresses how transnational actors connect formerly disparate entities and issues, so everything becomes relevant everywhere – again, a pattern of greater connectivity both encouraging and changing diffusion processes. Castells (1996) put forth the idea of a global 'network society' in which processes occur in a 'space of flows' rather than conventional geographic-political space. Another example of the implicit use of diffusion ideas in the globalisation literature is Beck (1999) who describes globalisation as transmission belts that intersect more frequently in some regions of the world than in others, thereby creating a pattern of varying density and centrality in terms of interactions and flows.

Empirical research of dissemination and globalisation has slowly followed, much of it inspired by the groundbreaking work of Rogers (2003) who presented a model of how innovations spread through social systems. Understanding how diffusion works is most critical if the information disseminated is of significance and has the potential for change. For this reason, researchers emphasize the link between innovation and diffusion. According to Rogers (2003: 12), an innovation is '... an idea, practice, or object that is perceived as new by an individual or other unit of adoption,' whereas diffusion is a particular type of communication about innovation, and the process in which an innovation is communicated through certain channels over time among the members of that system. In this sense, diffusion is the fourth consecutive component of innovation after the stages of initiation, creation and implementation.

It also helps to think of innovation in a broader sense. For example, an activist may succeed in linking local issues (like labour market policies perceived as discriminatory by youths in French suburbs) to global ones (perceived Western attempts to dominate Islam or the Middle East) in ways that are convincing to other local activists and potential followers, and in ways that make this 'message' of potential interest to other groups in France or elsewhere where conditions may be similar. Sociologists use the term 'framing' to show how activists turn complex political realities into 'sense-making' interpretations, and the term 'political opportunity structures' to illustrate how activities use such frames to create communicable themes around issues when attaching them to perceived weaknesses in the political system and its governance structure. For diffusion models it matters little if the idea, practice or object is truly new; what matters most is that 'something' is seen as worthy of adoption by others and therefore begins a process of spreading within and across populations.

A basic assumption of Rogers' diffusion model is that innovations spread along established lines of social interaction and institutional system, that is, they follow some structure. Research has confirmed this, and also demonstrated that globalisation greatly facilitates diffusion processes: Soule (1997), Strang and Soule (1998), Ayers (1999) and Chabot (2004) among others, have used Rogers' framework or aspects and modifications thereof to model the diffusion of global civil society process such as social movements, protests, and collective action. Tarrow (2001) argues that with the waning of the Cold War, the diffusion of transnational non-governmental organisations (NGOs) as a model of organising in the 1980s and 1990s opened up the field of transnational politics and took it in new directions. Potoski and Prakash (2004) examine how globalisation facilitated the broad diffusion of ISO 14001, the non-governmental regime of environmental standards, across many countries. They find that ISO diffusion is both a result of, and patterned by, economic globalisation in the form of trade flows, political globalisation in the form of transnational governmental and non-governmental networks, and the pervasiveness of the Internet as a vehicle to encourage self-regulatory regimes of compliance rather than third party control.

Diffusion models are also a useful response to address what methodologists have long identified as 'Galton's problem', which was posited as one of the main issues affecting research into globalisation and global civil society (Anheier and Katz 2005). Galton's problem concerns the analysis of social units and actors as if they are independent entities, while in actuality they are dependent on each other, and are part of a larger structure of relations that are activated or enacted through diffusion processes. According to Detlef (2006) dependence among units/entities is inherent in many diffusion processes, and analysing them takes into account the influences between actors and entities as part of a complex association between structures and flows. Thus, analysing diffusion in transnational settings can help identify the emergent systems of non-contiguous institutions, organisations and individuals of a globalising world. Against this background, we will explore some basic notions and components of diffusion models.[1]

Diffusion Models

Diffusion models have become a rather technical and statistically demanding field in a number of the social sciences, especially sociology and economics, with applications in communications research, marketing, and technological as well as economic development. The basic idea underlying diffusion models, however, is relatively simple: diffusion is the spreading of a phenomenon from one unit to another, and diffusion models analyse the dynamics, patterns and outcome of this process (Mahajan & Peterson 1985).

There are various ways in which the spread of a phenomenon can occur, in particular whether the diffusion process is exogenous (induced from the outside) or endogenous (from within) or both. Furthermore, the phenomenon spreading in diffusion models can be dichotomous or continuous in the sense that different entities can be more or less associated with the phenomenon in question.

Together these entities or units, whether they innovate, adopt, spread or block the innovation, comprise a system that defines the boundaries between exogenous and endogenous change. Entities within the system must have the potential capacity of incorporating or adopting the phenomenon; all others without such capacity are outside the system. However, system units do not need to be located in the same place; they may well be in non-contiguous spaces and located in rather different cultural, economic and political contexts. Methodologically speaking, the system is a set of entities actually or potentially being able to incorporate the object of diffusion, irrespective of their location in space (although spatial proximity may affect diffusion, a tendency that various diffusion methodologies take into account).

Another important element in diffusion models is the medium or the agent in and through which phenomena such as information or innovations 'travel.' This includes a wide range of agents, from exogenous influences such as advertising agencies, and communication and the media generally, to endogenous agents such as persons communicating with each other, gossip, organisations exchanging formal information via the Internet, or one NGO executive observing another at a professional meeting.

---

[1] *Diffusion models can also address another methodological issue raised by Anheier and Katz (2006) – the 'black box' problem. While often social science methodologies take an input-output approach that does not examine the processes between the input and the output (hence the 'black box'), diffusion models focus not only on structures and behaviours, but also on the actual causal process by which they are generated.*

The basic diffusion model

The basic diffusion model posits that the rate of diffusion is a function of the difference between the total number of possible adopters in the system and the number of previous adopters at that time. The diffusion occurs at a specific rate from one entity in the set to another without regard to variations in the units themselves. Such thinking has a mechanistic, even deterministic feel to it, and may not reflect reality very well.[2] However, the basic diffusion model is a useful staring point. This model is expressed as a differential equation that represents the rate of diffusion:

$$dN(t) / dt = g(t) [N' - N(t)],$$

where $N(t)$ are the number of entities that have incorporated the phenomenon at time t; N' is the total number of entities that could eventually adopt it, i.e. N' is the full set of units in the system; and $g(t)$ the coefficient of diffusion at a given time (see below). At time zero (t=0), $N(t)$ is equal to the number of entities in the system that have initially incorporated the phenomenon of diffusion either as innovators or first adaptors. Throughout the process, the rate of diffusion $dN(t)/dt$ will depend on the number of units that have not yet adopted the object of diffusion or remain resistant as such. Conceptually, the most critical component of the basic diffusion model is the coefficient of diffusion $g(t)$, which can be defined in different ways. As we will see, each definition gives way to different diffusion models that offer different conceptualisations of the very nature of the diffusion process.

The external-influence diffusion model

The simplest variant is to set $g(t)$ as a constant (k), which has the object of diffusion spread through the system at a set rate. Very likely, the constant k represents the influence of external agents rather than the rate of prior adoptions or their impact on non-adopters. Put differently, people or organisations are exposed to a constant flow of messages from outside, and this is what causes them to adopt an innovation, not direct interaction with previous

adopters. For this reason, the resulting pattern of the external-influence diffusion model is a decaying exponential diffusion curve for cumulative adoptions (inverted 'elbow' function), presented in Figure M1. Over time, the cumulative rate of adoptions increases, albeit at a constant rate, and the rate of diffusion at any given time is dependent only on the strength of external pressures at that moment.

The model is important for what it does not take into account: namely, interactions between prior, current and potential adopters among the entities in the system. For this very reason, the process is 'driven' by outside agents and their influences. Prime examples of this process are the effects of mass media communications (radio, TV, advertising, propaganda etc) on the diffusion of information and awareness-building campaigns across a given population. As a general rule, the external influence model is useful and appropriate when (a) entities in the system are relatively isolated and have little chance or interest of direct communication; (b) the phenomenon to be disseminated is rather simple and does not require inter-personal validation; and (c) adequate information about the phenomenon is mostly available outside the system (Mahajan and Peterson 1985).

The internal-influence diffusion model

Whereas the external-influence model assumes that all entities in the system are basically identical and in a similar structural position vis-à-vis the external agent in question, the internal-influence model takes a different starting point. Here, $g(t)$ is seen as an index of imitation (l), taking into account the interaction between prior adopters $N(t)$ and potential adopters $(N' - N(t))$. In this case, the rate of diffusion is interaction-based; it is a purely endogenous process, a form of communication in which entities transmit the object of diffusion to each other. The more units that incorporate the object, the greater the opportunity for further diffusion among the declining pool of potential adopters.

This is the process presented in Figure M2. The figure shows an S-shaped curve of cumulative adoptions along a time dimension, which depicts a characteristic pattern of diffusion processes. The reasons for this regularity are straightforward: since adoption is a result of interaction, initially only a few entities can adopt the innovation (Rogers 2003, refers to these as 'innovators'); over time the diffusion

---

[2] *More advanced models are stochastic and allow for variations in the probabilities associated with diffusion from one entity to another.*

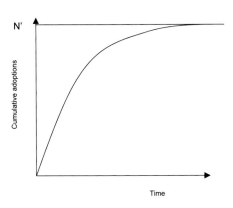

N'

Cumulative adoptions

Time

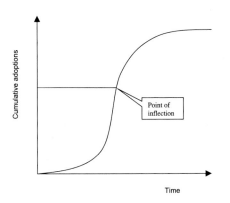

Cumulative adoptions

Point of
inflection

Time

process unfolds more fully as increasing numbers of previous adopters mean that more adoptions can take place. Finally, as more and more entities have adopted and fewer and fewer have not yet (or will not) (Rogers refers to these as 'laggards'), the increase in new adopters begins to slow, and the cumulative curve of adoptions eventually levels off. So, the internal diffusion curve starts with a rapid increase until a point of inflection where the number of entities that have incorporated the phenomenon equals the number that have not. After the inflection point the rate of diffusion decreases and begins to level off.

The internal-influence model describes a contagion process, and is most appropriate in cases where the innovation or the phenomenon to be adopted is both complex and visible, and the system is rather homogeneous, with a need for inter-personal validation and legitimating information (Mahajan and Peterson 1985).

Further expansions of diffusion models

The external and internal models are highly stylised versions of diffusion processes. In reality, it is probable that internal and external influences operate in tandem. Mixed models try to take account both processes, yielding many variations in both conceptual and mathematical terms that go well beyond what this Chapter can achieve. In mixed models, g(t) is a product m of the external constant k and the internal constant l, although the way the product is calculated depends on the specific model used. The mixed influence model also has a characteristic S-shaped curve.

Other models treat the fixed inflection point of .5 at which diffusion is maximised and the symmetry of cumulative adoptions in more flexible ways. This can be achieved either by adding an exponent to the basic diffusion rate equation (see above), or by adding a coefficient that varies the influence entities have over each other in the course of the diffusion process (thus making for a variable coefficient of diffusion). In one such modified model, early adopters have more influence over each other, and their influence decreases as more entities incorporate the innovation or information in question.

Another expansion of the basic models addresses the fixed number of entities in the system. It is often unrealistic to assume that N' is constant over the diffusion process, given the complexity of transnational systems and the frequent overlaps among groups from contiguous and non-contiguous settings. For example, as we will see below, the entities (number and types of groups and people) reacting to the Danish cartoons were not fixed but increased in number and changed in composition over time as the crisis unfolded. To take account of such developments, N' is seen as a function of factors relating to changes in population size and composition. These factors may be based on variables within the system itself (for example, the number of relations that groups have with outside organisations) as well as other systems (for example, organisations eager to join the system or that strategically employ diffusion processes for their own purposes).

The models briefly introduced above assume that diffusion processes are independent of each other. In reality, however, this may rarely be the case. The Danish Cartoons crisis did not occur in isolation from other processes such as the mobilisation of Islamic groups after the Iraq War, or the use of the Internet as a mode of communication for protest movements. A more obvious example would be the diffusion of personal computers, the Internet, WiFi, and telephony technologies as highly interdependent processes with partially overlapping time lines. Mahajan and Peterson (1985) suggest four different types of relationships among diffusion objects:

- Functionally independent but mutually enhancing, e.g. Islamic resurgence and anti-globalisation resistance
- Complementary, in that one enhances adoption of the other, such as the way that the spread of the social forums phenomenon enhances the emergence of the anti-globalisation movement and vice-versa
- Contingent, in that adoption of one depends upon incorporation of the other, such as with the emergence of the free software movement and the Internet
- Substitutable, in that one replaces the other, such as the way in which legal action has substituted the use of more traditional organising techniques such as mass mobilisation in some policy areas.

This perspective gives rise to multi-innovation diffusion models where adoption rates and the cumulative number of adoptions become contingent on multiple processes unfolding either simultaneously or partially separated in time but across similar non-contiguous spaces.

An important assumption in diffusion models is homogeneity of system entities, according to which it is assumed that individuals' preferences and incentives are uniform. This assumption runs up against two characteristics of social systems, their internal differences in terms of the values, norms, attitudes and behaviours; and the contingency of decision by individual and groups on others. Indeed, diffusion researchers like Rogers (2003) show how critical the degree of similarity among entities is for

accepting, rejecting or modifying innovations, including information generally. The terms homophily and heterophily are used to describe the extent to which entities are alike or unlike for diffusion purposes. Homophily is the degree to which two or more individuals who interact are similar in certain attributes, such as beliefs, education, socio-economic status etc. Sociological studies have shown that in free-choice situations, when individuals can interact with any one of a number of other individuals, the tendency is to select those who are similar. By contrast, heterophily is defined as the degree to which two or more individuals who interact are different in certain attributes (for a fuller discussion of homophily and heterophily see Burt 2005).

Clearly, homophilious communication processes yield diffusion patterns different from heterophilious ones. In the former, an innovation is more likely to remain within the defined social systems and would very likely give rise to the S-shaped curve, whereas in the latter, it is more likely to spread widely across systems but also more 'thinly,' slowly and unevenly. For example, the reactions to the Danish Cartoons crisis involved groups that were increasingly heterophilious, showing political and cultural 'jumps' and unevenness in geographical coverage and penetration. By contrast, we can assume that the suburban riots in French suburbs did not spread as much because protests remained with rather homophilious groups of disenchanted immigrant youths.

Threshold models address the presumed homogeneity in terms of individual decision making. Granovetter's (1978) groundbreaking work presents a model that attempts to capture a situation in which an individual or group makes a decision to adopt an innovation or any other object of diffusion only if a certain number of other entities incorporate it first. A threshold is the number of prior adoptions an individual requires before making the positive decision to adopt the object. With a small number of variables, threshold models can help shed light on seemingly enigmatic situations in crowd behaviour such as demonstrations and protest movements.

Granovetter (1978) presents a thought experiment where 100 people milling about a plaza have to make a decision whether to riot or not. In this crowd, each individual, having a unique number from 0 to 99, has a 'riot joining threshold' equivalent to their respective number. Thus, the individual with number 0 will immediately start a riot. Then individual 1, seeing person 0 rioting, will join in, followed by person 2 (needing two people to riot to make a decision to join in), will become part of the rioting group, and so on, until person 99 joins. It is a linear function of individual thresholds that very much like a domino effect turns a group of 'peaceful demonstrators' into a 'rioting menace' 100 strong.

Now imagine that individual 1 has a threshold of 2 instead of 1, but everybody else's threshold remains identical. Then, when person 0 start to riot, no one else will, as one individual's threshold, the critical link, has been changed. Thus, no riot will ensue, even though the distribution of thresholds changed only by 1%. Such cases can help understand why riots break out in some situations but not in others: very small changes in 'thresholds,' i.e. people's decisions, can have dramatic and massive implications. Moreover, thresholds may not be constant and reflect learned behaviour and experiences over time.

Analytic approaches to Diffusion Models

A major development since the 1990s has been to apply various analytic approaches and methodologies in the study of diffusion, and in particular spatial effects analysis models and event history analysis.

Spatial effects analysis focuses on the spatial aspects of social diffusion (Land and Deane 1992; Land, Deane, and Blau 1991; Tolnay 1995; Tolnay, Deane, and Beck 1996; Morenoff and Sampson 1997), and assumes that the diffusion process in a given system is affected by similar processes in nearby or adjacent areas. In a sense, spatial effects models view diffusion processes as part of macro contagion models, where one process can influence others as well as being influenced by them. Spatial effects models are sometimes combined with event history approaches, which allows diffusion models to take on a considerably more dynamic character, with multiple events unfolding along different dimensions (Strang and Tuma 1993; Greve et al. 1995). This research has produced evidence that contagion effects are indeed operating in waves rather than as isolated events (as shown, for example, by Tolnay et al. (1996) in their study of the impact of lynching events in southern counties of the US on subsequent events in neighbouring counties).

Event history analysis is an umbrella term for a set of procedures that analyse time-dependent processes. It is prominent in the field of international relations, where it has been used to examine the development of international conflicts. Regression models estimate the 'risk' of experiencing an event at a certain point in time, based on a set of covariates, with the assumption that both timing and spacing of observations become critical variables in their own right. The application of event history analysis to the modelling of diffusion is demonstrated in Soule's (1997) analysis of college anti-apartheid shantytown protests in the 1980s, and in Myers' studies of contagion effects in the racial riots of the 1960s (Myers 1996; 1997). In later work, Myers (2000) looks at characteristics of events (e.g. riots) and location (e.g. the city), and how these affect the contagious potential of the event. He examines the role of the communication system in places that would allow knowledge of events to spread to other places. Event history diffusion models allow four specific types of diffusion related predictors: intrinsic characteristics, infectiousness, susceptibility, and proximity (Strang and Tuma 1993; Strang 1995):

- **Intrinsic characteristics** are attributes of actors that increase or decrease their propensity to adopt behaviours, and include social characteristics of the population or local economic conditions (Olzak and Shanahan 1996). For example, the degree of ideological radicalisation of an organisation's membership will have an effect on its tendency to engage in a protest.

- **Infectiousness** involves an estimate of how influential the individual actor's adoption is on others. For example, Strang and Tuma (1993) found the magnitude of protest activity to be a strong indicator affecting further contagion in the analysis of riots. Similarly, the media exposure that the Seattle anti-WTO demonstrations received turned this event into a particularly powerful mobilising factor.

- **Susceptibility** is how responsive an individual actor is to others' adoption, and is measured using social, political and cultural characteristics. Some conservative religious communities, for example, are often resistant to new ideas and tend to attempt to isolate themselves from external connections.

- **Proximity** indicators have to do with the level of influence actors have on each other based on the closeness of their location. Proximity is related to structural attributes of physical distance and centrality (Strang and Tuma 1993; Myers 1996). For example, Minkoff (1997) uses organisational density as a factor affecting the successful diffusion of protest movements.

The diffusion of global protest – The Danish Cartoons Crisis

To illustrate how aspects of diffusion models can be applied to the study of global civil society, we use the protests sparked by the publication of 12 cartoons depicting the prophet Muhammad in a Danish newspaper, *Jyllands-Posten*, on 30 September, 2005. The publication of the controversial cartoons sparked protests not just in the predominantly Muslim countries of the Middle East but in Asia, Latin America, North America, and Europe. Protests occurred for over a year, driven in part by not just the initial publication but by subsequent reprints in other newspapers, news programmes, and television shows. Our rudimentary analysis presented here aims to demonstrate the logic, process, and application of diffusion models for the study of global civil society.

In terms of the diffusion models presented above, the Danish Cartoons Crisis would fit the mixed model, where both external and internal diffusion takes place: external, due to the extensive media attention the crisis received after the initial adoption of the object (i.e. concerns about the Cartoons and willingness to act), with a barrage of newscasts and repeated images on CNN, BBC World, Al-Jazeera, and many other international news services; and internal, because many of the groups participating in the protests were linked either personally or organisationally across locations that spanned large distances. Existing communication networks facilitated the spread of protests.

The first step in building a dataset for diffusion models is to construct a timeline of events with basic descriptive variables such as the date the protest began, the country/locality in which it took place, the number of protestors involved, and the length of the protest. One limitation of this kind of analysis,

however, is 'censoring.' Left censoring occurs when we do not have information about the beginning of an event, and right censoring occurs when we do not have information about the end of an event. In terms of the latter, the fact that our cut-off point for reported data was March 2006 means that the levelling-off phenomenon characteristic of the S-shaped curve beyond the inception point is less pronounced (see especially Figure M4). The source for most of this information was gleaned from Wikipedia (URL), which provides a detailed timeline of events, based on media coverage. Thus our data, which is dependent on events reported by the media that were recorded in Wikipedia, may not capture every incident relating to the Cartoons Crisis. It should also be noted that we did not cross-check and validate Wikipedia entries for the purposes of this exercise. Figure M3 shows a timeline of the number of protests, protestors and countries involved in the cartoon controversy, and the number of reprints of the cartoons. The protests peaked in February 2006, and occurred in many countries, including Hong Kong, New Zealand, Belgium, France, the UK and Finland.

Interestingly, no major protests took place in the United States with the exception of two minor protests that occurred on the college campuses of the University of Wisconsin and the University of California, Irvine. Since their initial publication in Denmark in September 2005, the cartoons were reprinted about 70 times in various newspaper and media outlets between October 2005 and February 2007, on average about eight reprints per month. As shown in Figure M3, approximately 75% (53) of these reprints appeared in February 2006, which may account for the large numbers of protests that occurred that month.

In terms of analysis, a second step is to determine the duration of time between events, in this case, protests. This time interval or period is called a 'spell' or diffusion period. In the public health field, if researchers are interested in death from AIDS, the spell may be the time between contraction of HIV and death from AIDS, and typically is measured in years. For shorter events, such as when radio stations first play a particular song, or when a video was first posted on the Internet, the spell may be measured in weeks, days, even hours. Given that this dataset concerns protests, which are normally thought of as daily occurrences, spells will be measured in days.

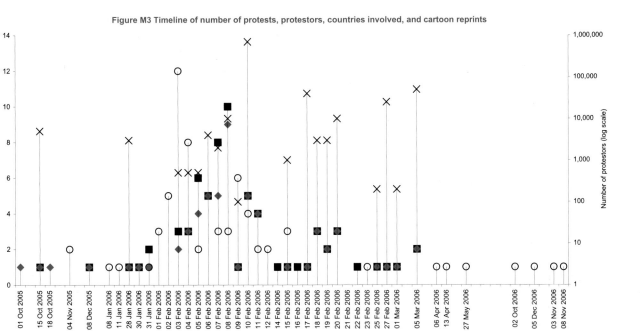

Figure M3 Timeline of number of protests, protestors, countries involved, and cartoon reprints

■ Protest ◆ Countries O Reprints ✕ Protestors

ce: Wikipedia, http://en.wikipedia.org/wiki/Timeline_of_the_Jyllands-Posten_Muhammad_cartoons_controversy

Specifically, there were 15 distinct spells and 31 events (see Table M1).

We apply event history analysis to model the diffusion of the protests listed above. We determine the risk set and the hazard rate similar to how we defined diffusion rates and potential adaptors in the external-influence model. The risk set is defined as, 'the set of individuals (or any subject of interest) who are at risk of event occurrence at each point in (discrete) time.' (Allison 1984: 16) The 'event' of interest or the adoption of the object of diffusion is the date when a protest first occurs. Note that only the date of the first protest in a given country is recorded, subsequent protests in the same country are not included in this analysis because the country is no longer at risk. For example, numerous protests occurred in Denmark after the initial one in October 2005, but only the date of the first protest is included in this analysis.

In this case, therefore, the risk set is the set of countries at potential risk of experiencing a protest - or the 208 member states of the UN. It is debatable whether all UN member countries are at risk of a protest, and there is an argument that the risk set

should be limited to countries where protest is politically feasible (that is, excluding Communist or other illiberal regimes where the act of protest may be circumscribed), or to countries with a large Muslim population. However, many countries in the major regions of the world did in fact experience protests; therefore, it is an appropriate assumption that all countries are at risk.

The hazard rate, in analogy to the diffusion rate, is defined as the probability that an event will occur during a particular period to a particular individual in the risk set (Allison 1984: 16). The hazard rate in the Danish Cartoons crisis is the ratio of the percentage of countries that have experienced a protest divided by the percentage of countries that have not experienced a protest (or those at risk). Table M1 lists the hazard rates along with the spell dates, cumulative percentages, and percentage of those at risk. Figure M4 shows a graphical representation of the cumulative adoptions, or countries experiencing protests.

Of particular interest is the question of what factors help predict the occurrence of protest events at the country level. Before we can estimate the regression models to do so, we need to create a dichotomous

Table M1 Jyllands-Posten cartoon protests, basic event history data structure

Date of First Protest	Number of Countries	Percentage of total	Cumulative percentage of countries	Percentage at risk (1-cumulative)	Hazard rate = (percentage of total / percentage at risk)
14 Oct 2005	1	0.5	0.5	99.5	0.5
7 Dec 2005	1	0.5	1.0	99.0	0.5
27 Jan 2006	1	0.5	1.4	98.6	0.5
2 Feb 2006	1	0.5	1.9	98.1	0.5
3 Feb 2006	2	1.0	2.9	97.1	1.0
4 Feb 2006	1	0.5	3.4	96.6	0.5
5 Feb 2006	4	1.9	5.3	94.7	2.0
6 Feb 2006	3	1.4	6.7	93.3	1.5
7 Feb 2006	5	2.4	9.1	90.9	2.6
8 Feb 2006	1	0.5	9.6	90.4	0.5
9 Feb 2006	3	1.4	11.1	88.9	1.6
11 Feb 2006	3	1.4	12.5	87.5	1.6
14 Feb 2006	1	0.5	13.0	87.0	0.6
17 Feb 2006	3	1.4	14.4	85.6	1.7
19 Feb 2006	1	0.5	14.9	85.1	0.6
Total	31				

dependent variable where 0 states that no protests took place, and 1 indicates their presence. Since this is a discrete time model,[3] we expand the original dataset in which the unique spell dates are repeated for each event. Recall from Table M1 that there are 15 spells, each corresponding to a unique date. Table A in the appendix shows the original dataset with protests occurring in 31 different countries. The expanded data set is listed alphabetically by country and the dependent variable is labeled 'event.' The date for each spell is repeated for each country, hence 465 observations (31 events multiplied by 15 spells); and for each given 'spell set' per country, recall that it is 15 each, event=1 for the date when the protest occurred in that country, event=0 for dates prior to the protest date, and event=. for dates after the initial protest date. Given this simple data structure, we can conduct logistic regression models with a dichotomous dependent variable.[4] The independent variables used in the regression include:[5]

- Level of economic development (low, middle, or high income countries, using World Bank country classifications based on per-capita income levels) as a control variable
- Percentage of total population that is Muslim, as a measure of the propensity of local protest potential (Wikipedia URL)
- INGO membership density per 1 million people, as an indicator of a country's integration in global civil society (Union of International Associations 2003).

Table M2 shows that, controlling for economy type and INGO membership density, the percentage of the population that is Muslim in a given country is a significant predictor. While this finding may not be surprising, it is interesting to note that the probability is fairly high (66%) regardless of a country's wealth. In fact, an odds ratio of 1.66 would suggest that a one percent increase in the Muslim population increases the likelihood of a protest by 22% (this is determined by calculating the log of the odds ratio result), net of economy type and global civil society integration. In

---

[3] There are two time models used in event history analysis, continuous and discrete time models, with different estimation procedures for each. Continuous time models have a data structure in which there are no breaks in time. Discrete time models take into account breaks and temporal discontinuities so that events are discrete in nature and often occur at specific points in time (i.e. a given year, week, or month).

[4] We provide here only a brief description of the expanded dataset; interested readers should contact the authors for more information or a copy of the expanded dataset used for analysis.

[5] For more details see Table A, available at www.lse.ac.uk/depts/global/yearbook08data.htm

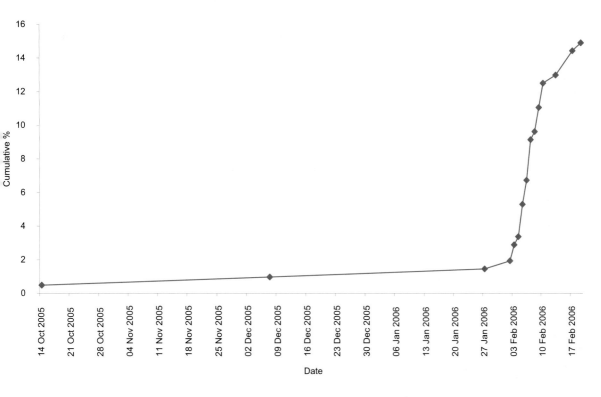

Figure M4 Cumulative diffusion of protests

Table M2 Logistic regression model predicting spread of protests (N=269)

Predictors		Coefficient	Standard error	p value	Odds ratio
Economy type:	Low income vs. middle income	-0.083	0.184	0.653	0.921
	Low income vs. high income	0.256	0.273	0.350	1.291
% Muslim		0.508	0.212	0.017	1.663
INGO membership density		0.001	0.001	0.254	1.001
Intercept		-2.403	0.154	0.000	

addition, our measure of global civil society integration is not significant, with about an even probability of a protest occurring, controlling for economy type and percent Muslim. The main diffusion agent may have been the media (external model), combined with efforts by local organisations (internal model), which jointly succeeded in mobilising a highly susceptible population by taking advantage of a very contagious or infectious event.

Using the widespread Danish cartoon protests as an example, we wanted to show what a diffusion analysis can achieve and what it looks like. This technique can be applied to other global civil society phenomena such as the

spread of social forums. In addition, the model presented in Table M2 can be expanded to include other predictors and control variables such as the number of civil society organisations in a given country or the density of international links between Muslim organisations, the number of media outlets that reprinted the cartoons in a given country and the rate of exposure to Arab media such as Al-Jazeera, regime types, and even a spatial measure of proximity to countries where protests already took place.

Conclusion

We agree with Levi-Faur (2005) that a diffusion perspective is important in globalisation research: whereas until recently social scientists were predominantly interested in explaining stability and exploring the variegated factors that contributed to the stability of the post-war order, since the late 1980s, and with the end of the Cold War, the focus has shifted to change, transformation, convergence as well as divergence. The analysis of structures, he adds, may capture some of the dynamics of these changes; yet structures typically cannot capture the socially and politically contested nature of change and the complex processes involved. In particular, a structural view often falls short in analysing how actors involved in the process of change imbue it with meaning, interpret and project it.

The growth and expansion of communication and transport technologies make it likely that interdependencies of events will become increasingly important drivers of change. Consequently, global networks become denser and wider in scope, and accordingly, diffusion processes can be expected to become more important. Thus, diffusion perspectives allows us 'to endogenize change, to see it in a social and network context and, most important, to look at the role of "knowledge actors" in its diffusion' (Levi-Faur 2005: 21). Likewise, Tarrow (2001) pleads for greater recognition of the mechanisms of diffusion that help create and change the structural aspects of globalisation. This Chapter, its brevity notwithstanding, takes a step towards this goal by suggesting the use of diffusion models as readily available options to scholars and students of globalisation generally and global civil society in particular. Diffusion models help uncover and understand the complex and often perplexing nature of a globalising world.

REFERENCES

Allison, P D (1984) *Event History Analysis*. London: Sage Publications.

Anheier, H K & Stares, S R (2002) 'Introducing the *Global Civil Society* Index' in Marlies Glasius, Mary Kaldor & Helmut K Anheier (eds) *Global Civil Society 2002*. Oxford: Oxford University Press.

Anheier, H K (2001) 'Measuring *Global Civil Society*' in Helmut K Anheier, Marlies Glasius & Mary Kaldor (eds) *Global Civil Society 2001*. Oxford: Oxford University Press.

Anheier, H K & Katz H, (2003) 'Mapping *Global Civil Society*' in Mary Kaldor, Helmut K Anheier & Marlies Glasius (eds) *Global Civil Society 2003*. Oxford: Oxford University Press.

Anheier, H K & Katz, H (2005) 'Network Approaches to *Global Civil Society*' in Helmut Anheier, Marlies Glasius and Mary Kaldor (eds) *Global Civil Society 2004/5*. Oxford: Oxford University Press.

Anheier, H K & Katz, H (2006) 'Learning from History? Comparative Historical Methods for Researching *Global Civil Society*,' in Marlies Glasius, Mary Kaldor, and Helmut Anheier, (eds) *Global Civil Society 2005/6*. London: Sage.

Ayers, J (1999) 'From Streets to the Internet, the Cyber-Diffusion of Contention', *The Annals of the American Academy of Political and Social Sciences*, 566: 132-143.

Beck, U (2002) 'The Cosmopolitan Society and its Enemies', *Theory, Culture and Society*, 19(1–2): 17–45.

Beck, U (1999) *What is Globalisation?* Cambridge: Polity Press.

Burt, R S (2005) *Brokerage and Closure: An Introduction to Social Capital*. Oxford: Oxford University Press.

Castells, M (1996) *Rise of the Network Society: The Information Age: Economy, Society and Culture*. Cambridge: Blackwell Publishers.

Center for Civil Society (2006) UCLA-UCSB International Data Conference. Proceedings available at http://www.spa.ucla.edu/ccs/ - under link 'Conferences and Proceedings'.

Centre for the Study of Global Governance (2001) 'Conference on Methodological Nationalism', London School of Economics. Proceedings available at http://www.spa.ucla.edu/ccs/ - under 'Conferences and Proceedings'.

Chabot, S (2004) 'Framing, transnational diffusion, and African American intellectuals in the Land of Gandhi', *International Review of Social History*, 49: 19-40.

Detlef, J (2006) 'Globalisation as 'Galton's Problem': The Missing Link in the Analysis of Diffusion Patterns in Welfare State Development', *International Organisation* 60: 401-431.

Giddens, A (1990) *The Consequences of Modernity*. Cambridge: Polity Press.

Granovetter, M (1978) 'Threshold Models of Collective Behavior', *American Journal of Sociology*, 83: 1420-1443.

Greve, H R, Strang D & Tuma, N B (1995) 'Specification and Estimation of Heterogeneous Diffusion Models', *Sociological Methodology*, 25: 377–420.

Harvey, D (1989) *The Conditions of Postmodernity: An Enquiry into the Origins of Cultural Change*. Oxford: Blackwell.

Held, D, McGrew, A, Goldblatt D, & Perraton, J (1999) *Global Transformations*. Cambridge: Polity Press.

Katz, H, Anheier, H K and Lam, M (2007) 'Fuzzy Set Approaches to the Study of Global Civil Society', in Mary Kaldor, Helmut Anheier and Marlies Glasius (eds) *Global Civil Society 2006/7*. London: Sage.

Land, K C & Deane G (1992) 'On the large-sample estimation of regression models with spatial- or network-effects terms: a two stage least squares approach', in P Marsden (ed) *Sociological Methodology*. San Francisco: Jossey-Bass.

Land, K C, Deane G & Blau J R (1991) 'Religious Pluralism and Church Membership: A Spatial Diffusion Model', *American Sociological Review* 56: 237–49.

Levi-Faur, D (2005) 'The global diffusion of regulatory capitalism', *Annals of the American Academy of Political and Social Science*, 598: 12-32.

Mahajan, V & Peterson R A (1985) *Models for Innovation Diffusion*. Newbury Park, CA: Sage Publications.

Minkoff, D C (1997) 'The Sequencing of Social Movements', *American Sociological Review*, 62:5, 779-799.

Morenoff, J D & R J Sampson (1997) 'Violent Crime and the Spatial Dynamics of Neighborhood Transition: Chicago, 1970-1990', *Social Forces*, 76/1: 31-64.

Myers, D J (1996) *The Diffusion of Collective Violence*. Paper presented at the 1996 Annual Meeting of the American Sociological Association, New York.

Myers, D J (1997) *Diffusion Models for Riots and Other Collective Violence*. PhD Dissertation, University of Wisconsin, Madison, Department of Sociology.

Myers, D J (2000) 'The Diffusion of Collective Violence: Infectiousness, Susceptibility, and Mass Media Networks', *American Journal of Sociology*, Volume 106(1), 173–208.

Olzak, S and Shanahan S (1996) 'Deprivation Race Riots: An Extension of Spilerman's Analysis', *Social Forces*, 74:931–61.

Potoski, M & Prakash, A (2004) *Globalisation(s) and the Diffusion of Non-Governmental Regimes: The Case of ISO 14001*. Paper presented at the annual meeting of the American Political Science Association, Chicago.

Rogers, E M (2003) *Diffusion of Innovations* [5th ed]. New York: Free Press.

Soule, S A (1997) 'The Student Divestment Movement in the United States and Tactical Diffusion: The Shantytown Protest', *Social Forces*, 75: 855-883.

Strang, D (1995) *Mhdiff: User Documentation*: Technical Report 95-3. Ithaca: Cornell University, Department of Sociology.

Strang, D & Meyer, J W (1993) 'Institutional Conditions for Diffusion' *Theory and Society* 22, 487-511.

Strang, D & Tuma N B (1993) 'Spatial and Temporal Heterogeneity in Diffusion', *American Journal of Sociology*, 99: 614-639.

Strang, D (1991) 'Adding Social Structure to Diffusion Models: An Event-History Framework', *Sociological Methods and Research*, 19: 324-53.

Tarrow, S (2001) 'Transnational Politics: Contention and Institutions in International Politics,' *Annual Review of Political Science*, 4: 1–20.

Tolnay, S E (1995) 'The Spatial Diffusion of Fertility: A Cross-Sectional Analysis of Counties in the American South, 1940', *American Sociological Review*, 60: 299–308.

Tolnay, S E, Deane, G and Beck, E M (1996) 'Vicarious Violence: Spatial Effects on Southern Lynchings, 1890–1919', *American Journal of Sociology* 102: 788–815.

Wikipedia, Islam by Country, http://en.wikipedia.org/wiki/Islam_by_country (consulted 15 July 2007).

Wikipedia, Timeline of the *Jyllands-Posten* Muhammad cartoons controversy http://en.wikipedia.org/wiki/Timeline_of_the_Jyllands-Posten_Muhammad_cartoons_controversy (consulted 15 July 2007).

Yergin, D A & Stanislav, J (1998) *The Commanding Heights: The Battle between Government and the Marketplace that is Remaking the Modern World*. New York: Simon and Schuster.

INDICATOR SUITES OF GLOBAL CIVIL SOCIETY
Hagai Katz

Introduction

Readers familiar with the Yearbook will notice that this year's Records section differs from the format presented since the inaugural edition in 2001. The new presentation comprises a set of thematic indicator suites, which as their name suggests, offer indications or insights into different aspects of a particular phenomenon. This style of presenting data is particularly appropriate for global civil society, which is an emerging and contested concept for which there is no established set of indicators. In this context, and with limited available data about global civil society, we offer this set of indicator suites as a way of enhancing our understanding of global civil society, its characteristics, processes, impacts, and the influences upon it.

The indicator system serves a slightly different function to the tables presented in previous Yearbooks. Rather than providing detailed, 'raw' data for specific variables and actors, an indicator suite summarises the key characteristics and trends of these data, at a higher level of abstraction. The indicator suites are intended to portray these central dimensions of global civil society in their broader context, rather than provide a comprehensive account of global civil society – thus, only a selection of indicators from available data are presented. We do not presume that we can highlight all aspects of global civil society, but we make a concerted effort to include in each suite indicators of action and the context of that action. In other words, indicators suites are not merely static representations of global conditions, but an account of how different actors perceive those conditions and respond to them. For example, in the indicators dealing with the environment, we show data on environmental deterioration, such as the levels of air pollution, and the responses of different actors including states, corporations and NGOs, as indicated by data on public environmental performance, ISO14000 accreditation and international environmental networks. Each indicator suite is accompanied by a brief description

highlighting some of the central characteristics and trends in the data, and is followed by a list of references to the original sources, where more detailed information about the data can be sought.

The structure of the data included in the Records varies between themes. Not all data are presented in a 'per country, per annum' configuration. In some cases this is because the data are simply not available in this form, while in others, it is because the main patterns and trends are better illustrated using different units of analysis. We make a particular effort to move away from the nation state as a taken-for-granted unit of analysis, in order to avoid the pitfalls of 'methodological nationalism'. So the units of analysis we employ include different actors and geographies at different levels of aggregation; from individuals to nation states, from cities to regions. Sometimes they break away from a geographical frame of reference, and follow a classification of, for example, types of ideas, or issues. For example, indicators of the role of global civil society in the global governance system involve different units of analysis, such as issues, organisations, funds, and events, which can be described in a variety of time frames. The heterogeneous structure and coverage of these data means that they are not amenable to formal statistical treatment, such as combining them into a single overall index – as is done, for example, in UNDP's Human Development Index.

The extent to which we can to avoid reliance on national-level data is, of course, dependent on the availability of data with different units of analysis, and on the coverage of national-level data to aggregate into summaries by region, by economy type, etc. As global data systems develop, this is becoming more feasible. In one sense, the indicator suites are a compromise insofar as they make the best of data that is empirically available, to reveal the 'story' that the data tells in diffrent formats, for various of audiences. In another sense, these varied formats allow a freer and potentially richer way of presenting data on the issues that concern us, because their heterogeneity illustrates rather than masks the inherent complexity of the issues, and allows for more nuanced presentation, description, and interpretation.

This set of indicator suites is the first step in an ongoing process of identifying the components and descriptors of global civil society and its context, which will be developed further in future editions of the Yearbook, alongside developments in theory and data availability, and consultation with experts in this field. In the development of the indicator suites we are dependent on the quality and coverage of existing data systems. We are constantly searching for new and better data systems in order to improve our understanding of global civil society. Readers with ideas for such data sources are invited to contact us - please email: katzh@bgu.ac.il

We welcome advice and constructive criticism on all aspects of the data programme, from experts, those who work on or with our data sources, and our readers, so we can improve our initial attempt to confront the challenges of providing data on global civil society.

General note on data:

- References to sources are found at the end of each record. All major terms used in the records are briefly defined in the Glossary, which is available online http://www.lse.ac.uk/depts/global /yearbook08data.htm

- Data reported are the most up to date available. Where data for a specific unit of analysis were not available for a particular year, we took the figure from the year before as an estimate. Entries based on such data are presented in the tables in italics. A blank entry indicates that the data are not available, not comparable, or otherwise of insufficient quality to be reported.

- Where the time frame of the data is not detailed, the references should be consulted for further information. Where the data have been taken from online sources, they were generally accessed in July 2007.

- When referring to countries, short or conventional country names are used. It is not the intention of the editors to take a position with regard to the political or diplomatic implications of geographical names or continental groupings used.

- Data are often presented in aggregations, by countries' regions and by their economy groups, defined by income levels. Where possible, the aggregations presented are taken directly from the original data source. Where we aggregate data ourselves, regions and economy groups are defined according to World Bank classifications. A general caveat applies to aggregations, since the coverage of countries is variable for different indicators and different groups. The reader is referred to the original references and data sources for information on country coverage in these summaries.

Economic globalisation, and particularly the global role of transnational corporations (TNCs), has a manifold role vis-à-vis global civil society. Global economic integration facilitates the growth of global civil society, but it is also one of the central issues around which resistance of global civil society actors is framed. This record shows selected indicators of economic globalisation, TNCs and global civil society response to economic globalisation.

The data show that however unequally, economic globalisation is on the rise – in the last decade trade has grown worldwide, even in Sub-Saharan Africa, and migrant workers' remittances have increased dramatically. At the same time, official aid has decreased in most parts of the world (1.1). Changes were most dramatic in the developing world (1.2). Developing nations' share of global trade has been on the rise since 2000 (1.3), although this is mostly explained by the economic boom in China (1.4). Yet, developing nations play a minor role in the global economy, as they host very few of the world's largest corporations (1.5, 1.9).

Global civil society plays a double role in the global economy. Some organisations like the International Chamber of Commerce promote trade (1.10,1.11) and others offer alternatives to the neo-liberal free-trade logic, for example, the fair trade movement (1.12), while INGOs such as the ICFTU monitor labour practices and promote workers' rights (1.13). Often the engagement of global civil society is mostly Western and Northern, but some networks are more representative of Southern audiences.

Notes: [1]Official development aid includes both official development assistance and official aid. [2]'Goods' excludes oil. [3]TNI = Transnationality Index (average of the ratios of foreign to total assets, sales and employment). [4] Spread Index = square root of proportion of all affiliates that are foreign, multiplied by the number of host countries. (Affiliates counted in this table refer to only majority-owned affiliates.)

Sources: Trade, Official development aid & Remittances: World Development Indicators 2005, WDI Online, World Bank. Foreign direct investment: UNCTAD **Foreign Direct Investment** database. **Share in trade:** World Economic Outlook, April 2007, World Economic and Financial Surveys, International Monetary Fund. **TNCs:** World Investment Report 2006, UNCTAD. **ICC:** http://www.iccwbo.org/ **ICFTU:** http://www.icftu-apro.org/index.html **Fair trade:** http://www.fairtrade.net/labelling_initiatives.html

1.1 Regional indicators of economic globalisation

Region	Trade — Total trade in % GDP			Official development aid[1] — Aid (% GNI)			Remittances — Outgoing total amount (US$ millions, current)			Remittances — Incoming total amount (US$ millions, current)		
	1995	2005	% change 1995-2005	1995	2005	% change 1995-2005	1995	2005	% change 1995-2005	1995	2005	% change 1995-2005
Low income	36.2	54.0	49	3.7	2.9	-21	1,342	3,379	152	12,776	48,188	277
Middle income	51.2	68.8	34	0.7	0.6	-17	11,161	34,784	212	45,021	144,716	221
Low & middle income	49.1	66.7	36	1.3	1.1	-16	12,503	38,163	205	57,797	192,904	234
East Asia & Pacific	58.7	86.7	48	0.8	0.3	-59	1,618	9,918	513	9,701	45,053	364
Europe & Central Asia	63.4	81.7	29	1.1	0.2	-78	5,024	13,420	167	8,120	31,363	286
Latin America & Caribbean	37.9	48.7	28	0.4	0.3	-30	1,142	2,288	100	13,420	48,201	259
Middle East & North Africa	56.0	72.7	30	1.5	3.9	152	2,239	8,014	258	13,358	24,001	80
South Asia	27.1	44.6	64	1.1	0.9	-16	475	1,338	182	10,005	35,558	255
Sub-Saharan Africa	59.4	67.3	13	6.1	5.5	-9	2,005	3,185	59	3,193	8,728	173
High income	40.6	49.4	22	0.0	0.0	-99	86,145	140,514	63	43,765	69,585	59
World	42.1	52.2	24	0.2	0.2	4	98,648	178,677	81	101,562	262,489	158

1.2 Dynamics of economic globalisation: fastest declining and fastest growing 5 countries, selected indicators

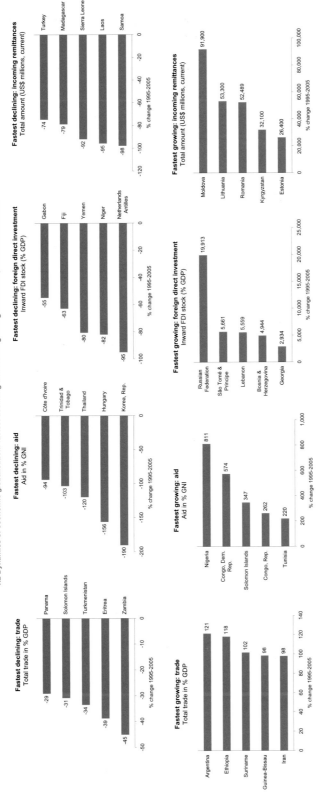

Fastest declining: trade
Total trade in % GDP

	% change 1995-2005
Panama	-29
Solomon Islands	-31
Turkmenistan	-34
Eritrea	-39
Zambia	-45

Fastest declining: aid
Aid in % GNI

	% change 1995-2005
Côte d'Ivoire	-94
Trinidad & Tobago	-103
Thailand	-120
Hungary	-156
Korea, Rep.	-190

Fastest declining: foreign direct investment
Inward FDI stock (% GDP)

	% change 1995-2005
Gabon	-55
Fiji	-63
Yemen	-80
Niger	-82
Netherlands Antilles	-95

Fastest declining: incoming remittances
Total amount (US$ millions, current)

	% change 1995-2005
Turkey	-74
Madagascar	-79
Sierra Leone	-92
Laos	-95
Samoa	-98

Fastest growing: trade
Total trade in % GDP

	% change 1995-2005
Argentina	121
Ethiopia	118
Suriname	102
Guinea-Bissau	98
Iran	98

Fastest growing: aid
Aid in % GNI

	% change 1995-2005
Nigeria	811
Congo, Dem. Rep.	574
Solomon Islands	347
Congo, Rep.	262
Tunisia	220

Fastest growing: foreign direct investment
Inward FDI stock (% GDP)

	% change 1995-2005
Russian Federation	19,913
São Tomé & Principe	5,661
Lebanon	5,559
Bosnia & Herzegovina	4,944
Georgia	2,934

Fastest growing: incoming remittances
Total amount (US$ millions, current)

	% change 1995-2005
Moldova	91,900
Lithuania	53,300
Romania	52,489
Kyrgyzstan	32,100
Estonia	26,400

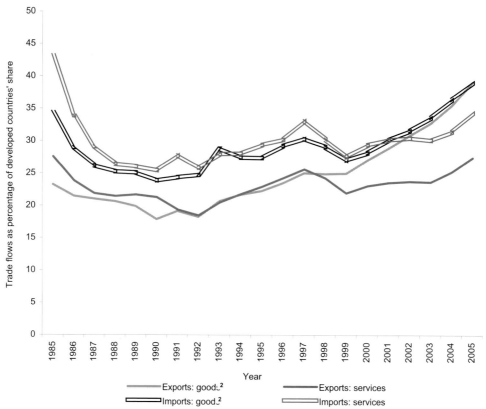

1.3 Developing countries' share in global trade, 1985-2005

Legend:
- Exports: goods[2]
- Imports: goods[2]
- Exports: services
- Imports: services

1.4 Manufacturing imports of advanced OECD economies: four sources, as percentage of total, 1990-2004

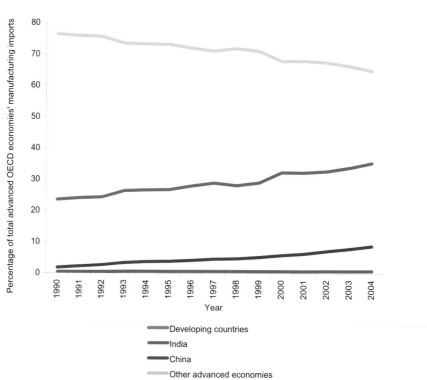

Legend:
- Developing countries
- India
- China
- Other advanced economies

1.5 Top 100 nonfinancial TNCs

Summary by home economies, ranked by foreign assets

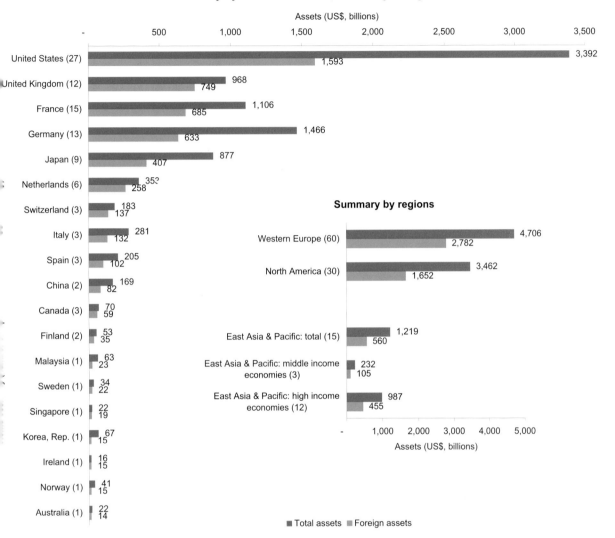

Assets (US$, billions)

	Total assets	Foreign assets
United States (27)	3,392	1,593
United Kingdom (12)	968	749
France (15)	1,106	685
Germany (13)	1,466	633
Japan (9)	877	407
Netherlands (6)	353	258
Switzerland (3)	183	137
Italy (3)	281	132
Spain (3)	205	102
China (2)	169	82
Canada (3)	70	59
Finland (2)	53	35
Malaysia (1)	63	23
Sweden (1)	34	22
Singapore (1)	22	19
Korea, Rep. (1)	67	15
Ireland (1)	16	15
Norway (1)	41	15
Australia (1)	22	14

Summary by regions

	Total assets	Foreign assets
Western Europe (60)	4,706	2,782
North America (30)	3,462	1,652
East Asia & Pacific: total (15)	1,219	560
East Asia & Pacific: middle income economies (3)	232	105
East Asia & Pacific: high income economies (12)	987	455

Assets (US$, billions)

■ Total assets ■ Foreign assets

1.6 Top 100 nonfinancial TNCs

Summary by industries, ranked by foreign assets

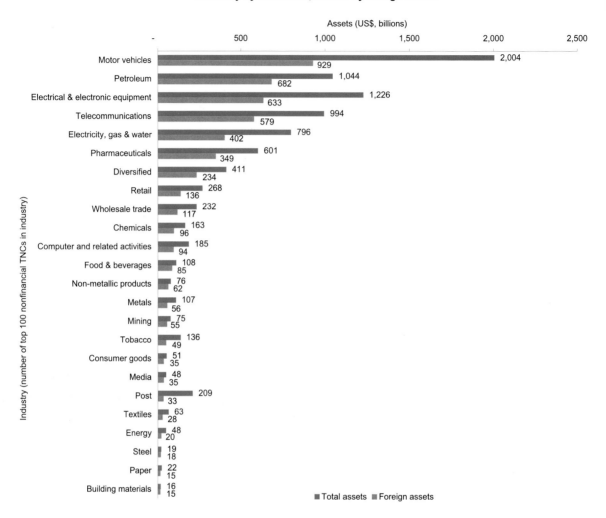

Assets (US$, billions)

Industry (number of top 100 nonfinancial TNCs in industry)	Total assets	Foreign assets
Motor vehicles	2,004	929
Petroleum	1,044	682
Electrical & electronic equipment	1,226	633
Telecommunications	994	579
Electricity, gas & water	796	402
Pharmaceuticals	601	349
Diversified	411	234
Retail	268	136
Wholesale trade	232	117
Chemicals	163	96
Computer and related activities	185	94
Food & beverages	108	85
Non-metallic products	76	62
Metals	107	56
Mining	75	55
Tobacco	136	49
Consumer goods	51	35
Media	48	35
Post	209	33
Textiles	63	28
Energy	48	20
Steel	19	18
Paper	22	15
Building materials	16	15

■ Total assets ■ Foreign assets

1.7 Top 50 financial TNCs

Summary by region

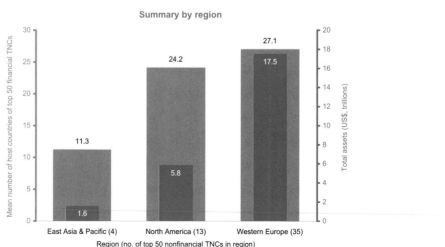

Region (no. of top 50 nonfinancial TNCs in region)	Mean number of host countries	Total Assets
East Asia & Pacific (4)	11.3	1.6
North America (13)	24.2	5.8
Western Europe (35)	27.1	17.5

■ Mean number of host countries ■ Total Assets

World ranking by TNI				Corporation & industry	Home economy	Assets (US$, millions)			Sales (US$, millions)			Employees (number)			TNI (%)
2001	2002	2003	2004			Foreign	Total	% Foreign	Foreign	Total	% Foreign	Foreign	Total	% Foreign	
2	2	1	1	Thomson Corporation *Media*	Canada	19,221	19,643	98	7,837	8,098	97	38,926	40,000	97	97.3
-	4	2	2	CRH Plc *Lumber & other building material dealers*	Ireland	15,192	16,165	94	14,920	15,918	94	57,882	60,411	96	94.5
20	46	15	3	Nestlé SA *Food & beverages*	Switzerland	65,396	76,965	85	68,586	69,778	98	240,406	247,000	97	93.5
13	11	7	4	Vodafone Group Plc *Telecommunications*	United Kingdom	247,850	258,626	96	53,307	62,494	85	45,981	57,378	80	87.1
-	16	8	5	Alcan Inc. *Metal and metal products*	Canada	25,455	33,341	76	23,381	24,885	94	71,000	82,000	87	85.6
-	-	19	6	Koninklijke Ahold *Retail*	United States/ Netherlands	24,659	28,202	87	51,668	64,567	80	206,057	231,003	89	85.6
7	10	6	7	Philips Electronics *Electrical & electronic equipment*	Netherlands	30,330	41,848	72	36,155	37,646	96	134,814	161,586	83	84
-	-	-	8	Nortel Networks *Telecommunications*	Canada	13,854	16,984	82	9,260	9,828	94	25,160	34,150	74	83.2
35	40	35	9	Unilever *Diversified*	United Kingdom/ Netherlands	38,415	46,141	83	44,361	50,121	89	171,000	223,000	77	82.8
15	14	10	10	British Petroleum Company Plc *Petroleum*	United Kingdom	154,513	193,213	80	232,388	285,059	82	85,500	102,900	83	81.5
-	-	-	11	Astrazeneca Plc *Pharmaceuticals*	United Kingdom	17,176	25,616	67	20,318	21,426	95	52,700	64,200	82	81.3
-	-	11	12	Lafarge SA *Non-metallic products*	France	30,127	33,742	89	15,146	17,925	84	52,365	77,075	68	80.6
38	27	23	13	Hutchison Whampoa *Diversified*	Hong Kong, China	67,638	84,162	80	17,039	23,037	74	150,687	180,000	84	79.3
5	6	4	14	Roche Group *Pharmaceuticals*	Switzerland	42,884	51,322	84	24,794	25,149	99	35,587	64,703	55	79
-	-	-	15	L'Air Liquide Groupe *Commodity chemicals*	France	17,166	19,648	87	9,053	11,642	78	24,412	35,900	68	77.7
-	-	41	16	Sanofi-Aventis *Pharmaceuticals*	France	82,612	104,548	79	15,418	18,678	83	68,776	96,439	71	77.6
-	-	-	17	Diageo Plc *Consumer goods/distillers & vintners*	United Kingdom	18,147	25,661	71	13,715	16,544	83	29,922	38,955	77	77
-	-	-	18	Mittal Steel Company NV *Steel*	Netherlands/ United Kingdom	17,720	19,153	93	20,186	22,197	91	150,437	164,000	92	77
18	17	14	19	Suez *Electricity, gas and water*	France	74,051	85,788	86	38,838	50,585	77	100,485	160,712	63	75.2
21	20	16	20	Total *Petroleum*	France	98,719	114,636	86	123,265	152,353	81	62,227	111,401	56	74.3

Spread Index 2004	2003	TNC	Home economy	Total assets (US$, millions)	Employees (number)	Total affiliates (number)	Foreign affiliates (number)	Host countries (number)
1	3	GE Capital Services	United States	566,708	76,300	425	85	55
2	1	Citigroup	United States	484,101	294,000	612	347	70
3	2	UBS	Switzerland	732,121	67,424	426	363	43
4	5	Allianz Group	Germany	302,894	162,180	778	569	47
5	11	BNP Paribas	France	230,071	94,892	622	403	53
6	6	Gruppo Assicurazioni Generali	Italy	372,996	58,354	368	323	39
7	4	Zurich Financial Services	Switzerland	346,083	53,246	358	345	34
8	24	Unicredito	Italy	359,903	68,571	44	998	31
9	9	HSBC Bank	United Kingdom	274,557	243,333	76	658	47
10	8	Société Générale	France	816,735	93,359	430	253	48

1.10 International Chamber of Commerce: affiliation by region

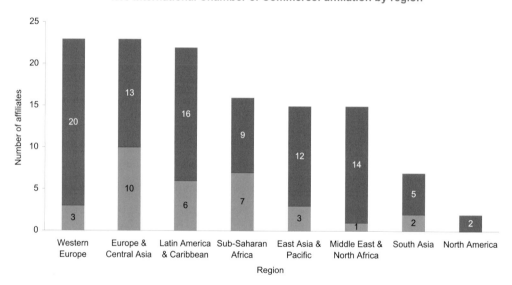

1.11 International Chamber of Commerce: affiliation by level of income

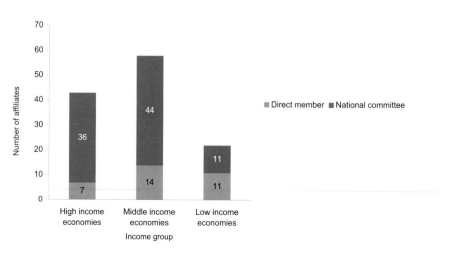

1.12 Fair trade labelling initiatives
by home country region and level of income

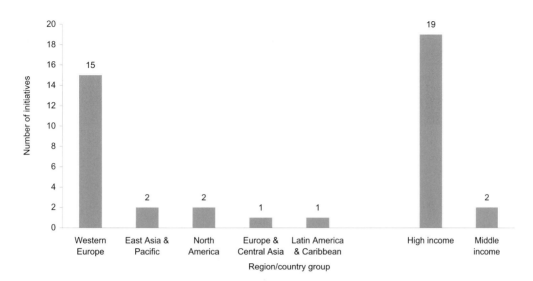

1.13 International Confederation of Free Trade Unions (ICFTU), members
by region and income level of home country

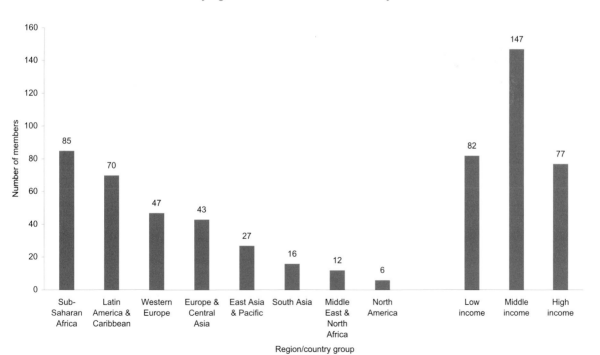

Increased opportunities for human interaction are a main force driving the development of global civil society. Migration, international travel and tourism, student exchanges and refugee flows increase the density of global links and ties, which are essential for the emergence of international movements and initiatives.

Global migration rose in the last decade, with movements predominantly from developing nations to rich economies, or within regions experiencing protracted conflicts (2.1, 2.2). Since the end of the slump in international air travel caused by 9/11, air travel has risen steadily. Regional airlines (such as RyanAir and EasyJet) now deliver a significant proportion of regional flights, whilst inter-regional travel remains mostly between developed nations (2.3, 2.4). Tourism has also increased generally, and is rapidly growing in developing nations (2.5, 2.6). Student exchanges and foreign study are facilitating the links: North America and Western Europe are hubs of the receiving end of this network, and East Asia and the Pacific are the main exporters (2.7, 2.8). Data on refugees show a general decline, both in flows and in total numbers of refugees (2.9). High numbers of refugees are indicative of conflict areas, as well as of countries willing to act as sanctuaries (2.10).

Sources: Migration: World Bank, World Development Indicators (WDI-Online). **Air travel:** *World Air Transport Statistics (WATS) 2006,* IATA International Air Transport Association, http://www.iata.org/index.htm **Tourism:** World Bank, World Development Indicators (WDI-Online). **Students:** UNESCO Institute for Statistics, Data Center, Table 18: International flows of mobile students at the tertiary level, http://stats.uis.unesco.org/unesco/ReportFolders/ReportFolders.aspx **Refugees:** World Development Indicators, WDI Online.

2.1 International migration

Region	International migration Total (1,000s)			International migration (% population)		
	1995	2005	% change 1995-2005	1995	2005	% change 1995-2005
Low income	30,421.0	27,119.7	-11	1.6	1.2	-26
Middle income	50,121.0	50,803.7	1	1.8	1.7	-8
Low & middle income:						
East Asia & Pacific	3,001.4	4,432.2	48	0.2	0.2	35
Europe & Central Asia	33,571.4	31,137.1	-7	7.1	6.6	-7
Latin America & Caribbean	5,348.5	5,776.9	8	1.1	1.0	-7
Middle East & North Africa	8,780.3	9,641.6	10	3.5	3.2	-9
South Asia	13,133.0	11,229.2	-14	1.1	0.8	-28
Sub-Saharan Africa	16,707.3	15,706.3	-6	2.9	2.1	-26
High income	84,234.3	112,282.3	33	9.2	11.4	24
World	164,776.3	190,205.7	15	2.9	3.0	2

2.2 International migration, 1995-2005

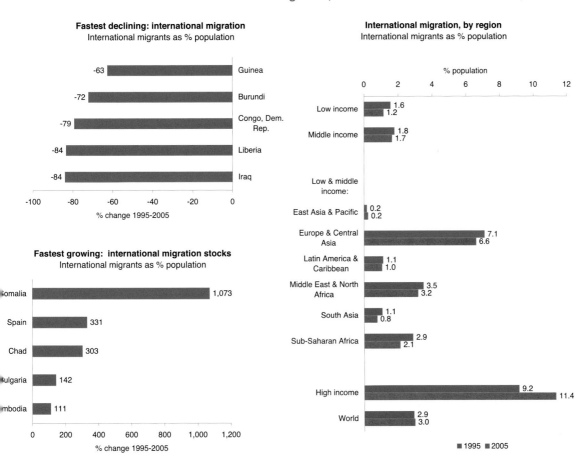

Fastest declining: international migration
International migrants as % population

-63	Guinea
-72	Burundi
-79	Congo, Dem. Rep.
-84	Liberia
-84	Iraq

% change 1995-2005

Fastest growing: international migration stocks
International migrants as % population

Somalia	1,073
Spain	331
Chad	303
Bulgaria	142
Cambodia	111

% change 1995-2005

International migration, by region
International migrants as % population

% population

Region	1995	2005
Low income	1.6	1.2
Middle income	1.8	1.7
Low & middle income:		
East Asia & Pacific	0.2	0.2
Europe & Central Asia	7.1	6.6
Latin America & Caribbean	1.1	1.0
Middle East & North Africa	3.5	3.2
South Asia	1.1	0.8
Sub-Saharan Africa	2.9	2.1
High income	9.2	11.4
World	2.9	3.0

■ 1995 ■ 2005

2.3 International air travel

Scheduled passengers carried, international flights
Top 10 airlines, 2006

Passengers (1,000s)

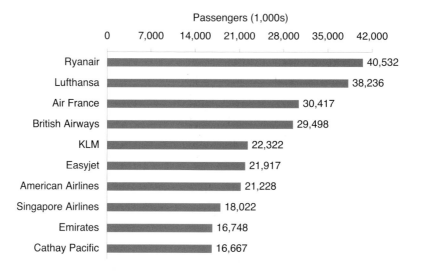

Ryanair	40,532
Lufthansa	38,236
Air France	30,417
British Airways	29,498
KLM	22,322
Easyjet	21,917
American Airlines	21,228
Singapore Airlines	18,022
Emirates	16,748
Cathay Pacific	16,667

Scheduled passenger-kilometres flown, international flights
Top 10 airlines, 2006

Kilometres (1,000s)

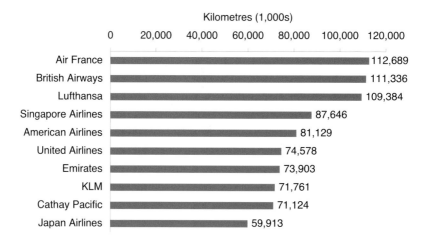

Air France	112,689
British Airways	111,336
Lufthansa	109,384
Singapore Airlines	87,646
American Airlines	81,129
United Airlines	74,578
Emirates	73,903
KLM	71,761
Cathay Pacific	71,124
Japan Airlines	59,913

Scheduled passenger-kilometres flown, by routes
% world total, October 2005

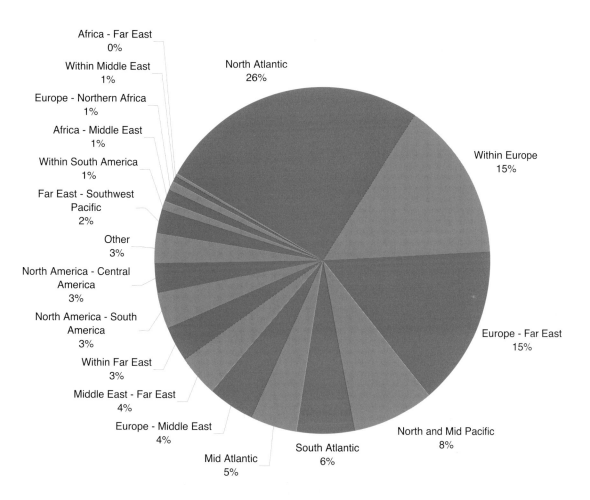

Africa - Far East
0%

Within Middle East
1%

Europe - Northern Africa
1%

Africa - Middle East
1%

Within South America
1%

Far East - Southwest
Pacific
2%

Other
3%

North America - Central
America
3%

North America - South
America
3%

Within Far East
3%

Middle East - Far East
4%

Europe - Middle East
4%

Mid Atlantic
5%

South Atlantic
6%

North and Mid Pacific
8%

North Atlantic
26%

Within Europe
15%

Europe - Far East
15%

2.4 Scheduled passenger-kilometres flown, international flights
Annual % change, 2002-2007

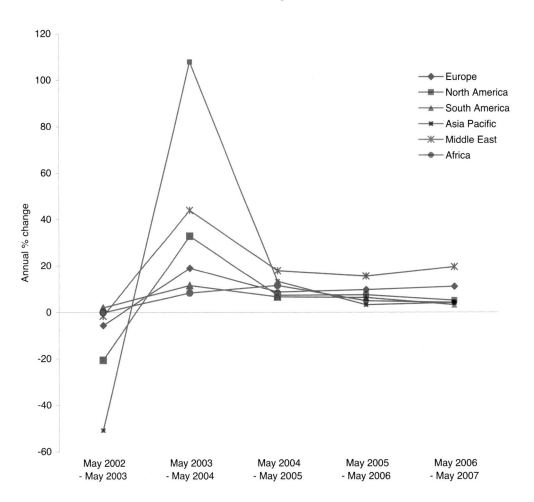

2.5 International tourism

| | Inbound tourists | | | | | Outbound tourists | | | | |
| | Total (1,000s) | | % change 1995-2005 | Per 1,000 population | | Total (1,000s) | | % change 1995-2005 | Per 1,000 population | |
Region	1995	2005		1995	2005	1995	2005		1995	2005
Low income	10,879	*17,998*	*65*	6	*8*		9,317			*4*
Middle income	159,782	265,628	66	57	86	208,088	*273,023*	*31*	75	*89*
Low & middle income:										
East Asia & Pacific	44,254	91,295	106	26	48	36,006	*81,084*	*125*	21	*43*
Europe & Central Asia	58,037	90,756	56	123	192	142,185	*161,107*	*13*	301	*341*
Latin America & Caribbean	39,667	54,142	36	83	98	21,025	32,407	54	44	59
Middle East & North Africa	13,420	27,605	106	53	90	11,226			44	
South Asia	3,744	6,254	67	3	4	4,522	*8,792*	*94*	4	6
Sub-Saharan Africa	12,119	*17,247*	*42*	21	*23*					
High income	353,399	456,818	29	382	452	214,294	365,507	71	232	361
World	524,060	736,109	40	93	114	427,305	568,830	33	76	88

2.6 Top 10 countries in international tourism, 2005

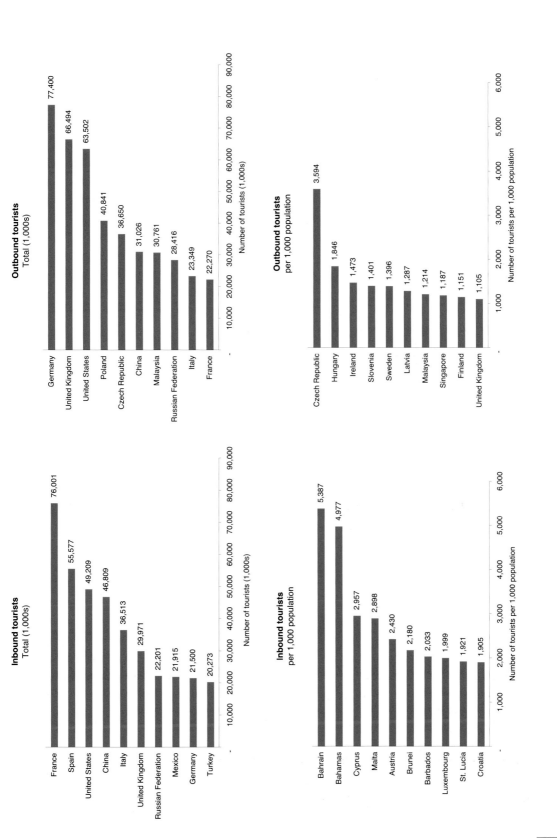

Inbound tourists
Total (1,000s)

Country	Number of tourists (1,000s)
France	76,001
Spain	55,577
United States	49,209
China	46,809
Italy	36,513
United Kingdom	29,971
Russian Federation	22,201
Mexico	21,915
Germany	21,500
Turkey	20,273

Outbound tourists
Total (1,000s)

Country	Number of tourists (1,000s)
Germany	77,400
United Kingdom	66,494
United States	63,502
Poland	40,841
Czech Republic	36,650
China	31,026
Malaysia	30,761
Russian Federation	28,416
Italy	23,349
France	22,270

Inbound tourists
per 1,000 population

Country	Number of tourists per 1,000 population
Bahrain	5,387
Bahamas	4,977
Cyprus	2,957
Malta	2,898
Austria	2,430
Brunei	2,180
Barbados	2,033
Luxembourg	1,999
St. Lucia	1,921
Croatia	1,905

Outbound tourists
per 1,000 population

Country	Number of tourists per 1,000 population
Czech Republic	3,594
Hungary	1,846
Ireland	1,473
Slovenia	1,401
Sweden	1,396
Latvia	1,287
Malaysia	1,214
Singapore	1,187
Finland	1,151
United Kingdom	1,105

2.7 International student flows, 2004

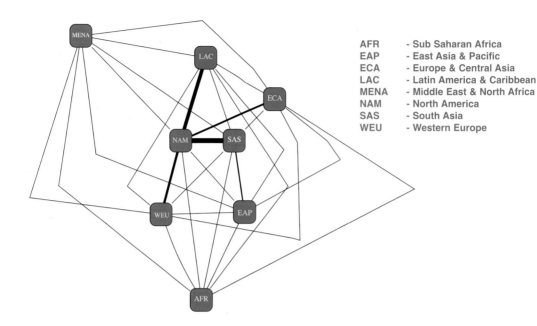

AFR — Sub Saharan Africa
EAP — East Asia & Pacific
ECA — Europe & Central Asia
LAC — Latin America & Caribbean
MENA — Middle East & North Africa
NAM — North America
SAS — South Asia
WEU — Western Europe

2.8 International students flows, 2004
Regional analyses

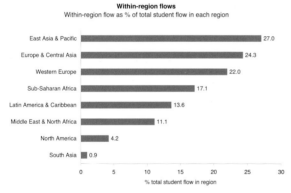

Within-region flows
Within-region flow as % of total student flow in each region

Region	% total student flow in region
East Asia & Pacific	27.0
Europe & Central Asia	24.3
Western Europe	22.0
Sub-Saharan Africa	17.1
Latin America & Caribbean	13.6
Middle East & North Africa	11.1
North America	4.2
South Asia	0.9

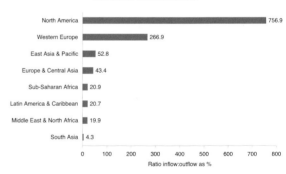

Importer or exporter?
Ratio of inflow to outflow of students

Region	Ratio inflow:outflow as %
North America	756.9
Western Europe	266.9
East Asia & Pacific	52.8
Europe & Central Asia	43.4
Sub-Saharan Africa	20.9
Latin America & Caribbean	20.7
Middle East & North Africa	19.9
South Asia	4.3

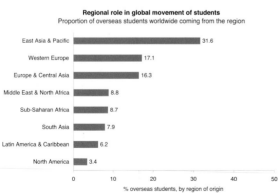

Regional role in global movement of students
Proportion of overseas students worldwide coming from the region

Region	% overseas students, by region of origin
East Asia & Pacific	31.6
Western Europe	17.1
Europe & Central Asia	16.3
Middle East & North Africa	8.8
Sub-Saharan Africa	8.7
South Asia	7.9
Latin America & Caribbean	6.2
North America	3.4

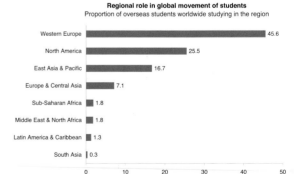

Regional role in global movement of students
Proportion of overseas students worldwide studying in the region

Region	% overseas students, by region of study
Western Europe	45.6
North America	25.5
East Asia & Pacific	16.7
Europe & Central Asia	7.1
Sub-Saharan Africa	1.8
Middle East & North Africa	1.8
Latin America & Caribbean	1.3
South Asia	0.3

DATA PROGRAMME

2.9 Refugee populations and flows

Region	Refugee poulations[1] Total (1,000s) 1995	2005	% change 1995-2005	per 1,000 inhabitants 1995	2005	% change 1995-2005	Refugee flows[2] (1,000s) Inflow 2005	Outflow 2005
Low income	7,304.1	4,255.5	-42	3.8	1.8	-52	-390.7	-641.6
Middle income	4,552.9	1,987.4	-56	1.6	0.6	-60	-550.4	-340.8
Low & middle income	11,857.0	6,242.9	-47	2.5	1.2	-54	-941.1	-982.5
East Asia & Pacific	447.0	464.5	20	0.3	0.2	-6	8.4	-2.3
Europe & Central Asia	1,436.9	484.1	41	3.0	1.0	-66	-172.5	-282.1
Latin America & Caribbean	93.9	37.7	-60	0.2	0.1	-65	1.6	10.8
Middle East & North Africa	2,510.4	1,323.3	-47	9.9	4.3	-56	-384.0	-70.7
South Asia	1,625.5	1,371.6	-16	1.3	0.9	-29	-227.5	-505.5
Sub-Saharan Africa	5,743.4	2,561.6	-55	9.8	3.5	-65	-167.1	-132.5
High income	3,039.1	2,147.5	-29	3.3	2.1	-35	-208.5	0.7
World	14,896.1	8,390.3	-44	2.6	1.3	-51	-1149.6	-981.6

2.10 Refugee numbers, top 10 host countries, 2005

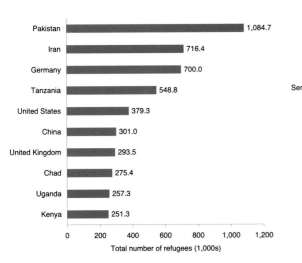

Total number of refugees (1,000s)

- Pakistan: 1,084.7
- Iran: 716.4
- Germany: 700.0
- Tanzania: 548.8
- United States: 379.3
- China: 301.0
- United Kingdom: 293.5
- Chad: 275.4
- Uganda: 257.3
- Kenya: 251.3

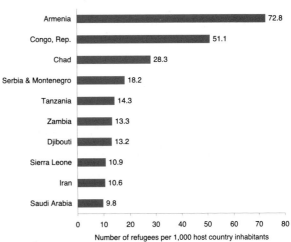

Number of refugees per 1,000 host country inhabitants

- Armenia: 72.8
- Congo, Rep.: 51.1
- Chad: 28.3
- Serbia & Montenegro: 18.2
- Tanzania: 14.3
- Zambia: 13.3
- Djibouti: 13.2
- Sierra Leone: 10.9
- Iran: 10.6
- Saudi Arabia: 9.8

The media and communications revolution has catalysed the 'network society' (Castells 2000), in which location matters less and action is based on flows rather than place. The network society can enable global civil society to flourish, for it democratises knowledge and facilitates interaction and exchange of information between non-contiguous actors. But the democratising effect of this revolution is hindered by the global divide, which is expressed clearly in the data in this record.

The media and communications industry is dominated by Northern TNCs (3.1-3.2); despite the rapid growth of communications in the developing world, the technological advantages remain with developing nations, and in the poorest countries, such as those in Sub-Saharan Africa and South Asia, cellular communications have increased significantly but landline communications infrastructure remains limited (3.3). The Internet revolution too is yet to have a dramatic impact. It does assist in interpersonal communication (3.10), but penetration of the Internet in developing regions remains low – too low to challenge the prominence of English language and Western-produced content on the worldwide web (3.4, 3.5, 3.9). In addition, wireless access is predominantly a Northern and commercial phenomenon (3.6-3.8). The rapid growth in blogs is often seen as a way of generally equalising and democratising media and news. Blogs are becoming important alternatives to a TNC-dominated media, but their global spread is uneven, and readership is strongly linked to gender, age and education (3.11-3.18).

Sources: Telecomm statistics: World Bank, World Development Indicators (WDI-Online), *World Telecommunications/ ICT Indicators,* March 2006, International Telecommunication Union (ITU). **Media & communications TNCs:** Special Report: *The Global 2000, Forbes,* 2007. **Blogs:** The Blog Herald, Perseus, http://perseus.com/blogsurvey/blog Blogads, 2006 blog reader survey results, http://www.blogads.com/survey/blog_reader_surveys_overview.html
Internet population: World Internet Usage and Population Statistics, http://www.internetworldstats.com/stats.htm **Internet languages:** Global Internet Statistics, http://global-reach.biz/globstats/evol.html **Wifi services:** JiWire WiFi HotStats, June 2007, http://www.jiwire.com/search-hotspot-locations.htm **Internet genres:** Nielsen NetRatings, http://www.adrelevance.com/intelligence/intel_dataglance.jsp?sr=36808&flash=false

3.1 Media TNCs - global top 10 by sales, 2006

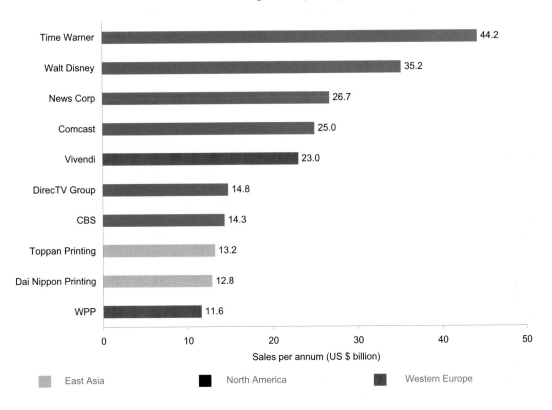

Company	Sales (US $ billion)
Time Warner	44.2
Walt Disney	35.2
News Corp	26.7
Comcast	25.0
Vivendi	23.0
DirecTV Group	14.8
CBS	14.3
Toppan Printing	13.2
Dai Nippon Printing	12.8
WPP	11.6

Sales per annum (US $ billion)

East Asia   North America   Western Europe

3.2 Telecommunication TNCs - global top 10 by sales, 2006

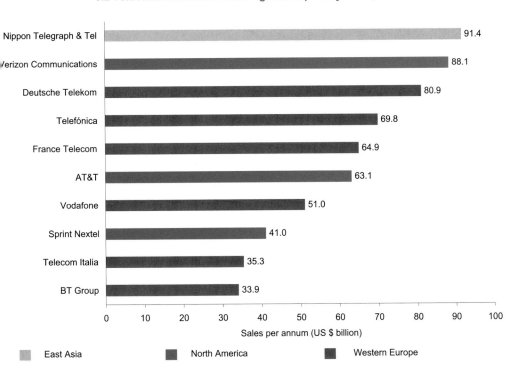

Company	Sales (US $ billion)
Nippon Telegraph & Tel	91.4
Verizon Communications	88.1
Deutsche Telekom	80.9
Telefónica	69.8
France Telecom	64.9
AT&T	63.1
Vodafone	51.0
Sprint Nextel	41.0
Telecom Italia	35.3
BT Group	33.9

Sales per annum (US $ billion)

East Asia   North America   Western Europe

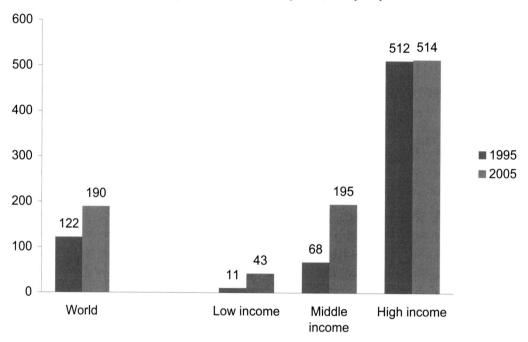

3.3 Telephone mainlines per 1,000 people

- 1995
- 2005

3.4 Cellular subscribers per 1,000 people

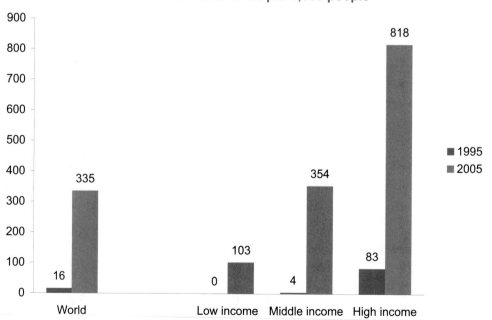

- 1995
- 2005

3.5 PCs per 1,000 people

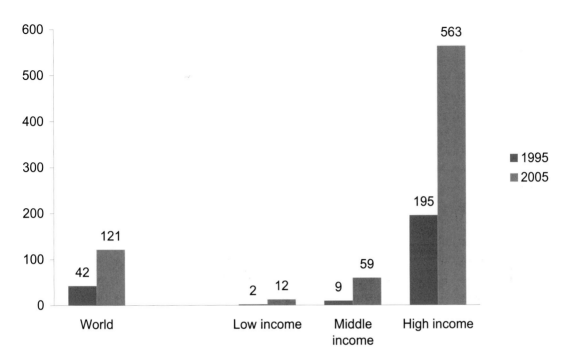

3.6 Internet users per 1,000 people

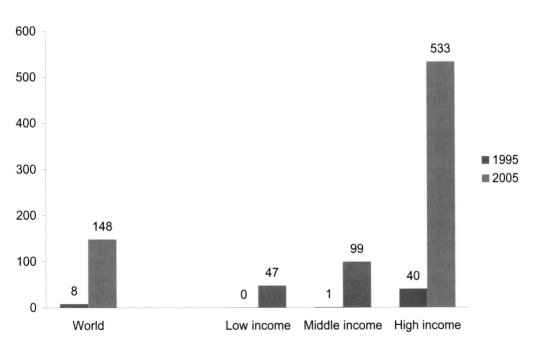

3.7 International Internet bandwidth (bits per person)

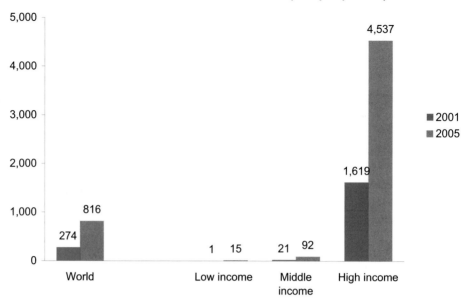

3.8 Internet usage and penetration

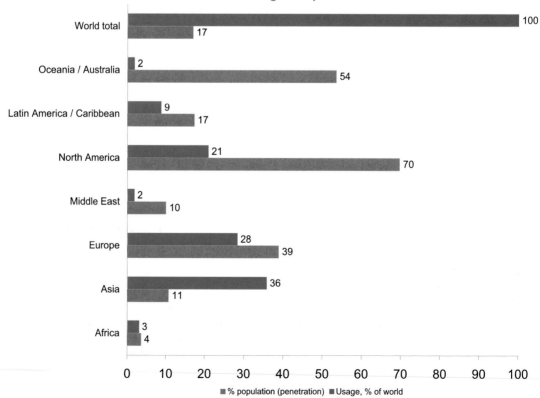

■ % population (penetration) ■ Usage, % of world

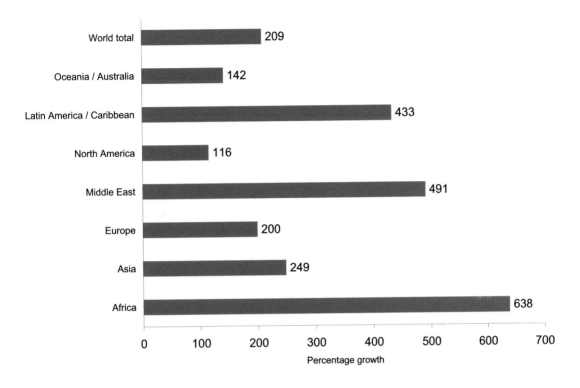

3.9 Internet usage growth 2000-2007

	Percentage growth
World total	209
Oceania / Australia	142
Latin America / Caribbean	433
North America	116
Middle East	491
Europe	200
Asia	249
Africa	638

Percentage growth

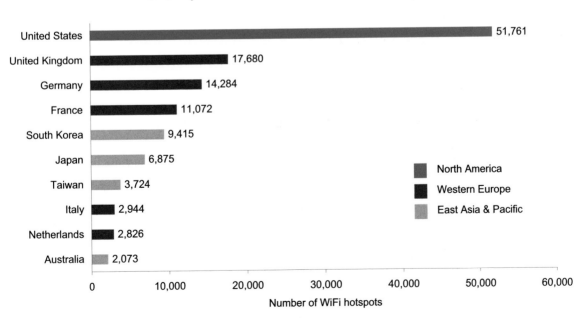

3.10 Top 10 countries with available WiFi service

Country	Number of WiFi hotspots
United States	51,761
United Kingdom	17,680
Germany	14,284
France	11,072
South Korea	9,415
Japan	6,875
Taiwan	3,724
Italy	2,944
Netherlands	2,826
Australia	2,073

North America
Western Europe
East Asia & Pacific

Number of WiFi hotspots

3.11 Top 10 cities with available WiFi service

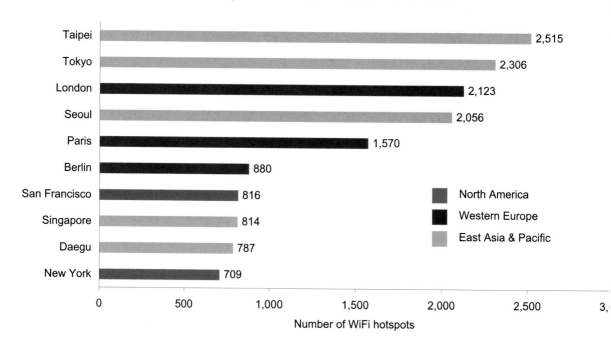

Number of WiFi hotspots

Taipei	2,515	East Asia & Pacific
Tokyo	2,306	East Asia & Pacific
London	2,123	Western Europe
Seoul	2,056	East Asia & Pacific
Paris	1,570	Western Europe
Berlin	880	Western Europe
San Francisco	816	North America
Singapore	814	East Asia & Pacific
Daegu	787	East Asia & Pacific
New York	709	North America

Legend:
- North America
- Western Europe
- East Asia & Pacific

3.12 Top 10 location types with available WiFi service

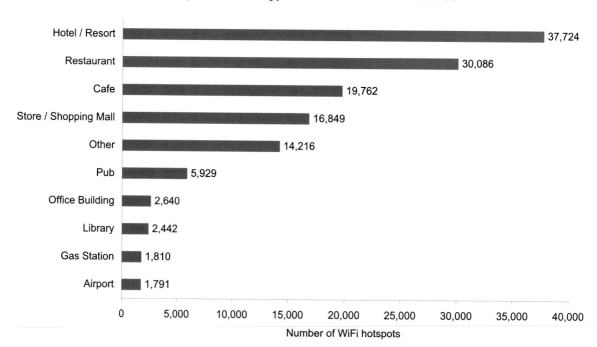

Number of WiFi hotspots

Location type	Value
Hotel / Resort	37,724
Restaurant	30,086
Cafe	19,762
Store / Shopping Mall	16,849
Other	14,216
Pub	5,929
Office Building	2,640
Library	2,442
Gas Station	1,810
Airport	1,791

3.13 Dynamics in Languages of the Internet, 2000-2005

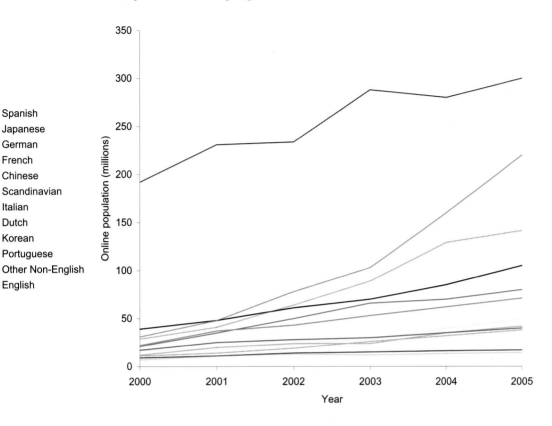

Legend:
- Spanish
- Japanese
- German
- French
- Chinese
- Scandinavian
- Italian
- Dutch
- Korean
- Portuguese
- Other Non-English
- English

Y-axis: Online population (millions)
X-axis: Year (2000, 2001, 2002, 2003, 2004, 2005)

3.14 Top Internet Web Site Genres
May 21-May 27, 2007

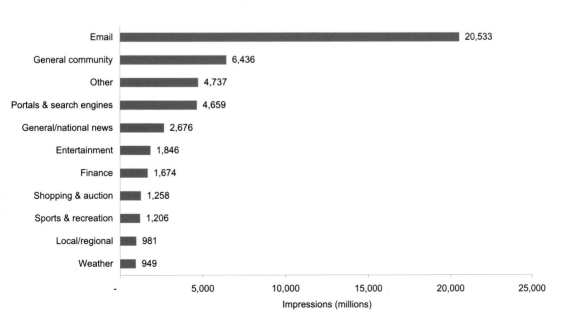

Genre	Impressions (millions)
Email	20,533
General community	6,436
Other	4,737
Portals & search engines	4,659
General/national news	2,676
Entertainment	1,846
Finance	1,674
Shopping & auction	1,258
Sports & recreation	1,206
Local/regional	981
Weather	949

X-axis: Impressions (millions)

3.15 Growth in the number of blogs worldwide, 2000-2005

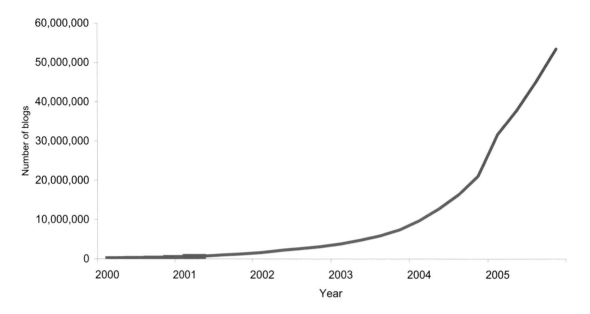

3.16 Distribution of blog authorship by region, July 2005

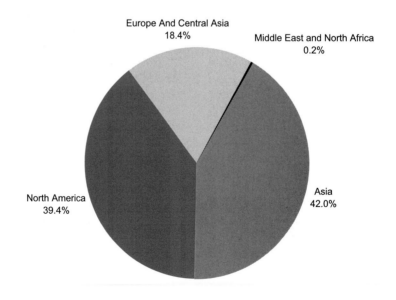

3.17 Age distribution of blog writers

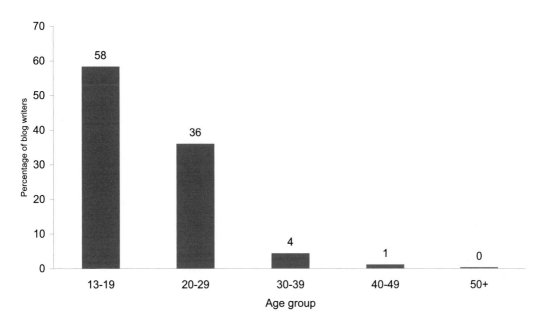

3.18 Gender distribution of blog writers

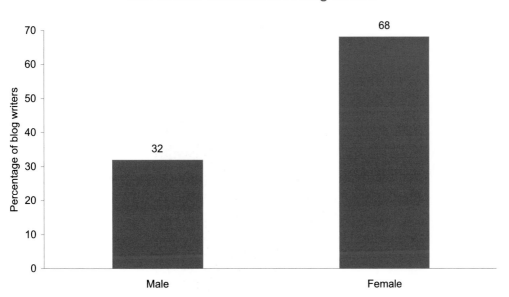

3.19 Ages of blog readers, by blog genre

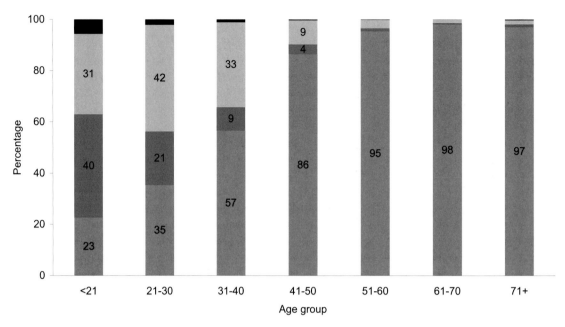

Percentage

| Age group | | | | | | |

■ Political blogs ■ Gossip blogs ■ Mom blogs ■ Music blogs

3.21 Education of blog readers, by blog genre

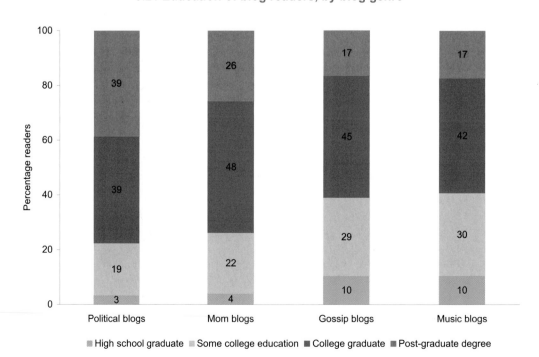

Percentage readers

■ High school graduate ■ Some college education ■ College graduate ■ Post-graduate degree

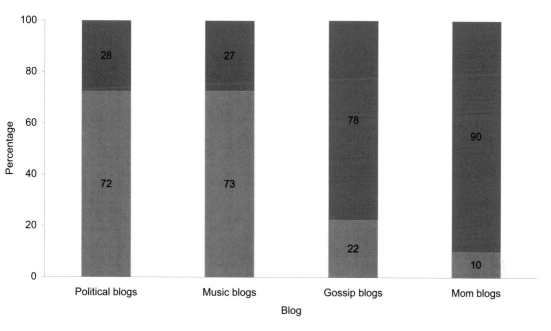

3.20 Gender of blog readers, by blog genre

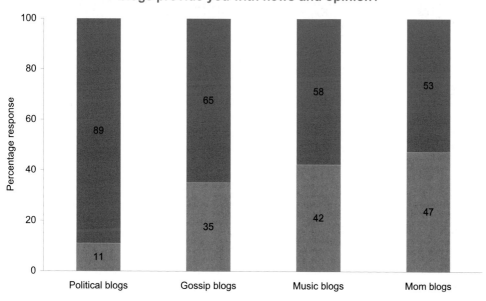

3.22 Readers' views of blog usefulness, by blog genre: how well do blogs provide you with news and opinion?

Political and governance systems that are stable and transparent, where corruption is minimised and governments provide a sound legal and administrative infrastructure of free association and enterprise, are conducive to a thriving civil society. At the same time, political and governance systems with the opposite characteristics provide an impetus for dissent and resistance by local and global civil society actors. Average country-level scores on governance indicators differ regionally, and are generally correlated with levels of economic development. This is true for perceptions of and estimated levels of government corruption and transparency (4.1), voice and accountability (4.3), and the degree to which a country's legal environment is conducive to business (4.5). The World Bank's Voice and Accountability scores also illustrate that differences between regions and economy groupings tend to be stable over time (4.3). The public integrity index data (4.4) show that different aspects of governance often vary widely not only between nations but also within nations. Transparency International's (TI) Corruption Barometer also reveals respondents' perceptions of the motivation and effectiveness of governments' actions on corruption are very low (4.2). Expert evaluations of corporate governance, as measured by sustainability reporting scores, tend to vary widely between and within nations, regions and industries (4.6, 4.7).

Dynamics in governance in recent years provide reasons for optimism: TI's Corruption Perceptions Index shows that perceived corruption in most regions is decreasing, and the World Bank's Control of Corruption Index shows a general increase in governments' efforts to combat corruption, excluding low-income economies in East Asia and Africa. Similarly, the Institute for Management Development's Bribing and Corruption and Transparency of Government measures indicate that, generally speaking, corruption is declining, and governments are becoming more transparent (4.1).

Corruption Perceptions Index: range = 0-10, low score = high corruption
Control of Corruption Index: range = –2.5-+2.5, low score = high corruption
Bribing and Corruption: range = 0-10, low score = high levels of bribing and corruption
Transparency of Government: range = 0-10, low score = low levels of transparency

Notes:[1] Figures for Australia, Netherlands and UK include companies that are bi-national and which were therefore counted twice in the data set.
Sources: Corruption and transparency: *Corruption Perceptions Index 2001, Corruption Perceptions Index 2006,* Transparency International, *Governance Matters VI: Governance Indicators for 1996–2006,* World Bank Institute, *World Competitiveness Yearbook 2007,* IMD International, Switzerland. **Public opinion on government efforts to fight corruption:** *Global Corruption Barometer 2006,* Transparency International. **Voice & Accountability:** *Governance Matters VI: Governance Indicators for 1996–2006,* World Bank Institute. **Public Integrity:** *Global Integrity Index, 2006,* The Center for Public Integrity. **Opacity:** 'The Opacity Index, The Global Costs of Opacity Measuring business and investment risk worldwide', *MIT Sloan Management Review,* By Joel Kurtzman, Glenn Yago and Triphon Phumiwasana, 2004. **Corporate sustainability reporting:** *Tomorrow's Value: The Global Reporters 2006 Survey of Corporate Sustainability Reporting,* UNEP, Standard & Poor's and SustainAbility.

4.1 Corruption and transparency of government

Region	Corruption Perceptions Index			Control of Corruption			Bribing and corruption			Transparency of government		
	2001	2006	% change 2001-2006	2000	2005	% change 2000-2005	2002	2007	% change 2002-2007	2002	2007	% change 2002-2007
Low income	2.4	2.5	4	-0.80	-0.86	-8	0.50	1.03	106	1.20	2.58	116
Middle income	4.0	3.7	-7	-0.17	-0.12	29	2.11	2.40	14	3.26	3.64	12
Low & middle income	3.5	3.2	-7	-0.45	-0.45	0	1.97	2.27	15	3.12	3.60	15
East Asia & Pacific	3.2	2.8	-12	-0.60	-0.63	-5	2.47	2.16	-13	4.08	4.15	2
Europe & Central Asia	3.6	3.5	-4	-0.40	-0.32	20	1.60	2.25	40	2.47	3.21	30
Latin America & Caribbean	3.7	3.5	-5	-0.22	-0.15	30	2.61	2.17	-17	3.70	3.22	-13
Middle East & North Africa	4.6	3.6	-21	-0.29	-0.28	5		4.43			5.13	
South Asia	1.8	3.2	77	-0.55	-0.54	1	1.54	1.67	8	3.70	4.54	23
Sub-Saharan Africa	3.1	2.8	-12	-0.60	-0.69	-15	2.82	2.19	-22	5.97	5.59	-6
High income	4.7	4.1	-14	-0.07	-0.06	16	4.30	4.28	0	4.49	4.67	4

4.2 Public opinion on government efforts to fight corruption
Average country % responses across economy groups

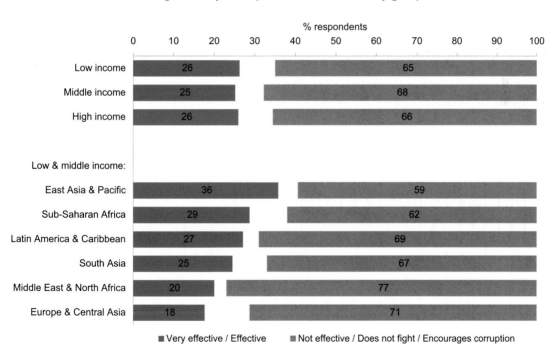

4.3 Voice and accountability scores

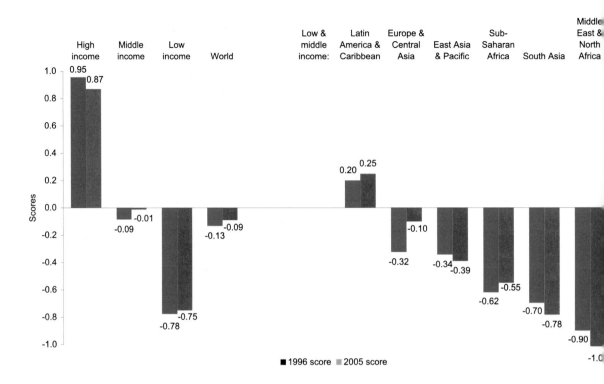

■ 1996 score ■ 2005 score

4.4 Public Integrity Index, 2006

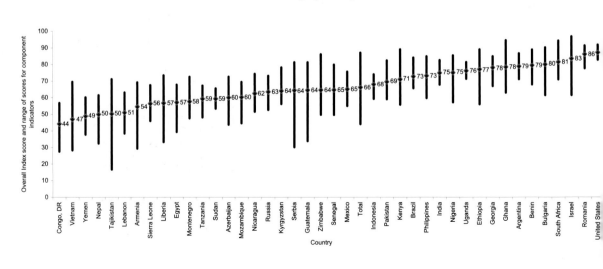

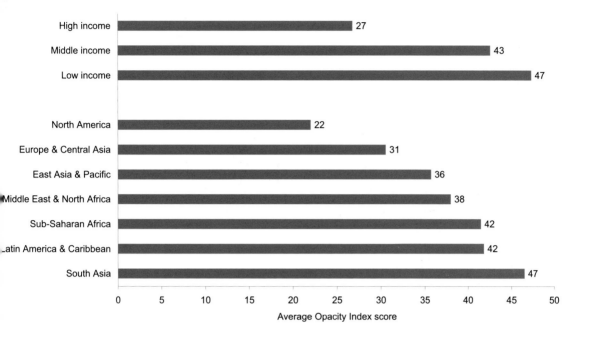

4.5 Opacity Index
Average of country index scores, by economy group and region

	Average Opacity Index score
High income	27
Middle income	43
Low income	47
North America	22
Europe & Central Asia	31
East Asia & Pacific	36
Middle East & North Africa	38
Sub-Saharan Africa	42
Latin America & Caribbean	42
South Asia	47

4.6 Corporate sustainability reporting scores 2006, by country and region

Region/country	Number of companies assessed	Number of industries assessed	Average company score
East Asia & Pacific	**11**	**9**	53
Australia[1]	4	2	58
Hong Kong	1	1	66
Japan	5	5	45
New Zealand	1	1	58
Europe & Central Asia	**28**	**18**	59
Denmark	1	1	64
Finland	1	1	58
France	3	3	52
Germany	3	3	50
Italy	1	1	48
Netherlands[1]	6	5	63
Norway	1	1	57
Spain	1	1	52
Sweden	1	1	52
Switzerland	1	1	51
United Kingdom[1]	11	7	65
Latin America & Caribbean	**2**	**2**	59
Brazil	2	2	59
North America	**8**	**8**	54
Canada	3	3	48
United States	5	5	40
Sub-Saharan Africa	**2**	**2**	59
South Africa	2	2	59

4.7 Corporate sustainability reporting scores 2006, by industry

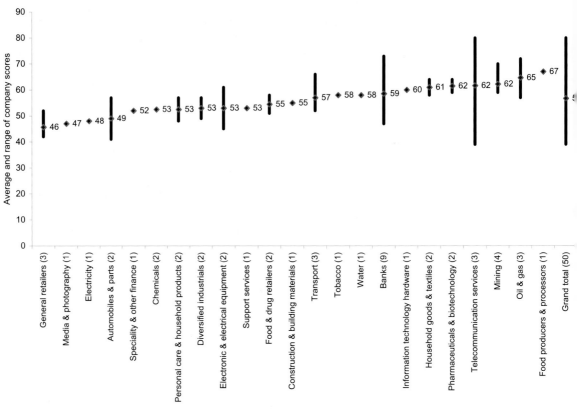

RECORD 5 RULE OF LAW

Global civil society is dependent on the international rule of law and is active in pushing for its adoption and enforcement. Global civil society actors play significant roles both initiating and promoting international treaties. They are instrumental in exposing human rights violations, which threaten the survival of local civil societies. The World Bank's general rule of law index scores and the Institute of Management Development's indices show that the rule of law is weak in the developing world, and that the global increase in the rule of law is mostly a result of the progress made in middle income economies, while developing nations show a general decline in the rule of law (5.1, 5.2). Trends vary among different aspects of the rule of law: the dynamics in respect of intellectual property rights are somewhat less positive than in other facets, for example (5.1).

Most countries have ratified the major international human rights, humanitarian, and environmental treaties, and ratifications of newer treaties (e.g. Kyoto Protocol and the International Criminal Court) are quickly catching up with more established ones (5.3, 5.4). Some countries have ratified few treaties overall, and/or in recent times, and could be described as resistant or laggard in this respect – for example, the US, countries in protracted conflicts (Iraq, Somalia), and a number of Central and East Asian nations (5.5).

Formal respect for human rights appears to be on the rise overall, but with some variations. Respect for human rights is particularly low in some Middle Eastern, East and South Asian, and African nations (5.6). Respect for physical integrity rights seems to have increased in most regions since 2000, but the trend regarding political empowerment rights is more mixed (5.7).

Sources: Rule of law: *Governance Matters VI: Governance Indicators for 1996–2006,* World Bank Institute; IMD World Competitiveness Online, Executive Opinion Survey http://www.worldcompetitiveness.com/online. **Treaty ratifications:** Office of the United Nations High Commissioner for Human Rights, http://www.ohchr.org/english/law/index.htm http://www.un.org/womenwatch/daw/cedaw/states.htm http://www.ohchr.org/english/countries/ratification/9.htm United Nations Treaties, http://untreaty.un.org/ENGLISH/bible/englishinternetbible/Bible.asp#partI Biological and Toxin Weapons Convention, http://www.opbw.org International Committee of the Red Cross, http://www.icrc.org/IHL.nsf **Human Rights:** CIRI Human Rights Data Project, http://ciri.binghamton.edu/index.asp

5.1 Institute of Management Development (IMD) rule of law indices

Region	Rule of law			Intellectual property rights			Ethical practices			Financial institutions' transparency		
	2000	2005	% change 2000-2005	2001	2006	% change 2001-2006	2001	2006	% change 2001-2006	2001	2006	% change 2001-2006
Low income	-0.87	-0.88	-1	2.62	2.75	5	3.00	3.28	9	3.59	3.84	7
Middle income	-0.16	-0.12	29	4.36	4.46	2	3.94	4.95	25	4.09	5.42	32
Low & middle income	-0.49	-0.47	4	4.17	4.27	2	3.84	4.76	24	4.04	5.24	30
East Asia & Pacific	-0.61	-0.35	43	5.16	4.64	-10	4.88	5.28	8	4.66	5.71	23
Europe & Central Asia	-0.41	-0.33	19	3.33	3.84	15	2.63	3.95	50	2.96	4.51	52
Latin America & Caribbean	-0.25	-0.32	-30	5.39	4.13	-23	5.70	5.50	-4	5.75	5.80	1
Middle East & North Africa	-0.18	-0.28	-50	0.00	5.96		0.00	5.79		0.00	6.49	
South Asia	-0.70	-0.40	42	4.34	5.21	20	4.55	5.95	31	6.23	6.57	5
Sub-Saharan Africa	-0.70	-0.77	-10	6.75	6.22	-8	6.36	6.09	-4	6.44	6.50	1
High income	1.44	1.32	-8	7.74	7.11	-8	6.71	6.82	2	6.74	6.67	-1
World	-0.11	-0.09	22	5.95	5.69	-4	5.28	5.79	10	5.39	5.95	11

5.2 Rule of law, 2000-2005

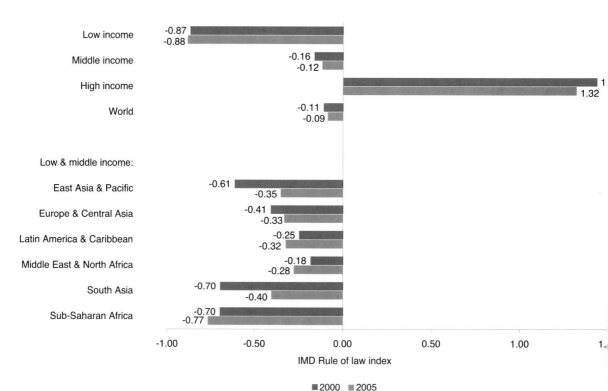

5.3 Ratifications of human rights, humanitarian, and environmental treaties
22 major treaties

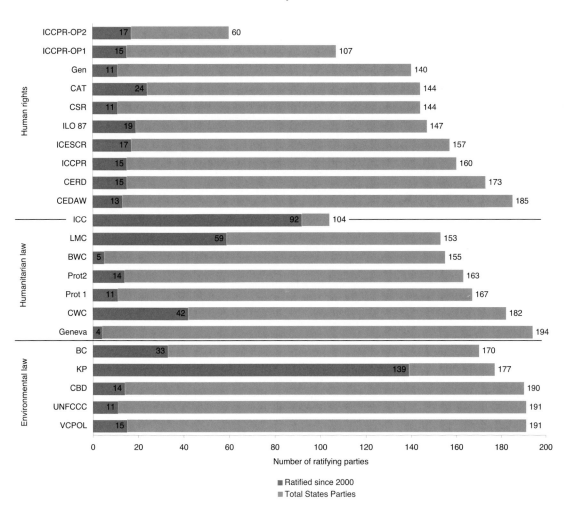

Number of ratifying parties

■ Ratified since 2000
■ Total States Parties

5.4 How many countries have ratified how many of the 22 treaties?

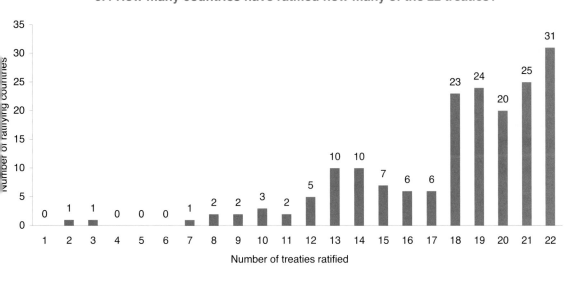

Number of treaties ratified

5.5 Record of treaties signed or ratified, by highest and lowest performers

Ratifications overall		Ratifications since 2000	
Ratified all 22 treaties	Ratified 10 treaties or fewer	Ratified more than 5 treaties	Have not ratified any treaties
Austria	Bhutan	Afghanistan	El Salvador
Belgium	Brunei	Azerbaijan	Iraq
Bosnia & Herzegovina	Indonesia	Bosnia & Herzegovina	United States
Bulgaria	Iraq	Cape Verde	Uzbekistan
Canada	Myanmar	Congo, Dem. Rep.	
Colombia	Singapore	Djibouti	
Costa Rica	Somalia	Equatorial Guinea	
Croatia	Timor-Leste	Eritrea	
Cyprus	Tonga	Ghana	
Denmark	United States	Haiti	
Ecuador		Indonesia & East Timor	
Estonia		Liberia	
Germany		Lithuania	
Greece		Montenegro	
Hungary		Serbia & Montenegro	
Iceland		Sierra Leone	
Ireland		St. Vincent & the Grenadines	
Italy		Sudan	
Lithuania		Swaziland	
Luxembourg		Turkey	
Macedonia		Yugoslavia	
Netherlands			
Norway			
Panama			
Paraguay			
Romania			
Slovakia			
Slovenia			
Spain			
Sweden			
Uruguay			

5.6 Record of respect for human rights, by highest and lowest performers

Average scores on Cingranelli-Richards (CIRI) Integrity Rights and Empowerment Rights indices

Declined more than 2 points, 1996-2004	Scored 1 or less in 2004	Consistently scored 8.5 or more in 1996, 2000 and 2004
Bangladesh	China	Belgium
Burundi	Congo, Dem. Rep.	Canada
Ethiopia	Ethiopia	Denmark
Laos	Iran	Finland
Malaysia	Iraq	Iceland
Mozambique	Korea, Dem. Rep.	Japan
Nepal	Myanmar	Luxembourg
Romania	Uzbekistan	Netherlands
Uzbekistan	Zimbabwe	New Zealand
Venezuela		Norway
Zimbabwe		Sweden
		Switzerland

5.7 Dynamics in respect of human rights, 1996-2004

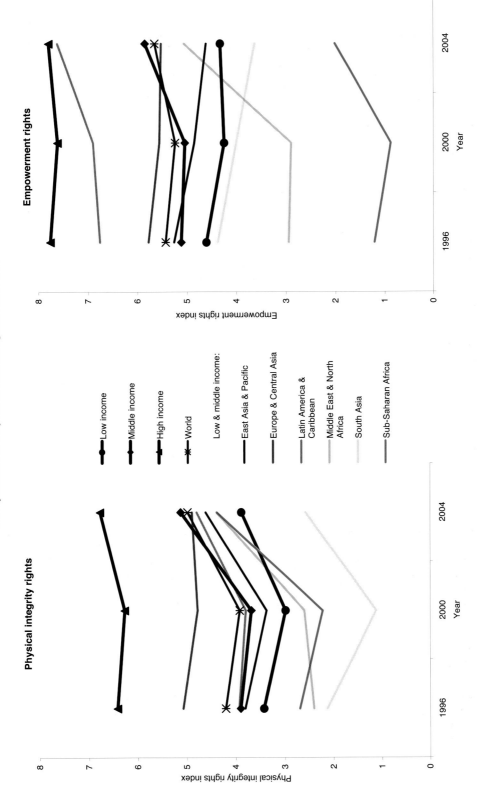

Social and economic rights are focal issues for global civil society. Basic needs such as food and shelter, education, social and health services are either not met, or met poorly in many parts of the world, and there remain great inequalities between countries and regions on these issues. Two general and well known patterns are illustrated by the data in this record. Levels of human development vary widely between countries, as captured in the UNDP's Human Development index (HDI); and although HDI is rapidly increasing in many developing nations, it remains low in Sub-Saharan Africa (6.1, 6.2). These patterns are replicated in other indicators of development, such as education (6.3-6.6), the prevalence of HIV (6.7), the prevalence of and success in combating tuberculosis (6.8, 6.9), numbers of slum dwellers (6.10) and nutrition (6.12). Developed nations provide assistance to developing countries in forms such as food aid (6.11), but debt service remains considerable, even though the burden of debt service payments has decreased in many countries between 1994 and 2004 (6.13).

Sources: HDI: *Human Development Report 2006, Cultural Liberty in Today's Diverse World,* New York: Oxford University Press. **Education:** UNFPA, *State of World Population 2006,* UNESCO, *Global Monitoring Report 2007,* World Bank, World Development Indicators (WDI-Online). **HIV/AIDS:** 2006 Report on the global AIDS epidemic, UNAIDS/WHO, May 2006. **TB:** *The Millennium Development Goals Report,* United Nations, 2006, UN Millennium Development Goal Indicators Database. **Slums:** Global Urban Observatory Statistics, http://ww2.unhabitat.org/programmes/guo/statistics.asp **Nutrition:** *Bread for the world, Hunger report 2007.* **Food aid:** FAO Statistics Division, http://www.fao.org/faostat/foodsecurity/Files/Food_aid_en.xls **Debt service:** UN Millennium Development Goal Indicators Database, http://millenniumindicators.un.org/unsd/mi/mi_indicator_xrxx.asp?ind_code=44

6.1 Human Development Index, 2004

Average country scores and ranges, by economy group and region

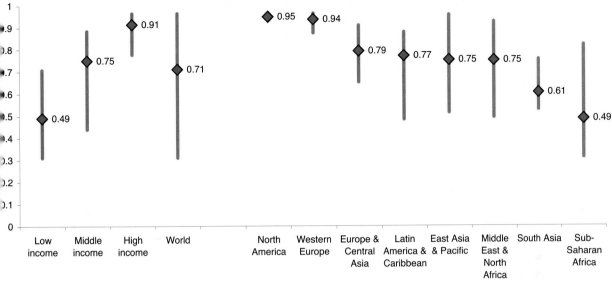

Economy group/region

6.2 Human Development Index trends, 1975-2004

Average scores by regions

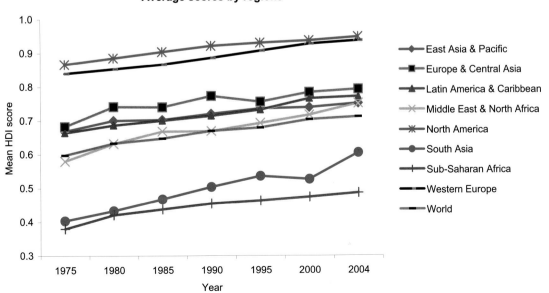

6.3 Access to public primary education
% enrolled in public schools

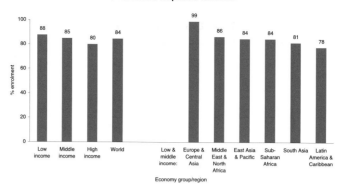

6.4 Public investment in education
% GDP per capita

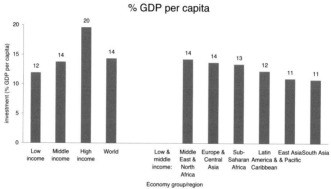

6.5 Teaching provision
Pupil-teacher ratio, 2004

6.6 Gender equality in access to primary education
Ratio of girls to boys, 2001-2005

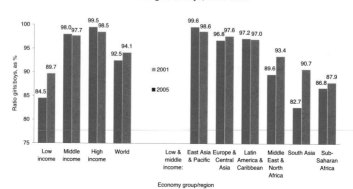

6.7 Prevalence of HIV
Estimated % population aged 15-49 with HIV

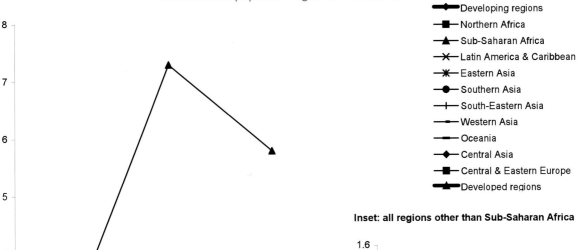

Legend:
- Developing regions
- Northern Africa
- Sub-Saharan Africa
- Latin America & Caribbean
- Eastern Asia
- Southern Asia
- South-Eastern Asia
- Western Asia
- Oceania
- Central Asia
- Central & Eastern Europe
- Developed regions

Inset: all regions other than Sub-Saharan Africa

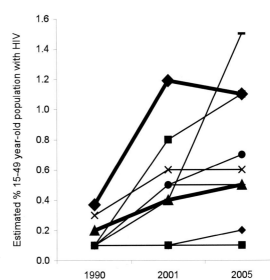

6.8 Tuberculosis prevalence, detection and deaths

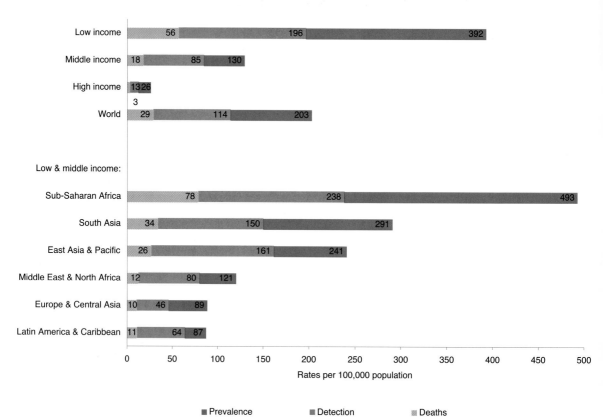

Rates per 100,000 population

■ Prevalence   ■ Detection   ■ Deaths

6.9 Tuberculosis treatment success rates

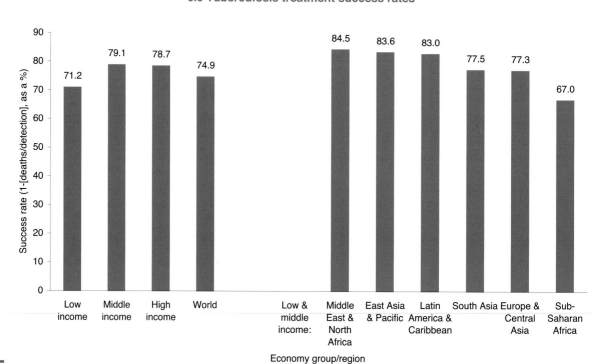

Economy group/region

6.10 Slum populations in regions, 1990-2005 and projection to 2020

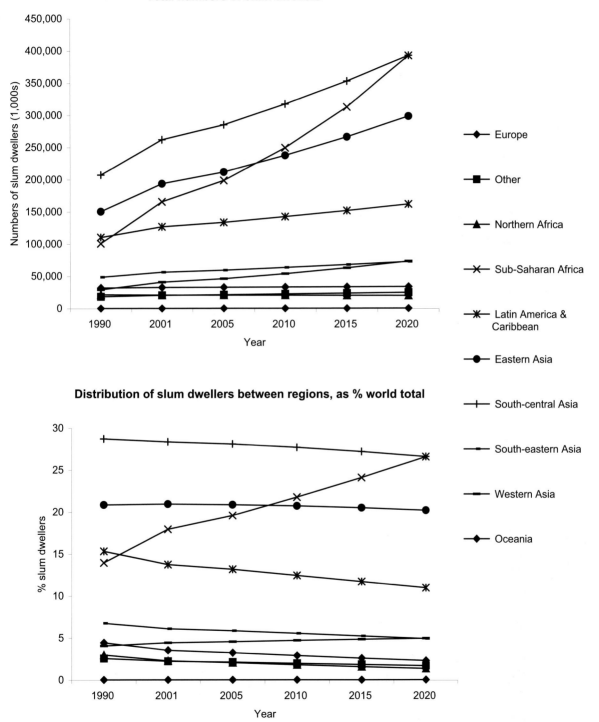

Total numbers of slum dwellers

Distribution of slum dwellers between regions, as % world total

Legend:
- ♦ Europe
- ■ Other
- ▲ Northern Africa
- ✕ Sub-Saharan Africa
- ✳ Latin America & Caribbean
- ● Eastern Asia
- ╂ South-central Asia
- ▬ South-eastern Asia
- ▬ Western Asia
- ♦ Oceania

6.11 Food aid shipments: cereals & non-cereals
Annual shipment in two time periods

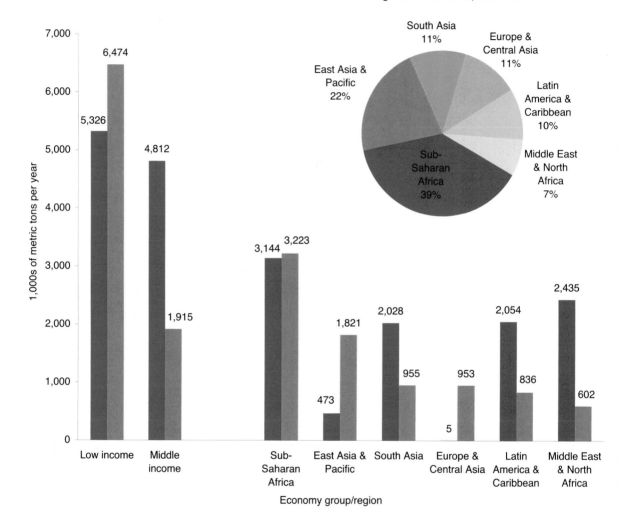

Regional distribution, 2001-2003

South Asia 11%
Europe & Central Asia 11%
East Asia & Pacific 22%
Latin America & Caribbean 10%
Sub-Saharan Africa 39%
Middle East & North Africa 7%

1,000s of metric tons per year

Economy group/region

■ 1990-1992 ■ 2001-2003

6.12 Per capita dietary energy supply, 2001-2003

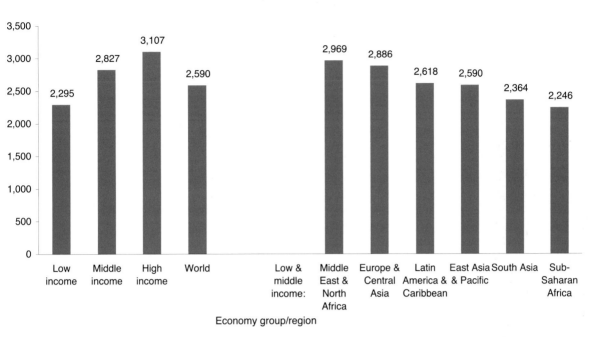

Economy group/region

6.13 Global inequality
Debt service as % exports of goods and services and net income from abroad

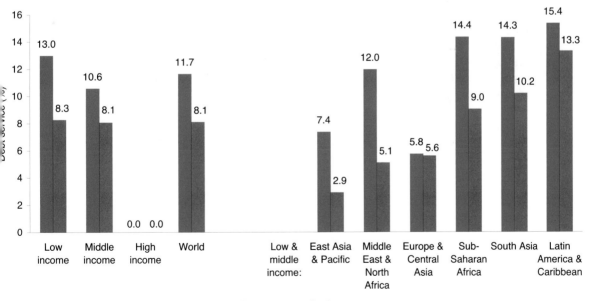

Economy group/region

■ 1994　■ 2004

War and conflict adversely affect practically any attempts to develop a more just and prosperous world; peacekeeping is a central task for humanity. The locations, time and duration of UN peacekeeping operations (PKO) signal which areas of the world suffer from intractable conflicts where the battling sides are unable to bridge their differences. Current PKO missions are predominantly in Sub-Saharan Africa, the Middle East, and in the post-Soviet world (7.1), while the largest numbers of PKO forces come from countries in South Asia and in Sub-Saharan Africa (7.2). The UN PKO timeline (7.3) shows the rise in the peacekeeping role of the UN – the number of missions has risen dramatically since 1988, although they tend to be shorter in duration than previously. In a survey of public opinion, conducted recently in fourteen countries, the idea of a standing UN peacekeeping force generally receives more support than opposition, although the level of support varies from country to country (7.4).

Sources: UN PKO: United Nations, Department of Peacekeeping Operations, www.un.org/Depts/dpko/dpko/contributors/index.htm http://www.un.org/Depts/dpko/dpko/timeline/pages/timeline.html **Attitudes towards UN PKO:** *The Chicago Council on Global Affairs, Public Opinion on the Future of the UN, May 2007,* http://www.worldpublicopinion.org/?nid=&id=&lb=hmpg

Peacekeeping forces, as of April 2007

Country/area of mission	Region	Name of mission	Start date	Total	Male	Female	% female	Approved resources, July 2006-June 2007 (US$)	Fatalities, as of April 2007
Burundi	Sub-Saharan Africa	BINUB	January 2007	4	4	0	0	45,935,000	14
Western Sahara	Middle East & North Africa	MINURSO	April 1991	228	223	5	2	489,207,100	27
Haiti	Latin America & Caribbean	MINUSTAH	June 2004	7,036	6,919	117	2	1,094,247,900	109
Congo, Dem. Rep.	Sub-Saharan Africa	MONUC	November 1999	17,318	17,017	301	2		7
Afghanistan	South Asia	UNAMA	March 2002	13	13	0	0		4
Iraq	Middle East & North Africa	UNAMI	November 2003	230	230	0	0	39,865,200	42
Golan Heights	Middle East & North Africa	UNDOF	June 1974	1,043	1,023	20	2	46,270,400	176
Cyprus	Europe & Central Asia	UNFICYP	March 1964	856	810	46	5	350,866,600	260
Lebanon	Middle East & North Africa	UNIFIL	March 1978	13,251	12,854	397	3		3
Sierra Leone	Sub-Saharan Africa	UNIOSIL	September 2006	14	14	0	0	137,385,100	19
Ethiopia/Eritrea	Sub-Saharan Africa	UNMEE	July 2000	1,706	1,689	17	1	217,962,000	47
Kosovo	Europe & Central Asia	UNMIK	June 1999	38	37	1	3	714,877,300	93
Liberia	Sub-Saharan Africa	UNMIL	September 2003	14,060	13,766	294	2		23
Nepal	South Asia	UNMIN	January 2007	97	89	8	8	1,079,534,400	2
Sudan	Sub-Saharan Africa	UNMIS	March 2005	9,398	9,276	122	1	170,221,100	11
Timor-Leste	East Asia & Pacific	UNMIT	August 2006	33	32	1	3		33
India/Pakistan	South Asia	UNMOGIP	January 1949	45	44	1	2	472,889,300	11
Côte d'Ivoire	Sub-Saharan Africa	UNOCI	April 2004	8,054	7,980	74	1	33,377,900	48
Georgia	Europe & Central Asia	UNOMIG	August 1993	132	125	7	5		
Middle East	Middle East & North Africa	UNTSO	May 1948	150	144	6	4		

7.2 Current UN peacekeeping forces, as of April 2007
By region and income group of country of origin

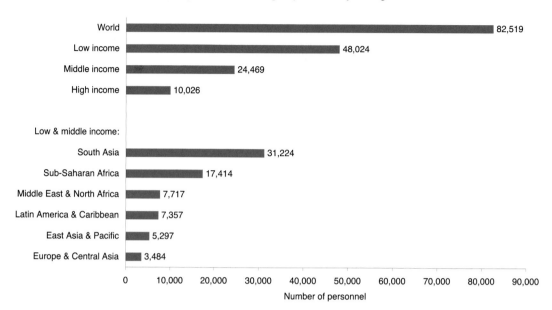

Number of personnel

7.3 UN peacekeeping missions timeline, 1948-2007

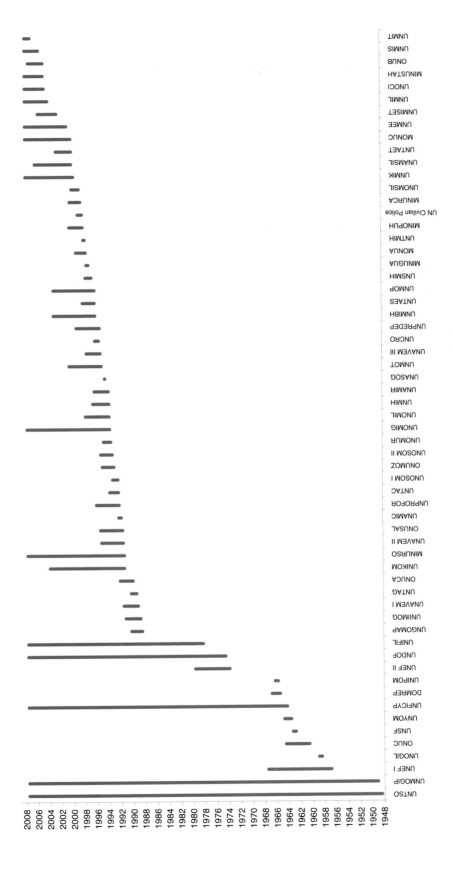

7.4 Public opinion on UN peacekeeping forces
'Do you favour or oppose having a standing UN peacekeeping force selected, trained and commanded by the United Nations?'

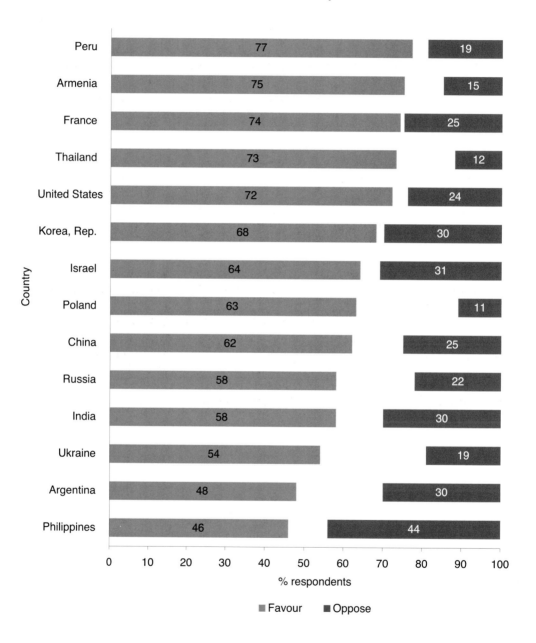

Environmental degradation and environmental governance are central concerns for many global civil society actors. This record presents a selection of indicators of environmental change, and of the practices of governments, corporations and global civil society in relation to environmental themes. An index to evaluate overall Environmental Performance per country has been constructed by Yale University. Countries with high income economies are awarded higher scores in this Index, on average, than those with low incomes (8.1). However, carbon dioxide emissions – a key concern in environmental debates – remain strikingly higher in per capita terms among high income economies than among developing countries (8.2). Energy consumption rates, especially from non-renewable sources, also vary markedly between regions (8.3). Two more positively framed indicators follow. Rates of recycling in paper production are changing, with notable increases in high income economies, and in South Asia (8.4). At the corporate level, the number of companies adopting ISO 14000 standards is increasingly rapidly; globally, the number of accredited companies in 2005 was nearly 26 times greater than in 1997 (8.5).

The increase in extreme weather incidents is often cited as an indicator of the effects of climate change, brought about by human-caused environmental degradation. The number of incidents and fatalities from such incidents appears to have risen steeply over the last twenty years (8.6). Civil society actors have played a significant role in raising concern about climate change as well as many other environmental issues. As an example of the global presence of environmentally focused INGOs, 8.7 summarises for three INGOs the locations of their constituent member groups and offices, and shows differing global distributions and regional foci.

Sources: EPI: *Environmental Performance Index,* Center for Environmental Law & Policy, Yale University, and Center for International Earth Science Information Network (CIESIN), Columbia University. **CO emissions:** World Bank, World Development Indicators (WDI-Online). **Energy consumption:** *BP Statistical Review of World Energy June 2006,* http://www.bp.com/statisticalreview **Paper production:** FAOSTAT database: http://faostat.fao.org/ **Extreme weather:** *Disaster Data: A Balanced Perspective, June 2007,* Centre for Research on the Epidemiology of Disasters (CRED), Université catholique de Louvain, Belgium. **ISO 14000:** ISO 14000 survey 2004: http://www.iso.org/iso/en/iso9000-14000/pdf/survey2005.pdf **NGOs:** FoEI, http://www.foei.org/en/who-we-are Greenpeace, http://www.greenpeace.org/international/about/worldwide WWF, http://www.panda.org/about_wwf/who_we_are/offices/index.cfm.

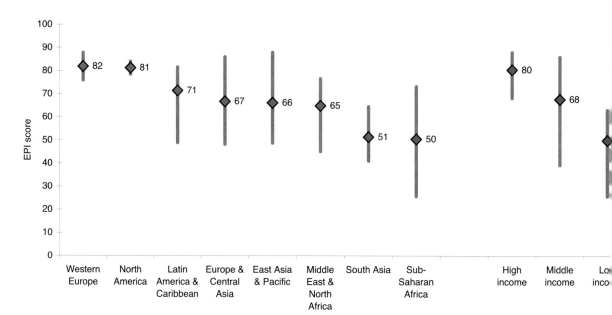

8.1 Environmental Performance Index, 2006
Mean scores and ranges for countries grouped by region and income level

8.2 Carbon dioxide emissions

	Metric tons per capita			kg per ppp$ of GDP		
	1993	2003	% change 1993-2003	1993	2003	% change 1993-2003
Low income	0.800	0.835	4	0.460	0.407	-12
Middle income	3.350	3.560	6	0.828	0.615	-26
Low & middle income:						
East Asia & Pacific	2.158	2.748	27	0.853	0.601	-30
Europe & Central Asia	8.288	6.921	-16	1.351	0.927	-31
Latin America & Caribbean	2.373	2.423	2	0.363	0.343	-5
Middle East & North Africa	2.675	3.441	29	0.643	0.714	11
South Asia	0.768	1.010	31	0.448	0.407	-9
Sub-Saharan Africa	0.804	0.751	-7	0.494	0.422	-15
High income	11.970	12.789	7	0.516	0.456	-12
World	3.937	4.300	9	0.610	0.507	-17

8.3 Energy consumption by fuel type
Summaries by region

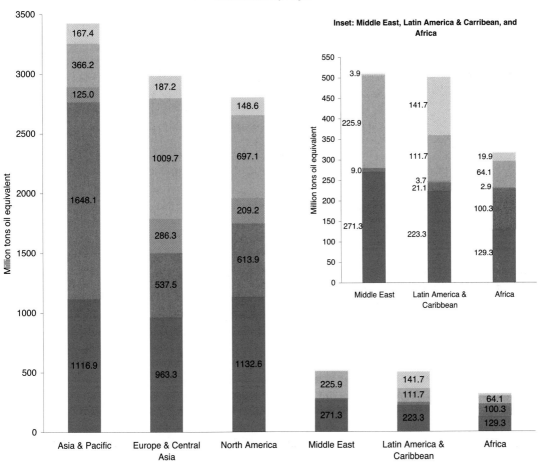

Inset: Middle East, Latin America & Carribean, and Africa

■ Oil ■ Coal ■ Nuclear energy ■ Natural gas ■ Hydro-electric

Proportions of energy consumed from different fuel types, worldwide

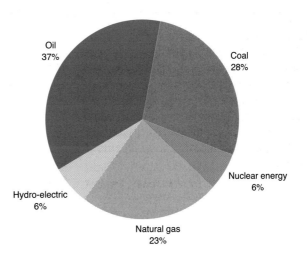

Oil 37%
Coal 28%
Nuclear energy 6%
Natural gas 23%
Hydro-electric 6%

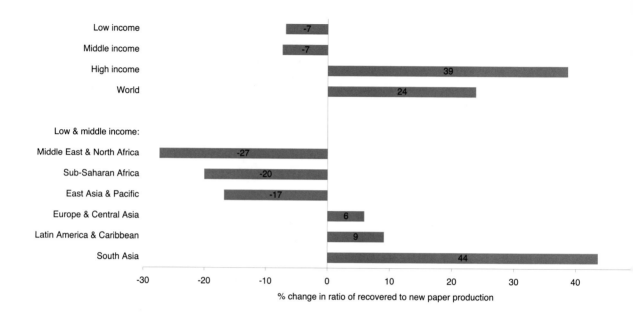

8.4 Recycling: ratio of recovered paper to new paper production
% change in ratio, 1995-2005

% change in ratio of recovered to new paper production

8.5 ISO 14000 accredited companies

Region	Number of ISO 14000 accredited companies		
	1997	2001	2005
Low income	75	707	2,689
Middle income	353	4,559	27,691
Low & middle income:			
East Asia & Pacific	175	2,326	15,574
Europe & Central Asia	81	1,214	7,487
Latin America & Caribbean	109	931	3,824
Middle East & North Africa	11	179	970
South Asia	30	418	1,814
Sub-Saharan Africa	22	198	711
High income	3,776	30,008	78,790
World	4,204	35,274	109,170

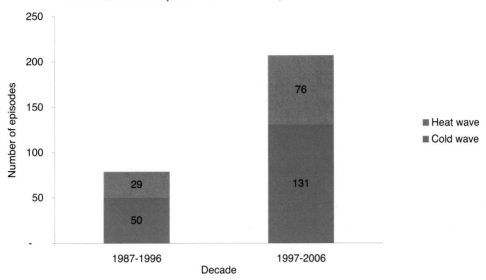

8.6 Extreme temperature disasters, 1987-2006

Number of episodes

- Heat wave
- Cold wave

Decade

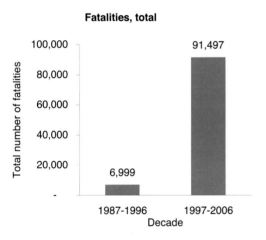

Fatalities, total

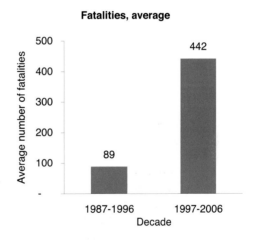

Fatalities, average

8.7 Global presence of international environmental NGOs
by regions and income groups

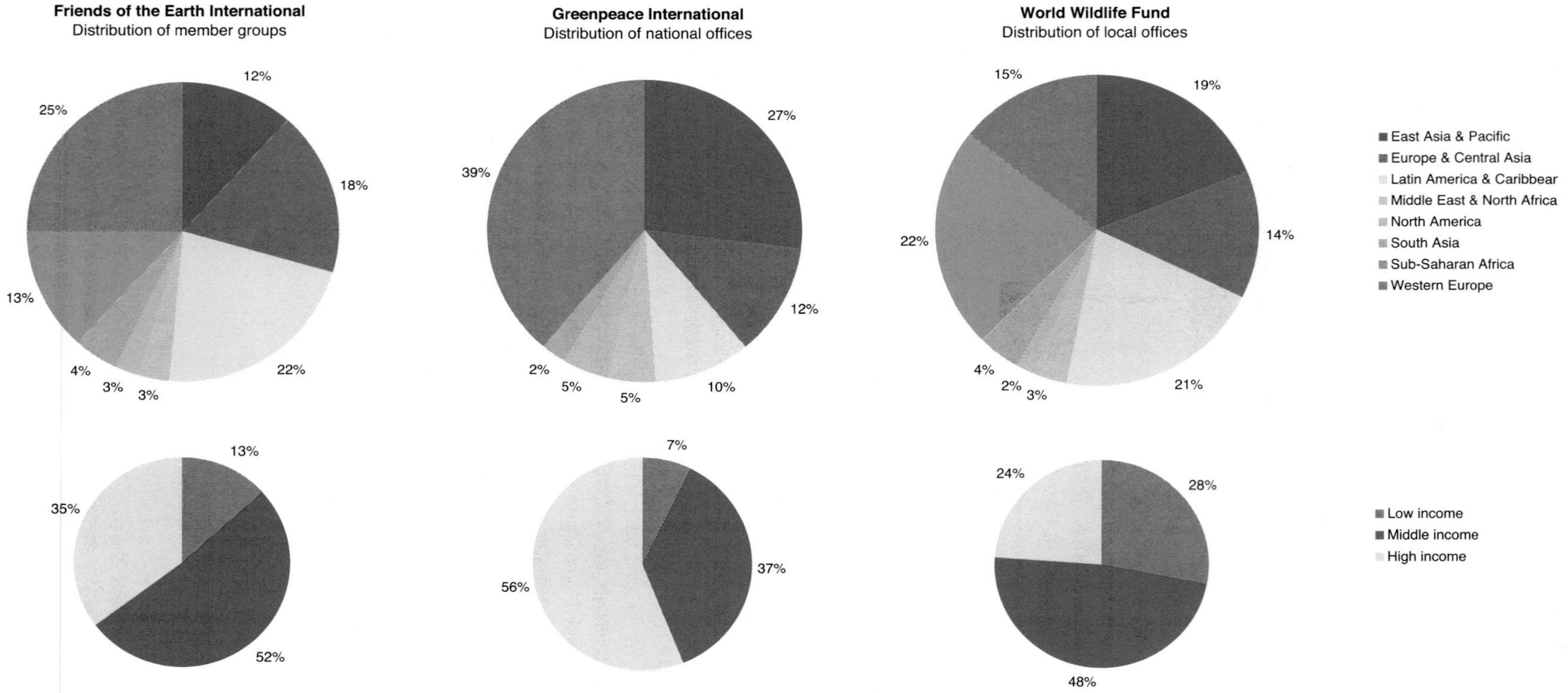
Friends of the Earth International
Distribution of member groups
12%
18%
22%
3%
3%
4%
13%
25%
13%
52%
35%
Greenpeace International
Distribution of national offices
27%
12%
10%
5%
5%
2%
39%
7%
37%
56%
World Wildlife Fund
Distribution of local offices
19%
14%
21%
3%
2%
4%
22%
15%
28%
48%
24%
East Asia & Pacific
Europe & Central Asia
Latin America & Caribbear
Middle East & North Africa
North America
South Asia
Sub-Saharan Africa
Western Europe
Low income
Middle income
High income

A multitude of international agents operate in the global public sphere. Inter-governmental organisations (IGOs) are some of the main instruments of global governance, and international NGOs (INGOs) are one of the most prominent manifestations of global civil society. INGOs and local NGOs participate in global governance institutions and processes in various ways. In addition, a variety of global civil society actors come together to organise their own forums – most notably the Social Forum movement, which includes local, regional, national, thematic, and world social forums.

International organisations continue to grow in numbers: the growth of INGOs in the last decade was 10 times that of IGOs. According to the Union of International Associations (UIA) classification, this growth is predominantly in INGOs that have a narrower scope (UIA types D-G), such as regional INGOs and internationally-oriented national organisations (9.1, 9.2). International organisations remain a mostly Northern phenomenon, characterised by a US and Western European prevalence, as seen in the statistics on country participation and meetings of international organisations (9.3-9.5). These different global civil society actors work on a huge variety of topics, as evidenced, for example, by the manifold activities at the World Social Forums (9.6).

NGOs play different roles in global governance institutions, including sharing information, engaging in consultations and collaborating on projects (9.9). The engagement of NGOs in global governance institutions is not uniform. On the one hand, the number of NGOs in consultative status with the UN's Economic and Social Council has increased at a steady rate since 1995 (9.7), and the number of NGOs with participatory status in the Council of Europe increased between 2005 and 2006 (9.10). On the other hand, there was a slight decrease in NGO participation in World Bank country assistance and poverty reduction efforts (9.8), as well as in WTO Ministerial conferences in 2005 (9.11).

Notes:[1] Calculated using 2007 populations of the countries included in this table in the UIA Yearbook, using the UN's medium population estimate variant. [2]Of the 3186 activities listed in the 2006 World Social Forum website, areas of interest were specified for 2000. [3]Data for Singapore 1996 contain one NGO related to both Singapore and India. [4]Data for Geneva 1998 contain one NGO related to both the US and Switzerland. [5]Data regarding Cancún include NGOs eligible to attend the Fifth WTO Ministerial Conference.

Sources: International organisations, meetings and country participation: *Yearbook of International Organizations*, 1996/97 and 2007/2008 editions, Union of International Associations, Brussels, http://www.uia.org/statistics/pub.php **WSF:** 2006 World Social Forum, http://www.wsf2006.org/org_activity_list.php **ECOSOC:** Peter Willetts (2002) *The Conscience of the World.* Washington: The Brookings Institution. http://www.staff.city.ac.uk/p.willetts/NGOS/NGO-GRPH.HTM UN DESA-NGO section, NGOs in consultative status with ECOSOC, http://www.un.org/esa/coordination/ngo/pdf/INF_List.pdf **World Bank:** *World Bank-Civil Society Engagement, Reviews of Fiscal Years 2002–2004 and 2005- 2006*, World Bank. Council of Europe: **Council of Europe:** http://www.coe.int/t/e/ngo/public/participatory_status/list_of_ngos/ WTO: World Trade Organization, http://www.wto.org/english/forums_e/ngo_e/ngo_e.htm

9.1 Number of international governmental organisations (IGOs) and international non-governmental organisations (NGOs) by UIA organisation type, 1996-7 and 2007-8

UIA organisation type	IGOs		NGOs		All international organisations	
	1996-7	2007-8	1996-7	2007-8	1996-7	2007-8
A. Federations of international organisations	1	1	39	35	40	36
B. Universal membership organisations	36	34	493	468	529	502
C. Intercontinental membership organisations	37	32	1,007	1,051	1,044	1,083
D. Regionally oriented membership organisations	186	175	3,933	5,963	4,119	6,138
E. Organisations emanating from places, persons, bodies	751	814	1,944	2,689	2,695	3,503
F. Organisations of special form	743	728	3,223	4,342	3,966	5,070
G. Internationally oriented national organisations	76	117	4,469	6,895	4,545	7,012
Total UIA types A - G	1,830	1,901	15,108	21,443	16,938	23,344

9.2 International organisations, 1996-2008
Total numbers of IGOs and NGOs

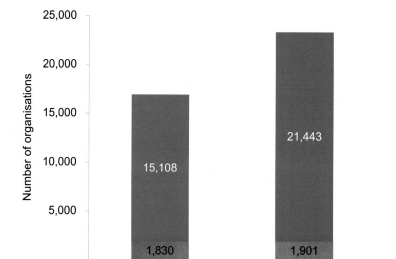

9.3 Country participation in international organisations, by UIA types, 2007-8

UIA organisation type groups	Conventional international bodies (A-D)			Organisations emanating from places, persons, bodies			Organisations of special form (F)			Internationally oriented organisations (G)			All A-G international organisations		
Continent	Number of organisation memberships	Memberships in region, as % total	Membership density per million of population [1]	Number of organisation memberships	Memberships in region, as % total	Membership density per million of population [1]	Number of organisation memberships	Memberships in region, as % total	Membership density per million of population [1]	Number of organisation memberships	Memberships in region, as % total	Membership density per million of population [1]	Number of organisation memberships	Memberships in region, as % total	Membership density per million of population [1]
Africa	25,537	13.1	26.5	9,470	15.7	9.8	17,471	17.2	18.1	3,013	17.2	3.1	55,491	14.8	57.5
America	33,316	17.1	36.6	10,292	17.1	11.3	18,533	18.3	20.3	3,830	21.9	4.2	65,971	17.6	72.4
Asia	34,433	17.6	8.7	9,550	15.9	2.4	17,436	17.2	4.4	3,614	20.6	0.9	65,033	17.4	16.5
Australasia & Oceania	7,323	3.8	213.0	2,297	3.8	66.8	4,071	4.0	118.4	815	4.7	23.7	14,506	3.9	421.8
Europe	94,606	48.5	105.0	28,612	47.5	31.8	43,837	43.3	48.7	6,240	35.6	6.9	173,295	46.3	192.4
World	195,215	100.0	28.9	60,221	100.0	8.9	101,348	100.0	15.0	17,512	100.0	2.6	374,296	100.0	55.5

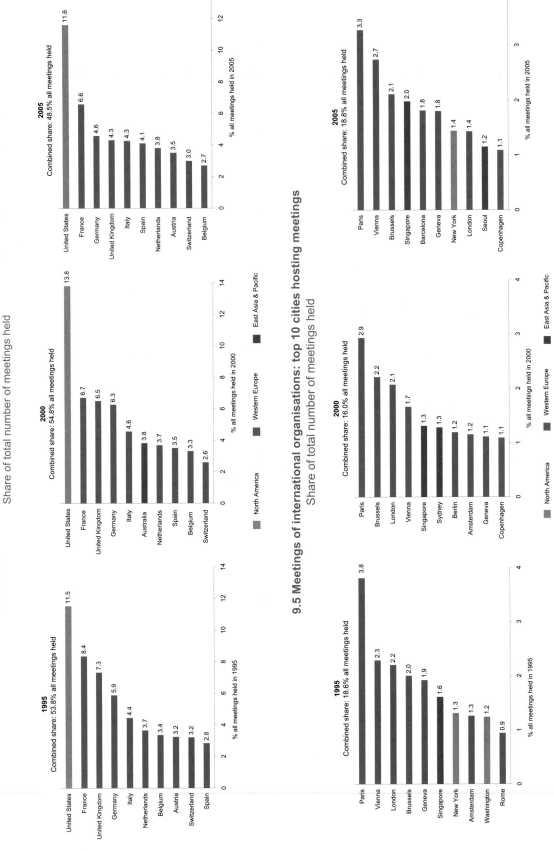

9.4 Meetings of international organisations: top 10 countries hosting meetings
Share of total number of meetings held

9.5 Meetings of international organisations: top 10 cities hosting meetings
Share of total number of meetings held

9.6 Prominent issues in 2006 World Social Forum

Issued mentioned more than 50 times as primary or secondary areas of focus in World Social Forum activities[2]

Issue	Number of mentions
Culture (counter-hegemony, cultural diversity, popular, identities, commodification)	181
The arts (education, awareness, social change)	136
Education (environment, popular, adults, distance, formal, non-formal, informal, formation)	125
Human rights (universalisation, to reproductive, economic, social, cultural)	125
Development (democratic, economical, social, local, sustainable)	105
Democracy (direct, participative, planetary, representative)	100
Social movements (grassroots, trade unions, student)	92
Citizenship (building, right of, world)	70
Empire, imperialism (hegemony, struggle against)	70
Agriculture (ecological, familiar, organic, sustainable, urban, earth)	68
Children and teenagers' rights	68
The arts (the performing arts, cinema, the visual arts, painting)	67
Democratisation (communication, knowledge, the state, economy)	63
Globalisation	62
Participation (social, citizen, local power, democracy, social control)	62
Work (condition of, right to, unemployment, infantile, of women, of slaves, domestic)	61
Latin America, Cone Sul, Mercosul	59
Youth	58
Peace (culture of, activism for)	57
Media (commodification, democratisation, alternative media)	55
Trade agreements (FTAA, NAFTA, GATS, TLCs, TRIPS, EU/Mercosul, AoA)	54
Advocacy	52
Discrimination and/or affirmation (ethnical, social, of gender, sexual orientation)	52
Economy (alternative, informal, sustainable, national, international, new economy)	51

9.7 NGOs at the United Nations
NGOs having consultative status with the UN Economic and Social Council (ECOSOC), 1946-2006

9.8 Engagement of civil society in World Bank projects, 2002-2006

Consulting civil society on country assistance strategies

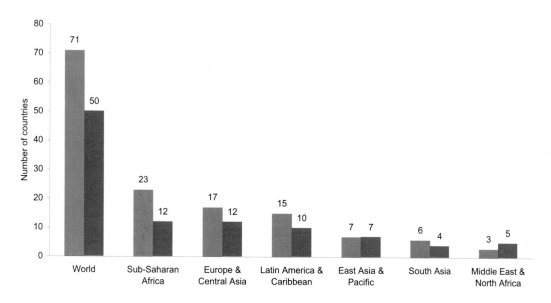

Civil society participation in poverty reduction strategy papers

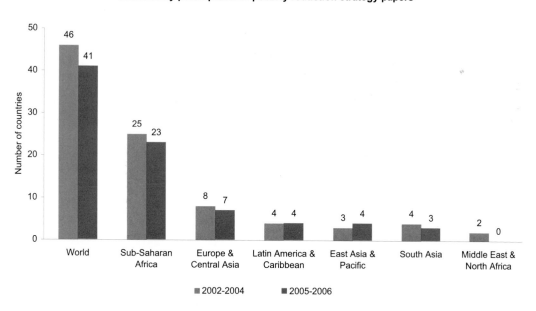

■ 2002-2004　　■ 2005-2006

9.9 Forms of civil society engagement in World Bank projects

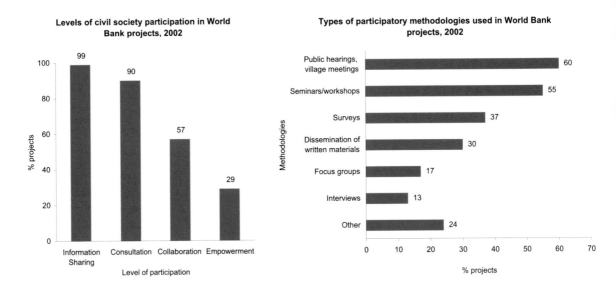

Levels of civil society participation in World Bank projects, 2002

Types of participatory methodologies used in World Bank projects, 2002

9.10 NGOs with participatory status with the Council of Europe, 2005/6
by economy group/region of organisations' host countries

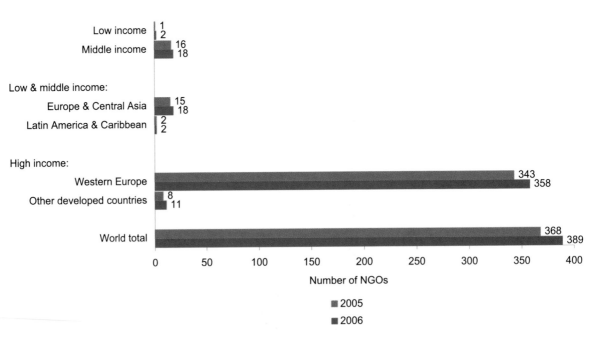

9.11 NGO participation in WTO ministerial conferences
Numbers of NGOs participating in six conferences

		Low income	**Middle income**	**Low & middle income**						**High income**	**World**
				East Asia & Pacific	Europe & Central Asia	Latin America & Caribbean	Middle East & North Africa	South Asia	Sub-Saharan Africa		
Singapore[3]	1996	6	10	5	0	4	0	7	0	90	108
Geneva[4]	1998	7	11	3	0	5	1	6	3	112	130
Seattle	1999	25	41	13	2	24	1	7	19	410	476
Doha	2001	101	140	32	6	87	10	49	57	708	949
Cancún[5]	2003	101	140	32	6	87	10	49	57	713	954
Hong Kong	2005	80	93	51	8	28	1	42	43	592	765

Bar chart: world totals

Social Forums, by type and year

This map updates research on the social forum phenomenon conducted for *Global Civil Society 2005/6* by Marlies Glasius and Jill Timms. More than six years after the first World Social Forum in Porto Allegre, we can cautiously conclude that social forums are likely to remain a significant part of the global civil society landscape. In most parts of the world, the founding of new social forums has slowed down from a peak in 2003/4, but in Africa and particularly in the United States, growth continues. Approximately two thirds of social forums endure in one form or other. National and local social forums are considerably more successful in this regard than the more ambitious regional and thematic forums, which in any case are perhaps not intended to become regular events.

This table and map, based on regular web searches undertaken between January 2003 and June 2007, has some methodological limitations. It only takes account of forums that have some form of presence on the Internet and in a language known to the researchers (Spanish, English, Russian, Polish, Italian, French, Dutch, Urdu, German and Portuguese). Other vibrant local social forums may well exist, particularly in developing countries, but without a web presence in one of the above languages we could not include them here. Moreover, local social forums in Italy and Greece have been excluded because at one point there were too many to consider and track over time. If you have information on a social forum not represented on this map, please let us know by contacting f.c.holland@lse.ac.uk

	Regional	Thematic	National	Local	Total
Founded in 2001					**5**
2001 only				1	1
2001-2002					
2001-2003					
2001-2004				1	1
2001-2005					
2001-2006					
2001-current	1	1		1	3
Founded in 2002					**50**
2002 only	1		3	7	11
2002-2003			1	3	4
2002-2004			1	6	7
2002-2005	1		1	3	5
2002-2006					
2002-current	2		7	14	23
Founded in 2003					**71**
2003 only	2	2	2	11	17
2003-2004			1	9	10
2003-2005				7	7
2003-2006				1	1
2003-current	1	2	14	19	36
Founded in 2004					**63**
2004 only	1	1	6	10	18
2004-2005	1			6	7
2004-2006					
2004-current	2	1	7	28	38
Founded in 2005					**25**
2005 only	2	1	2	5	10
2005-2006				1	1
2005-current		1	4	9	14
Founded in 2006					**27**
2006 only		1			1
2006-current	1		9	16	26
Founded in 2007			**3**	**7**	**10**
Total non-survivors	*8*	*5*	*17*	*71*	*101*
Total survivors	*7*	*5*	*44*	*94*	*150*

9.12 SOCIAL FORUMS BY TYPE AND YEAR

Official Development Aid (ODA) can be seen as an instrument of redistribution that reflects governments' commitments to tackling global inequalities. The years 2001-2005 witnessed rapid growth in ODA, but this decreased in 2006 (10.2). EU members of the OECD's Development Assistance Committee (DAC) provided over half of ODA donated by OECD countries in 2005, and almost all of the ODA that was channelled through NGOs. The latter constitutes only a miniscule share of ODA, reflecting the preference of donor governments for government-led programmes (10.1).

In relief funding, as reported by the UN's OCHA (Office for the Coordination of Humanitarian Affairs) the US plays a major role (10.5). Relief reflects a reactive style of funding in response to events as they occur and thus it tends to fluctuate (10.4, 10.6). On average it covers two-thirds of the funding requested by agencies providing relief on the ground (10.6). Humanitarian contributions are directed at a variety of needs, with food often representing the largest proportion of assistance (10.3).

International philanthropy from US foundations has been rising gradually in recent years (10.7). The contributions of the Gates Foundation account for a large share of the total value of funding from this source. The foundation's focus on health means that health issues in Sub-Saharan Africa, and Asia and the Pacific, receive a large proportion of the grants awarded by US foundations overall (10.8-10.10). European foundations award grants worth billions of Euros annually (10.11-10.13), with the numbers of foundations and funding from foundations varying from country to country. Unfortunately, available data do not indicate what proportion of the grants given by European foundations are directed towards recipients outside of the foundations' home countries.

Sources: OECD ODA: OECD Statistics, http://webnet4.oecd.org/wbos/default.aspx **Relief:** ReliefWeb, UN OCHA www.reliefweb.int **International Philanthropy:** *International Grant making Update, 2006*, Foundation Center, *Foundation Facts & Figures Across the EU – Associating Private Wealth for Public Benefit*, European Foundation Center, April 2005.

10.1 Overall Official Development Aid (ODA) and ODA channelled through NGOs, OECD countries, 2006

Total ODA from OECD countries

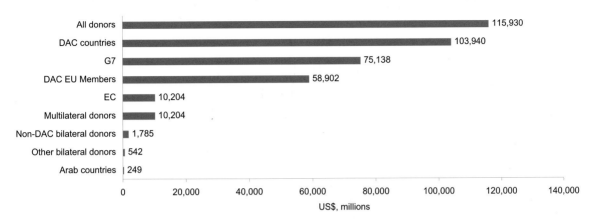

US$, millions

ODA from OECD countries channelled through NGOs

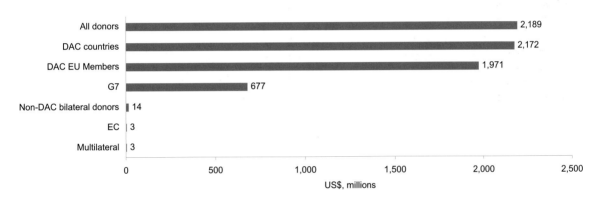

US$, millions

ODA channelled through NGOs, as % total ODA from OECD countries

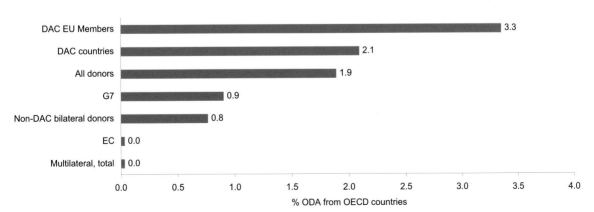

% ODA from OECD countries

10.2 Overall Official Development Aid (ODA) and ODA channelled through NGOs, OECD countries, 1994-2006

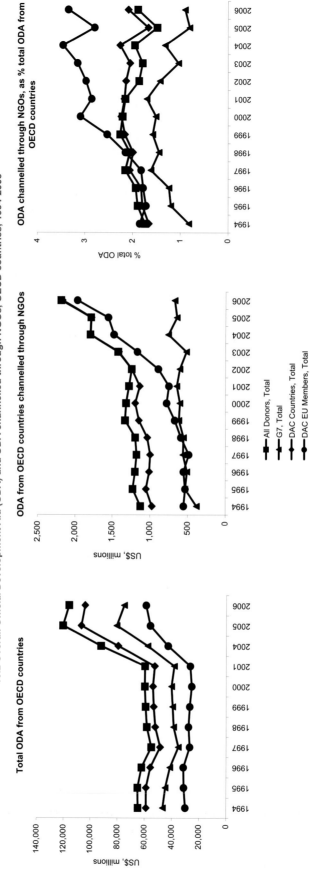

10.3 Global humanitarian contributions by sector, 2000-2007

Donor	Funding (contributions and commitments) US$, millions							
	2000	2001	2002	2003	2004	2005	2006	2007
Security	3.7	7.4	6.4	8.0	20.1	7.4	9.5	4.8
Education	18.0	27.7	99.8	125.0	67.0	215.1	107.6	30.0
Mine action	20.2	28.7	81.5	71.3	70.8	86.4	111.5	38.4
Shelter and non-food items	61.0	84.4	123.5	70.9	161.9	485.2	223.1	67.1
Agriculture	105.5	100.7	229.8	235.0	250.7	272.1	224.1	67.7
Economic recovery and infrastructure	25.7	35.7	92.8	929.5	151.9	763.7	323.4	76.7
Water and sanitation	15.1	36.8	55.2	105.0	148.7	331.1	216.5	96.3
Protection/Human rights/Rule of law	48.6	44.0	55.1	193.2	91.7	212.3	292.2	133.7
Coordination and support services	58.8	95.1	206.4	299.4	320.7	811.8	464.3	224.7
Health	149.1	214.3	326.5	403.0	478.1	1,051.4	515.8	279.6
Food	984.2	1,388.3	2,216.1	3,340.9	1,271.8	2,603.4	2,777.7	1,446.7
Multi-sector	515.9	1,759.1	1,664.6	1,869.8	1,292.7	4,324.9	1,274.7	496.3
Sector not yet specified			0.2	21.1	412.1	1,974.9	715.5	576.1
Total	2,005.7	3,822.1	5,158.0	7,758.8	4,737.9	13,139.6	7,256.0	3,538.4

10.4 Global humanitarian contributions: totals, 2000-2007

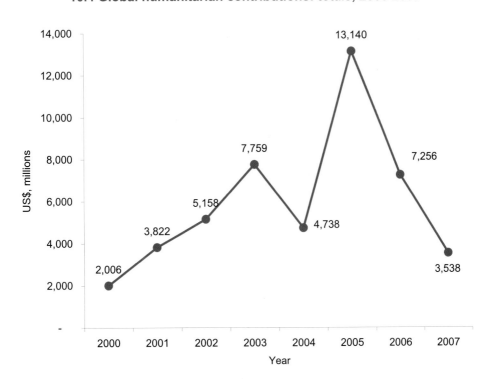

10.5 Global humanitarian contributions: top 10 donors, 2000-2007
Total funding

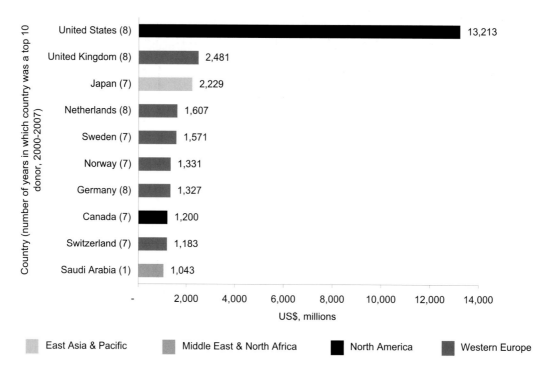

United States (8) — 13,213
United Kingdom (8) — 2,481
Japan (7) — 2,229
Netherlands (8) — 1,607
Sweden (7) — 1,571
Norway (7) — 1,331
Germany (8) — 1,327
Canada (7) — 1,200
Switzerland (7) — 1,183
Saudi Arabia (1) — 1,043

Country (number of years in which country was a top 10 donor, 2000-2007)

US$, millions

East Asia & Pacific   Middle East & North Africa   North America   Western Europe

10.6 International relief: UN consolidated inter-agency appeals
Requirements and actual funding, 1992-2007

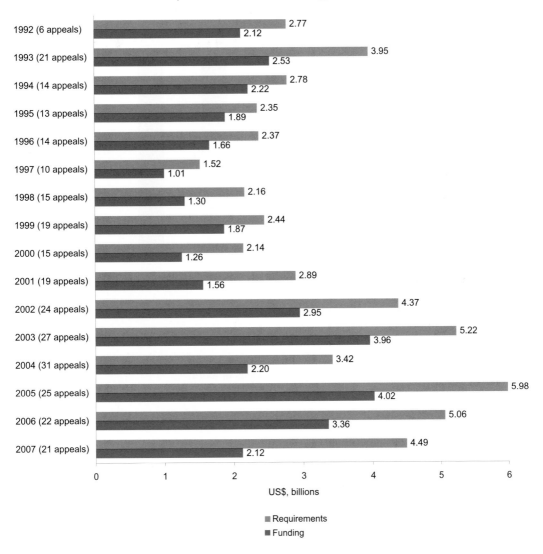

US$, billions

- ■ Requirements
- ■ Funding

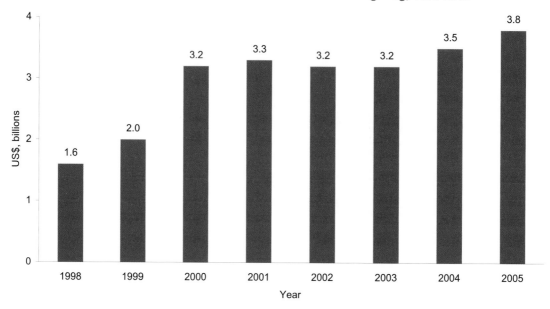

10.7 Total estimated US foundations' international giving, 1998-2005

US$, billions

1998 1.6
1999 2.0
2000 3.2
2001 3.3
2002 3.2
2003 3.2
2004 3.5
2005 3.8

Year

10.8 US foundations' international giving, by country of recipient, 2004
% total grants amount

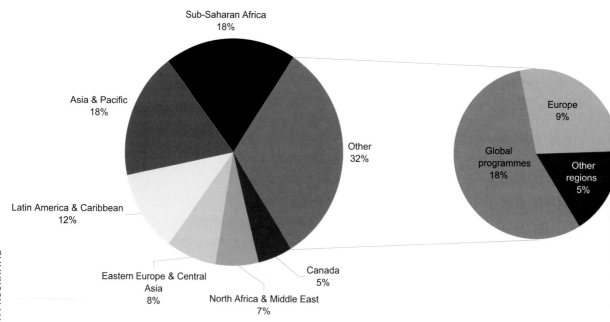

Sub-Saharan Africa
18%

Asia & Pacific
18%

Other
32%

Latin America & Caribbean
12%

Eastern Europe & Central
Asia
8%

Canada
5%

North Africa & Middle East
7%

Europe
9%

Global
programmes
18%

Other
regions
5%

10.9 US foundations' international giving, by target area, 2004
% total grants amount

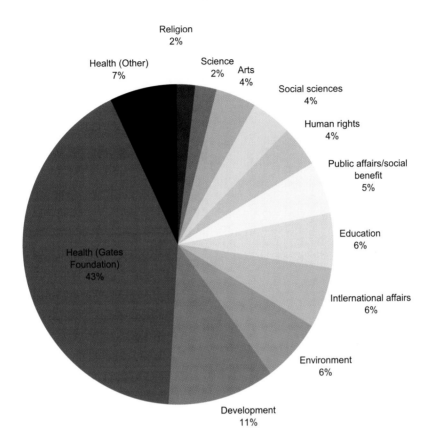

10.10 Top 15 US foundations by international giving, 2004

Foundation name	Number of international grants in 2004	Total international grants in 2004, US$	Primary international focus areas
Bill & Melinda Gates Foundation	134	1,233,160,002	Supports efforts to improve equity in global health through the prevention and treatment of infectious diseases in developing countries; and to bridge the global digital divide by providing access to knowledge through public libraries.
Ford Foundation	1,328	258,502,043	Seeks to strengthen democratic values, reduce poverty and injustice, promote international cooperation, and advance human achievement through programmes in asset building and community development; education; media; sexuality; religion; arts and culture; and peace and social justice.
Gordon and Betty Moore Foundation	79	83,184,068	Seeks to preserve the biodiversity and health of the environment in the Andes-Amazon region and the North Pacific, and supports scientific research through marine microbiology and conservation.
John D and Catherine T MacArthur Foundation	223	73,138,000	Seeks to promote conservation and sustainable development; human rights and international justice; international peace and security; and reproductive health.
Rockefeller Foundation	329	72,306,649	Seeks to improve the lives of poor people worldwide through programmes in the areas of food security; creativity and culture; global health equity; global inclusion; higher education in Africa; and regional programmes in Southeast Asia.
William and Flora Hewlett Foundation	165	56,595,034	Supports global development in the areas of education, population, environment and the performing arts.
WK Kellogg Foundation	122	56,315,269	Promotes regional development in Latin America & Caribbean and helps reduce poverty and improve quality of life in southern Africa's rural communities.
Freeman Foundation	223	53,456,718	Supports international exchange programmes, fellowships, and international studies, with a focus on Asia.
Carnegie Corporation of New York	113	42,415,000	Supports efforts for international peace and security, and seeks to strengthen international development in Sub-Saharan Africa by enhancing universities, women's opportunities, and libraries.
Starr Foundation	101	41,392,820	Supports efforts to provide healthcare to underserved communities, promote democratic values and international relations.

10.11 Number of foundations in the European Union

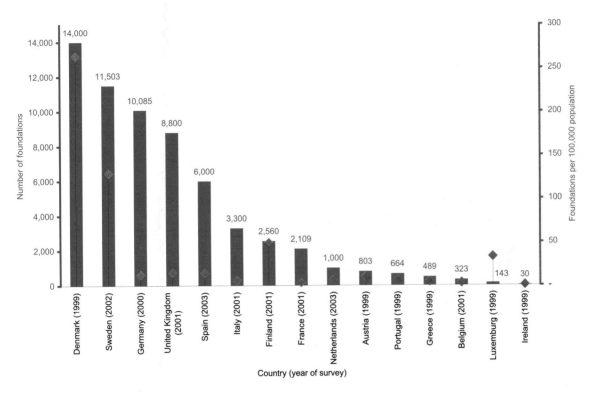

■ Number of foundations ◆ Foundations per 100,000 population

10.12 European foundations: expenditure
Total expenditure of foundations surveyed (€, millions)

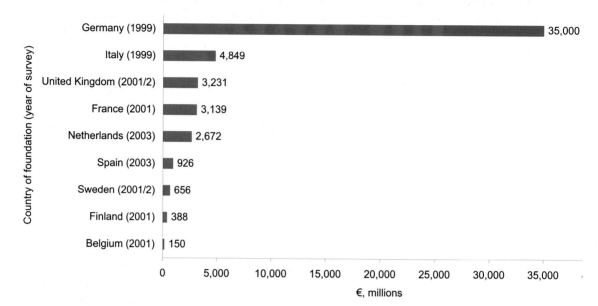

Global civil society is a normative phenomenon; an expression of humanistic and cosmopolitan values. It is enabled by a set of shared values, attitudes and social practices that generate the trust and social capital needed for collaborative action. There are clear differences in cultural traditions between regions (11.1) which appear to be relatively stable (11.3), but key cosmopolitan values such as tolerance seem to be gaining support worldwide (11.2).

Globalisation is increasingly a shared frame of reference for action in global civil society, either with a positive (one world) or a negative focus (the anti-globalisation movement). Support for globalisation has generally been rising in the developing world and declining in higher income economies (11.4). Among a selection of major global economic actors, the World Bank's global public image is more positive than that of the IMF or global companies (11.5). Contrastingly, attitudes towards the US, a major agent of globalisation, appear to be increasingly negative, while opinion broadly disfavours the US government's approach to a number of key international issues (11.6).

The social capital indicators presented here mostly demonstrate a considerable gap between developed and developing nations, and a general decline around the world. Compared to 20 years ago, people are less trusting of their fellow men (11.7), with lowest levels of generalised trust in Sub-Saharan Africa, Latin America and the Caribbean, and Europe and Central Asia. In developing regions political activism is the lowest globally, following a broad decline over the last 20 years, in contrast to an increase in political activism in high income economies (11.8). Data on the level of participation in social organisations shows a slightly different pattern, with some developed regions boasting levels of participation higher than those of Western Europe (11.9). One half of all memberships are in four types of organisations: education and cultural activities, labour unions, religious organisations and sports or recreation (11.10).

Sources: Values, Trust, Political activism and Social participation: World Values Survey, http://www.worldvaluessurvey.org **Attitudes:** *World Competitiveness Yearbook,* International Institute for Management Development, World Public Opinion: Global Public Opinion on International Affairs, Program on International Policy Attitudes (PIPA), http://www.worldpublicopinion.org/pipa/articles/btglobalizationtradera/index.php?nid=&id=&lb=btgl

11.1 Value sets of nations

Countries ranked by traditional/secular-rational and survival/self-expression values

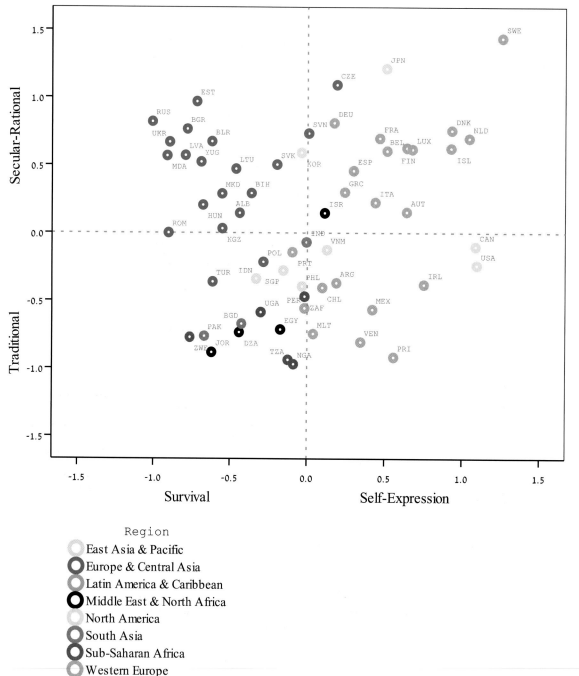

11.2 Cosmopolitan values: those selecting tolerance as an important quality to teach children

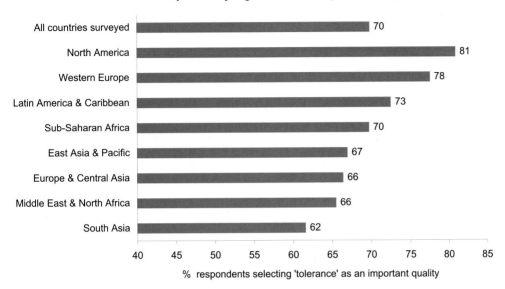

Responses by region, 1999-2004 (fourth survey wave)

Region	%
All countries surveyed	70
North America	81
Western Europe	78
Latin America & Caribbean	73
Sub-Saharan Africa	70
East Asia & Pacific	67
Europe & Central Asia	66
Middle East & North Africa	66
South Asia	62

% respondents selecting 'tolerance' as an important quality

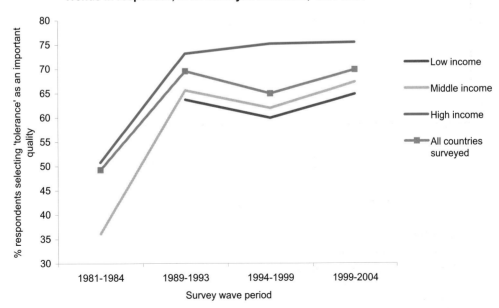

Trends in responses, in all surveyed countries, 1981-2004

% respondents selecting 'tolerance' as an important quality

Survey wave period

Low income
Middle income
High income
All countries surveyed

11.3 Post-materialist values

Trends in responses, in all surveyed countries, 1981-2004

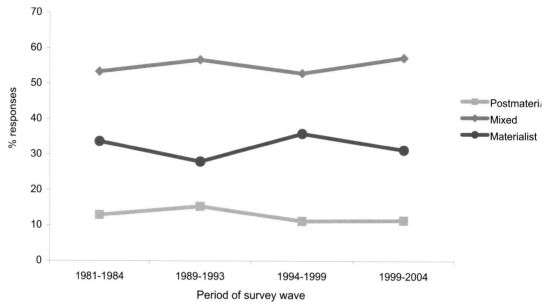

By economy group, 1999-2004 (fourth survey wave)

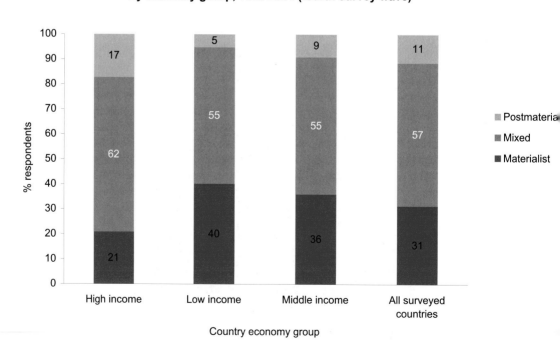

11.4 Attitudes towards globalisation, surveyed by the International Institute for Management Development (IMD)

Scores on the IMD's 9-point index (1=negative, 9=positive)

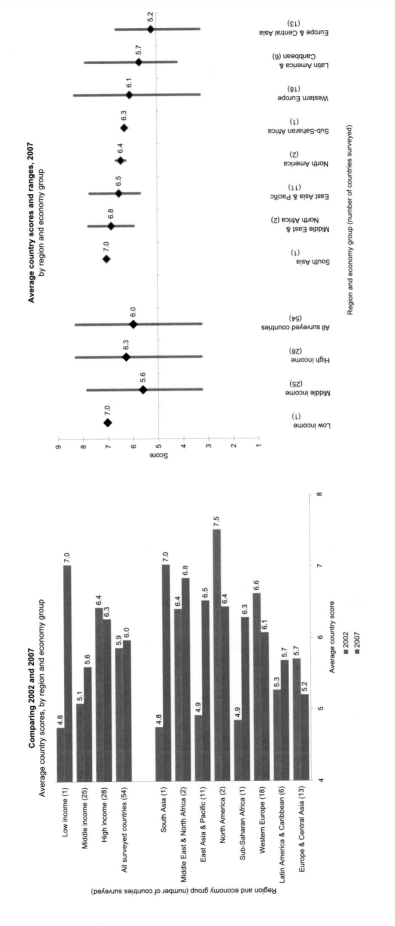

Average country scores and ranges, 2007
by region and economy group

Score

Europe & Central Asia (13) — 5.2
Latin America & Caribbean (6) — 5.7
Western Europe (18) — 6.1
Sub-Saharan Africa (1) — 6.3
North America (2) — 6.4
East Asia & Pacific (11) — 6.5
Middle East & North Africa (2) — 6.8
South Asia (1) — 7.0

All surveyed countries (54) — 6.0
High income (28) — 6.3
Middle income (25) — 5.6
Low income (1) — 7.0

Region and economy group (number of countries surveyed)

Comparing 2002 and 2007
Average country scores, by region and economy group

Region and economy group (number of countries surveyed)	2002	2007
Low income (1)	4.8	7.0
Middle income (25)	5.1	5.6
High income (28)	6.4	6.3
All surveyed countries (54)	5.9	6.0
South Asia (1)	4.8	7.0
Middle East & North Africa (2)	6.4	6.8
East Asia & Pacific (11)	4.9	6.5
North America (2)	6.4	7.5
Sub-Saharan Africa (1)	4.9	6.3
Western Europe (18)	6.6	6.1
Latin America & Caribbean (6)	5.3	5.7
Europe & Central Asia (13)	5.2	5.7

Average country score

11.5 Attitudes towards global economic actors, 2005/6

Overall attitudes towards three key economic actors
Average country % responses across all surveyed countries

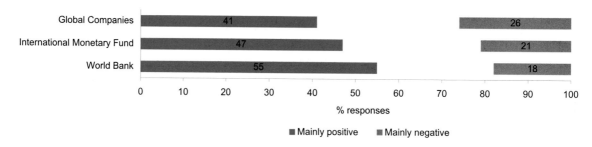

Attitudes towards the World Bank
Average country % responses, by regions and economy groups

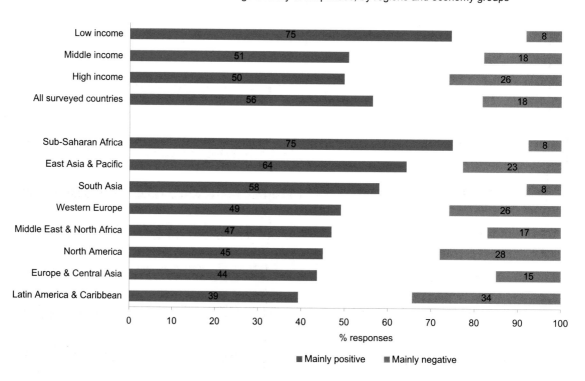

11.6 Attitudes towards the United States

Perceptions of the influence of US as 'mainly positive' versus 'mainly negative'
Average % responses in 18 countries, 2005-2007

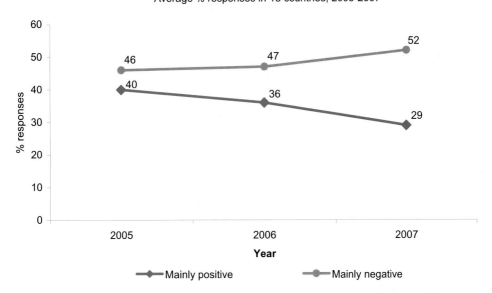

Opinions of the US Government's handling of...
Average % responses in 25 countries, Nov 2006-Jan 2007

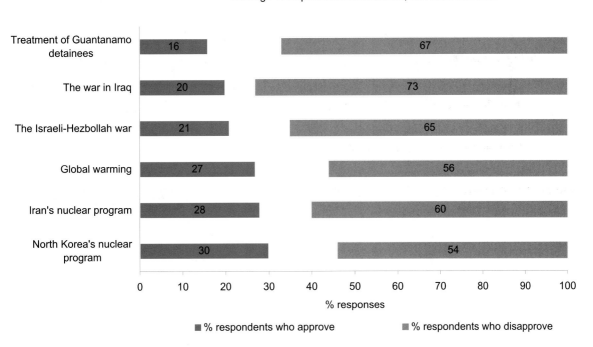

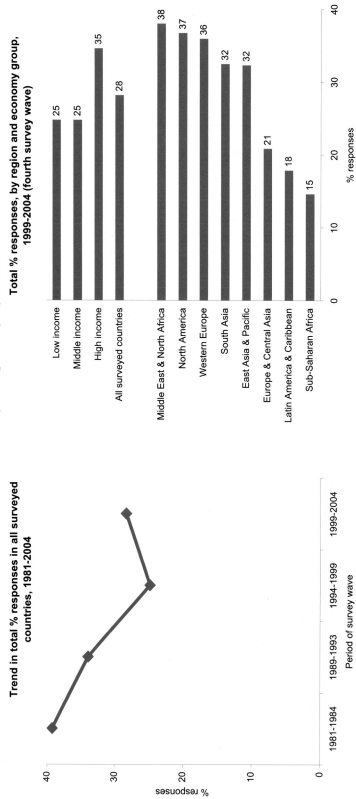

11.7 Generalised trust: % responding 'most people can be trusted'

Trend in total % responses in all surveyed countries, 1981-2004

Total % responses, by region and economy group, 1999-2004 (fourth survey wave)

11.8 Popular political engagement: % reporting high levels of political activism

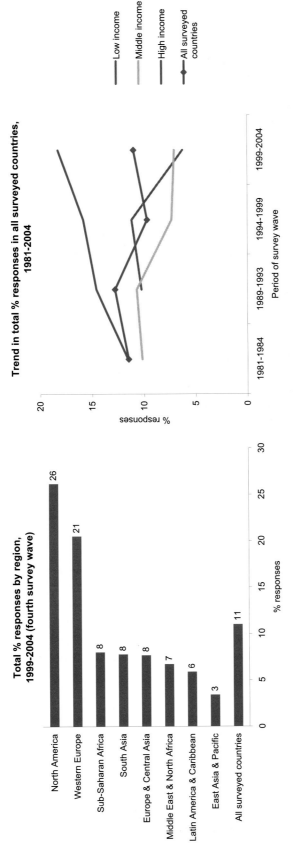

Total % responses by region, 1999-2004 (fourth survey wave)

Trend in total % responses in all surveyed countries, 1981-2004

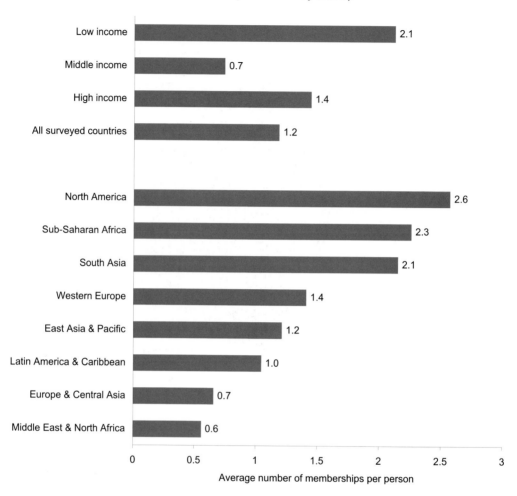

11.9 Membership in organisations
Average number of memberships per person in all surveyed countries, 1999-2004 (fourth survey wave)

Average number of memberships per person

11.10 Distribution of memberships across issues, survey wave 1999-2004

% memberships in each organisation type, in all surveyed countries

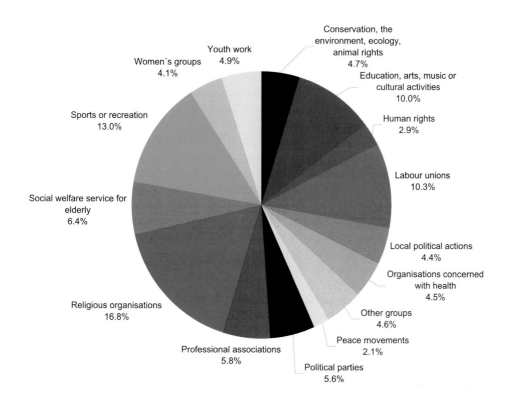

Conservation, the environment, ecology, animal rights
4.7%

Youth work
4.9%

Women´s groups
4.1%

Education, arts, music or cultural activities
10.0%

Human rights
2.9%

Sports or recreation
13.0%

Labour unions
10.3%

Social welfare service for elderly
6.4%

Local political actions
4.4%

Organisations concerned with health
4.5%

Religious organisations
16.8%

Other groups
4.6%

Peace movements
2.1%

Professional associations
5.8%

Political parties
5.6%

Issues with greatest share of total memberships

Total % memberships in labour unions; religious organisations; sport and recreation; education, arts, music or cultural activities, by regions

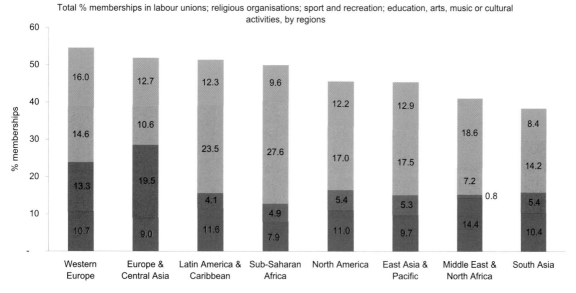

- Education, arts, music or cultural activities
- Labour unions
- Religious organisations
- Sports or recreation

The relationship between civil society and democracy is complex: often democracy is seen as a precondition for a flourishing civil society, and yet the lack of it can mobilise civil society activity. Civil society is sometimes described as a guardian of democracy and bulwark against the state. This record tracks recent dynamics in freedom, democracy and the support for democracy around the world.

The role of democracy as a mobilising frame for global civil society is illustrated in the NGO participation in the World Movement for Democracy. The members of this global movement are concerned with diverse issues that they link to the concept of democracy (12.1). Freedom is strongly associated with economic development, and those in developed economies enjoy generally higher levels of socio-political and economic freedom than do their developing world counterparts. However, higher levels of political freedom can also be found in some developing nations, as is the case in Latin American and Caribbean nations that rank highly on political freedom and freedom of the press (12.2-12.4). Political freedom and freedom of the press are strongly correlated with each other, and each is correlated rather strongly, though to a lesser extent, with economic freedom (12.5-12.7); we might suppose that the three are mutually supporting. Overall, the global trend in the last 30 years is a steady increase in political freedom (12.8).

The number of democratic elections has increased in recent decades (12.10), alongside regime changes in the former Soviet bloc and in Africa (12.11). The number of electoral democracies has remained more or less constant since the mid-1990s (12.9). Summarising voter turnout rates in parliamentary elections in the post-war years, voting rates can be seen to vary between regions – but not in a way that coincides with differences in economy groups (12.12). Popular support for democracy has increased slightly since the mid-1990s, albeit from a high base throughout the world (12.13-12.15).

Sources: World Movement for Democracy: http://www.ned.org/dbtw-wpd/textbase/participants-search.htm
Freedom: *Freedom in the World, 2007,* Freedom House, *Freedom of the Press 2006,* Freedom House, 2007 *Index of Economic Freedom,* Heritage Foundation. **Electoral democracies:** *Freedom in the World, 2007,* Freedom House. **Elections and turnout:** Voter turnout database, IDEA International Institute for Democracy and Electoral Assistance, http://www.idea.int/vt/index.cfm **Support of democracy, attitudes and preferences:** World Values Survey, http://www.worldvaluessurvey.org

12.1 NGO Participation in World Movement for Democracy

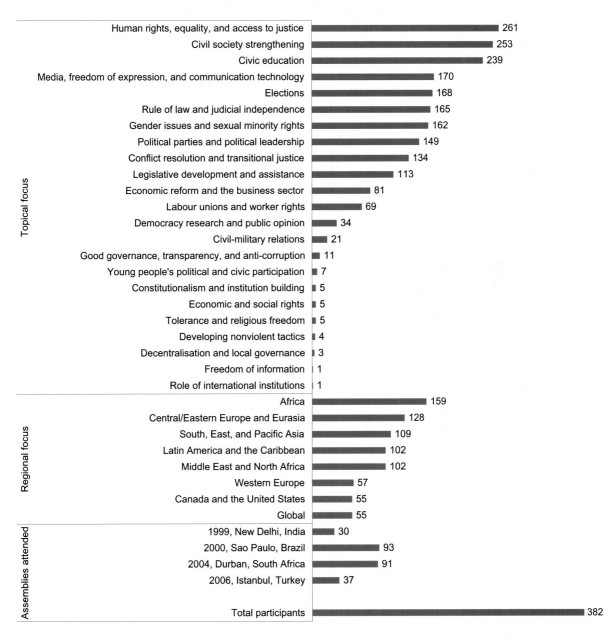

Number of participants (NGOs)

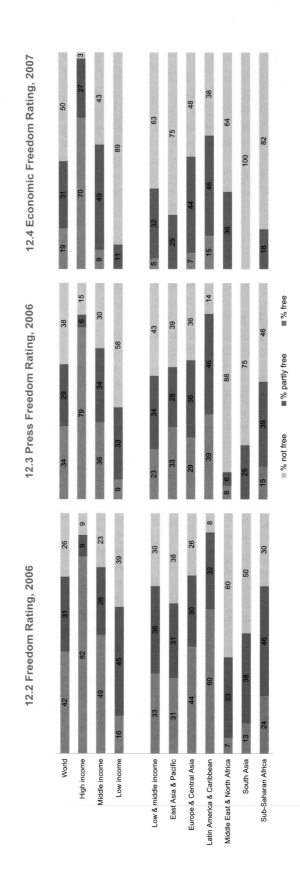

12.2 Freedom Rating, 2006

12.3 Press Freedom Rating, 2006

12.4 Economic Freedom Rating, 2007

■ % not free   ■ % partly free   ■ % free

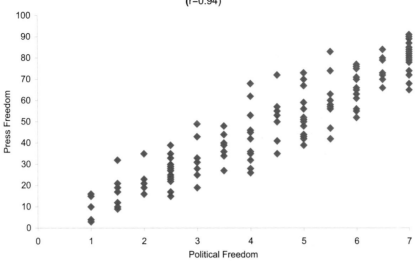

12.5 Press Freedom and Political Freedom
(r=0.94)

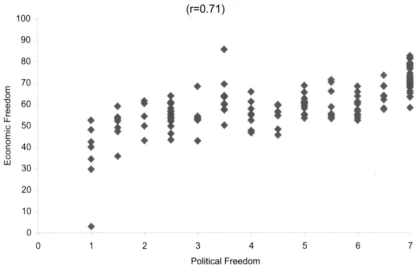

12.6 Economic Freedom and Political Freedom
(r=0.71)

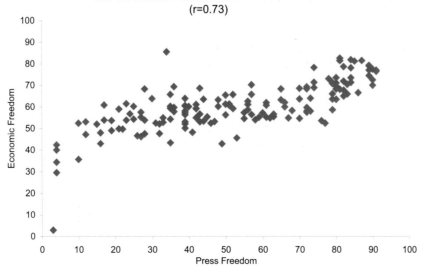

12.7 Economic Freedom and Press Freedom
(r=0.73)

12.8 Global trends in Political Freedom, 1976-2006

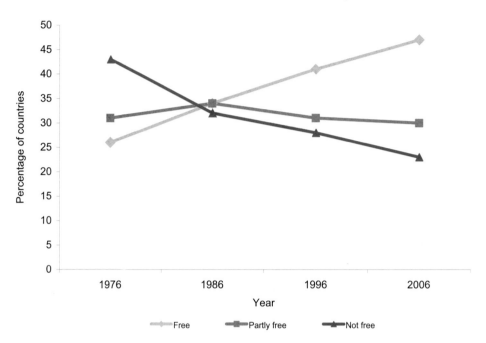

12.9 Tracing electoral democracy

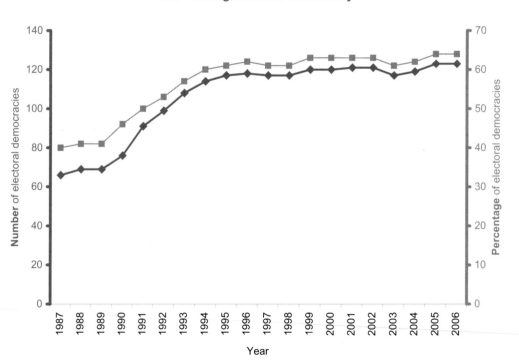

12.10 Growth in number of democratic elections, world total

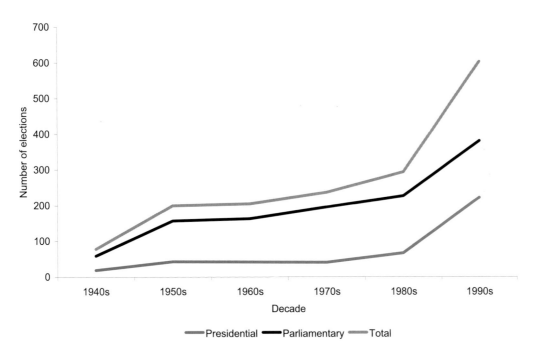

12.11 Growth in number of democratic elections, by region

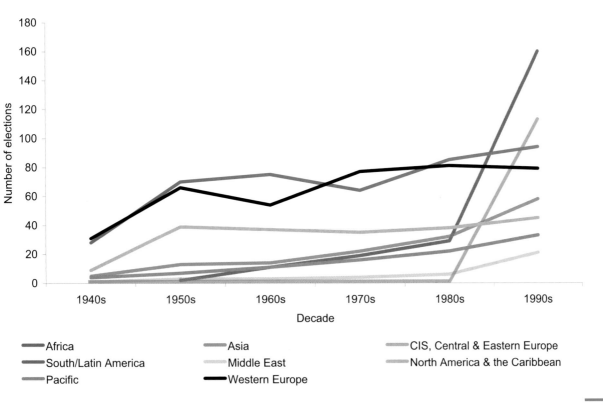

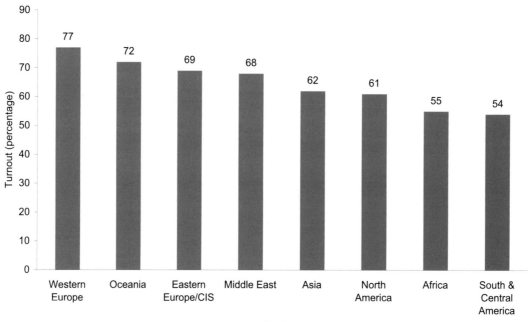

12.12 Voter turnout in parliamentary elections, 1945-97

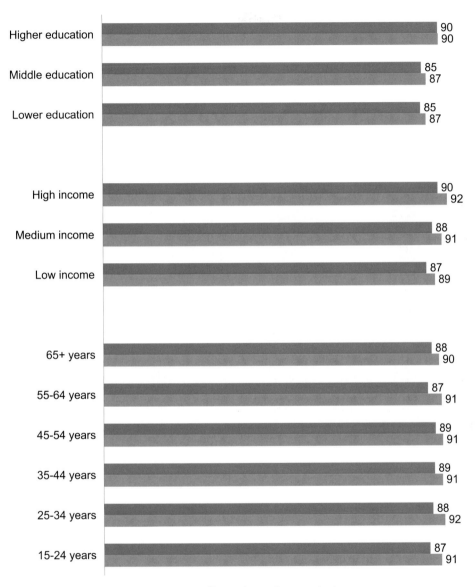

12.13 Support for democracy: percentage of respondents who would favour having a democratic political system

Higher education
90
90

Middle education
85
87

Lower education
85
87

High income
90
92

Medium income
88
91

Low income
87
89

65+ years
88
90

55-64 years
87
91

45-54 years
89
91

35-44 years
89
91

25-34 years
88
92

15-24 years
87
91

Percentage of respondents

■ Survey wave III: 1994-1999
■ Survey wave IV: 1999-2004

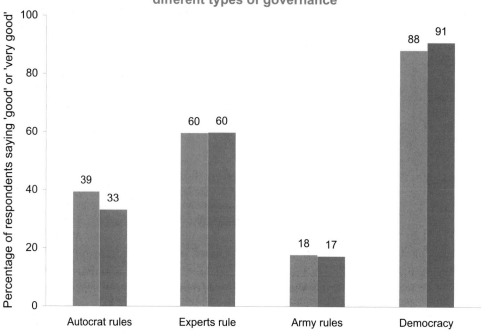

12.14 Political system preferences: percentages in favour of different types of governance

Percentage of respondents saying 'good' or 'very good'

- Autocrat rules: 39, 33
- Experts rule: 60, 60
- Army rules: 18, 17
- Democracy: 88, 91

■ Survey wave I: 1994-1999　■ Survey wave IV: 1999-2004

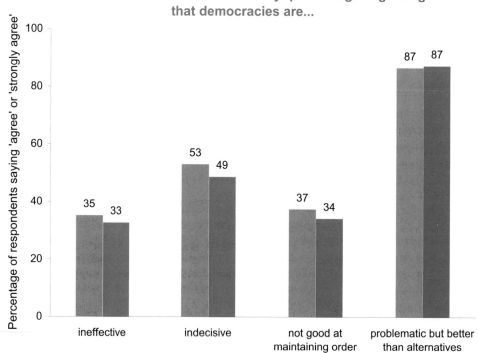

12.15 Attitudes towards democracy: percentages agreeing that democracies are...

Percentage of respondents saying 'agree' or 'strongly agree'

- ineffective: 35, 33
- indecisive: 53, 49
- not good at maintaining order: 37, 34
- problematic but better than alternatives: 87, 87

■ Survey wave III: 1994-1999　■ Survey wave IV: 1999-2004

Conflict and violence are often seen as the antitheses of global civil society; they are certainly inimical to its existence and philosophy. Whatever its complexities and causes, conflict represents a serious impediment to global civil society actors, who respond to it in various ways. Often they try to ameliorate the physical and social harm caused by conflicts – for example, by forging transnational links across cultural, political and ethnic divides, or by providing assistance to those affected by violence.

According to the Global Conflict Barometer, overall the number of conflicts, and specifically the number of violent conflicts, is increasing. While there were only slightly more ethnic domestic conflicts in the 1990s than in the 1980s, more of the conflicts in the 1990s were violent (13.2). Almost 60 per cent of conflicts in 2006 were located in Asia and Oceania and Sub-Saharan Africa. Most conflicts are internal, caused by struggles over ideology, attempts to achieve national dominance and competition for resources (13.1).

Terrorism increased in the twenty-first century, mostly due to activity in the Middle East, the Persian Gulf and South Asia (13.3). Most terrorist attacks are against police and private citizens. The number of attacks on NGOs increased in 2003 and have remained high since (13.4). Most terrorist incidents are perpetrated by groups with nationalist/separatist, religious, or Communist/socialist ideologies. They are responsible for a growing share of all terrorist attacks - up to 99 per cent of all incidents and fatalities in 2006 (13.5).

Following a general decrease during the 1980s and 1990s, the total value of the global arms trade has begun to rise again since 2000 (13.6). Developed and post-Communist nations are the main sellers of arms, and Middle Eastern and North African countries, as well East Asian and Pacific nations, are the main buyers (13.7)

Notes: [1]Figures are trend-indicator values expressed in million constant 1990 US$.
Sources: Global Conflict Barometer: *Conflict barometer 2006 - 15th annual conflict analysis*, Institute for International Conflict Research, University of Heidelberg. **Ethnic conflicts:** *Clash of Civilizations and Escalation of Ethnopolitical Conflict 1980-1999, June 2003*, by Philip G. Roeder, UCSD, http://weber.ucsd.edu/~proeder/data.htm. **Terrorism:** Terrorism Knowledge Base, the Memorial Institute for the Prevention of Terrorism (MIPT), http://www.tkb.org

13.1 Global conflict barometer: conflicts and conflict negotiations

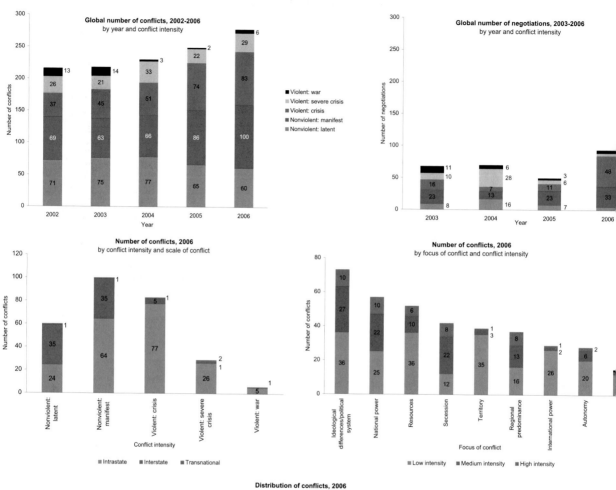

Global number of conflicts, 2002-2006
by year and conflict intensity

- Violent: war
- Violent: severe crisis
- Violent: crisis
- Nonviolent: manifest
- Nonviolent: latent

Global number of negotiations, 2003-2006
by year and conflict intensity

Number of conflicts, 2006
by conflict intensity and scale of conflict

- Intrastate
- Interstate
- Transnational

Number of conflicts, 2006
by focus of conflict and conflict intensity

- Low intensity
- Medium intensity
- High intensity

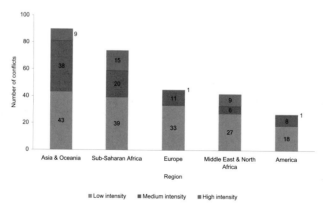

Distribution of conflicts, 2006
by region and conflict intensity

- Low intensity
- Medium intensity
- High intensity

13.2 Dynamics in number of ethnic conflicts, 1980s and 1990s

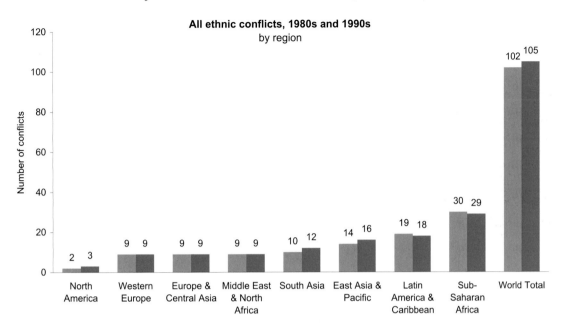

All ethnic conflicts, 1980s and 1990s
by region

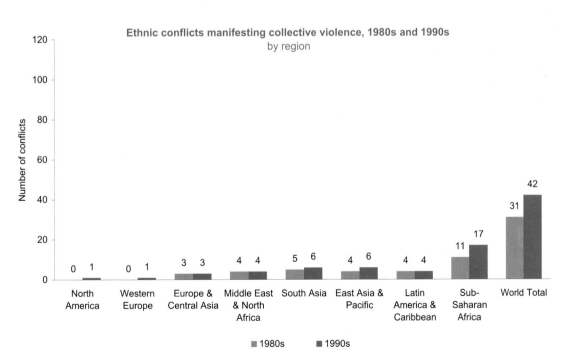

Ethnic conflicts manifesting collective violence, 1980s and 1990s
by region

■ 1980s   ■ 1990s

Terrorist incidents, injuries and fatalities, 2000-2007

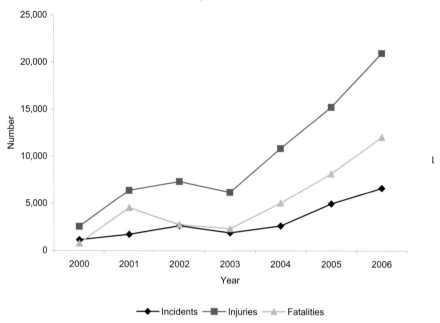

Terrorist incidents and fatalities, 2006
by region

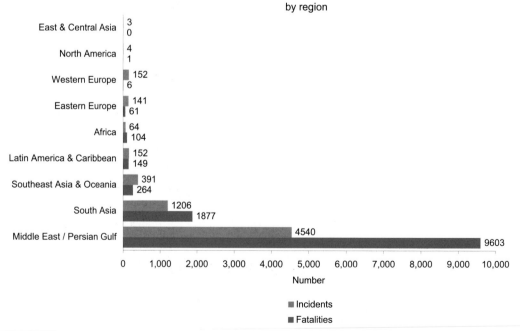

13.4 Targets of terrorist incidents, 2006

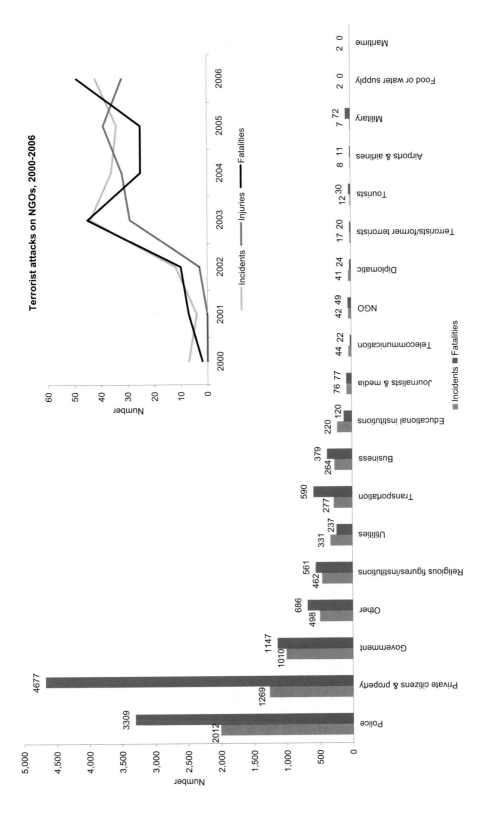

Terrorist attacks on NGOs, 2000-2006

Incidents   Injuries   ——— Fatalities

Maritime   2 0
Food or water supply 2 0
Military   7 72
Airports & airlines   8 11
Tourists   12 30
Terrorists/former terrorists 17 20
Diplomatic   41 24
NGO   42 49
Telecommunication   44 22
Journalists & media   76 77
Educational institutions 120 220
Business   264 379
Transportation   277 590
Utilities   237 331
Religious figures/institutions 462 561
Other   498 686
Government   1010 1147
Private citizens & property 1269 4677
Police   2012 3309

Incidents   Fatalities

13.5 Terrorist incidents, by type of terrorist group

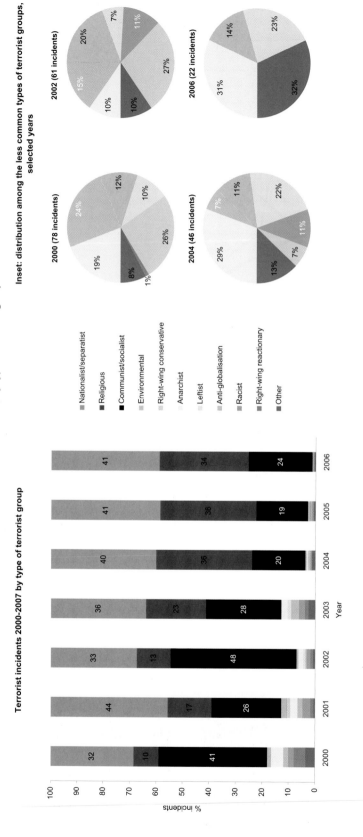

13.5 Terrorist incidents, by type of terrorist group

Terrorist incidents 2000-2007 by type of terrorist group

Inset: distribution among the less common types of terrorist groups, selected years

13.6 Total value of the global arms trade, 1976-2005
Estimate of constant 1990 US$, millions[1]

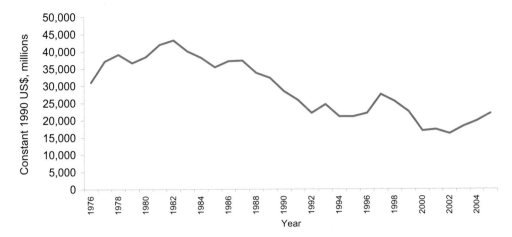

13.7 The global arms trade: regional distribution of buyers and sellers, 1976-2005
% total arms trade, 1976-2005

Regional totals of top 20 seller countries

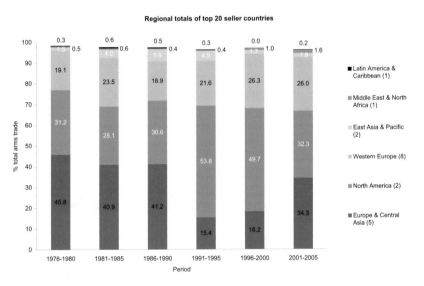

Regional totals of top 20 buyer countries

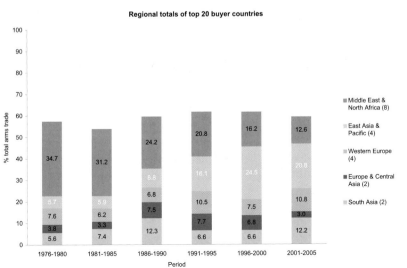

CHRONOLOGY OF GLOBAL CIVIL SOCIETY EVENTS

Compiled by Jill Timms

Contributors: Mustapha Kamel Al-Sayyid, Leighton Andrews, Baris Gencer Baykan, Nick Buxton, Giuseppe Caruso, Hyo-Je Cho, Bernard Dreano, Louise Fraser, Iuliana Gavril, Nihad Gohar, Vicky Holland, Deborah James, Jeffrey Juris, Bjarne Kristoffersen, Silke Lechner, Leeshai Lemish, Otilia Mihai, Alejandro Natal, Esther Nagle, Imogen Nay, Katarina Sehm Patomaki, Mario Pianta, Oscar Reyes, Asthriesslav Rocuts, Ineke Roose, Thomas Ruddy, Amade Suca, Katharine Talbot, Kate Townsend, Caroline Watt, Duccio Zola.

Introduction

Here we present an alternative record of global civil society through a chronology of diverse events that have involved or had significance for civil society beyond national borders. This chronology allows us to present qualitative descriptions of global civil society activity, data which are difficult to record statistically. Through this we aim to offer a flavour of the vast range of actions being employed to campaign, engage and protest. We also aim to highlight activity in areas of the world often not reported by the mainstream media.

This edition of the chronology records events that have taken place between May 2006 and April 2007. It is important to note that we present a sample of events to achieve the above aims, and due to the nature of the data we do not intend this chronology to be a comprehensive record of all global civil society actions. Instead, we hope that this resource will draw attention to the diversity of activity and offer an indication of major themes and sites of struggle. Our selection of events is partially limited by our reliance on reports from our global network of correspondents and the availability of information via the Internet in an accessible language. We continue to include the growth of social forums, as these are reported as being of significance. In addition to our descriptions of these in the chronology, please also see Map 9.12 on page 327.

Invitation to join our network of global civil society correspondents

The Global Civil Society Yearbook initiative has been interactive from the beginning. Engagement with civil society activists, policy makers, students and academics has been an integral part of each stage of the research, including, for example, a range of seminars in different parts of the world and public lectures. The chronology is an ongoing part of this engagement strategy. As well as welcoming feedback about the content of the chronology each year, we offer an open invitation to our readers to become one of our global civil society correspondents. We strongly urge you to consider joining our network.

The chronology is compiled largely from reports offered by our global network of correspondents. The network has been growing since 2000 and is mainly comprised of activists, journalists, academics, non-governmental organisation (NGO) workers, and students, who work, study or have an interest in civil society activity. We are keen to expand this network to as many parts of the world as possible. Each correspondent submits a short report of any event they believe should be recorded in the chronology.

Would you be interested in submitting an entry, or do you know someone who might be interested in joining the network? Every correspondent who has an entry published is acknowledged in the Yearbook and will receive a complimentary copy of *Global Civil Society 2008/9*. You will be making a valuable contribution to our understanding of changes in civil society. To find out more and to submit an event, please visit **http://www.lse.ac.uk/Depts/global/correspondents.htm**

Global Civil Society events
May 2006–April 2007

May 2006
1 May

International Labour Day inspires diverse actions around the globe to promote workers' rights. These include a march in Dhaka, Bangladesh to call for improvements to factory conditions and for the USA and Europe to drop import tariffs, which protesters claim are destroying the garment industry. Ten thousand people protest in Macau, China, calling for an end to corruption and improved working conditions. In Croatia a rally is held at a disused tobacco factory in solidarity with the 50 workers who barricaded themselves in to protest against the allegedly unlawful privatisation of the industry. In Cuba one million workers gather in Havana's Square of Revolution to hear President Fidel Castro, and are given red t-shirts by the government to celebrate Labour Day. In the EuroMayDay parade, a pan-European event in 22 European cities, 200,000 people demonstrate against social and economic precariousness. Protesters call for an end to the erosion of job security brought about by increased flexible, casual and temporary working practices. In Indonesia 100,000 hold a strike against the introduction of a new labour law that promotes flexible contracts and reduces job security. In Moscow 25,000 activists gather for a rally to promote workers' rights. Despite an official ban, protests are held throughout Iran against low pay, poor conditions and the persecution of workers. In Turkey, one million people take part in demonstrations to mark the 30th anniversary of the 1977 May Day march, which ended with 34 people being shot or trampled to death when a gunman opened fire on the crowd. In the USA 'A day without immigrants' is organised to highlight their poor working conditions and lack of rights. This is supported by a boycott of US goods called for by Sub Commandante Marcos in Mexico, who declares 'A day without gringos'. Workers and the unemployed in Harare, Zimbabwe, hold a rally to call for improved working conditions and some union leaders call for the removal of President Mugabe.

1 May

One hundred farmers in China's Guangxi province join an international relay hunger strike focusing on rights violations in China. Launched in February by human rights lawyer Gao Zhisheng, the relay hunger strike is for months joined by human rights activists and Chinese people across 29 provinces as well as members of Chinese communities overseas.

1 May

In Hyderabad, a counter-summit to the annual general meeting of the Asian Development Bank (ADB) is held as 97 civil society organisations from throughout Asia come together as the People's Forum against the ADB. The group criticises the policies of the ADB, claiming they are causing rather than alleviating poverty.

3 May

Eight weeks after news broke of how Chinese hospitals were killing thousands of detained Falun Gong practitioners for their organs, protests to bring this to international attention are held in Thailand, Malaysia, Taiwan, Singapore, Japan, and the USA. Some of these include mock organ-removal operations.

3–4 May

Activists in San Salvador Atenco, Mexico, hold a series of protests against the construction of an airport and the relocation on informal merchants. The movement receives immediate support from international human rights and environmental groups, including Human Rights Watch.

4–7 May

Some 35,000 people register to participant in the fourth European Social Forum. This takes place in Athens, Greece. Over 80,000 activists take part in the closing rally. A major theme throughout the event is the need for more cooperation between activist groups and the issue of whether political parties should be able to participate in the forum.

5–15 May

Farmland in Pyeongtaek, south of Seoul, becomes the centre of a standoff between the South Korean government and farmers and their supporters. The farmers are due to be evicted to facilitate the expansion of a US military base. The local Daechuri Elementary School becomes the makeshift headquarters of the activists attempting to protect the land from the authorities. The protest turns violent and over 100 demonstrators are arrested after 3,000 troops raid the school. Further protests are held throughout the country. Some 6,000 supporters of the farmers stage a candlelight vigil in Seoul demanding the cancellation of the US plan and the release of activists. A rally in the rural town brings together more than 3,500 activists and students, despite the deployment of 18,000 police to block all roads surrounding Daechuri.

6 May

Over 80 civil society organisations participate in the third Chicago Social Forum.

8 May

Women's rights groups organise in South Africa under the banner 'How free are we?' to protest against the acquittal of former Deputy President Jacob Zuma from a rape charge and to call for greater support for the victims of gender-based violence. Outside the courthouse demonstrators wear kangas, (wrap-around cloths), to protest at Zuma's argument that the complainant had provoked the sexual encounter by wearing such a cloth while she was a guest at his house. This is organised by the One in Nine Campaign, so named because only one in nine rapes are reported in South Africa.

8 May

In Saint-Malo, France, the local Pays de Saint Malo Social Forum is held. A major aim is to explore the effects of globalisation on the local population.

10–13 May

The second Alternative Summit of Social Movements from Latin America, the Caribbean and Europe, is held in Vienna, Austria, to coincide with a meeting of the heads of state. This four-day event focuses on social alternatives in a new era of Europe–Latin American relations.

11 May

Families exiled from the Chagos Islands in the Indian Ocean and their international supporters celebrate a victory after the UK High Court rules they were unlawfully removed and should be allowed to return to all but one of the Islands. This international campaign has been active since the islanders of the British colony were exiled in the 1960s and 1970s, when the UK government leased the largest island of Diego Garcia to the USA to use as an airbase.

11 May

Organisations campaigning for women's rights and protection against gender-based violence celebrate victory in Colombia, when the legal ban on abortion is partially lifted for cases when women have been raped.

14–18 May

In Jakarta, Indonesia, the Asia Pacific People's Conference on Rice and Food Sovereignty is held. Organised by La Via Campesina and the Federation of Indonesia Peasant Union, this event brings together peasants, land rights activists and NGOs from Asia and the Pacific region. The final declaration is entitled 'Rice is life, culture and dignity'.

17 May

2,000 people take part in the Pirkanma Social Forum in Tampere, Finland. This is the second time the forum has been held. It includes a 'Market of opportunities' to promote the work of civil society organisations.

18 May

In Turkey, over 25,000 demonstrators take to the streets to defend the country's secular status. This follows the murder of a leading judge who was involved in rulings that confirmed a ban on wearing the headscarf in public institutions and universities.

18 May

Following sustained pressure from the people of Nepal and international human rights organisations, Parliament votes overwhelmingly to strip King Gyanendra of his powers. The royal family will in future be subject to tax and the country officially becomes secular, rather than Hindu.

19–21 May

The Netherlands Social Forum is held in Nijmegen, The Netherlands. Dozens of workshops and debates take place, with the aim of reinforcing cooperation between people working to resist current forms of capitalist globalisation.

19–21 May

In Brisbane, Australia, the Brisbane Social Forum is held.

22 May

Following extensive campaigning against discrimination and social and cultural exclusion in Ecuador, the Collective Rights of Black and Afro–Ecuadorian Peoples law is promulgated.

25 May

The thematic social forum 'Gendering the WSF 2007 process' takes place in Nairobi in preparation for the world forum to be held there next January.

27 May

Human rights groups protest against the trade deal negotiated between the EU and Turkmenistan, claiming that the EU is ignoring the human rights abuses allegedly carried out under President Saparmurat Niyazov because it is interested in the country's gas reserves.

June 2006

2–3 June

The second la Vall Social Forum is held in la Vall d'Uixó-País Valencia, Spain.

4 June

Activists travel from South Korea to Washington, despite being warned against this by their government, to protest against negotiations taking place between the two countries regarding a free trade agreement. They are supported by US peace and social justice groups when they hold a demonstration outside the White House.

4 June

An estimated 44,000 Hong Kong residents, as well as activists in New York, London, and other cities, mark the 17-year anniversary of the massacre of students and others who demonstrated for greater democracy in Beijing in 1989. The vigils and rallies commemorate the hundreds who were killed. Demonstrators call upon the Chinese authorities to recognise the atrocities, to release all pro-democracy activists and compensate victims' families.

5–6 June

By exercising universal jurisdiction, a Spanish National Court judge begins hearing testimony in a lawsuit brought by a Tibetan human rights group against former Chinese leader Jiang Zemin and other top officials, over genocide and crimes against humanity in Tibet.

8 June

An international forum on the future of the UN is held in Seoul, focusing on the contribution of civil society organisations to promoting reform, transparency and accountability in the UN.

9 June

Over 1,000 anti-violence demonstrators dress in black and line the boardwalk in Copacabana, Brazil. The protestors lie down, playing dead, to represent the number of murders committed in the city so far this year.

10 June

In Poland over 2,500 campaigners take part in a lesbian and gay pride march, despite a two-year old ban on the event and threats from right-wing groups.

14–18 June

In France, the second Paris 14e (arrondissement) Social Forum is held.

15 June

An international day of action is held to demonstrate solidarity with 468 homeless families currently threatened with eviction from the empty building they have been occupying for the last four years in Sao Paolo, Brazil. Demonstrations are held outside Brazilian embassies in Paris, Tokyo and Lisbon.

15–17 June

The Austria Social Forum is held in Graz, Austria.

16–18 June

The Southeast Social Forum, held in Durham, North Carolina is attended by 550 participants. The focus is on building towards the first US Social Forum to be held next year and developing networks between people and organisations working for social justice.

18–20 June

An international forum on 'strategies for the debt repudiation' is held in Nairobi, Kenya. The Nairobi Declaration on Debt Repudiation is supported by activists from 35 countries in Africa, Asia, Latin America and the Caribbean, Europe and North America. The statement emphasises a series of challenges that need to be overcome and reinforces the determination of the groups to cooperate in this goal.

19 June

Rallies in over 25 countries mark the birthday of Burmese democracy leader Aung San Suu Kyi.

19–23 June

Environmentalists and activists from 18 countries come together to discuss and protest against the deterioration of the global eco-system during the fourth annual World Life Culture Forum in Ilsan, South Korea.

22–24 June

The second Migrations World Social Forum is held in Madrid, Spain, bringing together 3,391 participants from 870 organisations. These include people from 53 different countries. The main themes discussed are immigration and asylum, and political and social oppression.

23–25 June

In Barcelona, Spain, the second European Caravan for Freedom of Movement is organised by the No Borders network.

23–26 June

In Vancouver, Canada, the World Peace Forum is held under the banner 'Cities and communities: working together to end war and build a peaceful, just and sustainable world'.

28 June

Following sustained campaigning by women's rights groups, women in Kuwait stand in elections and vote for the first time.

July 2006

1 July

Whistles are given out to 50,000 pro-democracy demonstrators in Hong Kong, under the banner 'Make yourself heard'. This is the ninth anniversary of Hong Kong's return to China.

2–7 July

In Lille, France, a network of leftist activists from Brazil, Canada, France, Morocco, Niger, Israel, Palestine and South Africa, and partners in the Netherlands, Belgium, Turkey, Hungary, Russia, Pakistan and Algeria, meet for an intense summer school in civil society campaigning methods.

3 July

3,000 people take part in the second Democracy Social Forum held in Santiago, Chile. Over 200 organisations are brought together by the event.

5 July

Anti-American activists begin a five-day march over 91 km from Seoul to Pyeongtaek to protest against plans to expand a US military base south of Seoul.

5–9 July

The Caribbean Social Forum is held in Martinique, focusing on the key issues of Caribbean identity, the impact of imperialism and the Caribbean as a natural habitat in danger.

6–9 July

The second Midwest Social Forum is held in Milwaukee, USA. The 1,000 participants represent a doubling of numbers from the previous year. The proceedings include preparation for the first US Social Forum next year.

8 July

The global problem of access to water is the focus of an event in London bringing together international activists to network and coordinate strategies under the banner 'Challenging the corporate water takeover'.

11–13 July

In Korea 60,000 rally against free trade agreement negotiations with the USA, organised by 280 trade unions, farmer groups and civil society organisations. Some 100,000 union workers also take part in a one day strike in support of the protest.

11–15 July

Demonstrations are held as leaders of the G8 meet in St Petersburg, Russia, in which many of the protests focus on environmental issues. Activists condemn the 'commodification of the earth' through increased investment in oil, gas and coal production as well as the expansion of the nuclear energy under the banner of 'energy security'. Worldwide protests are coordinated against the G8 and climate change in at least 35 cities as part of an International Day of Direct Action against Climate Change. The rallies in St Petersburg are limited by the detention of hundreds on their way to the city and by a ban on planned marches. The second Russian Social Forum is held at Kirov Stadium, St Petersburg, to coincide with the event.

12 July–13 August

Peace and international human rights groups begin to coordinate global actions as bombing breaks out between Israel and Lebanon. During the next month of bloodshed, protests are held in cities throughout the world in solidarity with the many civilian casualties and in condemnation of the indiscriminate nature of the attacks.

15–17 July

A People's Forum is held in Gao, Mali. A major theme is the G8 summit and the consequences for Africa.

16 July

One million people demonstrate on the streets of Mexico City against alleged electoral fraud, as left-of-centre Andres Manuel Lopez Obrador is defeated by only 0.6 per cent by conservative Filipe Calderón.

20 July

Falun Gong adherents and supporters in at least 74 cities across 33 countries and six continents protest on the anniversary of seven years of the spiritual discipline's persecution in China. The demonstrations, torture re-enactments and candlelight vigils call for the release of all Falun Gong practitioners from labour camps and prisons, and commemorate the 3,000 followers who have been killed.

21–23 July

The second Triple Border Social Forum is held in Ciudad del Este, Paraguay. Civil society organisations from Argentina, Paraguay, Brazil and Uruguay take part to network and coordinate actions against militarisation and free trade treaties.

25–27 July

In Kaduna, Nigeria, the North West Zonal Social Forum is held.

26 July

Environment campaigners gather in Iceland to protest against the plan to build gigantic hydroelectric dams that are solely designed to fuel an Alcoa aluminium smelter. Environmentalists claim this will destroy the habitat of many endangered plants and animals. They stress the need to protect Europe's largest remaining wilderness as corporations seek to exploit its unique geothermal terrain.

27 July

As the Doha Round of the World Trade Organization's (WTO) negotiations break down in Switzerland, trade justice campaigners call attention to the continued poverty caused by WTO policies in the poorest regions of the world.

28–30 July

The Maine Social Forum takes place in Lewiston, Maine. The main theme is 'Reflecting the global in the local'.

29–30 July

The Western Kenya Social Forum takes place in the lakeside city of Kisumu with fisher folk, people living HIV/AIDS, small farmers, youth groups, community broadcasters, women and human rights activists as the main groups of participants.

August 2006

2 August

Humanitarian aid is sent to North Korea by South Korean NGOs for the first time since its suspension after the North's controversial missile testing programme. The aid is reinstated due to food shortages brought by severe flooding.

4–13 August

An anti-G8 camp is held in Heiligendamm, Germany. Activists come together, mainly from Europe, to prepare for the campaign against the G8 to take place in Germany in 2007.

7 August

Two years ahead of the scheduled 2008 Beijing Olympics a coalition of international human rights organisations issues a statement saying that the International Olympic Committee is failing to follow the Olympics' mission. The coalition further calls upon athletes, national committees and sponsors to take action in response to continuing human rights abuses in China.

8 August

International organisations working for gay and lesbian rights express outrage at the Ugandan national paper *Red Pepper*, when it publishes the names of 45 men it says are gay. The newspaper claims this is part of a campaign to 'rid our motherland of the deadly vice' and goes on to publish a similar list of alleged lesbians the next month.

14 August

Organisations campaigning for the rights of indigenous people celebrate victory as the Nukak tribe of Amazonian nomads return to Colombia. This isolated tribe fled after fighting engulfed their forest. However, under international pressure the Colombian government has created a safe haven for them. The tribe leader later commits suicide; his tribe continues to suffer from the consequences of the drugs wars, with the population dropping from 1,200 to 500 in 20 years.

16 August

La Via Campesina issue a statement to denounce the aggression against the civilian population of Lebanon, demanding an immediate halt to the war, the retreat of Israeli forces and the placement of an international peacekeeping force under the direction of the UN. This is an example of many such statements offered by global civil society groups to show solidarity with the Lebanese people and to contribute to a campaign of pressure on the Israeli government.

16 August

Indigenous rights groups condemn an amendment to the Aboriginal Land Rights Act in Australia that allows land to move into private ownership. Campaigners claim this will mean that ancestral land could now be bought by outsiders and call on the Australian government to overturn the change.

19 August–3 September

The fourth People's Global Action European Conference takes place in various cities throughout France.

21 August

Under pressure from humanitarian civil society organisations, particularly the Red Cross, the South Korean government agrees to provide one-time emergency aid to North Korea after recent devastating floods.

22 August

The Kibera Social Forum is held, focusing on housing, human rights and the how slum dwellers might be able to participate in the World Social Forum to be held in Kenya in January.

22 August

International human rights groups call for boycotts of Yahoo, Google and Microsoft after claiming that they have been complicit in politically repressive activities in China.

25 August

On the first anniversary of hurricane Katrina, which devastated parts of the United States, activists cycle through 22 cities as part of a critical mass against climate change and to demand 'Climate Justice'.

26 August–4 September

Environment campaigning groups and activists meet in Yorkshire, UK, to hold a camp for climate action. Over 100 workshops are held to share experience and knowledge, and promote cooperation, including training in non-violent direct action.

31 August–3 September

In Bari, Italy, representatives from 44 civil society groups come together under the banner 'The enterprise of a different economy' to demand alternative budget priorities in order to promote policies based on peace, environment, social justice and income redistribution issues.

September 2006

1–2 September

The Social Work Social Forum takes place in Santiago, Chile, the first to focus on the theme of social work. Events are organised under the banner 'Another world is possible and social work makes its contribution'

7–8 September

In Mexico City, the thematic Social Forum of Information, Documentation and Libraries is held, organised by Latin-American library and documentation associations.

8–10 September

The third regional Parana Medio Social Forum takes place in Argentina. A major focus is the issue of access to water.

9–24 September

The town of Die, in south-east France, holds an East–West cultural festival for intercultural dialogue and understanding. Participants come from Russia, the Balkans, Turkey, Caucasus, Georgia, Armenia and Azerbaijan.

13 September

A protest against violence in Colombia is led by the wives and girlfriends of gang members. The women in Pereira refuse to have sex with their partners until they commit to giving up violence, as part of the campaign, 'Violence is not sexy'.

13 September

The Chinese authorities begin a crackdown on civil liberties activists, arresting over 100 in a month, creating new media restrictions and starting investigations into any environmental and charity campaigners who have foreign funding. This is seen to be linked to the high-profile Olympics due to take place in Beijing in 2008.

13 September

In Mexico, environmental activists protest against a project by corporations including Monsanto and Dupont with the Mexican government, to define a bio-security framework for research with transgenic corn. Demonstrations are held under the banner 'Genetic independence cry', and a network of activists called 'In defence of corn' claim that transgenic corn imported from the USA is already polluting native grains.

14–16 September

The second Youth Social Forum is held in Paraná, in the Entre Ríos province of Argentina.

15–16 September

Mass demonstrations are held in Taiwan in response to corruption allegations against President Chan Shui-bian. On 15 September 400,000 Taiwanese demonstrate peacefully in Taipei, calling on the president to step down. The following day 200,000 rally in Chen's support without incident.

17 September

In Mombasa, Kenya, the Coast Social Forum takes place.

17–24 September

Days of protests throughout Hungary are held after a confession by Prime Minister Ferenc Gyurcsany is made public. He admits his government had 'lied morning, evening and night' to get re-elected. Far-right groups hijack early demonstrations leading to riots and over 150 people are arrested. At the largest protest 20,000 gather in the main square in Budapest to call for Gyurcsany's resignation.

18 September

To promote peace and co-existence, a convoy of five caravans arrive in Kampala from different parts of the country to begin the second Ugandan Social Forum. The events focus on the theme 'Build Uganda: our country, our struggles'.

18–24 September

In Nantes, France, the Pays Nantais Social Forum is held in a former cigarette factory. Major themes of the forum are the resurrection of democracy, human rights and political duties.

22 September

The first One Web Day takes place, with events and virtual events taking place around the world to draw attention to the impact of the worldwide web on daily life and to celebrate the achievements of web-based activism. Plans are laid to make this an annual event.

22–24 September

The first Saguenay-Lac-Saint-Jean Regional Social Forum is held in Quebec, Canada.

23 September

In Canada, the local Ottawa Social Forum takes place.

23 September–15 October

The Alpes-Maritimes Departmental Social Forum is held, focusing on social and immigration issues in southern France.

24 September

Environmental protestors breach security at Nottingham East Midlands Airport in the UK, making a chain across the runway and labelling all airports 'climate change factories'. A Baptist minister holds a remembrance service on the runway for the victims of climate change and preaches on the dangers of increased air travel from a mobile pulpit brought by the Plane Stupid activists.

25 September–15 October

The Alps Social Forum takes place in Valbonne, France, its third meeting.

30 September

In Harare, the Zimbabwe Social Forum is held, with strong youth involvement.

October 2006

2–4 October

Demonstrations against climate change are held in Mexico to coincide with the G8 + 5 Climate Summit. The actions begin with 10,000 pro-democracy activists marching through Mexico City to mark the 38th anniversary of the Tlatelolco Massacre, when the Mexican army and federal police opened fire on protesting students.

7 October

An International Day of Action and Mobilisation for Migrant Rights coordinates actions worldwide. Most of the demonstrations take place in Europe and Africa, calling for equal rights for migrants and the closure of all detention centres.

9 October

Protests are made around the world when North Korea carries out nuclear testing. Anti-nuclear campaigners, peace activists and environmentalists condemn the action and call for a renewed global effort to create a worldwide nuclear ban.

10 October

Child and labour rights campaigners mark a victory in India when a new law is established making it illegal for children under 14 to work in the service industry.

10 October

As part of the forth anniversary of the World Day Against the Death Penalty, an international human rights watchdog launches an anti-death penalty network in Seoul.

12–15 October

In Cochabamba, Bolivia, the first international Social Forum of Ancestral Wisdoms brings together activists and civil society organisations from throughout the Americas on the anniversary of Christopher Columbus' 'discovery' of the New World. Members of indigenous communities discuss struggles over identity and culture under the pressure of capitalist globalisation and the development of a network of indigenous lawyers, and a charter is signed pledging to spread the knowledge of ancient ways and wisdom for promoting sustainable living.

13–15 October

In Almada, the second Portuguese Social Forum takes place, with a focus on strengthening civil society.

13–15 October

The first Borders Social Forum is held in Cuidad Juarez, Mexico. This initiative came out of meetings between organisations and activists from Mexico and the USA at the World Social Forum in Venezuela. The forum protests against the 'wall of death' currently being built along the Mexican border by the US authorities and focuses on creating a space for integration and cooperation between social movements in the North and South.

14 October

The Turku Social Forum is held in Finland.

15–22 October

Artists and activists are brought together in Lima, Peru, for the third Solidarity Culture Forum. Events focus on promoting democracy and engagement through art and culture.

16 October

In Lilongwe, Malawi the Southern African Social Forum is held.

17 October

An International Day of Action in Solidarity with Bolivia takes place to generate a variety of activities across the globe in solidarity with the people of Bolivia.

18 October

International human rights group condemn the Chinese authority's ban on 'Snow Lotus', a university AIDS NGO working in the western region of Xinjiang, after the organisation publicises news that a local middle school had expelled students with hepatitis B.

19 October

The Russian government suspends the activities of more than 60 foreign NGOs, including Amnesty International and Human Rights Watch. The authorities claim that new procedures to allow the closer monitoring of NGO activity have not been followed by these organisations.

19–22 October

The Norwegian Social Forum takes place at the Oslo Congress Centre, with 17,000 participants and 40 civil society organisations taking part.

21–23 October

The national Thai Social Forum is held in Bangkok.

25–29 October

After three years of preparations, over 2,000 people participate in the first Mozambique Social Forum. This is held in Maputo, Mozambique. Workshops, seminars and cultural events are held under the banner 'Another Mozambique is possible'.

26 October

The Bahrain Centre for Human Rights website, together with another 21 sites, is blocked by Batelco, Bahrain's main Internet service provider, in what campaigner argue is an attempt to stifle criticism of the government ahead of the upcoming parliamentary elections.

27 October

In Nyeri, the Central Kenya Social Forum is held.

29 October

Rallies in Canada, the USA, Hong Kong, Indonesia and other countries are held in support of Jia Jia, a Chinese official seeking asylum in south-east Asia after he had promoted the Nine Commentaries, a book critical of the Chinese Communist Party, and called for the Party's disintegration.

November 2006

1 November

Human rights activists celebrate victory in China at the overturning of the conviction of Chen Guangcheng. This 'barefoot' rural lawyer, who is blind, has been responsible for exposing the forced abortions and sterilisations carried out by the authorities as part of the one-child policy of the Chinese government.

1–4 November

The thematic World Forum on Education is held in Caracas, Venezuela.

3–6 November

In Niamey, the national Niger Social Forum is held, although organisers claim the event is marred by a campaign of harassment by the authorities.

4 November

In Rome 200,000 people from social movements, trade unions, parties and groups on the left demonstrate to demand the protection and the extension of workers' rights.

4–5 November

The Aarhus Social Forum is held in Denmark.

5–6 November

In Coquimbo, Chile, the local Coquimbo and La Serena Social Forum is held with a strong focus on education.

6 November

A Senegalese women whose son drowned two months before trying to leave the country, claims that, she has since prevented all boats leaving her area loaded with would-be migrants trying to reach the Canary Islands.

7 November

As the death sentence is imposed on Saddam Hussein for crimes against humanity, protests are held in several cities. Lawyers in Jordan hold a one-hour strike, Palestinian schoolchildren march in Jenin and throughout Iraq people take to the streets, some in celebration. International human rights organisations call on leaders to condemn the use of the death penalty in all cases.

8 November

In Maldives, a mass march and other protests calling for constitutional reform are cancelled following what the organisers describe as sustained government harassment. It is rumoured that the protest could have initiated a military coup and over 100 activists were arrested during the preparations for it.

9–13 November

The Indian Social Forum takes place in Delhi. Participation by African NGOs helps to create strong networks and strategic alliances between Indian and African activists, in preparation for the next World Social Forum to take place in Nairobi.

11 November

The national Pakistan Social Forum is held in Lahore, with peace being a central focus.

12 November

The Libournais Social Forum is held. This is a sub-forum of the Gironde regional forum.

17 November

The Central Kenya Social Forum takes place in Whisper Park, Nyeri, Kenya. Many of the events focus on preparations for the World Social Forum to be held in Nairobi in January.

17–19 November

The first Puerto Rican Social Forum takes place in Rio Piedras. Building on the theme of the World Social Forum, the event uses the banner 'Another world is possible, another Puerto Rica is possible'. People from over 110 organisations take part.

17–19 November

In Heidelberg, the Network of Local Social Forums in Germany is held.

18 November

In Milan 50,000 people and in Rome 20,000 demonstrate and under the banner the 'Rally for peace and justice in the Middle East' organised by dozens of civil society groups, political parties and local authorities.

19 November

A G20 Alternative Forum is organised by the Melbourne Social Forum Organisation in Australia. This open public forum is held as a democratic alternative to the closed G20 meeting of trade ministers taking place simultaneously in Melbourne. The discussion and workshops focus on promoting alternative policies to address debt relief, poverty and climate change, and renewing strategies of the global justice/alter-globalisation movement.

19 November

Human rights activists are refused entry to Beijing's 'Human rights in China' exhibit. One protester is arrested for displaying a sign that reads: 'We wait with bitterness for human rights in China'.

21–24 November

In Lagos, the Nigerian and West African Social Forum is held. A major aim of the forum is to work towards a regional event.

22 November

The Association for the Struggle of Transvestites and Transsexual Identity in Argentina wins its legal battle when the Supreme Court rules that it must be afforded legal recognition.

23 November

Tens of thousands of Lebanese pay tribute to assassinated Christian politician Pierre Gemayel, turning his funeral into a display of defiance towards Syria and Hizbollah.

23–26 November

In Natal, Brazil the Potiguar Social Forum is held.

25 November

The first Araucania Social Forum takes place in Temuco in the south of Chile. The music of the Mapuche people opens this regional forum, with people from over 40 organisations taking part. The main areas of focus are the poverty and environmental conflict which affect the area.

25 November

Hundreds of veiled students demonstrate in Alexandria in protest against insulting comments made by the Egyptian Minister of Culture against the veil. The demonstrators demand the resignation of the minister.

25–26 November

The Chile Social Forum, the second national forum, is held in Santiago and begins with a 'Children's march for another world'. Over 170 self-organised events are held, including a mock judgement by environmental pressure groups against the multinational Barrick Gold Corporation to highlight alleged human rights violations during their mining in Chile.

26 November

25,000 demonstrate in Turkey against a visit by Pope Benedict XVI following his recent remarks on violence and the Prophet Muhammad.

29 November

In Bolivia, a major new land reform bill introduced by President Evo Morales is hailed as a progressive step by campesinos and indigenous peoples and their supporters. This will involve the redistribution of up to 20 million hectares of land and aims to undo some of the years of discrimination against indigenous peoples. The passing of the bill is the culmination of several weeks of protests both in favour of and against the change.

December 2006

1 December

Hizbollah joins its pro-Syrian allies to organise a protest in Egypt against the Lebanese govenment. Some 5,000 demonstrators camp overnight in central Beirut to block access to the governmental palace and 800,000 join the rally to call for the resignation of Prime Minister Fouad Siniora and what is described as his 'western-backed' government.

3 December

Protests are held outside Chinese embassies in Japan, Belgium, Germany, the UK and the USA against China's forced repatriation of North Korean refugees.

6–9 December

The Social Summit for Peoples Integration takes place in Cochabamba, Bolivia to coincide with the meeting of the South American Community of Nations Presidents. There are 5,000 participants from across Latin America, with areas of focus including access to water, native towns, the environment and alternatives to free trade agreements.

8 December

One of the key activists in the conception of the World Social Forum, Chico Whitaker, is presented with the Right Livelihood Honorary Award. The awards, described as an an alternative to the Nobel prize, aim to honour the vision of those working on behalf of the planet and its peoples.

10 December

The Bangladeshi Mohammed Yunus is awarded the Nobel Peace Prize for his pioneering microcredit finance schemes through which millions of impoverished people have been lent very small sums of money.

10 December

People take to the streets throughout Chile at the announcement of the death of the former dictator Captain General Augusto Pinochet. Some mourn and other celebrate, accusing him of being responsible for the disappearance of thousands of people and a catalogue of human rights abuses during his 17 years in power. The Chilean government deny him a full state funeral.

10–12 December

The Migrant Forum in Asia, a regional network of more than 260 migrant workers associations, NGOs and trade unions, organise an alternative ASEAN Film Festival on Migration in Cebu City, Philippines. The aim is to draw attention to issues of undocumented workers, forced migration and internally displaced persons.

11 December

In Paris, the Congress of the Association for the Taxation of Financial Transactions to Aid Citizens takes place, with a new leadership elected after a year of crisis. This is supported by a broad spectrum of NGOs and activists.

12 December

Over 4,000 people take part in the Social Summit for the Integration of Peoples held in Cochabamba in Bolivia. This coincides with the second Summit of the Presidents of the South American Community of Nations.

13 December

Indigenous rights groups and the Kalahari San Bushmen celebrate victory as the High Court in Botswana rules that their eviction from ancestral lands in the Central Kalahari Game Reserve was both unconstitutional and unlawful. The government had evicted the Bushmen four years ago, and although the case was fought by the poorest citizens of Botswana, it was the longest and most expensive in the country's history.

14–15 December

The first Algerian Social Forum takes place in Tipaza. A major aim is to facilitate the building of Algerian civil society and to link with the principles of the World Social Forum.

16 December

In Milan 20,000 people demonstrate in a rally 'For a new policy on immigration' to coincide with the International Day of Migrant People.

29–30 December

In Kathmandu the first Nepal Youth Social Forum is held with the aim of creating a 'youth vision for a new Nepal'. The forum focuses on building coalitions between existing social movements to raise collective campaigns for peace, inclusive democracy and sustainable development.

30 December–2 January

A first encounter of the Zapatista Communities with the Peoples of the World takes place in Chiapas, Mexico. The focus is on sharing ways to organise, confront and overcome neo-liberalism. Many of the participants, including children, attend wearing balaclavas to remain anonymous.

30 December

The execution of Saddam Hussain sparks protests in many parts of the world, by both his supporters and those who call for an end to the death penalty. Demonstrations include a rally by 3,000 in Jordan, violent clashes in Iraq and India, protests by the Vatican and a hunger strike by an Italian member of the European Parliament.

January 2007

12–14 January

The local Ivry Social Forum is held in France, a relatively small but very active forum.

15 January

Anti-war activist Brain Haw, who has been holding a vigil outside the Houses of Parliament in London for six years, has an exhibition of his protest installed in the internationally renowned Tate Britain art gallery. An official line, marking a new exclusion zone for unlicensed public protests close to parliament, falls within the gallery building. The exhibition of the protest falls half on one side and half on the other side of the line. Although the new law was developed in an attempt to stop protests such as Haw's, his demonstration continues in a scaled-back form.

19 January

People take to the streets in Istanbul to protest against the murder of Hrant Dink, a prominent Turkish–Armenian journalist who frequently wrote about one of the most sensitive issues in Turkey, the mass killing of Armenians during the final days of the Ottoman empire. Dink was shot outside the *Agos* newspaper offices where he had been editor-in-chief. Later, more that 100,000 people showed solidarity with his work for reconciliation by joining the five-mile funeral procession.

20–25 January

The seventh World Social Forum takes place in Nairobi, Kenya, under the banner 'People's struggles, people's alternatives'. Over 75,000 people attend from 110 countries and 1,400 organisations take part in the first WSF to be held solely in Africa. A whole range of issues are discussed and experiences shared, aiming to overcome neo-liberal globalisation and develop alternatives. Major themes are the principles of forum organisation, the future of the forum and and how to ensure it is accessible to as many participants as possible.

20 January

Tibetan Youth Congress activists arrive in New Delhi after a weeklong bicycle ride in protest against the 2008 Beijing Olympics. The group's core slogan is 'No Olympics in China until Tibet is free'.

20 January

The local Auxerre Social Forum is held in France.

24 January

The fifth Local Authorities Forum takes place in Nairobi as part of the seventh World Social Forum held in the city.

27 January

In Washington, 400,000 take part in a 'United for peace and justice' march to demand an end the Iraq war. This is one of the largest anti-war mobilisations in the USA in recent years and brings increased public interest through the participation of well-known figures such as Susan Sarandon, Jane Fonda, Danny Glover and Tim Robbins. Three Nobel peace laureates send their support in an open letter from the World Social Forum in Nairobi. The march is organised ahead of a Congress vote to send an additional 21,500 troops to Iraq.

February 2007

9 February

Around 16,000 workers in the textile and garment sector in Egypt end a one-week sit-in protest against the refusal of their management to pay them. The sit-in ends when the Egyptian Minister of Manpower and of Investment assists the company to make the payments.

9–10 February

Maghreb Social Forum takes place in Nouakchott, Mauritania. This is the second such forum held.

10 February

The fourth local Val de Bievre Social Forum is held in France.

14 February

Labour activists in Wales step up a global campaign against the closure of a Burberry factory in Treorchy, the Rhondda Valley. Demonstrations under the banner 'Keep Burberry British' are held simultaneously in London, New York, Chicago, Strasbourg and Las Vegas. The campaign brings together anti-corporate and labour rights groups and focuses on harnessing the global media, often via celebrities. The protesters argue that moving the factory to China is not only unethical, because the Treorchy plant is working at a considerable profit, but conflicts with the 'Britishness' which Burberry stresses throughout its marketing.

17 February

In Italy, 150,000 peace activists demonstrate in a rally under the banner 'Against the war and the war bases, for peace and justice: the future is in our hands'.

23 February

Every Friday approximately 100 Israeli, Palestinian and foreign protesters stage a demonstration in Bil'in against the West Bank barrier. This week, the second anniversary of the barriers construction is marked by hundreds more joining the protest. Israeli police use water cannons to disperse the rally. The International Court of Justice has ruled the barrier illegal, but the Israeli government claims it is necessary for security.

23–27 February

A World Forum for Food Sovereignty takes place in the village of Sélingué, Mali. Participants number 600 people from five continents and represent all sectors of society with an interest in agricultural and food issues. They aim to reaffirm the right to food sovereignty and to clarify its economic, social, ecological and political implications. Organisers give the forum the name 'Nyéléni 2007' after a legendary woman farmer in Mali.

22 February

Small shopkeepers and anti-globalisation protesters hold demonstrations in India as Wal-Mart executives visit the country ahead of a plan for the company to enter the retail sector there.

March 2007

1–4 March

More than 600 people are arrested as days of mass protests involving more than 4,000 turn violent in the Danish capital of Copenhagen. The demonstrations begin when left-wing activists are evicted from a youth centre they had been occupying since 1982. The site has been sold and legal protests that have been going on for several years over the squatters' right to stay have now failed.

3 March

Over 500 Chinese sent by the Beijing Tourism Bureau to parade for the 2008 Beijing Olympics in Hollywood are met by hundreds of human rights activists demanding 'Freedom before Games'. Event organisers attempt to block off the demonstrators by parking four large tourist buses in front of them and using high-decibel loudspeakers to block out the sounds of their protest.

4 March

In Tehran 33 women are arrested during a protest against discriminatory laws on child custody and polygamy and to show solidarity with five women arrested under these laws last year. Women's groups say they have been suffering increasing intimidation from the authorities since they launched a petition to challenge the laws.

4 March

More than 2,000 demonstrators in Jalalabad, Afghanistan, take to the streets to protest against the killing of at least eight civilians by US forces as part of an ambush. International peace and human rights groups express concern over alleged indiscriminate shooting by US soldiers following a suicide bomb attack.

5 March

Xanana Gusmao, the President of East Timor, threatens to use emergency measures to prevent further demonstrations in the capital of Dili. Thousands of protesters gather to express their concern over a raid by Australian-led peacekeepers on the base of the rebel leader Alfredo Reinado, during which four rebels were killed.

5 March

In Uganda judges and lawyers hold a strike to protest against raids on their courts by government troops. They claim these raids are threatening the independence of the country's judiciary.

5 March

Minghui Radio, a station set up and run by overseas Chinese and international volunteers, begins broadcasting into China 24-hours a day via a Eutelsat satellite. The broadcasts consist of information prohibited in China.

5 March

Violent protests erupt in Jharkhand, India, when a member of the national parliament is killed. Maoists are suspected of the murder of Sunil Mahato and widespread disruption ensues.

5–9 March

In Quito, Ecuador, activists come together to promote the abolition of foreign military bases. A coalition of anti-bases activists, individuals and organisations working in campaigns for disarmament, demilitarisation and peace and justice, coordinate a No Bases Network. The gathering particularly expresses its solidarity with the Ecuadorian people in their campaign against the Manta base.

7–9 March

Demonstrations are held in several parts of Brazil in the build up to President Bush's visit to the country. A mine, a bank and other corporate property are invaded to draw attention to the impact of corporate business on the poor. Over 15,000 activists are involved, including many landless farmworkers who march to Sao Paulo, where President Bush arrives to forge an ethanol energy alliance with Brazilian president.

8 March

International Women's Day is marked around the world by over 500 events in at least 49 countries. These include a silent protest against violence in Taipei, a march for equality in Brazil, an assembly of Manitoba chiefs in Canada, and a Right to Play campaign in Tanzania to promote female inclusion in sports. In Iran, a strong police presence disperses women trying to gather outside parliament in Tehran to demonstrate over the arrests of 33 women earlier in the week. These detained women are now on hunger strike over their treatment when they tried to protest against discriminatory laws.

10 March

In New York, hundreds of students and other activists form a human chain across 12 city blocks connecting the Sudanese and Chinese missions to the USA in an effort to highlight the Chinese Communist Party's backing of the genocidal Khartoum regime.

10–11 March

An international seminar on the Indo–US nuclear deal is held in Mumbai, India, organised by the Afro–Asian Peoples' Solidarity Organisation.

12 March–4 July

An international campaign is launched after BBC reporter Alan Johnson is kidnapped in Gaza City. He was the only journalist permanently based in the Gaza Strip. Many Palestinians support the campaign for his release and demonstrations are coordinated in cities around the world. The Hamas government helped to secure his eventual release after 114 days of captivity.

15 March

As the UK Parliament gets ready to vote on the future of the Trident nuclear weapons programme, large demonstrations are held by international disarmament campaigning groups and peace activists, including a peace camp at the Faslane, marches in central London and the unfurling of a banner on the Scottish Parliament building, which reads 'Whatever they vote, Trident is still wrong!'

17–20 March

Anti-war demonstrations are held in cities throughout the world to mark the fourth anniversary of the invasion of Iraq, including 20,000 marching for peace in Spain and over 1,000 protests, marches, demonstrations and vigils held across the USA calling for immediate troop withdrawal.

18 March

An estimated 5,000 people march through the streets of Hong Kong calling for universal suffrage. Of the seven million Hong Kong residents, only 800 individuals – mostly appointed by Beijing – are allowed to elect the Special Administrative Region's new leader.

19 March

A demonstration is held outside the European Commission's Trade Department in Brussels by international water activists. Under the banner 'Water out of free trade negotiations! Water is a human right!', they claim it is unfair for EU trade talks to demand that developing countries open up their water sector to European multinationals.

21 March

Anti-racism events are held in cities around the world to mark International Day for the Elimination of Racism on the anniversary of the Sharpeville massacre in South Africa. On this day in 1960, 69 anti-apartheid demonstrators were killed when they stood up against the pass laws which were designed to regulate the movements of black Africans.

21 March

An international campaign saves the life of Knut the polar bear who had been rejected by his mother. Some animal rights activists believe the bear should be killed as it would need to be reared 'unnaturally' by humans.

24 March

On the occasion of the 50th anniversary of the Rome treaty, the origin of the EU, a common declaration is made by international branches of the alter-globalist movement ATTAC, including Germany, Austria, Belgium, Denmark, Spain, Finland, France, Greece, Hungary, Italy, Jersey, Norway, The Netherlands, Poland, Sweden and Switzerland.

28 March

An international conference on participatory budgeting is held in Malaga, Spain, to share and respond to the conclusions of the Forum of Local Authorities for Social Inclusion and Participatory Democracy at the World Social Forum in Nairobi this year.

29 March–1 April

In Cairo, the Egyptian Social Forum is held.

April 2007

1 April

Protests are held in Iran, the largest outside the British Embassy, against what the Iranian authorities claim was a violation of Iran's territorial waters by British navel personnel. Fifteen personnel captured by Iranian forces are later released.

7–8 April

In Concarneau, France, the local Contre-Feux Social Forum is held.

12–14 April

The eighth International Free Software Forum is held in Porto Alegre, Brazil.

13–15 April

In Sweden, the regional Ostergotland Social Forum is held consecutively in the two towns of Norkoping and Linkoping.

20 April

A global day for trade justice is marked by demonstrations in many cities calling for an end to unfair EU trade deals with poor countries. As part of this, a march in London takes their message to all 26 EU embassies.

20–22 April

In Australia, the third Melbourne Social Forum takes place with the theme 'Change the political climate: turn up the heat!'.

21 April

The Freiburg Social Forum is held in Switzerland, including mobilisation for protests against the G8 summit to be held in Germany later in the year.

21–22 April

In Helsinki, Finland, the sixth national Finnish Social Forum takes place. A major focus is the Finnish government's asylum policy and the campaign against forced deportations.

21–22 April

In Germany, the local Berlin Social Forum is held.

24 April

Hundreds of activists gather in New York's Wall Street area to call upon Fidelity Investments to divest from PetroChina, a Chinese oil company believed to be helping to fund the genocidal Khartoum regime. In response to student pressure, Harvard University divested from PetroChina in 2005, an action that was later followed by dozens of other universities.

29 April

Over one million people take part in a rally in Istanbul in support of secularism and democracy. This is the largest in a series of actions in response to a tense stand-off between the Islamist-rooted government and the army, over presidential elections. Over 600 civil society organisations have been involved in planning the protests.